Park Campus
Library

Satisfaction

Satisfaction

A Behavioral Perspective on the Consumer

Second Edition

Richard L. Oliver

M.E.Sharpe
Armonk, New York
London, England

Library of Congress Cataloging-in-Publication Data

Oliver, Richard L.
  Satisfaction : a behavioral perspective on the consumer / by Richard L. Oliver. — 2nd ed.
      p. cm.
  Includes bibliographical references and index.
  ISBN 978-0-7656-1770-5 (cloth : alk. paper)
  1. Consumer satisfaction. 2. Consumer satisfaction—Evaluation. I. Title.

HF5415.335.O55 2009
658.8'12—dc22   2008039870

Printed in the United States of America

The paper used in this publication meets the minimum requirements of
American National Standard for Information Sciences
Permanence of Paper for Printed Library Materials,
ANSI Z 39.48-1984.

∞

CW (c)   10   9   8   7   6   5   4   3   2   1

CONTENTS

LIST OF TABLES

LIST OF FIGURES

PREFACE

As noted in the introduction to the first edition, an overarching purpose for writing the original and revised editions of this book is to explore a common human quest, the satisfaction of one's needs, wants, or desires. In one form or another, this goal has preoccupied humankind for thousands of years. Beginning with the necessity of mere survival to the present-day pursuit of material goods and hedonic pleasures, individuals have judged their outcomes in life as satisfactory or not, and institutions, organizations, and even governments have endeavored to best deliver satisfactory outcomes to their customers and constituencies.

Unfortunately, not all have succeeded. In part, this lack of success occurs because of production, delivery, and merchandising problems or competitive actions. Most probably, however, organizations fail because of a lack of understanding of how consumers actually form satisfaction judgments. In this sense, consumers may have "designed-in" dissatisfaction, an unintentional result of use of a thought process not immediately apparent to providers of goods and services. Thus, the goals of this new edition go beyond mere exploration. Rather, efforts will be made to describe the satisfaction process in a manner that both promotes an understanding of this complex phenomenon and, to the extent possible, makes this knowledge useful to those who would study satisfaction for its many implications.

BACKGROUND

Questions about the meaning, causes, and consequences of satisfaction have intrigued the author for over thirty-five years. I began study of the satisfaction phenomenon after teaching a consumer behavior course in the early 1970s. At that time, the topic was not well understood: the consumer behavior textbooks of the day did not address satisfaction to any degree, and the professional journals contained little on the topic. This situation persisted despite the continued importance placed on satisfaction by marketing management textbooks and readings.

Perhaps because of this lack of knowledge, consumer satisfaction researchers began in earnest to provide the consumer behavior discipline with insights into postpurchase phenomena. This trend began in the mid-1970s and continues in the present. Of interest is the fact that early writings on the topic in the academic literature focused on the consumerism movement and, particularly, complaining behavior. This early work tended to emphasize three themes: what caused consumers to be dissatisfied, how dissatisfied consumers reacted (e.g., complain—or not), and what the provider did in response to these consumer actions. These were worthy pursuits at the time, but the result was a focus on dissatisfying product feature performances or service provider behaviors and not necessarily the satisfying mental elements of provision. Indeed, marketers were still aligned with a production orientation whereby high quality (as defined by the provider) was, ipso facto, satisfying. Fortunately, as the field progressed, a more challenging set of questions emerged concerning *how* and *why* consumers became satisfied, as opposed to *what* it was about the product or service that consumers found satisfying or dissatisfying. Thus, the first purpose of this book is to expand on an accumulated knowledge base and provide readers with a more complete discussion of what is known of the satisfaction response and other postpurchase processes.

A second goal in writing this book and its revision is to assist the decision maker, program evaluator, and researcher with methodological and measurement suggestions specific to post-delivery and postconsumption environments. To this end, research approaches and measures, many unique to the first edition of this book or subsequently published by a large contingency of focused researchers, are provided in the hope that a broad array of marketers will benefit from a continuing and growing knowledge base in customer satisfaction. I would be remiss, however, if I did not acknowledge that satisfaction is no longer the ultimate goal of business. Loyalty, with its relation to satisfaction, is now considered the penultimate pursuit (second to profit for those organizations having monetary goals), and, as the reader will find, greatly expanded coverage of the loyalty response is provided here.

Like the first edition, this second edition summarizes the research findings to date, speculates on what is not yet known, and suggests where the field may be heading in the future. Also apparent from the prior edition, external literatures, primarily both pure and applied psychology, are referenced for their insight into satisfaction phenomena. The reader will discover, however, that in the interval since publication of the earlier volume, some very significant behavioral advances have taken place in the study of consumer satisfaction and, in particular, loyalty—resulting in much greater proportional reliance in the current edition on material in the consumer behavior field. Much of the credit for what is currently known extends to the authors of these efforts.

ACKNOWLEDGMENTS

In acknowledgment of these many individuals responsible for the progress made in understanding consumer satisfaction and postpurchase phenomena generally, I dedicate this book. It is the result of the author's and other's desires to understand the whys of consumer satisfaction and its elusive covariate, loyalty.

Appreciation is expressed to the Owen Graduate School of Management, Vanderbilt University, its Walker Management Library, and to all those who assisted in providing the resources necessary for the successful completion of this book. Because much of the work giving rise to the underlying logic and content provided here has taken place over the nearly twenty years the author has been in residence, the names are too numerous to cite. To these individuals, much gratitude is expressed.

Appreciation is also expressed to the many associates at M.E. Sharpe, without whom this second edition would not be possible. These include my Executive Editor Harry M. Briggs and Associate Editor Elizabeth Granda.

My hope is that readers find this book "satisfying," as this term is individually interpreted. A more specific hope is that it be found "more than satisfying," but I would not presume to be able to accomplish this even in this second effort at exposition. I ask readers to assist me in this task and I will do my best to make the next rendition even more fully satisfying.

Satisfaction

CHAPTER 1

INTRODUCTION

What Is Satisfaction?

In 1965, the Rolling Stones produced a hit song titled "Satisfaction." The lyrics contained the lament that, despite efforts to the contrary, the band members couldn't "get no satisfaction" even though they "tried and tried and tried." Just what is this quest that the Rolling Stones popularized with their hit? What, exactly, is that "satisfaction" that is so frustrating to attain? Even though these questions stem from the lyrics of a popular song, they·do reflect the difficulties that individuals encounter when they "try and try and try" to get satisfaction from consumption, institutions and governments, and relationships.

Shifting emphasis to the business side of providing satisfaction, what did Sears mean to imply when it offered its explicit warranty in the catchy motto "Satisfaction guaranteed or your money back"? Similarly, L.L. Bean, the formidable mail merchandiser in Freeport, Maine, offers a modern variation of this guarantee with a promise of "100% satisfaction in every way" by providing either a replacement or refund form of restitution.

These promises and others like them raise a number of questions. Can Sears, L.L. Bean, or any other firm *guarantee* satisfaction? Will a money-back guarantee provide an alternative means of satisfying customers? Are there strategies at the firm or individual consumer levels that can prevent dissatisfaction from occurring or that can turn dissatisfaction into satisfaction? Addressed specifically in later chapters, these and other questions contribute to the focus of this book.

This introductory section sets the stage for the book, describing its unique behavioral focus. In contrast to the specific approach taken here are a number of publications on "how to" satisfy customers. Some do not necessarily address satisfaction directly, but focus on related concepts such as value, quality, and loyalty. Others discuss specific strategies or activities that are thought to be satisfying to consumers, as opposed to framing the activities within the consumer's psyche.

Still other popular writings available in the marketplace attempt to describe organizational strategies and changes that are thought to make a firm more "customer-friendly." This movement, sometimes described as total quality management (TQM) and quality function deployment (QFD), has many adherents and has been institutionalized with the Malcolm Baldrige National Quality Award and the Deming Prize. In this context, customer satisfaction is thought to be a natural outgrowth of optimal organizational design and of instilling the appropriate organizational culture, personnel training, and customer responsiveness within employee ranks. In short, it is believed that the attainment of satisfaction will be enhanced if these practices are followed.

As will become evident throughout this book, however, these managerial practices cannot guarantee satisfaction any more than the best efforts of a good coach can guarantee consistent victories in sport. The reason is that, like the coach viewing the opposition across the field, management cannot see inside the heads of its constituents. Managers can only devise strategies that they hope will work based on the best data available at the time. By adopting a behavioral focus, however, management may be able to "see" the workings of the consumer's mind and thus be able to better satisfy customers.

This introduction begins by explaining satisfaction in evolutionary terms, describing how it was first construed as simple satiation and, given the added meaning of goods and services in industrialized economies, how it has now taken on more modern proportions. Essentially, consumers are now described as wanting more "satisfaction from their satisfaction" since "merely satisfying" the consumer may no longer provide a competitive advantage. Companies must struggle in today's markets to define what this means in the context of their industry.

This section also discusses various definitions and views, defining the pursuit of satisfaction in current terms as an essential human desire for fulfilling experiences in life. The discussion goes on to distinguish satisfaction from other provisions by business and society, such as quality, and also from other psychological responses, such as attitude and (perhaps surprisingly) loyalty and concludes by showing how involved the psychological mechanisms underlying satisfaction are and how the remaining chapters in the book will address these processes. A "map" in graphic form is provided, further illustrating the structure of the book and how it unfolds the satisfaction response. Part I of the book, which follows this introduction, will begin examination of the essential components of this response.

WHY STUDY SATISFACTION IN A CONSUMER CONTEXT?

In a word, satisfaction is fundamental to the well being of individual consumers, to the profits of firms supported through purchasing and patronization, and to the stability of economic and political structures. All of these entities benefit from the provision and receipt of satisfying life outcomes, particularly in the marketplace. Some reasons follow.

The Consumer's Perspective

Satisfaction can be likened to an individual pursuit, a goal to be attained from the consumption of products and the patronization of services. Few would disagree with the premise that consumers want to be satisfied. Why? Here are three possible answers:

- Satisfaction itself is a desirable end-state of consumption or patronization; it is a reinforcing, pleasurable experience.
- It obviates the need to take additional redress actions or to suffer the consequences of a bad decision.
- It reaffirms the consumer's decision-making prowess.

In this latter sense, a satisfactory purchase is an achievement; it signals that the consumer has mastered the complexity of the marketplace. Of course, not all purchases are achievements, but they are instances of reinforcement that provide stability and serenity in the consumer's life.

Additionally, satisfaction is one of the many life outcomes that provides a means of understanding the environment. In the human desire to make sense of reality, consumers can be viewed as drawing on their highly developed processing skills to update prior information and to discover new knowledge. One way of doing so is to rely on the occurrence and nonoccurrence of events (data) and to search for the reasons about their causes. Satisfaction (or the lack of satisfaction) is one such event that appears almost inevitably as a consequence of purchasing and consumption. While some purchase outcomes may be given little thought, those that are processed for the satisfaction they provide bring powerful insight into the workings of the marketplace.

The Firm's Perspective

Firms exist in capitalistic societies to make a profit. If the firm's product were viewed as a one-time-only purchase by consumers (e.g., novelty items such as the pet rock), if the level of performance were not subject to regulation, and if only limited cross-communication channels were open to consumers, then customer satisfaction would be an unimportant goal for the purely profit-oriented firm. Few producers, however, encounter these conditions. Most find that repeat purchasing is essential to a continued stream of profitability. Even for products with long purchase intervals (e.g., major appliances, automobiles), satisfaction is important because of word of mouth and the activities of numerous watchdog organizations, such as Consumers Union, that track reports of satisfaction over time. Now becoming more available, empirical data on the influence of satisfaction, quality, and other such measures are substantiating the long-held assumption that customer satisfaction is one key to profitability. Further elaboration is presented here and in Chapter 15.

The Industry Perspective

Entire industries, including, of course, the firms making up individual industries, have long been a subject of scrutiny for their ill or benign effects on consumers. Generally, the government has relied on documented harm to determine the extent of consumer "satisfaction." Many laws, such as the Agricultural Meat Inspection Act, the Food, Drug, and Cosmetic Act, the Flammable Fabrics Act, the Fair Packaging and Labeling Act, and the Child Protection Act, are a result of this process. Clearly, a consequence of consumer discontent directed at an industry is regulation and its attendant costs. Additionally, taxation (which is ultimately borne by the consumer) is another likely consequence, as in the raising of cigarette taxes to offset smoking-related health-care costs. Recently, a program to monitor industry satisfaction has been implemented in a number of countries by the University of Michigan's National Quality Research Center via its American Customer Satisfaction Index (ACSI);[1] other world locales and governments are beginning to follow suit, thereby making satisfaction with entire industries across countries a measurable phenomenon for input to regulatory policy.

The Societal Perspective

Research on the quality of life suggests quite strongly that satisfied members of society demonstrate better life outcomes, whether in health, social and mental adjustment, or finances.[2] While it is difficult to distinguish the direction of effect between favorable life outcomes and perceived quality of life, life satisfaction continues as a worthy goal for individuals in society and for governments desirous of reinstatement by constituents.[3] The previously mentioned customer satisfaction indices, now expanded beyond products and services to public sector organizations (e.g., postal services), is a step in the direction of monitoring broader arrays of satisfaction-inducing elements in life.

As mentioned, quality of life issues are inextricably intertwined with consumers' (citizens') satisfaction with public agencies. These include all government renderings including social security, defense, the legal system, the environment, taxation, and the like.[4] The issue takes on added complexity when the overlapping and sometimes overriding arenas of jurisdiction come into conflict, as with federal versus states' rights in the United States (e.g., controlled substances). Interestingly, a number of boundary-spanning agencies and regulated industries are beginning to recognize the wisdom of serving customers satisfactorily as the public is becoming more active in this regard. Public utilities, regulatory agencies (e.g., the Food and Drug Administration), and even the Internal Revenue Service are beginning to take note, and it is only a matter of time before the quest for satisfaction becomes part of their "business" model.

A DIVERSITY OF SATISFACTION DEFINITIONS

While most people would agree with the premise that satisfaction with consumption benefits consumers, firms, industries, and governments, few agree on what this concept called "satisfaction" is. Without a sense of resolution on this issue, little reason would exist to continue with the present discussion. Thus, it would be useful if some consensus existed on an early definition of what a promise of "satisfaction" means.

Satisfaction is derived from the Latin *satis* (enough) and *facere* (to do or make). Thus, satisfying products and services have the capacity to provide what is sought to the point of being "enough." Two related words are *satiation*, which loosely means enough up to the point of excess, and *satiety*, which can mean a surfeit or too much of enough, as if to say that too much is necessarily undesirable. These terms illustrate the point that satisfaction implies a filling or fulfillment, perhaps up to a threshold of undesirable effects (e.g., overindulging, such as credit purchasing beyond one's financial means).

As readers are no doubt aware, interpretations in the consumer domain allow for a greater range of favorable (and unfavorable) responses than mere fulfillment. Fulfillment implies that a satiation level is known, as in the basic needs of sustenance. However, observers of human behavior understand that these need levels can be and frequently are exceeded in various ways. Thus, consumer researchers have moved away from the literal meaning of satisfaction and now pursue this concept as the consumer experiences and describes it. Later chapters will elaborate on this concept, attempting to explain how more recent interpretations play into the consumption experience. For the present, discussion turns to attempts in the marketing literature to define what exactly it is that firms are supposed to do vis-à-vis their customers.

Pinning down a generally agreed-upon definition of consumer satisfaction is not as easy as it would first appear. To illustrate, the list below shows definitions that have been proposed in the past.[5] All, incidentally, remain valid today.

- "An evaluation rendered that the [consumption] experience was at least as good as it was supposed to be."
- "The summary psychological state resulting when the emotion surrounding disconfirmed expectations is coupled with the consumer's prior feelings about the consumption experience."
- "The consumer's response to the evaluation of the perceived discrepancy between prior expectations [or some other norm of performance] and the actual performance of the product as perceived after its consumption."

Note that these are not "dictionary" definitions. Rather, they are known as *process* definitions. That is, they define key concepts and the mechanisms by which these concepts interact. Unlike a dictionary entry, each of these recognizes that satisfaction is the summary-state of a psychological process. As such, satisfaction results at the end (or the current summation) of the consumer's

Figure 1.1   **Variants of "Satisfaction"**

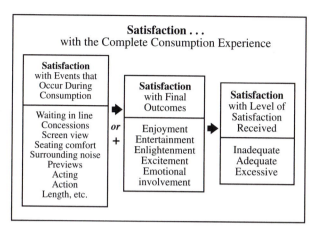

processing activities and not necessarily when product and service outcomes are immediately observed. This permits rapid judgments of the satisfaction rendered by quickly consumed products (e.g., a candy bar), as well as judgments of the satisfaction resulting from products with lengthy consumption periods (e.g., a satisfying vacation, satisfaction with owning and driving one's car, satisfaction with a college education)—a critical distinction for service providers.

It is also possible for consumers to give interim judgments of satisfaction, as when college students are asked how satisfied they are after the sophomore year of a four-year program. In this case, the students judge satisfaction on the basis of what is known to date. The same psychological process that will later determine satisfaction after graduation now generates this interim judgment. One may now begin to appreciate that the satisfaction process, or the process giving rise to satisfaction stages including choice, is also subject to satisfaction judgments.[6]

Figure 1.1 illustrates how interim and final stages of consumption are assessed in the context of attendance at a movie. Initially, elements of the movie experience, shown here as "events," are individually judged. Generally, consumers can state how satisfying each of these events is perceived to be. Collectively, the series of events constitutes the consumer's movie experience so that, at the movie's end, overall impressions of entertainment, excitement, and so on can also be assessed for their satisfaction potential. The resulting level of satisfaction can additionally be assessed on the basis of how satisfying it was. This is done in terms of the expected level of satisfaction anticipated by the consumer, a topic discussed in later sections of this book. Lastly, the entire experience, shown as the larger inclusive rectangle, can be similarly judged as satisfactory or not.

Thus, satisfaction can be viewed in terms of singular events leading up to a consumption outcome and as a collective impression of these events. Moreover, consumers can be satisfied or dissatisfied with the level of satisfaction received. In fact, one might argue that today's consumers desire more "satisfaction from their satisfaction," suggesting that current levels of consumer satisfaction may be dissatisfying at a higher level of abstraction. This duality of meaning is one of the intriguing aspects of satisfaction that makes definition difficult. Drawing an analogy in the form of a paraphrase from the emotion literature: "Everyone knows what [*satisfaction*] is, until asked to give a definition. Then it seems, nobody knows."[7]

From the preceding discussion, one can see that a good definition of satisfaction would require that it generalize satisfaction with individual elements of product or service delivery, final outcome satisfaction, and satisfaction with satisfaction. The definitions in the preceding list are a worthy start as they acknowledge psychological processes used by consumers in their satisfaction judgments. They fail, however, in specifying the consumer's summary judgment, described variously as an "evaluation," a "summary state," and a "response to the evaluation." It is as if this final judgment defies definition.

Satisfaction: A Formal Definition

In the first edition of this book and after much tribulation, I proposed a definition of satisfaction that appeared to be sufficiently general in scope so that it would relate to the many domains of satisfaction and, at the same time, would distinguish the concept of satisfaction from other behavioral responses engaged in by consumers. Others have adopted this definition to guide their work. While no claims of exclusivity are offered, it is repeated here in the hope that others will find it similarly helpful.

> *Satisfaction* is the consumer's fulfillment response. It is a judgment that a product/service feature, or the product or service itself, provided (or is providing) a *pleasurable* level of consumption-related fulfillment, including levels of under- or overfulfillment.[8]

Here, *pleasurable* implies that fulfillment gives or increases pleasure or reduces pain, as when a problem in life is solved (to be discussed in Chapter 5). Thus, individuals can be satisfied just to get back to normalcy or neutrality, as in the removal of an aversive state (e.g., pain relief). Moreover, fulfillment does not need to be constrained to the case of met needs. Overfulfillment can be satisfying if it provides additional unexpected pleasure; and underfulfillment can be satisfying if it gives greater pleasure than anticipated in a given situation (to be discussed in Chapter 4). These examples illustrate the need to more fully understand the complexities of the satisfaction process—how it evolves, maintains, and concludes.

Note that satisfaction has been explained with reference to fulfillment, as if this latter concept were more basic. In like manner, the notion of fulfillment requires further elaboration. More specifically, it implies that a goal exists, something to be met or filled. Thus, fulfillment (and satisfaction as explained later) can be judged only with reference to a standard. The standard forms the basis for comparison. This raises a very important point. A judgment of fulfillment and hence of satisfaction involves, at the minimum, two stimuli—an outcome and a comparison referent. This explains why consumers can be satisfied with the level of satisfaction received. Possible comparison referents include prior satisfaction or other people's satisfaction. Greater elaboration appears in Part I of this book.

Defining satisfaction in terms of pleasurable fulfillment explains types of consumption where apparently nothing of tangible value is received. For example, many people find satisfaction in altruistic "purchasing" such as donating to charity, volunteerism, and even a willingness to pay taxes. What is so satisfying about these activities? Perhaps it is because they are undertaken to purchase altruistic satisfaction. In terms of the definition of satisfaction presented here, altruistic satisfaction derives from the fulfillment of a moral or ethical obligation, which gives pleasure. The reason that so many individuals find taxation dissatisfying is that, to them, the fulfillment of this obligation is *unpleasant*. This illustrates the point that the pleasurableness of the fulfillment response is essential to the definition of satisfaction.

What About Dissatisfaction?

Note that it is not necessary to provide a separate definition of *dis*satisfaction. One need only substitute the word *unpleasant* for *pleasurable* in the (dis)satisfaction definition offered here. Thus, the displeasure of underfulfillment can be (and typically is) dissatisfying. More interesting,

Table 1.1

Vertical and Horizontal Views of Satisfaction

Viewpoint	Antecedents	Core concept	Consequences
Individual: One transaction	Performance or service encounter	Transaction-specific satisfaction	Complimenting, complaining, word of mouth
Individual: Time accumulated	Accumulated performance history	Summary satisfaction	Attitude, loyalty, switching
Firm's customers in the aggregate	Reputation, product quality, promotion	Average satisfaction, repurchase rates, competitive ranking	Share, profits
Industry or commercial sector	Average quality, monopoly power	Consumer sentiment	Regulation, taxation
Society	Product and service variety, average quality	Psychological well-being	Tranquility, productivity, social progress, alienation, consumerism

however, is that overfulfillment may be dissatisfying if it is unpleasant—as in the case of "too much of a good thing," as when a waitperson is too attentive to the point of annoyance. Later, in Chapter 4, the notion of satisfaction in the face of insufficient fulfillment and dissatisfaction in the face of adequate fulfillment will be entertained, again illustrating the necessity of including the extent of pleasure received in the satisfaction definition.

Interestingly, dissatisfaction may also be a goal of some marketing organizations. For example, governments may wish to demarket harmful products or behaviors by creating dissatisfaction with their use. Additionally, it is well known among marketers of fashion or style goods that one purpose of new products is to create dissatisfaction with the prevailing style, a common strategy of automobile companies through the release of new models. In fact, Charles Kettering, the general director of General Motors Research Laboratories in 1929, was reported to have said that the company's corporate mission was the "organized creation of dissatisfaction."[9] Fortunately (or unfortunately), the principles outlined in this book are just as valid for fostering dissatisfaction (if that is the firm's goal) as satisfaction. The two goals are strategic mirror images, and many firms have (re)discovered strategic methods to capitalize on this distinction. Taking cues from the fashion industry, it is now commonplace to see makers of even mundane products (e.g., toothbrushes) redesign products frequently to foster a sense of obsolescence. This issue, however, takes on political notes best served by those who have been debating the social negative consequences of these strategies for decades.

VERTICAL AND HORIZONTAL DISTINCTIONS

In addition to the various satisfactions consumers can experience during product or service delivery, with final consumption outcomes, and with satisfaction itself, other conceptual distinctions should be noted at different *vertical* and *horizontal* levels. In this context, vertical implies a level of abstraction along micro (individual) and macro (aggregate) dimensions, while a horizontal analysis examines the process by which antecedents or determinants cause satisfaction and the subsequent effects of satisfaction on other consumer thoughts and actions (see Table 1.1). Unfortunately, the term *satisfaction* is often used liberally to apply to the content of any of the cells in the table. This overgeneralization contributes to the confusion regarding the meaning of satisfaction. The following discussion is a brief attempt to clarify these vertical and horizontal levels.

Vertical Distinctions

At the micro level, the focus is on an individual consumer's state of satisfaction based on a single observation or transaction, sometimes called encounter or transaction-specific satisfaction. At a higher level of abstraction, one might be interested in the consumer's *accumulated* satisfaction over many samplings (occurrences) of the same experience. Going to a favorite restaurant is an example of this phenomenon. Sometimes, accumulated satisfaction is referred to as "long-term," "overall," "global," or "summary" satisfaction.[10] At a still higher level, interest would shift to the aggregated experiences of a firm's consumers for the net effect of these experiences on the firm. This has been referred to as "microeconomic" satisfaction and is thought to be related to the firm's profitability. At a still higher level of aggregation, one might investigate the aggregate experiences of consumers in a given industry or sector (e.g., products, retail services, government) where levels of satisfaction as well as aggregate causes of satisfaction might be found. Lastly, at the highest level of abstraction, the accumulated, aggregated experiences of consumers in a given social system (society or culture), the fourth reason for studying satisfaction, can be studied. This level speaks to a culture's well being and survivability and is related to the level of health, productivity, and consumer alienation in the social system.

The purpose of this book is not to discuss satisfaction at all of these levels. Rather, analysis will be largely restricted to the two consumer judgments of transaction-specific and summary satisfaction, although Chapter 15 provides some discussion of aggregate satisfaction effects on a firm's profitability. Surely efforts to satisfy individual consumers will have cumulative effects on the firm's outcomes. Beyond that, study of satisfaction as an aggregate industry or societal phenomenon is outside the present focus. Interested readers are referred to publications such as *Social Indicators Research*, a journal that focuses on this latter level of aggregation.

Horizontal Distinctions

At the horizontal level of analysis, interest is focused on the behavioral sequence leading up to and resulting from satisfaction. In effect, this is the process of satisfaction as it unfolds for an individual consumer or for a firm or government. In studying satisfaction from this perspective, a particular need arises for distinguishing satisfaction from seemingly identical concepts. This need stems from the ubiquitous use of a number of terms (to be discussed) that are used as proxies for satisfaction. While these proxies may be sufficient in a specific situation, these concepts are not satisfaction and do not operate in the same manner within the consumer mind-set.

Examples include product or service performance, its manifestation of excellence more commonly known as quality, and the still more complicated concept of value, which contains an implicit consideration of price. Other related psychological concepts include attitude, dissonance, and regret. In the emotion literature, concepts such as happiness, good feelings, and mood are found. And in still other literatures, the absence of complaints, loyalty, and repeat purchasing are used as if they were one and the same with satisfaction.

As seen in Table 1.1, confusion extends to the macro levels of firm and societal satisfaction, where some consequences noted earlier are shown. Here, there is no *one* satisfaction judgment of the firm's product mix or of society's offerings. Rather, aggregate manifestations of satisfaction such as repeat purchasing rates and mental health data may be more operational. This is not to say that the individuals forming the aggregate do not harbor satisfaction judgments; rather, managers of firms and government officials typically see individual behaviors through aggregate statistics provided by market research firms, consumer testing organizations, and government reports.

Do Firms Agree on Satisfaction as a Corporate Goal?

This wide variation in the interpretation of the concept of satisfaction has led to a great diversity of intended success standards for firms as described in their mission statements. A reasonable question concerns the lack of unanimity of opinion that satisfaction be a goal or even the ultimate goal of firms. Historically, satisfaction was thought to be the goal as firms transitioned from a production orientation to the era of the marketing concept. Now, customer retention and its psychological equivalent of loyalty may have superseded satisfaction, and it is the intent of this book to chronicle the emergence of loyalty and even to suggest a correspondence between satisfaction and loyalty. At this point, a review of the evidence is in order.

Two recent sources were used to inform this section.[11] The first is a compilation of the mission statements of 101 companies. The second is a content analysis of the annual reports of 76 companies in four industries. This diversity of these two approaches and information sources gives some perspective on the complexity of satisfaction focus and nonfocus in firms. Also included are other related goals, such as loyalty, where available.

The mission statement analysis (based on the author's reading where multiple goals were tabulated) found both traditional and contemporary goals among the top four statements with approximately thirty occurrences of the first (traditional) and twenty of the remaining three (contemporary). The first of the four was quality or excellence, the next two were the provision of value and superior service, the fourth, somewhat surprisingly was meeting and/or exceeding expectations. Apparently companies are beginning to capitalize on this central satisfaction concept in their dealings with customers.

Also surprising, albeit in a more reserved sense, was that satisfaction (or satisfying) was mentioned only about ten times, with fairness citations close behind. Rounding out the list were the goals of fulfilling needs and, most curiously, loyalty, mentioned only three times. Since the analysis was based on 101 companies, this implies that many used only operational descriptors ("to be the best" was common). Mission statements are not routinely revised; many of these had been constructed in times past. One can conclude, however, that there is scant agreement on what it is that the firm's mission seeks to accomplish.

In the analysis of company reports within four industries (household/personal and food products, banking and restaurant services), satisfaction was the central concept studied. No explicit mention of satisfaction was made in 25 percent of both the product and service categories. However, satisfaction was implied (e.g., delight, meeting needs) in 65 percent and 40 percent of the company categories respectively. In the remaining cases, either qualitative or quantitative satisfaction measurement was mentioned with only a small fraction reporting actual numbers (e.g., 9 or 10 on a 10-point scale). It was noted that satisfaction was largely subservient to more financially based measures.

Of interest is that both retention and loyalty were analyzed along with the financial measures. Retention was not mentioned in any of the product company reports and was referred to in less than 20 percent of the service company reports. Loyalty, in similar fashion, was mentioned in less than 10 percent of company reports and less than 15 percent of the service reports. This is consistent with the very low ranking of loyalty in the mission statements.

What is the takeaway of these methodologically distinct studies? It appears that satisfaction remains secondary to the traditional criteria of quality, value, and service, and that company reports are shareholder-driven with bottom-line (financial) results of greatest interest. Perhaps this is so because the links between satisfaction and profits (and especially loyalty and profits) are not well understood or appreciated. Thus, there is much to be gained from further study of satisfaction, and the goal of this book does not deviate to any degree from that in the previous edition. Much remains to be understood and implemented within firms. The last chapter on loyalty will make this point more strongly as loyalty will remain the ultimate goal of the firm with regard to its customers after satisfaction is more fully pursued.

CONSUMER SATISFACTION COMPARED TO SATISFACTION IN OTHER DOMAINS

As noted in the discussion of the vertical dimension of satisfaction, individual episodes of satisfaction can accumulate into summary or long-term states. This phenomenon provides the underlying basis for relating satisfaction across its many domains. For example, is the psychological process for satisfaction with a movie the same as it is for a dishwasher, a retirement home, a sports event, a vacation, a new car, and medical care? Granted, the facets used to infer satisfaction in each of these areas will be markedly different, but do the psychological mechanisms vary? A definitive answer awaits empirical testing, but my understanding of research findings across these domains points to the conclusion that the processes leading to the satisfaction response are essentially isomorphic. They differ only in the degree of episodic integration or "blending" (see Figure 1.2).

As shown in the figure, various human experiences are categorized in five approximations of customer contact. Each is further divided into simple and complex experiences. Simple experiences are those having few facets or dimensions, such as the purchase of a soft drink. Complex situations, such as a hospital stay, have many facets requiring separate integration mechanisms, discussed more fully in Chapter 2. Regardless of whether the consumption experience is simple or complex, consumer reactions can be based on a single unique encounter, on continual ongoing encounters, or on any frequency of contact between these two extremes.

Unique encounters stand out in isolation. In this case, satisfaction assessment is based on this one event. Repetitive episodes of a discretionary nature can be assessed either individually or over a longer time period, such as when a consumer goes to a particular movie theater only when a desirable movie is being shown. Some consumers may evaluate each movie experience separately because idiosyncratic elements (e.g., the movie itself, the crowd) may be more salient than the invariant characteristics of the theater (e.g., the location, concessions, seating). Other consumers, however, will assess the theater as an integrated experience, such as when it is their "favorite movie house" regardless of the nature of the film.

At a higher level of episodic blending, regular repetitive experiences will be evaluated. A favorite weekly TV series supplies a familiar example. Generally, consumers will view the series as an integrated whole and not as individual episodes. While it is true that each episode can be evaluated separately, consumers are known to take a liking or disliking to the series in general regardless of its weekly content. Job satisfaction is another frequently researched domain of a repetitive nature, although some would classify it in the following category.

At the next level of integration are continuing episodes with occasional lapses. Satisfaction with one's residence is an example; the lapses occur when one is away from home. Here, individual events (a leaking roof) are generally insignificant or fleeting relative to the holistic

Figure 1.2   **Domains of Satisfaction Based on Episodic Frequency**

Unique Episodes	**Discretionary Repetitive Episodes**	**Scheduled Repetitive Episodes**	**Continual Episodes**	**Constant Experiences**
Simple: Unrepeated trials Travel experiences Novelties Repairs	**Simple:** Favorite indulgences TV viewing Games	**Simple:** Everyday staples Weekly TV viewing Mail delivery Public transportation Exercise (aerobics)	**Simple:** Weather Household utilities Home furnishings	**Simple:** Air quality Prevailing law
Complex: Medical emergency Birth of child Dream vacation Olympics IRS Audit	**Complex:** Fine restaurant Local travel Recreation area Shopping mall Sporting events	**Complex:** Job Education Weekly night out Grocery shopping Driving (various)	**Complex:** Home Marriage Family Community Government	**Complex:** Health Well-being Life Spirituality

Episodic Blending →

nature of "consumption" for this category. Other representative experiences include a person's community and government. In this latter example, laws and regulations are ever present. The lapses are akin to "not thinking about it." In this sense, some would put government in the next category.

Last are those events that are constantly experienced. Life and health satisfaction are two examples. While there will be ups and downs, life is a continuous blend of all its facets. In fact, life satisfaction is frequently measured as a combination of most of the major domains (e.g., job, marriage) preceding it in Figure 1.2. Consistent with the definition of satisfaction presented here, life satisfaction can be modeled as the degree to which a person's wants in life are fulfilled.[12]

All these examples illustrate the common theme that satisfaction is the degree of fulfillment provided by experiences in life, regardless of how frequently they are encountered. More frequent encounters simply provide aggregate fulfillment. At the limit, experiences blend together until fulfillment can be gauged only against broad, general goals or desires.

Because of the structural similarities in the satisfaction response across domains, examples will be freely drawn from among them when it is appropriate to do so. For now, discussion turns to greater elaboration of the horizontal dimension of satisfaction as shown in Table 1.1.

SATISFACTION COMPARED TO RELATED CONCEPTS

One of the goals of this chapter and of this book is to disentangle the confusion of terms surrounding the concept of satisfaction by pursuing it as a central concept in a myriad of responses that consumers might make to consumption events. Instead of a detailed discussion of the differences among these concepts here, a glossary has been provided at the end of this introductory chapter, defining a number of common terms used in place of satisfaction, as mentioned in the previous section. This glossary may help to eliminate some early misgivings about what satisfaction is and what it is not. Additionally, the following vignettes of likely purchase scenarios will serve to position each term within this cluster of associated responses.

A First-Time Consumer

Imagine a consumer with no experience in buying a particular product. Having an interest in its purchase, the consumer might read advertisements and consumer guides to acquire information. This information, usually regarding benefits (and some drawbacks) that the product will deliver, provides the consumer with *expectations* about the product's likely performance. Moreover, the consumer may have specific *needs* that the product should fulfill.

Because a number of suitable alternatives are available, this consumer must choose among them—a difficult choice because the alternatives often have mutually exclusive, but desirable features. Thus, choosing one alternative requires that the consumer forgo the unique features of the others. This creates two problems. First, the consumer may anticipate *regret* if the chosen alternative does not work out as well as others might have. Second, until the consumer has consumed, used, or sufficiently sampled the product's performance (as in driving a car over a period of time), an apprehension or tension, known more commonly as *dissonance*, will exist over whether the choice was best. States of dissonance are very likely for products having great financial outlays (purchase of a home), personal significance (choice of a college or whether to go to college), or which require lengthy prepossession or usage periods (mail-order, custom-designed articles, pre-planned vacations). Concurrent with the apprehensions comprising dissonance, the consumer may also relish *anticipation* of ownership or usage of the product. Such anticipations are now becoming widely known as motivators of purchase. Although more will be said about this in Chapter 3, it is sufficient to say that pleasant anticipations may be more satisfying than actual usage of the consumable itself.

Once the product is used and its *performance* evident, the consumer is now in a position to compare actual performance with expectations, needs, or other standards, resulting in an *expectation-performance discrepancy*. For example, the consumer may have expected an automobile to deliver thirty miles per gallon and finds that, under the best of conditions, the mileage only reaches twenty-five. The discrepancy is a (negative) five miles per gallon. This comparison, which results in a better-than-expected, same-as-expected, or worse-than-expected summary judgment, is referred to as *disconfirmation*. Additionally, the consumer may be able to make a judgment of perceived *quality*—how the product compares against standards of excellence for the product class, and a judgment of *value*—quality received relative to the outlays, frequently measured as cost or price of the product.

Consumers often think about why consumption outcomes occurred in the manner that they did. When consumers generate reasons or assign responsibility for purchase outcomes, this process is referred to as *attribution*, as in "to what do I attribute this outcome?" Based on these attribution judgments, consumers may experience certain *emotions*—specific human *affects* resulting from, for example, blame or gratitude. Emotions resulting from attributions could be anger, directed at the manufacturer for producing a defective product; guilt, or a feeling of self-blame for making a bad decision; or delight over the choice of an exceptionally or surprisingly good product.

Without explicit reference to expectations or standards of excellence, the consumer might just observe product or service performance and *evaluate* it on purely functional dimensions. That is, does the product do what it is supposed to do and is this good or bad? In this sense, performance goodness is an implicit comparative standard, frequently referred to as an *attitude*. This evaluation might be of the nature of a success or failure or of degrees of success. This primary evaluation is likely to result in a more basic and less complex primary affect, such as simple pleasure or displeasure over the purchase.

The net result of all these possible postpurchase responses is *satisfaction*—the degree to which the product provided pleasurable levels of fulfillment. *Dissatisfaction* would result if the level of fulfillment (probably unfulfillment or underfulfillment) were unpleasant. Note that satisfaction is a summary judgment of all these processes or at least those used by a particular consumer. It is not simply performance processing or disconfirmation processing or even emotion states such as happiness. More specifically, it contains components of judgment (e.g., cognition) *and* affect (e.g., emotion).

Repeat Purchasing, Consumption, or Patronization

Having purchased a product previously, the consumer has more than likely developed an attitude toward it. As suggested previously, an attitude is a fairly stable liking or disliking toward the product based on prior experience (e.g., previous satisfaction). It is also possible that an attitude can develop based on prior information without experience, as when consumers develop biases for or against brands based on their image (or the manufacturer's reputation) in the marketplace. This attitude now forms the basis for the consumer's expectation in the next product encounter. It is also likely that the attitude is tied fairly strongly to the consumer's *intention* to repurchase the product or repatronize the service in the future. Additionally, the consumer's attitude may be closely linked in tone to the consumer's general perception of the quality of the good or service.[13]

At this point, the consumer may be fairly insensitive to a single shortfall in product performance. In fact, the consumer may endure several shortfalls, particularly if they are easily attributed to external causes such as fate or random chance. This consumer would be described as possessing brand or service *loyalty* and would also be expected to have a deeply held commitment to continue buying the brand in the future. Consumers in this frame of mind may remain loyal despite repeated performance failures—up to a point.

Loyalty in the face of repeated failures represents an extreme response. The average consumer may require only a few failures before discontinuing use of the brand. The first of the performance failures would be manifest as negative disconfirmation—a shortfall in performance when compared to expectations. Initially there might be *disappointment* and then dissatisfaction. The level of dissatisfaction would act on the prior attitude, revising it downward, and with it, intention to repurchase. Finally, purchasing would cease or would shift to another brand.

A Note on the "Nonprocessing" of Satisfaction

The scenarios in the previous section assume that the consumer harbors certain types of thoughts and feelings in responding to products and services. Could it be that a subset of consumers is so uninvolved in the performance of a particular product that they do not assess performance unless the product becomes dysfunctional and creates harm? Introspection on the reader's part would probably bring specific product categories and experiences to mind. For example, common utilities, including water and natural gas and even the postal service, may fit this situation for many consumers.

Rather than focus on the percentage of consumers who do not evaluate consumption, it would be helpful to understand why (and when) they do not. Specifically, consider the possibility that some consumers do not evaluate consumption outcomes because of their low or passive *involvement* with the product or service. Here, low involvement denotes a disinterest in predecision product knowledge and postdecision consequences, while passive involvement denotes a disinterest in *processing* the consequences; predecision processing may, in fact, have been high. This latter situation of the lack of involvement within passive processing will receive some attention here.[14]

Thus, in various sections of the book and more specifically in Chapter 13, the "behavior" of nonprocessing will be examined. This does not imply that uninvolved consumers will have no satisfaction; rather, their satisfaction (or dissatisfaction) may be latent or passive. For example, satisfaction with the provision of electricity is not normally processed beyond its obvious availability. Power outages are required to get the consumer's attention. This state of nature contains information for the marketer, however, and requires study. As will be discussed, nonprocessing consumers ("I never think about this product") do report levels of satisfaction that can be compared to other consumer segments with greater degrees of product interest.

THE STRUCTURE OF THIS BOOK

To address the issues raised in this introductory chapter, this book has been structured as shown in Figure 1.3. The chapters, portrayed as rectangles of various sizes, are positioned roughly according to the time line (shown as a gray outline arrow) leading up to and following the satisfaction response. The present chapter, which describes the meaning of satisfaction, is located in the second column from the right. As satisfaction is the core concept addressed by this book, all topics to its left are viewed as antecedents, while those to the right are consequences.

Generally, the chapters follow a roughly similar pattern. Each opens with an introductory example or examples. Next, either a historical view of the focal chapter concept is presented or a theoretical framework is outlined. The reader will find that some have been more fully developed since the first edition while others have been out of favor, so to speak. Depending on this developmental evolution, findings from empirical studies of the concept, demonstrating its links to satisfaction, follow, as do studies unique to the consumer domain. Measurement suggestions appear in the later sections of the chapters unless they are necessary for illustrative reasons earlier in the discussion. Managerial implications may appear throughout the chapters as concepts are brought into focus, but are usually reserved for later sections. Lastly, the chapters conclude with speculative suggestions for future work in the content area where appropriate and with links to later chapters in the book. Readers who seek information on specific topics, such as measurement, may wish to skim the early chapter sections and jump instead to issues of greater relevance to their field.

The Essentials of the Satisfaction Response

Part I, which includes Chapters 2, 3, and 4, discusses the immediate causes of satisfaction, first, according to current practice and, second, according to emerging theory and leading-edge practice. Chapter 2 acknowledges the current (and historic) attention paid to physical (tangible) features of products and specific actions of service providers to satisfy consumers. In discussing this traditional approach, the inadequacies of *attribute* performance analysis, particularly as currently practiced, will be noted. These inadequacies highlight the need to develop a greater appreciation of the consumer's thought process. Essentially, product features have no meaning to consumers unless they are interpreted within a mental framework. This chapter also explores the meaning of importance within satisfaction. It makes the infrequently understood point that what is important in purchasing a product is not necessarily what is important in forming judgments of satisfaction or dissatisfaction. Importance as a momentary shortfall and not a requirement is also discussed.

The two remaining chapters of Part I move much beyond a product feature or product development standpoint and discuss the psychological events, as interpretations of physical events, which shape satisfaction responses. Specifically, Chapter 3 provides the background for the expectancy

Figure 1.3 **The Satisfaction Process**

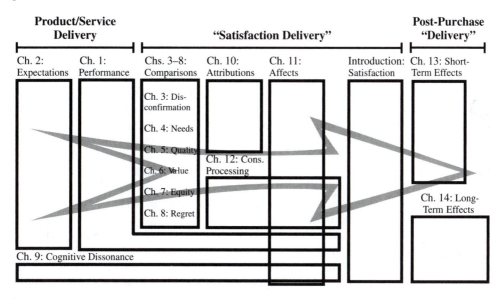

disconfirmation model of satisfaction by establishing the role of expectations or standards by which later performance comparison processes are formed. The case is made that, without a standard of comparison, satisfaction as a consumption response cannot occur. For example, in the case of need fulfillment (elaborated more fully in Chapter 5), the consumer's present experienced deficit is the baseline standard. This chapter on expectations explores not only the various levels of comparison, such as ideal and predicted levels, but also a number of factors that influence these standards. The content of this chapter necessarily precedes that of Chapter 2 (performance) in time, but follows it in the book outline (see Figure 1.3). This is so because the role of pre-existing performance standards in the satisfaction judgment was not acknowledged and operationalized in satisfaction measurement until the study of satisfaction emerged from its performance roots.

Chapter 4, one of the six discussing comparison operations, describes the origins, development, and current status of the expectancy disconfirmation model of consumer satisfaction, now the dominant theoretical paradigm in many satisfaction fields. Expectancy disconfirmation involves a comparison of performance observations to expectations and a subsequent judgment of the degree of discrepancy (disconfirmation). Evidence in support of this paradigm, or variations thereof, is now very compelling, and industry is now making greater use of its principles, particularly in advertising and promotion. The somewhat complex process is discussed in detail and apparent anomalies in its operation are explained. Different types of disconfirmation are presented and their implications suggested. A new addition to this chapter includes a discussion of delight, a (positive) comparison to the latent standard of normalcy. Having surprise as a central component, delight has also been adopted by business as a promotional vehicle.

Chapter 4 completes Part I of the book, but coexists with Chapters 5 through 9 as comparison operations in Figure 1.3. This is necessary to demonstrate the dual role of expectancy operations. At the same time that disconfirmation completes the sequence of "expectation formation → performance → comparison of performance to expectation," it is also one of the other comparison operations that may occur within the satisfaction response. Each of these other comparisons also has standards that exist prior to consumption (e.g., needs, excellence, fairness), but the consumer satisfaction literature has not elaborated on these mechanisms to the same extent that it has on disconfirmation.

Comparison Operators

Part II of the book is devoted to these alternative comparison operations, as illustrated in Figure 1.4. The first of these is expectancy disconfirmation, as noted, and the last is shown as a noncomparison. Known in the literature as "unappraised cognition," this last operation acknowledges the possibility that performance can affect satisfaction directly if no comparison operators are considered.

Beginning with Chapter 5, the oldest of the comparison operations, known in many fields as need fulfillment, is discussed from both a historical and current perspective. Generally, it will be suggested that product and service needs are frequently discovered with the identification of critical attributes emerging from traditional pilot study techniques discussed in Chapter 2. While the possibility of discovering relevant needs through critical attributes analysis is likely, it is not necessarily so. Insights from earlier work in the needs area are highlighted, suggesting that present-day researchers may benefit from a reintroduction to basic need concepts. Generally, higher-order consumer goals, which exist at the pinnacle of many need hierarchies and are sometimes referred to as values (a term subject to multiple interpretations, as Chapter 7 will discuss), are generally overlooked in satisfaction studies, but nonetheless provide a basis for understanding the underlying reasons for all consumption activities. Also discussed in Chapter 5 is the Japanese Kano model, used in quality control strategies and named after its contributor, Noriaki Kano. Because it shows considerable correspondence to the need fulfillment model, it is discussed here rather than in the next chapter on quality.

Chapters 6 and 7 discuss two judgments of a comparative nature, both of which are steeped in the history of consumer response. The first, previously defined as a comparison to engineering standards and now more generally considered as a comparison to the consumer's excellence standards, is the judgment of quality. The definition of quality is undergoing revision, particularly within the services field, where objective "engineering" standards are not easily applied. The present discussion defines quality as a comparison to consumer ideals and explores a number of comparison operations suggested in the literature. The role of quality within the expectancy disconfirmation process is also elaborated. Chapter 7 continues this tradition with a discussion of value, previously thought of as a comparison of benefits to costs. In addition to its meaning within a goal hierarchy (discussed in Chapter 5), value takes on additional import as an experiential consumption outcome based on interpretation along intrinsic/extrinsic and proactive/reactive dimensions. Of necessity, this will require greater levels of analysis including attribution, discussed in Chapter 11.

Equity/inequity and fairness are often discussed but little understood concepts in consumer transactions. Chapter 8 elaborates on consumer inequity and how it differs from job or workplace inequity, where much of the original research was performed. Generally, the notion of a fair exchange or "fair deal" is explored and found to be different from equity explanations in other disciplines. Equity notions such as fairness and "equitable unfairness" are discussed as antecedents of consumer satisfaction and are distinguished from the disconfirmation response. Additionally, the targets of various equity operations are elaborated, including comparisons to the outcomes of other buyers, the outcomes of salespeople, and the outcomes of dealers and firms (e.g., price and profit).

Chapter 9, the last chapter in this section, discusses regret or "buyer's remorse." Regret—the comparison of what is to what might have been—lacked development in the consumer satisfaction literature until recently. Much greater interest has been shown in the consumption area since

Figure 1.4 **The Comparison Operators**

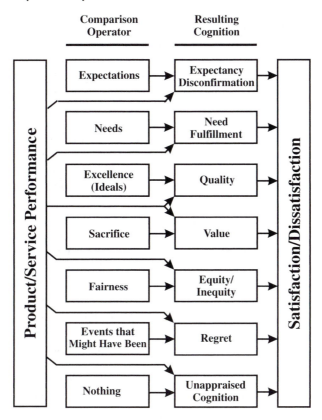

the first edition of this book, and this literature will provide a more developed basis for further applications to consumption. A related concept, referred to as hindsight bias, is also discussed and its implications for consumer satisfaction noted.

Integrative Psychological Processes

Part III, the next major section of the book, describes the manner in which consumers come to translate the antecedent states discussed in Parts I and II into satisfaction judgments. Moving beyond mere description, this section elaborates on the psychological mechanisms, particularly with regard to high-level mental operations, that result in the states causing satisfaction judgments. These processes, although less observable than those discussed previously, are essential to an understanding of the satisfaction process.

Chapter 10 returns to the original notion of cognitive dissonance as a precursor of satisfaction or dissatisfaction. This perspective, one of the earliest topics studied in post-Freudian psychology, provided consumer researchers with early insights into the satisfaction process. It continues to be a currently under researched topic—needlessly so. The concept is just as viable as ever for three reasons. First, dissonance exists as an apprehension in the prepurchase phase of consumption along with other prepurchase cognitions such as expectations. Second, it continues as a force after consumption as it acts both to create tension if not resolved and to reduce tension if resolved. Lastly, it can continue into prolonged consumption experiences (e.g., owning and driving an automobile), as long as future performance is anticipated. This duration of effect is why cognitive dissonance is shown as an elongated influence in Figure 1.3. Of interest is the fact that it can be viewed as an integral process incorporating regret and attribution elements, discussed next.

In Chapter 11, individuals' attribution processes are described whereby consumers select and assign apparent reasons or causes for the outcomes of consumption. Using a commonly accepted attribution framework, the various causes can be described as having dimensions based on the causal entity (e.g., consumer, product, dealer), whether or not the cause is likely to recur (i.e., stability), and whether or not the cause is controllable (by the consumer or others). Although these attribution judgments do not affect satisfaction directly, the attribution process is critical to the entire satisfaction sequence. For example, attribution is triggered by disconfirmation (as in "why did this negative discrepancy between my expectations and performance happen?"), and various attributions (e.g., a manufacturing defect) are known to cause certain emotional responses (e.g., anger). The importance of understanding attribution in satisfaction is stressed and its role in mediating performance assessments is explained.

Chapter 12 describes one of the later and potentially most important developments in satisfaction research, the role of consumer emotion or "affect." The chapter begins by describing the different forms of affect and examines a number of representations of affect in the psychology literature. Here, the concept of cognitive appraisal is introduced to explain how specific emotions occur with some regularity after different outcomes in life are assessed (appraised) for their effect on the individual. Later, the content of this very broad area will be limited to the context of satisfaction judgments in order to determine where satisfaction is located within the affect representations. Recent models of satisfaction that include affect will be discussed in order to estimate what part of satisfaction is affective and what part is cognitive.

The last chapter in this section (Chapter 13) brings everything together into an integrative framework. The central focus of this chapter is on the author's Consumption Processing Model of satisfaction, which explains that satisfaction cannot be assumed to be one thing, but rather involves various modes of "satisfaction responding." That is, consumers may (and do) mean different things when they proclaim that they are "satisfied" within different contexts and situations. Essentially consumers can opt to engage in nonprocessing, whereby they become passive acceptors of consumption outcomes. Beyond this, each successive stage of involvement brings to bear greater processing of the various concepts described in this book until the complete model of consumption processing is accessed. In this "full" model, consumers are described as processing every determinant of satisfaction, including expectations, performance, disconfirmation, equity, attribution, and affect. Of course, few consumers would be expected to do this, and a methodology is described to determine the composition of a firm's customer base in terms of the percentage of those who use disconfirmation, those who use equity, and so on. Unique to this chapter is an appraisal-affect model of satisfaction that suggests direct links between various states of expectancy disconfirmation and the appearance of specific affects.

Figure 1.3 shows an intentional parallel and/or overlap between the processing of consumption, direct performance influences (represented by the extension of the performance rectangle), and future performance apprehensions with the content of the attribution and affect chapters. This is meant to imply that processing states, performance, and apprehensions can have independent effects on satisfaction operating in parallel with attribution and affect, issues that will be discussed later in this book.

Note also, that the sequence of antecedents leading up to satisfaction is labeled with two headings. The expectation and performance categories represent what will be called "product/

service delivery" as this is what the consumer brings to the purchase and observes. In contrast, the remaining categories are referred to as "satisfaction delivery" as these processes determine the satisfaction response within the consumer's mind. Thus, product/service delivery is a physical process while satisfaction delivery is a psychological process.

Consequences of Satisfaction

Lastly, Part IV discusses two sets of satisfaction consequences, those that occur shortly after satisfaction or dissatisfaction is experienced and those that develop over time. Chapter 14 addresses the short-term consequences of both satisfaction (complimenting, positive word of mouth) and, perhaps more important for management, dissatisfaction (complaining, negative word of mouth, third-party action, subterfuge). Work on these topics actually predates many of the writings on the psychology of satisfaction. One goal of this chapter is to show how the prior chapters, particularly those in Part II, can be useful in understanding consumer responses to dissatisfaction. For example, a complaint-handling model based on expectancy disconfirmation principles is introduced. An extended discussion of word of mouth or "buzz" is new to this chapter.

The final chapter discusses satisfaction in the context of longer-term consequences. As opposed to the temporal process driving satisfaction within one consumer's postpurchase decision, discussed in the previous chapter, Chapter 15 elaborates satisfaction changes over multiple purchase decisions. Here, the effects of satisfaction on later satisfaction, on attitude-like structures, and on loyalty are discussed. Although readings on these phenomena are becoming commonplace, data attesting to these influence sequences are not abundant and permit only a limited, albeit reasonable set of conclusions. A loyalty sequence presented in this chapter, culminating with a stage referred to as action loyalty, is augmented by further work integrating the proposed loyalty stages with the presence or absence of a social network or "community" supporting the degree of loyalty held by any one consumer. Early data attesting to this stage-by-support representation are discussed.

Finally, the indirect effect of satisfaction on the firm's profits is discussed, based on recent findings. Previously, researchers could only hypothesize a correspondence between these concepts because available data at the time were inconclusive. After the aforementioned customer satisfaction indexes were examined, however, specific results are now known. The data show wide support for the supposition that satisfaction results in excess profit returns to the firm that excels among and against its competition. These data, however, do not speak directly to loyalty effects. Mention is made of loyalty programs, although their influence is equivocal. This topic, which continues to be less than fully understood, is of extreme importance to management. The answer, as will be suggested, lies in better measurement of "true" consumer loyalty.

GLOSSARY

Affect (primary affect). Generally, a valenced (i.e., positive or negative) feeling of a nonthinking nature, although it may be caused by specific thoughts. This category of affective response, which has been variously described as containing moods, feelings, emotions, and attitudes (the latter involving cognitive thought), presents a major definitional problem to the behavioral community. In consumer behavior, affective response is generally taken to subsume only emotion, and it is this latter a perspective that is taken here. A primary affect in a consumer is a fairly nonspecific positive or negative feeling state most typically represented by labels such as happiness or sadness, pleasure or displeasure, as a result of initial observations of product performance.

Appraisal. An evaluation of the significance or worth of an event to oneself, especially to one's well being.

Attitude. A relatively stable affect-like judgment that a product (or object) has desirable or undesirable properties. The judgment takes the form of a liking or disliking, and is based on many separate evaluations of product features that are combined using various heuristics. Whereas affect can exist as pure feeling, attitudes are thought to result from deliberate processing of product- or service-related information. Although not discussed here in detail, it is possible for attitudes to be conditioned in a noncognitive manner such as when advertising depicts a product in a universally pleasant environment.

Attributes. Product or service features or dimensions, including benefits and drawbacks.

Attribution. An inference about what caused observed events (a causal agent) either as a specific reason (e.g., poor quality construction) or as a dimension (e.g., internal to the consumer versus an external entity such as the manufacturer). If one were to ask "why did this outcome occur?" or "to what do I attribute this outcome?" the answer would represent an attribution.

Brand equity. See **equity**.

Brand loyalty. See **loyalty**.

Cognition. Thought and reason involving the conscious retrieval and processing of information.

Contentment. A placid state of acceptance whereby "more" or "better" is not currently relevant (although it is in the realm of the feasible). It is a low-arousal manifestation of satisfaction, but is not "satisfaction."

Delight. An extreme expression of positive affect resulting from surprisingly good performance. Currently thought to be a stated expression of very high satisfaction, delight is a high-arousal manifestation of satisfaction, but is not "satisfaction."

Disappointment. A mild expression of negative affect resulting from performance below rather high expectations so that the summary judgment is positive, but less so than it would have been had expectations been met. Not to be confused with dissatisfaction, which is a negative summary judgment.

Disconfirmation (expectancy disconfirmation). Technically, the result of a comparison between what was expected and what was observed. In current satisfaction theory, it more commonly refers to the psychological interpretation of an expectation-performance discrepancy. Consumers would describe this concept in terms of the performance of a product or service being better or worse than expected.

Dissatisfaction. The negative satisfaction state, when the consumer's level of fulfillment is unpleasant.

Dissonance (cognitive dissonance). A state of psychological discomfort, tension, or anxiety brought about by uncertainty over the outcomes of a decision; an apprehension. Usually a postchoice and preusage condition, but may exist during consumption of events that are prolonged over a period of time (e.g., a vacation) so that future performance is as yet unknown.

Emotions. Valenced reactions to events, agents, or objects resulting in both somatic and mental changes in disposition, depending on the level of arousal involved. Emotions are more spontaneous and less deliberate than attitudes. Certain basic emotions such as anger and joy are thought to have biological origins, while others require additional cognitive processing, such as when joy attributed to the actions of others results in gratitude. Clusters of emotions with the same polarity are frequently referred to as positive or negative affects (but see the preceding definition of *affect*).

Equity (inequity). As discussed here, fairness. The degree to which the proportionate input-to-outcome ratio of one entity compares to that of another. Equity assumes comparative equality whereas inequity occurs when these ratios are disparate, either in a positive sense (favoring the actor—"preference") or in a negative sense (disadvantaging the actor). Not to be confused with *brand equity*, which is the economic value accruing to a manufacturer from the worth of its marque in accounting or market valuation terms. *Behavioral* brand equity can be represented by perceptions of loyalty, quality, and recognition.

Evaluation (primary evaluation). As used here, an initial judgment of an outcome based on its facilitation or frustration of the consumer's goals, usually in the form of a valenced reaction such as good or bad performance. Not to be confused with satisfaction, which is the summary fulfillment judgment by the consumer.

Expectancy disconfirmation. See **disconfirmation**.

Expectation. A prediction, sometimes stated as a probability or likelihood, of attribute or product performance at a specific performance level. Includes *anticipations*, which may be positive (e.g., hope), and *apprehensions*, which are usually negative (e.g., fear or dread).

Expectation-performance discrepancy. An objective or calculated (usually subtractive) difference between expectation levels and performance levels, sometimes referred to as a *gap*. Not to be confused with the more psychological "better/worse than" disconfirmation concept, although when coupled with emotional tone or labeling, it may precede "true" disconfirmation.

Happiness. A generally positive affective state, less enduring and extreme than *delight*, but more arousing and outwardly visible than mere *contentment*. Recent thinking distinguishes *eudaimonia*, an ongoing state of blissful experience, from hedonic enjoyment resulting from a more specific pleasure state. Both can be considered manifestations of happiness.

Hindsight. A reconstructed mental state of understanding concerning an event after the fact. In psychology, a counterfactual or remembrance not in accord with historical accuracy.

Intention. A stated likelihood to engage in a behavior.

Involvement. A focused orientation toward specific products and services of a more intense nature, consisting of greater prepurchase behavior (e.g., search), greater attention to the act of consumption, and greater processing of consumption outcomes. Low levels of involvement are akin to disinterest.

Loyalty (brand loyalty). A deeply held psychological commitment to repurchase a product or repatronize a service in the future despite obstacles or disincentives to achieve the consumption goal. Not to be confused with repeat purchasing, which may involve constrained or happenstance (e.g., random) repetitive behavior.

Need. A requirement to fulfill a goal. May be innate (e.g., physiological) or learned.

Performance (performance level). The perceived amount of product or service attribute outcome or overall outcome delivered and/or received, usually reported on an objective scale bounded by good and bad levels of performance (e.g., courteous/discourteous service, terrific/terrible product).

Primary affect. See **affect**.

Quality. A judgment of performance excellence; thus, a judgment against a standard of excellence. Although frequently confused with satisfaction, recent theory and evidence suggest the concepts are separate and distinct. Like *attitude*, quality judgments can be made in the absence of consumption behavior.

Regret. A judgment of perceived loss, sometimes referred to as an opportunity cost, due to "what might have been" had the consumer purchased a forgone alternative. *Anticipated* regret is a predecision, probabilistic expectation of the regret outcome, having the capacity to thwart the decision altogether.

Satiation. Technically, the terminal state of full or complete satisfaction. Its opposite, *insatiation*, implies that this state has not been or cannot be attained.

Satisfaction (dissatisfaction). As discussed here, the consumer's fulfillment response, the degree to which the level of fulfillment is pleasant or unpleasant.

Valence. Polarity; the positivity or negativity of a state of nature.

Value. Normally, a judgment comparing what was received (e.g., hedonic or utilitarian performance) to the acquisition costs (e.g., financial, psychological, or physical effort). A frequently used example is a comparison of the quality received to the price of a good or service. Also, as used here, a high (or ultimate) level of achievement in a consumption goal hierarchy; alternatively, any of a number of states of nature constituting the raisons d'être of consumption.

NOTES

1. Anderson and Fornell, "Foundations of the American Customer Satisfaction Index"; Cassel and Eklöf, "Modelling Customer Satisfaction and Loyalty on Aggregate Levels"; Johnson et al., "Evolution and Future of National Customer Satisfaction Index Models"; Johnson, Herrmann, and Gustafsson, "Comparing Customer Satisfaction across Industries and Countries."

2. Di Tella, MacCulloch, and Oswald, "Macroeconomics of Happiness"; Helliwell, "How's Life?"; Lance and Sloan, "Relationships between Overall and Life Facet Satisfaction"; Layard, *Happiness.*

3. Later, the distinction between quality of life or "happiness with life" and satisfaction will be elaborated, particularly in Chapter 5. Brief mention is made in the Glossary to this chapter.

4. Dagger and Sweeney, "Effect of Service Evaluations on Behavioral Intentions and Quality of Life"; Myers and Lacey, "Consumer Satisfaction, Performance and Accountability in the Public Sector"; Younis, "Customers' Expectations of Public Sector Services."

5. These are attributed, respectively, to Hunt, "CS/D: Overview and Future Directions," p. 459; Oliver, "Measurement and Evaluation of Satisfaction Processes in Retail Settings," p. 27; and Tse and Wilton, "Models of Consumer Satisfaction Formation," p. 204.

6. Bolton, "Dynamic Model of the Duration of the Customer's Relationship with a Continuous Service Provider"; Heitman, Lehmann, and Herrmann, "Choice Goal Attainment and Decision and Consumption Satisfaction"; Tse, Nicosia, and Wilton, "Consumer Satisfaction as a Process"; Wright, "Satisfaction with Home Ownership"; Zhang and Fitzsimons, "Choice-Process Satisfaction."

7. Fehr and Russell, "Concept of Emotion Viewed from a Prototype Perspective," p. 464.

8. Oliver, *Satisfaction*, p. 13 (italics in original).

9. This oft-cited quote can be found in Rifkin, *End of Work*, p. 20. However, although Kettering does say that consumers "must accept this reasonable dissatisfaction with what [they] have and buy the new thing, or accept hard times" (p. 79) and other like statements, the phrase as quoted does not appear in his original article, "Keep the Consumer Dissatisfied."

10. See Bitner and Hubbert, "Encounter Satisfaction Versus Overall Satisfaction Versus Quality"; and Jones and Suh, "Transaction-specific Satisfaction and Overall Satisfaction."

11. Abrahams, *101 Mission Statements from Top Companies*; Jones, "Content Analysis of Customer Satisfaction in Annual Reports." Readers may also be interested in Morgan, Anderson, and Mittal, "Understanding Firms' Customer Satisfaction Information Usage."

12. Lance, Mallard, and Michalos, "Tests of the Causal Directions of Global-Life Facet Satisfaction Relationships."

13. Note, however, that attitude is not satisfaction and exists within a separate cognitive schema. Although the attitude literature is referenced in this book from time to time, readers will find it more fully accessed elsewhere. See Eagly and Chaiken, *Psychology of Attitudes*; Oskamp and Schultz, *Attitudes and Opinions*.

14. See Babin, Griffin, and Babin, "Effect of Motivation to Process on Consumers' Satisfaction Reactions."

BIBLIOGRAPHY

Abrahams, Jeffrey. *101 Mission Statements from Top Companies*. Berkeley, CA: Ten Speed Press, 2007.

Anderson, Eugene W. "Cross-Category Variation in Customer Satisfaction and Retention." *Marketing Letters* 5, no. 1 (January 1994): 19–30.

———, and Claes Fornell. "Foundations of the American Customer Satisfaction Index." *Total Quality Management* 11, no. 7 (September 2000): S869–S882.

Babin, Barry J., Mitch Griffin, and Laurie Babin. "The Effect of Motivation to Process on Consumers' Satisfaction Reactions." In *Advances in Consumer Research*, ed. Chris T. Allen and Deborah Roedder John, 21: 406–411. Provo, UT: Association for Consumer Research, 1994.

Bitner, Mary Jo, and Amy R. Hubbert. "Encounter Satisfaction versus Overall Satisfaction versus Quality: The Customer's Voice." In *Service Quality: New Directions in Theory and Practice*, ed. Roland T. Rust, and Richard L. Oliver, 72–94. Thousand Oaks, CA: Sage, 1994.

Bolton, Ruth N. "A Dynamic Model of the Duration of the Customer's Relationship with a Continuous Service Provider: The Role of Satisfaction." *Marketing Science* 17, no. 1 (1998): 45–65.

Cassel, Claes, and Jan A. Eklöf. "Modelling Customer Satisfaction and Loyalty on Aggregate Levels: Experience from the ECSI Pilot Study." *Total Quality Management* 12, nos. 7 & 8 (December 2001): 834–841.

Dagger, Tracey S., and Jillian C. Sweeney. "The Effect of Service Evaluations on Behavioral Intentions and Quality of Life." *Journal of Service Research* 9, no. 1 (August 2006): 3–18.

Di Tella Rafael, Robert J. MacCulloch, and Andrew J. Oswald. "The Macroeconomics of Happiness." *Review of Economics and Statistics* 85, no. 4 (November 2003): 809–827.

Eagly, Alice H., and Shelly Chaiken. *The Psychology of Attitudes*. Fort Worth, TX: Harcourt Brace Jovanovich, 1993.

Fehr, Beverley, and James A. Russell. "Concept of Emotion Viewed from a Prototype Perspective." *Journal of Experimental Psychology: General* 113, no. 3 (September 1984): 464–486.

Gardial, Sarah Fisher, Daniel J. Flint, and Robert B. Woodruff. "Trigger Events: Exploring the Relationships Between Critical Events and Consumers' Evaluations, Standards, Emotions, Values and Behavior." *Journal of Consumer Satisfaction, Dissatisfaction and Complaining Behavior* 9 (1996): 35–51.

Heitman, Mark, Donald R. Lehmann, and Andreas Herrmann. "Choice Goal Attainment and Decision and Consumption Satisfaction." *Journal of Marketing Research* 44, no. 2 (May 2007): 234–250.

Helliwell, John F. "How's Life? Combining Individual and National Variables to Explain Subjective Well-Being." *Economic Modeling* 20, no. 2 (March 2003): 331–360.

Hunt, H. Keith. "CS/D—Overview and Future Research Directions." In *Conceptualization and Measurement of Consumer Satisfaction and Dissatisfaction*, ed. H. Keith Hunt, 455–488. Cambridge, MA: Marketing Science Institute, 1977.

Johnson, Michael D., Anders Gustafsson, Tor Wallin Andreassen, Line Lervik, and Jaesung Cha. "The Evolution and Future of National Customer Satisfaction Index Models." *Journal of Economic Psychology* 22, no. 2 (April 2001): 217–245.

————, Andreas Herrmann, and Anders Gustafsson. "Comparing Customer Satisfaction across Industries and Countries." *Journal of Economic Psychology* 23, no. 6 (December 2002): 749–769.

Jones, Michael A. "A Content Analysis of Customer Satisfaction in Annual Reports." *Journal of Consumer Satisfaction, Dissatisfaction and Complaining Behavior* 19 (2006): 59–75.

————, and Jaebeom Suh. "Transaction-specific Satisfaction and Overall Satisfaction: An Empirical Analysis." *Journal of Services Marketing* 14, no. 2 (2000): 147–159.

Kettering, Charles F. "Keep the Consumer Dissatisfied." *Nation's Business* 17, no. 1 (January 1929): 30–31, 79.

Lance, Charles E., Alison G. Mallard, and Alex C. Michalos. "Tests of the Causal Directions of Global-Life Facet Satisfaction Relationships." *Social Indicators Research* 34, no. 1 (January 1995): 69–92.

————, and Christopher E. Sloan. "Relationships between Overall and Life Facet Satisfaction: A Multitrait-Multimethod (MTMM) Study." *Social Indicators Research* 30, no. 1 (September 1993): 1–15.

Layard, Richard. *Happiness: Lessons from a New Science.* New York: Penguin, 2005.

Morgan, Neil A., Eugene W. Anderson, and Vikas Mittal. "Understanding Firms' Customer Satisfaction Information Usage." *Journal of Marketing* 69, no. 3 (July 2005): 131–151.

Myers, Ronald, and Robert Lacey. "Consumer Satisfaction, Performance and Accountability in the Public Sector." *International Review of Administrative Sciences* 62, no. 3 (September 1996): 331–350.

Oliver, Richard L. "Measurement and Evaluation of Satisfaction Processes in Retail Settings." *Journal of Retailing* 57, no. 3 (Fall 1981): 25–48.

————. *Satisfaction: A Behavioral Perspective on the Consumer.* New York: McGraw-Hill, 1997.

Oskamp, Stuart, and P. Wesley Schultz. *Attitudes and Opinions.* 3rd ed. Mahwah, NJ: Lawrence Erlbaum, 2005.

Rifkin, Jeremy. *The End of Work: The Decline of the Global Labor Force and the Dawn of the Post-Market Era.* New York: G.P. Putnam's Sons, 1995.

Tse, David K., Franco M. Nicosia, and Peter C. Wilton. "Consumer Satisfaction as a Process." Psychology & Marketing 7, no. 3 (Fall 1990): 177–193.

————, and Peter C. Wilton. "Models of Consumer Satisfaction Formation: An Extension." *Journal of Marketing Research* 25, no. 2 (May 1988): 204–212.

Wright, Newell D. "Satisfaction with Home Ownership: An Evolutionary Process." *Journal of Consumer Satisfaction, Dissatisfaction and Complaining Behavior* 9 (1996): 178–189.

Yi, Youjae. "A Critical Review of Consumer Satisfaction." In *Review of Marketing 1990,* ed. Valarie A. Zeithaml, 68–123. Chicago: American Marketing Association, 1990.

Younis, Talib. "Customers' Expectations of Public Sector Services." *Total Quality Management* 8, no. 4 (August 1997): 115–129.

Zhang, Shi, and Gavan J. Fitzsimons. "Choice-Process Satisfaction: The Influence of Attribute Alignability and Option Limitation." *Organizational Behavior and Human Decision Processes* 77, no. 3 (March 1999): 192–214.

PART I

BASIC SATISFACTION MECHANISMS

This section of the book, consisting of three chapters, explains the essential building blocks of the satisfaction response. Although consumers initially process expectations as a starting point for satisfaction judgments, the section begins with a discussion of product and service performance because performance measurement remains the approach most commonly taken in satisfaction surveys.

Chapter 2 begins by discussing performance assessment from a historical perspective, explaining why it is so fully entrenched in satisfaction measurement, and then elaborates on the different forms of performance scales. Some scale formats are judged as more appropriate than others if satisfaction measurement and prediction are the researcher's goal. The argument is then made that performance is an incomplete proxy for satisfaction because it omits consideration of other key elements of the satisfaction response, referred to as "black box" concepts. Without a comparative referent, such as a consumer's expectation set for the product or service, actual performance is arguably a sterile benchmark, at least conceptually. Reasons are given for this conclusion, although an attempt is made to show how a performance-only survey can yield insight if that is all that the researcher is able to measure.

A central argument of this chapter is that performance "importance," although widely measured, may have less information value than many suspect. A number of arguments are given for this assertion. The chapter is especially critical of the use of "importance-performance" analysis whereby satisfaction is inferred without the actual measurement of the satisfaction construct. The technique is not inherently flawed; it is the methodology most used to tease out satisfaction implications that is suspect. With the addition of even the simplest of satisfaction measures, however, a modification of this technique can increase its validity.

In an attempt to more fully elaborate the psychology behind customer satisfaction, Chapter 3 discusses expectations at both the macro and micro levels and how they have come to be known as a key ingredient in the satisfaction response. The definition of expectations, their sources, the measurement of expectations (when and how), and their role in the satisfaction response are given detailed coverage. Additionally, this chapter provides somewhat intricate explanation regarding levels of expectation (e.g., ideal, deserved, predicted) and how one would use multiple standards in practice, as well as the author's expectation framework based on the holding of active/passive, knowable/unknowable, and probability/uncertainty dimensions.

New to the current edition is an elaboration of anticipation and the role of various forms of anticipation (anticipated satisfaction and even anticipation of evaluating satisfaction) in the final satisfaction judgment. It is argued that expectations (of satisfaction) may perform a very important function in preconsumption processing, as affecting postpurchase response, in addition to their traditional role as performance comparators.

The last topic of this section, expectancy disconfirmation, is introduced in Chapter 4. Currently the most popular and robust paradigm for explaining satisfaction, the expectancy disconfirmation model has found application in many satisfaction research domains (e.g., consumer, life, patient, marital). The chapter begins by describing the background of the disconfirmation concept and then explains the necessity for treating it as a conceptually distinct variable apart from expectation and performance. A simple thought experiment illustrates how performance can fail as a satisfaction substitute when two consumers receive identical performance, yet respond to these identical situations in a diametrically opposite manner. An understanding of the role of disconfirmation is shown to fully explain this anomaly. Appropriate measurement of the disconfirmation concept is discussed as are research findings showing representative support for its role in predicting satisfaction later in the chapter.

Chapter 4 also discusses a "gap" model whereby arithmetic differences between expectations and performance are used as proxies for disconfirmation; offers an extended exposition of the role of surprise in the disconfirmation response and how it contributes to form delight, new to this edition; and explains the dual interplay of delight and disconfirmation in satisfaction and re-patronage intention. Different performance-based comparators, including the distinction between benefits and problems, individual dimensions, and information "performance" (e.g., marketing communication effects) versus product performance are introduced as alternatives to the mostly attribute performance-based model.

A central component of this chapter is the operation of the expectancy disconfirmation model illustrated via two examples, one of dominating expectation effects and one of dominating disconfirmation effects. These examples allow the reader to address some common misconceptions in the popular press, including the belief that exceeding expectations will universally guarantee satisfaction. The chapter concludes with discussion of how consumers may selectively use combinations of performance, expectations, and disconfirmation in forming satisfaction judgments, and studies from the literature demonstrating these various combinations are provided.

CHAPTER 2

THE PERFORMANCE OF ATTRIBUTES, FEATURES, AND DIMENSIONS

"Less filling, tastes great," "Melts in your mouth, not in your hands," "Gets the red out," "For virtually spotless dishes," "Tastes as good as it smells," "The most accurate watch in the world," "Keeps babies drier," "Cuts grease quicker," "Locks in freshness," "Nothing protects food better," "Softens your hands while you do the dishes," "Gives you 'sex appeal'," "Personalized service that comes to your home," "Kills bad breath, but doesn't taste mediciney," "Gets your whole wash clean," "Helps stop the greasies," "Kills bugs dead."[1]

The advertising slogans in the preceding paragraph illustrate the marketing fascination with product (or service) performance. This attention to performance is not surprising since consumers do buy products to "do something" (e.g., "kill bugs") and to do it better than the alternatives (e.g., "the most accurate watch"). For this reason, measurement of product performance has dominated satisfaction surveys for some time. In focusing only on performance, however, researchers have assumed a direct link from product attribute performance to satisfaction, a linkage that will be questioned here and elsewhere in this book.

This chapter has a number of related goals: to show different perspectives of measuring performance, to show how current practice has and has not related performance to satisfaction, and to suggest the limitations of a performance-only approach. Later chapters will elaborate on how one might begin to move beyond these limitations.

TRADITIONAL SATISFACTION ANALYSIS

In an all-too-familiar research scenario, much of satisfaction research is conducted according to the following format: A list of key product or service features is generated which, it is hoped, contains an exhaustive set of factors thought to cause satisfaction and dissatisfaction. In a fairly direct manner, consumers are asked to rate the importance of these features and to retrospectively rate the product or service on the degree to which each of the features was delivered.[2] At the same time, the consumer may be asked to rate the product on an overall basis. This overall score, which may or may not be a measure of satisfaction, is used to represent the consumer's mental summary state of experience with the product. It becomes the standard against which the feature ratings are compared. An assumption of this technique is that those features which are most aligned with the overall score across consumers (high feature scores corresponding to satisfaction, low feature scores to dissatisfaction) are those that have the greatest impact on satisfaction.

Despite the ubiquity of this method, a number of problems are inherent in its implementation. First, the list of features cannot be exhaustive for all consumers. Survey length restrictions and the inability to adequately sample the full population of consumers, particularly in the pretest stages of survey construction, are likely to cause the researcher to overlook some critical elements of the purchase that will therefore not be represented in the feature list. These will show up as "noise" in the researcher's analysis, preventing a complete understanding of the causes of satisfaction or dissatisfaction. In part, this problem can be addressed by using the proper level of feature abstraction when the attribute list is prepared (to be discussed). Another problem, also discussed, concerns the relevance of features at different stages of decision-making.

Second, the questioning of feature importance is typically made without qualification, as in "Please rate the following on their importance (to you)." A reasonable question, then, is: Important for what? Often the importance question is qualified in terms of "buying this product." However, if the research goal is an understanding of consumer satisfaction, then importance in product choice is an inappropriate context; rather, the concern should center on importance in delivering satisfaction. This example illustrates the relevancy issue at different stages of decision-making noted in the previous paragraph. Later in this chapter, a number of other issues will be discussed on the matter of importance.

Third, the summary measure collected in the survey is frequently not satisfaction. Rather, it could be a liking or disliking, a judgment of goodness or badness, a quality scale of the poor-fair-good-excellent (pfge—or "fudge") variety, a "will you shop here again?" measure, or any of the "sound-alike" terms discussed in the Introduction (Chapter 1). In the worst-case scenario, no summary measure is used at all; instead, an additive sum of the feature scales is constructed to represent the consumer's overall judgment. The researcher is then put in the tenuous position of using individual equally weighted features to predict their summation. The point here is that if the researcher is interested in predicting satisfaction, then the feature measures should relate to satisfying and dissatisfying properties of products and, as a minimum, an overall satisfaction scale should be included in the survey. If an attitude, quality, or other purchase criterion is of interest, then attitude-specific or quality- or value-specific measures (see Chapters 6 and 7) should be used.

Descriptive Statistics

At the next phase of the typical satisfaction study, an initial analysis of feature performance data may be performed with the calculation of descriptive statistics (e.g., averages, distributions of replies); often the analysis stops at this point. If historical data are available, the new data can be compared to historical averages, and then a determination can be made regarding trends and whether or not the current averages are acceptable to the firm. This latter step is known as benchmarking, a procedure used to not only compare the same critical levels (e.g., satisfaction) over time, but also to different measures or metrics of satisfaction at the same point in time, to compare steps in the satisfaction delivery process against established criteria, and to compare satisfaction levels with those of competitors.[3]

Descriptive data, when not properly analyzed, introduce a fourth problem, if it is assumed that high scores on performance ratings mean that these features are "key" in providing satisfaction. In fact, high scores mean little in the analysis unless they are compared to the overall satisfaction score (and competitors' scores, if available) through a correlation analysis. If the researcher were to plot each respondent's attribute performance rating on the x (horizontal) axis and satisfaction score on the y (vertical) axis of an xy graph, resulting in a configuration of points commonly called a scatterplot, the relationship between performance and satisfaction would be observed (see Figure 2.1). Note that performance, the causal agent, is on the x axis and satisfaction, the effect, is on the y axis. This particular labeling is by convention as researchers are typically concerned with how

Figure 2.1 **A Satisfaction-Performance Scatterplot**

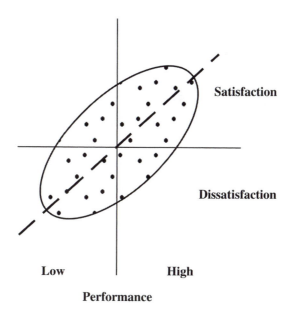

the effect varies with given values of the cause—performance in the present case. When neither variable is "causal," the axis orientation is not important.

The relation in Figure 2.1 can be summarized statistically through calculation of the correlation coefficient, available in most spreadsheet and statistical packages. The strength of this coefficient assesses whether the feature performance scores and the overall measure of satisfaction covary, that is, move in the same direction so that individuals with high (low) feature scores tend to also provide high (low) satisfaction scores. This type of relationship is approximated by the dashed line (also called a regression line) in the scatterplot. At this point, the researcher can assume that the intersection of the midpoint of the performance-based horizontal axis with the regression line breaks the vertical axis into satisfaction and dissatisfaction regions. This, however, is merely a function of the descriptors used for satisfaction and performance scaling in the analysis and is not necessarily accurate. Inspection of the scale midpoints is required to draw conclusions.

Importance-Performance Analysis

Frequently the satisfaction issue is sidestepped through an importance-performance (IP) analysis. In the classic IP analysis, each attribute is rated by the consumer on an importance scale (e.g., not important = 1, very important = 5) and on performance (e.g., poor = 1, excellent = 5).[4] The arithmetic averages or means for each attribute are then calculated over respondents for both importance and performance. This results in an attribute-specific importance mean and an attribute-specific performance mean for every attribute used in the study. Interestingly, neither overall performance nor satisfaction is used! Thus the popularity of this technique may arise from instances where researchers have omitted or were unable to collect an overall measure.

The importance and performance means for each attribute are then plotted on an *xy* graph. Typi-

Figure 2.2 **Importance-Performance Grids Showing Interpretive Regions**
(Attribute Means Not Shown)

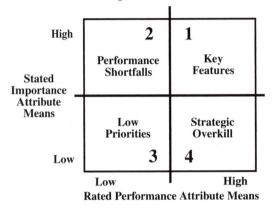

Panel A: Stated Importance vs. Rated Performance

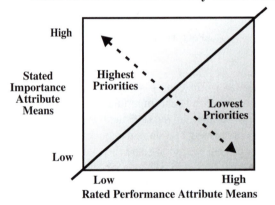

Panel B: Dichotomous Priority-Based Grid

cally, the two axes are split into high and low importance and good and bad performance, resulting in four attribute categories, although more categories can be used if desired (see Figure 2.2, Panel A). Unfortunately, guidelines for these dichotomous splits are murky. Researchers sometimes use the scale midpoints (3 on a 1-to-5 point scale) or the mean or median values of the two variables. Note that Figure 2.2 portrays performance on the *x* axis and importance on the *y* axis. In this case, neither variable is assumed to be causal and positioning is arbitrary.

The four categories of attributes in the four quadrants (cells) are given various names, but essentially result in the following interpretations:

1. *High importance, high performance.* These attributes are assumed to be *key features* (promoting satisfaction); management is advised to continue the current level of emphasis devoted to delivering these features.

2. *High importance, low performance.* These attributes are considered to have critical *performance shortfalls*; management must mobilize efforts to attack these problem areas.

3. *Low importance, low performance.* These are *low-priority* areas that are apparently not a problem.

4. *Low importance, high performance.* Attributes in this cell are identified as areas of *strategic overkill*; management may wish to reallocate resources to other areas in need of improvement.

In yet another interpretation of this same matrix, some have drawn a diagonal from the low-low region to the high-high region so that two areas result, an "upper diagonal" and a "lower diagonal"[5] (see Figure 2.2, Panel B). These areas are shown as separated by a solid 45° line in the figure and represent low priority attribute locations (where performance is high on unimportant attributes) and high priority locations (where performance is low on important attributes).

These various interpretations notwithstanding, however, without knowledge of the relation between performance and satisfaction and the reasons why features are or are not considered important by consumers, there is little more that can be said about the IP technique. It is intuitively attractive, but not empirically defensible. However, a more acute issue with the use of this technique involves the interpretation of importance, both by the consumer and by the researcher.

Earlier, the issue of "important for what?" was introduced. Here, a second, related issue is that there may be a difference between importance as a requirement (it must be there) and importance as a temporary shortfall (It's not there, and I miss it). In the latter case, importance will be short-lived because it will diminish as soon as the feature is restored to its proper level. In the prior case, important required features are frequently "not important" because firms must deliver these features or else the product will not survive in the marketplace. Thus, consumers will expect that all competitive entries will have the feature, and it will lose its importance as a key attribute.

This latter example illustrates an apparent paradox for researchers. Once an attribute becomes "unimportant" as a choice determinant because all competitive offerings possess the attribute to the same degree, it will become even more "important" as a dissatisfaction driver if the purchased brand fails to deliver this feature. For the consumer not only has suffered a loss of utility, but also will feel regret from knowing that all other options would have provided the benefit. This again illustrates the case where importance for choice and importance for satisfaction are not necessarily congruent. More will be said on interpreting importance later in this chapter where the traditional importance-performance analysis will be adjusted so that the problems noted here are mitigated. For now, discussion continues on current methodologies in satisfaction research.

Regression Analysis

Researchers wishing to go beyond the analysis of descriptive statistics typically calculate the statistical impact of the individual feature scores on the overall satisfaction score through regression analysis, also available in major spreadsheet and statistical packages. This analysis reveals which of the features are most highly correlated with the overall scores when the effects of other investigated variables are controlled—that is, whether they make distinct and nonoverlapping contributions to satisfaction. These features, then, are marked as predictors or key drivers of satisfaction or dissatisfaction for the product or service under study. This analysis can be represented by the graphic in Figure 2.3.

Still other variants of this technique exist. Frequently, factor analysis—another commonly available statistical technique—is used to reduce the dimensionality (i.e., number of predictors) of the feature list. Because many of the features will be highly related (e.g., the size and gas mileage of a car, the ambiance and prices in restaurants), regression will single out one

Figure 2.3 **The Common "Performance Causes Satisfaction" Model Showing Correlated Features**

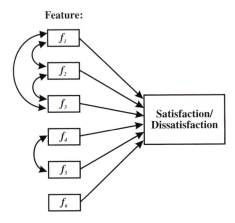

Figure 2.4 **The "Performance *Dimension* Causes Satisfaction" Model**

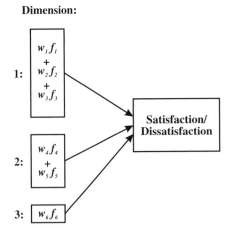

to the exclusion of the other. This is shown in Figure 2.3 through the use of double-headed arrows linking certain features. These features are said to be correlated with each other, or *multicollinear*, and hence are not independent. Multicollinearity in a data set may obscure the contribution of one or more highly correlated predictors and affect the numeric output in strange ways.

In the example in the figure, features 1, 2, and 3 are correlated, as are features 4 and 5. Feature 6 appears as a unique, uncorrelated product attribute. To allow for multicollinearity, the correlated features can be combined into a higher-order factor or dimension, and the dimension score can be used to represent the underlying tie that the correlated features have with one another. The overall satisfaction score can then be regressed on the factor scores to reveal the drivers of customer satisfaction at a more aggregated level. This is shown in Figure 2.4, where the w_i values represent weights determined by the factor analysis.

A Fundamental Shortcoming of Performance Analysis

Aside from the problems noted in the preceding discussion, what is wrong with the fundamental theme underlying the approaches discussed here? The paradoxical answer to this question is everything and nothing. At an operational level, the approach outlined in the preceding discussion is better than conducting no research at all. At the very least, the firm will benefit from insights gained as to the levels and potential causes of satisfaction. To a firm that has never applied satisfaction analysis to its consumer base, some very interesting and revealing results may emerge. And, for the most part, the features that are identified in the analysis will probably be those that should receive attention. Thus, in a sense, traditional analysis is a first step in identifying likely candidates that may have an influence on satisfaction. When one is aided by subjective interpretation of the performance data and corroborating follow-up validation of this interpretation, then, perhaps, nothing may be wrong with this approach—if that is all the firm wishes to do.

Then why, at the same time, is everything wrong with this approach? Quite simply, because feature ratings do not explain why the particular feature is a problem (or a benefit) for the consumer. That is, they do not reveal the psychological intricacies the consumer brings to the firm's product or service. Levels of performance exist only as external stimuli to consumers; the methods described up to this point do not explain how consumers interpret these stimuli.

In short, satisfaction is an internal frame of mind; it is tied only to mental interpretations of performance levels. Fortunately for the numerous firms that conduct surveys in the traditional manner, consumers do bring their psychological interpretations to performance ratings. At the same time, it is impossible to know just what that interpretation is at the level of the individual consumer. For example, if a consumer rates the service in a restaurant as poor, does that rating result because the service was actually good but below expectations (a state that is known as negative disconfirmation—see Chapter 4)? Does it result because service at the next table was more prompt (an inequity judgment—see Chapter 8)? Is it because the consumer wishes to have gone to another restaurant where the service is imagined to be better (regret—see Chapter 9)? Or is it because service was perceived to be objectively bad that evening? The last explanation is probably what the restaurateur will conclude for lack of more useful and incisive data.

Having only the observation that service is a problem, the researcher can speculate about the reasons for the consumer's response. These speculations can be corroborated with anecdotal accounts of service personnel or with ex post facto queries from consumers. However, these may not be the same consumers who participated in the survey. Other errors of consumer recall or obfuscation may enter in the explanations at this point as well.

Thus, the approach used by many firms ignores the psychological processing of performance. In a sense, it provides little insight into the workings of the consumer's mind. These workings are sometimes known as a "black box" because an observer can see only what goes in and what comes out, not what occurs inside. As suggested in the Preface, the overarching goal of this book is to open that box and unravel the mental processing of feature performance. An expanded framework of the direct performance-to-satisfaction interpretation provides the underlying structure for the subsequent chapters.

Picture a black box positioned between performance and satisfaction, to imply that the consumer's psychology mediates the impact of performance observations on satisfaction judgments. Picture, also, a number of antecedent states acting on and within the black box that "prime" the consumer to respond in a particular way. Product or service expectations generated by promotional messages are one likely example, as would be prior experience with the brand. It should be noted that a potential direct effect of performance levels is not ignored. As has been alluded to previously, performance itself can carry psychological overtones. It is also likely, in unique situations, that objective performance is the only satisfying element sought by the consumer; this was referred to as unappraised cognition in the Introduction. Money outcomes, such as stock market gains or gambling winnings, might be an example of this phenomenon.

It may appear that the previous discussion advocates the elimination of performance measurement in satisfaction surveys. This would be hardly advisable, however, as feature performance is one of the inputs to the black box. It follows that performance measurement should not be overlooked in satisfaction surveys if diagnostic information is to be attained and used to improve satisfaction levels. This begs the question of what features to include.

DETERMINING AND MEASURING FEATURE PERFORMANCE

This section discusses features from the perspective of useful techniques to derive feature lists, including the determination of an appropriate level of specificity. In doing so, a number of approaches and variations thereof will be explained. Some readers will be familiar with many of these while others will not. The measurement or scaling of performance is also discussed, and a number of scaling issues are addressed.

It is important to note that the present focus is on techniques and strategies for determining feature lists, and not on particular lists of features. Attempts to find common dimensions of products and services that generalize across large product or service categories have not been universally successful. Unlike the areas of job and life satisfaction, where some progress on finding common facets, particularly among core elements (e.g., pay, health), has been achieved, product and service categories are too diverse and emerge or mutate too rapidly for this strategy to maintain its validity. Even for those areas where some agreement exists, as in the much-used SERVQUAL instrument designed for the measurement of service quality (to be discussed),[6] there seem to always exist "fringe" dimensions unique to a particular industry that are not captured in the core dimensions.

Satisfaction Drivers Versus Choice Criteria

In pursuing the reasons for the consumer's satisfaction response, it should be borne in mind that the researcher's goal is to determine the correct feature list of satisfaction drivers, as opposed to product or service choice criteria. As noted, a common mistake is to assume that the features consumers use in selecting a product from a list of alternatives are identical to the set of features that play into satisfaction and dissatisfaction judgments. Although many of the choice features will also be those used in forming satisfaction judgments, the assumption that the choice feature set and the satisfaction set are identical or even similar has recently been shown to be incorrect.

In an early study attesting to this distinction, consumers were probed as to their thoughts regarding the stages of selecting a product, evaluating its performance, and judging their satisfaction with it.[7] The authors' results showed "important differences" in the criteria used at the prepurchase and postpurchase phases. Specifically, prepurchase thoughts centered on ideal characteristics and specific attributes of the between-brand variety, whereas postpurchase thoughts were more abstract, focusing on the goal outcomes of the purchase. Satisfaction thoughts were similar to evaluation thoughts, as might be expected, but were more oriented to a comparison against standards—a point elaborated at length in later chapters of this book. More recent studies have reasserted these observations.[8]

Figure 2.5 illustrates how features used as choice criteria and those used as satisfaction drivers may interact. Some features, such as f_1, are used by the consumer only in the choice phase

Figure 2.5 **Choice Criteria Versus Satisfaction Drivers**

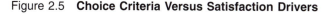
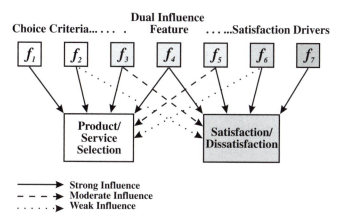

of decision-making. The cost of an airline ticket is an example. A consumer may shop for the lowest fare. Once found, the cost ceases to be a factor in satisfaction with the flight, which may be months away.

Feature f_7 is an example of a pure satisfaction driver. In the case of the airline trip, a rough flight due to turbulence is an example of this situation. The turbulence could not have been predicted previously, and any air flight by any carrier may be randomly subject to this effect.

Features f_2 through f_6 are examples of mixed influence. The feature position and the strength of the arrows—shown as strong, moderate, and weak—determine the degree of influence on choice and/or satisfaction. Some features will be used in choice, but will have only modest effects on satisfaction, while others will have the reverse effect. The air carrier's on-time arrival record might be an example of the former, while the courteousness of the flight staff would conform to the latter. Arrival time accuracy could influence choice heavily, but would only affect satisfaction through the peace of mind the traveler would have during the flight, particularly if a connection were involved. Courtesy would surely affect satisfaction, but only a general impression of the courtesy of the carrier's flight staff would affect choice. The actual courtesy experienced cannot be known until the flight begins.

Finally, f_4 is shown as a dual-influence feature affecting both choice and satisfaction to the same degree. The type of aircraft and its seat layout are an example of this phenomenon. Plane designs are known for their cramped seating, which both deters choice and frustrates travelers in flight.

An illustration of these various influences appears in a study investigating commercial vendor selection and vendor switching in the purchase of high-end workstations.[9] Here, vendor selection represents the choice phase while vendor switching is used as a proxy for dissatisfaction. The same set of predictor variables was used to predict both dependent variables. The significant findings are shown in Table 2.1. Other early data from a study of ad agency clients are similarly convincing.[10] When the respondents were asked why they chose and why they switched agencies, both sets of answers pointed to an agency's creativity as the critical dimension. In a follow-up one year later to identify clients who switched during the year, the two prominent reasons given for changing agencies were media buying skills and lack of attention to the client's account. Clients that switched actually expressed greater satisfaction with the prior agency's creativity than those clients who retained their original agency! In addition to supporting the premise that reasons for choice (i.e., creativity in the present context) differ from causes of dissatisfaction leading to switching, these

Table 2.1

Choice Versus Satisfaction Influences: High-End Workstation Purchasing

| Predictor | Size of influence | | Nature of influence |
	Choice	Satisfaction	
Equipment compatibility	Large	Zero	Pure choice criterion
Decision importance	Large	Not significant	Mostly a pure choice criterion
Vendor switching costs	Large	Moderate	Mixed effect, greater on choice
Pace of technological change	Moderate	Moderate	Dual influence
Buying process formalization	Small	Large	Mixed effect, greater on satis-faction
Centralized buying authority	Not significant	Large	Mostly a pure satisfaction driver
Prior buying experience	Zero	Large	Pure satisfaction driver

Source: Heide and Weiss, "Vendor Consideration and Switching Behaviors for Buyers in High-Technology Markets."

findings also show that anecdotal accounts of reasons for switching are frequently misleading.

Still another reason why satisfaction drivers may be different from choice determinants is that researchers and consumers often cannot foresee all possible problems (and sometimes benefits) that may arise in consumption. This is so because there is a diversity of consumption settings and product use, because technological advances are designed into products that are well beyond the ability of consumers to understand, because certain problems are sufficiently rare as to be undocumented, because the manufacturer has not been forthcoming about potential hazards, or because the delivery of a service is entirely controlled by a provider whose own behavior is subject to whim and unpredictability. The frequent expression "Never in my wildest dreams did I expect this to happen!" is testimony to this problem.

A number of deeper psychological factors predispose consumers to focus or increase the salience of predecision versus postdecision attributes. Here salience is used interchangeably with importance as discussion focuses on the presence or absence of a factor and not on its degree of influence. It has been shown that the mere suggestion of a factor to a respondent can cause focused attention. For example, simply asking respondents to elaborate their experience when purchasing versus using can direct thought.[11] Similarly, because predecision processing is based on assumed benefits or "capability," a different set of factors can be expected to be salient than when "usability" is primed in the consumer's mind. Within usage, it can be shown that the relevant satisfaction factors can change both within a consumption episode and over a consumer's relationship with a firm. And, in an electronic commerce example, where "consumption" consists of both website navigation and purchase culmination (check-out), wide differences have been found over salient attributes.[12]

Thus, for all the preceding reasons, researchers are advised to determine satisfiers and dissatisfiers independently of choice determinants. Additionally, the prior discussion illustrates why it is critical that a satisfaction measure, and not one of attitude or quality, be used to determine the features that relate to choice criteria and those that relate to satisfaction. Both attitude and quality judgments are used in choice and thus may give a distorted picture of the features most strongly related to satisfaction.

Levels of Feature Abstraction

An additional concern early in the satisfaction measurement process is determination of how specific the feature list should be. This issue addresses whether the list is to contain detailed micro dimensions of a product or micro behaviors of a service provider, or if it is to contain more general macro dimensions of higher abstraction. An example may be helpful at this point.

Micro Dimensions

Suppose a consumer takes his or her car in for an oil change or repair and finds the shop area dirty, greasy, and strewn with tools and discarded parts. Moreover, service personnel uniforms are soiled and not standardized so that some repairers wear jackets, others wear shirts, and still others wear jeans instead of slacks. To make matters worse, the customer waiting room is cold, cramped, and stocked with months-old, tattered magazines, and the vending machines are either inoperable or out of stock. This sorry situation can be summarized exactly as described, and consumers can be asked to rate all dimensions of the cleanliness of the repair area, the neatness of the person-nel, and the comfort of the waiting room. In fact, waiting room comfort can be analyzed in still greater detail on the basis of the temperature of the room, the comfort of the chairs, the variety and condition of the magazines, and so forth.

This example illustrates the point that situations can be presented to the respondent in minute detail for rating. However, an obvious drawback to the micro-dimension approach is that the list of features presented to consumers becomes overly long, although it will contain maximum di-agnostic value—value deriving from the fact that specific details of a dissatisfying situation will be singled out for study.

Macro Dimensions

In an alternative approach operating at a higher level of abstraction, the researcher can simply have consumers rate the repair area, the service personnel, and the waiting room on scales bounded by clean/dirty, neat/messy, or pleasant/unpleasant. Note, however, that this simple list of the three main features of the repair experience does not provide details about the repair area, personnel, or waiting room that generate the consumer responses. At an even higher level of abstraction, the researcher can ask consumers to rate the "facilities" on a poor-fair-good-excellent "fudge" scale. At this point, however, virtually no diagnostic information content is available to the researcher except that something about the repair facilities is problematic to the consumer. This leaves the researcher with no real actionable conclusions.

The answer to the question "What is the appropriate level of abstraction?" lies in two areas. The first area relates to the progress made in determining key features—that is, whether the re-searcher is still in the early exploratory phases of discovery or whether the analyses are closer to pinpointing critical problem dimensions. Greater specificity should be more appropriate at the exploratory study phases. Later, techniques such as factor analysis can be used to reduce the fea-ture dimensionality and increase the level of abstraction as needed. In a still broader, but related context, the level of analysis within the product category may be of relevance. Research shows that generic product evaluation generally results in (and requires) more abstract dimensions while brand differences require greater specificity, since competing brands already have many dimen-sions in common.[13]

The second area reflects a more practical concern. Greater specificity requires longer lists of features. If issues of questionnaire length, respondent apathy or fatigue, and inadequate incentives are in play, then shorter, more abstract feature lists are required. The lack of diagnosticity will have to be compensated for in other ways, such as open-ended sections of the survey.

Factor analysis is the preferred method of reducing the dimensionality (increasing the level of abstraction) of attribute lists. As noted, factor analysis searches for highly correlated responses, indicating that consumers see certain features in similar light, and creates weighted composites of the variables generating the similarities of response. In the car repair example, it was assumed that the composites or dimensions were based on entities (the repair area, personnel, and waiting area). This would suggest that all dimensions of the entity (e.g., the temperature, chair comfort, and magazine variety of the waiting room) were equally neglected. It could also happen that a common theme existed across all entities. For example, all could be described as dirty or messy. In this latter case, dimensions of cleanliness or neatness would appear as opposed to dimensions representing specific entities.[14]

What Features?

Three general approaches to feature list determination are discussed here. The first relies on broad-based general principles that are thought to be true by virtue of the fact that they are universally accepted and difficult to refute. The second uses generally accepted feature lists, usually at a fairly high level of abstraction; and the third is consumer-driven and may be constructed at any level, or at mixed levels of abstraction. Not recommended are approaches based on "intuition," executive or otherwise. In a recent example of this latter failing, GTE Directories reported that its management believed "quality" to the advertising client meant no smeared ink and hard-to-rip directory pages.[15] Millions of dollars were spent on printing refinements to achieve these goals. Later, research showed that all that clients wanted were value, good business relations, and great customer service; the quality of the directories was not considered "important."

Feature Categories Based on General Principles

Perhaps one of the earliest conceptualizations in marketing, that of the total product as a unitary, invariant concept, has been challenged via the so-called rings model.[16] This model traces the evolution of a product or service using ripples of growth similar to the growth rings of a tree. Typically, the ripples are concentric, drawn in the manner of a bull's-eye target. A similar conceptualization is shown in Figure 2.6. For reasons to be explained, the rings are deliberately drawn off-center in the manner of a fried egg. The innermost ring defines the generic product—an undifferentiated, bare-bones, commodity-like market offering. Beyond this first ring is the expected product, which encompasses consumer expectations for delivery (provision) of the product to the consumer. To illustrate, if ordinary gasoline were used as an example of a generic product, then consumer-friendly, hand-operated pumps would be, at a minimum, the expected product.

Surrounding the expected product is the augmented product, consisting of embellishments to the consumer's expectation set. Clean restrooms, a weather-protected pumping area, and an on-site mini-market with concessions would be additions within this latter product extension. Finally, there exists the potential product, or what is feasible to attract and hold customers. Something on the order of an Acme Gasoline Buyers Club, similar to a frequent-flyer club, might be an example of this latter extension. Whereas most competitors find equilibrium at the level of the augmented product, those that will succeed in the future will be among the first to define the potential product for consumers.

Figure 2.6   **The "Rings" Model of Product and Service Attributes**

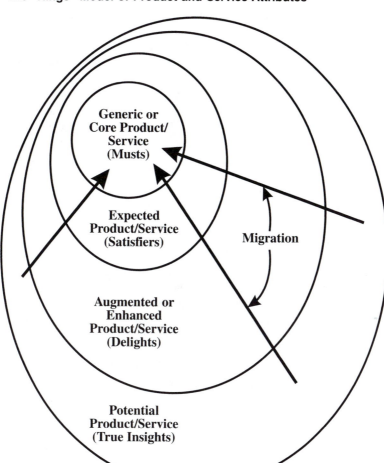

Based on the product analogy, a rings conceptual model for services is also evident. Like the innermost ring for the core product, a generic core for the basic service anchors the growth curves. In service provision, the second ring is service support, while the outermost ring is reserved for enhanced service. Because services most often provide extended interactions with a provider, an outside ring has been proposed as consisting of a relationship of trust or affinity with the agent.[17] In the securities brokerage industry, for example, the basic service might be the buy/sell trade execution, service support would be information and accurate accounting including monthly statements, while enhanced service could include checking accounts, retirement planning, and personalized tax planning. The investor's personal relation with the account manager would correspond to the affinity aspect of this particular service.

Observers of the various ring frameworks have noted, however, that although the ring labels do not change, the feature (attribute) content of each does over time. Some have called the respective rings in the three-ring model *musts*, *satisfiers*, and *delights*, implying that provision of the basic service (first ring) only serves to preclude dissatisfaction. The content of the second ring, if delivered, guarantees satisfaction, while elements of the third ring go beyond satisfaction to delight. This is consistent with the psychological mechanism of need fulfillment, discussed in Chapter 5, whereby satisfied needs serve to redirect focus to other, usually higher-order pursuits. Unexpected deficits in previously satisfied needs have the opposite effect of causing regression to the lower-level, newly activated need.[18] The current reactivated cycle of gasoline shortage is a case in point as consumer focus has shifted (once again) to fuel-efficient small cars with corresponding sacrifices in size, power, and other creature comforts generally.

In another influence, competitive actions often cause the content of the outer rings to migrate to the center over time, as all competitors eventually mimic the provision of delights, thereby raising consumer expectations for what the basic service should constitute. This motivates innovators to draw on their understanding of a potential product or service, offering it as a new enhancement and thereby demonstrating true insight, the label of the fourth ring in the figure. This competitive phenomenon has deep roots in human behavior where it has been known for some time that similarity is effective indistinguishability, causing focus to redirect to innovative differences.[19] It cannot be expected, however, that all competitive enhancements will migrate at the same rate; migration is shown by different-length arrows in Figure 2.6, explaining the elliptical ring shapes. Firms should understand the timing and degree to which their enhancements will be mimicked in order to prepare for introduction of the potential product.

Still another very abstract scheme is based on the motivation hierarchy of Abraham Maslow.[20] As covered in greater detail in Chapter 5, Maslow proposed five stages of human development that are approached hierarchically, as described previously. In order of priority, these are physiological (e.g., food, water), security or freedom from physical and psychological threat, affiliation (e.g., love, belongingness), self-esteem, and self-actualization (self-fulfillment).

Some have likened product or service purchasing to fulfillment of specific levels of this hierarchy. For example, the ownership and display of an expensive car may signify to others "I've made it, and I want others to know it," thereby fulfilling all goals embedded in the hierarchy. Historically, this scheme has been aligned with job satisfaction and has not been widely adopted in the study of consumer behavior. Apparent applications of the Maslow hierarchy are found from time to time in advertising (e.g., "Because you love someone"), but it has not been shown that this framework is capable of generating an exhaustive set of satisfaction drivers or even choice criteria.

One problem with frameworks based on general principles is that they do not, a priori, define the content of the rings or of specific motives. Researchers must determine what these are in individual product or service contexts. The next section discusses two frameworks that provide feature content irrespective of context.

Standard Categories and Lists

As suggested, approaches based on standard feature categories are successful only at a fairly high level of abstraction because consumers view attributes at lower levels of abstraction idiosyncratically. For example, reliable mail service may mean delivery at the same time every day; reliable trash pickup may mean that the trash is picked up on a given day at any time; and a reliable recycling center is one that is open when convenient for the customer. All three may be evaluated on a scale labeled only as "reliable/unreliable service." However, the phrases "prenoon delivery," "no missed pickups," and "open when convenient" would not generalize across the three contexts. Unfortunately, the more abstract phrase "reliable service" does not specify what exactly is reliable or unreliable about the service across different consumer interpretations.

Of the generally accepted higher-order categorizations, one very useful classification scheme is that of utilitarian versus hedonic product outcomes. In this scheme, utilitarian features (also referred to as instrumental features) are those that provide the basic functions that the product is required to deliver. Examples are the passenger compartment size and gas mileage of an automobile. Hedonic features or outcomes, in contrast, are those that provide intangible pleasures such as styling and the admiration of others. Online, consumers might consider the utilitarian values of price savings and the hedonic values of entertainment. And, in the context of "bricks" shopping, it has been found that the hedonistic "joy" of shopping often competes with the utilitarian "tedium" of this activity.[21] As the reader may have noted, there are obvious parallels to the basic or core product and enhanced product levels in the ring frameworks. Overlaps such as these between feature conceptualizations are not uncommon.

While the utilitarian/hedonic breakdown is helpful, particularly in reminding researchers that there are two sides to consumption and that the feature list should contain elements of both, this framework remains in very general form. Although it seems to provide for an unambiguous categorization of product attributes, some features, such as the comfort and the sound system in a car, are both utilitarian and hedonic. Moreover, the relation of either category to satisfaction and dissatisfaction is not well specified.

A good operational example of the standardized frameworks is SERVQUAL in the context of service delivery.[22] Discussion of this instrument is of value because it is a reasonable illustration of the programmatic development of a universal list of service dimensions. Additionally, it shares some correspondence with satisfaction measurement, which will be discussed in later chapters. The impetus behind the SERVQUAL instrument was to determine common dimensions of service delivery as opposed to product usage. Beginning with focus group interviews of consumers' experiences with four service sectors (retail banking, credit cards, securities brokerage, and product repair and maintenance), its authors discovered ten general dimensions that they labeled tangibles, reliability, responsiveness, competence, courtesy, credibility, security, access, communication, and understanding. Without further analysis, these ten aspects might be viewed as singular, yet potentially correlated dimensions of service performance as depicted in Figure 2.3. Later investigation showed that, in fact, some of the ten were correlated; refinements were made until the instrument was composed of five higher-order dimensions that subsumed the previous ten. This dimensionality of the SERVQUAL instrument is shown in Figure 2.7. Note that the instrument is designed to predict service quality, not satisfaction. This issue awaits further discussion in Chapter 6.

SERVQUAL's authors acknowledge that the five summary service dimensions are general dimensions relating to a large component of services but that specific criteria within each dimension may vary. By this, they mean that the micro determinants of what defines courtesy, for example, will be different for different service environments. In a fine-dining experience, courtesy includes respect and pleasantness; however, a courteous trash collector might only have to put the lid back on the container. Moreover, for services without much human involvement (a cash or vending machine), courtesy is not so relevant a dimension although visual or voice commands and "thank you" messages are quite common.

The universal nature of the SERVQUAL dimensions has been tested in a number of studies and the number has grown since the first edition of this book.[23] As before, all report the necessity of amending the instrument prior to its final administration so that both superfluous and omitted critical dimensions are identified. Some studies find that the SERVQUAL dimensions overlap, others find that the dimensions split into subdimensions, while still others find that additional dimensions of a product- or service-specific nature are needed to more fully account for quality or satisfaction responses. It is also the case that other scales, tested in tandem, can be used to augment or supplant the service quality instrument.[24]

Figure 2.7 **The Dimensionality of the SERVQUAL Instrument**

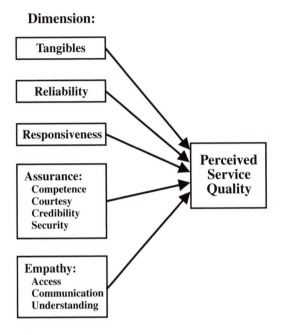

Consumer-Generated Lists

Arguably, the most common technique used to determine key performance dimensions is the focus group. Focus groups are unstructured or semistructured gatherings of six to ten individuals who discuss a product or service topic in the presence of a moderator. Usually, these sessions are repeated with different consumers until the information obtained becomes redundant. The participants' comments are summarized, coded, and interpreted by the researcher and then are used to define the key performance dimensions of the product or service. This technique is largely qualitative, but useful. The main caution regarding its use is that conclusions must be viewed as tentative until later validation is attempted. Nonetheless, in cases where little other basis for discovering performance dimensions is available, this approach is recommended.

Two very helpful structured approaches may be used to assist the researcher in identifying key satisfaction determinants from consumer responses. The first approach was actually designed to understand how consumers process information in buying and using, rather than to discover how consumers form satisfaction and dissatisfaction judgments. This method is easily modified to reveal satisfiers and dissatisfiers, however. The second approach directly targets satisfying and dissatisfying purchase factors.

Laddering

This technique, also known as means-end chain analysis or hierarchical value analysis, is a probe-driven method of determining the hierarchy of benefits (and some drawbacks) that consumers see in products and services, as well as the level of abstraction used by consumers in this process.[25] The benefits are seen as ranging from the concrete, tangible attributes of the product or service

Figure 2.8   **A Means-End Hierarchy for Fruit Juice**

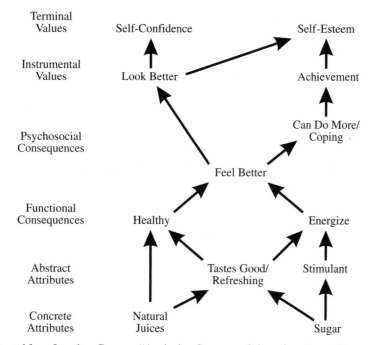

Source: Adapted from Jonathan Gutman, "Analyzing Consumer Orientations Toward Beverages Through Means-End Chain Analysis," *Psychology and Marketing,* 1 (Fall/Winter 1984): 34, by permission of John Wiley & Sons.

up through the values individuals pursue (e.g., a sense of achievement). The manner in which consumers make linkages between attributes and other reasons for purchasing, including values, is elicited through direct questioning of the "Why is that?" or "Why is that important to you?" or "What does that mean to you?" variety. Consumers are asked what they see in products and then are asked to explain the significance of the benefit or problem that they have just named. They may also be asked to describe what the *lack* of an attribute means to them.

In the classic description of this hierarchy of benefits, consumers are believed to link three levels of product knowledge with three levels of self-knowledge in the following manner (coffee is used here as an example): Coffee contains natural caffeine (a concrete attribute), which is known to be a stimulant (an abstract attribute). Stimulants, in turn, are known to prevent drowsiness (a functional consequence). Prevention of drowsiness will allow the consumer to remain energized and alert (a psychosocial consequence). Being alert allows the consumer to perform daily activities more accurately and rapidly (an instrumental value), which enables the accomplishment of more goals in life (an end or terminal value). This sequence of events is the ladder or means-end chain that this hypothetical consumer uses to justify the consumption of coffee. To provide another example, a graphical representation of a means-end hierarchy for fruit juice is shown in Figure 2.8.

Variations of this technique have been proposed that substantially broaden its versatility. For example, given foreign language equivalency, cultural differences in "value logic" can be determined. Moreover, it can be shown that diagnoses of involvement effects reveal greater linkages for more highly involved consumers and, also, that more abstract interpretations are found for more affectively oriented products and respondents.[26]

Although designed for understanding purchase motivation, the technique is easily adapted to the consumer's reasons for postpurchase satisfaction or dissatisfaction. Instead of consumers being asked questions about the benefit of a product, which they could answer vicariously in the absence of experience, consumers could be asked what satisfactions or dissatisfactions they derived from its use. In a manner similar to the standard technique, the consumer would be probed with "Why?" queries until a hierarchy of satisfactions emerged. The purchase decision phase of usage relates to extended purchase scenarios where the acquisition of a consumable is secondary to its lifetime provision of consumer experience. Individuals do not buy power hand tools to "own" (although some do for bragging rights). Rather the satisfaction derives from the ability of the tool to build and construct, solve problems, save time and money, and provide emergency relief, among other functions, many of which are unanticipated. In fact, many sporting paraphernalia provide only the means and not the ends to the excitement of participation.[27]

Would the results of this variation in technique yield materially different results? Perhaps or perhaps not, depending on the consumer's level of experience with the product. After all, satisfactions are benefits. What laddering possibly avoids are the standard answers that consumers are known to give, based on knowledge common to all individuals. Moreover, as noted earlier, the reasons for satisfaction and dissatisfaction are not necessarily those for considering or selecting a product. This satisfaction-driven variation may also elicit the unanticipated, surprising consumption outcomes that consumers would not have considered in the purchase of that same product. In fact, the technique is so sufficiently versatile that it has been applied in such diverse contexts as ethics in selling and political campaign issues.[28]

Critical Incidents

In a more direct technique, the method of critical incidents, including those of an affective nature, has been applied to satisfaction with a fair amount of success.[29] In this approach, consumers who have experienced the product or service are asked to describe a particularly satisfying or particularly dissatisfying encounter and to explain why they feel as they do about this experience. Via this elegantly simple technique, the responses can be categorized into characteristics of the product, its delivery, the personnel, or even external entities such as advertising claims or the experiences of other purchasers. More importantly, the impact of these events on catastrophic behaviors, such as abrupt termination of a service contract, or, conversely, "customer for life" epiphanies can be diagnosed. Of interest is the fact that the researcher can ensure that satisfying elements as well as dissatisfying elements will be elicited.

Other time-tested elicitation methods are also available to the researcher, such as projective techniques whereby consumers respond to ambiguous but product-related stimuli without understanding fully the nature of the task.[30] These procedures, however, do not specifically target the satisfaction response, and their ability to do so remains unknown.

Scaling Performance

Because perceived performance is measured ex post facto in satisfaction surveys, the questions are typically worded in the past tense. Other, more pressing measurement issues also require attention.[31] These are the polarity of the performance items, the related issue of "ideal" performance, and whether one wishes to also include the valence (positivity or negativity) of the performance rating. Further, one could address the number of scale points and secondarily a preference for whether the number should be odd or even.

Polarity

All performance dimensions have some ability to underperform or to negatively perform. Take the case of a denture whitener, and assume that "whitens teeth" is the basic performance dimension. (It is recognized, of course, that other attributes, such as stain removal, grittiness, and taste may be equally important and, in fact, may be correlated in consumers' minds with whitening.) Consider the following scales:

1. Partially whitened _____Completely whitened
2. No whitening effect_____Completely whitened
3. Yellowed_____Whitened

In practice, researchers put numbers under the horizontal lines or boxes between the endpoints. These endpoints are referred to as poles, and the issue here is whether the negative pole should be truly negative or something less than that.

Scale 1 assumes that the worst the whitener can do is to only partially brighten teeth. In other words, in the worst-case scenario, using the dentifrice would have some minimal effect on whiteness. Scale 2 presumes that the dentifrice may be perceived as having no effect, that the consumer's teeth are no better off than before. In contrast, scale 3 assumes that some consumers might actually believe that a dentifrice on the market would actually leave teeth less white or more off-white than they were originally.

Which scale assumption should be followed? The best answer is that the scale should encompass the experience of the consumers responding to the survey. If consumers are queried after a professional treatment in a dentist's office, then scale 1 might be best. If consumers are surveyed after using over-the-counter preparations sold in tooth care aisles in stores, then 2 may be more appropriate. However, if one is sampling consumers with the potential for poor hygiene habits, then it does not matter what dentifrice is used and scale 3 may be necessary.

Handling the Case of an Ideal Point

Often, the desired performance level exists at some level less than maximum performance. The carbonation level of a soft drink is an often-cited example. Consider, again, alternative scales:

1. Not carbonated _____ xxxXxx _____Highly carbonated
2. Not carbonated_____Ideally carbonated

In scale 1, the "positive" pole has been labeled as the extreme or maximum level of performance (as in as much carbonation as the liquid can contain). The capital X marks an individual consumer's preferred level of carbonation, at least subjectively, while the lowercase x's represent the range of other consumers' preferred ideals. Scale 1 has little value if the range of the x's is not known to the researcher. In fact, a high maximum score on this scale may be interpreted as maximum performance when, in fact, it represents a level of carbonation that is excessive to most consumers. Scale 2 overcomes this problem if the researcher wishes high scores to represent maximum performance as viewed by the consumer but unfortunately does not inform the researcher as to what the "ideal" level of carbonation is, particularly at the market level. Experimentation is necessary to further explore this phenomenon.

Valence

Note that no mention has been made of how good (or bad) denture whitening is to the consumer. In many cases, the feature itself connotes a goodness or badness, "pearly white" connoting a desired feature level and, for example, "yellowed" connoting an undesired level. For this reason, most surveys do not separately measure the valence of performance. However, there are many other situations in which a valence must also be measured. The carbonation example illustrates one such case. If a consumer finds carbonation undesirable, then the only favorable rating for this consumer is the not-carbonated pole on the scale. The researcher, however, may interpret this as a negative response. Thus the consumer must also be asked if the degree of carbonation is good or bad or likable or not, as shown in the following two scales:

This level of carbonation is:

Bad _____Good
Undesirable_____Desirable

The separate measurement of valence can be avoided if the researcher is able to include valence in the feature description. Consider the two scales that follow:

Low gas mileage_____ High gas mileage
Poor gas mileage_____ Good gas mileage

Although these two alternatives appear almost identical and in practice may yield equivalent results, there is a subtle distinction between them. In the first, the researcher is not able to determine if high gas mileage is believed to be desirable to the respondent. Few would question that it is, of course, but the example makes the point.

The Number of Scale Points

For predictive purposes, a minimum of 3 scale points is recommended. As the number of points becomes large, exceeding 10, problems of interpretation are introduced.[32] The reason is that individual consumers tend to use subintervals of very long scales, such as restricting responses to an interval of 5 points on a 10-point scale. Thus, one respondent's rating of 7 may be another's 9 for the same perceived performance level. In effect, these consumers are interpreting the scale's meaning in a manner not known to the researcher. An exception is the "chances in 10" scale. When percentages have clear meaning in a particular context, the resulting 11-point scale (0 percent to 100 percent in 10 percent increments) is admissible. This permits interpretation of "50–50" as representing a true midpoint, one easily understood by respondents.

As a practical matter, three-point scales should be reserved for situations, such as telephone interviewing, when the respondent would be expected to encounter difficulty visualizing many descriptors or even the scale itself. Because much satisfaction-related data is behaviorally oriented and not subject to strict numeric interpretation, 5- and 7-point scales have become somewhat standardized in the field. Web surveys often restrict the response range to one or the other of these two possibilities. By tradition, the "strongly agree/strongly disagree" scales (Likert scaling) are typically 5 points in length with a "neither" category in the center. Seven-point scales are more versatile descriptively, however. In the end, the researcher must make a judgment call for any and all measure lengths in the survey.

Odd or Even Number of Items: The Issue of a Midpoint

Debate exists over whether there should be an even or odd number of items in a scale. Consider the following two alternatives:

1.	Bad	1	2	3	4	5	6		Good
2.	Bad	1	2	3	4	5	6	7	Good

In scale 1, there is no midpoint, and respondents who believe that the feature is neither bad nor good are forced to commit themselves to answering with a 3 or with a 4, the first suggesting modestly negative feelings and the second, modestly positive. In scale 2, these consumers can comfortably respond with a 4. Opponents of the second scale argue that there is no information in fence-sitting and that few, if any consumers are really neutral toward features and products. This author disagrees. The degree of neutrality is information, and the percentage of respondents who feel this way may provide the researcher with additional insight. For these and perhaps other reasons, most researchers use 5 to 7 points. Because consumers tend to rate consumables positively, most ratings are skewed, with the bulk of responses in the positive half of the scale. This tendency is more pronounced for scales with a smaller number of points (say, 3 and 4). Further discussion of scores follows shortly.

Given the potential additional insight provided by neutral midpoints, what explains the popularity of even-numbered scales? A seemingly cynical answer relies on the positivity bias noted in the preceding paragraph. Fence-sitters will be more likely to move to the positive side of the scale than to the negative, thereby elevating the percentage of positive responses. There are perhaps occasions when a neutral position is not meaningful, however, and even-numbered scales can be used. These involve dimensions that are unipolar—that is, they have no negative pole. Likelihood scales are a good example, as negative likelihoods are not possible. Thus, the following scale, used when the researcher wishes to know if consumers believe that a product is likely to have a given attribute, has met with little resistance:

Unlikely	1	2	3	4	5	6	Likely

Despite this apparent correctness, what rating do consumers give if they believe that the odds are even (for example, 50–50)?

A "Good" Satisfaction Score?

The ratings positivity bias alluded to previously is not unique to satisfaction distributions, occurring in many behavioral score distributions, perhaps due to a yea-saying response style or a sense of generally positive well-being.[33] Product and/or service satisfaction, however, is particularly susceptible to this bias because most consumables that make it to market under current regulatory and competitive forces are, in fact, well designed, engineered, and tested. Even services, where the human element is much less controllable, suffer from positivity because individuals are likely to give others the benefit of the doubt or harbor a "that could be me" mind-set or assign an external attribution (see Chapter 11) to the failings of others. For all these reasons, the positivity bias in satisfaction surveys is well documented.[34]

This general bias provides an answer to a question this author has fielded on numerous occasions. Specifically, researchers wish to know what numeric level is associated with a "good" satisfaction score. Obviously, this number is a function of the number of scale points, but the specific number does not matter! Because of the positivity bias, it is the shape (actually the mode) of the satisfaction

Figure 2.9   **Distributions of Satisfaction Scores for "Poor," "Good," and "Excellent" Results**

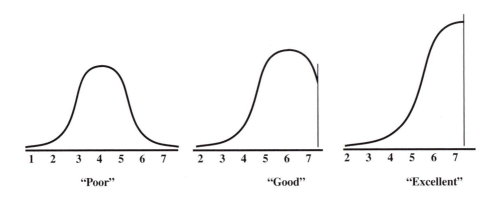

score distribution that is most diagnostic. Poor scores are represented by a normal (bell-shaped) distribution peaking at the scale midpoint; good scores peak near—but not at—the upper (positive) endpoint and then decline before reaching this extreme; excellent scores rise continuously up to the positive extreme without falling (see Figure 2.9).

Perhaps it will now become clear why most satisfaction summaries cite satisfaction scores in the upper 80 to 90th percentiles. This result harkens back to the old paper-and-pencil days when boxes were used on surveys to capture respondent scores, as follows:

| Very dissatisfied | Dissatisfied | Neither | Satisfied | Very satisfied |

It is no wonder that the "top two box" score has become the industry standard for reporting satisfaction levels. The reader only has to superimpose the "good" distribution from Figure 2.9 on top of the box responses. A mental transformation will serve to convert the seven points in the figure to the five boxes as shown here.

Feature or Attribute Importance

Once a list of key performance aspects is generated, researchers often wish to determine the importance of these aspects in driving the satisfaction response. The most direct and common approach is to have consumers rate each of the performance features on a scale of importance, usually ranging from not important to very important. As may be evident from previous mentions of the issue of importance in this chapter, it is this author's feeling that this task inordinately consumes the respondent's time and increases the survey's length. The reason is straightforward but requires elaboration beyond that provided in prior sections. In short, importance is an ambiguous and unreliable concept.

Reasons for Ambiguity and Unreliability in Importance Measures

Consider the following arguments against measuring importance. All involve potential misinterpretation either by the respondent vis-à-vis the survey or by the researcher vis-à-vis the respondent.

1. If some consumers interpret importance as meaning "essential," then all requisite features of the product, such as bicycle brakes and shifters (early bicycle versions—high wheelers— had neither), become very important. All such features will be rated high on importance, and no variance in the ratings will occur. This is a frequent problem with measures of importance. Alternatively, if another segment of respondents interprets importance as referring to a special preference, then some features will be singled out to the exclusion of others. For example, if the bicycle consumer is only interested in the type of bike (road, mountain, or hybrid), then such things as the design of the handlebars and pedals will be unimportant as long as they conform to the bike's configuration. These two consumer mind-sets reflect the use of different personal definitions of importance.

2. It is not clear, when a consumer scales a feature as important, whether the feature is important for its presence or its absence. The no-smoking policies in restaurants, for example, are extremely important to both smokers and nonsmokers, but for entirely different reasons.

3. A feature may be important to the extent that all alternative offerings have reliably incorporated it into their product or service design. At this point, it remains important, but consumers will have become acclimated to it to the point of indifference. They may, however, continue to describe the feature as important. For example, do consumers still ponder over whether refrigerators maintain constant temperatures, whether their telephone service will generate a dial tone, or whether the air bags in their car will reliably deploy? Although some tiny percentage of consumers surely will ponder each of these examples, the average consumer does not. This is an example of the migration of features described earlier in the rings model.

4. Satisfied features or goals tend to diminish in importance, particularly as new goals are pursued. This truism lies at the base of the hierarchical value models discussed earlier. A central tenet of goal hierarchies is that satisfied states of life are no longer salient. This is a particular problem for the pursuit of satisfaction from the firm's perspective. As a company resolves issues and upgrades its product or service design, previously important features will become less so up to the point of total indifference noted in the preceding paragraph.

5. Importance is subject to context effects and other extraneous influences. It has already been noted that features important in considering the need for a product may be different from those important in choosing between alternatives and in evaluating the product during and after consumption. The explanation is that different goals come into play at each of these stages. When considering a product for purchase, consumers are interested in knowing whether the product will satisfy basic needs and desires in their lives. When choosing among alternatives, consumers are interested in differences across brands. At this point, many of the essential features become unimportant because all brands being considered have these features to equivalent degrees. In both instances of consideration and evaluation, certain features are known with certainty (e.g., the styling of a car), and the importance of these features is, likewise, fairly stable.

Importance Changes After Survey Administration

When a consumer is evaluating the product after use, three events can potentially change importance ratings and, hence, the impact of the relevant features on satisfaction. This is another case of the instability of importance ratings over time, with the first being the stage of decision making. Here, however, the possibility is entertained that some consumers will change their emphasis on features, while others will not. Discussion of events follows:

1. Feature performance that could not be sampled before use now becomes known during use, as do the consequences of this performance. The difficulty of finding a willing number of "family and friends" for participation in a long-distance telephone-calling circle is one example of this.

A more poignant example is given in a study of patients at a fertility clinic where the researchers found that the success of the procedure moderated the impact of outcomes on satisfaction.[35] For those patients who became pregnant, the core service (pregnancy) was dominant over all process variables such as physician or staff and patient interaction. However, for those who did not, the process variables assumed primary importance in predicting satisfaction.

2. Unanticipated problems may be encountered, such as the incidence of new-car breakdowns and repairs. In both this and the previous example, these newly discovered relevant features become salient or differentially important because of their immediacy, thereby shifting the importance ratings in unknown ways. Research also shows that communication interventions such as advertising and new information can also temporarily change importance levels.[36] Again, importance levels can be fickle concepts at best.

3. Importances can be changed by administration of a postpurchase survey itself, as noted. For example, in studies of the effects of satisfaction survey responding, it was found that, when compared to a control, consumers who were contacted and replied with feedback reported more positive future purchase intentions, were less likely to defect, and generated more favorable profitability metrics.[37] Presumably, this occurred because the firm's display of concern motivated a greater sense of relationship bonding on the part of the respondent.

"Range of Affect" Influences

Perhaps the most convincing evidence for the futility of importance measurement in satisfaction studies comes from early work in job satisfaction. In this field, it has long been known that measuring importance and then factoring importance scores into satisfaction assessments have not been fruitful. In particular, multiplicative or other combinatorial techniques of integrating importance with job facet satisfactions have not improved the prediction of overall satisfaction. The reasons for this are now generally recognized.

The explanation is that, psychologically, importance is already factored into feature satisfactions and dissatisfactions. In short, individuals assign more extreme positive and negative ratings—the range of affect—to more important attributes. Unimportant features have unimportant performance implications. Thus, measuring importance would be akin to double-counting. Similarly, in a consumer context, it has been found that consumers tend to focus on and exaggerate experiences with important attributes and minimize experiences involving unimportant attributes when forming satisfaction judgments and that attempts to improve satisfaction prediction by weighting performance by importance is not productive.[38] Simply put, importance as evaluated by the consumer does not add to predictability in satisfaction models and unduly adds to the survey length.

Alternative Measures of Importance for Satisfaction

Given this spate of evidence, how does one assess the importance of features *as to their impact on satisfaction?* This is a separate issue from that of attribute importances generally, a point emphasized in this chapter. The accepted procedure is to rely on the statistical coefficients generated in a regression of satisfaction on the performance ratings (see Figure 2.3) or dimensions (Figure 2.4). Because importance is implicit in the attribute ratings, the coefficients will provide some testimony as to how importance is woven into the attribute judgments. The debate continues, however. In a recent study of services, direct measures were compared to a variety of regression and related techniques with varied results largely favoring the statistical procedures. More advanced discussions of various importance-determining techniques in regression can be found in more involved examinations.[39]

Figure 2.10   **Alternative Importance-Performance Grids**

Panel A: Stated Importance vs. Rated Performance

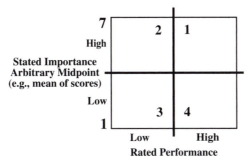

Panel B: Derived Importance vs. Rated Performance

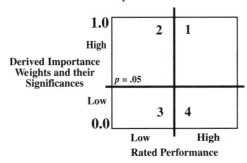

Although not widely used in customer satisfaction studies, another form of reflecting attribute importance into predictions of satisfaction is a respondent's stated interest in particular attributes of a product or, perhaps, the frequency of mention. While attribute interest, measured in various forms, displayed some promise in one study, "regrettably" frequency did not. However, in another study, a multiplicative combination of frequency and (aggregate) importance appeared to be theoretically justifiable. In this latter approach, the consumer's experience could be described in terms of how many times the product delivered a desired (as measured by importance) level of performance.[40]

IMPORTANCE-PERFORMANCE ANALYSIS REVISITED

Given the shortcomings of importance analysis, what, then, can firms do to take advantage of the inherent information in performance ratings and the various measures of importance, if that is all they choose to do? Traditional importance-performance (IP) analysis has been discussed earlier in this chapter. Here, another version of this analysis is presented after some recapitulation.[41] Recall that the traditional IP approach results in four quadrants (cells) as shown in Figure 2.10, Panel A. Respectively, these are key features or drivers (cell 1), performance shortfalls (cell 2), low priority (cell 3), and strategic overkill (cell 4).

As noted, without knowledge of the relation between performance and satisfaction and why features are considered important or not by consumers, interpretation becomes ambiguous. Consider some possibilities. Quadrant 1 could refer to a core attribute, such as air bag protection, which is provided by all competitors. Hence it is actually not a driver of satisfaction, although no firm would be advised to decrease emphasis on its obvious necessity.

In quadrant 2, it appears that low performance on an important attribute signals trouble. However, these low-performance attributes could actually be subconsciously unimportant if the high-importance ratings result from socially acceptable or "politically correct" responses. For example, high nutrition is important in foods, but most junk food "junkies" would rate their favorite snack low on this dimension.

Quadrant 3 could be problematic if the low importance rating results from a previously important attribute that has been superseded by a more cogent need. Given that the splits between important and unimportant attributes are usually relative, previously important features can be "bumped down" as others become prominent. Many communities, for example, face a plethora of social, environmental, school, and transportation problems of varying degrees of seriousness. If there is a crime wave, previously important problems such as road repair become temporarily suspended in the community's collective mind. The earlier concerns have not disappeared, however. When the crime wave is subdued, the previous problems will resume their important status.

Finally, the same logic could apply to the low importance–high performance cell in quadrant 4. This could result in future problems for the firm if the focal feature is labeled unimportant only because it has reached a level of superior performance that is now considered "normal" as in "the norm" (see the migration example, discussed previously in the rings model). When these superior levels are compromised or can no longer be maintained, dissatisfaction sentiments are sure to surface.

What, then, can improve on the basic IP technique? A more acceptable variation uses *derived* versus stated (rated) importance. Derived importance relies on an actual assessment of how each attribute relates to satisfaction. The preferred technique is to regress the overall satisfaction score on each attribute rating. The empirically derived importance estimate for each attribute (see Figures 2.3 and 2.4) can be either the correlation of attribute performance with satisfaction or the multiple regression weight (which controls for the dependence/independence of attributes). Note that this "weight" takes into account both performance and satisfaction. The same four-cell *xy* graph would be constructed using performance and derived importance scores (weights in the latter case). The vertical axis would now contain fractional weights ranging from zero to one, with higher weights indicating greater "importance." Additionally, significance levels of the weights can now be reported at desired cutoff levels. See Figure 2.10, Panel B ($p = 0.05$ used for illustration).

As an aside, there are not-so-subtle differences when using correlations versus regression weights of satisfaction and the attribute performance ratings. Attribute correlations with performance are calculated independently of one another while regressions weights, in effect, partial out the influence of other attributes when the weights are calculated; hence, individual attribute influences are obscured. This author prefers correlations when performing individual attribute versions of IP analysis *only* and not in interpreting dimensional effects. To ensure independence of attribute *set* influences, a factor analysis should be performed and attribute *dimensions* used in the IP analysis. As a further aside, negative weights are possible; typically they reverse the influence of an attribute on satisfaction and may be rescaled to maintain consistency, remembering the attribute's inverse influence.

The locations of the attribute cell identities will change somewhat in this new analysis depending on the significance cutoff used. Cells 1 and 3 will require continued emphasis and de-emphasis, respectively, as before. Here, both cell 1 and cell 2 with significant derived importances are "important" (for different reasons) because the attributes in these cells correlate strongly with satisfaction. Likewise, cells 3 and 4 contain features not significantly correlated with satisfaction and may be de-emphasized as appropriate.

The reader may have noted that the cell interpretations have not changed from the basic analysis using only importance and performance scores alone. What has changed, however, is the incorporation of satisfaction into the analysis! Although satisfaction is not represented on either axis, it is contained implicitly in the derived importance estimates. What this graphical view does do is focus management's attention on the significance of specific attributes and where they operate within the constellation of all product or service attributes, thereby enlarging the viewer's perspective on attribute performance, the topic of this chapter. A potentially more enlightening discussion of this perspective is reserved for Chapter 5, where the Kano technique is presented.

CONCLUSION

This discourse temporarily postpones the discussion of performance analysis as it may affect satisfaction directly or, alternatively, without the aid of other satisfaction influences or moderators. Additionally, it notes some advantages and disadvantages of measuring attribute performance using various scaling techniques. More to the point, however, it emphasizes that some performance analyses do not consider actual satisfaction scores in the procedure, doing so only through stated importance. For example, missing from the discussion is consideration of the inputs to the black-box model (i.e., unknown antecedent mechanisms) of satisfaction processing as well as the content of the black box itself. The next chapter begins this examination by exploring what consumers bring to the consumption experience. What do they want? What do they expect? For now, the assumption is that purchases are made because products and services are expected to satisfy wants. This topic of the role of expectations in satisfaction formation is addressed next.

NOTES

1. In order, these slogans represent the following products: Miller Lite beer, M&Ms candy, Visine eye solution, Cascade dishwashing detergent, Maxwell House coffee, Bulova watches, Huggies diapers, S.O.S. scouring pads, Tupperware containers, Saran Wrap, Palmolive dish detergent, Ultra-Brite toothpaste, Avon home products, Scope mouthwash, Wisk laundry detergent, Agree shampoo, and Raid insecticide.

2. Readers interested in a comparison of direct and less direct importance measures may wish to see Chrzan and Golovashkina, "An Empirical Test of Six Stated Importance Measures."

3. See, e.g., Camp, *Benchmarking*; Mentzer, Bienstock, and Kahn, "Benchmarking Satisfaction"; and Sharma, Niedrich, and Dobbins, "A Framework for Monitoring Customer Satisfaction." The "perils" of benchmarking are discussed in Denrell, "Selection Bias and the Perils of Benchmarking."

4. See Martilla and James, "Importance-Performance Analysis."

5. Bacon, "Comparison of Approaches to Importance-Performance Analysis"; Sampson and Showalter, "Performance-Importance Response Function." An interesting use of IP analysis in both the pre- and postusage stages of consumption can be found in Duke and Mount, "Rediscovering Performance-Importance Analysis of Products."

6. Parasuraman, Zeithaml, and Berry, "SERVQUAL."

7. Gardial et al., "Comparing Consumers' Recall of Prepurchase and Postpurchase Product Evaluation Experiences."

8. Bassi and Guido, "Measuring Customer Satisfaction"; Posselt and Gerstner, "Pre-Sale vs. Post-Sale e-Satisfaction."

9. Heide and Weiss, "Vendor Consideration and Switching Behavior for Buyers in High-Technology Markets."

10. Henke, "Longitudinal Analysis of the Ad Agency-Client Relationship."

11. Borle et al., "Impact of Survey Participation on Subsequent Customer Behavior"; Dholakia and Morwitz, "Scope and Persistence of Mere-Measurement Effects"; Morwitz and Fitzsimons, "Mere-Measurement Effect."

12. See, respectively, Huffman, "Elaboration on Experience"; Mittal, Katrichis, and Kumar, "Attribute Performance and Customer Satisfaction Over Time"; Mittal, Kumar, and Tsiros, "Attribute-Level Performance, Satisfaction, and Behavioral Intentions Over Time"; Thompson, Hamilton, and Rust, "Feature Fatigue"; and Posselt and Gerstner, "Pre-Sale vs. Post-Sale e-Satisfaction."

13. See Johnson et al., "Attribute Abstraction, Feature-Dimensionality, and the Scaling of Product Similarities"; and Snelders and Schoormans, "Exploratory Study of the Relation Between Concrete and Abstract Product Attributes."

14. Examples of both types of factor solutions can be found in Carman, "Consumer Perceptions of Service Quality."

15. *Executive Report on Customer Satisfaction*, "Align Quality Programs with Customers' Expectations."

16. One of the earliest treatises on this topic is Levitt, *Marketing Imagination*, pp. 78–85.

17. Brechan, "Different Effect of Primary and Secondary Product Attributes on Customer Satisfaction"; Clemmer, *Firing on All Cylinders*; Taher, Leigh, and French, "Augmented Retail Services."

18. Brendl, Markman, and Messner, "Devaluation Effect"; Dagger and Sweeney, "Service Quality Attribute Weights."

19. Mellers and Biagini, "Similarity and Choice."

20. Maslow, *Motivation and Personality*.

21. See, e.g., Batra and Ahtola, "Measuring the Hedonic and Utilitarian Sources of Consumer Attitudes"; Childers et al., "Hedonic and Utilitarian Motivations for Online Retail Shopping Behavior"; Chitturi, Raghunathan, and Mahajan, "Form Versus Function"; Crowley, Spangenberg, and Hughes, "Measuring the Hedonic and Utilitarian Dimensions of Attitudes Toward Product Categories"; Lee and Overby, "Creating Value for Online Shoppers"; and Voss, Spangenberg, and Grohmann, "Measuring the Hedonic and Utilitarian Dimensions of Consumer Attitude."

22. Parasuraman, Zeithaml, and Berry, "SERVQUAL."

23. For more recent reviews, see Asubonteng, McCleary, and Swan, "SERVQUAL Revisited"; Buttle, "SERVQUAL"; Coulthard, "Measuring Service Quality"; Dabholkar, Shepperd, and Thorpe, "Comprehensive Framework for Service Quality"; Finn and Kayandá, "Service Quality Measurement Literature"; Smith, "Measuring Service Quality"; and for a review in electronic commerce, see Wolfinbarger and Gilly, "eTailQ."

24. Gounaris, "Measuring Service Quality in b2b Services"; Lassar, Manolis, and Winsor, "Service Quality Perspectives and Satisfaction in Private Banking."

25. See Gutman, "Exploring the Nature of Linkages between Consequences and Values"; Gutman and Haley, "Integrating Cues into Means-End Chain Models"; and Reynolds and Gutman, "Laddering Theory, Method, Analysis, and Interpretation."

26. Botschen and Hemetsberger, "Diagnosing Means-End Structure to Determine the Degree of Potential Marketing Program Standardization"; Valette-Florence, "Causal Analysis of Means-End Hierarchies in a Cross-Cultural Context"; Claeys, Swinnen, and Vanden Abeele, "Consumers' Means-End Chains for 'Think' and 'Feel' Products"; Gengler, Klenosky, and Mulvey, "Improving the Graphic Representation of Means-End Results"; Grunert and Bech-Larsen, "Explaining Choice Option Attractiveness by Beliefs Elicited by the Laddering Method."

27. Gutman, "Means-End Chains as Goal Hierarchies"; Pieters, Baumgartner, and Allen, "Means-End Chain Approach to Consumer Goal Structures."

28. See Bagozzi and Dabholkar, "Discursive Psychology"; and Pitts, Wong, and Whalen, "Consumers' Evaluative Structures in Two Ethical Situations."

29. For a review with further suggestions, see Edvardsson and Roos, "Critical Incident Techniques." Applications can be found in Arnold et al., "Customer Delight in a Retail Context"; Bitner, Booms, and Tetreault, "Service Encounter"; Friman, "Structure of Affective Reactions to Critical Incidents"; Gardial, Flint, and Woodruff, "Trigger Events"; Grace, "How Embarrassing!"; and Keaveney, "Customer Switching Behavior in Service Industries."

30. See, e.g., Mick, DeMoss, and Faber, "Projective Study of Motivations and Meanings of Self-Gifts."

31. For elaboration and discussion of this and other issues in this section, see Devlin, Dong, and Brown, "Selecting a Scale for Measuring Quality," and commentary from others, including Danaher and Haddrell, "Comparison of Question Scales Used for Measuring Customer Satisfaction"; and Scherpenzeel and Saris, "Validity and Reliability of Survey Questions."

32. See, e.g., Coelho and Esteves, "Choice Between a Five-Point and a Ten-Point Scale in the Framework of Customer Satisfaction Measurement."

33. Diener and Diener, "Most People Are Happy"; Knowles and Condon, "Why People Say 'Yes.'"

34. Danaher and Haddrell, "A Comparison of Question Scales Used for Measuring Customer Satisfaction"; Hazelrigg and Hardy, "Scaling the Semantics of Satisfaction"; Hurley and Estelami, "Alternative Indexes for Monitoring Customer Perceptions of Service Quality"; Johnson, Garbarino, and Sivadas, "Influences of Customer Differences of Loyalty, Perceived Risk and Category Experience on Customer Satisfaction Ratings"; Peterson and Wilson, "Measuring Customer Satisfaction."

35. Lytle and Mokwa, "Evaluating Health Care Quality."

36. See Shavitt and Fazio, "Effects of Attribute Salience on the Consistency Between Attitudes and Behavior Predictions."

37. Dholakia and Morwitz, "Scope and Persistence of Mere-Measurement Effects." See, also, Borle et al., "Impact of Survey Participation on Subsequent Customer Behavior."

38. See Bridges, "Service Attributes"; Cronin and Taylor, "Measuring Service Quality"; McAlexander, Kaldenberg, and Koenig, "Service Quality Measurement"; and Mittal, Katrichis, and Kumar, "Attribute Performance and Customer Satisfaction Over Time."

39. See Gustafsson and Johnson, "Determining Attribute Importance in a Service Satisfaction Model"; and Budescu, "Dominance Analysis."

40. See Griffin and Hauser, "Voice of the Customer"; and Dolinsky, "Consumer Complaint Framework with Resulting Strategies."

41. For additional analyses, see Chu, "Stated Importance Versus Derived Importance Customer Satisfaction Measurement"; and Yavas, "Importance-Performance Analysis."

BIBLIOGRAPHY

Arnold, Mark J., Kristy E. Reynolds, Nicole Ponder, and Jason E. Lueg. "Customer Delight in a Retail Context: Investigating Delightful and Terrible Shopping Experiences." *Journal of Business Research* 58, no. 8 (August 2005): 1132–1145.

Asubonteng, Patrick, Karl J. McCleary, and John E. Swan. "SERVQUAL Revisited: A Critical Review of Service Quality." *Journal of Services Marketing* 10, no. 6 (1996): 62–81.

Bacon, Donald R. "A Comparison of Approaches to Important-Performance Analysis." *International Journal of Market Research* 45 (Quarter 1, 2003): 55–71.

Bagozzi, Richard P., and Pratibha A. Dabholkar. "Discursive Psychology: An Alternative Conceptual Foundation to Means-End Chain Theory." *Psychology & Marketing* 17, no. 7 (July 2000): 535–586.

Bassi, Francesca, and Gianluigi Guido. "Measuring Customer Satisfaction: From Product Performance to Consumption Experience." *Journal of Consumer Satisfaction, Dissatisfaction and Complaining Behavior* 19 (2006): 76–85.

Batra, Rajeev, and Olli T. Ahtola. "Measuring the Hedonic and Utilitarian Sources of Consumer Attitudes." *Marketing Letters* 2, no. 2 (April 1990): 159–170.

Bitner, Mary Jo, Bernard H. Booms, and Mary Stanfield Tetreault. "The Service Encounter: Diagnosing Favorable and Unfavorable Incidents." *Journal of Marketing* 54, no. 1 (January 1990): 71–84.

Borle, Sharad, Uptal M. Dholakia, Siddharth S. Singh, and Robert A. Westbrook. "The Impact of Survey Participation on Subsequent Customer Behavior: An Empirical Investigation." *Marketing Science* 26, no. 5 (September–October 2007): 711–726.

Botschen, Günther, and Andrea Hemetsberger. "Diagnosing Means-End Structure to Determine the Degree of Potential Marketing Program Standardization." *Journal of Business Research* 42, no. 2 (June 1998): 151–159.

Brechan, Inge. "The Different Effect of Primary and Secondary Product Attributes on Customer Satisfaction." *Journal of Economic Psychology* 27, no. 3 (June 2006): 441–458.

Brendl, C. Miguel, Arthur B. Markman, and Claude Messner. "The Devaluation Effect: Activating a Need Devalues Unrelated Objects." *Journal of Consumer Research* 29, no. 4 (March 2003): 463–473.

Bridges, Eileen. "Service Attributes: Expectations and Judgments." *Psychology & Marketing* 10, no. 3 (May–June 1993): 185–197.

Budescu, David V. "Dominance Analysis: A New Approach to the Problem of Relative Importance of Predictors in Multiple Regression." *Psychological Bulletin* 114, no. 3 (November 1993): 542–551.

Buttle, Francis. "SERVQUAL: Review, Critique, Research Agenda." *European Journal of Marketing* 30, no. 1 (1996): 8–32.

Camp, Robert C. *Benchmarking: The Search for Industry Best Practices That Lead to Superior Performance*. Milwaukee, WI: ASQC Quality Press, 1989.

Carman, James M. "Consumer Perceptions of Service Quality: An Assessment of the SERVQUAL Dimensions." *Journal of Retailing* 66, no. 1 (Spring 1990): 33–55.

Childers, Terry L., Christopher L. Carr, Joann Peck, and Stephen Carson. "Hedonic and Utilitarian Motivations for Online Retail Shopping Behavior." *Journal of Retailing* 77, no. 4 (Winter 2001): 511–535.

Chitturi, Ravindra, Rajagopal Raghunathan, and Vijay Mahajan. "Form Versus Function: How the Intensities of Specific Emotions Evoked in Functional Versus Hedonic Trade-Offs Mediate Product Preferences." *Journal of Marketing Research* 44, no. 4 (November 2007): 702–714.

Chrzan, Keith, and Natalia Golovashkina. "An Empirical Test of Six Stated Importance Measures." *International Journal of Market Research* 48, no. 6 (2006): 717–740.

Chu, Ray. "Stated Importance Versus Derived Importance Customer Satisfaction Measurement." *Journal of Services Marketing* 16, no. 4 (2002): 285–301.

Claeys, C., A. Swinnen, and P. Vanden Abeele. "Consumers' Means-End Chains for 'Think' and 'Feel' Products." *International Journal of Research in Marketing* 12, no. 3 (October 1995): 193–208.

Clemmer, Jim. *Firing on All Cylinders: The Service/Quality System for High-Powered Corporate Performance*. Homewood, IL: Business One Irwin, 1992.

Coelho, Pedro S., and Susana P. Esteves. "The Choice Between a Five-Point and a Ten-Point Scale in the Framework of Customer Satisfaction Measurement." *International Journal of Market Research* 49, no. 3 (2007): 313–339.

Coulthard, Lisa J. Morrison. "Measuring Service Quality: A Review and Critique of Research Using SERVQUAL." *International Journal of Market Research* 46 (4th Quarter 2004): 479–497.

Cronin, J. Joseph, Jr., and Steven A. Taylor. "Measuring Service Quality: A Reexamination and Extension." *Journal of Marketing* 56, no. 3 (July 1992): 55–68.

Crowley, Ayn E., Eric R. Spangenberg, and Kevin R. Hughes. "Measuring the Hedonic and Utilitarian Dimensions of Attitudes Toward Product Categories." *Marketing Letters* 3, no. 3 (July 1992): 239–249.

Dabholkar, Pratibha A., C. David Shepperd, and Dayle I. Thorpe. "A Comprehensive Framework for Service Quality: An Investigation of Critical Conceptual and Measurement Issues Through a Longitudinal Study." *Journal of Retailing* 76, no. 2 (Summer 2000): 139–173.

Dagger, Tracey S., and Jillian C. Sweeney. "Service Quality Attribute Weights: How Do Novices and Longer-Term Customers Construct Service Quality Perceptions?" *Journal of Service Research* 10, no. 1 (August 2007): 22–42.

Danaher, Peter J., and Vanessa Haddrell. "A Comparison of Question Scales Used for Measuring Customer Satisfaction." *International Journal of Service Industry Management* 7, no. 4 (1996): 4–26.

Denrell, Jerker. "Selection Bias and the Perils of Benchmarking." *Harvard Business Review* 83, no. 4 (April 2005): 114–119.

Devlin, Susan J., H.K. Dong, and Marbue Brown. "Selecting a Scale for Measuring Quality." *Marketing Research* 15, no. 3 (Fall 2003): 13–16.

Dholakia, Utpal M., and Vicki G. Morwitz. "The Scope and Persistence of Mere-Measurement Effects: Evidence from a Field Study of Customer Satisfaction Measurement." *Journal of Consumer Research* 29, no. 2 (September 2002): 159–167.

Diener, Ed, and Carol Diener. "Most People Are Happy." *Psychological Science* 7, no. 3 (May 1996): 181–185.

Dolinsky, Arthur L. "Consumer Complaint Framework with Resulting Strategies: An Application to Higher Education." *Journal of Services Marketing* 8, no. 3 (1994): 27–39.

Duke, Charles R., and Andrew S. Mount. "Rediscovering Performance-Importance Analysis of Products." *Journal of Product & Brand Management* 5, no. 2 (1996): 43–54.

Edvardsson, Bo, and Inger Roos. "Critical Incident Techniques: Towards a Framework for Analysing the Criticality of Critical Incidents." *International Journal of Service Industry Management* 12, no. 3 (2001): 251–268.

Executive Report on Customer Satisfaction. "Align Quality Programs with Customers' Expectations." 8 (May 31, 1995): 1–4.

Finn, Adam, and Ujwal Kayandá. "The Service Quality Measurement Literature: A Generalizability Perspective." In *Advances in Services Marketing and Management*, ed. Teresa A. Swartz, David E. Bowen, and Stephen W. Brown, 7:97–130. Greenwich, CT: JAI Press, 1998.

Friman, Margareta. "The Structure of Affective Reactions to Critical Incidents." *Journal of Economic Psychology* 25, no. 3 (June 2004): 331–353.

Gardial, Sarah Fisher, D. Scott Clemons, Robert B. Woodruff, David W. Schumann, and Mary Jane Burns. "Comparing Consumers' Recall of Prepurchase and Postpurchase Product Evaluation Experiences." *Journal of Consumer Research* 20, no. 4 (March 1994): 548–560.

Gardial, Sarah Fisher, Daniel J. Flint, and Robert B. Woodruff. "Trigger Events: Exploring the Relationships Between Critical Events and Consumers' Evaluations, Standards, Emotions, Values and Behavior." *Journal of Consumer Satisfaction, Dissatisfaction and Complaining Behavior* 9 (1996): 35–51.

Gengler, Charles E., David P. Klenosky, and Michael S. Mulvey. "Improving the Graphic Representation of Means-End Results." *International Journal of Research in Marketing* 12, no. 3 (October 1995): 245–256.

Gounaris, Spiros. "Measuring Service Quality in b2b Services: An Evaluation of the SERVQUAL Scale vis-à-vis the INDSERV Scale." *Journal of Services Marketing* 19, no. 6 (2005): 421–435.

Grace, Debra. "How Embarrassing! An Exploratory Study of Critical Incidents Including Affective Reactions." *Journal of Service Research* 9, no. 3 (February 2007): 271–284.

Griffin, Abbie, and John R. Hauser. "The Voice of the Customer." *Marketing Science* 12, no. 1 (Winter 1993): 1–27.

Grunert, Klaus G., and Tino Bech-Larsen. "Explaining Choice Option Attractiveness by Beliefs Elicited by the Laddering Method." *Journal of Economic Psychology* 26, no. 2 (April 2005): 223–241.

Gustafsson, Anders, and Michael D. Johnson. "Determining Attribute Importance in a Service Satisfaction Model." *Journal of Service Research* 7, no. 2 (November 2004): 124–141.

Gutman, Jonathan. "Exploring the Nature of Linkages between Consequences and Values." *Journal of Business Research* 22, no. 2 (March 1991): 143–148.

———. "Means-End Chains as Goal Hierarchies." *Psychology & Marketing* 14, no. 6 (September 1997): 545–560.

———, and Russell Haley. "Integrating Cues into Means-End Chain Models." *Journal of Promotion Management* 4, no. 1 (1996): 13–25.

Hazelrigg, Lawrence E., and Melissa E. Hardy. "Scaling the Semantics of Satisfaction." *Social Indicators Research* 49, no. 2 (February 2000): 147–180.

Heide, Jan B., and Allen M. Weiss. "Vendor Consideration and Switching Behavior for Buyers in High-Technology Markets." *Journal of Marketing* 59, no. 3 (July 1995): 30–43.

Henke, Lucy L. "A Longitudinal Analysis of the Ad Agency-Client Relationship: Predictors of an Agency Switch." *Journal of Advertising Research* 35, no. 2 (March–April 1995): 24–30.

Huffman, Cynthia. "Elaboration on Experience: Effects on Attribute Importance." *Psychology & Marketing* 14, no. 5 (August 1997): 451–474.

Hurley, Robert F., and Hooman Estelami. "Alternative Indexes for Monitoring Customer Perceptions of Service Quality: A Comparative Evaluation in a Retail Context." *Journal of the Academy of Marketing Science* 26, no. 3 (Summer 1998): 209–221.

Johnson, Mark S., Ellen Garbarino, and Eugene Sivadas. "Influences of Customer Differences of Loyalty, Perceived Risk and Category Experience on Customer Satisfaction Ratings." *International Journal of Market Research* 48, no. 5 (2006): 601–622.

Johnson, Michael D., Donald R. Lehmann, Claes Fornell, and Daniel R. Horne. "Attribute Abstraction, Feature-Dimensionality, and the Scaling of Product Similarities." *International Journal of Research in Marketing* 9, no. 2 (May 1992): 131–147.

Keaveney, Susan M. "Customer Switching Behavior in Service Industries: An Exploratory Study." *Journal of Marketing* 59, no. 2 (April 1995): 71–82.

Knowles, Eric S., and Christopher A. Condon. "Why People Say 'Yes': A Dual-Process Theory of Acquiescence." *Journal of Personality and Social Psychology* 77, no. 2 (August 1999): 379–386.

Lassar, Walfried M., Chris Manolis, and Robert D. Winsor. "Service Quality Perspectives and Satisfaction in Private Banking." *Journal of Services Marketing* 14, no. 3 (2000): 244–271.

Lee, Eun-Ju, and Jeffrey W. Overby. "Creating Value for Online Shoppers: Implications for Satisfaction and Loyalty." *Journal of Consumer Satisfaction, Dissatisfaction and Complaining Behavior* 17 (2004): 54–67.

Levitt, Theodore. *The Marketing Imagination*. New York: Free Press, 1983.

Lytle, Richard S., and Michael P. Mokwa. "Evaluating Health Care Quality: The Moderating Role of Outcomes." *Journal of Health Care Marketing* 12, no. 1 (March 1992): 4–14.

Martilla, John A., and John C. James. "Importance-Performance Analysis." *Journal of Marketing* 41, no. 1 (January 1977): 77–79.

Maslow, Abraham H. *Motivation and Personality*. 2nd ed. New York: Harper & Row, 1970.

McAlexander, James H., Dennis O. Kaldenberg, and Harold F. Koenig. "Service Quality Measurement." *Journal of Health Care Marketing* 14, no. 3 (Fall 1994): 34–39.

Mellers, Barbara A., and Karen Biagini. "Similarity and Choice." *Psychological Review* 101, no. 3 (July 1994): 505–518.

Mentzer, John T., Carol C. Bienstock, and Kenneth B. Kahn. "Benchmarking Satisfaction." *Marketing Management* 4, no. 1 (Summer 1995): 41–46.

Mick, David Glen, Michelle DeMoss, and Ronald J. Faber. "A Projective Study of Motivations and Meanings of Self-Gifts: Implications for Retail Management." *Journal of Retailing* 68, no. 2 (Summer 1992): 122–144.

Mittal, Vikas, Jerome M. Katrichis, and Pankaj Kumar. "Attribute Performance and Customer Satisfaction Over Time: Evidence from Two Field Studies." *Journal of Services Marketing* 15, no. 5 (2001): 343–356.

Mittal, Vikas, Pankaj Kumar, and Michael Tsiros. "Attribute-Level Performance, Satisfaction, and Behavioral Intentions Over Time: A Consumption-System Approach." *Journal of Marketing* 63, no. 2 (April 1999): 88–101.

Morwitz, Vicki G., and Gavan J. Fitzsimons. "The Mere-Measurement Effect: Why Does Measuring Intentions Change Actual Behavior?" *Journal of Consumer Psychology* 14, nos. 1 & 2 (2004): 64–74.

Parasuraman, A., Valarie A. Zeithaml, and Leonard L. Berry. "SERVQUAL: A Multiple-Item Scale for Measuring Consumer Perceptions of Service Quality." *Journal of Retailing* 64, no. 1 (Spring 1988): 12–40.

Peterson, Robert A., and William R. Wilson. "Measuring Customer Satisfaction: Fact and Artifact." *Journal of the Academy of Marketing Science* 20, no. 1 (Winter 1992): 61–71.

Pieters, Rik, Hans Baumgartner, and Doug Allen. "A Means-End Chain Approach to Consumer Goal Structures." *International Journal of Research in Marketing* 12, no. 3 (October 1995): 227–244.

Pitts, Robert E., John K. Wong, and D. Joel Whalen. "Consumers' Evaluative Structures in Two Ethical Situations: A Means-End Approach." *Journal of Business Research* 22, no. 2 (March 1991): 119–130.

Posselt, Thorsten, and Eitan Gerstner. "Pre-Sale vs. Post-Sale e-Satisfaction: Impact on Repurchase Intention and Overall Satisfaction." *Journal of Interactive Marketing* 19, no. 4 (Autumn 2005): 35–47.

Reynolds, Thomas J., and Jonathan Gutman. "Laddering Theory, Method, Analysis, and Interpretation." *Journal of Advertising Research* 28, no. 1 (February–March 1988): 11–31.

Sampson, Scott E., and Michael J. Showalter. "The Performance-Importance Response Function: Observations and Implications." *Service Industries Journal* 19, no. 3 (July 1999): 1–25.

Scherpenzeel, Annette C., and Willem E. Saris. "The Validity and Reliability of Survey Questions: A Meta-Analysis of MTMM Studies." *Sociological Methods & Research* 25, no. 3 (February 1997): 341–383.

Sharma, Subhash, Ronald W. Niedrich, and Greg Dobbins. "A Framework for Monitoring Customer Satisfaction: An Empirical Illustration." *Industrial Marketing Management* 28, no. 3 (May 1999): 231–243.

Shavitt, Sharon, and Russell H. Fazio. "Effects of Attribute Salience on the Consistency between Attitudes and Behavior Predictions." *Personality and Social Psychology Bulletin* 17, no. 5 (October 1991): 507–516.

Smith, Anne M. "Measuring Service Quality: Is SERVQUAL Now Redundant?" *Journal of Marketing Management* 11, nos. 3–4 (April 1995): 257–276.

Snelders, Dirk, and Jan P.L. Schoormans. "An Exploratory Study of the Relation Between Concrete and Abstract Product Attributes." *Journal of Economic Psychology* 25, no. 6 (December 2004): 803–820.

Taher, Ahmed, Thomas W. Leigh, and Warren A. French. "Augmented Retail Services: The Lifetime Value of Affection." *Journal of Business Research* 35, no. 3 (March 1996): 217–228.

Thompson, Debora Viana, Rebecca W. Hamilton, and Roland T. Rust. "Feature Fatigue: When Product Capabilities Become Too Much of a Good Thing." *Journal of Marketing Research* 42, no. 4 (November 2005): 431–442.

Valette-Florence, Pierre. "A Causal Analysis of Means-End Hierarchies in a Cross-Cultural Context: Methodological Refinements." *Journal of Business Research* 42, no. 2 (June 1998): 161–166.

Voss, Kevin E., Eric R. Spangenberg, and Bianca Grohmann. "Measuring the Hedonic and Utilitarian Dimensions of Consumer Attitude." *Journal of Marketing Research* 40, no. 3 (August 2003): 310–320.

Wolfinbarger, Mary, and Mary C. Gilly. "eTailQ: Dimensionalizing, Measuring and Predicting etail Quality." *Journal of Retailing* 79, no. 3 (2003): 183–198.

Yavas, Ugur. "Importance-Performance Analysis: An Exposition and Illustration." *Journal of Professional Services Marketing* 20, no. 1 (1999): 23–35.

CHAPTER 3

EXPECTATIONS AND RELATED COMPARATIVE STANDARDS

In 1952, George Katona constructed the first version of the Index of Consumer Sentiment (ICS) in an effort to predict the direction of the economy. Conducted by the Survey Research Center at the University of Michigan, it now consists of five questions. Three specifically address consumer expectations for the future. The first asks whether the respondent will be better or worse off one year from now; the second asks whether business conditions in the economy will be better or worse in one year's time; the third extends the time interval in this second query to a five-year time horizon. Studies have shown that this index is a valid predictor of aggregate future business activity, particularly for purchases of durables.[1]

While few would question the power of an individual consumer's expectations in determining this individual's willingness to buy, could it also be the case that the aggregated satisfaction of consumers is influenced by their collective expectations? The answer, which may be surprising to some, is yes.[2] Expectations are predictive of satisfaction both in the aggregate and at the individual level. The mechanisms differ somewhat; the explanation for individual-level effects is provided in later sections of this chapter.

The role of collective expectations in aggregate satisfaction stems from the fact that they reflect prior levels of performance (e.g., quality) and satisfaction delivered by firms or industries. Because the average quality of a firm's products does not vary greatly in the short term, consumers will observe repetitive cycles of high quality from better-performing firms and low quality from poorly performing firms (see Figure 3.1).

The figure shows the mirror-image satisfaction and dissatisfaction cycles for high- and low-quality firms. Collectively, consumers will accurately perceive the high and low quality provided by these firms (an assumption that is not necessarily true at the individual level) and will form respective satisfaction and dissatisfaction judgments. The satisfaction or dissatisfaction experienced will create expectations for similar levels of quality-related satisfaction in the future. Because the firms' performances are relatively stable, these expectations will be confirmed in the next round of product or service experience, thereby initiating a new cycle. Thus, the satisfaction resulting from quality performance promotes expectations of future satisfactory performance for those firms or industries most capable of providing high performance levels. A similar logic obtains for firms not able to provide high-quality performance.

These observations have recently been supported in a study of 241 products in forty-six categories over a twelve-year horizon.[3] The researchers discovered that, among other findings, negative quality changes are reflected more quickly and in larger decrements than are equivalent movements for positive changes. Moreover, high-reputation brands are rewarded

Figure 3.1 **Operation of Expectations at the Macro Level**

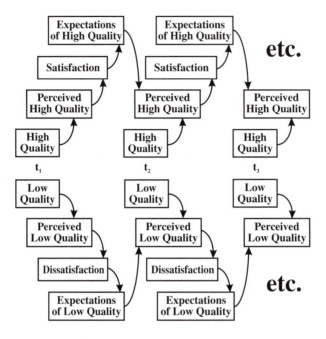

three times quicker for positive increments than are punished for negative decrements when compared to low-reputation brands. Generally the findings were consistent with the central tenets of the model.

Although the focus of this book is on the individual consumer and not aggregate consumption, the aggregate findings are instructive for two reasons. First, they suggest that expectations play a role in satisfaction formation by suggesting levels of anticipated satisfaction to the consumer and, thus, may add to the prediction of satisfaction beyond the contribution of performance measures. Second, the aggregate explanation is reported to emphasize that large numbers of consumers do harbor expectations and that these expectations are subject to marketing strategy over extended time periods. In fact, expectations permeate everyday life. Consumers have expectations of their future well-being, of their willingness to buy products and consume services, of the degree to which these products and services will satisfy their needs, and of redress procedures should those wants and needs not be fulfilled. Without expectations, markets such as securities exchanges could not operate, wagers would not take place (since both parties to the bet must have differing expectations), and politicians would not be elected (or defeated).

How, then, do consumers form and use their expectations in consumption and in judging consumption outcomes? And how can management measure the expectations of its customer base and act on that information? These questions form the basis for this chapter. Initially, it will be suggested that consumers use expectations as a basis for comparing performance outcomes. Then, after a discussion of the definition and dimensionality of an expectation, sources of expectations are explored and measurement options suggested. The chapter culminates with a discussion of how expectations directly influence satisfaction at the individual level.

WHAT IS AN EXPECTATION?

The concept of an expectation most likely dates back many thousands of years to early species where it could only be felt subconsciously as an anticipation (of food, water, sex, and even rain, sunrises, and summer solstices). The first written expression of this concept is probably lost in history. Within the behavioral area, one might argue that individuals learn of potential consequences of their actions and subsequently behave to realize (and avoid) these outcomes. Thus, an expectation is an "anticipation of future consequences based on prior experience, current circumstances, or other sources of information."[4]

Some have distinguished between an expectation and an *anticipation*, another comparative standard, and others use them interchangeably. As used here and elaborated further, an anticipation differs on two dimensions from an expectation more generally. First, an anticipation may be seen as a weak form of a strong expectancy where something is thought to occur in response to vague conditions, as in "I'm anticipating bad weather on this trip." An expectation is more direct and may be estimated as a probability of occurrence, as when the weather report assigns a 40 percent chance of rain on a given day. In this sense, it is more cognitive and amenable to measurement on a "chances in ten" scale or something similar. In a second and even paradoxical difference, an anticipation connotes action in the form of forestalling or preventing a negative outcome, where it begins to assume volitional tendencies. In contrast to either, a *propensity* is a subjective disposition to favor future events under intentional control, as in "I'm predisposed to go golfing only if the chance of rain is 30 percent or less." Individuals can harbor all these variations regarding the same target.

The notion of a vague expectation and, in some sense, an undefined expectation is becoming more prominent within marketing circles. Based on early ethnographic studies in consumption, consumers are known to engage in "experiential consumption" or "extraordinary experience" whereby only a general sense of what is to occur is known. Illustrations can be found in the activities of white-water rafting, motorcycle rallying, and even bird-watching.[5] These situations will present certain difficulties of measurement although some will be surmounted when affective expectations and emotional responding are analyzed within the satisfaction process. For now, it can be said that experience may mitigate these measurement difficulties when repetitions accumulate, as in the case of analyzing visits to the same theme park over and over again.

As used in consumption, however, an expectation is more than a subjective probability of events. In fact, some would not use the term *expectation* at all. The reason is that many researchers focus on the *function* of expectations within the satisfaction response. An expectation's function relates to why it is engaged by the consumer—what it does or what it is intended to do. By shifting emphasis to function and not definition, the term *expectation* broadens to include other concepts that also perform the same function. *Expectation*, then, becomes only one of many terms that can be used in its place. This discussion begs the question, "What is this function?"

The answer appeared throughout Chapter 2. Performance alone is an unreferenced concept. Meaning is attached only when performance can be compared to some standard. In an elementary sense, the adjectives *good* and *bad* suggest the operation of a "goodness" standard, although they provide little diagnostic value to management because the terms have highly variable meanings across consumers. Diagnosticity is increased as the standard becomes less ambiguous and more objective to the point that it can be measured. Thus, the standard of comparison or comparative referent becomes a key concept to those interested in the function of an expectation.

Despite this difference of perspective on expectations and anticipations versus their use as comparative referents, the fundamental notion of an expectation and its variants remains the focus of this chapter. As will be argued later, any number of referents can be used in satisfaction assessments, but all become channeled into expectations, broadly defined, when the product or service is purchased. Chapter 5 will discuss the concept of needs, one of the many referents available to consumers. Need-oriented consumers, however, will pursue only those products that they expect to fulfill their needs. Thus, the expectation, not the need, is what the consumer brings to the purchase. Often the expectation and need will overlap exactly, becoming interchangeable. For example, consumers buy can openers because they need an efficient device to remove the lid from cans; it is also their expectation that the purchased product will do so.

MORE ON VARIETIES OF EXPECTATIONS AND PERFORMANCE REFERENTS

The next chapter will discuss the widely adopted expectancy disconfirmation model of consumer satisfaction. The focus of the present chapter is on the first sequence in that model, the formation of expectancies or expectations, as they are referred to here. As noted, some have objected to the use of the word *expectancy* in general and as it is used in this model in particular, because it would seem to imply that the standard of comparison or referent for performance is—and can only be—expectations. This is an unfortunate generalization stemming from the widespread belief that expectations are limited to predictions of future performance. In fact, it has already been said that anticipations may perform this function in a less exact or measurable manner. Thus, expectancies can be many things, including hopes and wishes and, as noted and discussed next, anticipations.

Anticipations as Expectations: Affective Expectations

The notion of anticipation is fairly new to the satisfaction literature, sharing commonalities with affect in consumption; the reason resulting from the fact that the two are related in some sense. If one were to scour the satisfaction literature for occurrences of *anticipation* one would find it linked to affective outcomes of consumption, such as disappointment, regret, joy, and even satisfaction itself (which, as argued later, is only partly affective). Although affect is discussed in much greater detail in Chapter 12, some aspects can be discussed in the present context.

Generally, affect cannot be pinpointed to an exact value for three reasons. First, it blends across its spectrum of related affects (e.g., contentment and serenity) and, second, its measurement is inexact. Even the best measures require either intensity qualifiers (strong or weak anger?) or frequency qualifiers (happy some days or most days?). More importantly, affect is *subjective experience*—a third reason estimation is difficult.

This discussion leads to two lines of discourse. First, are affective expectations processed? And, second, what are the most common consumption contexts in which they are relevant? The answer to the first is straightforward. A number of studies have found evidence (both anecdotal and empirical) showing consequences of pre-encounter states coupled with affective expectations (i.e., anticipations). For example, anticipated negative outcomes such as injury are preceded by apprehension, anxiety, and fear, while anticipated pleasure is preceded by optimism and hope. In all cases, significant effects of expectation-related consequences, including satisfaction, are observed.[6] Marketers and advertisers, of course, have known this for some time; anecdotal evidence is now supported by empirics too numerous to cite.[7] The barrier to greater specification has been more precise measurement, where strides are taking hold.

Regarding context, the two most prevalent areas of prepurchase anticipation as it affects postexposure evaluation are regret and satisfaction itself. The regret literature, elaborated more fully in Chapter 9, is replete with discussions of anticipated regret. In fact, the phenomenon is so robust that it has been shown to affect willingness to exercise a purchase decision via forestalling, mentioned earlier, as well as eventual satisfaction. High levels of anticipated regret may actually preclude a decision and hence its satisfaction outcome entirely. In this sense, the topic would not normally appear in this volume, except, of course, individuals can become (dis)satisfied with their *decision* to purchase or not.[8]

In the second area, that of satisfaction, two decision modalities have been studied. The first is that of expecting to provide (anticipating) an evaluation of satisfaction; the second is anticipating (in a predictive sense) the state of satisfaction itself. Research shows that evaluation expectations decrease satisfaction, perhaps because the consumer becomes primed to (negative) critical incidents.[9] Other research illustrates the indirect effect of various anticipations on satisfaction via mediating variables, such as expectancy disconfirmation, which have yet to be covered here.[10] The findings presented in this section suggest quite strongly that anticipations, like more formal expectations, are instrumental in satisfaction formation and deserve greater emphasis in fuller accounts of postpurchase responding.

Expectations of What?

Assume in what follows that anticipations and expectations act similarly in the processing of satisfaction; more specifically, both are either loose or more concrete predictions of future events. Then what exactly should the consumer predict in consumption? Up to the recent past, the most common answer would have been product performance. For example, consumers may invest in a security because they predict (and expect and hope) that it will go up in price, that it will perform well. This example of a price (or monetary return) expectation is one of the more easily operationalized expectations in consumption. Consumers, however, may view purchase outcomes in terms of higher-order abstractions.

The issue here is similar to that raised in the previous chapter, namely, the level of abstraction that is used by consumers. If consumers focus on attribute performance, then that is what they expect. If consumers focus on higher-order outcomes such as value, quality, or even self-actualization, then that is what is expected. And, as discussed, expectations may involve anticipated satisfactions. Thus, a consumer is able to predict a purchase outcome, but only anticipate a level of satisfaction that will accrue. The notion of an anticipated satisfaction, however, opens up the question of what it is about the product that is anticipated as satisfaction, a somewhat circular line of logic.

Also as noted in the prior chapter, the issue of the proper level of abstraction, or even of agreement on anticipated satisfactions, is intractable over a large sample of consumers. It is difficult to equate individuals on the basis of any one abstraction or satisfaction level. Perhaps this is why attribute performance is measured so often, as there is general agreement on what performance means. However, in doing so, the researcher incurs the risk of assuming that the meaning to the consumer is inherent in the attribute itself, a process referred to as reification.[11] Reification implies that the attribute is the "reality" sought by the consumer when, in fact, it may be a higher-order abstraction such as aesthetics or pleasure.

The pleasure example shows how this issue can become still more complicated. It may be that, for certain consumers, expectations will reference the consumer's affective anticipation of product performance. In fact, the product may not be processed directly or even at all if the consumer's only concern is the feeling generated by the product. A consumer who expects to enjoy a movie, for example, can make an enjoyment assessment without consciously processing the producing, directing, editing, or even the acting! In this example, expectations existed at the level of the consumer's affective response and were no more detailed than that. Recognition of nonperformance and noncognitive expectations was a fairly new phenomenon when the first edition of this book was composed, and work on this topic undoubtedly will continue.[12]

It should be clear that there is no simple answer to the question, Expectations of what? Expectations can always be reduced to the levels of product or service attributes, but the researcher will not be in a position to retranslate these attribute responses to higher-order abstractions or satisfactions. The issue does not end here, however. Even if it were possible to find the optimal abstraction level for each attribute, the researcher would still not know exactly which level of desire intensity the consumer holds as a standard, as discussed next.

Expectation Referents Categorized by Level of Desire

Shortly, we will examine the types of hierarchical expectations that consumers bring to product experiences. It has been recognized for some time that various expectation modalities vary by level of desire. For example, one might be the ideal or wished-for level; the second the expected or predicted level; and a third the minimum tolerable or lowest acceptable level. Generally, predicted levels will fall between the ideal and minimally tolerable, although often consumers will have no other option than to "tolerate" expected levels below the minimum tolerable. This could happen in business monopoly situations, such as in the service of a public utility. Lastly, a fourth might be the deserved level, stemming from what consumers think is appropriate based on investments, rights, and so on. Each of these levels can be given a short "be" label to enhance understanding. Respectively, they may be referred to as *can, will, must,* and *should* (or ought to be) levels.

Of note is that researchers often use a consumer's desired level of performance, or simply desire, as a performance referent.[13] Desires can be used along with expectations on the same attribute (to be discussed as dual- or multiple-level expectations) or on separate attributes when it is thought that predicted attribute levels versus desired attribute levels are more appropriate in a given context. And they can converge to the same level so that they become interchangeable. Moreover, both can be used when comparing competing purchase alternatives where desires apply to both, but predictions differ. As noted, more will be said on this, as the issue is intertwined with more abstract comparative operations, including equity and regret.

Tolerance and Indifference Zones

The phenomenon of event zones for expectations (and other concepts) has its roots in the intersection of a probability distribution with an ordering of event desirability. In a sense, it is a probability of winning different amounts of prize. This conception, however, is too pedestrian, as the prize itself has a distribution of desirability including the negative extreme of undesirability (the booby prize), while the upper, positive extreme is not necessarily most desirable for any one consumer. Whereas early treatments in satisfaction assumed that this underlying joint distribution contained discrete, identifiable levels (e.g., ideal, predicted), recent treatments recognize "vague" levels as might be more readily adapted for anticipations.[14] The remaining discussion will entertain the more easily described point levels, although vague levels are no less realistic. Later, the notion of undefined expectations will be introduced, a key concept for understanding consumer delight.

Current writings now recognize that the various expectation zones, as described earlier, are bounded by a level of perfection known as the ideal and a minimally acceptable level. Unacceptable levels are recognized as possibilities, but are viewed as situations to be avoided. The more probable levels expected in consumption are described as falling into an area bound by "adequate" and "desired" performance. More specifically, the range in between the desired and adequate levels is referred to as the *zone of tolerance* or, in a more restrictive case, a zone of indifference.[15] According to this view, the expected or predicted level is akin to the adequate level while the high end of the range is based on excellence or superiority.

It is unfortunate that the phrase *tolerance zone* has become accepted to describe the adequate-to-desired range because the literal meaning of *tolerance* is endurance or sufferance, as in a prescription drug being well tolerated. This author prefers to refer to the tolerance zone as the low or very low end of a product or service delivery range. Consumers must tolerate many offerings in life including regulated utilities, near monopolies (hubbed air transport), local unavailabilities of preferred products, entertainment availabilities, and so on. This is the convention assumed here. It is also possible to shift emphasis in the expectation range from personal desires to the basket of product offerings. Using this approach, another early paper described expectations as bounded by the "best brand" in the product class, through the brand-set norm (average), to the most unappealing of the offerings. This listing is a viable alternative that has been tested successfully by its proponents.[16]

Generally, researchers can choose the levels of greatest interest or strategic importance (e.g., competitive superiority). Although the entire range of expectations will not have been studied, more insight will be gained than if expectations had been omitted from the study or, worse, inferred without data. And, as noted previously, other related standards not technically falling into the category of pure expectations can be used to replace the expectation moniker. Candidates for this approach include strong desires more commonly known as wants (and even cravings), needs, values, and other competitive benchmarks.[17]

Figure 3.2 shows the full range of levels derived from these perspectives. The left side of the rectangle containing the range of expectations shows likely differences between what the consumer strongly desires (wants) in an objective sense and what the consumer speculates as the range of more likely (realistic) outcomes. Thus, the ideal vacation would have 100 percent sunny days and no rainy or cloudy days; the desired might be 90 percent; the deserved, based on the cost and time invested, might be 60 percent; 50 percent might be adequate; and anything less than that would have, in retrospect, voided the vacation location altogether.

These percentages loosely correspond to what are referred to here as desired expectation levels, as in "This is what I expect the product to deliver to satisfy me" or "This is what I know I want." Overlapping with the lower bound of the want expectations are levels that might reasonably be predicted to occur and that, by virtue of this fact, can only be held with uncertainty. Thus, the wanted levels are those that motivate the consumer to purchase or patronize; the predicted levels are those that might occur in an imperfect world and may be held as anticipations or apprehensions by the consumer.

Note that the wanted and predicted expectation levels are viewed as ranges with indefinite overlap. The range of wanted levels is intentionally higher than that of predicted levels, to indicate that consumers probably desire more than they know they will receive, due to the inability of businesses to prevent shortfalls in product and, especially, service delivery. It is unlikely that consumers would patronize an establishment where intolerable service is expected. However, there may very well be a nonzero prediction that intolerable service will be received, even if it is not expected. Also shown are brand-based norm levels that will be idiosyncratic to the tested context.

Figure 3.2 also shows two hypothetical tolerance zones and a potentially narrower zone of indifference. The upper tolerance zone encompasses the adequate–desired range while the lower range corresponds to the meaning preferred by the author. Reasons for distinguishing between

Figure 3.2   **Expectations According to Level of Desirability With Descriptive Ranges**

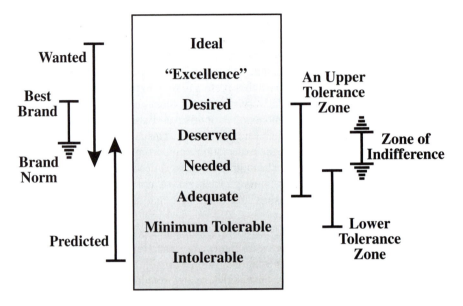

the tolerance and indifference ranges relate to the inherent separate meanings of tolerance and indifference. Consumers are not indifferent to what they must tolerate. Nor are they indifferent to excellent products or services; rather they are appreciative. This has been shown empirically where excellent service was consistently rated higher than normal service, which, in turn, was rated higher than adequate service.[18] Thus, tolerance zones are bounded by "the best I can expect to get to fulfill my desires" versus "the worst I will accept as barely fulfilling my needs," while indifference zones are bounded by an unspecified range of a lack of evaluative differences on the part of individual consumers.

Note at this point that consumers frequently refer to low expectations: "My expectations weren't too high" (as if to say they were low). This is not the same as saying that they were poor, for the word *poor* assumes a negative valence. Many products are profitably sold on the basis of low expectations, such as budget airlines, no-frills service, and other bare-bones offerings. Obviously and oftentimes the fulfillment of low expectations can be satisfying (but not so for "poor"), as will be explained in the next chapter. This, again, illustrates the fine semantic distinctions researchers must make when teasing out the true motivations underlying consumption.

Use of Multiple Standards

The previous discussion illustrates the difference between consumer desires and likely outcomes. If both are actively processed, the researcher may have to allow for the use of multiple expectation levels. A number of research investigations have established that consumers recognize and use multiple levels of expectations or standards. These studies have investigated the influence of predicted and normative (should) expectations; expected and ideal referents; and expected, ideal, and deservedlevels.[19]

In an early test of the influence of will (i.e., predicted) expectations and should (i.e., desired or deserved) expectations in two studies, the results were similar and representative of those to come.[20] In the first study, when the ideal or should level of expectations was the referent, satisfaction was lower than when the expected, predicted, or will-expectations were used. Apparently, high expectations can frustrate satisfaction attainment. In the second study, both desired and predicted levels were tested, with the result that desires were more compatible in an expectancy disconfirmation framework (to be discussed) than were predicted levels. Moreover, the studies generally concluded that consumers do entertain multiple standards and that inclusion of more than just the predicted level may improve a model's ability to predict satisfaction. And, in still another test of multiple expectations, it was found that some consumers have what might be termed "tentative" expectations. The authors speculated that buyers may harbor (in the authors' terms) "as-if" expectations, implying that consumers may predict one outcome but "would be satisfied if" a lesser outcome occurred.[21]

Selecting a "Best One" From Multiple Standards

In yet another study, this in the context of satisfaction with negotiation outcomes, negotiators were asked to report the levels of their very best, most likely, and rock-bottom profit outcomes expected in a forthcoming negotiation.[22] The most-likely expectation came closest to the actual outcome received by both buyers and sellers, lending substance to the assertion that predicted or expected outcomes have validity as comparative referents. Moreover, a comparison of the three outcome levels within a broader satisfaction paradigm (the expectancy disconfirmation model, to be discussed in the following chapter) showed that predicted outcomes generated the greatest explained variance estimates.

This study illustrates the use of direct questioning to discover multiple expectation levels. However, this task was facilitated in the negotiation study because there was only one critical attribute—financial gain. Had there been ten important attributes, then thirty separate questions would have had to be posed to get high, low, and predicted expectation levels, placing an onerous burden on the respondent. Note that this approach is perfectly general; as long as measures of differing levels of expectation, as well as the criterion variable of interest (e.g., satisfaction, quality) are taken, the most predictive of the expectations levels will be discovered. Two examples, one of an early test and one performed later, attest to this approach.[23]

Referents Categorized by Level of Abstraction

In an effort to show that expectations do not have to exist as concrete levels or even as likelihoods of known levels, a conceptual discussion of expectations couched in terms of whether the expectations were active or passive, knowable or unknowable, and certain, uncertain, or without a probability distribution whatsoever has been proposed.[24] This framework is presented in Figure 3.3.

Passive Versus Active Expectations

In the first column of the figure, expectations are viewed as either passive or active (active in the sense that they are cognitively processed). That is, when expectations are active, thought is given to the occurrence of outcomes regardless of whether the likelihoods are known. Thus, the likelihood of repairs, and even their cost, can be forecast at the macro level for a particular car model (and has been by Consumer's Union, publisher of *Consumer Reports*). Other outcomes, such as a fire in the engine compartment, are in a different category. Consumers would view this as a pos-

Figure 3.3   **The Oliver and Winer Expectation Framework**

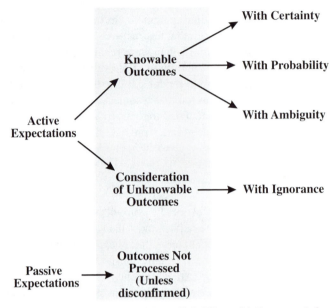

Source: Adapted from Richard L. Oliver and Russell S. Winter, "A Framework for the Formation and Structure of Consumer Expetations: Review and Propositions," *Journal of Economic Psychology,* 8 (December 1987): 488, by permission of Elsevier.

sible outcome because they have seen such occurrences on the freeway or on the news. But for an individual consumer, these events are assumed to be improbable and are not processed.

Similarly, other plausible outcomes may not be processed because they have become permanently coded into the consumer's view of the product; the consumer has adapted to a usual or static level of product performance. For example, consumers probably do not entertain the cognition that a refrigerator could maintain anything other than low operating temperatures. This becomes a passive expectation. Yet refrigerators do break down, and the likelihood of warm temperatures and spoiled food is real—it is plausible.

These latter expectations are the most difficult to ferret out because consumers do not process them until the underlying event is realized. For example, although the likelihood of being served unhealthy food (e.g., high fat and cholesterol) at a restaurant is probably an active expectation for many, the thought of dangerous food is not, thereby explaining the newsworthiness of food poisoning episodes.

Knowable Versus Unknowable Outcomes

The second level of analysis, shown in the second column of Figure 3.3, is the knowability of outcomes. Most consumers are not product designers and cannot know all the possible consequences of using products and services. Automobile rollovers may be improbable and may not be processed, but they are acknowledged as likely events when they occur. However, certain outcomes that have resulted during automobile ownership, such as fuel tanks exploding in accidents, transmissions jumping into and out of gear, and grossly premature engine wear (e.g., the first rotary engines), are not considered because they are not within the normal experience of automobile ownership. Innovations, including computer system upgrades, are particularly prone to this phenomenon. It is not unusual for computer users to feel shock and despair when they lose files without backups. Who would have thought this would happen?

Perhaps more so than with passive expectations, consumers will not have the foresight or wisdom to anticipate unknowable outcomes. This begs the question of how one can refer to them as expectations at all. The answer to this is that the component of an expectation set reflecting unknowable outcomes is not attribute-specific. Rather it exists as an apprehension, an anxiety, or, in the worst case, a dread (see Chapters 10 and 12). Frequently individuals will refer to this anxiety with phrases like "knocking on wood," "keeping my fingers crossed," or "waiting for the other shoe to drop." Not knowing for sure what will happen, they exhibit an apprehensiveness nonetheless. It should be clear that no attribute list will draw out this type of expectation. And for products susceptible to this problem, the expectation set will always be incomplete, and reasons for reluctance to buy will not be completely understood. This discussion has not touched on a broader set of phenomena where individuals have no apparent expectations; that is, they do not entertain future events at all. This will be discussed shortly.

Certainty, Uncertainty, Ambiguity, and Ignorance

The last column in Figure 3.3 shows that outcomes can be framed in terms of the degree to which the frequency distribution of the outcome is known. For example, some consequences of purchase and patronage are known with certainty. Perhaps the best example is cost, if one narrowly defines it as price. Most retail purchases involve fixed prices at a given establishment (but not necessarily across outlets), and little or no variance exists in the probability distribution of price paid. The price of a first-class postage stamp at a particular time is a good example of invariant cost across most postal service outlets.

The second category of outcome distributions involves uncertainty with a known distribution of outcomes. Games of chance (e.g., cards, bingo) are the best examples. In roulette, the payoff odds of every possible bet are known precisely. Odd or even bets on a zero, double-zero wheel give the bettor a .476 chance of winning double the bet. Other "near examples" include certain securities derivatives, such as options, and even the weather on a particular day.

Most products fall into the third category, which is referred to as ambiguity. This term implies that although the possible outcomes of a purchase are known, the probabilities of their occurrence are not. Consider a dining-out example. What are the probabilities of traffic being light or heavy, of parking being easy or hard, of the wait being long or short, of the available tables being well situated or not, of the service being courteous or rude or slow or prompt, of the meal being good or so-so, of the other patrons being noisy or subdued? Even if all these individual distributions were known, the joint distribution would still be ambiguous.

Finally, there exists ignorance, which implies that no distribution of outcomes can be ascertained, perhaps because there is no historical precedent for the outcomes or because the outcomes are subject to a random process. This occurs in conjunction with unknowable outcomes, discussed previously, and is not all that uncommon in societies with rapid innovation and experimentation. For example, pharmaceuticals, medical procedures, biogenetics, social reform, social experimentation, and politics are subject to these processes. Often the outcomes of novelty cannot be anticipated and are surprising, even to those who pioneered the innovation. To take an unfortunate example, it could not have been anticipated that asbestos, one of the most noncombustible, nonconducting, and insulating of materials, would later prove to be one of the most dangerous carcinogens.

The previous discussion attempts to make the point that expectations contain elements that are not tangible and cannot be easily quantified. Unknowables, uncertainties, vague probabilities, and affective anticipations including apprehensions and passive tranquility are part of this process. Researchers are not oblivious to these states, for the surprise of unanticipated consumer response is disheartening to the profession as well. The literature is somewhat piecemeal on this, perhaps because the occurrence of errant expectations is found under a mix of situations. For example, low involvement, unfamiliar, infrequent, nonroutine, and complex products and purchases and those having ambivalent or meaningless features all pose conceptual and measurement difficulties. To this end, a variety of examples is provided.[25]

Referents Categorized by Focal Comparison Object

At this point, attribute levels and their accompanying expectations psychology have been discussed. The attribute itself, the level of abstraction at which the attribute is processed, the level of desired performance, and the uncertainty surrounding attainment of the attribute level are all dimensions within this concept. A remaining dimension concerns the high likelihood that attribute performance will be compared to something else; that is, the product or service or its attribute set is expected to outperform or meet the performance of an alternative or comparative referent object. Thus, the expectation initiates a comparison operation of the "better than" variety.

A number of writings have provided insights, and in some cases, empirically based propositions, concerning to what consumers compare candidate products. These comparative referents are intertwined with the expectation process and cannot be omitted. In particular, they determine the relative level of the expectation in a "better than," "same as," or "worse than" sense and form the basis for regret (see Chapter 9). In this sense, the consumer is saying, "I expect that the product I select will be better than one I forgo" or "I expect that this version of the product will be better than the one I bought before" or "I expect that this product will be better than the one my neighbor bought."

Early efforts to formally address this issue proposed that expectations could be framed on the basis of historical norms or experience.[26] This view speaks to the sources of expectations, suggesting that comparisons against other brands in the product class may be more germane to satisfaction judgments than are ordinary predictions of attribute performance. Specifically, for commonly patronized establishments that have attained only subtle differentiation, such as fast-food restaurants where burgers and fries are the mainstay, it has been found that, in addition to predictive expectations, a best-brand norm (the best in its class) and a product norm (an average for the class) all played a role in satisfaction judgments. Other studies have found similar effects in other contexts. These involved situations where consumers could make judgments comparing a best brand versus competitive brands (banks, B2B consulting services) or comparisons between same-form product brands versus alternative forms (exercise equipment, wines). The results of all these studies were instructive in that satisfaction levels were sensitive to both comparisons where each added to explained variance.[27]

Using a more elaborate exposition of many and varied comparisons consumers may make to a single product selection, an open-ended format protocol analysis was conducted on a small sample of new users of a fitness center.[28] This study revealed a number of distinct categories of comparison referents used in selecting and evaluating the facility. In order of mention, these were (1) other products or services, either directly competitive or substitutable (e.g., another fitness club or an organized sport such as cycling); (2) other situations, such as when the center is crowded versus when it is not, or on weekends versus after work; (3) other people, such as others in the center (e.g., fitness "jocks") or others not working out; (4) other times, such as prior to beginning a fitness program; (5) internal standards, such as specific personalized desires (e.g., clean locker

Table 3.1

Hypothetical Expectation Set for a Family Shopping for a New Home

Expectation dimension	Type of attribute				
	Knowable with certainty	Knowable with probability	Knowable with ambiguity	Unknowable	Passive
Attribute/level of abstraction	Property taxes	Location	Style/design	Hidden problems	Availability of utilities/services
Level of desire	Minimally tolerable	"Best"	Desired	Minimal	Not processed
Level of uncertainty	None	Low	High	Very high	Not processed
Comparative referent	Higher than previous	Better than previous	Better than neighbors	No more than normal	Not processed

rooms, specific equipment); and (6) marketer-supplied standards such as promotional claims (e.g., lose weight, tone muscles). This study, more so than most, illustrates the complexity of studying expectations in actual consumer environments.

One can conclude from the preceding discussion that both brand differences and product form differences that perform the sought-after performance function should be studied for a better understanding of postpurchase responses. The discussion also illustrates the many and varied referents available to consumers and the many dimensions of an expectation. To recap, expectations can exist at any level of want or desire, in a concrete or very ambiguous level of abstraction, and can be held in regard to products, other people, situations, internal standards, and external claims.

An Applied Example

As an example of the many combinations of expectation possibilities, consider a family prospecting for a new home in a new geographic location. A home purchase is a very complex decision, and many factors are considered. Thus, the family's expectation set may be very involved and may encompass all the combinations of expectation dimensions discussed here. A hypothetical limited set is shown in Table 3.1.

The table shows five attributes with different expectation properties. These correspond to the five examples in Figure 3.3. In the first, the shopper expects to pay property taxes of a known amount, this amount is "minimally tolerable," and the rate is higher than that paid in the previous residence. Although this is a perfectly known aspect of moving to the new location, it nonetheless qualifies as a valid expectation. In all likelihood, it will be exactly achieved. The effect of this outcome on satisfaction awaits analysis in the next chapter where confirmed tolerably negative expectations are discussed.

The second example, that of location, illustrates an attribute with a high expectation likelihood. Under many circumstances, the number of available homes in certain neighborhoods is known with precision. If the family narrows the search to a subset of communities, the a priori likelihood of finding a home in each is proportional to the number of available homes specific to each area. Therefore, the shopper can expect to find a home in a "best" neighborhood with a particular "high-likelihood" probability. If the shopper intends the candidate neighborhoods to be in the upper reaches of those formerly resided in, then it can be said that the shopper expects to find a home potentially better than those owned previously.

The third case shows an example of a "hope" expectation, one with a high uncertainty but a high return if achieved. Here, the family hopes to find a home with a desirable architectural design that would make the home a showcase in the neighborhood. The family has no sense of the likelihood of finding such a house because the outcome is contingent on two events—finding a desirably styled house and finding it in a neighborhood where all other houses are less desirably styled. This expectation is a long shot, but it exists in the consumer's expectation set nonetheless.

The fourth example shows a "fear" expectation. Because all homes, even newly constructed ones, can be expected to develop problems, home purchases come with apprehensions. Here, the level of uncertainty is very high because problems can go undetected prior to purchase, they can develop after purchase due to normal deterioration, or they can be caused by some unanticipated external event (e.g., an earth tremor). The shopper's expectation, however, is that these problems will be minimal or "no more than normal." Despite this wish, the level of uncertainty cannot be assessed.

Finally, the last column depicts the typical passive expectation, which the shopper takes for granted and does not process. The example here is the availability of public utilities and services. It would be rare, indeed, for an established neighborhood not to have water, gas, electricity, fire protection, police, and sanitary services. Imagine the shock if a new-home purchaser were to find that the trash contractor went bankrupt and no ready replacement were available. The expectation would go unprocessed until this event occurred; then it would be processed extensively.

The "Best" of the Expectation-Based Comparative Referents

Earlier, the notion of a "best" expectation *level* was discussed. Here, one questions whether any particular expectation is the best comparison standard or *referent* for use in satisfaction models. Note, correctly, that the most common interpretation of the word *expectation* is a consideration of future events, particularly as to the likelihood of occurrence of these events. The origins of this notion are manifold, but are especially prevalent in economic models where the terms *rational expectations* and *expected utility* abound. Theoretically, individuals take actions, including the purchase of products and services, because they expect that the product will maximize their "utility." The intended purpose of this section is to unravel this issue and to formally argue that predictive expectations capture a greater variety of what purchasers desire in a consumable than do other terms.

The argument begins by acknowledging that consumers do buy products and patronize services to fulfill their desires, to "satisfy" needs, and to achieve valued end states of consumption, such as achievement and well being. Their desires, needs, and/or values are preexisting and may be seen as antecedent conditions. Once actively aroused, however, these same desires, needs, and values prompt consumers to seek out products that have desire-fulfilling, need-fulfilling, and value-fulfilling properties. Thus, individuals pursue products that they expect will satisfy, and these expectations are the immediate translations of the basic needs. Thus, needs, values, and desires all operate to influence the "expectations" the consumer would have for a candidate purchase; each would constitute a different category of the consumer's expectation set.[29]

It follows that if a consumer has a particular desire and believes (expects) that a product will fulfill that desire, the consumer cannot be faulted for buying it. Now, if the product fails in its promise to fulfill these expectations, the consumer will, in all likelihood, be dissatisfied with it (see the next chapter for exceptions). The consumer may also be frustrated that his or her desires were not quelled, that needs were not fulfilled, and that values were not achieved. However, these additional frustrations have already been reflected in the fact that the expectation set, deriving from needs, values, and desires, has not been fulfilled. Thus, the underfulfillment of expectations captures all the derivative elements that were considered in the expectation formation process itself.

Acknowledging this, there will be situations where consumers may process expectations and needs separately. Research findings presented earlier have shown, for example, that desires or should expectations may operate in tandem with predictive expectations. What would explain this? A speculation is that this situation is more likely to occur when the outcomes of processing the two referents are incongruent so that, in an apparent paradox, the consumer may express satisfaction and dissatisfaction at the same time. Assume that it is known that a product, the best on the market, will only partially satisfy the consumer, but that the consumer's desire is full satisfaction. This same product may perform exactly as promised and may even overperform. However, that level of performance was known a priori to be less than fulfilling, so that the consumer is satisfied with the product and dissatisfied with the lack of complete fulfillment.

Using an example from the previous chapter, dentifrice whiteners do lighten teeth, but it is rare that they would result in teeth as white as pearls. So a consumer could be "happy" with the improvement, but not with the fact that pure whiteness was not achieved, resulting in a state of "unsatisfaction" as opposed to dissatisfaction. This example shows the operation of multiple expectation levels, one a desire or wished-for level and the other a predicted or will level. If a survey were to ask only one expectation question without a stated should or would referent, the researcher would not be able to tie any one respondent's answer to multiple comparison levels and the interpretation of the results would be incomplete or perhaps muddled.

Thus, the issue of the "best" referent is now further extended. Whereas the examples in Table 3.1 assumed different referents for different attributes, it now appears that, under special circumstances, there may be more than one correct referent for the same attribute, as noted earlier. Generally, however, multiple expectations tend to exist on the level-of-desire dimension, rather than on other dimensions such as uncertainty.

It is the researcher's responsibility to determine when the operation of multiple comparison standards occurs and if this is relevant to the research context. As noted later in this chapter, this will require two sets of expectation measures. If the researcher is confident that one referent is sufficient or if survey parsimony is a concern, then the author's preferred method is to measure the preconsumption comparative referent as a predictive expectation. The logic for this conclusion derives from the inclusive nature of an expectation.

Note that discussion has been limited to expectation-based comparative referents. As explained in the Introduction, Part II of this book discusses referents that rely on different comparative logic. The possible exception to this is need fulfillment, the subject of Chapter 5. This topic is central to the satisfaction response, however, and requires detailed treatment, presented later.

SOURCES OF REFERENTS AND REASONS FOR THE LEVEL OF ABSTRACTION

The previous discussion explored in depth the concept of an expectation. At this point, a reasonable question is "How does information available to the consumer come to form the expectation set?" Although one would assume that much is known about this matter from anecdotal accounts and generalities, the available writings do not bear this out.[30] What follows is a brief overview. Discussion begins by considering the external factors that create expectations in consumers' minds.

External Sources

Promotional Claims

Expectations deriving from sources external to the consumer are not limited simply to promotional claims such as advertising and sales statements, although these do constitute the majority of corporate communications received. Due to the obvious commercial nature of these statements, some would argue that such claims are subject to greater consumer scrutiny than other sources. Generally, however, it should be acknowledged that consumers may very well believe the manufacturer's and provider's product and service claims, frequently taking them at full measure and using them to create expectations of the product's likely performance. For example, it has been theoretically and empirically shown that advertising may be particularly important if the consumer has no other information sources or experience on which to draw.[31]

Word of Mouth

Another very potent source of information is word of mouth. Some researchers have argued that the experiences of other consumers carry much greater weight than other information sources due to the degree of similarity between recipient and communicator and the lack of a financial motive on the part of the other person. In fact, one study found that the importance of the opinions of referent others varied in terms of how closely the person was related to the recipient. In this study, spouses' opinions were more important than those of relatives, which, in turn, were more important than those of friends. It is also the case, however, that consumers do not require that the referent person be known to them; simple evaluations by others may be sufficient to generate expectations.[32]

Third-Party Information

Consumers frequently rely on independent reports of product quality and transform these ratings into an expectation. The well-known Consumer's Union publication *Consumer Reports* is one such example. Government testing, such as the National Institute of Traffic and Highway Safety crash fatality tests, is another source. Files of the local Better Business Bureau provide other reports, as do the increasingly popular exposé TV programs at both the local and network levels. Specialty magazines, such as *Motor Trend*, *Bicycling*, and *Skiing*, also provide comparative data.

Product Cues

From a behavioral perspective, the more interesting issue concerns how consumers utilize various cues that have only an indirect relation to product attribute expectations. Five of these that have received much attention in the literature are price, scarcity, brand name, store image, and advertising expenditures—the latter more so than advertising repetition. Regarding price, a history of research suggests that a high price relative to other brands implies quality or general performance excellence in the minds of consumers. Reviews of this literature reveal the following generalizations.[33]

First, it appears that reference prices—the prices of like goods—are used as a price expectation so that price begets price. Also, and as one would expect, some, but not all, consumers do use price as an indicator of overall quality, particularly if other information is not available. Interestingly, some consumers actually use quality as an indicator of price. To the extent that product knowledge and the availability of other cues increase, the influence of price decreases. Because price is a surrogate for the quantity and quality of the inputs to production, consumers feel some justification for this belief. Also of interest is that studies of price and objective quality often find only weak relations for some product categories, particularly durables, and near-zero relations for others.[34] This latter anomaly has been explained in a comprehensive review of the literature. The authors show that one can only expect a positive price-quality relation when one or more of the following conditions are present: the quality determinants are clearly visible, the cost of obtaining quality information is low, the price is high, the item is purchased frequently, and the consumption period is long. Interestingly, "prestige" goods tend to exhibit a negative relationship.[35]

In a related manner, a product's scarcity or unavailability connotes value, a sense of quality, and generally high price to those who would invest in this product category.[36] Art, collectibles, antiques, limited editions, and one-of-a-kinds all benefit from this phenomenon. The reasons go beyond mere supply and demand. Due to the awe and mystery of a rare item, individuals tend to make extreme evaluations. When values are placed on scarcity, the value tracks the extremity of the evaluation in the direction of its valence so that rare "good things" can be expensive and rare "bad things" may be avoided. Interestingly, initially ambiguous items have no evaluative extremity until some authority places a value on their goodness or badness. For example, the famous upside-down airplane on a misprinted U.S. postage stamp did nothing to increase the stamp's face value until it was decided that this stamp was a worthy collectible. Stamp buyers at the time of its issue may have shunned it as defective.

Brand name is yet another powerful influence on expectations. In fact, in a recent cross-cultural comparison of signals of product quality, brand name dominated price (which ranked second) consistently across four global cultural regions. Research on this topic, now discussed under the heading of brand equity, is growing to show that brand names can transfer meaning to new products for which no information is yet available to the consumer. In a variation of this theme, a well-known brand and a lesser-known brand (to consumers) may pair to form a brand alliance, such as IBM and Intel, Diet Coke and NutraSweet, and Kellogg and Healthy Choice. The effect may diminish, however, when little correspondence exists between the old and new, although sequential, intermediate brand extensions may be helpful in this regard.[37] Store image follows a similar logic.

The relation between the level of advertising (expenditures, repetitions) and perceptions (expectations in the present case) of quality was first proposed in the 1970s. It was argued that producers of high-quality goods will reap greater benefits from advertising because consumers will more rapidly become familiar with and motivated to use the product, will find that it lives up to its claims, and will encourage others to try it. Thus, consumers will learn to impute quality through frequent advertising, a conclusion reinforced by macrolevel analyses cited earlier. Although this sequence of events has face validity, at least one study shows that advertising level effects may be U-shaped if consumers begin to question the advertiser's confidence in its product.[38]

Internal Sources

It is widely acknowledged that the consumer's past experience with the focal product and those of its competitors become internalized as norms and are coded as normative expectations.[39] A number of studies use these as proxies for what the consumer may or may not believe to be true regarding current or future experience. These phenomena partially explain the carryover effects of the past on current perceptions, as mentioned in the introduction to this chapter, and account for the dilemma of the poor quality producer and the competitive advantage held by the leading firm.

For the same reason, information stored from personal and impersonal communications, apart from direct experience, plays an important, but somewhat intuitive role in expectation formation. A more complex treatment of this topic requires examination of the retrieval mechanisms that consumers use when formulating expectations from memory. For some time, researchers have known that the retrieval process is subject to subtle distortions and to specific strategies to conserve mental effort. Two of these are the ease of recall and the vividness of the events being recalled.

Ease of Recall

Whenever a product category is unimportant to the consumer, a phenomenon known as low involvement, consumers will not expend great amounts of cognitive effort to process it. Particularly in such cases, the information used by the consumer will generally be that which is most easily retrieved, a strategy referred to as availability or accessibility. Use of availability will cause consumers to access the most immediate information in memory. This example is often referred to as a recency phenomenon.

One reason for effects such as recency in product or service performance recall is that consumers appear unable to process a long history of performance experience in a manner similar to a moving average. Rather, they are thought to focus on memorable or distinctive moments from the past or to update a summary of past experience with their most recent exposure. While some researchers have tried to model this process with sophisticated mathematical terms, generally consumers are found to give inordinate weight to the most recent occurrence of product performance. As discussed at the beginning of this chapter in a macro context, prior satisfaction has a potent effect on future expectations. A study at the individual level shows this same effect. In a model of expectation influences, the coefficient due to prior satisfaction exceeded that of store image and word of mouth.[40]

For a number of reasons, negative events are more available in memory than positive events; in fact, research shows that negativity exerts inordinate influence at the earliest stages of processing. Individuals are thought to attend to and encode negative information more rapidly because such processing has the potential to prevent harm through avoidance of negative stimuli, people, products, and so on. Generally, individuals are prone to take immediate action to avoid losses, but can pursue pleasure at a more leisurely pace. When the greater vigilance directed at negative information is paired with the willingness of consumers to overweigh more recent information, one can see the danger for firms that permit a dissatisfying service experience to go unresolved. Not only do dissatisfied consumers communicate their feelings to others at a rate estimated to be many times that of satisfied consumers, but the recipients of the negative reports will, in all likelihood, use them in their own expectation formation thoughts.

Vividness of Recall

Apart from the recency effect, the second factor facilitating recall is the distinctiveness or vividness of the events that have occurred. In a sense, negative information appears as more distinctive than positive information and thus may be subject to both influences discussed here. Surprising events also appear as unique and distinctive, fostering attention and further mental processing.[41]

Imagery or imaginal processing has been shown to enhance vividness, partly because it is more colorful than semantic content (words and descriptions). Advertising has such an effect, particularly if it has a high percentage of visual stimuli. It has been argued that imagery is also more available than semantics in that it is easier to retrieve, thus providing a dual pathway for its effect. As an added benefit, imagery in the processing of advertising has been shown to be positively related to affect, whereas a more semantic analysis of advertising content had an adverse impact.[42]

Numerous other influences and heuristics are known to affect expectations directly or to influence the retrieval of expectation-relevant material from memory. This discussion serves only to provide an introduction to the complexity of the phenomenon. Attention turns now to the actionable side of the expectation concept, namely, measurement. In doing so, it is assumed that the list of key performance dimensions or attributes has been previously assessed, as discussed in the previous chapter.

MEASURING EXPECTATIONS: HOW AND WHEN

The measurement of expectations (or expectancies, as found in other sources) has been discussed at length in various literatures. Whether the probabilities of future events are referred to as odds, as is common in games of chance and sports, or as subjective probabilities, the measurement of expectations essentially asks consumers to place likelihood estimates on specific occurrences of product or service performances in the future. Consumers may also be asked to place likelihood estimates on events that have already occurred, a practice necessitated in many customer environments, such as pedestrian (as opposed to online) retailing, where the identity of clientele cannot be known a priori. Discussion centers first on the measurement of actual *predictive* expectations, those that are estimated before the occurrence of an event.

Predictive Expectations

As formulated in many disciplines, expectations are essentially probabilities or likelihoods without a valence (positivity or negativity), as in the odds of drawing a jack in a deck of cards. Without further knowledge of the card player's wishes, it is not known whether drawing a jack is good or bad. Even if it were known that the jack was needed to fill an inside straight, the likelihood of doing so would not change.

In most consumption situations, however, consumers will hold valenced expectations, since the basis of purchase and acquisition is to obtain products with pleasant consequences and to avoid those with potentially unpleasant outcomes. In fact, the following definitions of high and low expectations were proposed in an early paper by the author.[43]

High expectations:	Desirable events will occur.
	Undesirable events will *not* occur.
Low expectations:	Desirable events will *not* occur.
	Undesirable events will occur.

Note that the valence is clearly included in these statements, phrased as desirabilities or undesirabilities. In practice, the valence component of the expectation generally will be implied in the wording of the expectation item on a survey. For example, questions might refer to "good" gas mileage or use words with a positive or negative connotation such as praise from friends, courteous servers, or delays on airline departures. For purposes of illustration, the possibility that affective outcomes, such as joy, are part of the consumer's goal set will be suspended. Rather, concern will focus only on the performance component of expectations—the predicted performance level. It will be assumed that the performance referent is phrased in properly valenced fashion.

In measuring expectations before purchase or patronization, one must be careful to ensure that the consumer sample has some basis for forming an expectation set. Consumers probably do go into many purchases without complete expectation knowledge, but it would be rare for consumers not to have any awareness of the product at all. At the minimum, the brand and price will be known to the consumer, and some individuals will use these to infer the remaining performance characteristics.[44] Because of the possibility that some elements of the expectation set will not be known to all consumers, however, it would be wise to include a "don't know" category in the expectation section of the survey.

Examples of Measures

The types of expectation measures available to the researcher are straightforward. A number of variations are shown here, including the familiar Likert version in agree/disagree format.

If I complain, I will get a response (times in 10):	0 1 2 3 4 5 6 7 8 9 10
Brand X has (possesses) feature Y:	Unlikely_____Likely
Company X will refund my money:	No chance_____50/50_____Certain
Brand X will satisfy my needs:	Disagree_____Neither_____Agree

There is no evidence that any one measure is better than another. Rather, the context of the investigation should dictate the question format. For example, a chances-in-ten scale is most useful when the consumer has had a chance to sample the product over multiple purchases. A household staple and a familiar restaurant both qualify as examples. In contrast, a likelihood format could be used for a first-time purchase, as could the agree/disagree and no chance/certain scales.

Of interest is the fact that expectation questions typically ask only for the uncertainty dimension of an expectation. The attribute level, level of desire, and comparative referent are phrased into the stem of the question, as in the following (from Table 3.1):

Finding a desired architectural style more attractive than the surrounding homes:
Unlikely_____Likely

If the qualifier "more attractive than the surrounding homes" in this example were omitted, the meaning of the question would change to merely finding a desired architectural style. This illustrates the necessity of including in the question all specific meaning intended by the researcher. The question would also change if the word *adequate* or *ideal* were substituted for *desired* or if no adjective were used at all. This minor but important variation changes the degree of want (see Figure 3.2) implied in the expectation.

Note that no example of "raw" product performance has been suggested, as in "The car will average 35 miles per gallon." There are two problems with the use of such measures. First, 35 miles per gallon is a point estimate, and for any one consumer, expected performance could be above or below this level. Second, it is not known whether this is a good or poor level of performance in the consumer's mind. As noted, consumer research requires that the expectation have a connotation of valence so that the pull or push of the expectation for purchase can be gauged. The first problem might be mitigated if the item were reworded to say "at least" 35 miles per gallon, but, again, it is not known whether all consumers use this cutoff to determine acceptable versus unacceptable performance. Perhaps the best way of handling this situation is to phrase the question in terms of good or high mileage and to permit the consumer to use an internal standard of what good mileage is.

Measuring Ideal, Should, and Desired Expectations

A potential problem exists if the researcher wishes to tap expectations of excellence. In short, excellence or ideal levels frequently run up against the well-known ceiling effect, where respondents may wish to check a scale response higher than the scale allows (e.g., wishing to check 8 on a 1-to-7 scale). Because expectations are measured on bounded scales, consumers frequently use the extreme positive pole to represent ideal levels. Thus, expected ideal performance is perfect or 10-in-10 performance, or it is at the upper range of the performance scale. For example, the SERVQUAL method asks consumers to describe how excellent service firms should perform on seven-point scales where 7 is the highest positive value.[45] Critiques of this type of scale have pointed out that ideal levels of excellence may have little or no variance and contribute minimally to quality or satisfaction models.[46] Nonetheless, should expectation levels are of value to management and can be measured if the researcher takes care to word the measure so that ceiling effects are minimized, as will be illustrated. The actual wording is probably idiosyncratic to a context, however, so that few guidelines can be offered. Further insights for individual readers may be found in Chapter 6 on quality.

Practical Issues in the Measurement of Multiple Standards

Although some writers have decried the use of predictive expectations and have shown that alternative standards and referents perform better in individual studies, it has been argued here that predicted levels incorporate other standards such as desires and needs and hence provide the most consistent meaning across consumers. Different consumers may use different standards to form predicted levels, but these predicted levels are the standards they take into consumption.

There is some merit, however, in assessing the two levels of desired and adequate performance, as these bound a large section of the tolerance region (see Figure 3.2) where predicted or expected levels most surely can be found. This strategy will require that consumers complete two lists of expectation questions, along with the other questions needed to study satisfaction. The survey may therefore suffer from length and fatigue considerations. Including other standards, such as ideals, compounds the problem.

One solution is to use multiple samples of respondents whereby one sample completes a survey with desired expectations and another with predicted expectations. While this method will provide insight on each separately, the researcher will not be able to calculate the zone of tolerance on an individual level and must rely on descriptive comparisons across the two samples.

Another solution is to place the desired and predicted scales side by side, as in these two examples:

Medicine X: Easy to Swallow

Should be					Will be				
Hard				Easy	Hard				Easy
1	2	3	4	5	1	2	3	4	5

Courier X: Speed of Delivery

Desired					Adequate				
Slow				Fast	Slow				Fast
1	2	3	4	5	1	2	3	4	5

While this format provides some space-saving economies, the close juxtaposition of the two forms of expectation questions may introduce a fairly obvious interaction. The researcher's goal, under this format, is somewhat more transparent than if the two sections were widely separated. This is so because consumers may adopt a halo response set whereby the should questions are always scored high and the will questions are scored, for example, two scale units below. This two-column format (and three-column, to include performance) has been tested.47 Reliabilities and validities appear not to be compromised. However, a two-column format has not been tested against a sequential format where the should questions are asked in one section and the would questions in another. This comparison awaits further testing.

Measuring Expectations After the Fact: Retrospective Expectations

Very frequently in satisfaction studies (and possibly in every instance, depending on the industry), the researcher cannot identify purchasers before consumption and is therefore constrained to measure expectations concurrently as the level of satisfaction is assessed. In this event, the expectation section of the survey should appear before any other material, especially satisfaction. The wording of the question would conform to the following general format: "Referring to the time you first purchased the product (engaged the service), what were your expectations at that time?" The subsequent list of attribute expectations would then be worded in the following tense: "At the time I purchased the car, I believed that it would give me high gas mileage."

Although this usage does not tap predictive expectations and raises some fairly important issues (to be discussed), three reasons account for the majority of cases when the researcher is forced to rely on expectations ex post facto. The first is simply neglect; the researcher was not aware of or saw no need for expectation measurement prior to purchase and use, and was content to make interpretations from the performance ratings alone. The second reason is that some firms may not wish to suggest possible product experience—for example, the probability of breakdown and repair or of complaining outcomes—to consumers before use.

The third reason is due to necessity; most firms cannot predict and do not have access to their customers prior to purchase of the product. Virtually all tangibles sold at retail fit this description. Producers first learn who (a fraction of) their buyers are when warranty cards are returned. Services provide greater latitude because the consumer can be intercepted prior to the service episode. However, it is still true that the consumer, in most cases, has made an earlier decision to patronize the service, and this decision may affect expectation measurement in subtle ways. In these cases the researcher must rely on the ability of consumers to reflect back on what they thought the product or service would deliver. A number of problems now become evident.

Recall the earlier discussion of consumer retrieval mechanisms. The retrieval biases of availability and vividness may play a role in recollection. Another problem is even more severe. Generally, consumers will have already experienced the product's performance. In this case, what they have experienced and what they recall will be confounded. Most probably, the recalled expectations will be biased in response to the experienced performance. In tests of this hypothesis, two studies found that recalled expectations were higher for dissatisfied than for satisfied consumers. The explanation is that a negative product experience would create higher expectancies in retrospect to justify the dissatisfaction (unmet expectations) and that positive experiences would move recalled expectations lower, as if to imply that expectations were exceeded. Moreover, when this "recall error" in expectations is examined over desired (ideal) and predicted (will) variations, the will expectations are affected to a greater extent, presumably because desires, being high-level goals, are less mutable.48

One explanation for findings such as these is that consumers with ill-defined expectations, perhaps because they are unfamiliar with the product or service category, will construct data-driven or bottom-up strategies for responding to expectations ex post facto. This may be especially true if consumers feel that ill-formed expectations reflect poorly on their judgment or decision-making skills, or if the survey appears to assume that consumers are "supposed to have" expectations.

This phenomenon has also been recently explored with reference to the consistency or inconsistency between predictions and outcomes. It had been thought that outcome-consistent expectancies would be more easily retrieved. Later evidence showed that outcome-inconsistent expectancies were also likely to be accurately remembered due to the attention-getting properties of an expectancy violation, suggesting a U-shaped effect. Evidence now suggests that vague, one-sided claims, such as found in fortune cookies ("Good luck will come your way"), are remembered only when actualized; the default outcome—the status quo—is not processed. Alternatively, events that have clear, two-sided outcomes that are focused in time, such as a gain or loss in a security at the end of a year, result in accurate expectation remembrances if either event materializes.[49] Thus, there may be greater validity in retrospective reports of expectations than most are willing to concede, particularly if the predictions are clear and relate to a particular point in consumption. Research awaits this issue.

Updating Expectations During Consumption

Are expectations updated during consumption? Most assuredly. The issue of expectation changes during consumption pervades extended consumption situations, such as those encountered for services. Because transaction satisfaction is most accurately measured at the conclusion of the transaction, the expectation referent relevant to satisfaction analysis is the one actually used by the consumer in satisfaction formation, not necessarily the one measured before consumption. As intuitive as this conclusion may appear, however, the evidence is mixed. Some studies in which expectations were measured (or manipulated) both before and after consumption found that the after measures predicted satisfaction more accurately. This result, known as "backward assimilation" (referred to as hindsight in Chapter 9), would be expected given the psychological biases just discussed. In another study, however, the reverse "forward assimilation" effect occurred where preexpectations dominated, although the backward effect was evident to a lesser extent.[50]

In yet another study of restaurant dining, participants were asked to record expectations of a novel restaurant experience, patronize the establishment, and complete a second survey of recalled expectations and satisfaction. This study, described more fully in the next chapter, illustrated that, although expectations are updated, they do not necessarily have differential effects on satisfaction or other criteria. The correlation between pre- and postratings was on the order of 0.7, varying over features. That between preexpectations and performance was 0.3, which rose to 0.45 when performance was related to postexpectations. Neither pre nor post, however, were markedly different in their relation with satisfaction (0.2 versus 0.3).[51]

These studies illustrate to greater or lesser degrees the inevitable confounding of expectations and performance once performance observations have begun. In measuring revised expectations, the researcher must realize that they may have been influenced by observed performance up to the updating. Thus, it is more accurate to say that the revised expectations are "performance-amended" or some such term. The studies do illustrate, however, the need to explore the updating phenomenon more thoroughly. Moderating conditions such as feature abstraction, involvement, and ambiguous or vague performance may play a role. This issue is confounded with the role of expectations in both performance and disconfirmation judgments, discussed more fully in the next chapter and alluded to in the following sections.

THE FUNCTION OF EXPECTATIONS IN SATISFACTION FORMATION

Why has so much time been allocated to expectations, which, prior to recent experience, have not been typically measured in satisfaction surveys? There are two answers to this question. The first is covered here and the second in the following chapter. For the present, a hasty prelude to the second answer is that consumers are thought to combine expectations and performance to form a conclusion about the degree to which their expectations were fulfilled.

The first answer is that expectations, alone, play a role in satisfaction formation, as noted in the introduction to this chapter (see Figure 3.1). That is, without observing performance, expectations may have already predisposed the consumer to respond to the product in a certain way, a phenomenon known by various terms including that of a *confirmation bias*.[52] There are two opposing arguments for the direction of effect.

Expectations as Assimilation Agents

Perhaps the oldest known rendition of the effect of expectations comes under the umbrella term *placebo effect*, whereby inert substances in the physical form of medications, palliatives, or elixirs bring on a cure or lessening of symptoms when compared to the actual medicine itself. The evidence for this phenomenon is overwhelming to the extent that placebo effects sometimes rival the actual medication in clinical trials. This "mysterious" effect has been well documented and studied and a more "scientific" explanation has been forthcoming. In a review of the concept, authors have attributed this phenomenon to conditioning, self-confirming explanations of somatic effects, and goal activation whereby individuals become motivated to achieve the intended result through any mental mechanism available, conscious or subconscious. In fact, the anticipation of an event has been found to be processed in disparate brain regions from the event itself.[53] A frequent application in marketing is that of price effects on quality judgments. In a discussion, including debate and rejoinder of a placebo ("activation of expectancies") explanation for this well-known observation, the authors find that consumers do form correlated judgments from price cues.[54]

In other cases, expectations may be held with extreme confidence. Additionally, consumers may have publicly or otherwise committed themselves to believing that a certain performance level will occur. In such cases, they may not wish to test performance in the apprehension that their expectations will be inaccurate. This behavioral tendency is described by assimilation theory. This framework assumes that individuals are reluctant to acknowledge discrepancies from previously held positions and therefore "assimilate" judgment toward their initial feelings for an object or event. Thus, in an ego-protective sense, observed performance may be assimilated into the prior expectation level. In fact, consumers may intervene, consciously or subconsciously, in the consumption process, in a manner similar to the well-known self-fulfilling prophecy, in order to guarantee that their predictions come true.[55] For example, a consumer might engage in a physical fitness program in addition to a dietary regimen in order to achieve a predicted weight loss goal, or rationalize a bad movie starring a favorite performer.

In still other instances, products may have ambiguous performance dimensions, such as the elegance of a fine restaurant, or have performance dimensions of a low-involvement nature, such as the refresh rate of a computer screen. In these cases, the consumer would be neither able nor willing to measure performance and would thereby rely on expectations for a guide to performance. In these examples and others too numerous to cite, the expectation level becomes the standard for judging performance. That is, the consumer begins the performance assessment process with an initial assumption that performance will map expectations as originally formulated.

Figure 3.4   **Operation of Expectations Under Adaptation**

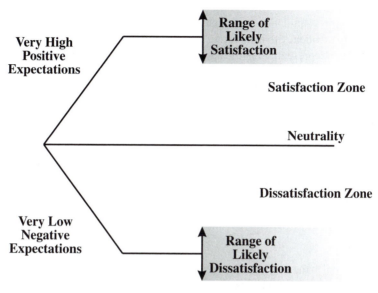

There are parallels here to a framework known generally as adaptation level theory whereby consumers, having adapted to a certain level of performance, use that level as a baseline for judgment. Thus, if they were initially very positive toward a product and find it less than fully satisfying, they may lower their judgment of the product somewhat from its elevated initial level. However, because the starting position was high, the final judgment remains similarly high, though lower than it was predicted to be. The consumer remains satisfied, but less than anticipated. In the same manner, very low expectations in the face of better performance may keep the final judgment in the unfavorable region of dissatisfaction because of the very low initial position. The examples used here assume that the observed performance was counter to the high or low initial expectations level. Performance consistent with the valence of the expectation level would have similar but marginal effects on judgment (see Figure 3.4). Whether expectations are measured or manipulated, such assimilation effects are frequently found. Generally, satisfaction ratings track the level of expectation so that the higher (lower) the expectations, the higher (lower) the satisfaction. Greater elaboration of this process is covered in the next chapter, where citations to representative studies are provided.

For now, a study is described because its unusual nature provides both an illustration of the present material and a segue to the material to come, which states an opposing point of view. In the study, the authors used consumer moods as affective expectation levels to demonstrate the effect of assimilation on postconsumption judgments of taste-altered and unaltered peanut butter.[56] Music was used to induce positive and negative moods among the participants. The results showed that postconsumption ratings of the peanut butter varied in the direction of the initial mood for neutral consumption experiences (unaltered product). This effect was not observed, however, when the experiences evoked strong positive or negative responses from the altered versions, one made to taste better and one to taste worse. In the latter case, the experience itself determined the resulting attitude. This finding is in accord with a contrast interpretation of expectation effects, discussed next.

Expectations as Contrast Agents

As an alternative to the assimilation or adaptation-level effect, the contrast effect as proposed in social psychology is a tendency to exaggerate the discrepancy between a person's initial position on an object and later representations of that object. As presented in the consumer satisfaction literature, this theory predicts that product performance below expectations will be rated more poorly than it is in reality, while performance above expectations will be rated more highly than justified. In effect, consumers would be thought to magnify ratings in the direction of the performance discrepancy. Thus, the contrast-influenced consumer will respond quite differently from the assimilation-influenced individual if these response tendencies operate as described.

The contrast effect, then, is actually a form of discrepancy reaction whereas assimilation may be viewed as the lack of a meaningful reaction to the same discrepancy. As such, these very disparate reactions provide an introduction to the next chapter, which focuses on like phenomena explicitly. In a sense, expectations act only as primes for more complicated processes to follow.

CONCLUSION

Expectations are central to the satisfaction response because, in their many variations, they provide a standard for later judgments of product performance. The variations, however, pose conceptual and measurement difficulties because the researcher cannot know what level of abstraction, what level of desire, what level of certainty, and what comparative object(s) are used by individual consumers. Pretesting may uncover the particular set of expectations encompassing the most frequently used combination of these issues. When this set is worded in the predictive sense, researchers will have covered as many bases as they could hope to accomplish. In situations where the use of dual expectations is prominent, two or more sets of expectation responses will be required, and where expectations change over unfolding phases of consumption, frequent monitoring of expectations may be required if feasible.

The role of expectations, first as anticipations and later as assimilation agents, provides the mechanisms by which expectations may influence satisfaction directly. Consumers not wishing to process performance, due to lack of motivation or lack of ability, may simply rely on prior expectations for their satisfaction judgments. This possibility adds to the necessity of collecting information on this critical variable, one of many yet to come.

NOTES

1. See Huth, Eppright, and Taube, "Indexes of Consumer Sentiment and Confidence"; and Eppright, Arguea, and Huth, "Aggregate Consumer Expenditure Indexes as Indicators of Future Consumer Expenditures."

2. Anderson and Salisbury, "Formation of Market-Level Expectations and Its Covariates"; Andreassen and Lindestad, "Effect of Corporate Image in the Formation of Customer Loyalty"; Hellofs and Jacobson, "Market Share and Customers' Perceptions of Quality"; Johnson, Anderson, and Fornell, "Rational and Adaptive Performance Expectations in a Customer Satisfaction Framework."

3. Mitra and Golder, "How Does Objective Quality Affect Perceived Quality?"

4. Tryon, "Expectation," p. 313.

5. Arnould and Price, "River Magic"; McAlexander, Schouten, and Koenig, "Building Brand Community"; Swan, Martin, and Trawick, "Compensatory Satisfaction."

6. Brown and Kirmani, "Influence of Preencouter Affect on Satisfaction with an Anxiety-Provoking Service Encounter"; Cowley, Farrell, and Edwardson, "Role of Affective Expectations in Memory for a Service Encounter"; DeSteno et al., "Discrete Emotions and Persuasion"; Griffin, Babin, and Attaway, "Anticipation

of Injurious Consumption Outcomes and Its Impact on Consumer Attributions of Blame"; Klaaren, Hodges, and Wilson, "Role of Affective Expectations in Subjective Experience and Decision-Making"; MacInnis and de Mello, "Concept of Hope and Its Relevance to Product Evaluation and Choice"; Zhang, Fishbach, and Dhar, "When Thinking Beats Doing."

7. Desai and Mahajan, "Strategic Role of Affect-Based Attitudes in the Acquisition, Development, and Retention of Customers"; Kopalle and Lehmann, "Strategic Management of Expectations"; Lemon, White, and Winer, "Dynamic Customer Relationship Management"; Sheppard, Sweeney, and Cherry, "Influencing Audience Satisfaction by Manipulating Expectations."

8. Heitmann, Lehmann, and Herrmann, "Choice Goal Attainment and Decision and Consumption Satisfaction"; Hetts et al., "Influence of Anticipated Counterfactual Regret on Behavior"; McConnell et al., "What If I Find It Cheaper Someplace Else?"; Simonson, "Influence of Anticipating Regret and Responsibility on Purchase Decisions"; Zeelenberg, "Anticipated Regret, Expected Feedback and Behavioral Decision Making"; Zeelenberg et al., "Consequences of Regret Aversion."

9. Lane and Keaveney, "Negative Effects of Expecting to Evaluate"; Ofir and Simonson, "Effect of Stating Expectations on Customer Satisfaction and Shopping Experience" and "In Search of Negative Customer Feedback"; Shiv and Huber, "Impact of Anticipating Satisfaction on Consumer Choice."

10. Phillips, "Anticipating the Future"; Simintiras, Diamantopoulos, and Ferriday, "Pre-Purchase Satisfaction and First-Time Buyer Behaviour"; and Zhang and Fishbach, "Role of Anticipated Emotions in the Endowment Effect."

11. Howard, *Consumer Behavior*, p. 28.

12. See Wilson et al., "Preferences as Expectation-Driven Inferences"; Wilson and Klaaren, "'Expectation Whirls Me Round'"; Wirtz, Mattila, and Tan, "Moderating Role of Target-Arousal on the Impact of Affect on Satisfaction"; and Wood and Bettman, "Predicting Happiness."

13. See Dröge, Halstead, and Mackoy, "Role of Competitive Alternatives in the Postchoice Satisfaction Formation Process"; Perugini and Bagozzi, "Distinction between Desires and Intentions"; Pieters, Bottschen, and Thelen, "Customer Desire Expectations about Service Employees"; and Spreng and Olshavsky, "A Desires Congruency Model of Consumer Satisfaction."

14. Kuhn, "Communicating Uncertainty"; Rust et al., "What You *Don't* Know about Customer-Perceived Quality"; and Wirtz and Bateson, "Introducing Uncertain Performance Expectations in Satisfaction Models for Services."

15. Early references to tolerance zones as the difference between desired and adequate service appears in Parasuraman, Berry, and Zeithaml, "Understanding Customer Expectations of Service"; and Zeithaml, Berry, and Parasuraman, "The Nature and Determinants of Customer Expectations of Service." A comprehensive exposition of tolerance zones inclusive of indifference zones can be found in Strandvik, *Tolerance Zones in Perceived Service Quality*, where many of the concepts discussed here were empirically tested. Later references include Teas and DeCarlo, "Examination and Extension of the Zone-of-Tolerance Model"; and Yap and Sweeney, "Zone-of-Tolerance Moderates the Service Quality-Outcome Relationship."

16. Cadotte, Woodruff, and Jenkins, "Expectations and Norms in Models of Consumer Satisfaction"; Woodruff, Cadotte, and Jenkins, "Modeling Consumer Satisfaction Processes Using Experience-Based Norms."

17. Hine, *I Want That!*

18. Strandvik, *Tolerance Zones,* pp. 104–52.

19. Caruana, Ewing, and Ramaseshan, "Assessment of the Three-Column Format SERVQUAL"; Dean, "Rethinking Customer Expectations of Service Quality"; Dion, Javalgi, and Dilorenzo-Aiss, "Empirical Assessment of the Zeithaml, Berry and Parasuraman Service Expectations Model"; Parasuraman, Zeithaml, and Berry, "Alternative Scales for Measuring Service Quality"; Schommer, "Roles of Normative and Predictive Expectations in Evaluation of Pharmacist Consultation Services." For an overview of standards from many theoretical perspectives, see Ngobo, "Standards Issue."

20. Boulding et al., "Dynamic Process Model of Service Quality"; Wirtz and Mattila, "Exploring the Role of Alternative Perceived Performance Measures and Needs-Congruency in the Consumer Satisfaction Process."

21. Kopalle and Lehmann, "Effects of Advertised and Observed Quality on Expectations about New Product Quality."

22. Oliver, Balakrishnan, and Barry, "Outcome Satisfaction in Negotiation."

23. Cadotte, Woodruff, and Jenkins, "Expectations and Norms in Models of Consumer Satisfaction"; Park and Choi, "Comparison Standards in Consumer Satisfaction Formation."

24. Oliver and Winer, "Framework for the Formation and Structure of Consumer Expectations."

25. Respectively, these are Park and Choi, "Comparison Standards in Consumer Satisfaction Formation"; McGill and Iacobucci, "Role of Post-Experience Comparison Standards in the Evaluation of Unfamiliar Services"; Johnson, Nader, and Fornell, "Expectations, Perceived Performance, and Customer Satisfaction for a Complex Service"; Dasu and Rao, "Dynamic Process Model of Dissatisfaction for Unfavorable, Non-Routine Service Encounters"; Otnes, Lowrey, and Shrum, "Toward an Understanding of Consumer Ambivalence"; and Carpenter, Glazer, and Kent, "Meaningful Brands from Meaningless Differentiation."

26. Cadotte, Woodruff, and Jenkins, "Expectations and Norms in Models of Consumer Satisfaction"; Woodruff, Cadotte, and Jenkins, "Modeling Consumer Satisfaction Processes Using Experience-Based Norms." See, also, Johnson and Mathews, "Influence of Expectations on Service Expectations."

27. Respectively, these include Gupta and Stewart, "Customer Satisfaction and Customer Behavior"; Patterson and Johnson, "Focal Brand Experience and Product-Based Norms as Moderators in the Satisfaction Formation Process"; Giese, Cote, and Henderson, "Effect of Product-Level Standards of Comparison on Consumer Satisfaction"; and Landon and Smith, "Use of Quality and Reputation Indicators by Consumers."

28. Gardial et al., "Comparison Standards."

29. For a review of many of the concepts here, see Halstead, "Use of Comparison Standards in Customer Satisfaction Research and Management."

30. See, e.g., Grewal, "Product Quality Expectations"; Kirmani and Rao, "No Pain, No Gain"; Steenkamp, *Product Quality;* and Zeithaml, Berry, and Parasuraman, "Nature and Determinants of Customer Expectations of Service."

31. Bebko, Sciulli, and Garg, "Consumers' Level of Expectation for Services and the Role of Implicit Service Promises"; Deighton, "Interaction of Advertising and Evidence"; Hoch and Ha, "Consumer Learning"; Kopalle and Lehmann, "Effects of Advertised and Observed Quality on Expectations about New Product Quality"; McDougall and Levesque, "Customer Satisfaction with Services"; Sorescu, Shankar, and Kushwaha, "New Product Preannouncements and Shareholder Value."

32. Bagozzi and Dholakia, "Antecedents and Purchase Consequences of Customer Participation in Small Group Brand Communities"; Herr, Kardes, and Kim, "Effects of Word-of-Mouth and Product-Attribute Information on Persuasion"; John, "Referent Opinion and Health Care Satisfaction"; Sweeney, Johnson, and Armstrong, "Effect of Cues on Service Quality Expectations and Service Selection in a Restaurant Setting"; Wooten and Reed, "Informational Influence and the Ambiguity of Product Experience."

33. Dodds, Monroe, and Grewal, "Effects of Price, Brand, and Store Information on Buyers' Product Evaluations"; Rao, "Quality of Price as a Quality Cue"; Rao and Monroe, "Effect of Price, Brand Name, and Store Name on Buyers' Perceptions of Product Quality"; Teas and Agarwal, "Effects of Extrinsic Product Cues on Consumers' Perceptions of Quality, Sacrifice, and Value."

34. Chang and Wildt, "Impact of Product Information on the Use of Price as a Quality Cue"; DelVecchio, Krishnan, and Smith, "Cents or Percent?"; Mazumdar, Raj, and Sinha, "Reference Price Research"; Moon, Russell, and Duvvuri, "Profiling the Reference Price Consumer"; Noël and Hanna, "Benchmarking Consumer Perceptions of Product Quality with Price"; Suter and Burton, "Believability and Consumer Perceptions of Implausible Reference Prices in Retail Advertisements"; Thomas and Menon, "When Internal Reference Prices and Price Expectations Diverge."

35. Hanf and von Wersebe, "Price, Quality, and Consumers' Behaviour."

36. Ditto and Jemmott, "From Rarity to Evaluative Extremity"; Lynn, "Psychology of Unavailability"; Lynn, "Effect of Scarcity on Anticipated Price Appreciation."

37. Respectively, Dawar and Parker, "Marketing Universals"; Erdem and Swait, "Brand Equity as a Signaling Phenomenon"; Rao, Qu, and Ruekert, "Signaling Unobservable Product Quality Through a Brand Ally"; Keller and Aaker, "Effects of Sequential Introduction of Brand Extensions"; Yeung and Wyer, "Does Loving a Brand Mean Loving Its Products?"

38. Kirmani, "Advertising Repetition as a Signal of Quality."

39. See Clow and Beisel, "Managing Consumer Expectations in Low-Margin, High-Volume Services"; and John, "Patient Satisfaction."

40. Ito et al., "Negative Information Weighs More Heavily on the Brain"; Pratto and John, "Automatic Vigilance."

41. Gendolla and Koller, "Surprise and Motivation of Causal Search"; Schützwohl and Borgstedt, "Processing of Affectively Valenced Stimuli."

42. MacInnis and Price, "Role of Imagery in Information Processing"; Oliver, Robertson, and Mitchell, "Imaging and Analyzing in Response to New Product Advertising."

43. Oliver, "Measurement and Evaluation of Satisfaction Processes in Retail Settings," p. 34.

44. For discussion, see Söderlund, "Retrospective and the Prospective Mind and the Temporal Framing of Customer Satisfaction."

45. Parasuraman, Zeithaml, and Berry, "SERVQUAL."

46. See, e.g., Babakus and Boller, "An Empirical Assessment of the SERVQUAL Scale."

47. Parasuraman, Zeithaml, and Berry, "Alternative Scales for Measuring Service Quality."

48. Clow, Kurtz, and Ozment, "Longitudinal Study of the Stability of Consumer Expectations of Service"; Halstead, "Exploring the Concept of Retrieved Expectations"; Hamer, Liu, and Sudharshan, "Effects of Intraencounter Changes in Expectations on Perceived Service Quality Models"; Liu, Sudharshan, and Hamer, "After-Service Response in Service Quality Assessment." Also see Swan, Martin, and Trawick, "Compensatory Satisfaction," where respondents actually changed the main focus of their expectations to attain consistency.

49. McGill and Iacobucci, "Post-Experience Comparison Standards in the Evaluation of Unfamiliar Services"; Madey and Gilovich, "Effect of Temporal Focus on the Recall of Expectancy-Consistent and Expectancy-Inconsistent Information"; Stangor and McMillan, "Memory for Expectancy-Congruent and Expectancy-Incongruent Information."

50. Cowley, Farrell, and Edwardson, "Role of Affective Expectations in Memory for a Service Encounter"; Hamer, Liu, and Sudharshan, "Effects of Intraencounter Changes in Expectations on Perceived Service Quality Models"; Monga and Houston, "Fading Optimism in Products"; Yi and La, "What Influences the Relations Between Customer Satisfaction and Repurchase Intention?"; Zwick, Pieters, and Baumgartner, "On the Practical Significance of Hindsight Bias"; Kopalle and Lehmann, "Effects of Advertised and Observed Quality"; Pieters, Koelemeijer, and Roest, "Assimilation Processes in Service Satisfaction Formation."

51. Oliver and Burke, "Expectation Processes in Satisfaction Formation."

52. Hamer, "Confirmation Perspective on Perceived Service Quality."

53. Geers et al., "Goal Activation, Expectations, and the Placebo Effect"; O'Doherty et al., "Neural Responses during Anticipation of a Primary Taste Reward."

54. Shiv, Carmon, and Ariely, "Placebo Effects of Marketing Actions" and "Ruminating about Placebo Effects of Marketing Actions."

55. See Hart, "Naturally Occurring Expectation Effects"; and Levine, "Reconstructing Memory for Emotions."

56. Miniard, Bhatla, and Sirdeshmukh, "Mood as a Determinant of Postconsumption Product Evaluations."

BIBLIOGRAPHY

Anderson, Eugene W., and Linda Court Salisbury. "The Formation of Market-Level Expectations and Its Covariates." *Journal of Consumer Research* 30, no. 1 (June 2003): 115–124.

Andreassen, Tor Wallin, and Bödil Lindestad. "The Effect of Corporate Image in the Formation of Customer Loyalty." *Journal of Service Research* 1, no. 1 (August 1998): 82–92.

Arnould, Eric J., and Linda L. Price. "River Magic: Extraordinary Experience and the Extended Service Encounter." *Journal of Consumer Research* 20, no. 1 (June 1993): 24–45.

Babakus, Emin, and Gregory W. Boller. "An Empirical Assessment of the SERVQUAL Scale." *Journal of Business Research* 24, no. 3 (May 1992): 253–268.

Bagozzi, Richard P., and Utpal M. Dholakia. "Antecedents and Purchase Consequences of Customer Participation in Small Group Brand Communities." *International Journal of Research in Marketing* 23, no. 1 (March 2006): 45–61.

Bebko, Charlene P., Lisa M. Sciulli, and Rajendar K. Garg. "Consumers' Level of Expectation for Services and the Role of Implicit Service Promises." *Services Marketing Quarterly* 28, no. 2 (2006): 1–23.

Boulding, William, Ajay Kalra, Richard Staelin, and Valarie A. Zeithaml. "A Dynamic Process Model of Service Quality: From Expectations to Behavioral Intentions." *Journal of Marketing Research* 30, no. 1 (February 1993): 7–27.

Brown, Tom J., and Amna Kirmani. "The Influence of Preencounter Affect on Satisfaction with an Anxiety-Provoking Service Encounter." *Journal of Service Research* 1, no. 4 (May 1999): 333–346.

Cadotte, Ernest R., Robert B. Woodruff, and Roger L. Jenkins. "Expectations and Norms in Models of Consumer Satisfaction." *Journal of Marketing Research* 24, no. 3 (August 1987): 305–314.

Carpenter, Gregory S., Rashi Glazer, and Kent Nakamoto. "Meaningful Brands from Meaningless Differentiation: The Dependence on Irrelevant Attributes." *Journal of Marketing Research* 31, no. 3 (August 1994): 339–350.

Caruana, Albert, Michael T. Ewing, and B. Ramaseshan. "Assessment of the Three-Column Format SERVQUAL: An Experimental Approach." *Journal of Business Research* 49, no. 1 (July 2000): 57–65.

Chang, Tung-Zong, and Albert R. Wildt. "Impact of Product Information on the Use of Price as a Quality Cue." *Psychology & Marketing* 13, no. 1 (January 1996): 55–75.

Clow, Kenneth E., and John L. Beisel. "Managing Consumer Expectations in Low-Margin, High-Volume Services." *Journal of Services Marketing* 9, no. 1 (1995): 33–46.

Clow, Kenneth E., David L. Kurtz, and John Ozment. "A Longitudinal Study of the Stability of Consumer Expectations of Service." *Journal of Business Research* 42, no. 1 (May 1998): 63–73.

Cowley, Elizabeth, Colin Farrell, and Michael Edwardson. "The Role of Affective Expectations in Memory for a Service Encounter." *Journal of Business Research* 58, no. 10 (October 2005): 1419–1425.

Dasu, Sriram, and Jay Rao. "A Dynamic Process Model of Dissatisfaction for Unfavorable, Non-Routine Service Encounters." *Production and Operations Management* 8, no. 3 (Fall 1999): 282–300.

Dawar, Niraj, and Philip Parker. "Marketing Universals: Consumers' Use of Brand Name, Price, Physical Appearance, and Retailer Reputation as Signals of Product Quality." *Journal of Marketing* 58, no. 2 (April 1994): 81–95.

Dean, Alison M. "Rethinking Customer Expectations of Service Quality: Are Call Centers Different?" *Journal of Services Marketing* 18, no. 1 (2004): 60–77.

Deighton, John. "The Interaction of Advertising and Evidence." *Journal of Consumer Research* 11, no. 3 (December 1984): 763–770.

DelVecchio, Devon, H. Shanker Krishnan, and Daniel C. Smith. "Cents or Percent? The Effects of Promotion Framing on Price Expectations and Choice." *Journal of Marketing* 71, no. 3 (July 2007): 158–170.

Desai, Kalpesh Kaushik, and Vijay Mahajan. "Strategic Role of Affect-Based Attitudes in the Acquisition, Development, and Retention of Customers." *Journal of Business Research* 42, no. 3 (July 1998): 309–324.

DeSteno, David, Richard E. Petty, Derek R. Rucker, Duane T. Wegener, and Julia Braverman. "Discrete Emotions and Persuasion: The Role of Emotion-Induced Expectancies." *Journal of Personality and Social Psychology* 86, no. 1 (January 2004): 43–56.

Dion, Paul A., Rajshekhar Javalgi, and Janet Dilorenzo-Aiss. "An Empirical Assessment of the Zeithaml, Berry and Parasuraman Service Expectations Model." *Service Industries Journal* 18, no. 4 (October 1998): 66–86.

Ditto, Peter H., and John B. Jemmott, III. "From Rarity to Evaluative Extremity: Effects of Prevalence Information on Evaluations of Positive and Negative Characteristics." *Journal of Personality and Social Psychology* 57, no. 1 (July 1989): 16–26.

Dodds, William B., Kent B. Monroe, and Dhruv Grewal. "Effects of Price, Brand, and Store Information on Buyers' Product Evaluations." *Journal of Marketing Research* 28, no. 3 (August 1991): 307–319.

Dröge, Cornelia, Diane Halstead, and Robert D. Mackoy. "The Role of Competitive Alternatives in the Postchoice Satisfaction Formation Process." *Journal of the Academy of Marketing Science* 25, no. 1 (Winter 1997): 18–30.

Eppright, David R., Nestor M. Arguea, and William L. Huth. "Aggregate Consumer Expenditure Indexes as Indicators of Future Consumer Expenditures." *Journal of Economic Psychology* 19, no. 2 (April 1998): 215–235.

Erdem, Tülin, and Joffre Swait. "Brand Equity as a Signaling Phenomenon." *Journal of Consumer Psychology* 7, no. 2 (1998): 131–157.

Gardial, Sarah Fisher, Robert B. Woodruff, Mary Jane Burns, David W. Schumann, and Scott Clemons. "Comparison Standards: Exploring Their Variety and Circumstances Surrounding Their Use." *Journal of Consumer Satisfaction, Dissatisfaction and Complaining Behavior* 6 (1993): 63–73.

Geers, Andrew L., Paul E. Weiland, Kristin Kosbab, Sarah J. Landry, and Suzanne G. Helfer. "Goal Activation, Expectations, and the Placebo Effect." *Journal of Personality and Social Psychology* 89, no. 2 (August 2005): 143–159.

Gendolla, Guido H.E., and Michael Koller. "Surprise and Motivation of Causal Search: How Are They Affected by Outcome Valence and Importance?" *Motivation and Emotion* 25, no. 4 (December 2001): 327–349.

Giese, Joan L., Joseph A. Cote, and Pamela W. Henderson. "The Effect of Product-Level Standards of Comparison on Consumer Satisfaction." *Journal of Consumer Satisfaction, Dissatisfaction and Complaining Behavior* 10 (1997): 15–25.

Grewal, Dhruv. "Product Quality Expectations: Towards an Understanding of Their Antecedents and Consequences." *Journal of Business and Psychology* 9, no. 3 (March 1995): 225–240.

Griffin, Mitch, Barry J. Babin, and Jill S. Attaway. "Anticipation of Injurious Consumption Outcomes and Its Impact on Consumer Attributions of Blame." *Journal of the Academy of Marketing Science* 24, no. 4 (Fall 1996): 314–327.

Gupta, Kamal, and David W. Stewart. "Customer Satisfaction and Customer Behavior: The Differential Role of Brand and Category Expectations." *Marketing Letters* 7, no. 3 (July 1996): 249–263.

Halstead, Diane. "Exploring the Concept of Retrieved Expectations." *Journal of Consumer Satisfaction, Dissatisfaction and Complaining Behavior* 6 (1993): 56–62.

———. "The Use of Comparison Standards in Customer Satisfaction Research and Management: A Review and Typology." *Journal of Marketing Theory and Practice* 7, no. 3 (Summer 1999): 13–26.

Hamer, Lawrence O. "A Confirmation Perspective on Perceived Service Quality." *Journal of Services Marketing* 20, no. 4 (2006): 219–232.

Hamer, Lawrence O., Ben Shaw-Ching Liu, and D. Sudharshan. "The Effects of Intraencounter Changes in Expectations on Perceived Service Quality Models." *Journal of Service Research* 1, no. 3 (February 1999): 275–289.

Hanf, C.-Hennig, and Bernhard von Wersebe. "Price, Quality, and Consumers' Behaviour." *Journal of Consumer Policy* 17, no. 3 (September 1994): 335–348.

Hart, Allen J. "Naturally Occurring Expectation Effects." *Journal of Personality and Social Psychology,* 68, no. 1 (January 1995): 109–115.

Heitmann, Mark, Donald R. Lehmann, and Andreas Herrmann. "Choice Goal Attainment and Decision and Consumption Satisfaction." *Journal of Marketing Research* 44, no. 2 (May 2007): 234–250.

Hellofs, Linda L., and Robert Jacobson. "Market Share and Customers' Perceptions of Quality: When Can Firms Grow Their Way to Higher Versus Lower Quality?" *Journal of Marketing* 63, no. 1 (January 1999): 16–25.

Herr, Paul M., Frank R. Kardes, and John Kim. "Effects of Word-of-Mouth and Product-Attribute Information on Persuasion: An Accessibility-Diagnosticity Perspective." *Journal of Consumer Research* 17, no. 4 (March 1991): 454–462.

Hetts, John J., David S. Boninger, David A. Armor, Faith Gleicher, and Ariel Nathanson. "The Influence of Anticipated Counterfactual Regret on Behavior." *Psychology & Marketing* 17, no. 4 (April 2000): 345–368.

Hine, Thomas. *I Want That! How We All Became Shoppers.* New York: Perennial/HarperCollins, 2002.

Hoch, Stephen J., and Young-Won Ha. "Consumer Learning: Advertising and the Ambiguity of Product Experience." *Journal of Consumer Research* 13, no. 2 (September 1986): 221–233.

Howard, John A. *Consumer Behavior: Application of Theory.* New York: McGraw-Hill, 1977.

Huth, William L., David R. Eppright, and Paul M. Taube. "The Indexes of Consumer Sentiment and Confidence: Leading or Misleading Guides to Future Buyer Behavior." *Journal of Business Research* 29, no. 3 (March 1994): 199–206.

Ito, Tiffany A., Jeff T. Larsen, N. Kyle Smith, and John T. Cacioppo. "Negative Information Weighs More Heavily on the Brain: The Negativity Bias in Evaluative Categorizations." *Journal of Personality and Social Psychology* 75, no. 4 (October 1998): 887–900.

John, Joby. "Patient Satisfaction: The Impact of Past Experience." *Journal of Health Care Marketing* 12, no. 3 (September 1992): 56–64.

———. "Referent Opinion and Health Care Satisfaction." *Journal of Health Care Marketing* 14, no. 2 (Summer 1994): 24–30.

Johnson, Cathy, and Brian P. Mathews. "The Influence of Experience on Service Expectations." *International Journal of Service Industry Management* 8, no. 4 (1997): 290–305.

Johnson, Michael D., Eugene W. Anderson, and Claes Fornell. "Rational and Adaptive Performance Expectations in a Customer Satisfaction Framework." *Journal of Consumer Research* 21, no. 4 (March 1995): 695–707.

Johnson, Michael D., Georg Nader, and Claes Fornell. "Expectations, Perceived Performance, and Customer Satisfaction for a Complex Service: The Case of Bank Loans." *Journal of Economic Psychology* 17, no. 2 (April 1996): 163–182.

Keller, Kevin Lane, and David A. Aaker. "The Effects of Sequential Introduction of Brand Extensions." *Journal of Marketing Research* 29, no. 1 (February 1992): 35–50.

Kirmani, Amna. "Advertising Repetition as a Signal of Quality: If It's Advertised So Much, Something Must Be Wrong." *Journal of Advertising* 26, no. 3 (Fall 1997): 77–86.

———, and Akshay R. Rao. "No Pain, No Gain: A Critical Review of the Literature on Signaling Unobservable Product Quality." *Journal of Marketing* 64, no. 2 (April 2000): 66–79.

Klaaren, Kristen J., Sara D. Hodges, and Timothy D. Wilson. "The Role of Affective Expectations in Subjective Experience and Decision-Making." *Social Cognition* 12, no. 2 (Summer 1994): 77–101.

Kopalle, Praveen K., and Donald R. Lehmann. "The Effects of Advertised and Observed Quality on Expectations about New Product Quality." *Journal of Marketing Research* 32, no. 3 (August 1995): 280–290.

———. "Strategic Management of Expectations: The Role of Disconfirmation Sensitivity and Perfectionism." *Journal of Marketing Research* 38, no. 3 (August 2001): 386–394.

Kuhn, Kristine M. "Communicating Uncertainty: Framing Effects on Responses to Vague Probabilities." *Organizational Behavior and Human Decision Processes* 71, no. 1 (July 1997): 55–83.

Landon, Stuart, and C.E. Smith. "The Use of Quality and Reputation Indicators by Consumers: The Case of Bordeaux Wine." *Journal of Consumer Policy* 20, no. 3 (September 1997): 289–323.

Lane, Vicki R., and Susan M. Keaveney. "The Negative Effects of Expecting to Evaluate: Reexamination and Extension in the Context of Service Failure." *Psychology & Marketing* 22, no. 11 (November 2005): 857–885.

Lemon, Katherine N., Tiffany Barnett White, and Russell S. Winer. "Dynamic Customer Relationship Management: Incorporating Future Considerations into the Service Retention Decision." *Journal of Marketing* 66, no. 1 (January 2002): 1–14.

Levine, Linda J. "Reconstructing Memory for Emotions." *Journal of Experimental Psychology: General* 126, no. 2 (June 1997): 165–177.

Liu, Ben Shaw-Ching, D. Sudharshan, and Lawrence O. Hamer. "After-Service Response in Service Quality Assessment: A Real-Time Updating Model Approach." *Journal of Services Marketing* 14, no. 2 (2000): 160–177.

Lynn, Michael. "The Psychology of Unavailability: Explaining Scarcity and Cost Effects on Value." *Basic and Applied Social Psychology* 13, no. 1 (March 1992): 3–7.

———. "The Effect of Scarcity on Anticipated Price Appreciation." *Journal of Applied Social Psychology* 26, no. 22 (November 1996): 1978–1984.

MacInnis, Deborah J., and Gustavo E. de Mello. "The Concept of Hope and Its Relevance to Product Evaluation and Choice." *Journal of Marketing* 69, no. 1 (January 2005): 1–14.

MacInnis, Deborah J., and Linda L. Price. "The Role of Imagery in Information Processing: Review and Extensions." *Journal of Consumer Research* 13, no. 4 (March 1987): 473–491.

Madey, Scott F., and Thomas Gilovich. "Effect of Temporal Focus on the Recall of Expectancy-Consistent and Expectancy-Inconsistent Information." *Journal of Personality and Social Psychology* 65, no. 3 (September 1993): 458–468.

Mazumdar, Tridib, S.P. Raj, and Indrajit Sinha. "Reference Price Research: Review and Propositions." *Journal of Marketing* 69, no. 4 (October 2005): 84–102.

McAlexander, James H., John W. Schouten, and Harold F. Koenig. "Building Brand Community." *Journal of Marketing* 66, no. 1 (January 2002): 38–54.

McConnell, Allen R., Keith E. Niedermeier, Jill M. Leibold, Amani G. El-Alayli, Peggy P. Chin, and Nicole M. Kuiper. "What If I Find It Cheaper Someplace Else? Role of Prefactual Thinking and Anticipated Regret in Consumer Behavior." *Psychology & Marketing* 17, no. 4 (April 2000): 281–298.

McDougall, Gordon H.G., and Terrence Levesque. "Customer Satisfaction with Services: Putting Perceived Value into the Equation." *Journal of Services Marketing* 14, no. 5 (2000): 392–410.

McGill, Ann L., and Dawn Iacobucci. "The Role of Post-Experience Comparison Standards in the Evaluation of Unfamiliar Services." In *Advances in Consumer Research,* ed. John F. Sherry Jr. and Brian Sternthal, 19:570–578. Provo, UT: Association for Consumer Research, 1992.

Miniard, Paul W., Sunil Bhatla, and Deepak Sirdeshmukh. "Mood as a Determinant of Postconsumption Product Evaluations: Mood Effects and Their Dependency on the Affective Intensity of the Consumption Experience." *Journal of Consumer Psychology* 1, no. 2 (1992): 173–195.

Mitra, Debanjan, and Peter N. Golder. "How Does Objective Quality Affect Perceived Quality? Short-Term Effects, Long-Term Effects, and Asymmetries. *Marketing Science* 25, no. 3 (May–June 2006): 230–247.

Monga, Ashwani, and Michael J. Houston. "Fading Optimism in Products: Temporal Changes in Expectations About Performance." *Journal of Marketing Research* 43, no. 4 (November 2006): 654–663.

Moon, Sangkil, Gary J. Russell, and Sri Devi Duvvuri. "Profiling the Reference Price Consumer." *Journal of Retailing* 82, no. 1 (2006): 1–11.

Ngobo, Paul V. "The Standards Issue: An Accessibility-Diagnosticity Perspective." *Journal of Consumer Satisfaction, Dissatisfaction and Complaining Behavior* 10 (1997): 61–79.

Noël, Mark, and Nessim Hanna. "Benchmarking Consumer Perceptions of Product Quality with Price: An Exploration." *Psychology & Marketing* 13, no. 6 (September 1996): 591–604.

O'Doherty, John P., Ralf Deichmann, Hugo D. Critchley, and Raymond J. Dolan. "Neural Responses during Anticipation of a Primary Taste Reward." *Neuron* 33, no. 5 (February 2002): 815–826.

Ofir, Chezy, and Itamar Simonson. "The Effect of Stating Expectations on Customer Satisfaction and Shopping Experience." *Journal of Marketing Research* 44, no. 1 (February 2007): 165–174.

———. "In Search of Negative Customer Feedback: The Effect of Expecting to Evaluate on Satisfaction Evaluations." *Journal of Marketing Research* 38, no. 2 (May 2001): 170–182.

Oliver, Richard L. "Measurement and Evaluation of Satisfaction Processes in Retail Settings." *Journal of Retailing* 57, no. 3 (Fall 1981): 25–48.

Oliver, Richard L., P.V. (Sundar) Balakrishnan, and Bruce Barry. "Outcome Satisfaction in Negotiation: A Test of Expectancy Disconfirmation." *Organizational Behavior and Human Decision Processes* 60, no. 2 (November 1994): 252–275.

Oliver, Richard L., and Raymond R. Burke. "Expectation Processes in Satisfaction Formation: A Field Study." *Journal of Service Research* 1, no. 3 (February 1999): 196–214.

Oliver, Richard L., Thomas S. Robertson, and Deborah J. Mitchell. "Imaging and Analyzing in Response to New Product Advertising." *Journal of Advertising* 22, no. 4 (December 1993): 35–49.

Oliver, Richard L., and Russell S. Winer. "A Framework for the Formation and Structure of Consumer Expectations: Review and Propositions." *Journal of Economic Psychology* 8, no. 4 (December 1987): 469–499.

Otnes, Cele, Tina M. Lowrey, and L.J. Shrum. "Toward and Understanding of Consumer Ambivalence." *Journal of Consumer Research* 24, no. 1 (June 1997): 80–93.

Parasuraman, A., Leonard L. Berry, and Valarie A. Zeithaml. "Understanding Customer Expectations of Service." *Sloan Management Review* 32, no. 3 (Spring 1991): 39–48.

Parasuraman, A., Valarie A. Zeithaml, and Leonard L. Berry. "Alternative Scales for Measuring Service Quality: A Comparative Assessment Based on Psychometric and Diagnostic Criteria." *Journal of Retailing* 70, no. 3 (Fall 1994): 201–230.

———. "SERVQUAL: A Multiple-Item Scale for Measuring Consumer Perceptions of Service Quality." *Journal of Retailing* 64, no. 1 (Spring 1988): 12–40.

Park, Jong-Won, and Jiho Choi. "Comparison Standards in Consumer Satisfaction Formation: Involvement and Product Experience as Potential Moderators." *Journal of Consumer Satisfaction, Dissatisfaction and Complaining Behavior* 11 (1998): 28–39.

Patterson, Paul G., and Lester W. Johnson. "Focal Brand Experience and Product-Based Norms as Moderators in the Satisfaction Formation Process." *Journal of Consumer Satisfaction, Dissatisfaction and Complaining Behavior* 8 (1995): 22–31.

Perugini, Marco, and Richard P. Bagozzi. "The Distinction between Desires and Intentions." *European Journal of Social Psychology* 34, no. 1 (January–February 2004): 69–84.

Phillips, Diane M. "Anticipating the Future: The Role of Consumption Visions in Consumer Behavior." In *Advances in Consumer Research*, ed. Kim Corfman and John Lynch, 23:70–75. Provo, UT: Association for Consumer Research, 1996.

Pieters, Rik, Günther Bottschen, and Eva Thelen. "Customer Desire Expectations about Service Employees: An Analysis of Hierarchical Relations." *Psychology & Marketing* 15, no. 8 (December 1998): 755–773.

Pieters, Rik, Kitty Koelemeijer, and Henk Roest. "Assimilation Processes in Service Satisfaction Formation." *International Journal of Service Industry Management* 6, no. 3 (1995): 17–33.

Pratto, Felicia, and Oliver P. John. "Automatic Vigilance: The Attention-Grabbing Power of Negative Social Information." *Journal of Personality and Social Psychology* 61, no. 3 (September 1991): 380–391.

Rao, Akshay R. "The Quality of Price as a Quality Cue." *Journal of Marketing Research* 42, no. 4 (November 2005): 401–405.

Rao, Akshay R., and Kent B. Monroe. "The Effect of Price, Brand Name, and Store Name on Buyers' Perceptions of Product Quality: An Integrative Review." *Journal of Marketing Research* 26, no. 3 (August 1989): 351–357.

Rao, Akshay R., Lu Qu, and Robert W. Ruekert. "Signaling Unobservable Product Quality Through a Brand Ally." *Journal of Marketing Research* 36, no. 2 (May 1999): 258–268.

Rust, Roland T., J. Jeffrey Inman, Jianmin Jia, and Anthony Zahorik. "What You *Don't* Know about Customer-Perceived Quality: The Role of Customer Expectation Distributions." *Marketing Science* 18, no. 1 (1999): 77–92.

Schommer, Jon C. "Roles of Normative and Predictive Expectations in Evaluation of Pharmacist Consultation Services." *Journal of Consumer Satisfaction, Dissatisfaction and Complaining Behavior* 9 (1996): 86–94.

Schützwohl, Achim, and Kirsten Borgstedt. "The Processing of Affectively Valenced Stimuli: The Role of Surprise." *Cognition and Emotion* 19, no. 4 (June 2005): 583–600.

Sheppard, James A., Kate Sweeney, and Lisa C. Cherry. "Influencing Audience Satisfaction by Manipulating Expectations." *Social Influence* 2, no. 2 (2007): 98–111.

Shiv, Baba, Ziv Carmon, and Dan Ariely. "Placebo Effects of Marketing Actions: Consumers May Get What They Pay For." *Journal of Marketing Research* 42, no. 4 (November 2005): 383–393.

———. "Ruminating about Placebo Effects of Marketing Actions." *Journal of Marketing Research* 42, no. 4 (November 2005): 410–414.

Shiv, Baba, and Joel Huber. "The Impact of Anticipating Satisfaction on Consumer Choice." *Journal of Consumer Research* 27, no. 2 (September 2000): 202–216.

Simintiras, Antonis, Adamantios Diamantopoulos, and Judith Ferriday. "Pre-Purchase Satisfaction and First-Time Buyer Behaviour: Some Preliminary Evidence." *European Journal of Marketing* 31, nos. 11–12 (1997): 857–872.

Simonson, Itamar. "The Influence of Anticipating Regret and Responsibility on Purchase Decisions." *Journal of Consumer Research* 19, no. 1 (June 1992): 105–118.

Söderlund, Magnus. "The Retrospective and the Prospective Mind and the Temporal Framing of Customer Satisfaction." *European Journal of Marketing* 37, no. 10 (2003): 1375–1390.

Sorescu, Alina, Venkatesh Shankar, and Tarun Kushwaha. "New Product Preannouncements and Shareholder Value: Don't Make Promises You Can't Keep." *Journal of Marketing Research* 44, no. 3 (August 2007): 468–489.

Spreng, Richard A., and Richard W. Olshavsky. "A Desires Congruency Model of Consumer Satisfaction." *Journal of the Academy of Marketing Science* 21, no. 3 (Summer 1993): 169–177.

Stangor, Charles, and David McMillan. "Memory for Expectancy-Congruent and Expectancy-Incongruent Information: A Review of the Social and Social-Developmental Literatures." *Psychological Bulletin* 111, no. 1 (January 1992): 42–61.

Steenkamp, Jan-Benedict E.M. *Product Quality: An Investigation into the Concept and How It Is Perceived by Consumers.* Assen/Maastricht, Netherlands: Van Gorcum, 1989.

Strandvik, Tore. *Tolerance Zones in Perceived Service Quality.* Helsinki, Finland: Swedish School of Economics and Business Administration, 1994.

Suter, Tracy A., and Scot Burton. "Believability and Consumer Perceptions of Implausible Reference Prices in Retail Advertisements." *Psychology & Marketing* 13, no. 1 (January 1996): 37–54.

Swan, John E., Warren S. Martin, and I. Frederick Trawick. "Compensatory Satisfaction: An Ethnography of Avoiding Disappointment and Producing Satisfaction in Birding." *Journal of Consumer Satisfaction, Dissatisfaction and Complaining Behavior* 16 (2003): 157–165.

Sweeney, Jillian C., Lester W. Johnson, and Robert W. Armstrong. "The Effect of Cues on Service Quality Expectations and Service Selection in a Restaurant Setting." *Journal of Services Marketing* 6, no. 4 (Fall 1992): 15–22.

Teas, R. Kenneth, and Sanjeev Agarwal. "The Effects of Extrinsic Product Cues on Consumers' Perceptions of Quality, Sacrifice, and Value." *Journal of the Academy of Marketing Science* 28, no. 2 (Spring 2000): 278–290.

Teas, R. Kenneth, and Thomas E. DeCarlo. "An Examination and Extension of the Zone-of-Tolerance Model: A Comparison to Performance-Based Models of Perceived Quality." *Journal of Service Research* 6, no. 3 (February 2004): 272–286.

Thomas, Manoj, and Geeta Menon. "When Internal Reference Prices and Price Expectations Diverge: The Role of Confidence." *Journal of Marketing Research* 44, no. 3 (August 2007): 401–409.

Tryon, Warren W. "Expectation." In *Encyclopedia of Human Behavior*, ed. V.S. Ramachandran, 2:313–319. San Diego, CA: Academic Press, 1994.

Wilson, Timothy D., and Kristen J. Klaaren. "'Expectation Whirls Me Round': The Role of Affective Expectations in Affective Experience." In *Review of Personality and Social Psychology,* vol. 14, ed. Margaret S. Clark, 1–31. Newbury Park, CA: Sage, 1992.

Wilson, Timothy D., Douglas J. Lisle, Dolores Kraft, and Christopher G. Wetzel. "Preferences as Expectation-Driven Inferences: Effects of Affective Expectations on Affective Experience." *Journal of Personality and Social Psychology* 56, no. 4 (April 1989): 519–530.

Wirtz, Jochen, and John E.G. Bateson. "Introducing Uncertain Performance Expectations in Satisfaction Models for Services." *International Journal of Service Industry Management* 10, no. 1 (1999): 82–99.

Wirtz, Jochen, and Anna Mattila. "Exploring the Role of Alternative Perceived Performance Measures and Needs-Congruency in the Consumer Satisfaction Process." *Journal of Consumer Psychology* 11, no. 3 (2001): 181–192.

Wirtz, Jochen, Anna Mattila, and Rachel L.P. Tan. "The Moderating Role of Target-Arousal on the Impact of Affect on Satisfaction: An Examination in the Context of Service Experience." *Journal of Retailing* 76, no. 3 (Fall 2000): 347–365.

Wood, Stacy L., and James R. Bettman. "Predicting Happiness: How Normative Feeling Rules Influence (and Even Reverse) Durability Bias." *Journal of Consumer Psychology* 17, no. 3 (2007): 188–201.

Woodruff, Robert B., Ernest R. Cadotte, and Roger L. Jenkins. "Modeling Consumer Satisfaction Processes Using Experience-Based Norms." *Journal of Marketing Research* 20, no. 3 (August 1983): 296–304.

Wooten, David B., and Americus Reed II. "Informational Influence and the Ambiguity of Product Experience: Order Effects and the Weighting of Evidence." *Journal of Consumer Psychology* 7, no. 1 (1998): 79–99.

Yap, Kenneth B., and Jillian C. Sweeney. "Zone-of-Tolerance Moderates the Service Quality-Outcome Relationship." *Journal of Services Marketing* 21, no. 2 (2007): 137–148.

Yeung, Catherine W.M., and Robert S. Wyer Jr. "Does Loving a Brand Mean Loving Its Products? The Role of Brand-Elicited Affect in Brand Extension Evaluations." *Journal of Marketing Research* 42, no. 4 (November 2005): 495–506.

Yi, Youjae, and Suna La. "What Influences the Relations Between Customer Satisfaction and Repurchase Intention? Investigating the Effects of Adjusted Expectations and Customer Loyalty." *Psychology & Marketing* 21, no. 5 (May 2004): 351–373.

Zeelenberg, Marcel. "Anticipated Regret, Expected Feedback and Behavioral Decision Making." *Journal of Behavioral Decision Making* 12, no. 2 (June 1999): 93–106.

Zeelenberg, Marcel, Jane Beattie, Joop van der Pligt, and Nanne K. de Vries. "Consequences of Regret Aversion: Effects of Expected Feedback on Risky Decision Making." *Organizational Behavior and Human Decision Processes* 65, no. 2 (February 1996): 148–158.

Zeithaml, Valarie A., Leonard L. Berry, and A. Parasuraman. "The Nature and Determinants of Customer Expectations of Service." *Journal of the Academy of Marketing Science* 21, no. 1 (Winter 1993): 1–12.

Zhang, Ying, and Ayelet Fishbach. "The Role of Anticipated Emotions in the Endowment Effect." *Psychology & Marketing* 15, no. 4 (2005): 316–324.

Zhang, Ying, Ayelet Fishbach, and Ravi Dhar. "When Thinking Beats Doing: The Role of Optimistic Expectations in Goal-Based Choice." *Journal of Consumer Research* 34, no. 3 (December 2007): 567–578.

Zwick, Rami, Rik Pieters, and Hans Baumgartner. "On the Practical Significance of Hindsight Bias: The Case of the Expectancy-Disconfirmation Model of Consumer Satisfaction." *Organizational Behavior and Human Decision Processes* 64, no. 1 (October 1995): 103–117.

CHAPTER 4

THE EXPECTANCY DISCONFIRMATION
MODEL OF SATISFACTION

The reader may have noticed continuing frequent references in the promotional media to products and services delivering "unexpected pleasure" or "unexpected taste" (True cigarettes); increasingly popular claims by firms that they will "meet your expectations" or "deliver more than you bargained for" (GMC Trucks); and imperatives such as "allow us to exceed your expectations" (Celebrity Cruises). In still other versions of this theme, Holiday Inns promises prospective guests that they would encounter "no surprises," while other firms offer assurances that the consumer will encounter no "hidden charges." And, of course, let us not forget the Target motto, "Expect More. Pay Less." What do all these promises have in common? They guarantee that product or service performance will contrast favorably with the expectations that the consumer is likely to have had prior to purchase.

Note that in the first examples, those of unexpected pleasure and exceeding expectations, the consumer has been promised more positive performance than normally anticipated. In fact, at least one automaker has taken this promise to excess, literally. In an ad for a Toyota model, the bold copy read, "It is pure excess." The ad goes on to claim that this car delivers the highest horsepower-to-weight ratio in its class and can accelerate to sixty miles per hour in under five seconds. Whereas racing buffs might find this level of performance ordinary, the advertiser probably hoped that this same performance would be perceived as exceeding expectations for this type of car in the minds of sports car consumers.

In contrast, the implicit promise made in the claims of no surprises and no hidden charges is that the provider will not deliver a level of more negative performance than is normally anticipated. This is an effort to allay consumers' fears or apprehensions of negative surprises—anticipations of unforeseeable outcomes, as discussed in the previous chapter.

These examples illustrate the recent interpretation of postpurchase or postusage response as involving a comparison to expectations or to other judgmental standards. This approach makes the nature of the consumer's rating explicit so that when a consumer assigns a negative or positive rating to performance, the researcher is in a position to answer the question: Compared to what? The following discussion presents a brief review of the origins of this notion.

DISCREPANCY MODELS OF SATISFACTION

Although comparative models of satisfaction date back many years, most notably in the job satisfaction literature, the suggestion that individuals make performance judgments with reference to a standard is not unique to any one field, and no one discipline can lay claim to it. Generally, this concept is contained under the umbrella term discrepancy theory, and applications appear in literatures other than those relating to one's place of work. For example, in the quality-of-life literature, these concepts are referred to as what one has (in life) versus what one wants, deserves, or expects now and in the future. In the self-concept literature, the discrepancy investigated is between one's self-image and one's ideal self. In the information technology field, discrepancies are studied between data required for an effort or decision, and what a user has or is provided. And, with regard to specific dimensions of life, income satisfaction has been found to be based on comparisons to that of others, known and unknown to the respondent.[1]

One unfortunate aspect of the use of the term *discrepancy* in the many fields in which it appears (and of *disconfirmation*, as it is more commonly called in consumer behavior) is that it carries a negative connotation in the minds of individuals. Phrases such as *discrepant from* and *disconfirmed expectations* usually imply a negative comparison, in that what was received is usually less than what was ordinary or expected. This is an important issue in consumer satisfaction, as negative discrepancies would appear to operate only as a tendency toward dissatisfaction.

While preventing dissatisfaction is a worthy and necessary goal, management should be more interested in what it can do to foster satisfaction. Even more important is the question of what the marketer can do to gain a competitive advantage by providing more satisfaction than the competition. This issue has even greater relevance today. Unfortunately, the notion of providing more satisfaction than one's competitors is foreign to the concept of need satiation (fulfillment) discussed in the Introduction and to need satisfaction models generally.

How *does* greater satisfaction than mere satiation occur, and how can management bring this situation about? An attempt at answering these questions will be made throughout this book. For now, it can be said that this issue is implicitly addressed in the adaptations of discrepancy theory used in the consumer behavior literature. This is not to say that consumer researchers have qualitatively better models; rather, they approach the issue from a standpoint that reflects consumer experiences with products and services in the marketplace, as opposed to the workplace or other environments.

THE CONSUMER BEHAVIOR APPROACH

The first behavioral work in consumer satisfaction dates to the 1970s. At that time, researchers attempted to apply dissonance theory (discussed more fully in Chapter 10) to consumer satisfaction in the belief that shopping effort would cause consumers to become committed to their expectations for products. Researchers argued that, in effect, shopping effort generates knowledge and a degree of confidence in that knowledge. Under these conditions, product performance not matching the consumer's expectations will create psychological discomfort (dissonance) because this purchase outcome will reflect poorly on the consumer's decision in light of the effort expended. Therefore, consumers were thought to reinterpret performance so as to be consistent (or nearly so) with their expectations as a dissonance reduction strategy. Interestingly, this same interpretation was given to situations where the product exceeded the consumer's expectations.

This focus on expectations—and the counterintuitive (to some) notion that consumers would disbelieve poor performance when their expectations were high and, even more astoundingly, disbelieve good performance when their expectations were low—sparked a search for alternative interpretations of how consumers evaluate purchase outcomes. Thought to be especially promising at the time was the hybrid framework of assimilation-contrast theory, borrowed from the literature on the effect of communicator-recipient similarity as an influence on attitude change.

Shortcomings of Assimilation Versus Contrast Interpretations

Briefly, research supporting the assimilation effect suggested that communicators sharing something in common with members of an audience (e.g., views, values, lifestyles) were frequently judged to be similar or "just like me." This perceived similarity facilitated communicator effectiveness, as the audience would assimilate the communicator's viewpoints into its own. Thus, the assimilation framework, like dissonance theory, emphasizes reluctance on an individual's part to acknowledge discrepancies from a previously held position. It relies on individuals' ability to explain away (rationalize) apparent discrepancies.[2]

The contrast effect is quite the opposite. It has been described as a tendency to "exaggerate the discrepancy between one's own attitudes and the attitudes represented by opinion statements endorsed by other people with opposing views."[3] Thus, when exposed to a communicator or communication perceived as different, according to contrast theory, individuals will exaggerate the discrepancy, making it larger than it is in reality. In effect, if contrast were applied to a consumption context, then poor performance would be worse than simply poor and good performance would be better than a rating of good would suggest. Satisfaction researchers were, not unexpectedly, taken with this interpretation as it both complemented and contradicted assimilation theory. Why was this advantageous to the development of the field? The answer is that it sparked controversy and testing in a number of early studies.[4]

One shortcoming of assuming that one or the other of assimilation and contrast theories operated is that only two variables of a three-variable framework were of interest. Most of the early studies manipulated (or measured) expectations, usually through product information, and also manipulated the performance level (although not in every study). What these prior studies omitted, however, was the third concept of interest—the perceived discrepancy between expectation and performance; no direct manipulations or measures of this difference were attempted. Thus, the discrepancy as perceived by the subject was inferred by the researcher and could not be investigated as an independent concept. It was not surprising, then, that an assimilation-to-expectations effect, for example, was frequently reported, since the operation of the expectancy discrepancy was masked or absorbed within the observed effects.

This misunderstanding about how discrepancies affect satisfaction judgments was brought to light by two developments. The first was provided by the observation, noted in the previous paragraph, that prior research had omitted measurement of discrepancy as a separate key variable. Researchers had been assuming that the nature of the perceived discrepancy could be derived from the following arguments:

1. A poor outcome, given high expectations, results in a negative discrepancy and disappointment.
2. A good outcome, given low expectations, results in a positive discrepancy and glee.

These arguments reflect the familiar "ceiling-and-floor" effects where, in the context of the present discussion, expectations "at the ceiling" can be confirmed or disconfirmed only in a negative direction. Similarly, expectations "at the floor" can be confirmed or disconfirmed only in a positive direction. These commonly held beliefs are reinforced by familiar, seemingly valid statements such as "stocks are so low that they can only go up" and vice versa, as well as product names indicating "top," such as zenith, acme, apex, ultra, peerless, and nonpareil. However, consumer responses are not bounded by absolute zero nor infinity and can be psychologically "bested." Even games with maximum scores (e.g., bowling's 300) can be extended to tournaments, team scores, and runs of perfect games.

To fully understand the operation of disconfirmation, one needs to relax these conventions and allow for "better than best" and "poorer than poor." For example, prognostications of the "saturation" of product design and ownership include the miniaturization and speed of electronics and the number of residences with TVs (now calculated as the number of TVs per residence). Like inventiveness, the human mind is versatile. Unfortunately, as will be seen, researchers must rely in most cases on numerically bounded scales, but this does not change the conceptual underpinnings of disconfirmation, which will be shown graphically later.

With this in mind, a strong case for the operation of a discrepancy, operating separately and apart from expectations and outcomes, required investigation. In an ingenious card game experiment, where discrepancy was objectively manipulated independently of expectations and performance, researchers were able to show the unique discrepancy effect.[5] In this study, participants predicted whether they would win or lose a card hand. Using a marked deck, the researchers caused confirmed expectancies and positive and negative discrepancies in a prespecified order. The outcome (performance) versus the prediction (expectation) was thought to be sufficiently "obvious" that subjects could not misinterpret or confuse these with the state of discrepancy. The predicted independent discrepancy effect was supported, thereby calling into question the two arguments listed previously.

The second development appeared in consumer satisfaction research (variations can be found elsewhere) and involved direct measurement of the expectancy discrepancy. Rather than simply assuming that consumers see discrepancies as intended by the researcher's manipulations, this new phase of research asked consumers to scale their discrepancy feelings as to direction and strength. Two of the most common forms of this scale are as follows:[6]

My expectations for this product/service were:

Too high			Accurate		Too low	
It was *poorer* than I thought.			It was just as I thought.		It was *better* than I thought.	
1	2	3	4	5	6	7

Overall, this product or service or feature or attribute was:

Much worse than expected			Just as expected		Much better than expected	
1	2	3	4	5	6	7

These scales are generic and have numerous applications. For example, the entire consumption experience can be judged on the degree to which it was better or worse than expected, as can individual attributes. In air travel, for example, the entire trip can be assessed, as can each minute element of the trip, from the ticket agent's speed, to the waiting area, to the food in flight, to the landing.[7] Other possibilities, which are discussed later, include dimensions (attribute groups) of performance and the benefits (good things) reaped from consumption as separate from the problems (bad things) encountered.

Disconfirmation Elaborated

The preceding scales represent the consumer response of disconfirmation, more specifically disconfirmation of preperformance standards. Because the early work in consumer satisfaction was

Table 4.1

Categories of Disconfirmation Related to Experiential States of Nature

State of disconfirmation	Consumer's experience
Positive	Low-probability desirable events occur and/or high-probability undesirable events do not occur.
Zero	Low- and high-probability events do or do not occur as expected.
Negative	High-probability desirable events do not occur and/or low-probability undesirable events occur.

conducted with predictive expectations as a standard, the phrase *disconfirmation of expectations* or *expectancy disconfirmation* has come to apply to this concept. As noted in the previous chapter, many standards that consumers bring to the consumption experience can be disconfirmed, so an alternative phrase to describe the discrepancy from standard could be simply *disconfirmation*. In this chapter and throughout this book, the phrases *expectancy disconfirmation* and *disconfirmation* will be used interchangeably, unless otherwise stated.

Note that the disconfirmation scales are two-sided, or bipolar. This convention permits disconfirmation to take on a positive as well as a negative value. In the same way that product performance can be worse than expected, it can also be better than expected. Because the phrase *disconfirmation* without the valence qualifier is ambiguous as to direction, the phrase *negative disconfirmation* will refer to the negative discrepancy that occurs when performance is below standard, and *positive disconfirmation* will refer to the positive discrepancy that occurs when performance is above standard. When performance is equal to standards or expectations, a zero disconfirmation or, simply, a confirmation of expectations exists.

In a previously noted article on the topic, this author proposed conditions that can give rise to the three states of positive, zero, and negative disconfirmation in terms of valenced expectations and the occurrence of outcomes, as shown in Table 4.1.[8] Disconfirmation actually has three components: the event, its probability of occurrence, and its desirability or undesirability. As noted in Chapter 2, the valence of the event is frequently taken as a given or as known. Some illustrations of the conditions for disconfirmation follow.

Negative Disconfirmation

Because the ordinary interpretation of disconfirmation is typically negative, discussion of the negative disconfirmation state will provide a familiar starting point. Under the common interpretation of negative disconfirmation, performance falls short of expectations in an absolute sense. To illustrate, a student may expect a B in a course. Receiving a C (or worse) would be perceived as a negative disconfirmation by the student. This is an example of the most common form of disconfirmation, that of comparing a received performance level to one that was expected with near certainty.

In the more complex case, however, performance falling short of expectations must be qualified with the likelihood of this event occurring and the valence of the performance level. Table 4.1 shows that negative disconfirmation includes both the nonoccurrence of highly probable, desirable events and the occurrence of remote-probability negative events. Thus, a poor acting performance by a top-rated movie star or a boring movie from an Oscar-winning director illustrates the first case. Similarly, a 6.5 Richter scale earthquake in a low-risk residential location with no prior quake activity illustrates the second. Admittedly, these are extreme cases, but they make the point.

Positive Disconfirmation

Positive disconfirmation, where performance exceeds expectations, is subject to the same interpretation. As with the negative case, performance exceeding expectations is exemplified by the student in the preceding example receiving an A after expecting a B. Table 4.1 shows, however, that positive disconfirmation is also exhibited when highly probable undesirable events do not occur or when very improbable desirable events do. Getting through a winter flu season without so much as a cold is an example of the first case, while winning a lottery illustrates the second.

Zero Disconfirmation

Last, confirmation obtains when high-probability events occur and low-probability events do not, in about the frequency one would predict, regardless of the valence of the event. As noted previously, both desirable and undesirable events are equally confirmable if they occur as expected. Thus, receiving gifts from family members on one's birthday and enduring cold temperatures in the dead of winter are confirmations despite their opposing valences.

As disconfirmation measurement is practiced, it is common to assume the valence of the event and to allow the consumer to mentally factor in the event's prior probability in response to a better than/worse than scale. Although it is possible to measure valences and probabilities and combine them, as was done in a rather involved study by the author, the results were not greatly superior to the better than/worse than scale.[9] If greater diagnostic information is required to more fully interpret the meaning of disconfirmation in a particular context, the more complicated valenced approach may prove fruitful.

Objective Versus Subjective Disconfirmation

Measurement Issues: A Diversion

The better than/worse than scales shown here are usually completed as self-reported scores on a survey or as verbal responses to a personal or phone interview. Both are subjective measures in that no actual numeric comparison is made to the expectation level. This issue has a long history. All comparative assessments require that two variables be contrasted in some manner. The point here is that behavioral scientists have had an initial inclination to quantify comparisons subtractively. Consumers, however, are prone to "measure" symbolically, verbally, or qualitatively unless, of course, they have reasons to be more precise. Researchers, at times, have such reasons and must coax numeric conversions out of qualitative expressions by respondents. This brings up the current discussion of how best to quantify disconfirmation respondents. Since expectancy discrepancies (d) are differences between performance (p) and prior expectations (e), researchers can use either (p-e) or more simply (d). This issue pervades just about all topics in this book, including the comparative processes (see Figure 1.4) discussed in this chapter and in Part II of this book. Especially relevant are the topics of need fulfillment (what I have versus what I need) and quality (what I get and what I desire as an ideal).

Further issues will appear in the remaining chapters where the baseline of the discussed concepts is psychological zero (e.g., zero emotion, zero complaining, zero loyalty, and so on). Some of these concepts will have obvious zero points, such as complaining, while others will have negative reverse images, such as pleasure/displeasure. Still others will have ambiguous zero meanings. For example, is disloyalty the negative image of loyalty or is it zero loyalty? Unfortunately, many of these topics do not have satisfactory resolutions and will be pursued according to current convention. This approach will suffice, for now.

Consumer Perceptions of Disconfirmation

In light of the preceding discussion, one might question whether consumers actually make numeric comparisons (e.g., subtracting an expectation score from a performance score—known as a "gap") in a product or service evaluation. Although there is no direct evidence of this, intuition and anecdotal testimony would suggest that many do not and others do, at least for some products and events. For example, the job of a comedian is to generate laughs in an audience, but audience members are not known to count laughs or gauge their intensity. After the performance, however, most are able to say whether the comedian was funnier or less humorous than expected. Alternatively, a consumer might reflect on memories of being short-changed or given too much change in a purchase transaction. How would the consumer know that this had occurred unless the correct change were held as an expectation and comparisons were made to this amount? In this example, a comparison to expectations is most assuredly made.

How would one know if consumers made numeric comparisons? Consider the following hypothetical example. Assume that both consumer A and consumer B evaluate only one critical attribute in purchasing an automobile, gas mileage in miles per gallon. Assume also that both buy identical cars that yield identical gas mileage and that this mileage is typical for this brand of car. At this point, the naive observer might assume that both consumers would have identical satisfaction levels. To the observer's chagrin, however, the consumers could not be further apart in their judgments: consumer A claims that the car's performance is "great," while consumer B is "mad as hell" with the car's performance. As an aside, this example illustrates the typical failing of a performance-only measurement system. (A problem with matching bipolar scale end-points is also evident.)

One likely answer to this paradox can be found in Table 4.2, where the consumers have provided a more complete accounting of their mental processes. The table provides an explanation for the very divergent summary feelings of the two consumers. For any number of reasons, some of which were noted in the previous chapter, these consumers had very different expectations of what they were to receive. (At this point, it does not matter how or where these expectations originated.) It appears that both consumers are diligent measurers of the one dominant attribute, gas mileage, and that they calculated the actual difference between their expectations and their outcomes. This is how they arrived, respectively, at the +5 and –5 differences shown in the table. When asked to interpret these differences, consumer A replied that the outcome was better than expected, and B described the outcome as worse than expected. In all likelihood, this is the reason for the differing satisfaction levels.

A reasonable question at this point is, Why is the subjective interpretation needed if the calculation is available to the consumer and, thus, to the researcher? A first answer is that the numeric expectation level, the numeric performance level, and the consumer's calculation (and even its accuracy) are typically *not* performed by the consumer. In fact, many product and service attributes are not subject to numeric evaluation at all. How, for example, do consumers quantify the comfort level of the car's seating or the richness of the upholstery? If the consumer cannot quantify or scale expectations and performance, then disconfirmation can exist only at the subjective level.

A second answer to this question is that only the consumers can attach the proper amount of valence to the differences they calculate or assume. This valence, then, determines how much

Table 4.2

Consumers With Identical Outcomes and Different Satisfactions

"Calculation" components	Consumer A	Consumer B
Expectation	20 miles per gallon	30 miles per gallon
Performance outcome	25 miles per gallon	25 miles per gallon
Numeric difference	+5 miles per gallon	−5 miles per gallon
Subjective disconfirmation	Better than expected	Worse than expected
Expressed (dis)satisfaction	"Great"	"Mad as hell"

better or worse performance is perceived to be; the consumer then scales the amount of perceived positive or negative disconfirmation on the better than/worse than scale.

In an example of the first scenario, assume that consumers are less than diligent and fail to maintain the proper records for calculating gas mileage, a step that requires a log of distance traveled and a measure of the volume of gasoline used. Can the consumer still respond to the subjective disconfirmation query? Most certainly, as long as a perception of better than/same as/ worse than is *sensed.* This "sense" has been shown to exist in many studies (to be discussed) and can exist for purchases having no objective performance dimensions at all—for example, artwork bought for the purpose of aesthetic pleasure, insurance bought in the absence of a claim to achieve a sense of security, and contributions to charity (an intangible "purchase") made for the purpose of altruistic personal satisfaction. In fact, in an early investigation, the author studied the subjective disconfirmation of individuals receiving a flu inoculation against the threat of swine flu in 1976, an epidemic that did not occur in the United States where the study was performed.[10] Many of these individuals expressed positive disconfirmation as a result of receiving this protection, which, in fact, did not protect them against the nonappearing flu or, for that matter, other strains of the flu. Still other individuals reported negative disconfirmation with getting the shot, even though they could not have caught (and did not catch) swine flu. Where did these sham perceptions originate? They were apparently (and wrongly) sensed.

In the second example, researchers may be able to infer disconfirmation by collecting only expectation and performance data—in effect, data on the first two rows of Table 4.2. Could assumptions be made regarding the subjective disconfirmation and, hence, satisfaction of the two consumers? Perhaps, as we have done here, but not necessarily. The researcher would be able to calculate objective differences between these values if they were numeric "true" scores. If, instead, the numbers were subjective interpretations of a qualitative variable such as comfort on a seven-point comfortable/uncomfortable scale, this difference could still be calculated. Unfortunately, however, both differences exist only as a *managerial* calculation and may not be as revealing as the consumer would necessarily find them. Three reasons for inaccuracy in the manager's calculation exist.

Lack of Precision in the Translation of Numeric Scores to Subjective Meaning

Consider the previous example of the subjective automobile attribute, comfort, and assume that both the expectation and performance judgments are obtained on an uncomfortable/comfortable 1-to-7 scale such as the following:

		Uncomfortable			Comfortable		
1	2	3	4	5	6	7

Because comfort, like most luxury attributes, is not quantifiable by the consumer, there is little precision here, for it is not known exactly what the middle scale point (or any other for that matter) represents on a "true" comfort continuum. Additionally, researchers refer to this measure as an ordinal scale because the intervals between the numbers cannot be assumed to be constant on a "true" scale. Thus, any difference score calculated by using this scale reflects the imprecision in both the expectation and the performance numbers. The issue of the unreliability of difference scores is also a problem, having been discussed at length in the psychometric literature.[11] For now, researchers must live with this problem as it pervades many measures of concepts discussed in this book.

Implicit Weightings of Expectations and Performance

A second reason why a difference score may not reflect a consumer-generated subjective score is that the consumer may implicitly weight either expectations or performance more highly than the other. For example, expectations may be only vaguely recalled because of the time interval between purchase and use. This example of ease of recall or *availability*, mentioned in the previous chapter, is one of many consumer decision-making strategies. Unequal weightings could also arise because of the difference in the way consumers who assimilate (thereby placing greater weight on expectations) and consumers who contrast (thereby placing greater weight on performance) make judgments.

Valence

Finally, as noted, the raw difference score does not contain the consumer's valence toward the discrepancy. To return to the gas mileage example, the five miles per gallon (positive) difference may be only slightly better than expected for one consumer but may considered much, much better by another. The subjective difference score clearly accounts for this difference in interpretation and implicitly takes a consumer's ideal point into consideration (discussed in Chapter 6).

Predicting Satisfaction: Calculated or Subjective Disconfirmation?

Is there evidence for the superiority of subjective disconfirmation over calculated disconfirmation in the prediction of satisfaction? Yes. A number of studies have examined both the calculated and single-score varieties of disconfirmation, most using rating scale scores and one using objective calculations of disconfirmation in dollars of profit.[12] The results of all studies were similar, with the great majority of the evidence suggesting that the subjective version of disconfirmation correlates more highly with the satisfaction scales than do the difference scores. Moreover, when analyzed in an ordering of cause and effect, the following configuration of concepts has consistently been found to best fit the data:

"Calculated" disconfirmation → Subjective disconfirmation → Satisfaction

This sequence of events forms the basis for the expectancy disconfirmation model of consumer satisfaction to be presented here. As shown, this sequence portrays a calculated expectation-

Figure 4.1   **A Simplified Expectancy Disconfirmation Framework**

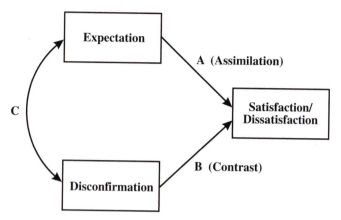

performance difference or gap (if performed) as input to the consumer's subjective interpretation of this difference. The subjective interpretation then becomes the most immediate antecedent of satisfaction. If no objective score is available, then a subjective judgment is "sensed." Expectations and performance are implicitly incorporated into the disconfirmation judgment in this sequence.

This discussion of disconfirmation has not explicitly considered the assimilation effect observed in a number of studies. The assimilation phenomenon has not been forgotten, just suspended. The following discussion considers its role in the satisfaction response. In doing so, it becomes necessary to reconcile the differences, if any, between the role of assimilation and contrast in satisfaction versus the differences between expectation and disconfirmation.

Expectation and Disconfirmation as Proxies for Assimilation and Contrast

As noted in the discussion of assimilation and contrast, early theorists assumed that the effects of these two influences were mutually exclusive. That is, either consumers were exclusively assimilation-oriented or contrast-oriented, or they assimilated for performance close to expectations and contrasted for performance more distant. In a sense, this assumption made the two strategies negatively correlated in that the presence of one implied the absence of the other, and vice versa. To test this notion, it is necessary to measure consumers' use of these strategies.

Since measures of both expectation and disconfirmation are available, it is possible to test for their dependence or independence. More specifically, it is possible to test for the validity of the two arguments posed earlier in this chapter. These contain an implicit assumption of a negative correlation between expectation and disconfirmation. This assumption results from the nature of the arguments themselves, namely, that expectation levels that are unreasonably high will always produce a negative disconfirmation and levels that are too low will always produce a positive disconfirmation. At these extremes, it is assumed that performance cannot exceed or fall short of the respective expectation levels.

This assumption of a negative correlation was tested in an early study by the author.[13] From a sample of students who rated a new automobile model before inspecting and driving it, actual predictive expectations were obtained. After the inspection and test-drive, subjective disconfirmation scores and an overall summary rating representing satisfaction were measured. The conceptual framework underlying this simplified scheme (i.e., performance is omitted) appears in Figure 4.1.

Note that three relations are displayed. Relation A is the expectation (assimilation) effect, relation B is the disconfirmation (contrast) effect, and relation C is the correlation between expectation and disconfirmation. Before examining the results, it is instructive to explore the three possible outcomes of relation C.

Relation C Is Negative

This is known as the previously mentioned ceiling-and-floor effect. The higher the consumer's expectations, the greater the likelihood of negative disconfirmation due to the increasing inability of performance to match extreme (i.e., ceiling) expectation levels. Similarly, the lower one's expectations, the greater the likelihood of positive disconfirmation, as performance is less likely to reach the floor.

Relation C Is Positive

This possibility has been alluded to briefly in an earlier part of this chapter under the labels "better than best" and "poorer than poor." Here, high expectations encourage positive disconfirmation, and low expectations encourage negative disconfirmation. A likely explanation for this phenomenon is the common halo effect, whereby consumers bring overall positive or negative biases to the judgment task.[14] Thus, high-expectation consumers will see only positive, better-than-expected outcomes, and low-expectation consumers will see only negative results.

Relation C Is Zero

Under this condition, the expectation level says little about the positivity or negativity of disconfirmation. High (or low) expectations are equally likely to precede negative as well as positive disconfirmation. This allows for performance to exceed even very high expectations ("beyond my wildest dreams!") and to fall short of very low expectations ("worse than I ever could have imagined!"). Thus, the conditions are independent and will require separate strategies.

As was found in the previously cited automobile study, the following correlations (using overall scales) emerged, corresponding to the relations in Figure 4.1: correlation A = 0.39, correlation B = 0.61, and correlation C = 0.01. The first two correlations were highly significant; the third was obviously not. This evidence suggests that two phenomena were generating the results in this study. First, there appeared to be no necessary relation between expectation level and the subjective disconfirmation as reported by individuals. Second, expectation and the positivity or negativity of disconfirmation apparently operated in tandem to jointly (and independently) determine satisfaction levels. This latter conclusion is readily apparent from a tabular presentation of cell means from the same findings that generated the correlations, as shown in Table 4.3.

A number of new insights emerge from the tabular presentation of the data. First, the independent operations of expectation and disconfirmation are clearly visible from the row and column marginals. (The marginals are the row and column averages, so called because they are reported in the table margins.) Ceteris paribus, an increase in expectations from low to high results in a 0.83 point increase (4.80 − 3.97) in the mean satisfaction rating. More influential is the increase in ratings as one moves from negative disconfirmation to confirmation (a 0.89 increase) and from confirmation to positive disconfirmation (a 1.10 increase).

Second, the best and worst expectation and disconfirmation combinations for firms are now visible. If one can generalize from these data, it is clear that consumers will be most dissatisfied if

Table 4.3

Tabular Results Cross-Classified by Expectation and Disconfirmation Levels

Respondent expectation level	Respondents reporting			Row marginals
	Negative disconfirmation	Confirmation	Positive disconfirmation	
Low	2.97	3.88	5.06	3.97
High	3.87	5.06	5.93	4.80
Column marginals	3.57	4.46	5.56	4.46

Source: Richard L. Oliver, "Effect of Expectation and Disconfirmation on Postexposure Product Evaluations: An Alternative Interpretation," *Journal of Applied Psychology* 62, no. 4 (August 1977): 485.
Note: 1–7 scale; cell means are not equal; total $n = 243$.

they enter into a purchase with low expectations and receive a product that is worse than expected. Is this possible? Examples such as dental root-canal procedures, IRS audits, and low-budget movies come to mind. An explanation for the best combination rests on similar logic whereby high expectations coupled with positive disconfirmation result in the highest satisfaction levels. Examples of delighting experiences (e.g., one's favorite sports team winning the World Series or Super Bowl) qualify here.

In one of the few reported replications of this analysis, almost identical results appear in a study of hotel visits.[15] On seven-point scales of satisfaction with the hotel stay, the marginals for high and low expectations were 5.29 versus 3.54, respectively, while the marginals for positive, zero, and negative disconfirmation were 6.31, 4.64, and 1.77, respectively. Both sets of figures contain significant differences across levels, and the cell means mapped the data in Table 4.3 very closely.

What Does This Imply for Managerial Strategy?

These data immediately raise the critical question of how firms can maximize satisfaction. The answer, evident from Table 4.3, is that management must instill high (but not ideal) expectations and then provide a product or service that is able to exceed them. This goal may sound paradoxical, but it is achievable. This is a managerial issue, involving managerial strategy. Management must decide the appropriate level of (high) expectations that it will promise, keeping in mind that exceeding this level in the eyes of the consumer must still be possible.

This dictum illustrates the problem with a firm's promise of "ideal" performance. Ideal-level expectations simply cannot be exceeded. And what happens if high expectations cannot be exceeded? As shown in Table 4.3, the best that this firm can expect to achieve is represented by the high-expectations zero-disconfirmation (confirmation) cell. According to the data reported here, the ratings will be equal to those obtained when consumers held low expectations and found that they were exceeded.

The Role of Confirmation

What does confirmation of expectations do? Unfortunately, very little—nothing much beyond the effect of the expectation level that already exists.[16] If consumers expect a pleasant dining

Figure 4.2   **Operation of an Indifference Zone in Expectancy Disconfirmation**

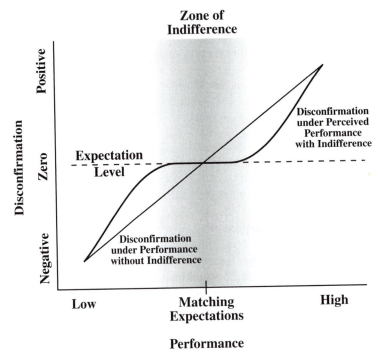

experience and receive exactly that, they will report that the experience was pleasant. Similarly, if consumers expect to be dissatisfied with a company's response to a legitimate complaint because the company's policy is generally known as unresponsive, they will be dissatisfied when it is later found that the company ignored the complaint, just as expected. Unfortunately, some literatures proclaim that meeting expectations is the key to satisfaction. Even given the presumption that these expectations were not negative, this is still a suboptimal proposition. At best, this strategy may merely stave off dissatisfaction. The competitor that has positioned itself to exceed customers' expectations will dominate the firm that merely meets them.

Another aspect of confirmation also requires consideration. The previous chapter discussed the notion of a zone of indifference. This zone, which is also called a latitude of acceptance in the assimilation-contrast literature and shares similarities with but remains different from the tolerance zone, surrounds a range of performance that is acceptable to the consumer because performance in this range essentially fulfills the consumer's needs.[17] An example might be a promised pizza delivery time of thirty minutes; most consumers would not be terribly upset if the pizza arrived as late as forty minutes or as early as twenty minutes. The general operation of indifference zones is shown in Figure 4.2.

The figure assumes a preset expectation level, shown by the dashed horizontal line. Given this level, the horizontal axis shows performance ranging from below expectations through matching expectations to exceeding expectations. Likewise, the vertical axis shows disconfirmation ranging from negative disconfirmation through zero disconfirmation (confirmation) to positive disconfirmation. The straight line running from the origin at 45° shows how disconfirmation will increase from negative to positive as performance goes from low to high. The curve snaking around this straight line shows the distortion that would be created by an indifference zone. The zone of indifference, shown as the gray shaded area, defines the range of performance both below and above the expectation level that consumers would accept as essentially meeting expectations. As a result, positive disconfirmation and negative disconfirmation first appear at greater performance discrepancies than would occur if no indifference zone were operating.

The implication of this phenomenon for the firm is that exceeding expectations may be more difficult to the extent that the acceptance region is large. If consumers are willing to give the firm the benefit of the doubt for small shortfalls in performance, they may also be equally insensitive to a range of performance exceeding expectations. In fact, if the distorted disconfirmation curve shown in Figure 4.2 can be considered the general case, then both positive and negative disconfirmation will lag straight-line disconfirmation until the two become psychologically identical, located at the two ends of the performance range shown in the figure.

To clarify an earlier point, note that the zone of indifference is not identical to this author's definition of a tolerance zone, discussed in the previous chapter. The upper and lower boundaries of a tolerance zone reflect the (usually lower) range of performance the consumer will find as minimally fulfilling needs. Minimal need fulfillment, such as might occur when a traveler expecting a limousine at the airport ends up taking a taxi, can be much below expectations and extremely frustrating. Guidelines for determining limits of the tolerance or indifference zones using desired (should) and adequate (will) levels were provided in the previous chapter.

The Role of Extremes of Disconfirmation

Moving from confirmation to what may be referred to as its polar opposite(s), the extremes of the disconfirmation regions are approached. At this point or points, the consumer's response is thought to turn from positive or negative reaction, as shown in Figure 4.2, to extraordinary emotional states. That is, disconfirmation may take on a greater role in the consumer's psyche than the cognitive state of disconfirmation would suggest.[18] Although more information will be provided later in this book when consumers' emotions are discussed, we can broach the topic of *delight* as commonly found in the practitioner literature. This is, of course, the reaction at the positive extreme. Its polar opposite goes by many names; one frequently used is *outrage*. In fact, the study of extreme negative responding in the consumer literature actually preceded that of delight when early studies of reactions in dissatisfaction and complaining were performed in the 1970s.

Delight has been explored more scientifically in the consumer affect literature. Based on earlier work by this author and colleagues, delight in consumption has been described as "a profoundly positive emotional state generally resulting from having one's expectations exceeded to a surprising degree."[19] The origins of this response in consumption arise partly from a "consumption processing" model proposed by this author and elaborated later in Chapter 13. One of the consumption prototypes in the original work was "satisfaction-as-surprise," whereby unexpected outcomes were categorized into those resulting from success and failure. Specific emotions were proposed for each of these outcome states. The success emotions included such intense emotions as amazement and astonishment but not, at the time, delight.

Delight is difficult to discuss in isolation because it is a primitive, but complex emotion. In its most simple terms, it is unexpected pleasure, or, as described in a well-known typology, surprising joy.[20] Thus, it contains elements of the surprise and pleasure emotions. As discussed by this author and colleagues, unexpectedness is also inherent in its meaning and unexpectedness as used here entails disconfirmation. It also contains attribution, but for now this element of the response is suspended.[21]

In 1989, the author discussed two categories of disconfirmation, "normal" and "surprise." Normal includes the zone of indifference and those levels thought to arise within the range of likely experience that consumers have encountered. This experience of course includes vicarious information and that from perceived authoritative sources. Surprise disconfirmation falls outside of this range, resulting in extremes of emotional responses. It is these totally unexpected outcomes that elicit delight (or rage), summed up as a response state the author originally referred to as "satisfaction-as-novelty."

In the second, later paper, two tandem sequences were proposed and substantiated through testing. One consisted of satisfaction deriving from processing within the normal disconfirmation range, while delight followed a pathway with extranormal performance resulting in a high aroused processing state akin to extreme surprise, then of focus. These pathways are shown in the sequences below. The first is the "satisfaction sequence," with disconfirmation influencing both positive affect (Chapter 12) and then satisfaction (with the disconfirmation-to-satisfaction link not shown for brevity). The second is the "delight sequence," whereby the surprise inherent in consumption influences delight through arousal. Both have been reconfirmed in a replication study using website participation with nearly identical results. Quadratic and interactive effects were also included but did not alter the basic framework.[22]

The satisfaction sequence:

$$Disconfirmation \rightarrow positive\ affect \rightarrow satisfaction$$

The delight sequence:

$$Surprising\ consumption \rightarrow arousal \rightarrow delight$$

Technically, then, delight is not on the same planar dimension as is satisfaction, although researchers and consumers may describe it as such, often using it to anchor the positive pole of a satisfaction scale. This difference will become clearer in Chapter 13, where the state of delight is further elaborated. For now, suffice it to say that delight is not simply a state of "very satisfied," which is how it is operationalized when researchers attempt to tease its meaning from simple five-point satisfaction scales. In fact, in one study, repurchase intention was found to be a function of delight and not "mere" high satisfaction levels.[23]

Thus, understanding delight requires greater elaboration along emotional integration lines. It also requires an appreciation for the role of surprise in its development, a topic to be covered next. Not much has been said of the negative surprise pole of outrage. This will be covered in greater detail in Chapter 14 under the rubric of "grudging."

Surprise and Disconfirmation in the Consumption Response

Surprise is now recognized as a viable tactic or strategy for marketers. The current emphasis on consumption surprise is interesting as it is clearly not new within purchasing, being an essential ingredient in gift-giving, for example. History buffs will recall the favorite snack of lore and baseball, Cracker Jack. One wonders how many fewer boxes of this product would have been sold over the years (since 1912) were it not for the famous promise: "Toy Surprise Inside."

Surprise is a basic emotion that is, as has been noted, central to the delight response. By definition, it entails unexpectedness. Actually, it is also or most frequently encountered as *mis*expectedness. This is something of a tautology since unexpectedness is also a misexpectation in that the consumer expected normalcy or adaptation. More confusingly, consumers can also have an expectation of unexpectedness when they "purchase" the right to be surprised. Examples include horror films; entertainment venues where surprise is part of the performance, such as circuses; "experiential" consumption where the nature of the experience has high variability, as in white-water rafting; spectator events where the performance, including the outcome, is unexpected or misexpected (sports); and numerous provisions, many of them sensory, where surprise encounters, surprisingly rare discoveries, and surprise endings occur (mystery novels). To be surprising, the event cannot become routine to the consumer (although it will be to the producer, designer, choreographer, etc.). Hence the popularity of "variations on a theme," including movie sequels.

Experiential consumption of this nature relies on the basic nature of the human surprise response. Surprise has been studied extensively and its phases are known.[24] First there is a recognition of a discrepancy from a baseline level of performance or the sequence of events processed as a script. This recognition, however, must be relevant to the consumer in that ongoing processes including thought are disrupted. For example, surprising events happen in traffic everywhere; seasoned commuters do not notice. At a second level, there is an orienting response where the individual categorizes the event as at variance with expectations or completely different from expectations, such as when a purchaser expects to obtain A and receives B (a variation of bait and switch), or receives B, expecting nothing (e.g., gifts) and vice versa. A third phase is referred to as updating, either in terms of event probabilities, their variance, or in terms of possible event outcomes themselves. Because surprise within the expectancy disconfirmation model has already been elaborated, the following discussion turns to situations where no expectations exist, where they are latent or unconscious, or where a consumer has distinct expectations of encountering surprise. Lastly, the possibility that disconfirmation and surprise can be experienced independently will be entertained, followed by implications of engendering surprise in marketing activities.

Surprise in consumption can be viewed from two levels. The first, as in the Cracker Jack example, is of surprise in consumption. This is usually a fairly mundane surprise gift to the consumer for patronizing or purchasing over time (e.g., an unexpected coupon inserted in a package without messaging on the container, or a greeting card on a patron's birthday).[25] It could be a surprise sale event at a store in an off-season period when sales are not usually expected. It could be an unanticipated treat after a purchase ordeal such as a token toy after a child's dentist appointment. Or it could be an unexpected extra, such as undercoating, added to a new car purchase free of charge. At the other extreme, we move from surprise in purchasing to the purchase or provision of surprise.

The provision of "pure" surprise consumption requires design. Excluding the initial sensation of delight, much if not most consumption is designed so as to be *non*surprising. Imagine what life would be like if common everyday necessities held surprises, items like refrigerators, microwaves, even cars after the initial "new car novelty" wears off. Generally consumers desire order in their environment, excepting positive surprises and delights. If they wish surprise in consumption (and *as* consumption), they can choose to patronize surprise providers. Surprise merchants have an intimate knowledge of the boundaries of human experience and seek to exceed these in positive and, in some cases, negative ways for the ensuing relief (e.g., peril and fright experiences, such as haunted houses and slasher movies).[26] In this sense, even surprise is subject to disconfirmation. In some cases, consumers seek out environments where surprise happens naturally (or does not), such as zoos, safaris, paint-ball combat, and casinos (to management, surprise is created with exact design parameters). In other cases, such as the cinematography industry and video games, the surprise is "designed in."

Are surprise and disconfirmation related? Yes. Can they be disentangled? Yes. It's all in the design. Surprise exists in isolation when expectations are zero or certain. Disconfirmation without surprise exists when expectations are disconfirmed in the latitude of acceptance. Surprise and disconfirmation (surprise disconfirmation) exist when events fall outside of this latitude but short of zero or certain. When events are not within a person's comprehension or simply cannot happen and do, or when events are certain to occur and do not, surprise occurs.

In concluding this section, let us assess the consequences of surprising consumption. They are as we would expect. The direction of effect is that of expectancy discrepancies generally or of good and bad performance *consequences* if expectations are not relevant in consuming a surprise deliverable. Surprise, however, changes the intensity of effect within consumer responses. Research shows that all affects are enhanced when surprise is one of the causal agents. Called "response contagion" or "excitation transfer" effects, positive experiences become delightful and negative experiences dreadful.[27]

THE RELATIVE INFLUENCES OF EXPECTATION OR DISCONFIRMATION: WHEN WOULD ONE DOMINATE THE OTHER?

The reader may have noticed that, in the example of auto test-drive experiences, the incremental return due to increasing the positivity of disconfirmation (i.e., moving from left to right in Table 4.3) appeared to generate greater increases in satisfaction than that of increasing the level of expectations from low to high. This result could have been predicted from the correlations corresponding to the relations in Figure 4.1, where the disconfirmation-satisfaction correlation was 1.5 times that of the expectation-satisfaction correlation. That is, satisfaction was found to respond more forcefully to increases in the positivity of disconfirmation than to increases in the level of expectation, a phenomenon known as "disconfirmation sensitivity."[28] Is this generally true? It depends.

A scorecard of data has not yet been compiled, but a sufficient number of studies have been performed to provide some initial and intuitive insights. For now, assume two opposite scenarios, one where the expectation effect is known to dominate disconfirmation and the other where disconfirmation is known to dominate expectation. Discussion begins with the first scenario.

When Expectations Dominate

For expectations to dominate a satisfaction decision, the processing of expectations must be more salient to the consumer than is the processing of performance or of comparing expectations to performance. It has been said that it is not necessary that the consumer have objective measurements of performance for a disconfirmation judgment to occur. If the dominant expectations scenario is to be useful, it must also be assumed that a subjective performance judgment that would give rise to a strong or salient disconfirmation perception is not or cannot be made. Three reasons may explain why consumers do not attend to performance and, hence, disconfirmation. First, they may be unable to judge performance; second, they may not do so as a practical matter; third, they may not wish to judge performance as an ego-defensive tactic.[29]

Measurement Difficulties

When are consumers unable to judge performance? Three answers are: (1) whenever no objective performance can be observed, (2) whenever performance is an ambiguous concept,[30] or (3) whenever measurement is so technically involved that the consumer would not even be aware of the procedures. The first two cases could be represented by "alternative" medications, "health" foods, and aesthetics such as artwork, while the third could pertain to any of a number of high-technology items such as computers, chemical water treatments and sanitizers, and any number of diagnostic measurements in medicine (e.g., cholesterol testing). After all, does a leading bathroom disinfectant really "kill germs dead?"

Impracticality

The case of the consumer's disinterest in testing performance is also an intriguing phenomenon. Some products have performance dimensions that are measurable, but the actual measurement procedures may be too intrusive, cumbersome, or inconvenient. For example, a manufacturer promises that a long-life lightbulb will last for an average of 1,500 hours. But consumers do not keep logs of the times that lamps were lit or put recording monitors on their lamps. When the bulb burns out, it is unlikely that the actual bulb life is known. What is the only number of hours that will be recalled by the consumer?

Unwillingness

Finally, some consumers are unwilling to measure performance because they fear that the result will be confusing or disturbing, will reflect poorly on their decision-making ability, or will contradict a previously drawn conclusion. Such a confirmation bias, noted earlier, pervades many decisions, especially those of an ego-involving nature.[31] One example might be found in security investing when a particular return is expected within a specific time frame. Many investors are known not to "test" interim performance for fear that their predictions will be proved wrong.[32] Thus, for this and the previous two reasons, expectations may quite routinely dominate the satisfaction decision.

Figure 4.3 illustrates graphically the operation of the expectancy disconfirmation model under strong expectation effects and, for the sake of discussion, weak disconfirmation effects. This model assumes an additive interpretation, as shown in the results displayed in Table 4.3. Location 1 represents hedonic neutrality, an emotionless consumer. At location 2, one consumer is given reason to hold high expectations, while a second consumer at location 3 is primed to hold low expectations. Now, if both consumers receive exactly what they expected, then the high-expectation consumer remains "satisfied" at location 4 and the low-expectation consumer remains "dissatisfied" at location 5.

Locations 6 and 9 represent the two situations of dual parallel effects. Position 6 occurs when a consumer expecting high performance receives a positive disconfirmation—a product better than expected, the most satisfying combination. Position 9, similarly, is the worst possible case whereby low expectations are negatively disconfirmed. Compare this combination to the product rating in the low-expectation negative-disconfirmation cell in Table 4.3. Firms should seek to avoid this possibility in all business matters.

In contrast to the complementary effects, positions 7 and 8 provide countervailing interpretations and paradoxical results. Position 7 portrays a negative disconfirmation under high expectations, yet the consumer's final resting place is in the region of satisfaction. How can this be? The reason is that the high (and strong) expectation effect overwhelmed the much weaker disconfirmation effect and maintained the satisfaction level, albeit at a lower level. This consumer is still satisfied, even given a product performing more poorly than expected, but is less satisfied than if expectations had been met (i.e., position 7 is lower than position 4). In fact, there is a descriptive name for this state of nature, one where poorer-than-expected performance remains satisfying, but less so than anticipated or desired. A commonly used term is *disappointment.* It applies when a favorite performer appears in a movie or concert, but the performance was not up to standard, or when a

Figure 4.3   **Operation of Expectancy Disconfirmation Under Strong Expectation and Weak Disconfirmation Effects**

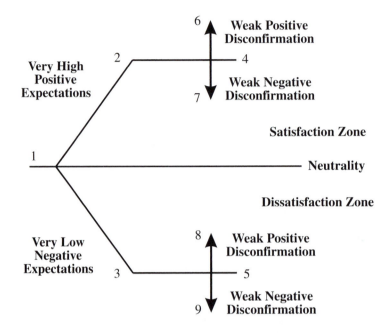

pet soils the carpet. The consumer's reaction is probably disappointment, but overall (and lower) satisfaction is felt nonetheless.

Consider now the case where strong low expectations are coupled with a weak, but positive disconfirmation (position 8). This is one example of dissatisfaction with a better-than-expected product, and it begs the question, Why isn't the consumer satisfied with a product that exceeded expectations? The answer, again, is that the low prior expectation was excessively dominant and prevented the positive disconfirmation from moving the consumer upward, crossing neutrality into the satisfaction region. This is the lament of the low-image producer trying to improve its product.

The U.S. automobile industry in the 1980s was probably an example of this latter situation. The *Consumer Reports* annual automobile issues had noted the improving quality of U.S. cars relative to those of foreign producers for some time before domestic consumers began to trust the quality of American-made cars. Responses by individuals to a product that remains dissatisfying, but is somewhat better than expected, are interesting because of their ambivalence. Phrases like "improving," "gratifying that it wasn't as bad as I thought," and "bad, but not terribly bad" come to mind.

These two situations at positions 7 and 8 should dispel a misconception heard numerous times from business practitioners and academics alike. It is frequently claimed that positive disconfirmation results in satisfaction and negative disconfirmation results in dissatisfaction. These statements are simply not true under the conditions underlying the responses in Figure 4.3, and such blanket, oversimplified renditions of the expectancy disconfirmation model only serve to confuse. Situations where this interpretation is accurate, however, will be described shortly.

In summary, expectation effects are pervasive when they obscure or overwhelm the processing of

Figure 4.4 **Operation of Expectancy Disconfirmation Under Weak Expectation and Strong Disconfirmation Effects**

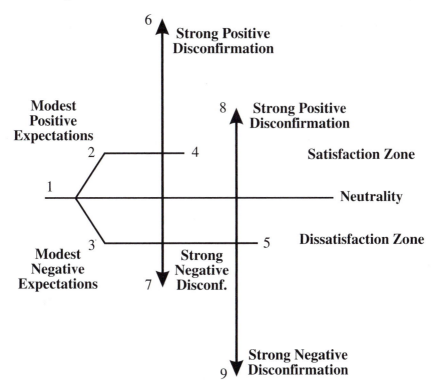

performance so that disconfirmation is not sensed. If performance is obscure, it will be absorbed into expectations via assimilation so that disconfirmation is technically zero. This statement assumes no disconfirmation influences whatsoever. If we relax this strong condition so that some disconfirmation effect operates, it will be weak relative to the influence of expectation. This phenomenon has been noted in countless literatures where first impressions in, for example, education, employee selection, stereotypy, profiling, and macroeconomics are studied, as noted in the introduction to the last chapter. It is up to marketers to determine whether this situation operates to their advantage or not.

As a final point in this section, the reader may have noted that the locations of the final positions in Figure 4.3 do not correspond to the order of the cell means in Table 4.3. The reason for this apparent anomaly is simple. The illustrative example assumed that the expectation effect was stronger than the effect of disconfirmation, while the results giving rise to the data in Table 4.3 are from a data set where the reverse is true. This situation is now presented.

When Disconfirmation Dominates

Figure 4.4 illustrates a response quite opposite to the previous example—strong disconfirmation in the presence of weak expectations. As before, one neutral consumer at location 1 is given favorable expectations but much weaker than shown in Figure 4.3 while another is given a similar level of unfavorable weak expectations so that the first consumer is now at location 2 and the second at location 3. Note that the disconfirmation effects, represented by the vertical lines, are stronger (longer). As before, when the two influences are in the same direction (favorable expectations, positive disconfirmation; unfavorable expectations, negative disconfirmation), the effects are cumulative, and the best and worst possible situations are again apparent at positions 6 and 9.[33] Additionally, confirmation of either favorable or unfavorable expectations (locations 4 and 5) simply maintains the previous level of expected satisfaction.

The effect of countervailing influences is now very visible in this second example. Here, favorable expectations in the face of a negative disconfirmation do result in dissatisfaction (position 7), as the negative disconfirmation influence drags the consumer's judgment across neutrality into the dissatisfaction region. One might liken this situation to shock or betrayal, as if the consumer were set up with overhyped product claims. Similarly, a strong positive disconfirmation given unfavorable expectations (position 8) is now sufficient to reverse the prior negative feelings, causing satisfaction. This situation illustrates what companies with negative images must do to jump-start the consumer. Expressions of surprise, including amazement, would pertain here, as in "I simply didn't realize how good this product is!"

The resting places of the four expectation-disconfirmation combinations (represented by the locations of the arrowheads) now roughly correspond to the cell means in Table 4.3. Be aware, however, that the means will differ for every unique situation, and Table 4.3 and Figure 4.4 are presented as actual and hypothetical illustrations, respectively, of one product and one consumer setting. Studies of expectation and disconfirmation effects produce differing results depending on numerous idiosyncratic variables, and researchers must calculate these effects on an individual product or service basis.

Conditions Favoring Strong Disconfirmation Effects

When does disconfirmation dominate the expectation (assimilation) effect? The literature is now more persuasive on this matter. Obviously, the consumer would need to be aware (cognizant) of a departure from expectations. As discussed, surprise qualifies as a departure as long as it is of the normal variety. All expectation deviations become more poignant, however, if the expectation is embedded in a script—a series of expected events as in a fine dining experience. Now, any nonconforming part of the script is capable of violating the entire expectation sequence.[34] For example, if guests are accustomed to a complimentary morning newspaper at a swank hotel, it becomes obvious that something is changed or amiss if the paper is not there on a particular morning and even more frustrating if the hotel has changed its policy so that papers are no longer provided.

Another answer addresses the role of involvement. More involved consumers have been found to report higher levels of (positive) disconfirmation and of satisfaction. And at least one study finds that involvement enhances the effect of *both* positive disconfirmation and negative disconfirmation, so that negative disconfirmation, in particular, under high involvement has a more deleterious effect on satisfaction than it would if involvement were not operating. Generally, any concept that affects the salience of performance to the consumer should increase the degree to which disconfirmation, more so than expectation, affects satisfaction. This includes the correlates of involvement, including familiarity and experience with the product category and confidence in assessing its features, as well as the technical complexity of the category.[35]

Still another explanation relates to the degree to which expectations can be recalled, are prone to decay, or are overridden, particularly by subsequent performance. While recall may be an idiosyncratic issue, decay proneness is not. It is subject to many factors, the most obvious of which is the passage of time. For example, in a study of complaining, the authors found that complainers' satisfaction responded to both expectations and disconfirmation, while the satisfaction of noncomplainers was influenced only by disconfirmation. The authors argued that the lengthy time frame before recall caused the noncomplainers' recollection of their expectations to decay. Complainers, perhaps because they were more involved, held their expectations actively in memory.[36] Thus, a declining memory for expectations may cause satisfaction to be dominated by disconfirmation only. As noted in the previous discussion, it is not necessary to know precise expectation levels in order to form a judgment of better than/worse than expected and, corresponding with this, cognition appears to "best" affect as time and product experience progress.[37]

This phenomenon is a particular problem when the consumption situation is prolonged as many services are, either because they are extended encounters, such as a vacation, hospital stay, or education, or because consumption consists of many repetitions, such as with a housekeeper. Research shows that memory for extended encounters relies heavily on the most extreme or last episode, referred to as duration neglect or lack of attention to the passage of time coupled with a "peak-end" recollection heuristic.[38] Here, a clear inattention to prior expectations is fostered by memorable experiences of an unusual and recent nature.

Lastly, as is found in many studies, actual performance observations may obscure or override expectations that may have existed. This situation was alluded to in the previous chapter where the necessity of collecting retrospective expectations was discussed. Performance often causes consumers to believe that their prior dispositions were correct in that performance confirms their predictions. Sometimes called the "I knew it all along effect," this hindsight bias is pervasive. Even when the expectation decay is measured with two survey administrations, the performance effect is easily verified, as it was in a restaurant dining field experiment by this author (to be discussed).[39]

As specifics of the preceding suggest, negative disconfirmation has been found to have effects much more severe than an equivalent amount of positive disconfirmation has in the favorable direction. This has been known for some time, as discussed previously in the context of the disproportionate influence of negative information generally. The effect here is directly analogous. Disconfirmation can be viewed as a gain or loss from expectations, and, when compared side by side with the same absolute deviations in "utility," the loss function is steeper than the gain function.[40]

Not surprisingly, researchers in the satisfaction area find this effect as well. When compared to positive disconfirmation influences, negative disconfirmation exerts a profoundly more significant effect on satisfaction, intention, and other postpurchase phenomena (e.g., repeat purchase, word of mouth). Not only is the magnitude of impact more severe, but also the slope of the response curve is steeper and nonmonotonic.[41] In terms of the curves in Figure 4.2, the straight line at 45° would actually break more sharply downward in the performance shortfall region as would its tandem mirror curve in the presence of an indifference region. Although no evidence exists to support the following claim, it would not be too speculative to state that the indifference region to the left of met expectations would be less extensive, if it existed at all. Once again, firms are advised to use expectation management strategies in order to avoid, if at all possible, the bane of negatively disconfirming consumer expectations.

EVIDENCE FOR THE EXPECTANCY DISCONFIRMATION MODEL

A number of reviews have documented the increasing acceptability of the expectancy disconfirmation model in describing postpurchase evaluation. These were documented in the first edition of this book. Since that time, a number of additional tests and reviews of a more specialized nature have emerged.[42] At this point, the applicability of the theory is widely recognized. Although none of these reviews questions the ability of the expectancy disconfirmation model to predict satisfaction, each notes that various elements of the model are in need of greater specification in terms of when variations are appropriate. The reviewers provide legitimate and important observations on the limitations of the expectancy disconfirmation model. Each is covered in different parts of this book. The following chapters discuss other satisfaction comparison models that will be shown to operate in parallel with expectancy disconfirmation, including need fulfillment, quality, value, equity, regret, and affect. Lastly, it must be admitted that there are some issues for which researchers have no answers; these await further research. The interplay of the antecedents of satisfaction is an example of one such issue.

PERFORMANCE INFLUENCES IN THE EXPECTANCY DISCONFIRMATION MODEL

Performance-only influences are, perhaps, among the most primitive predictors of satisfaction in most disciplines; affect probably shares this distinction. As noted in Chapter 2, raw performance statements are of the nature of a description, as in "quarter-pounder." This provides the researcher with little actionable information unless consumers are asked to state their liking or disliking for this level of performance. This begs the question, Is large better? We can complicate this issue by adding phrases such as "on a sesame seed bun" or by adding a qualifier such as "juicy." The problem here is that good and bad levels of performance, such as good and bad mileage, already have the comparative referent attached: goodness or badness in general, special or plain as in the bun example, or a juicy versus dry meat patty. This problem will pose a rather severe dilemma when performance is input to a predictive equation that also contains other evaluative statements representing other constructs such as equity (fair or unfair). The problem becomes even more intractable when one of these evaluators is performance-based, such as disconfirmation. Thus, all research testing the comparative effects of performance is tainted with this confound.

This problem has been noted and empirically addressed in an ingenious experiment using satisfaction evaluations of courier service.[43] Here, actual performance was measured in terms of the arrival date in days before a deadline when the recipient absolutely needed the parcel. Subjective performance was scaled as "extremely slow" to "extremely fast." When two models were estimated, first with subjective performance and then with objective performance, the coefficient for the performance-to-satisfaction link was much attenuated when objective performance was used. In fact, when the authors tested a need-fulfillment model (see Chapter 5), the performance-to-satisfaction link washed out when objective performance was used. More critically, however, when the authors tested an expectancy disconfirmation model, the disconfirmation link was obscured when subjective performance was used in tandem; when objective performance was substituted, the disconfirmation linked emerged in robust form, as the model would predict. This study drives home the point that it is subjective performance with the attendant respondents' goodness-badness associations that confound models containing both subjective performance and disconfirmation. Objective performance avoids this confound.

At the risk of being repetitive, the role of performance in a disconfirmation model is confounded by the fact that it also plays a part in determination of the disconfirmation concept itself, exacerbating the problem already evident with evaluative measures of performance. Early studies often found one effect (disconfirmation or performance) to the exclusion of the other.[44] With the exception of purely affective products and services, such as those falling in the category of experienced surprise, generalizations are possible as follows.

If performance is analyzed so that its *key* dimensions or attributes are identified (see Chapter 2) and stated in evaluative form—usually with the good and bad poles labeled as such—it is rare that a significant relation between satisfaction and each measure will not be found at the zero-order, correlational level, whether dimension by dimension or attribute by attribute. If these dimensions are input to a regression simultaneously, multicollinearity will obscure some of these effects, depending on how correlated each one is with another. It is up to the researcher to tease out these dependent effects. Regardless of the amount of data sifting, the resulting relations with satisfaction only speak to the goodness or badness, likability or unlikability, or favorableness or unfavorableness of a particular attribute. The details will not be revealed by the data. This is how performance-based studies "succeed." They almost always provide some significant findings.

Unfortunately, this same problem plagues correlated *conceptual* dimensions as well. Performance and disconfirmation will be correlated by virtue of the fact that, even at the subjective level, disconfirmation takes performance comparisons into account. In fact, in the courier study, performance and disconfirmation were correlated at a mean level of 0.60 over all model variations tested. To disentangle these effects, two approaches can be taken (plus a number of statistical manipulations not discussed). In the first, the researcher can simply run two models, the first excluding performance, thereby revealing the disconfirmation effects. The second would include performance to the exclusion of disconfirmation. The researcher could then compare influences across analyses on an attribute dimension basis. In the second, an experiment can be conducted whereby these two concepts are manipulated independently. This procedure has been tested by the author and the effects were found to be additive on satisfaction; in fact, disconfirmation dominated performance by some margin.[45]

A number of other studies have been conducted since the first edition of this book, supporting the symbiotic relation between these two related concepts to varying degrees and in varying ways. Some illustrate tandem influences whereby one variable has effects exceeding the other. Interestingly, it is not known when the significance of performance or disconfirmation will exceed the other; the competing forces are not quite as clear as they are for the expectation versus disconfirmation effects described previously. One exception to this can be stated, however. If an individual has no confidence in judging the product or if no expectations are possible, such as in rare one-time experiences having no precedent, it is likely that performance will be processed in isolation.[46]

Still other studies show indirect performance effects that are fully mediated through disconfirmation so that the performance effect is absorbed within disconfirmation, or combined direct effects on satisfaction with indirect influences through disconfirmation, which then affects satisfaction. Three studies, one on a large sample of telephone users, another on a countrywide sample of citizens across a large number of product categories, and another in the context of business professional services, showed these combined effects.[47] Still another study on satisfaction with simulated stock market decisions, performed at the level of the individual consumer, showed consumer-specific effects and will be discussed in greater detail shortly.

At this point, it is possible to augment the elementary expectancy disconfirmation model in Figure 4.1 with the following disconfirmation sequence—calculated disconfirmation $(p-e) \rightarrow$ subjective disconfirmation $\rightarrow$ satisfaction—and with what is known about the tandem operation of performance with disconfirmation. Doing so results in the current version of the expectancy disconfirmation (including performance) model shown in Figure 4.5.

The figure begins with a bidirectional arrow between expectations and performance. This convention implies that the actual correlation between these two variables cannot be specified beyond the assumption that a relationship exists. This is so because the expectation-performance relation is idiosyncratic to the stage of consumption in which it is being measured and to the idiosyncrasies of the product or service being investigated. The first condition is, perhaps, more critical. The relation could be positive whereby consumers either perceive consistent performance in a self-serving sense (the confirmation bias) or have some volitional control over their performance outcomes (e.g., participative sports). It could also be positive in the early phases of consumption

Figure 4.5   **The Complete Expectancy Disconfirmation With Performance Model**

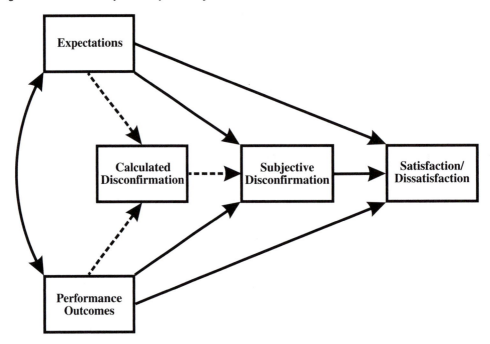

when expectations have not had time to adjust as performance is sampled and, paradoxically, even in later phases if performance is now instrumental in causing retrospective interpretations of what expectations might have been in hindsight (see Chapter 9).

Alternatively, the relation could be zero when performance is completely outside the control of the consumer, as it might be for games of chance; and it could be negative if, for example, extremely high (low) expectations cause the consumer to view highly likely moderate performance levels as poor or, in the second case, as very good (*assuming* the ceiling-and-floor effect is operating). Also note that, if one were researching multiple purchase occasions, the arrow very well could reverse over time as prior performance would influence later expectations.[48]

The other relations are as described previously. Expectations and performance combine to form the objective disconfirmation level, if quantified or measurable *and* measured; objective disconfirmation provides the basis for a subjective interpretation of this expectation-performance difference; and subjective disconfirmation is directly antecedent to satisfaction. As positioned in the upper chain of events, the direct link between expectations and satisfaction represents the assimilation effect *on satisfaction*. This implies that expectations are fairly pervasive throughout the satisfaction process, affecting possibly multiple subsequent variables. Finally, the lower performance-satisfaction link represents the direct effect of performance not mediated by disconfirmation, also as discussed previously. This graphic, which represents the most current version of disconfirmation theory, has been called the expectancy disconfirmation with performance model.

MODEL VARIATIONS

Although Figure 4.5 shows a fairly complete representation of the operation of all concepts in the expectancy disconfirmation model, it must be emphasized that not all the variables operate as shown or at all in individual contexts. There are a number of reasons for this; the possibility that certain concepts, such as performance or expectations, are not processed has already been discussed. This section entertains the possibility that particular groups of individuals respond to the variables differently. Another possibility is that certain attribute sets have different response characteristics.

Sample Versus Individual Influences

Up to now, the operation of the expectancy disconfirmation model has been discussed in aggregate form. That is, it has been assumed that the variable relations represent degrees of influence shared by all consumers. For example, if the disconfirmation influence is stronger than the expectation influence as determined by regression coefficients, then it can be assumed that this is so for all consumers in the sample. This conclusion is unlikely, although current convention embraces this interpretation. It would be very useful for segmentation purposes if researchers could separate consumers who rely mostly on disconfirmation from those who rely mostly on expectation, further analyzing their background variables, media habits, and so on.

One study by the author and a colleague answers the first part of this question concerning the proportion of consumers who rely more on expectations, on disconfirmation, or on performance than on the other variables. This study, using simulated stock purchase scenarios, manipulated expectation, disconfirmation, performance, and two other satisfaction influences in an experimental investigation of stock market trade outcomes.[49] The particular design employed ensured that the three primary influences (expectation, disconfirmation, and performance) were independent of one another, so that each had an equal and unfettered chance to influence satisfaction. Moreover, this procedure also allowed determination of the degree of influence on an individual basis.

The results showed that, on an aggregate basis, the disconfirmation effect dominated the performance effect in the prediction of satisfaction, which, in turn, was stronger than the effect of expectation. All effects were significant. On an individual basis, however, only fifteen of forty respondents used all three variables. Of the remainder, nine used performance and disconfirmation without expectation, nine used disconfirmation only, five used expectation and disconfirmation without performance, one used performance only, and the remaining individual used another of the study variables (equity, to be discussed in Chapter 8).

These findings lead to the conclusion that, ultimately, the tendency (or choice) to use one or the other of the model variables exists at the individual level, which, in the aggregate, results in sample-specific average coefficients. Unfortunately, moderating conditions such as the meaning of the security purchase to the respondent or the situation were not investigated. Nor were the authors able to find background variables that correlated with these response tendencies; other researchers pursuing this research direction, however, most surely will.

Other Disconfirmable Comparative Referents

Benefits and Problems as Separate Disconfirmation Influences

Earlier, it was suggested that the disconfirmation concept is sufficiently versatile that it can be applied to the entire consumption experience as well as groups of attributes or the individual attributes themselves. Here, discussion centers on the different influences of the benefits received by the consumer versus the problems encountered. At a more emotionally laden level, research-

Table 4.4

Separate Disconfirmation Effects of Benefits and Problems

Benefit/problem	Expectation	Actual performance	Disconfirmation	Result
Benefits	Courteous attendants	Delightful attendants	Better than expected	More joy
	Current release movie	Old B movie	Worse than expected	Less joy
Problems	"Airline" food	"Decent" food	Better than expected	Less frustration
	Wait for luggage	Stolen luggage	Worse than expected	More frustration

ers might wish to investigate delightful versus terrible experiences, and there is literature in both camps.[50] Why would we want to make this distinction?

The answer is inherent in the very different influences of positive versus negative reinforcement, discussed more fully in the next chapter, and of punishment. The relation to satisfaction versus dissatisfaction would appear to be direct, but may not be inherent; elaboration is provided as the topic is revisited. For now, the following examples will illustrate the likely consumer responses to the positive and negative disconfirmation of attribute benefit sets and problem sets. Given, again, an air travel example, let us assume that the main benefits sought are a comfortable trip from one city to another with courteous treatment from the attendants. Potential problems include lost luggage and substandard food. The air traveler is realistic and does not expect a perfect flight, accepting some number of mishaps as inevitable. Table 4.4 ranks the various disconfirmation scenarios in order of their potential to please and frustrate.

As can be seen in Table 4.4, benefits disconfirmation operates on positive experiences anticipated by the consumer, causing them to be more or less joyful. In contrast, problems disconfirmation operates on the negatives, causing them to be more or less frustrating. Thus, the effect of a worse-than-expected experience is attribute-specific. When this effect manifests itself for benefit attributes, the experience is less joyful than expected. When this occurs for a problem attribute, the experience is more frustrating than anticipated.

Measurement of separate problems and benefits disconfirmation is straightforward:[51]

Considering only the *benefits received* from this product, were they:

Much worse (less) than expected			Just as expected		Much better (more) than expected	
1	2	3	4	5	6	7

Considering only the *problems encountered* with this product, were they:

Much more (worse) than expected			Just as expected		Much less (better*) than expected	
1	2	3	4	5	6	7

*Not recommended; see the following discussion.

The author is aware of only one study that tested the separate components of this breakdown separately.[52] Most studies combine these scales with one of overall disconfirmation to form a three-item disconfirmation scale. In the single study in which benefits and problems were treated separately, the authors found that the satisfaction of high-involvement automobile consumers, those with greater-than-average interest in their cars, was affected by benefits disconfirmation early in ownership and by problems disconfirmation later. The satisfaction of low-involvement consumers was equally affected in both time periods. Thus, the more involved consumer is likely to derive joy from early ownership experiences that are better than expected and frustration from unanticipated later problems.

Traditionally, studies focus solely on the different effects of positive versus negative disconfirmation.[53] This technique essentially collapses the four-row structure in Table 4.4 into two rows, so that the first and third rows are joined, as are the second and fourth. The studies found results similar to those stated previously. When expressed in terms of the magnitude of influence, negative disconfirmation played a greater role in decreasing satisfaction than positive disconfirmation did in increasing it, again displaying the disproportionate influence of negative information, a point noted in this and the previous chapter.

On a cautionary note, care must be taken in editing the benefits-received and problems-encountered scales when applied to usage situations. While the benefits scale reflects the overall scale in the scale point descriptions of "better than" and "worse than," the problems scale changes to the preferred "more than" and "less than." The "better than" descriptor is problematic in this case because individuals do not usually refer to problems as "better than expected." What is a "better than" problem? If the reliability of a three-item scale including the overall disconfirmation measure fails, the offending item will most likely be "better than" problems.

Alternative Performance Comparatives: Desires

Some have criticized the use of expectations in the expectancy model, commenting that individuals are not motivated to purchase contemplating only expectations; rather they seek to fulfill desires in consumption. This author has no quarrel with that argument and has previously suggested that the motivation behind consumption, in this case desire or need fulfillment, leads to a quest to find venues for such consumption in product and service purchasing. Once suitable alternatives are found, consumers should expect that the alternatives will serve their intended purpose; these expectations, then, follow from the original motivations guiding the consumer. In fact, in a recent study, the authors compared four variations of prepurchase comparables over two product categories; the variations were needs, wants, predictive expectations, and desired (should) expectations. The results showed that "consumers tend to assimilate disconfirmation judgments into a single construct" and that when unique effects were compared, predictive expectations had the greatest impact in both research contexts studied.[54]

In the first edition and now in the revision of this book, need fulfillment is covered in the next chapter. However, because desires, a corollary of needs, have aroused such great attention within the discrepancy model, they are discussed here, as are other performance comparables. Bear in mind that two comparative concepts can operate in tandem and have been shown to do so, as in the operation of both "will" and "should" expectations, discussed in the preceding chapter.

The proponents of the desires approach refer to the discrepancy score as "desires congruency," or the mapping of what is received against what is desired. This conceptualization resulted from work showing that the term *expectations*, when used without further clarification, could be ambiguous and subject to multiple interpretations. Further research illustrated that, indeed, a desires format would be valid in its own right or, when used together, augmented the expectations approach in tandem fashion. In the latter case, the prediction of satisfaction is typically enhanced.[55]

The desires approach has been applied with regard to the information sought in making a purchase decision. In this sense, it is applied to the search phase of purchasing or, more specifically, to the promotional claims provided by the marketer or its agents and partly addresses the sources of expectations the consumer accesses. Results of this hybrid model have been encouraging, with both desires congruency and expectancy congruency (disconfirmation) jointly influencing attribute and desires satisfaction, with both of the latter influencing overall satisfaction. Generally, information satisfaction follows the discrepancy approach outlined in this chapter.[56]

Reviewers and proponents of the needs approach have noted conditions in which a congruency model may be more predictive of satisfaction or would enhance prediction when paired with other comparative forms.[57] These include cases where attributes are processed at higher levels in the value hierarchy or when ideals are accessed as the comparative referent. In such cases, the word *desired* would be substituted for *expected* as in "better/worse than desired." There is, however, a potential problem here if desires are at ideal levels, in which case "better than desired" would actually be a negative state. Solutions for this situation are presented in the next two chapters, where need levels and ideal levels are assessed. Desires may also prove fruitful if nonproduct attributes are central to the deliverable. For example, information needs are frequently stated as desires and dual information-attribute models have been successfully applied. An extension to online purchasing would be a natural venue for this approach.

Dimension- or Attribute-Specific Disconfirmation

In a 1980 paper, this author argued that "disconfirmation ultimately takes place at the individual attribute level."[58] Could it be that the expectancy disconfirmation model also operates at accumulations of attribute levels in the same way as it operates at the individual attribute or dimension levels? Numerous findings now suggest that this is so. In fact, one can construct a hierarchy of disconfirmations whereby satisfaction is regressed on overall disconfirmation, which is then regressed on benefits and problems disconfirmation, as in Table 4.4, which in turn is regressed on individual attribute disconfirmations. The results are revealing. A few representative studies are cited, one of which includes satisfaction with police practice. Others include comparisons to nonproduct dimensions such as trust, context, and competition.[59]

Figure 4.6 graphically models this dimension-specific possibility for three attribute dimensions and for all three predictors of satisfaction discussed in the expectancy disconfirmation model—expectation, disconfirmation, and performance. This is the more general case. For simplicity, each variable is portrayed as a simple, uncorrelated predictor. Additionally, each is shown with a corresponding satisfaction weight w_{ij}, where subscript i denotes the dimension and subscript j denotes the expectation, disconfirmation, or performance predictor.

This model could be tested in two stages. First, the three variables constituting each dimension (or attribute), such as the expectation score, disconfirmation score, and performance score from Dimension 1, are entered as predictors of satisfaction in a regression analysis. This will determine on a dimension-by-dimension basis which variation of the expectancy model operates for each dimension. The possibilities are shown in Table 4.5. It is this author's experience that any of these combinations is possible and that none can be ruled out (or assumed) a priori.[60] As shown in the simulated stock market study, discussed earlier, individual respondents in the experiment exhibited disconfirmation only, disconfirmation with expectation, disconfirmation with performance, and full model effects.

Figure 4.6   **Dimension- or Attribute-Specific Operation of the Expectancy Disconfirmation Model**

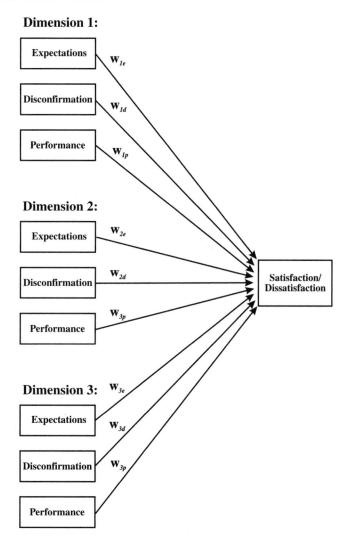

Once the dimension-specific results have been obtained, the researcher is ready for the second stage of the analysis. At this point, all the significant variables, and only the significant variables from each of the dimensions, are included as predictors in a final regression analysis with satisfaction as the dependent variable. This stage is necessary to ferret out lingering multicollinear effects across dimensions. The remaining significant predictors will be those most strongly related to satisfaction. Some may be expectations, others may be disconfirmations, and still others may be performance variables. There will be a set of significant predictors, however, given an adequate sample size.

A scheme corresponding to Figure 4.6 was tested in a previously described restaurant patronage study by this author and illustrates many of these variations.[61] When satisfaction was regressed on

Table 4.5

Possible Expectancy Disconfirmation Model Outcomes

Significant coefficients/findings	Model variation
Expectation only	Expectation (assimilation) model
Performance only	Raw performance model
Disconfirmation only	Disconfirmation (contrast) model of fully mediated expectation and performance effects
Expectation and performance	Noncomparative expectation and performance model
Expectation and disconfirmation	Expectancy disconfirmation model with fully mediated performance (see Figure 4.1)
Performance and disconfirmation	Performance and disconfirmation model with fully mediated expectations
Expectation, disconfirmation, and performance	Full expectancy disconfirmation with performance model (see Figure 4.5)

expectation, disconfirmation, and performance using summed attribute scores and overall scores for the entire sample, disconfirmation and performance operated in parallel in all variations; the expectation effect was not significant. When the attribute list was factored, the dimensions found were ambience, food, and service. The ambience dimension illustrated the operation of all three expectation, disconfirmation, and performance dimensions. Food yielded a performance-only effect, while service showed no significant effects.

Multicollinearity between performance and disconfirmation was a contributing contaminant, as has been discussed. The correlation between the two variables at the overall level was on the order of 0.8. When performance was removed so that satisfaction was regressed on expectation and disconfirmation only for each attribute dimension (see Figure 4.1), both expectation and disconfirmation predictors were significant for all attribute dimensions including service. These findings suggest that satisfaction increased as expectations increased (a positive relation so that higher expectations generated higher satisfaction) and as the positivity of disconfirmation increased. The performance effect was also positive. As an aside, the expectation-disconfirmation correlation (relation C in Figure 4.1) was effectively zero using predictive expectations and marginally positive using retrospective expectations for the overall measures only. This study is instructive as it shows the action of the model variants across attributes and model subsets.

CONCLUSION

The origins, development, and present status of the expectancy disconfirmation model have been discussed. Consisting of expectations, performance, and the outcome of their comparison—disconfirmation, the model has been shown to adequately account for one major mechanism by which consumers form satisfaction judgments. Although some consumers are known to use all elements of the model, others selectively base their satisfaction decisions on one or more of its components. Also discussed are extremes of the disconfirmation continuum, particularly with regard to delight and its major component of surprise. This discussion was considered necessary to fully account for the idiosyncrasies that occur when disconfirmation is taken to its limits. Surprise, in particular, is worthy of further study as it is now becoming part of managerial strategy, as in promises of "surprisingly excellent performance."

Generally, model variations will explore the expectancy disconfirmation with performance model fully. Research efforts could conceivably end here if there were no known remaining influences on satisfaction that were not accounted for in the disconfirmeting model. Unfortunately, that is not likely to be the case. Part II of this book begins discussion of other comparative standards that have been found to operate in parallel with disconfirmation and in addition to performance itself. These include needs, quality, values, inequity, and regret. Generally, some or all of these will not be accounted for in a list of performance dimensions or in the expectancy disconfirmation analysis, and it is for this purpose that discussion continues in Part II of this book.

NOTES

1. For respective reviews, see Michalos, "Multiple Discrepancies Theory (MDT)"; Rice, McFarlin, and Bennett, "Standards of Comparison and Job Satisfaction"; Meadow et al., "Life Satisfaction Measure Based on Judgment Theory"; Higgins, "Self-Discrepancy"; Mussweiler, "Comparison Processes in Social Judgment"; Jiang, Klein, and Crampton, "Note on SERVQUAL Reliability and Validity in Information System Service Quality Measurement"; and Solberg et al., "Wanting, Having, and Satisfaction."

2. This tendency, known as confirmation bias, is thoroughly reviewed in Nickerson, "Confirmation Bias."

3. Dawes, Singer, and Lemons, "Experimental Analysis of the Contrast Effect and Its Implications for Intergroup Communication and the Indirect Assessment of Attitude," p. 281.

4. For citations to these early studies, see Oliver, *Satisfaction*, p. 127, notes 18 and 19.

5. Weaver and Brickman, "Expectancy, Feedback, and Disconfirmation as Independent Factors in Outcome Satisfaction."

6. To this author's knowledge, use of an overall scale similar to the first example in the text initially appeared in the consumer behavior literature; see Oliver, "Effect of Expectation and Disconfirmation on Postexposure Product Evaluations," p. 483; the second, in wider, but limited use, is shown in Oliver, "Measurement and Evaluation of Satisfaction Processes in Retail Settings," p. 40.

7. For an example covering sixty-five features of the airport itself, see Fodness and Murray, "Passengers' Expectations of Airport Service Quality."

8. Oliver, "Measurement and Evaluation of Satisfaction Processes in Retail Settings," p. 35.

9. Oliver, "Conceptualization and Measurement of Disconfirmation Perceptions in the Prediction of Consumer Satisfaction."

10. Oliver, " Cognitive Model of the Antecedents and Consequences of Satisfaction Decisions."

11. Collins and Horn, eds., *Best Methods for the Analysis of Change.*

12. See the references in Oliver, *Satisfaction*, p. 128, note 29, and the following: Dabholkar, Shepherd, and Thorpe, "Comprehensive Framework for Service Quality"; Dion, Jivalgi, and Dilorenzo-Aiss, "Empirical Assessment of the Zeithaml, Berry and Parasuraman Service Expectations Model"; Oliver, Balakrishnan, and Barry, "Outcome Satisfaction in Negotiation"; Page and Spreng, "Difference Scores Versus Direct Effects in Service Quality Measurement"; and Wu and Padgett, "Direct Comparative Framework of Customer Satisfaction."

13. Oliver, "Effect of Expectation and Disconfirmation on Postexposure Product Evaluations."

14. Cooper, "Ubiquitous Halo."

15. Iacobucci, Grayson, and Ostrom, "Calculus of Service Quality and Customer Satisfaction."

16. This statement should be tempered somewhat. Often, simply meeting expectations is modestly but surprisingly positive, as if the consumer were to say, "I didn't think you could do even that." See Coughlan and Connolly, "Predicting Affective Responses to Unexpected Outcomes."

17. See Oliver, *Satisfaction*, p. 129, notes 36 and 37. Strandvik's monograph, *Tolerance Zones in Perceived Service Quality*, remains perhaps the most comprehensive treatment, although, here and elsewhere, the difference between tolerance and acceptance is used somewhat interchangeably. Readers may also wish to see alternative treatments provided by Teas and DeCarlo, "Examination and Extension of the Zone-of-Tolerance Model"; and Yap and Sweeney, "Zone-of-Tolerance Moderates the Service Quality-Outcome Relationship."

18. See Andreassen, "From Disgust to Delight."

19. Oliver, "Processing of the Satisfaction Response in Consumption"; Oliver, Rust, and Varki, "Customer Delight"; Rust and Oliver, "Should We Delight the Customer?" where the definition of delight cited in the chapter can be found at p. 86. Discussion in this section largely derives from these three sources.

20. Plutchik, *Emotion*, p. 162.

21. Tsiros, Mittal, and Ross, "Role of Attributions in Customer Satisfaction." Attribution can be found embedded within surprise and disconfirmation, however. See Stiensmeier-Pelster, Martini, and Reisenzein, "Role of Surprise in the Attribution Process."

22. Finn, "Reassessing the Foundations of Customer Delight." The satisfaction sequence is replicated in Wirtz and Bateson, "Consumer Satisfaction with Services."

23. Hicks et al., "Delighted Consumers Buy Again." See, also, McNeilly and Barr, "I Love My Accountants—They're Wonderful."

24. Gendolla and Koller, "Surprise and Motivation of Causal Search"; Meyer, Reisenzein, and Schützwohl, "Toward a Process Analysis of Emotions"; Reisenzein, "Subjective Experience of Surprise"; Schützwohl and Borgstedt, "Processing of Affectively Valenced Stimuli"; Vanhamme and Snelders, "Role of Surprise in Satisfaction Judgements."

25. Heilman, Nakamoto, and Rao, "Pleasant Surprises."

26. Andrade and Cohen, "On the Consumption of Negative Feelings."

27. Gorn, Pham, and Sin, "When Arousal Influences Ad Evaluation and Valence Does Not (and Vice Versa)"; Mellers, Schwartz, and Ritov, "Emotion-Based Choice"; Vanhamme and Snelders, "Role of Surprise in Satisfaction Judgements."

28. Kopalle and Lehmann, "Strategic Management of Expectations."

29. See Martin, Seta, and Crelia, "Assimilation and Contrast as a Function of People's Willingness and Ability to Expend Effort in Forming an Impression."

30. Hoch and Ha, "Consumer Learning."

31. Jones and Sugden, "Positive Confirmation Bias in the Acquisition of Information"; Nickerson, "Confirmation Bias"; and Sanbonmatsu, Akimoto, and Biggs, "Overestimating Causality."

32. Northcraft and Ashford, "Preservation of Self in Everyday Life."

33. Additive cumulative effects can be found in Feinberg, Widdows, and Steidle, "Customer (Dis)Satisfaction and Delays."

34. Stangor and McMillan, "Memory for Expectancy-Congruent and Expectancy-Incongruent Information"; Stayman, Alden, and Smith, "Some Effects of Schematic Processing on Consumer Expectations and Disconfirmation Judgments."

35. Babin, Griffin, and Babin, "Effect of Motivation to Process on Consumers' Satisfaction Reactions"; Morgan, Attaway, and Griffin, "Role of Product/Service Experience in the Satisfaction Process"; Patterson, "Contingency Approach to Modeling Satisfaction with Management Consulting Services"; Richins and Bloch, "Post-Purchase Product Satisfaction"; Söderlund, "Customer Familiarity and Its Effects on Satisfaction and Behavioral Intentions"; Spreng and Page, "Impact of Confidence in Expectations on Consumer Satisfaction."

36. Dröge and Halstead, "Postpurchase Hierarchies of Effects."

37. Homburg, Koschate, and Hoyer, "Role of Cognition and Affect in the Formation of Customer Satisfaction."

38. Dubé and Menon, "Multiple Roles of Consumption Emotions in Post-Purchase Satisfaction with Extended Service Transactions"; Frederickson and Kahneman, "Duration Neglect in Retrospective Evaluations of Affective Episodes"; Kahneman, "Objective Happiness."

39. Oliver and Burke, "Expectation Processes in Satisfaction Formation." In addition, also in a restaurant setting, see Yi and La, "What Influences the Relations Between Customer Satisfaction and Repurchase Intention?"

40. Kahneman and Tversky, "Choices, Values, and Frames."

41. Jun et al., "Relative Influence of Affective Experience on Consumer Satisfaction under Positive Versus Negative Discrepancies"; Mittal, Ross, and Baldasare, "Asymmetric Impact of Negative and Positive Attribute-Level Performance on Overall Satisfaction and Repurchase Intentions"; Yoon and Kim, "Empirical Validation of a Loyalty Model Based on Expectation Disconfirmation."

42. The early reviews were those of Erevelles and Leavitt, "Comparison of Current Models of Consumer Satisfaction/Dissatisfaction"; Tse, Nicosia, and Wilton, "Consumer Satisfaction as a Process"; and Yi, "Critical Review of Consumer Satisfaction." More recent reviews of a fairly comprehensive basis include Halstead, "Use of Comparison Standards in Customer Satisfaction Research and Management"; Spreng and Page, "Test

of Alternative Measures of Disconfirmation"; Szymanski and Henard, "Customer Satisfaction"; and Teas and Palan, "Disconfirmed Expectations Theory of Consumer Satisfaction." This latter source lists studies addressing each linkage in the expectancy disconfirmation model.

43. Wirtz and Mattila, "Exploring the Role of Alternative Perceived Performance Measures and Needs-Congruency in the Consumer Satisfaction Process," where the experimental details are discussed. In a second study, actual versus perceived performance was compared in predicting satisfaction using delivery damage rates to car dealers. Both were significant, with perceived performance dominating prediction; disconfirmation was not measured, however. See Burton, Sheather, and Roberts, "Reality or Perception?"

44. See the summary of studies in Oliver, *Satisfaction*, p. 130, notes 50–54.

45. Oliver and DeSarbo, "Response Determinants in Satisfaction Judgments."

46. Spreng and Page, "Impact of Confidence in Expectations on Consumer Satisfaction"; Dasu and Rao, "Dynamic Process Model of Dissatisfaction for Unfavorable, Non-Routine Service Encounters."

47. Bolton and Drew, "Multistage Model of Customers' Assessments of Service Quality and Value"; Anderson and Sullivan, "Antecedents and Consequences of Customer Satisfaction for Firms"; and Patterson, Johnson, and Spreng, "Modeling the Determinants of Customer Satisfaction for Business-to-Business Professional Services."

48. Wood and Moreau, "From Fear to Loathing?"; Yi and La, "What Influences the Relations Between Customer Satisfaction and Repurchase Intention?"

49. Oliver and DeSarbo, "Response Determinants in Satisfaction Judgments."

50. Arnold et al., "Customer Delight in a Retail Context"; d'Astous, "Irritating Aspects of the Shopping Environment." See, also, the critical incidents studies in Chapter 2.

51. The problems and benefits variations were initially reported in Oliver, "Cognitive Model of the Antecedents and Consequences of Satisfaction Decisions," p. 463. When combined with an overall disconfirmation item, the resulting scale forms a composite disconfirmation index. See Oliver and Westbrook, "Factor Structure of Satisfaction and Related Postpurchase Measures," pp. 11–14.

52. Richins and Bloch, "Post-Purchase Product Satisfaction."

53. Anderson and Sullivan, "Antecedents and Consequences of Customer Satisfaction for Firms"; DeSarbo et al., "On the Measurement of Perceived Service Quality"; Mittal, Ross, and Baldasare, "Asymmetric Impact of Negative and Positive Attribute-Level Performance on Overall Satisfaction and Repurchase Intentions"; Jun et al., "Relative Influence of Affective Experience on Consumer Satisfaction under Positive Versus Negative Discrepancies"; Yoon and Kim, "Empirical Validation of a Loyalty Model Based on Expectation Disconfirmation."

54. Niedrich, Kiryanova, and Black, "Dimensional Stability of the Standards Used in the Disconfirmation Paradigm," p. 49.

55. Dröge, Halstead, and Mackoy, "Role of Competitive Alternatives in the Postchoice Satisfaction Formation Process"; Spreng, MacKenzie, and Olshavsky, "Reexamination of the Determinants of Consumer Satisfaction"; Spreng, Mackoy, and Dröge, "Confounds in the Measurement of Predictive Expectations"; Spreng and Olshavsky, "Desires-as-Standard Model of Consumer Satisfaction"; and Wirtz and Mattila, "Exploring the Role of Alternative Perceived Performance Measures and Needs-Congruency in the Consumer Satisfaction Process."

56. Spreng, MacKenzie, and Olshavsky, "Reexamination of the Determinants of Consumer Satisfaction"; Spreng and Dröge, "Impact of Managing Attribute Expectations."

57. Halstead, "Use of Comparison Standards in Customer Satisfaction Research and Management"; Solberg et al., "Wanting, Having, and Satisfaction"; Gardial et al., "Comparing Consumers' Recall of Prepurchase and Postpurchase Product Evaluation Experiences."

58. Oliver, "Cognitive Model of the Antecedents and Consequences of Satisfaction Decisions," p. 467.

59. Dröge, Halstead, and Mackoy, "Role of Competitive Alternatives in the Postchoice Satisfaction Formation Process"; Grewal, Gotlieb, and Marmorstein, "Moderating Effect of the Service Context on the Relationship Between Price and Post-Consumption Perceptions of Service Quality"; Halstead, Hartman, and Schmidt, "Multisource Effects on the Satisfaction Formation Process"; Oliver and Burke, "Expectation Processes in Satisfaction Formation"; Reisig and Chandek, "Effects of Expectancy Disconfirmation on Outcome Satisfaction in Police-Citizen Encounters"; Singh and Sirdeshmukh, "Agency and Trust Mechanisms in Consumer Satisfaction and Loyalty Judgments"; Wu and Padgett, "Direct Comparative Framework of Customer Satisfaction."

60. Representative studies were cited in the first edition of this book: Oliver, *Satisfaction*, p. 131, notes 65–71. The list is not updated due to the many and varied studies performed to date.

61. Oliver and Burke, "Expectation Processes in Satisfaction Formation."

BIBLIOGRAPHY

Anderson, Eugene W., and Mary W. Sullivan. "The Antecedents and Consequences of Customer Satisfaction for Firms." *Marketing Science* 12, no. 2 (Spring 1993): 125–143.

Andrade, Eduardo B., and Joel B. Cohen. "On the Consumption of Negative Feelings." *Journal of Consumer Research* 34, no. 3 (October 2007): 283–300.

Andreassen, Tor Wallin. "From Disgust to Delight: Do Customers Hold a Grudge?" *Journal of Service Research* 4, no. 1 (August 2001): 39–49.

Arnold, Mark J., Kristy E. Reynolds, Nicole Ponder, and Jason E. Lueg. "Customer Delight in a Retail Context: Investigating Delightful and Terrible Shopping Experiences." *Journal of Business Research* 58, no. 8 (August 2005): 1132–1145.

Babin, Barry J., Mitch Griffin, and Laurie Babin. "The Effect of Motivation to Process on Consumers' Satisfaction Reactions." In *Advances in Consumer Research*, ed. Chris T. Allen and Deborah Roedder John, 21:406–11. Provo, UT: Association for Consumer Research, 1994.

Bolton, Ruth N., and James H. Drew. "A Multistage Model of Customers' Assessments of Service Quality and Value." *Journal of Consumer Research* 17, no. 4 (March 1991): 375–384.

Burton, Suzan, Simon Sheather, and John Roberts. "Reality or Perception? The Effect of Actual and Perceived Performance on Satisfaction and Behavioral Intention." *Journal of Service Research* 5, no. 4 (May 2003): 292–302.

Collins, Linda M., and John L. Horn, eds. *Best Methods for the Analysis of Change.* Washington, DC: American Psychological Association, 1991.

Cooper, William H. "Ubiquitous Halo." *Psychological Bulletin* 90, no. 2 (September 1981): 218–244.

Coughlan, Richard, and Terry Connolly. "Predicting Affective Responses to Unexpected Outcomes." *Organizational Behavior and Human Decision Processes* 85, no. 2 (July 2001): 211–225.

Dabholkar, Pratibha A., C. David Shepherd, and Dayle I. Thorpe. "A Comprehensive Framework for Service Quality: An Investigation of Critical Conceptual and Measurement Issues Through a Longitudinal Study." *Journal of Retailing* 76, no. 2 (Summer 2000): 139–173.

d'Astous, Alain. "Irritating Aspects of the Shopping Environment." *Journal of Business Research* 49, no. 2 (August 2000): 149–156.

Dasu, Sriram, and Jay Rao. "A Dynamic Process Model of Dissatisfaction for Unfavorable, Non-Routine Service Encounters." *Production and Operations Management* 8, no. 3 (Fall 1999): 282–300.

Dawes, Robyn M., David Singer, and Frank Lemons. "An Experimental Analysis of the Contrast Effect and Its Implications for Intergroup Communication and the Indirect Assessment of Attitude." *Journal of Personality and Social Psychology* 21, no. 3 (March 1972): 281–295.

DeSarbo, Wayne S., Lenard Huff, Marcelo M. Rolandelli, and Jungwhan Choi. "On the Measurement of Perceived Service Quality: A Conjoint Analysis Approach." In *Service Quality: New Directions in Theory and Practice,* ed. Roland T. Rust and Richard L. Oliver, 201–222. Thousand Oaks, CA: Sage, 1994.

Dion, Paul A., Rajshekhar Jivalgi, and Janet Dilorenzo-Aiss. "An Empirical Assessment of the Zeithaml, Berry and Parasuraman Service Expectations Model." *Service Industries Journal* 18, no 4 (October 1998): 66–86.

Dröge, Cornelia, and Diane Halstead. "Postpurchase Hierarchies of Effects: The Antecedents and Consequences of Satisfaction for Complainers versus Non-Complainers." *International Journal of Research in Marketing* 8, no. 4 (November 1991): 315–328.

Dröge, Cornelia, Diane Halstead, and Robert D. Mackoy. "The Role of Competitive Alternatives in the Postchoice Satisfaction Formation Process." *Journal of the Academy of Marketing Science* 25, no. 1 (Winter 1997): 18–30.

Dubé, Laurette, and Kalyani Menon. "Multiple Roles of Consumption Emotions in Post-Purchase Satisfaction with Extended Service Transactions." *International Journal of Service Industry Management* 11, no. 3 (2000): 287–304.

Erevelles, Sunil, and Clark Leavitt. "A Comparison of Current Models of Consumer Satisfaction/Dissatisfaction." *Journal of Consumer Satisfaction, Dissatisfaction and Complaining Behavior* 5 (1992): 104–114.

Feinberg, Richard A., Richard Widdows, and Robert Steidle. "Customer (Dis)Satisfaction and Delays: The Robust Negative Effects of Service Delays." *Journal of Consumer Satisfaction, Dissatisfaction and Complaining Behavior* 9 (1996): 81–85.

Finn, Adam. "Reassessing the Foundations of Customer Delight." *Journal of Service Research* 8, no. 2 (November 2005): 103–116.

Fodness, Dale, and Brian Murray. "Passengers' Expectations of Airport Service Quality." *Journal of Services Marketing* 21, no. 7 (2007): 492–506.

Fredrickson, Barbara L., and Daniel Kahneman. "Duration Neglect in Retrospective Evaluations of Affective Episodes." *Journal of Personality and Social Psychology* 65, no. 1 (July 1993): 45–55.

Gardial, Sarah Fisher, D. Scott Clemons, Robert B. Woodruff, David W. Schumann, and Mary Jane Burns. "Comparing Consumers' Recall of Prepurchase and Postpurchase Product Evaluation Experiences." *Journal of Consumer Research* 20, no. 4 (March 1994): 548–560.

Gendolla, Guido H.E., and Michael Koller. "Surprise and Motivation of Causal Search: How Are They Affected by Outcome Valence and Importance?" *Motivation and Emotion* 25, no. 4 (December 2001): 327–349.

Gorn, Gerald, Michel Tuan Pham, and Leo Yatming Sin. "When Arousal Influences Ad Evaluation and Valence Does Not (and Vice Versa)." *Journal of Consumer Psychology* 11, no. 1 (2001): 43–55.

Grewal, Dhruv, Jerry Gotlieb, and Howard Marmorstein. "The Moderating Effect of the Service Context on the Relationship Between Price and Post-Consumption Perceptions of Service Quality." *Journal of Business and Psychology* 14, no. 4 (Summer 2000): 579–591.

Halstead, Diane. "The Use of Comparison Standards in Customer Satisfaction Research and Management: A Review and Typology." *Journal of Marketing Theory and Practice* 7, no. 3 (Summer 1999): 13–26.

Halstead, Diane, David Hartman, and Sandra L. Schmidt. "Multisource Effects on the Satisfaction Formation Process." *Journal of the Academy of Marketing Science* 22, no. 2 (Spring 1994): 114–129.

Heilman, Carrie M., Kent Nakamoto, and Ambar G. Rao. "Pleasant Surprises: Consumer Response to Unexpected In-Store Coupons." *Journal of Marketing Research* 39, no. 2 (May 2002): 242–252.

Hicks, Jessica M., Thomas J. Page Jr., Bridget K. Behe, Jennifer H. Dennis, and R. Thomas Fernandez. "Delighted Consumers Buy Again." *Journal of Consumer Satisfaction, Dissatisfaction and Complaining Behavior* 18 (2005): 94–104.

Higgins, E. Tory. "Self-Discrepancy: A Theory Relating Self and Affect." *Psychological Review* 94, no. 3 (July 1987): 319–340.

Hoch, Stephen J., and Young-Won Ha. "Consumer Learning: Advertising and the Ambiguity of Product Experience." *Journal of Consumer Research* 13, no. 2 (September 1986): 221–233.

Homburg, Christian, Nicole Koschate, and Wayne D. Hoyer. "The Role of Cognition and Affect in the Formation of Customer Satisfaction: A Dynamic Perspective." *Journal of Marketing* 70, no. 3 (July 2006): 21–31.

Iacobucci, Dawn, Kent Grayson, and Amy Ostrom. "The Calculus of Service Quality and Customer Satisfaction: Theoretical and Empirical Differentiation and Integration." In *Advances in Services Marketing and Management: Research and Practice*, ed. Teresa A. Swartz, David E. Bowen, and Stephen W. Brown, 3:1–67. Greenwich, CT: JAI Press, 1994.

Jiang, James J., Gary Klein, and Suzanne M. Crampton. "A Note on SERVQUAL Reliability and Validity in Information System Service Quality Measurement." *Decision Sciences* 31, no. 3 (Summer 2000): 725–744.

Jones, Martin, and Robert Sugden. "Positive Confirmation Bias in the Acquisition of Information." *Theory and Decision* 50, no. 1 (February 2001): 59–99.

Jun, Sunkyu, Yong J. Hyun, James W. Gentry, and Chang-Seok Song. "The Relative Influence of Affective Experience on Consumer Satisfaction under Positive Versus Negative Discrepancies." *Journal of Consumer Satisfaction, Dissatisfaction and Complaining Behavior* 14 (2001): 141–153.

Kahneman, Daniel. "Objective Happiness." In *Well-Being: The Foundations of Hedonic Psychology,* ed. Daniel Kahneman, Ed Diener, and Norbert Schwarz, 3–25. New York: Russell Sage Foundation, 1999.

Kahneman, Daniel, and Amos Tversky. "Choices, Values, and Frames." *American Psychologist* 39, no. 4 (April 1984): 341–350.

Kopalle, Praveen K., and Donald R. Lehmann. "Strategic Management of Expectations: The Role of Disconfirmation Sensitivity and Perfectionism." *Journal of Marketing Research* 38, no. 3 (August 2001): 386–394.

Martin, Leonard L., John J. Seta, and Rick A. Crelia. "Assimilation and Contrast as a Function of People's Willingness and Ability to Expend Effort in Forming an Impression." *Journal of Personality and Social Psychology* 59, no. 1 (July 1990): 27–37.

McNeilly, Kevin M., and Terri Feldman Barr. "I Love My Accountants—They're Wonderful: Understanding Delight in the Professional Services Arena." *Journal of Services Marketing* 20, no. 3 (2006): 152–159.

Meadow, H.L., J.T. Mentzer, D.R. Rahtz, and M.J. Sirgy. "A Life Satisfaction Measure Based on Judgment Theory." *Social Indicators Research* 26, no. 1 (February 1992): 23–59.

Mellers, Barbara, Alan Schwartz, and Ilana Ritov. "Emotion-Based Choice." *Journal of Experimental Psychology: General* 128, no. 3 (1999): 332–345.

Meyer, Wulf-Uwe, Rainer Reisenzein, and Achim Schützwohl. "Toward a Process Analysis of Emotions: The Case of Surprise." *Motivation and Emotion* 21, no. 3 (September 1997): 251–274.

Michalos, Alex C. "Multiple Discrepancies Theory (MDT)." *Social Indicators Research* 16, no. 4 (May 1985): 347–413.

Mittal, Vikas, William T. Ross Jr., and Patrick M. Baldasare. "The Asymmetric Impact of Negative and Positive Attribute-Level Performance on Overall Satisfaction and Repurchase Intentions." *Journal of Marketing* 62, no. 1 (January 1998): 33–47.

Morgan, Marcy J., Jill S. Attaway, and Mitch Griffin. "The Role of Product/Service Experience in the Satisfaction Process: A Test of Moderation." *Journal of Consumer Satisfaction, Dissatisfaction and Complaining Behavior* 9 (1996): 104–114.

Mussweiler, Thomas. "Comparison Processes in Social Judgment: Mechanisms and Consequences." *Psychological Review* 110, no. 3 (July 2003): 472–489.

Nickerson, Raymond S. "Confirmation Bias: A Ubiquitous Phenomenon in Many Guises." *Review of General Psychology* 2, no. 2 (June 1998): 175–220.

Niedrich, Ronald W., Elena Kiryanova, and William C. Black. "The Dimensional Stability of the Standards Used in the Disconfirmation Paradigm." *Journal of Retailing* 81, no. 1 (2005): 49–57.

Northcraft, Gregory B., and Susan J. Ashford. "The Preservation of Self in Everyday Life: The Effects of Performance Expectations and Feedback Context on Feedback Inquiry." *Organizational Behavior and Human Decision Processes* 47, no. 1 (October 1990): 42–64.

Oliver, Richard L. "A Cognitive Model of the Antecedents and Consequences of Satisfaction Decisions." *Journal of Marketing Research* 17, no. 4 (November 1980): 460–469.

———. "Conceptualization and Measurement of Disconfirmation Perceptions in the Prediction of Consumer Satisfaction." In *Refining Concepts and Measures of Consumer Satisfaction and Complaining Behavior,* ed. H. Keith Hunt and Ralph L. Day, 2–6. Bloomington: Foundation for the School of Business, Indiana University, 1980.

———. "Effect of Expectation and Disconfirmation on Postexposure Product Evaluations: An Alternative Interpretation." *Journal of Applied Psychology* 62, no. 4 (August 1977): 480–486.

———. "Measurement and Evaluation of Satisfaction Processes in Retail Settings." *Journal of Retailing* 57, no. 3 (Fall 1981): 25–48.

———. "Processing of the Satisfaction Response in Consumption: A Suggested Framework and Research Propositions." *Journal of Consumer Satisfaction, Dissatisfaction and Complaining Behavior* 2 (1989): 1–16.

———. *Satisfaction: A Behavioral Perspective on the Consumer.* New York: Irwin/McGraw-Hill, 1997.

Oliver, Richard L., P.V. (Sundar) Balakrishnan, and Bruce Barry. "Outcome Satisfaction in Negotiation: A Test of Expectancy Disconfirmation." *Organizational Behavior and Human Decision Processes* 60, no. 2 (November 1994): 252–275.

Oliver, Richard L., and Raymond R. Burke. "Expectation Processes in Satisfaction Formation: A Field Study." *Journal of Service Research* 1, no. 3 (February 1999): 196–214.

Oliver, Richard L., and Wayne S. DeSarbo. "Response Determinants in Satisfaction Judgments." *Journal of Consumer Research* 14, no. 4 (March 1988): 495–507.

Oliver, Richard L., Roland T. Rust, and Sajeev Varki. "Customer Delight: Foundations, Findings, and Managerial Insight." *Journal of Retailing* 73, no. 3 (Autumn 1997): 311–336.

Oliver, Richard L., and Robert A. Westbrook. "The Factor Structure of Satisfaction and Related Postpurchase Measures." In *New Findings on Consumer Satisfaction and Complaining,* ed. Ralph L. Day and H. Keith Hunt, 11–14. Bloomington: Foundation for the School of Business, Indiana University, 1982.

Page, Thomas J., and Richard A. Spreng. "Difference Scores Versus Direct Effects in Service Quality Measurement." *Journal of Service Research* 4, no. 3 (February 2002): 184–192.

Patterson, Paul G. "A Contingency Approach to Modeling Satisfaction with Management Consulting Services." *Journal of Service Research* 3, no. 2 (November 2000): 138–153.

Patterson, Paul G., Lester W. Johnson, and Richard A. Spreng. "Modeling the Determinants of Customer Satisfaction for Business-to-Business Professional Services." *Journal of the Academy of Marketing Science* 25, no. 1 (Winter 1997): 4–17.

Plutchik, Robert. *Emotion: A Psychoevolutionary Synthesis.* New York: Harper & Row, 1980.

Reisenzein, Rainer. "The Subjective Experience of Surprise." In *The Message Within: The Role of Subjective Experience in Social Cognition and Behavior,* ed. Herbert Bless and Joseph P. Forgas, 262–279. Philadelphia: Psychology Press, 2000.

Reisig, Michael D., and Meghan Stroshine Chandek. "The Effects of Expectancy Disconfirmation on Outcome Satisfaction in Police-Citizen Encounters." *Policing: An International Journal of Police Strategies & Management* 24, no. 1 (2001): 88–99.

Rice, Robert W., Dean B. McFarlin, and Debbie E. Bennett. "Standards of Comparison and Job Satisfaction." *Journal of Applied Psychology* 74, no. 4 (August 1989): 591–598.

Richins, Marsha L., and Peter H. Bloch. "Post-Purchase Product Satisfaction: Incorporating the Effects of Involvement and Time." *Journal of Business Research,* 23, no. 2 (September 1991): 145–158.

Rust, Roland T., and Richard L. Oliver. "Should We Delight the Customer?" *Journal of the Academy of Marketing Science* 28, no. 1 (Winter 2000): 86–94.

Sanbonmatsu, David M., Sharon A. Akimoto, and Earlene Biggs. "Overestimating Causality: Attributional Effects of Confirmatory Processing." *Journal of Personality and Social Psychology* 65, no. 5 (November 1993): 892–903.

Schützwohl, Achim, and Kirsten Borgstedt. "The Processing of Affectively Valenced Stimuli: The Role of Surprise." *Cognition and Emotion* 19, no. 4 (June 2005): 583–600.

Singh, Jagdip, and Deepak Sirdeshmukh. "Agency and Trust Mechanisms in Consumer Satisfaction and Loyalty Judgments." *Journal of the Academy of Marketing Science* 28, no. 1 (Winter 2000): 150–167.

Söderlund, Magnus. "Customer Familiarity and Its Effects on Satisfaction and Behavioral Intentions." *Psychology & Marketing* 19, no. 10 (October 2002): 861–880.

Solberg, Emily Crawford, Ed Diener, Derrick Wirtz, Richard E. Lucas, and Shigehiro Oishi. "Wanting, Having, and Satisfaction: Examining the Role of Desire Discrepancies in Satisfaction with Income." *Journal of Personality and Social Psychology* 83, no. 3 (September 2002): 725–734.

Spreng, Richard A., and Cornelia Dröge. "The Impact of Managing Attribute Expectations: Should Performance Claims Be Understated or Overstated?" *Journal of Retailing and Consumer Services* 8, no. 5 (September 2001): 261–274.

Spreng, Richard A., Scott B. MacKenzie, and Richard W. Olshavsky. "A Reexamination of the Determinants of Consumer Satisfaction." *Journal of Marketing* 60, no. 3 (July 1996): 15–32.

Spreng, Richard A., Robert D. Mackoy, and Cornelia Dröge. "Confounds in the Measurement of Predictive Expectations." *Journal of Consumer Satisfaction, Dissatisfaction and Complaining Behavior* 11 (1998): 1–7.

Spreng, Richard A., and Richard W. Olshavsky. "A Desires Congruency Model of Consumer Satisfaction." *Journal of the Academy of Marketing Science* 21, no. 3 (Summer 1993): 169–177.

———. "A Desires-as-Standard Model of Consumer Satisfaction: Implications for Measuring Satisfaction." *Journal of Consumer Satisfaction, Dissatisfaction and Complaining Behavior* 5 (1992): 45–54.

Spreng, Richard A., and Thomas J. Page Jr. "The Impact of Confidence in Expectations on Consumer Satisfaction." *Psychology & Marketing* 18, no. 11 (November 2001): 1187–1204.

———. "A Test of Alternative Measures of Disconfirmation." *Decision Sciences* 34, no. 1 (Winter 2003): 31–62.

Stangor, Charles, and David McMillan. "Memory for Expectancy-Congruent and Expectancy-Incongruent Information: A Review of the Social and Social Developmental Literatures." *Psychological Bulletin* 111, no. 1 (January 1992): 42–61.

Stayman, Douglas M., Dana L. Alden, and Karen H. Smith. "Some Effects of Schematic Processing on Consumer Expectations and Disconfirmation Judgments." *Journal of Consumer Research* 19, no. 2 (September 1992): 240–255.

Stiensmeier-Pelster Joachim, Alice Martini, and Rainer Reisenzein. "The Role of Surprise in the Attribution Process." *Cognition and Emotion* 9, no. 1 (January 1995): 5–31.

Strandvik, Tore. *Tolerance Zones in Perceived Service Quality.* Helsinki, Finland: Swedish School of Economics and Business Administration, 1994.

Szymanski, David M., and David H. Henard. "Customer Satisfaction: A Meta-Analysis of the Empirical Evidence." *Journal of the Academy of Marketing Science* 29, no. 1 (Winter 2001): 16–35.

Teas, R. Kenneth, and Thomas E. DeCarlo. "An Examination and Extension of the Zone-of-Tolerance Model: A Comparison to Performance-Based Models of Perceived Quality." *Journal of Service Research* 6, no. 3 (February 2004): 272–286.

Teas, R. Kenneth, and Kay M. Palan. "Disconfirmed Expectations Theory of Consumer Satisfaction: An Examination of Representational and Response Language Effects." *Journal of Consumer Satisfaction, Dissatisfaction and Complaining Behavior* 16 (2003): 81–105.

Tse, David K., Franco M. Nicosia, and Peter C. Wilton. "Consumer Satisfaction as a Process." *Psychology & Marketing* 7, no. 3 (Fall 1990): 177–193.

Tsiros, Michael, Vikas Mittal, and William T. Ross Jr. "The Role of Attributions in Customer Satisfaction: A Reexamination." *Journal of Consumer Research* 31, no. 2 (September 2004): 476–483.

Vanhamme, Joëlle, and Dirk Snelders. "The Role of Surprise in Satisfaction Judgements." *Journal of Consumer Satisfaction, Dissatisfaction and Complaining Behavior* 14 (2001): 27–45.

Weaver, Donald, and Philip Brickman. "Expectancy, Feedback, and Disconfirmation as Independent Factors in Outcome Satisfaction." *Journal of Personality and Social Psychology* 30, no. 3 (March 1974): 420–428.

Wirtz, Jochen, and John E.G. Bateson. "Consumer Satisfaction with Services: Integrating the Environment Perspective in Services Marketing into the Traditional Disconfirmation Paradigm." *Journal of Business Research* 44, no. 1 (January 1999): 55–66.

Wirtz, Jochen, and Anna Mattila. "Exploring the Role of Alternative Perceived Performance Measures and Needs-Congruency in the Consumer Satisfaction Process." *Journal of Consumer Psychology* 11, no. 3 (2001): 181–192.

Wood, Stacy L., and C. Page Moreau. "From Fear to Loathing? How Emotion Influences the Evaluation and Early Use of Innovations." *Journal of Marketing* 70, no. 3 (July 2006): 44–57.

Wu, Jianan, and Dan Padgett. "A Direct Comparative Framework of Customer Satisfaction: An Application to Internet Search Engines." *Journal of Interactive Marketing* 18, no. 2 (Spring 2004): 32–50.

Yap, Kenneth B., and Jillian C. Sweeney. "Zone-of-Tolerance Moderates the Service Quality-Outcome Relationship." *Journal of Services Marketing* 21, no. 2 (2007): 137–148.

Yi, Youjae. "A Critical Review of Consumer Satisfaction." In *Review of Marketing,* ed. Valarie A. Zeithaml, 68–123. Chicago: American Marketing Association, 1990.

Yi, Youjae, and Suna La. "What Influences the Relations Between Customer Satisfaction and Repurchase Intention? Investigating the Effects of Adjusted Expectations and Customer Loyalty." *Psychology & Marketing* 21, no. 5 (May 2004): 351–373.

Yoon, Sung-Joon, and Joo-Ho Kim. "An Empirical Validation of a Loyalty Model Based on Expectation Disconfirmation." *Journal of Consumer Marketing* 17, no. 2 (2000): 120–136.

ALTERNATIVE AND SUPPLEMENTARY COMPARATIVE OPERATORS

Chapter 4 discussed the operation of comparison mechanisms, primarily with reference to the process of expectancy disconfirmation. It was acknowledged, however, that referents other than expectations are known to affect satisfaction decisions and are therefore likely to play a role in the consumer's satisfaction response. Part II of this book focuses on five of these referents, five that are steeped in the history of satisfaction within the various disciplines that study it.

The first chapter in this section discusses need fulfillment as developed primarily in the aligned fields of motivation. Needs are central to all dimensions of life. Writings on techniques of satisfying consumers frequently begin with the ever-popular need hierarchy framework that describes how individuals first fulfill basic needs and then go on to pursue higher-order goals. To bridge the gap to the consumer domain, these needs and goals are typically linked to the delivery of products or services.

Study of the needs literature reveals that little is understood about basic (or not so basic) needs and that any presumptions about the needs concept in consumption may be premature. Two prominent need theories are showcased, those of Maslow and Herzberg, and their relevance to marketing addressed. The Maslow framework, in particular, raises a number of issues not easily applied to consumer contexts. For example, do individuals always move from the satisfaction of one need to the pursuit of satisfaction of another in an orderly fashion, as prescribed by need hierarchy theory? The literature is equivocal about the legitimacy of this theory, and Chapter 5 provides an overview and summary of what is known. In contrast, Herzberg's two-factor theory has proven useful to marketers, although it will require much greater testing before it is more widely accepted.

It is also noted that the need-fulfilling function of product performance is often treated as if it were intuitively obvious. One might ask, then, why so little empirical work beyond that of Herzberg attests to the origin of needs and how they operate in the customer satisfaction response. One possible answer to this apparent lack of attention is that products are designed to fulfill needs, so that product feature performance is identical with need provision. Although this assumption is in "need" of further exploration, readers will find that quality control management in Japan has already operationalized a need fulfillment variation showing great promise. Attributed to Noriako Kano, this technique, new to this edition, is elaborated fully with measurement suggestions.

In Chapter 6, the concept of quality is discussed in light of its role in consumer satisfaction. Here, three issues are addressed. First, is quality synonymous with satisfaction? Second, if not, which comes first, satisfaction or quality? Third, is quality as important a concept as satisfaction, or more important or less important? These issues are aired in order to respond to the current, extremely popular emphasis on total quality in manufacturing and service delivery. There is no question that quality remains a critical determinant of demand; the issue is whether satisfaction is the criterion of interest in consumers' minds. Are firms focusing on the wrong concept? Interestingly, readers may desire that a specific position be taken in this chapter; this requires, however, that the concept of quality be developed along with its relation to satisfaction. A partial response is provided with a model at the end of the chapter, although not all readers will be "satisfied" with this attempt at a resolution.

Chapter 7, new to this edition, tackles the difficult topic of value. Virtually all enterprises, of course, promise to deliver value to their customers, typically framed in terms of attributes or benefits—leading to a difficult choice as to whether quality or value should take precedence in the order of the chapters. To address this conundrum, part of a more complex, "axiomatic" framework of value, presented in the chapter, is explored at a higher level of abstraction than mere delivery of performance. It will be suggested that value can span many levels of understanding up to what some would refer to as "ethereal." The chapter concludes that value delivery is typically satisfying but that satisfaction can result from value fulfillment, a tautology that will be addressed but not answered fully.

Chapter 8 discusses consumer equity. The concept of equity was first developed in the job satisfaction and legal literatures where fairness (or justice) matters were self-evident. Matters of inequity in the workplace were thought to result in decreased productivity, while inequity in the courts had obvious implications for societal harmony in general. But do consumers consider equity (or inequity) when buying products? The question comes up frequently in matters of pricing, as in being charged a "fair price." However, this topic does not represent the bulk of the literature on consumer equity. Rather, equity is explored in the context of fair dealings; that is, are the consumer's efforts and outlays fairly reimbursed in terms of the product's utility and dealer's efforts as well as equal (fair) distribution of the same product to others in similar circumstances? Attention also focuses on two other equity matters: the *process* of delivering the product or service, sometimes referred to as procedural justice, and the *nature* of the delivery process in terms of courtesy and understanding, known as interactional justice. All three "justice" sources (distributive, procedural, and interactional) will be found necessary to account for equity influences in consumption.

Finally, in Chapter 9, buyer's remorse is discussed. More commonly known in the literature as regret, this concept involves a comparison to "what might have been." Here, the consumer is believed to make a comparison not to expectations or other comparison standards, but to an imagined set of outcomes that could have occurred if another alternative had been selected, or even to the possibility that no purchase had been made at all. Since the first edition of this book, the study of regret has resulted in a substantial body of new literature in the consumer domain. It should come as no surprise that regret has been shown to be a powerful factor in the satisfaction response. Of interest is the fact that *anticipated* satisfaction is also known to be influenced heavily by anticipated regret. Consumers are now observed to utter the phrases "I'm going to regret this" or "If only I had . . ."

The last part of this chapter completes the regret phraseology with the lament "I knew this would happen." This phenomenon, known as hindsight bias, acts as a palliative for negative events after the fact. Little has been done on this topic in consumption, but one can easily see the positive effects on outcome satisfaction if the bad outcome was a foregone conclusion. This is, in fact, what this chapter concludes.

CHAPTER 5

NEED FULFILLMENT IN A
CONSUMER SATISFACTION CONTEXT

Companies frequently claim that they "fulfill needs" for consumers. Still other companies claim that they will "address all your needs satisfactorily," or they guarantee that they will "satisfy your every need." Others use the concept of need in advertising slogans such as "The closer you shave, the more you need Noxzema," "All the business news you need—when you need it" (*The Wall Street Journal*), "Thanks, I needed that" (Mennen Skin Bracer), and "Sometimes you need a little Finesse—sometimes you need a lot." In fact, the concepts of need and need satisfaction have been proposed as central to the very definition of marketing. According to one textbook, "Marketing is the performance of activities that seek to accomplish an organization's objectives by anticipating customer or client needs and directing a flow of need-satisfying goods and services from producer to customer or client."[1]

Just what is this concept of need satisfaction, and how does it differ, if at all, from need fulfillment or even consumer satisfaction in general? The answer at first appears intuitively obvious—namely, that they are all identical goals. After all, are not marketing efforts intended to generate profits by satisfying needs? Is not that what firms are in the business of doing? If so, then why are there so few articles written on need satisfaction in marketing? A search of every article published in the *Journal of Consumer Satisfaction, Dissatisfaction and Complaining Behavior* (volumes 1–19, 1998–2006), a journal solely devoted to consumer satisfaction matters, and all prior consumer satisfaction conference proceedings from 1976—nearly 500 articles in all—revealed no papers with either "need satisfaction" or "need fulfillment" in the title. There was only one instance of an article (in a proceedings volume) with "needs" in the title relating to business and government information needs. Thus, it appears that the concept is almost too intuitively obvious, so much so that consumer researchers do not feel compelled to conceptualize it theoretically or to test it empirically.

This enigma is one of the reasons for this chapter. Here, needs, need fulfillment, and the relationship between need fulfillment and customer satisfaction are explored. The first part of this chapter examines the concept of need fulfillment from a historical perspective. The later part discusses applications of need theory in consumer environments.

BASICS OF NEED

Restoration and Enhancement

Why do consumers purchase products? One obvious answer is acquisition—to own. Ownership, in turn, is pursued in order to fulfill a perceived need to own. But what is the basis of this need? There are two fundamental answers to this question. The first is that a deficit exists in the consumer's life and the consumer wishes the deficit removed. This example involves purchase for the purpose of restoration—bringing the consumer back to a perception of wholeness. Acquiring a high school equivalency degree after dropping out of school might be an example of this phenomenon.

The second answer is that consumers see acquisition as enhancement—adding to the positive value of their lives. In this case, the "deficit" is created by their imagination of the future utility of possession. That is, consumers construct a life with the acquisition added to the bundle of "things" that constitute their existence. For example, a second home on the lake may be purchased for the anticipation of idyllic evenings and momentous sunsets reflecting off the water, experiences not now available to the consumer. These two conceptual interpretations of need fulfillment—restoration and enhancement—provide the basis for further discussion. They also provide a distinction between needs and wants.

In short, needs are more aligned with deficits. Consumers expressing unfulfilled needs lack essentials in their lives and thus pursue restoration. Wants, in contrast, result from desired enhancements. Many observers of the human condition consider wants to be superfluous desires that are not essential to human existence. It is easy to envision, however, how wants can be redefined as needs as the wants become integrated into "existence." This idea will be more formally presented later.

Services fit into this discussion in much the same way, although at a more intangible level. Many services, such as home repair, health care, and legal redress, are restorative. Others, such as common residential utilities, security services, and government, simply maintain the status quo. Still others, such as travel, the arts, and entertainment, add value to an already satisfactory lifestyle. In general, little additional analysis is required here, although the process of delivering the service becomes an important element of the consumer's satisfaction judgment. Process considerations will be set aside in this chapter, so that discussion can focus on what the consumer gets from consumption and how this acquisition is mentally processed into a satisfaction judgment.

Reinforcement

The notions of restoration and enhancement are actually special cases of reinforcement. Generally speaking, reinforcement is a reward that has the property of sustaining behavior, of informing the organism that its response to a stimulus (i.e., its behavior) is "correct." Assume, first, a consumer at rest. Here, the phrase *at rest* implies a sort of contentment, a state of passive satisfaction in which all needs are met and additional hedonic pursuits are not entertained. The analogy of the contented cat, fully fed and serene in the sun, is direct here. Psychologists call this state of nature *hedonic neutrality.*

Assume, further, that this situation is upset by introducing a deficit from neutrality. Hunger in the case of the cat is one example, as are cold, rain, a breach of security by a neighbor's dog, causing fear, and any other of the possible physiological and psychological shortcomings that organisms can experience. The deficit now becomes a need, an actively processed drive to bring the situation back to neutrality. In the consumer domain, products or services will be purchased to provide the proper level of restoration. Interestingly, the psychology literature refers to this restoration as one of negative reinforcement. This term, which causes much confusion when presented to lay audiences, stems from early work in "rat psychology" where laboratory rats were motivated to learn tasks through the mechanism of removal of an aversive (negative) stimulus (e.g., an electric shock), used as a "reinforcer." An example of negative reinforcement is portrayed graphically in Figure 5.1.

Restoration brings with it a feeling of relief. This type of alternative "satisfaction" will be more

Figure 5.1   **The Reinforcements**

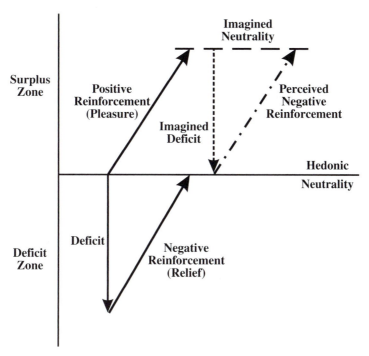

formally proposed in Chapter 13. Normally, relief is an end state in that the consumer, happy to be rid of the deficit, goes on with life. There are few, if any, motivational properties remaining, for relief satisfies the psychological longing to fill the deficit.

Given this outcome, there are two exceptions worthy of note. The first is that some consumers will actively take steps to avoid a recurrence of the deficit state in the future. For these consumers, avoidance may be satisfying for its own sake, as when a person leaves work early or late to avoid rush hour traffic. The second exception is that some consumers will begin to enjoy (i.e., find satisfying) the deficit-relief cycle, originally thought to be a clinical issue, but now known to involve high-risk consumption activities.[2]

In contrast, reinforcement that results in an addition (enhancement) to a consumer's contentment state is referred to as positive reinforcement. Shown as pleasure in Figure 5.1, this reinforcement provides a different sort of satisfaction, for the consumer's life is now enriched, not restored. In the words of an economist, it provides additional utility to an otherwise fulfilled consumer. Note, however, that both positive reinforcement and negative reinforcement provide a positive increase in the consumer's hedonic state, although the description of the end state is quite different. Whereas restoration results in relief and a return to neutrality, positive reinforcement results in pleasure, joy, and perhaps elation. A simple way of distinguishing positive from negative reinforcement is that negative reinforcement always begins in "negative territory" in the deficit zone, while positive reinforcement begins at neutrality or from a lower state of pleasure. It is also possible, of course, that relief can be coupled with enhancement, as when a consumer is given additional compensation in a redress situation such as "double your money back if not satisfied."

A second interesting aspect of positive reinforcement is also shown in Figure 5.1. If consumers perceive a yet-to-be-acquired product as essential to their lives, they have, in effect, elevated the level of neutrality to include the anticipated item. In doing so, they construct an imagined and immediate deficit. This may cause the process of positive reinforcement to be interpreted as negative reinforcement! For example, a teenager, hearing of the latest fad or fashion, proclaims, "I can't live without it!" Typically, the teen's life was perfectly satisfactory before learning of the new consumable. This example explains why parental gifts to assuage an "I must have" request result in minimal or no gratitude on the part of the teen recipient. From the parents' view, the gift provides positive reinforcement, adding to a benefit set. The teenager, however, views it as mere restoration from the imagined (then real) deficit.

This example describes an interesting aspect of positive reinforcement—its effect on the redefinition of neutrality. The World War I–era song lyric "How Ya Gonna Keep 'Em Down on the Farm (After They've Seen Paree)?" would seem to apply here. Consumers can become accustomed to higher levels of product performance, service, and so on, thereby redefining levels of normalcy. What was previously viewed as a level of pleasurable positive reinforcement now becomes a state of neutrality, and shortfalls from this higher level of product performance become deficit situations to be restored. In effect, this process ensures that individuals will find themselves in a continual pursuit of higher states of satisfaction, referred to as the "hedonic treadmill" or, more aptly, the "satisfaction treadmill."[3] This escalation appears to be orderly, however, and will be described under the topic of hierarchical need theories.

The preceding discussion sets the stage for an examination of still different interpretations of need fulfillment and of satisfaction. Through the use of need theory, hierarchical notions of need predominance will be discussed. All these theories have in common the characteristic that satisfaction (fulfillment) of lower-level (restorative or deficit) needs results in the emergence of salient higher-level needs. This process is thought to persist until the consumer attains satisfaction of ultimate goals in life, such as values. In examining these need hierarchies, the reader will note the correspondence of need dominance to the issue of salient attributes, as discussed in Chapter 2. In effect, this discussion will shed insight on the question of why certain product attributes are more salient than others.

NEEDS IN THE SATISFACTION PROCESS

The reader may have wondered why something so basic to consumption as need satisfaction has been relegated to the second part of this book. As perplexing as this may sound, the answer is that the conceptual basis of human needs, whether basic needs, universal needs, and so on, is in dispute. In fact, even the existence of needs, being largely unobserved, is debated. The managerial implications of need fulfillment strategies thus may be as ambiguous as the concept of need satisfaction itself.

In pursuing this topic, attention shifts to those theories, one of motivation and two of satisfaction, that have been operationalized by researchers for the specific prediction of satisfaction. It should be noted at this point that the relationship between motivation, a goal-directed pursuit state, and satisfaction are inextricably intertwined. Interestingly, separate literatures have emerged, but a close reading of either will confirm this last assertion. Goal striving has not been as widely studied in consumption behavior under strict interpretation, but that is only because the topic has been subsumed under the satisfaction umbrella. Discussion of two-factor theory, which follows in this chapter, is a case in point.[4]

In beginning this section, it may be helpful to graphically portray three conceptual versions of the role of needs in satisfaction and in the related field of motivation. Panel A of Figure 5.2 shows the classic need satisfaction model whereby need deprivation causes that need to become

Figure 5.2   **Operation of Needs in Satisfaction and Motivation**

(A) Need Satisfaction:

Deprivation » Dominance » Gratification » Homeostasis

(B) Motivation:

Deprivation » Dominance » Gratification » Reactivation

Dominance » Gratification » Reactivation, etc.

(C) Hierarchical Motivation:

Level 1 Need:
Deprivation » Dominance » Gratification » Homeostasis

Activation

Level 2 Need:
Deprivation » Dominance » Gratification » Homeostasis

Activation

Level 3 Need:
Deprivation » Dominance » Gratification » Reactivation

"dominant." After activities are undertaken to relieve the state of deprivation, hedonic neutrality, referred to here as homeostasis, is again attained. This "need" is motivating only in the sense that the individual is driven to attain an end state—need fulfillment. Once it is fulfilled (gratified), the motivating properties of the need are extinguished. This form of need satisfaction clearly corresponds to negative reinforcement as portrayed in Figure 5.1.

Panel B displays the classic motivation model whereby deprivation results in a dominating drive to fulfill the need as before. Once it is fulfilled, however, the need does not extinguish for at least two possible reasons. First, the need could be a stable personality trait of the individual, such as the need to achieve. In this case, a single achievement only serves to reactivate the need so that it can be achieved again. Solving a favorite puzzle, such as Rubik's cube, is an example. Second, the individual may be motivated to exceed each prior achievement, such as when a bridge player achieves increasing levels of mastery in the game or a runner exceeds a personal record in a fixed-distance footrace. In both of these examples, the prior accomplishment fulfills the need only temporarily or fleetingly, so that the need becomes reactivated after a short time. This continual redefining or respecifying of goals is similar to the positive reinforcement example in Figure 5.1. In these cases, reward may serve only to rekindle the desire to acquire the reward again, or it may result in a redefinition of the level of homeostasis (neutrality).

Finally, panel C draws on the now generally accepted deprivation → dominance → gratification → activation model to display hierarchical motivation. In motivation hierarchies, needs are ordered on the basis of their role in attaining and maintaining the physical and psychological health of the individual. Needs essential to the preservation of life are considered lower-order in that they are biological or instinctual. Higher-order needs are essential for the growth of the individual along social, psychological, or spiritual lines. One characteristic of hierarchical theories is that higher-order needs cannot be activated unless lower-order needs are fulfilled. Thus, the pursuit and attainment of higher-order needs are contingent on lower-order need fulfillment, a concept known as "prepotence."

In panel C, the early stages of the hierarchical model begin as simple need satisfaction. Once the need is fulfilled, however, the lower-order (level 1) needs attain homeostatic levels and are no longer prepotent. Their gratification, however, activates the dominance of the next higher need, its deprivation state having been dormant. Note that one cannot activate a higher-order need unless a latent state of deprivation was already present. This process of activating newly dominant needs continues until the highest-order needs are dominant. These ultimate-level needs, according to theory, cannot be sated and will continue to reactivate and remotivate the individual. Thus, hierarchical models actually provide the basis for linking need satisfaction models and motivation models in a coherent framework.

Discussion now proceeds to three motivation-satisfaction models that have implications for consumer satisfaction. Later, the evidence to date regarding the usefulness of these models in furthering an understanding of the consumer satisfaction response is discussed. In addition, the more general usefulness of need models will be explored, as will some problematic issues in their implementation.

Two Popular Need Satisfaction Models

Maslow's Need Hierarchy

In 1943, Maslow published a commanding article on human motivation, based on his earlier work in clinical psychoanalysis. Subsequent works elaborated on his theory and constitute the bulk of writings that prompted early research in job satisfaction and other areas.[5] Maslow's propositions, following the classic need hierarchy process outlined in panel C of Figure 5.2, consist of five levels. The "basic" needs existing at each level, which Maslow referred to as "instinctoid," are now lore in the motivation literature and consist of the following stages:

1. *Physiological needs*: sustenance requirements of the human body such as vitamins and minerals and the drives whose satisfaction maintains these necessary body composition levels, such as hunger, thirst, and reproductive tendencies.
2. *Safety needs*: freedom from threat of body or mind, including the needs for order, structure, and predictability; also, freedom from the psychological states resulting from such threat, including fear, anxiety, and apprehension.
3. *Affiliation needs*: possession of a sense of companionship, belonging, affection, love, and their expression through sexuality.
4. *Esteem needs*: a category that consists of two needs that Maslow did not order on prepotency: first, a sense of personal esteem, including confidence, strength, and achievement, that one bestows on oneself; second, the esteem that others bestow on the receiver, such as prestige, recognition, attention, and appreciation.
5. *Need for self-actualization*: the need for self-fulfillment, to become everything that one is capable of becoming, as in the U.S. Army recruiting slogan "Be all that you can be."[6]

Later, Maslow added a sixth need, which has been largely ignored in the research spawned by his original theory. Self-transcendence refers to the need to integrate with the human community rather than to remain as an individualist, pursuing self-goals.

Thus, according to interpretation, there are five or six need categories hypothesized in the Maslow hierarchy. As stated by Maslow, all these needs are present at any one time, differing only in prepotency or the dominance of one over the others. Lower-order need prepotency always dominates higher-level needs, so that a momentary shortfall in a previously gratified, but lower-order need will cause the individual to revert to a lower-order striving. For example, loss of one's residence in a hurricane would, under most circumstances, cause an individual to put career achievements aside until the residence and essential belongings were restored. At the highest level of the hierarchy, the need for self-actualization (and presumably self-transcendence) is never or rarely fulfillable, providing a source of continual activation for those who have adequately satisfied all lower-order needs. Philanthropists, for example, rarely seem to fulfill their need to help others.

Interest in Maslow's theory, both theoretical and empirical, was pronounced, and it did not abate until the topic of motivation ran its course around 1980. Before that point, numerous empirical studies and reviews of Maslow's conclusions appeared. These studies were universally nonsupportive of the Maslow hierarchy in its entirety, although subcategories of the "basic" five levels showed promise. Reasons given were both empirical and conceptual, as follows.[7]

Beginning with empirical efforts, little support from factor analysis findings (see Chapter 2) was found for Maslow's five need categories. Items reflecting both adjacent and nonadjacent need categories sometimes loaded together, and frequently only two factors—consisting of categories 1, 2, and 3 as the first, and 4 and 5 as the second—appeared as distinct. In a second problem area, the deprivation/domination aspect of Maslow's theory received mixed support at best. This element of his theory argues that deprivation of a lower-order need causes the quest for fulfillment of that need to dominate motivation. Thus, the need with the lowest gratification (highest deprivation) should also have the highest need strength or importance to the individual. Results showed that this appeared partially to be the case only for autonomy and self-actualization and not for security (safety), social (love), and esteem needs.

In yet another area, the gratification/activation aspect of Maslow's theory likewise received mixed to limited support. This postulate of the theory argues that gratification of a lower-order need reduces its importance and activates the next higher-order need, thereby increasing its importance to the individual. Unfortunately, data showed no such logical progression. Rather, self-actualization and security, at opposite ends of the hierarchy, tended to be the least satisfied needs, while social needs were the most satisfied. Generally, no pattern of findings supporting Maslow's theory could be found. Similarly, the order of needs in Maslow's hierarchy was questioned. Do all individuals progress in the same manner? Could some individuals pursue esteem before affiliation? As noted in the research findings, scant evidence has been found for an ascendance in importance of higher needs as a result of the fulfillment of lower needs.

Other writers questioned the very core of Maslow's theory—the existence of "basic" needs. In particular, they argued that Maslow, in relying on clinical observation, had no "proof" of needs or of their universality. For example, do all individuals have a need for self-actualization or even prestige, the "esteem" that others bestow on the individual? It appears that Maslow described needs that were socially acceptable by the standards of the day. Still other criticisms questioned the distinction between needs, desires, and values, three items that are frequently confused. Needs are elements missing from one's life, desires are temporal wants that may or may not have a biological basis, and values are worthy goals or representations of what is moral or right. Some have argued that needs may be ignored in the pursuit of wants (e.g., luxury cars purchased by the poor) or even values, such as when one leads a life of celibacy in order to pursue spirituality or a life of poverty in order to pursue a particular social goal. In still another sense, needs are thought to be universal, while wants and values may be more heterogeneous across cultures. It would be much less common to find similar value structures across diverse elements of humanity than to find similar need structures. Thus, interpretations of the higher-order needs in Maslow's hierarchy as values, such as self-transcendence, contribute to this problem of confusion in terms.

Further, Maslow's theory assumes that individuals with similar needs will pursue similar paths to fulfill those needs. Again, assuming that needs are somewhat universal, if different actions are taken by different individuals to fulfill the same need, then the corresponding managerial strategy will be multifaceted, diffuse, or, even worse, impossible to formulate. Finally, Maslow assumes that a satisfied need is not a motivator. Yet many of the lower-order and middle needs require continual satisfaction. Thus, all previously "fulfilled" needs may require some continued attention. Although Maslow did allow for operation of some levels of all needs at any one time, this last criticism does diminish the prepotency argument somewhat and requires that attention be paid to the maintenance of lower-order needs as one pursues higher-order needs.

Lastly, critics have questioned what type of mental "euphoria" people attain when they reach the ultimate pinnacle of achievement in Maslow's hierarchy. Is it satisfaction, happiness, or the catchier category of being all that one can be? Recent theorizing suggests that what Maslow was conceptualizing some sixty years ago was a fairly new version of positive affect referred to as *eudaimonia*.[8] Eudaimonia is a state of peaceful harmony of a long-lasting nature, a sort of blissful existence resulting from having attained an ultimate, but cogent, state of living. This would appear to be the frame of mind that Maslow was describing when he conceptualized his sixth level of self-transcendence. Happiness or hedonic enjoyment is more transitory, resulting from more immediate sources of pleasure. It, too, can be of a lasting nature, but may be subject to spats of apprehension that the state of happiness will not last or will be interrupted. Is either one *the* satisfaction as defined and described in this book? This author thinks not, although hedonic enjoyment certainly overlaps with many satisfactions in life. The eudaimonia literature is fairly recent and is mentioned here only to provide a comparison as "satisfaction" becomes more clearly defined and distinguished from these "close cousins." The remaining sections of this book will, I hope, shed more light on this major issue.

Thus, despite many criticisms and this most recent twist on what Maslow attempted to construct, studies show limited success with the Maslow hierarchical categories, primarily in contexts outside the job satisfaction environment where much of the research had been performed. Research in consumer behavior has not been forthcoming to any degree.[9] However, two recent studies have attempted to apply Maslow's ideas in the field of services.[10]

In the first, parallels to other works that identified service dimensions were used to show that stages in service delivery could be viewed as loosely corresponding to those in Maslow's hierarchy. The translation was not as close as one would prefer, but was reasonable given the context. Readers may wish to view this source for a service-specific scale (SQ-NEED) that the authors constructed showing favorable validation parameters. In the second, four needs loosely based on Maslow (security, self-esteem, justice, and trust) were measured and compared across four industries (hotel, airline, retail, finance). The results showed priority divergences that were explained ex post. Nonetheless, each of these studies does address a needs hierarchy within service provision and demonstrates that the basic premise of need fulfillment as a consumption goal remains as one to be explored in specific areas. Discussion now turns to a framework having more precise application to marketing. The reader should not expect, however, that this next approach would prove to be the panacea all may have hoped for. That possibility is reserved for the last section of this chapter.

Herzberg's Dual-Factor Theory

A second need satisfaction theory was proposed by Herzberg, who created a great amount of controversy in the job satisfaction area.[11] Unlike Maslow's hierarchy, which was intended to be a general theory of human (need) motivation, Herzberg did his original research and theorizing in the work environment with the intent of discovering "satisfiers." Although Herzberg's conceptualization theory is work-oriented, one might wonder why it would be covered here, if its satisfier/dissatisfier classification under this theory relates to job outcomes and not consumption outcomes. The answer is that consumer researchers have actually put this theory to empirical test in consumer contexts, while only anecdotal effort, primarily within the advertising community, had been described for the Maslow theory of needs. Moreover, as will be discussed, Herzberg's theory stimulated product design in Japan that has now been adapted by the global marketing community.

Herzberg employed the critical-incident technique (see Chapter 2) to discover the events that cause respondents to be exceptionally satisfied and, separately, dissatisfied with their jobs. Content analysis of these "storytelling" episodes, as some critics have called them, revealed two sets of factors—one predominant in the incidences of satisfaction and the other predominant in the incidences of dissatisfaction.

The dissatisfiers consisted primarily of job *context* factors such as working conditions, company policy, and relations with superiors, while the satisfiers consisted primarily of job *content* factors such as the work itself, achievement, and responsibility. Herzberg argued that these two categories had separate and distinct influences on workers. Specifically, context factors could only cause dissatisfaction in their absence or dysfunction. Because these factors, when at appropriate levels, are ordinary components of any job, their presence is expected; thus they have no satisfying consequences when fulfilled. Herzberg referred to these as "maintenance" or "hygiene" factors as if to imply that they are essential to a worker's ordinary homeostatic "health." Others in the literature referred to them as extrinsic needs, as they are elements outside a person's psyche.

In contrast, satisfiers such as achievement serve to satisfy and motivate. The absence of these "motivators" does not cause dissatisfaction; rather a neutral state is manifest. Both (job) satisfaction and motivation were described as contingent on the availability of responsibility, achievement, and other such intrinsic sources of fulfillment.

Herzberg referred to his process as a two-factor, dual-factor, or motivator-hygiene theory. He argued that satisfaction (resulting from attainment of a motivator need) and dissatisfaction (resulting from frustration of a hygiene need) could not be considered as bipolar, or two opposite poles of the same continuum, as shown in Example 1. Instead, satisfaction and dissatisfaction were viewed as unipolar and somewhat independent, as shown in Examples 2 and 3.

Example 1.

	Dissatisfaction				Satisfaction	
1	2	3	4	5	6	7

Example 2.

	No satisfaction				Satisfaction	
1	2	3	4	5	6	7

Example 3.

	Dissatisfaction				No dissatisfaction	
1	2	3	4	5	6	7

Figure 5.3 **Overlap in the Herzberg Two-Factor Framework**

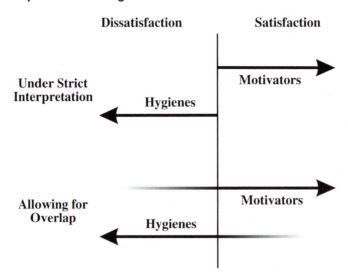

In present contexts, this interesting interpretation allows for simultaneous satisfaction and dissatisfaction. For example, jobholders can be dissatisfied with their coworker relations, but at the same time satisfied with their responsibility for independent thought and action. This interpretation also allows for the independent removal of dissatisfying elements, serving only to decrease dissatisfaction, and the addition of satisfying elements as separate motivators. Further, motivation can still be achieved in the face of intractable dissatisfiers (e.g., inclement or dangerous working conditions).

Herzberg's theory spawned numerous conceptual and empirical criticisms that are summed up in a number of sources, some drawing a nonsupportive conclusion, others showing support, and still others taking a more neutral stance, contending that the theory had not been adequately tested. Since these reviews were written, very little has appeared in the job satisfaction literature to support or refute the theory.[12]

Generally, the conceptual criticisms are of two kinds. The first notes that the dichotomies of motivators and hygiene factors are not mutually exclusive, as shown in the top half of Figure 5.3, but actually overlap to the extent that some motivators can produce dissatisfying experiences and some hygiene factors can be satisfying, as shown in the bottom half of the figure. For example, advancement is one often-cited motivator, but a worker's failure to be promoted can have extremely dissatisfying effects. Similarly, a move to more spacious office with windows and a view can indeed be a satisfying element of a person's job. In defense, Herzberg did acknowledge this overlap phenomenon, arguing only that motivators are more likely than hygiene factors to enhance satisfaction and that hygiene factors are more likely than motivators to cause dissatisfaction.

A second criticism, which will be detailed later, is that the two-factor theory is an oversimplification of a more complex interplay between satisfaction and motivation. Noting correctly that satisfaction and dissatisfaction are judgments of an attained or unattained state in the past or leading up to the present, while motivation is a current state of activated purpose that is expected to continue until that purpose is achieved, writers have questioned how the theory can predict both satisfaction and motivation. An attempt at an answer to this paradox will be provided but for now, attention turns to those studies in consumer behavior that have attempted to apply the two-factor framework.

Marketing Efforts to Apply Two-Factor Theory

After the publication of the Herzberg critiques, two articles appearing in the consumer satisfaction literature directly tested two-factor theory, using the critical-incidents technique. The first tested two-factor theory in the context of judgments of clothing satisfaction.[13] Subjects were asked to "think about a specific item of clothing that has been especially satisfactory and an item that has been especially dissatisfactory" and then to respond to the query, What happened to make you satisfied (dissatisfied) with this item?

Using an instrumental and expressive classification scheme (see Chapter 2) rather than hygiene factors and motivators, coders categorized answers into those that pertained to purely functional attributes (e.g., durability, fit, warmth) and to purely aesthetic features (e.g., styling, color, praise from others). The authors concluded that two-factor theory was supported, as more instrumental comments were reported in the dissatisfying situations and more expressive comments were reported in the satisfying situations.

In a second study, the researcher broadened the number of products to twelve, selecting from categories of clothing, personal care, food, and durables.[14] A predetermined number of thirty-six attribute descriptors was used and later divided into the same instrumental and expressive divisions used in the previous study. Employing an identical analysis, the author found that, for attributes having unambiguous instrumental or expressive identifications, two-factor theory was largely supported. However, the strength and consistency of results depended on the product category. For durables, the two-factor theory was robust; for personal-care items, it was most inconsistent. Thus, the findings suggest that two-factor theory may be a better description of satisfaction and dissatisfaction for high-involvement products or those requiring considerable information processing than for more mundane products. And, although not intended as a test of two-factor theory, a recent study in the banking area found that "tangibles" and "process" dimensions acted as hygiene factors and motivators in the same manner as those of the previous two studies.[15]

Despite these somewhat encouraging findings, two-factor theory has not received great attention from consumer researchers. Deferring, for now, the quality design analogy to satisfier-dissatisfier themes, let us look at three studies of more recent vintage. In the first two, the ever-popular critical-incidents technique was used in studies of bank services and pizza parlors.[16] The authors found remarkably similar results, in accord with the bottom overlap panel of Figure 5.3, that three attribute categories could be identified: satisfiers, dissatisfiers, and those that possessed both properties. Attentiveness, friendliness, and care were frequently cited satisfiers; availability, reliability, and integrity were frequent dissatisfiers; and responsiveness played both roles. In another study, this of website design, more than forty features were investigated along similar lines.[17] Generally, satisfiers concerned skill and knowledge learning, enjoyment, and website credibility, while dissatisfiers included appearance, navigation, and functionality. Dual features were more difficult to interpret, but included privacy and empowerment.

Thus, two-factor theory would appear to have great intuitive appeal, as it clearly fits the positive/ negative reinforcement distinctions in Figure 5.1. Moreover, anecdotal evidence and self-reflection would suggest that some aspects of products are not processed unless the item malfunctions, such as when an air conditioner ceases to operate. Other aspects are unexpected pleasures that are not processed until they are recognized or appreciated. A hidden cents-off coupon inside a food package is one such example.

The next section is a digression, of sorts, to summarize what has been covered. Following this, a major conceptual advance will be introduced with an accompanying methodology that has much to offer. As the reader will see, it greatly extends a similar perspective offered in this author's first edition.

Need Gratification Theory Elaborated

The inconsistent results found in both the job and consumer satisfaction literatures on need satisfaction have prompted writers to attempt to reconcile the various need theories proposed in the literature with the somewhat inconsistent findings. One proposed conclusion is that the operation of satisfiers or dissatisfiers or of motivation or hygienic factors is idiosyncratic, but with some orderly generalizations.[18] This perspective can be described as follows:

- When an individual's lower-order needs are unfulfilled, both satisfaction and dissatisfaction result from fluctuations in the degree of fulfillment of these needs.
- When lower-order needs are partially satisfied, higher-order needs will provide sources of satisfaction and dissatisfaction, except that threats to the fulfillment of lower-order needs will induce dissatisfaction.
- When lower-order needs are unconditionally satisfied, satisfaction and dissatisfaction will derive from higher-order needs.
- Ceteris paribus, satisfaction results from the gratification of a need.
- Ceteris paribus, dissatisfaction results from the frustrated gratification of an active need or the threatened frustration of a previously fulfilled need.
- In contrast to satisfaction, motivation results from the perceived opportunity to gratify a need through (consumption) behavior.

Thus, it appears that viewpoints are beginning to converge on the interplay of satisfaction and motivation and that extrapolations to product and service environments are warranted and overdue. Specifically, satisfaction in the context of negative reinforcement, satisfaction of true deficits, and satisfaction of instrumental necessities for a well-functioning product are end states, resulting in fulfillment with little further motivation potential. In contrast, positive reinforcement and satisfaction of higher-level goals, pleasures, and delights result in a desire (motivation) to repursue these same states of nature. The means of determining product and service characteristics that fall into the two (and other) categories are discussed next.

A CONSUMER PERSPECTIVE ON NEED SATISFACTION THEORY

The long discourse on need theories now begs the question of how to tailor the prior conclusions to consumer products and services. This section attempts to answer this question by considering two frames of reference. If the focus is on the product itself, then the attributes of the product can be analyzed like the facets of a job, and researchers can investigate the degree to which these attributes are similar to hygiene factors or motivators. This procedure will result in a list of attributes focusing on what the product has (or does not have). Alternatively, researchers can focus on what the consumer gets; the frame of reference is now on the consumer, and the list of attributes is now phrased in terms of consumer benefits. Generally, what the product has will operate at lower-level need fulfillment, and what the consumer gets will operate at higher-level need fulfillment. The reason is that the translation of product attribute performance to higher-order need fulfillment is made by the consumer. Lower-order needs tend to be functional in nature, and it is the product features that give the product its ability to perform its function. Unfortunately, these two reference frames are frequently confused and mixed in the same survey. The parallels here to laddering and the rings model in Chapter 2 are self-evident.

For example, consider the automobile attributes of miles per gallon and frequency of repair. These are what the automobile delivers in a physical sense. The consumer's needs (desires) are actually economical transportation or perhaps a long cruising range before fill-ups in the case of miles per gallon, and minimal downtime, freedom from worry of breakdown, or simple reliability in the case of repair frequency. This means-end chain logic was previously discussed in Chapter 2. However, the point here is that these two attributes are capable of being easily translated in either direction. That is, high gas mileage translates to economical transportation, and economical transportation is defined in one sense by high gas mileage at the physical attribute level. Both these elements are capable of generating both satisfaction and dissatisfaction because of this ease of translation. For example, economical operation (or its counterpart, high mileage) is a source of satisfaction, as is freedom from worry over repairs. However, low gas mileage due to the need for a tune-up, causing frequent need for fill-ups and eventual downtime for repair, would be dissatisfying to most car owners.

Now consider purely mundane aspects of a car that are essential components but are not processed by consumers. Engine technology, electronic circuitry, and emissions paraphernalia come to mind. Unless these malfunction in some way, they are largely incapable of affecting the consumer's satisfaction with the car. A malfunction, however, is most assuredly a dissatisfier. In Herzberg's terminology, these are hygiene factors. They are elements that the product has, whether known or unknown to the consumer.

Now consider those aspects of automobiles that give owners a psychological boost. These might include pride of ownership, the knowledge that the car can exceed the speed limit by a factor of 3, having the only car of its kind in the country club, and the ability to hear a pin drop at 75 miles per hour. These are elements the consumer gets, and they would be motivators or satisfiers in Herzberg's framework, because a shortfall in any of these (exceeding the speed limit only by a factor of 2, having one of two in the country club, and a tiny amount of road noise at speed) is unlikely to be a cause of dissatisfaction—perhaps less satisfaction, but not dissatisfaction.

These examples illustrate the three types of need categories that operate in analogous fashion to the job satisfaction categories. Based on their operation, they can be referred to as the following:

1. Bivalent satisfiers: the upward and downward translatable attributes that can cause both satisfaction and dissatisfaction.
2. Monovalent dissatisfiers: essential but unprocessed attributes capable of causing dissatisfaction only when flawed.
3. Monovalent satisfiers: psychological "extras" processed at a higher level of the need hierarchy.

The operation of the three satisfier categories is shown in Figure 5.4. It can be seen that monovalent dissatisfiers provide the bulk of ill feelings toward products, monovalent satisfiers provide the greatest source of satisfaction, and bivalent satisfiers provide intermediate amounts of both.

This graphic has intentionally been drawn so that bivalent satisfiers provide near-linear responses to need fulfillment. In contrast, the monovalent effects are more exponential and rise (fall) asymptotically toward satisfaction neutrality. Under this strict interpretation, monovalent dissatisfiers, when fulfilled, can never contribute to satisfaction and monovalent satisfiers, when

Figure 5.4   **Operation of Three Need Categories on Overall Satisfaction/Dissatisfaction**

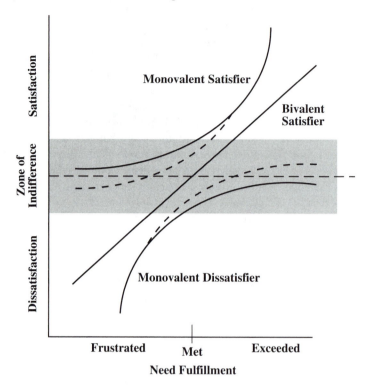

frustrated, can never contribute to dissatisfaction. The dashed lines in the graph show what might happen if modest monovalent crossover effects are allowed. Here, fulfilled (and overfulfilled) dissatisfiers can produce modest amounts of satisfaction, and frustrated monovalent satisfiers can generate modest amounts of dissatisfaction. Additionally, a shaded zone of indifference (see Chapter 4) is shown, to illustrate the point at which just-met needs begin to lose their satisfying and dissatisfying properties. Future research efforts will be necessary before it will be known whether the strict or more relaxed interpretations maintain and whether the indifference zone operates as shown. Two studies, one descriptive and one correlational, speak to the broader issue of bivalent satisfiers versus monovalent satisfiers and dissatisfiers. This is followed by discussion of the Kano technique, which will take this analysis to a new level.

Descriptive and Correlational Data

In an early study in the consumer satisfaction area, letters of complaining and complimenting for two industries (restaurant and lodging) were categorized as to the focal service dimension giving rise to the positive or negative sentiment.[19] Based on frequencies of mention, the authors found four categories of service attributes. Those with the capability of engendering complimenting but not complaining were referred to as *satisfiers*; those with only complaining potential were called *dissatisfiers*; those with the potential to create either complaints or compliments were dubbed *criticals*; while those having neither potential were *neutrals*.

In accord with two-factor theory, a group of satisfiers emerged (e.g., neatness and spaciousness) that were high on the list of compliments, but low or absent on the list of complaints. Similarly, a group of dissatisfiers (e.g., parking availability) were high on complaints and low on compliments. Also present were criticals (e.g., service quality) that were high on both, and neutrals (e.g., advertising) that were low or absent on both lists. (Interestingly, neutrals would appear as a horizontal straight line corresponding to neutrality in Figure 5.4.) Unfortunately, the authors did not take this analysis further in an attempt to predict overall satisfaction or need fulfillment, but these results are, nonetheless, wholly in line with need theory as developed here.

In another study, by the author, which is representative of a number of others appearing in the literature in various fields, registered pharmacists reported on their degree of fulfillment for drug information needs as part of their work.[20] This was assessed as the degree to which a drug information manual (the focal product used in the study) fulfilled the pharmacist's requirements for information on each of a large category of needs (e.g., brands available, dosage, contraindications, drug interactions). Generally, these needs were of the objective and functional variety and had no intrinsic properties that might provide elements of motivation. The information need categories constituted one element of the attribute set for this particular product.

Additionally, perception of overall need fulfillment, as provided by the information manual in its entirety, was assessed on a multi-item scale. The scale used for both attribute-specific and overall need fulfillment (to be discussed) ranged from "fell short of my needs" (scaled 1) through "met my needs" (4) to "exceeded my needs" (7). Analysis of the data showed, first, that attribute need fulfillment was related to satisfaction only through the mediating influence of overall need fulfillment, which significantly predicted satisfaction as follows:

Attribute need fulfillment → overall need fulfillment → satisfaction

Because the correlation between overall need fulfillment and satisfaction was significant, one might conclude that the information elements of the product were bivalent satisfiers. However, when three curvilinear transformations were applied to the overall need fulfillment variable, significant improvements in the need fulfillment-satisfaction fit were obtained in every case. The greatest improvement occurred when a simple "plateau" transformation was applied at the point of just fulfilling needs. That is, all overfulfillment response categories (scale points 5, 6, and 7) were scaled at the same numeric level as mere fulfillment (scaled 4). This suggests that the functional form of information category need fulfillment best fitting the data was that of the monovalent dissatisfaction curve in Figure 5.4. Apparently, other aspects of the information manual that were not studied (e.g., price, binding, monthly updates) provided the roles of bivalent or monovalent satisfiers.

Although not reported in the published article, additional data from the same study pitted need fulfillment against disconfirmation in the prediction of satisfaction. The respective regression coefficients showed that the disconfirmation weight was twice as large as that of need fulfillment (0.40 versus 0.20). Very similar results were reported in another study testing need satisfaction (which the authors referred to as value-percept disparity) in a product context.[21] Here, the disconfirmation coefficient again dominated that of need fulfillment (0.53 versus 0.18). The question arises, then, why researchers would focus on need fulfillment when disconfirmation measures are so easily obtained.

The answer is that additional information about the causes of consumer satisfaction is available from need fulfillment measures. If this were not the case, then the regression coefficients for the need fulfillment variable in the two previous examples would be zero. In fact, it is not uncommon for marketers to advertise that their services will *both* "meet your needs and exceed your expectations." This example makes it clear that more research on the role of need satisfaction in consumer behavior would be helpful, both to define the concept and to identify how it performs against other predictors of satisfaction.

Typically, any information pertaining to need fulfillment in satisfaction surveys becomes muddled within lists of product features, as noted in Chapter 2. If insights on need fulfillment are desired, one way to begin is to determine specific attributes modeled by the three need categories in Figure 5.4. This knowledge can be obtained with the addition of need fulfillment measures in satisfaction surveys. This brings us to the Kano methodology, as discussed next.

The Kano Approach to Satisfiers and Dissatisfiers

Kano and colleagues in Japan published a paper detailing a unique approach to the identification of need-fulfilling product features, similar to the operation of the three satisfaction categories in Figure 5.4.[22] They proposed the three states of "must-be" quality (the monovalent dissatisfiers), "one-dimensional" quality (bivalent satisfiers—this author would refer to these as "two-dimensional," a distinction no doubt fraught with translation nuances), and "attractive" quality (monovalent satisfiers). This latter category is frequently labeled "delight" or "delighters" by other writers. This is not a problem; delight has appeared within high positive states of (surprise) disconfirmation and will appear again in the discussion of emotion. The subject benefits from all these perspectives.

Must-be or monovalent dissatisfiers are those features that are basic to the function of the consumable; they are implied, taken for granted, self-evident, and therefore rarely mentioned in consumer responses unless specifically prodded for. Who, for example, would mention basic braking on an automobile? Bivalent satisfiers are functional features with variance in performance so that they can operate at a poor, average, or exceptional level. They are typically measurable, sometimes technical (e.g., the fidelity of a sound system), and rarely *not* mentioned. Attractive or monovalent satisfiers are delighters, pleasant surprises, and often wishes—stated or unstated, extras, and enigmatically often not stated. Consumers cannot know of that which they are unaware, which is why these features are often "surprises," as described in the previous chapter. In this author's experience, a surprise in automobile technology was variable speed windshield wiper control that responded to rain intensity automatically (but be wary of commercial car-washes).

The Kano technique has many variations, and a typical application will be presented here.[23] Once the feature list is developed using any of the methods in Chapter 2, both a functional and a "dysfunctional" description is constructed for each. For example, the automatic shift in a car could be described as "slow and jerky" or "smooth as silk." Then, both these descriptions would be assessed on the "scale" that follows. This scale is not intended to be linear, but it does approximate a continuum of sorts. Respondents are asked to check one and only one category for the functional and dysfunctional variations of each attribute. After the first entry in each category, this author has presented "acceptable" alternatives, although they should be of the same tone, tense, and so on.

- I like it that way; I would enjoy it that way; this would be very helpful to me.
- It must be that way; I expect it to be that way; this is a basic requirement for me.
- I am neutral; this would not affect me.
- I can live with it that way; I can tolerate it; this would be a minor inconvenience.
- I dislike it that way; I cannot accept it; this would be a major problem for me.

Table 5.1

Sample Kano Evaluation Table

Customer requirements		Dysfunctional				
		Like	Must-be	Neutral	Live with	Dislike
Functional	Like	Q	Q	A	A	O
	Must-be	Q	Q	M	M	M
	Neutral	R	R	I	I	M
	Live with	R	R	I	I	M
	Dislike	R	R	R	I	Q

Legend: A = attractive; M = must-be; O = one-dimensional; I = indifferent; R = reverse; Q = questionable.

Table 5.2

Hypothetical Kano Summary Table

Customer requirement	A (%)	M	O	I	R	Category
Gas mileage	17	22	53	7	1	O
Brakes	9	65	25	1	0	M
Full airbag system (e.g., side)	50	33	17	0	0	A or M
Retracting radio antenna	27	19	12	17	25	A or R or M

Legend: A = attractive; M = must-be; O = one-dimensional; I = indifferent; R = reverse.

In a sense, each attribute is defined by the pattern of responses by the sample as a whole or by significant subsets (e.g., male/female, age categories). One looks for the patterns (or a close approximation), organized in Table 5.1. There is not universal agreement on all categories, but the must-be (M), attractive (A), and bivalent (O, for one-dimensional) are clearly defined. The indifferent (I) categories typically include neutrals, while some require soul-searching, marked by a questionable (Q) designation (e.g., liking both the functional and dysfunctional variations of an attribute).

Finally, there is an R (reverse) category that can occur when subsegments are compared. I use an actual example from my own experience. My preference is that a car have an electronic antenna that rises and retracts as the radio is turned on and off. This feature prevents vandalism and accidents. Off-roaders prefer fixed antennas that are designed to be sufficiently rigid so as not to break when flexed. The reason, as they have discovered, is that repairs to the damaged automatic antenna run in the hundreds of dollars. Damage can occur in the outdoors (via tree limbs) and in car washes. It is all a matter of preference for these two consumers with opposite preferences.

A hypothetical data set is shown in Table 5.2 (an actual example is shown later). Note that the percents are run horizontally across features and that none are "clear" cases, including the antenna example, and that the Q column is intentionally omitted. The preponderance of the data suggests the conclusion in the last column. The analysis does not stop here, however.

Figure 5.5   **Kano-Based Satisfaction/Dissatisfaction Indices**

$$\frac{Satisfaction}{Potential} = \frac{A + O}{A + O + M + I}$$

$$\frac{Dissatisfaction}{Potential} = \frac{(-1) \, x \, (O + M)}{A + O + M + I}$$

Figure 5.6   **Satisfier/Dissatisfier Potentials by Product Feature: Ski Example**

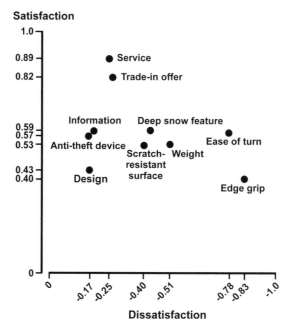

Source: Adapted from Kurt Matzler et al., "How to Delight Your Customers," *Journal of Product and Brand Management,* 5, 2 (1996): 15, by permission of Emerald.

A reasonable question at this point is the extent to which the features compare in their ability to satisfy or dissatisfy or the degree to which they can operate to both satisfy and dissatisfy. Kano and colleagues have provided formulas that are elegant in their simplicity. Since attractive features can only satisfy, must-be features can only dissatisfy, and bivalent (one-dimensional) features can do both, the equations in Figure 5.5 result. The numerators contain the A + O categories for satisfaction potential and the M + O for dissatisfaction potential. Both have all categories in the denominator (excluding Q and R). This results in feature scores that are easily plotted on an *xy* graph. The (–1) multiplicand for the dissatisfaction score is a mere formality to indicate negative potential.

Figure 5.6 shows an actual example from the literature using snow skis as the product of interest.[24] The feature locations correspond to the indices calculated from Figure 5.5 from data in the original article. Here, it can be seen that edge grip has the greatest dissatisfaction potential and, coincidentally, the least satisfaction potential, whereas service has the greatest satisfaction potential with lower-than-average dissatisfaction qualities. Those in the middle of the scatterplot (e.g., weight) have roughly equal potential to satisfy and dissatisfy.

PRACTICAL IMPLICATIONS OF THE NEED
SATISFACTION PERSPECTIVE

As noted, the Kano method shows great promise in assessing the ability of features to satisfy and dissatisfy. The reader will have already noted that the technique is more practical than a purist's definition of psychological need satisfaction would warrant. This chapter began with discussions of reinforcement theory, Maslow, and Herzberg—on which Kano is based. Kano's method also corresponds to this author's work on mono- and bivalent satisfiers, although it takes this topic much further in the direction of application. Indeed, NASA has used the Kano technique in designing various science programs.[25] And even the use of the technique in discovering delighting attributes is a worthy extension of its merits. Discussion of Kano's categories as presented here does suggest that many of the characteristics of delight are similar if not isomorphic to those of attractive features.

Application Implications

In exploring further applications, consider the typical satisfaction survey. Which of the three need categories is (are) most likely to be sampled in the attribute list? Given the long history of product feature dominance in satisfaction surveys, this author's guess would be the monovalent dissatisfier group and the bivalent satisfier group. One reason for this prediction is that these two categories represent actionable problem areas. If there is a shortfall in the performance of some product dimension, engineering or operations can "tweak" the specifications, production tolerances, or instructions to cause the product to fall within consumers' indifference zones. Perhaps this explains why simply meeting expectations was considered the path to success in satisfaction for such a long time.

As discussed in this chapter, the more intrinsic, higher-level needs provide a different type of satisfaction, one with motivating properties. Here, consumer motivation does not have direct parallels to motivation in the job satisfaction literature. In that literature, a motivated worker was thought to produce more, to innovate more, to solve problems better, to be absent less, and to generally pursue the "correct" organizational goals.

In consumer behavior, motivation might be redefined as *enthusiasm*. A consumer who is enthusiastic about an especially satisfying product that allows for the satisfaction of higher-level needs would be expected to purchase the product or service more regularly, to spend more effort acquiring it, to "talk it up" more, to protect it from its detractors, and to exclude competitive offerings from consideration regardless of incentives to switch (see Chapter 15). In other words, the consumer knows that purchasing or patronizing this particular product or service is a means to fulfilling needs beyond those at the functional level.

If this is so, why are not more higher-order needs used in marketing? They are, but at the prepurchase phases of consumption, primarily in advertising. Consumers are told that they will achieve, accomplish, and attain their wildest dreams if they buy the firm's product. How often are "benefits" of this nature placed on satisfaction surveys? Because the market research function is typically disjoint from the promotional function of the organization, higher-order needs rarely appear on surveys. Consumers in the prime of their consumption roles usually are not all that focused on self-actualization.

Measurement and Analysis

This chapter has suggested two potentially fruitful directions that management might pursue to assess need fulfillment, including Kano as an extension of the second. The first is the discovery of a needs hierarchy for specific products along the lines of Maslow, but without the strict categorizations of physiological needs, safety, and so on. One reason for relaxing this constraint is that products, unlike jobs, typically do not encompass the full range of needs in the hierarchy. Whereas a job can provide the means of supplying all needs from the physiological to self-actualization, products may target only one or two of these. For example, basic foods relate mostly at the physiological level, home security systems at the safety level, and fashion and personal grooming at the affiliation level.

Chapter 2 described the means-end hierarchy technique, which is ideally suited for identifying the characteristics of products and services that operate at various levels, as well as the manner in which these characteristics link up with more (and less) abstract benefits at other levels. Many of these will be explicit needs (e.g., nutrition, a sense of well-being), while others will be wants or needs as means to wants (e.g., an expensive set of titanium golf clubs that conveys a sense of mastery of the sport). The degree to which these attributes fit neatly into Maslow's or other hierarchies is not as important as identifying the key attributes impacting satisfaction and dissatisfaction.

This takes discussion to the second implication that can be drawn from the research and theorizing presented here. Shifting focus to the manner in which the various needs or need-related attributes affect satisfaction and dissatisfaction, as opposed to the needs themselves, provides a clearer understanding of the satisfaction process. This is best approached from the three-need categorization of monovalent and bivalent satisfaction attributes. In short, management should identify needs falling in all three categories, using a need fulfillment measure similar to the disconfirmation measure presented in Chapter 4. Rather than asking whether performance exceeded or fell short of expectations, however, the question here is whether performance met, fell short, or exceeded the consumer's needs. This scale appears as follows:

Fell short of my needs		Just met my needs			Exceeded my needs	
1	2	3	4	5	6	7

There are two items to note about this scale. First, like disconfirmation, it requires an odd number of scale points to appropriately accommodate the midpoint. Second, it is not clear in all instances whether "exceeded my needs" has positive or negative valence. Although the following discussion will assume that need overfulfillment is positive for the sake of illustration, a bifurcated scale may be needed. For example, points 5, 6, and 7 may have to appear twice, once as "exceeded my needs in a good way" and "exceeded my needs in a bad way." This ideal point situation is discussed more fully in the next chapter, but requires mentioning here. Indeed, in the two studies cited earlier, one of pharmacists and one of auto drivers, scales truncated at "met my needs" were more predictive of satisfaction.[26]

The Kano approach has been elaborated as a valuable extension to this need perspective, but it is not without its shortcomings. First, two scales are required for each attribute, one functional and one dysfunctional. Also, the scale points are not necessarily linear and may not be intuitive to some consumers. At the same time, some attribute combinations, such as "bad brakes," may be too obvious and may have adverse effects on consumer responses. Thus, as with any technique, care must be taken in pretesting within context.

In lieu of a Kano method or in the likely case of previously collected data or an unwillingness to engage the full Kano model, the relation between overall satisfaction and the need fulfillment properties of each specific attribute requires examination. When this relation is plotted on an xy graph, four possibilities may emerge, including one suggestive of no relationship between the need and satisfaction variables (see Figure 5.7).

Figure 5.7 **Likely Scatterplots Corresponding to Various Need Fulfillment Response Functions**

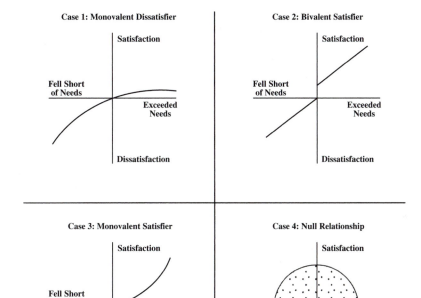

In case 1, the monovalent dissatisfier scatterplot (shown here as a best-fitting line) would occupy the lower left quadrant and level off on the horizontal axis when crossing the met-needs midpoint. These attributes are those that can only cause dissatisfaction when not met and which are unlikely to contribute to satisfaction even when exceeded. In the restaurant and lodging example mentioned previously, the availability of parking, the number of credit cards accepted, and the accuracy of the bill were examples of monovalent dissatisfiers. Inadequate parking, rejection of the consumer's preferred credit card, and inaccurate bills are definitely irritants. In contrast, having excessive parking, accepting numerous credit cards, and providing perfectly accurate bills do nothing, or very little, to enhance satisfaction.

Case 2 shows the bivalent satisfier plot, which rises steadily from left to right, from the dissatisfaction region through the satisfaction region. In this situation, the attribute is a cause of both dissatisfaction when needs are not met and higher levels of satisfaction when the needs are exceeded. In Figure 5.7, the plot is shown as purposely disjoint at the met-needs point. The graph was portrayed this way because the literature to date is not clear as to whether just meeting needs results in minimal satisfaction (i.e., neutrality) or satisfaction at some higher level. This author suspects that higher satisfaction levels will occur more often when there is a history of not meeting needs than when needs have been routinely met, but this is a speculative assumption at this point. Examples of attributes from the restaurant and lodging study that are clearly bivalent satisfiers include service quality, employee knowledge, and cleanliness.

Case 3 shows the monovalent satisfier, a mirror image of the monovalent dissatisfier. Here, the attributes can only enhance satisfaction. Examples from the same study include employee helpfulness, spaciousness, and neatness (as distinct from cleanliness). It should be pointed out that attributes in this category are more difficult to identify because they tend to be unexpected pleasant surprises. As such, they do not appear in complaint communications and frequently are not mentioned in operations manuals. Further, consumers may not be able to elicit them in means-end exercises until they have personally experienced the pleasantly surprising product or service features. As noted in Chapter 2, the critical-incidents technique is better than others in drawing these out, but only if the consumer can describe situations in which they occurred.

Finally, case 4 shows the likely appearance of null relationship attributes. Instead of a best-fitting line (for there is no fit), the plot is shown as a circle encompassing the data points. For these attributes, the degree of need fulfillment, including under- and overfulfillment, is not related to satisfaction. Attributes such as these would be considered low priority as satisfaction drivers, but may be related to other key variables such as reputation. Examples from the lodging industry include the quality of advertising, appearance uniformity across locations, and service variety.

As with the use of all techniques, the specific attributes that fall in each category will be idiosyncratic to a particular industry and, perhaps, to separate geographic regions within the same industry. Therefore, management must conduct separate analyses for its various constituencies.

CONCLUSION

This discussion of need fulfillment as one of the comparative processes giving rise to the satisfaction response shows that need analysis may offer insights beyond those of disconfirmation. Indeed, the question of falling short of, meeting, or exceeding needs may, in all likelihood, yield different predictions of satisfaction than the question of falling short of, meeting, or exceeding expectations. As shown in the pharmacist study and through additional analysis of this study presented here, disconfirmation and need fulfillment can both relate to satisfaction in an independent and additive fashion, thereby providing two analytical approaches to the satisfaction response.

In an extension of this basic approach, this chapter has described the Kano method, detailing its unique measurement methodology and the calculations needed to plot the degrees of satisfaction and dissatisfaction potential. Based on roots in quality research, it enlightens need analysis and should be of future value to research in the area. Readers will find, however, that the technique comes at some cost, as each feature must be analyzed twice for functional and dysfunctional operations in a comparative sense. The next chapter expands on the nature of comparative referents and addresses yet another approach, the quality judgment.

NOTES

1. Perreault, Cannon, and McCarthy, *Basic Marketing*, p. 6.
2. Solomon, "Opponent Process Theory of Acquired Motivation"; Celsi, Rose, and Leigh, "Exploration of High-Risk Leisure Consumption through Skydiving."
3. This process, discussed in terms of raising expectations in Chapter 3 and in the context of delight in Chapter 4, is now seen to be a fairly ubiquitous behavioral response to fulfillment generally. In the absence of control mechanisms, such as occur with thirst and hunger, individuals have the potential to acclimate to pleasurable experiences. See Frederick and Loewenstein, "Hedonic Adaptation"; and Schwartz, *Paradox of Choice*, p. 232.
4. One of the few studies expressly addressing goal-striving, using the arts as a research vehicle, is Garbarino and Johnson, "Effects of Consumer Goals on Attribute Weighting, Overall Satisfaction, and Product Usage." Readers interested in the interplay of motivation and satisfaction are directed to Austin and Vancouver, "Goal Constructs in Psychology"; and Sheldon and Elliot, "Goal Striving, Need Satisfaction, and Longitudinal Well-Being."

5. Maslow, "Theory of Human Motivation." This article was followed by many more publications, including *Motivation and Personality, Toward a Psychology of Being,* and *The Farther Reaches of Human Nature.* The latter book introduces a sixth need, self-transcendence.

6. The U.S. Army used this as its recruiting slogan for twenty years beginning in 1981.

7. See Kleinginna and Kleinginna, "Categorized List of Motivation Definitions, with a Suggestion for a Consensual Definition." All sources used in this section can be found in the author's first edition of *Satisfaction*, pp. 159–160, notes 15–19.

8. Ryan and Deci, "On Happiness and Human Potentials"; Waterman, "Two Conceptions of Happiness."

9. For an apparent verification of many of Maslow's tenets in the quality-of-life area, see, e.g., Hagerty, "Testing Maslow's Hierarchy of Needs." Readers may also wish to see Sheldon et al., "What Is Satisfying About Satisfying Events?" which is a good segue from Maslow to Herzberg in the immediate next section. Shortly after the first edition of this book went to press, a "tombstone" Maslow article appeared in the marketing field. See Soper, Milford, and Rosenthal, "Belief When Evidence Does Not Support Theory."

10. Chiu and Lin, "Service Quality Measurement Derived from the Theory of Needs"; Chung-Herrera, "Customers' Psychological Needs in Different Service Industries."

11. Herzberg, Mausner, and Snyderman, *Motivation to Work*; Herzberg, *Work and the Nature of Man* and "One More Time."

12. See the citations for this section in the first edition of *Satisfaction*, pp. 160–161, notes 24–27.

13. Swan and Combs, "Product Performance and Consumer Satisfaction."

14. Maddox, "Two-Factor Theory and Consumer Satisfaction."

15. Yap and Sweeney, "Zone-of-Tolerance Moderates the Service Quality-Outcome Relationship."

16. Johnston, "Determinants of Service Quality"; and Johns and Howard, "Customer Expectations Versus Perceptions of Service Performance in the Foodservice Industry."

17. Zhang and van Dran, "Satisfiers and Dissatisfiers."

18. Wolf, "Need Gratification Theory," pp. 92–93.

19. Cadotte and Turgeon, "Dissatisfiers and Satisfiers."

20. Oliver, "Attribute Need Fulfillment in Product Usage Satisfaction." See also Spreng's work, cited in the previous chapter, on the topic of desires congruency, where information needs are specifically addressed. External literatures where similar analyses can be found, including entire methodologies for information needs analysis, include the areas of information technology, information architecture, library systems, and organizational needs assessment.

21. Westbrook and Reilly, "Value-Percept Disparity." These authors also truncated their study at the "exactly what I need level."

22. After the first edition of this book was published in 1997, the author became aware of work by Noriako Kano and colleagues in Japan. The first English translation of his work was circulated as Kano et al., "Attractive Quality and Must-Be Quality," in 1984. His thesis of interpreting attribute meanings, although from a quality perspective, was identical to that presented in my first edition and it was with some chagrin that I realized that even the graphics in Fig. 4.4 were unmistakably similar. Without this author's knowledge, Kano's ideas and techniques, as presented here, had been circulating among quality circles, resulting in a 1993 journal volume devoted to his work which included contributions by a consortium of authors; see Berger et al., "Kano's Methods for Understanding Customer-defined Quality." With some humility, this author presented the Kano method to the marketing community in September 2000 in Oliver, "Kano Approach to Customer Delight." It is not known whether others had done so previously. That paper's contents are presented in their entirety in this chapter. They are not otherwise available. Kano himself critiqued the American quality industry in 1993 in "Perspective on Quality Activities in American Firms."

23. For an excellent and thorough discussion of the many variations, see Berger et al., "Kano's Methods for Understanding Customer-defined Quality."

24. Matzler et al., "How to Delight Your Customers." The complete analysis with tables appears in this work.

25. Lee and Newcomb, "Applying the Kano Methodology in Managing NASA's Science Research Program" and "Applying the Kano Methodology to Meet Customer Requirements." See, also, Matzler and Hinterhuber, "How to Make Product Development Projects More Successful by Integrating Kano's Model of Customer Satisfaction into Quality Function Development."

26. Oliver, "Attribute Need Fulfillment in Product Usage Satisfaction"; Westbrook and Reilly, "Value-Percept Disparity."

BIBLIOGRAPHY

Austin, James T., and Jeffrey B. Vancouver. "Goal Constructs in Psychology: Structure, Process, and Content." *Psychological Bulletin* 120, no. 3 (November 1996): 338–375.

Berger, Charles, Robert Blauth, David Boger, Christopher Bolster, Gary Burchill, William DuMouchel, Fred Pouliot, Reinhart Richter, Allan Rubinoff, Diane Shen, Mike Timko, and David Walden. "Kano's Methods for Understanding Customer-defined Quality." *Center for Quality of Management Journal* 2, no. 4 (Fall 1993): 3–36.

Cadotte, Ernest R., and Normand Turgeon. "Dissatisfiers and Satisfiers: Suggestions from Consumer Complaints and Compliments." *Journal of Consumer Satisfaction, Dissatisfaction and Complaining Behavior* 1 (1988): 74–79.

Celsi, Richard L., Randall L. Rose, and Thomas W. Leigh. "An Exploration of High-Risk Leisure Consumption through Skydiving." *Journal of Consumer Research* 20, no. 1 (June 1993): 1–23.

Chiu, Hung-Chang, and Neng-Pai Lin. "A Service Quality Measurement Derived from the Theory of Needs." *Service Industries Journal* 24, no. 1 (January 2004): 187–204.

Chung-Herrera, Beth G. "Customers' Psychological Needs in Different Service Industries." *Journal of Services Marketing* 21, no. 4 (2007): 263–269.

Frederick, Shane, and George Loewenstein. "Hedonic Adaptation." In *Well-Being: The Foundations of Hedonic Psychology,* ed. Daniel Kahneman, Ed Diener, and Norbert Schwarz, 302–329. New York: Russell Sage Foundation, 1999.

Garbarino, Ellen, and Mark S. Johnson. "Effects of Consumer Goals on Attribute Weighting, Overall Satisfaction, and Product Usage." *Psychology & Marketing* 18, no. 9 (September 2001): 929–949.

Hagerty, Michael R. "Testing Maslow's Hierarchy of Needs: National Quality-of-Life Across Time." *Social Indicators Research* 46, no. 3 (March 1999): 249–271.

Herzberg, Frederick. "One More Time: How Do You Motivate Employees." *Harvard Business Review* 46, no. 1 (January–February 1968): 53–62.

———. *Work and the Nature of Man.* Cleveland, OH: World Publishing, 1966.

Herzberg, Frederick, Bernard Mausner, and Barbara B. Snyderman. *The Motivation to Work.* 2nd ed. New York: Wiley, 1959.

Johns, Nick, and Antony Howard. "Customer Expectations Versus Perceptions of Service Performance in the Foodservice Industry." *International Journal of Service Industry Management* 9, no. 3 (1998): 248–265.

Johnston, Robert. "The Determinants of Service Quality: Satisfiers and Dissatisfiers." *International Journal of Service Industry Management* 6, no. 5 (1995): 53–71.

Kano, Noriaki. "A Perspective on Quality Activities in American Firms." *California Management Review* 35, no. 3 (Spring 1993): 12–31.

Kano, Noriaki, Nobuhiko Seraku, Fumio Takahashi, and Shinichi Tsuji. "Attractive Quality and Must-Be Quality" (English translation). *Quality: The Journal of the Japanese Society for Quality Control* 14, no. 2 (April 1984): 39–48.

Kleinginna, Paul R., Jr., and Anne M. Kleinginna. "A Categorized List of Motivation Definitions, with a Suggestion for a Consensual Definition." *Motivation and Emotion* 5, no. 3 (September 1981): 263–291.

Lee, Mark C., and John F. Newcomb. "Applying the Kano Methodology in Managing NASA's Science Research Program." *Center for Quality of Management Journal* 5, no. 3 (Winter 1996): 13–20.

———. "Applying the Kano Methodology to Meet Customer Requirements: NASA's Microgravity Science Program." *Quality Management Journal* 4, no. 3 (April 1997): 95–106.

Maddox, R. Neil. "Two-Factor Theory and Consumer Satisfaction: Replication and Extension." *Journal of Consumer Research* 8, no. 1 (June 1981): 97–102.

Maslow, Abraham H. *The Farther Reaches of Human Nature.* Hammondsworth, Middlesex, England: Penguin Books, 1971.

———. *Motivation and Personality.* New York: Harper, 1954.

———. "A Theory of Human Motivation." *Psychological Review* 50, no. 4 (July 1943): 370–396.

———. *Toward a Psychology of Being.* 2nd ed. Princeton, NJ: Van Nostrand, 1968.

Matzler, Kurt, and Hans H. Hinterhuber. "How to Make Product Development Projects More Successful by Integrating Kano's Model of Customer Satisfaction into Quality Function Development." *Technovation* 18, no. 1 (January 1998): 25–37.

Matzler, Kurt, Hans H. Hinterhuber, Franz Bailom, and Elmar Sauerwein. "How to Delight Your Customers." *Journal of Product & Brand Management* 5, no. 2 (1996): 6–18.

Oliver, Richard L. "Attribute Need Fulfillment in Product Usage Satisfaction." *Psychology & Marketing* 12, no. 1 (January 1995): 1–17.

———. "The Kano Approach to Customer Delight." Paper presented at the Ninth Annual AMA/INFORMS Frontiers in Services Conference, September 2000, Nashville, TN.

———. *Satisfaction: A Behavioral Perspective on the Consumer.* New York: Irwin/McGraw-Hill, 1997.

Perreault, William D., Jr., Joseph P. Cannon, and E. Jerome McCarthy. *Basic Marketing: A Marketing Strategy Planning Approach.* 16th ed. Boston: McGraw-Hill/Irwin, 2008.

Ryan, Richard M., and Edward L. Deci. "On Happiness and Human Potentials: A Review of Research on Hedonic and Eudaimonic Well-Being." *Annual Review of Psychology* 52, (2001): 141–166.

Schwartz, Barry. *The Paradox of Choice: Why More Is Less.* New York: Ecco, 2004.

Sheldon, Kennon M., and Andrew J. Elliot. "Goal Striving, Need Satisfaction, and Longitudinal Well-Being: The Self-Concordance Model." *Journal of Personality and Social Psychology* 76, no. 3 (March 1999): 482–497.

Sheldon, Kennon M., Andrew J. Elliot, Youngmee Kin, and Tim Kasser. "What Is Satisfying About Satisfying Events? Testing 10 Candidate Psychological Needs." *Journal of Personality and Social Psychology* 80, no. 2 (February 2001): 325–339.

Solomon, Richard L. "The Opponent Process Theory of Acquired Motivation: The Costs of Pleasure and the Benefits of Pain." *American Psychologist* 35, no. 8 (August 1980): 713–728.

Soper, Barlow, Gary E. Milford, and Gary T. Rosenthal. "Belief When Evidence Does Not Support Theory." *Psychology & Marketing* 12, no. 5 (August 1995): 415–422.

Swan, John E., and Linda Jones Combs, "Product Performance and Consumer Satisfaction: A New Concept." *Journal of Marketing* 40, no. 2 (April 1976): 25–33.

Waterman, Alan S. "Two Conceptions of Happiness: Contrasts of Personal Expressiveness (Eudaimonia) and Hedonic Enjoyment." *Journal of Personality and Social Psychology* 64, no. 4 (April 1993): 678–691.

Westbrook, Robert A., and Michael D. Reilly. "Value-Percept Disparity: An Alternative to the Disconfirmation of Expectations Theory of Consumer Satisfaction." In *Advances in Consumer Research*, ed. Richard P. Bagozzi and Alice M. Tybout, 10:256–261. Ann Arbor, MI: Association for Consumer Research, 1983.

Wolf, Martin G. "Need Gratification Theory: A Theoretical Reformulation of Job Satisfaction/Dissatisfaction and Job Motivation." *Journal of Applied Psychology* 54, no. 1 (February 1970): 87–94.

Yap, Kenneth B., and Jillian C. Sweeney. "Zone-of-Tolerance Moderates the Service Quality-Outcome Relationship." *Journal of Services Marketing* 21, no. 2 (2007): 137–148.

Zhang, Ping, and Gisela M. von Dran. "Satisfiers and Dissatisfiers: A Two-Factor Model for Website Design and Evaluation." *Journal of the American Society for Information Science* 51, no. 14 (December 2000): 1253–1268.

CHAPTER 6

QUALITY

The Object of Desire

"Quality is Job 1," "Quality never goes out of style," "The quality goes in before the name goes on," "America's quality cigarette," "Quality means the world to us."[1] Like performance claims, such quality claims are common. Likewise, the concept of quality has been incorporated into many brand names. For example, the reader may be familiar with Quality Inn, Quality Shoe, Quality Food, Quality Products, and other regional and local firms with the word *Quality* in their names. And a little-known fact is that the common Q-Tip was named for—what? Guess!

The previous chapter examined the concepts of need and need fulfillment. It was noted that many consumers consider the ability to fulfill needs the essential requirement of a product or service offering. Although need theories can be extended to include higher-order pursuits such as values, primary needs exist at a more basic level and represent levels of fulfillment that must be present if a product is to be at all satisfying. In contrast to a basic and middle-level need focus, this chapter leaps to what some have considered and still consider to be the ultimate goal of product or service provision—quality. The next chapter on value will provide a different perspective on this premise, however.

The content of this chapter also differs from that of Chapter 2, which examined product or service performance as an isolated concept. This chapter takes a broadened view of product and service provision in an attempt to describe the comparison referents that consumers use to infer quality from performance judgments. The relationship between quality and satisfaction will then be explored in a manner similar to the discussion of satisfaction's relation to disconfirmation and need fulfillment. It will be argued that quality, like other attribute-based concepts, is itself subject to disconfirmation and may attain the status of an additional consumption goal to many consumers. The chapter also entertains suggestions for the measurement of overall quality as distinct from attribute-based quality.

TECHNOLOGICAL REFERENTS: THE HISTORICAL APPROACH

Historically, quality was believed to derive from technological excellence in manufacturing. Top producers of all eras have gone to great lengths to ensure that their products were designed and manufactured precisely to technical specifications. This approach, known as conformance quality, still permeates much of operations management today, and it is not uncommon to find companies touting the fact that they follow a 6σ (6-sigma) program. Adherence to this goal requires that the number of manufacturing rejects or defects be less than the number of production units six standard deviations (sigmas) from the mean level of production (resulting in no more than 3.4 defects per million units of production).

Although the premise of this chapter is that quality is a consumer-generated comparative judgment, since individuals have no implicit sense of quality unless a standard of comparison is provided, it can also be argued that historical or technical definitions of quality employ comparative referents. For example, the 6σ program uses minimization of defects as the standard. Unfortunately, these technological referents operate in background mode vis-à-vis consumer experiences in that they exist as design, scientific, engineering, manufacturing, or production standards and not as actual consumer judgments. To an extent, these comparisons do share some correspondence with consumer preferences, for much effort is devoted to "design in" quality based on consumer input. The fact remains, however, that as long as consumers are capable of envisioning the characteristics of a technologically better product—the fourth circle in the rings model in Figure 2.6—management's operationalization of quality will lag consumer preferences. For example, many consumers desire the automotive technology—such as stability control, GPS, back-up cameras, lane tracking, and automatic parallel parking—that they know is in design or prototype phases, or available as options on top-of-the-line vehicles, but not yet available on more modest models.

Thus, only a brief discussion of the engineering and manufacturing definition of quality will be presented here. Some discussion is necessary, however, as the technical design phase of satisfying the consumer is essential and cannot be overlooked regardless of the behavioral sophistication of the firm's marketing staff. The reader is directed to articles discussing the now-popular "house of quality" where the many technical quality comparisons are explicitly detailed.[2] This "movement" has now been formalized with a number of coveted industry awards, including the International Organization for Standardization (ISO) series, the Malcolm Baldrige National Quality Award, and the J.D. Power and Associates Awards. Interestingly, the future prospects of the winning companies have been empirically tested and found to be mixed. This seeming paradox awaits further study.[3]

Technical Comparisons

Figure 6.1 shows a number of quality comparisons used in design and manufacturing. As displayed, two variables are assumed as given from the standpoint of the firm. These are customer needs/requirements/desires, and competitive offerings. To these, one can add technological science—the state of the art of production or provision for this particular product or service. The base of each arrowhead in Figure 6.1 indicates the source of the comparison (the entity making it), and the arrowheads indicate the target comparison object. Thus, the firm forms its technical specifications around what is needed by the target market, what is offered by the competition, and what is scientifically feasible. As is frequently the case, these comparisons often cannot be met, so that technically imperfect or deficient quality may be "designed in."

Note, also, that consumers are shown as monitoring the competition for a sense of what is available. In this manner, their needs and desires are shaped by the marketplace. A technological advance by one firm may, and frequently does, raise the stakes for others. This provides yet another reason why consumer definitions of quality should lead the efforts of any one firm in nonmonopolistic industries.

After consumer and competitive perspectives are surveyed, the next stages in the quality design process includes comparisons of (1) technical requirements with component characteristics (parts design), (2) component characteristics with process characteristics, and (3) process with process control characteristics—all of which can be compared to competitive standards. The double-headed arrows in this sequence of steps are meant to indicate a back-and-forth, give-and-take

Figure 6.1   **Technical Excellence Quality Comparatives**

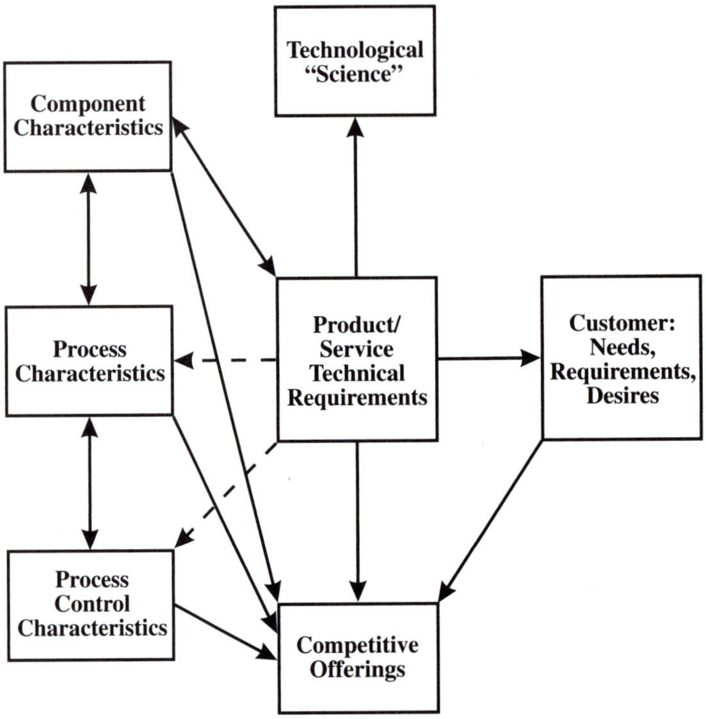

set of compromises between what should be and what can be in the technical manufacturing (or service engineering) process. The dashed arrows imply less formal assessments.

Consumer Perceptions of Quality

The preceding discussion provides a background to traditional treatments of quality, which go by such diverse names as manufacturing-based quality, objective quality, and production management quality.[4] The present focus, however, is on perceived or subjective quality. More importantly, it is on how consumers form quality perceptions. Some companies operate under their own interpretation of high quality, based on consumer need analysis, but are still unable to satisfy consumer definitions of quality. For example, call centers frequently define quality as the number of calls answered in x rings or y seconds or less. Analysis typically shows that agents accomplish this goal by abruptly terminating calls in progress, thereby alienating customers. When makers of "quality" commercial products attempt to enter the consumer market, they may fail to understand what their new customers want. For example, consumers were unimpressed with the heft, durability, and price of professional tree cutter saws for yard work they might perform once or twice a year.[5]

Similar failings of a management definition of quality versus that of the consumer are aptly demonstrated by other examples in the service industries. In a novel study of consumer perceptions of service quality in the airline industry, the authors found that consumer quality judgments were sensitive to the level of advertising expenditure in a positive manner and to passenger congestion as measured by the carrier's load factor (percentage of plane seating capacity filled) in a negative manner. No widely adopted traditional measure of quality for that industry (including on-time arrivals, problem-free baggage handling, and minimal flight cancellations) was related to these two variables.[6] Thus, this example shows that the consumer's view of quality can often differ from technical definitions. It also shows that consumer perceptions of quality can actually be at odds with management's profit goals. In the airline industry, flyers desire less passenger congestion while the airlines desire full loads and, therefore, full congestion. No wonder that the load factor is not reported as a quality dimension by the airlines.

Similarly, another study compared industry-determined dimensions of software quality with those of four other dimension lists, including SERVQUAL, proposed in the various quality literatures. It was found that only one dimension, reliability, was common to the software dimensions and to those listed in just two of the four quality frameworks. Numerous examples of this phenomenon occur in the online and technology areas generally: while management pursues technical and presentation quality, consumers become weary of constant upgrades and the attendant relearning required.[7] Again, quality appears to be elusive as a universal concept.

The next major section of this chapter discusses broader product and service abstractions that may be used as cues for inferring quality. Some more specific cues, such as price, were briefly discussed in Chapter 3 and are discussed here as needed; impressive summaries are available in other sources.[8] A comprehensive review of the quality literature, as it pertains to marketing, can be found in a highly recommended volume.[9]

QUALITY ABSTRACTIONS FROM THE CONSUMER'S PERSPECTIVE

Single-Stimulus Definitions

As discussed here, a single-stimulus definition entails what one might term a synonym or phrase-like synonym. When used to define characteristics of products and services, such singular definitions generally suffer from the same drawbacks as raw performance measures noted in Chapter 2—they have an indefinite referent. (This issue will reappear in the next chapter on value.) Consider some possible definitions for product quality: "detailed construction," "precision-crafted," and "simply exquisite." Operationally, these definitions would require greater elaboration: How finely detailed? How well crafted? How exquisite? While some terms used in surveys to convey quality have an implicit referent, such as the word *good* from the poor-fair-good-excellent scale—where *good* can be interpreted as good *for me*—others such as *fair* and *worth* do not.[10]

At this point, technical definitions of quality are put aside so that the appropriateness of some singular meanings of quality to the consumer can be entertained. Each will be shown to have an implied referent at either the conscious or subconscious level. Unfortunately, these will not lend themselves to a high level of measurement because the referent cannot be accessed objectively. Nonetheless, singular definitions are the mainstay of current quality measurement and require discussion so that their deficiencies relative to two- or multicomponent measures can be appreciated.

Ethereal Quality

Before subjective quality representations are introduced, one might ask if the notion of quality exists as a universally agreed-upon concept. That is, could it be that quality, like spirituality, is ethereal? According to some, quality is metaphysical or transcendental and defies definition. Writers on quality frequently cite Pirsig's *Zen and the Art of Motorcycle Maintenance*, in which Phaedrus

Table 6.1

Single-Stimulus Definitions of Quality

Terms connoting *attainment*
- Innate excellence
- Superiority
- Highest achievement
- Uncompromising standards

Terms connoting *desirability*
- Preference
- Value
- Worth
- Affordable excellence

Terms connoting *usefulness*
- Fitness for use
- Capacity to satisfy wants
- Possessing desired characteristics

pursues the nonpareil meaning of quality only to ultimately fail. Proponents of this metaphysical approach take the position that quality exists at a level not accessible to human understanding and, more certainly, measurement. "I know it when I see it, but I can't describe it when I do" might paraphrase this perspective. An unfortunate aspect of the metaphysical perspective, however, is that managers would derive little diagnostic information from this approach to quality.[11]

This ethereal notion of quality derives its meaning from the Greek word for "ideal"—*areté* (excellence). Interestingly, both ideal and excellence versions of quality are now operational, and researchers have models that assess these levels of performance. The ancient Greeks, however, had no behavioral or mathematical quality models; their use of the term and its implicit meaning transcended models or definitions, particularly in matters of morality, art, and philosophy.

Excellence-Based Terms

The notions of excellence and ideal performance do, however, provide an introduction to other definitions or subjective interpretations of quality commonly found in the literature. Generally, these terms can be placed into three categories, labeled attainment, desirability, and usefulness, and appear in various sources (see Table 6.1).[12]

Here, attainment refers to the achievement of a high-level standard of unspecified dimensions. Desirability refers to a more personal level of attractiveness to the consumer, again of unspecified dimensions. Lastly, usefulness refers to the ability of the product or service to "serve" the consumer's needs, which similarly are left unspecified.

Note, also, that the list includes terms, such as *value*, which will be described in the next chapter as encompassing the concept of quality; in an elementary sense, value refers to the quality received at a particular price or outlay. Other definitions, such as possession of desired characteristics, access the level of attribute or feature possession and can be viewed as more in line with the product cue interpretation of quality (see Chapter 2). Thus, these terms are useful in defining quality from a conceptual standpoint, but do not individually reflect the many uses of quality as a concept.

The difficulty in defining quality should now be apparent. Table 6.1 virtually exhausts the single-stimulus definitions proffered in the literature. Each of these phrases can be included on a survey in bipolar form and used as a measure of quality, as in the following example:

Unfit for use   Fit for use

| 1 | 2 | 3 | 4 | 5 |

And, as simple observation would demonstrate, the word *quality* itself is frequently used in a similar manner:

Low quality   High quality

| 1 | 2 | 3 | 4 | 5 |

The previous discussion illustrates the tautological nature of the various representations of quality in Table 6.1. Each of these phrases, ignoring for the minute the subtle distinctions between them, can be used as proxies for quality itself. This observation will prove to be useful later, when an effort to construct a global (overall) quality scale is presented.

There is a more important point to be made here. While these and other singular definitions are available to the researcher or to management, they are incomplete representations of the quality concept because they do not specify the comparison referent. For example, the list in Table 6.1 categorizes quality into dimensions of attainment, desirability, and usefulness. What, exactly, has been attained? What is it about the product or service performance that is desirable? And for what is this performance useful? In a partial answer to these questions, the standards that have been offered in the literature are explored next.

Dual-Stimulus Definitions

Some of the single-stimulus definitions discussed previously hinted at a comparison referent. For example, the phrase *affordable excellence* implies that excellence is achieved at a cost that is reasonable to the consumer and, hence, represents value. Similarly, even the word *superiority* implies that something must be inferior. Presumably, the superiority/inferiority referent is the set of competitive offerings available to the consumer. Generally, quality can exist only if something else is available to provide at least one other basis for comparison.

Consider a very common and essential staple in human existence—water. Although environmentally sophisticated consumers cognitively evaluate the drinking water available to them, most consumers probably do not. The quality of tap water is rarely questioned because, in the absence of strong local odors due to mineral or chemical impurities, most large municipal water utilities scrub, filter, and purify their water until little taste remains (pure water is both odorless and tasteless). Now, of course, the selection of flavored and enriched waters has proliferated; the basic concept remains the same, however.

Why do so many consumers accept tap water unconditionally? Because it does not enter their consciousness that local tap water is a variable, at least from the perspective of everyday life. In short, for most people, there is no observable variation in water, nothing to compare it against. This situation remains so until variation is introduced, through visits to other municipalities, the tasting of bottled or flavored waters, noticeable deterioration in the water supply, or sources of information from watchdog groups or vendors. When comparisons are introduced, quality becomes an issue because the previously accepted status quo can now be ranked on a superiority/inferiority or other preference scale. Moreover, the dimensions on which the tap water is to be judged can be presented to the consumer for evaluation. At this point, the local tap water can now be judged against excellence standards for quality.

One way of viewing a solution to the single-stimulus definition problem is to view quality as performance compared to a standard of whatever quality criterion management finds useful for its needs (e.g., excellence). Generally, the single-stimulus definitions focus either on the performance part of the quality "equation" or on the quality standard. For example, achievement or simple performance scores taken alone access only the performance dimension. In contrast, excellence and value sample the standards dimension. Some examples, such as affordable excellence, appear to have dual components, but limit the performance dimension to one standard, such as affordability.

If a comparison is the basis for quality judgments, then what do consumers compare against to infer quality? As one would expect, any number of feature cues have been documented in the literature, such as price, brand, store image, design, packaging, country of origin, and even perceived difficulty of manufacture; online purchasing adds still others to traditional, pre-Internet sets.[13] However, these are surrogate cues of quality. The task here is to ascertain the psychological basis for use of these surrogates. Generally, price, brand, and so on allude to a conceptual "something" at a higher level of abstraction. That higher level of abstraction, then, becomes the comparative basis on which quality judgments are made. Discussion now turns to the two most common comparative abstractions found in the literature, ideals and expectations of excellence.

Ideals as the Quality Standard

Perhaps the earliest notion of a comparative standard in marketing is an ideal point. Used almost from the inception of consumer study in the context of predictive models of attitude, the ideal product is one that possesses ideal levels of all its relevant features. What follows is a conceptual discussion of how one might operationalize this concept in the measurement of quality, using some basic arithmetic notation. In doing so, it will be assumed that the relevant attribute set has already been specified.

If it is assumed that the consumer is able to assess probabilities of the product or service possessing each of its attributes, and that all attributes are equally weighted (salient) to the consumer, then the predictive equation under ideal-point conditions for this consumer's quality judgment is

$$Q_j = 100 - \Sigma(pr_{ij} \, |P_{ij} - I_i|), \tag{6.1}$$

where

Q_j = quality judgment of brand j
100 = arbitrary constant to ensure positive-numbered judgments
Σ = summation over all attributes
pr_{ij} = probability that brand j possesses attribute i
Pi_j = performance level of brand j on attribute i
I_i = ideal level of attribute i
$| \, |$ = absolute value indicators

A number of details about this formulation can be noted. First, although most brand attributes will fall short of ideal levels, some may exceed these levels, such as when foods are too sweet, too spicy, or generally have "too much of a good thing." Thus, the absolute value designation around the $P_{ij} - I_i$ difference guarantees that negative and positive deviations from ideal levels are equally undesirable to the consumer. These differences, then, should detract from the brand's value to the consumer, hence the minus sign before the summation operator. Second, the arbitrary constant of 100 ensures that quality scores will be positive, that higher scores will correspond to brands nearer to the ideal, and that "perfect" brands having ideal attribute levels will score 100. Third, the probability weight pr_{ij} allows for uncertainty in the consumer's mind as to whether the brand does possess or will deliver the attribute under consideration.

However, because interest centers on postpurchase processes, one can assume that the consumer has previously observed performance levels and now holds them with some degree of certainty so that $pr_{ij} = 1$. The equation now appears as

$$Q_j = 100 - \Sigma |P_{ij} - I_i|. \tag{6.2}$$

Further, the ideal brand would possess all $P_{ij} = I_i$; this can be designated as Q_{ideal}.

The measurement scales for this formulation are straightforward, as follows:

(*P*)   Brand *j*'s performance on attribute *i*:

Low				High
1	2	3	4	5

(*I*)   My ideal brand's performance on attribute *i*:

Low				High
1	2	3	4	5

Here, it is assumed that the ideal brand does not necessarily possess the highest level of performance available on the scale, although often it does for individual consumers.

It follows that *if* (and this is a big *if*) attribute performance is the correct index for quality judgments, then $Q_{ideal} - Q_j =$ the quality deficit for brand *j*. That is, brand *j* is less than perfect in quality to the extent that the difference $Q_{ideal} - Q_j$ is large.

However, recall the water example. Assume that no consumer has ever experienced Q_{ideal} and that only Q_j exists for inspection. Assume, further, that Q_j appears as the paramount brand; there is none better. Now Q_j is the standard for quality against which all other brands are judged. This case probably describes the situation for most products and services. Lacking perfect products and services that give "all things to all people," the consumer has only reasonably perfect prototypes as examples of the highest quality items in the marketplace.

In this example, the dual stimuli used for quality judgments at first appear to be the ideal level and the perceived performance level. However, there are actually two stages to this process, each consisting of two stimuli. The first stage consists of a comparison of the ideal against a good prototype brand, an exemplar of what most now refer to as a *best brand* in class. The second is a comparison of other brands to the best brand. However, to the average consumer, the best brand may be the best that can be offered and appears as the marketplace ideal. At this point, one can take the position that the best brand is a proxy for the ideal standard.

Use of Excellence as the Quality Standard: SERVQUAL Revisited

In the original version of SERVQUAL, expectations were measured in terms of what companies should do to be perceived as high-quality service deliverers. Use of should or desired levels of expectations (see Chapter 3) was thought to access the correct referent for quality judgments at the time. However, problems with the directive of what companies should do (e.g., should do for what purpose?) led the authors to reformulate the manner in which expectations were measured.

Recognizing that, even though consumers can only perceive real-world offerings, they also have the capacity to imagine better offerings, the authors proposed assessing performance against standards of excellent (service) companies. Here, excellent companies could be either real or imagined. The specific wording of the question appeared as follows:[14]

> Please think about the kind of [service] company that would deliver excellent quality of service. Think about the kind of [service] company with which you would be pleased to do business. Please show the extent to which you think such a [service] company would possess the feature described by each statement. If you feel a feature is *not at all essential* for excellent [service] companies such as the one you have in mind, circle the number 1. If you feel a feature is *absolutely essential* for excellent [service] companies, circle [the highest scale point].

Note that the authors refer to two concepts in an effort to define the prototypical best brand in the service category under consideration—delivering excellence and possessing essential features. Because the SERVQUAL instrument is designed to measure feature levels that are later summed into dimensions, the referent used in this framework is an imagined or real company possessing essential and excellent (not ideal) levels of features. SERVQUAL's authors recommend the following formula for calculating a SERVQUAL score:

$$Q_j = \Sigma(P_{ij} - E_i) \tag{6.3}$$

where

Q_j = quality "gap" for company j
Σ = summation over all dimensions, features, or attributes
P_{ij} = performance perception for company j on dimension i
E_i = excellence expectation for dimension i

As in the ideal model representation, the measurement scales for this formulation are similarly straightforward, as follows:

(P)   Company j's performance on attribute i:

Low				High
1	2	3	4	5

(E)   An excellent firm's performance on attribute i:

Low				High
1	2	3	4	5

Again, it is assumed that excellent companies do not necessarily possess the highest level of performance available on the scale.

Inspection of equation 6.3 shows a number of differences from equation 6.2. First, equation 6.3 is a representation of quality shortfalls (and excesses) from excellence expectations, and not dissimilarity from an ideal. Thus, a presumption is made that ideals are not necessarily the proper consumer referent, even for quality judgments. Second, the performance-excellence deviations are called gaps in the SERVQUAL model. As such, they are more likely to take on both negative and positive raw differences, as excellence judgments are not as likely to come up against the ceiling effect commonly observed with ideal ratings. Third, no absolute value sign is needed or intended because it is desired that firms exceed expectations. In such cases, the $P_{ij} - E_i$ difference or gap score is positive. Positive scores are interpreted as good in the gap model and bad in the ideal-point model.

Despite these differences, the ideal-point model and the SERVQUAL model share common elements, the most important of which is that they compare observations of performance against standards, ideals in the first case and expectations of excellence in the second. These conceptualizations would be close approximations of each other were it not for the differences in the standard of comparison. It has already been noted that the ideal referent is one step removed from the best-brand standard. However, other differences are evident, as noted next.

Quality Response Functions

Generally, a response function is a trace of data reflecting the manner in which one variable moves or responds as it is affected by another. Response functions can be straight lines, curves, or kinked lines in the shape of an elbow. To illustrate, ideal-point models can be described as having three types of response functions, defining the manner in which increases in attribute performance translate to quality changes. In the first functional form, the consumer's sense of an ideal is a straight-line vector, an ever-increasing (decreasing) function much like an arrow pointed upward (downward). Thus, under this form, more of an attribute (or set of attributes) is always better, suggesting that manufacturers should strive to provide ultimately high levels of this attribute. At the extreme, this might be typified by the Midas complex, where the mythical king could not get enough gold—more was always better.

It is hard to imagine this infinite quest in the consumer domain, but lottery winnings and investment returns might qualify without running into the "too much of a good thing" ceiling. A more mundane example would be a manufacturer's lifetime guarantee of the durability of roofing materials or house paints, except that most know that durability beyond the typical home dweller's length of ownership adds unnecessary cost to materials and thus is suboptimal from the manufacturer's standpoint and is typically just "trade-talk." Nonetheless, this form of response to attribute performance is shown in Figure 6.2, panel A.

In what is perhaps a more common response form, consumers may be envisioned as harboring a finite ideal level, as shown in panel B, beyond which performance loses its utility. Carbonation in beverages, courtesy or attention of waitpersons, and length of movies are everyday examples. Thus, performance above the optimal level is dysfunctional and lowers, not raises, quality for the consumer.

Last, in what is probably the most typical case, the best brand in a product class possesses a suboptimal attribute set so that consumers can still envision a prototype that can exceed the best attributes of the best brand. This is referred to as a feasible ideal point (as in feasibly attainable) and is represented in panel C. Note that if the true ideal is sufficiently extreme (far to the right in panels A and B), the vector representation and the ideal variations generate the same result, as a practical matter.

Figure 6.2   Relationship Between Attribute Performance and Attribute Quality Under Three Ideal-Point Assumptions

Panel A: Vector Representation

Panel B: Classic Ideal Point

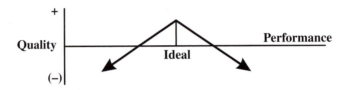

Panel C: Feasible Ideal Point

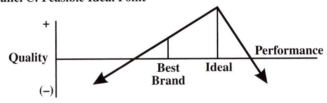

In exchanges with the SERVQUAL authors, other researchers have noted that the $(P - E)$ designation may fail to accurately represent quality when the following three conditions are simultaneously present: (1) the classic ideal point (Figure 6.2, panel B) is in effect, (2) $E = I$, and (3) P exceeds E (and I).[15] This is so because the positive $P - E$ difference under these circumstances is actually reflective of lower quality, not higher quality as SERVQUAL intends. Thus, the ideal level is another critical element of the quality formula and must be considered alongside P and E, giving rise to a three-component definition of quality that may improve on the SERVQUAL formulation when ideal feature levels are relevant to the context of the research. In most consumption situations, when consumers believe the best brand and the ideal are "close" or that the ideal is unattainable, sufficiently realistic results will be obtained. This is an interesting speculation that will require further research before it is resolved.

Are Importances Useful in a Quality Model?

Probably not. In further analyses described in the aforementioned exchange, which included importance-weighted and unweighted versions of the $P - E$ model, a normed quality formula (a variant of the ideal model) and an evaluated performance score that is similar to equation 6.1 in the preceding discussion were tested. It was found that, generally, no weighted version of any quality variant outperformed its unweighted version (in accord with the discussion in Chapter 2). As importances appear not to play a role in quality judgments, the issue at hand is whether one can represent quality as a performance-only or a performance-compared-to-general-ideals judgment. This would distinguish quality from other comparative performance judgments, such as need fulfillment. However, to compare quality to other concepts involved in the consumer's satisfaction response, including satisfaction itself, it is necessary to have valid measures of quality.

MEASURING QUALITY AS AN ENCOUNTER OR GLOBAL CONCEPT

In attempting to separate the concept of quality from others such as satisfaction, one first needs to separate short-term, encounter, or transaction-specific reactions from longer-term, overall, or global judgments deriving from the cumulative experience of many samplings of the concept.[16] As noted in the Introduction, a transaction-specific judgment is rendered during or immediately following a particular service provision or product consumption episode and is based on that experience only. Overall or global judgments are based on reflections or current memories of past experiences as interpreted by a summary judgment. If individuals have no experience with the product or service, then this summary judgment can only be based on external information or vicarious experience.

Quality Measurement at the Encounter Level

The measurement of encounter-specific or short-term quality has already been described with reference to the three response functions in Figure 6.2. The vector model is actually a performance-only model; quality rises or falls as performance rises or falls. Thus, a summation of performance ratings ($\sum P_{ij}$) or an empirically weighted model will provide a good proxy for quality under the vector model assumptions.

Both the ideal-point model ($\sum |P_{ij} - I_i|$) and the SERVQUAL model using expectations of excellence [$\sum (P_{ij} - E_{ij})$] are also quality proxies, if a researcher wishes to account for the influence of quality standards. Researchers should be aware, however, that the expectation of excellence model shares the same mathematical form as the inferred expectancy disconfirmation model (where the researcher infers the consumer's subjective judgment from the P_i and E_i subparts). Thus, use of predictive expectations instead of excellence expectations will most probably tap satisfaction with quality and not quality itself (to be discussed).

At an intermediate level of experience, when multiple samplings of performance have been observed, the $|P_{ij} - I_i|$ and $P_{ij} - I_i$ difference scores can be modified by the probability coefficient pr_{ij}, in equation 6.1. In this way, the consumer can indicate the likelihood of receiving the rated performance level. This will require a separate set of consumer judgments in the satisfaction survey, however, and may add to respondent fatigue. Nonetheless, this is the traditional manner in which uncertainty over outcomes is handled in such models.

Some authors recommend satisfaction scales and better/worse than expected (disconfirmation) scales as proxies for quality measures. This practice is misguided. Unless a researcher is sampling global quality where overall satisfaction and global quality take on similar properties (to be discussed), neither of these scale variants will provide true quality assessment. Use of satisfaction scales or disconfirmation scales at the encounter level will provide estimates of attribute satisfaction and disconfirmation, respectively, and not quality.

Quality Measurement at the Global Level

Less has been done in measuring quality at the global level. Global-level measurement is typically dimension-free. That is, specific quality attributes are not considered, so no one attribute can inordinately influence the consumer's judgment. Two such one-item measures are repeated here, the ubiquitous poor-fair-good-excellent scale and the low/high quality scale:

This product or service is (Circle one number):

	Poor	Fair	Good	Excellent	
	1	2	3	4	
Low quality					High quality
1		2	3	4	5

The first scale has no known metric (the numeric translation of each of its four components is ambiguous despite the fact that the coding format is numeric for arithmetic purposes) and is not recommended. In fact, boxes are preferred. The second scale appears to have a unit metric, but does not, as consumers will assign idiosyncratic meanings to the psychological differences separating the numbers. Nonetheless, use of this latter scale is very common. Another problem with both scales is that neither can be assessed for reliability unless it is readministered to the same sample over time, typically an impractical matter.[17]

Reliable global scales have multiple items so that a statistical reliability coefficient can be calculated. At the minimum, preferably three are required. An example of a six-item quality scale, reported in a paper by this author and shown here, displayed a reliability of 0.90 (the second, fourth, and last items are reverse-scored).[18]

Please rate this product or service on the following scales:

Poor				Excellent
1	2	3	4	5
One of the best				One of the worst
1	2	3	4	5
Inferior				Superior
1	2	3	4	5
Good value				Poor value
1	2	3	4	5
Low standards				High standards
1	2	3	4	5
High quality				Low quality
1	2	3	4	5

Note that the related concept of value is included in the list of items. This strategy implicitly injects a judgment of product or service value into the quality measure; reasons why this might be advisable (or not) are provided in the next chapter. In the context of the study in which this scale was used, however, this was not considered problematic. If a separate measure of value were needed, however, the inclusion of a value term in the list of quality items may not be appropriate if one believes they are truly separate and distinct constructs.

A number of quality scales of various types are used in the literature and can be found in a compilation of marketing scales.[19] All either include specific references to product dimensions or mix other concepts such as trial likelihood and cannot be considered to be true global quality measures. Including a repurchase item, or even a satisfaction item, would cause the scale to be considered a hybrid measure of quality, and the external concept, in much the same way as the scale just reported is a hybrid of quality and value. It should be noted, however, that quality scales are ubiquitous and are developed as new product venues and variations arise. All suffer from the same distraction from overall quality, re-elaborated next.[20]

This section on quality measures points to how little attention is paid to the measurement of overall quality beyond the simple summation of attribute ratings. The two-component measurement of quality that uses performance and ideal or excellence referents is a step in the correct direction at the encounter level. Much further work is needed to assess overall quality through multi-item scales that are attribute- or dimension-*neutral*. As long as attributes or dimensions are present in the measure, whether it is one- (e.g., performance-only) or two-dimensional, global measurement will be compromised by implicit weighting of dimensions by individual consumers.

As noted previously, proper measurement of quality permits investigation of its dependence/independence with other concepts, most notably value and, ultimately, satisfaction. Many practitioners and authors in the popular press assume that these are nearly identical concepts, as their perspective is generally more cumulative (long-term) in nature. Interestingly, data suggests that there may be some validity to this assumption.[21] Similarly, academics are prone to make the same assumption, although at the encounter-specific level. For example, it has been noted that this problem is so prevalent within academia that one may feel justified in referring to both quality and satisfaction as evaluations, thereby obviating the need to draw a distinction between the two.[22] This would be a mistake, indeed.

As noted, others, particularly proponents of the total quality management (TQM) approach, assume that high-quality provision translates directly to consumer satisfaction. As a result, separate measures are considered redundant and, therefore, unnecessary. In contrast, the view taken here is that assumptions regarding similarities between quality and satisfaction require further analysis, as the literature has not fully converged on distinction between them. To provide a perspective on this issue, the following discussion compares quality and satisfaction in greater detail than has been done so far.

QUALITY AND SATISFACTION: SIMILARITIES AND DIFFERENCES

Conceptual Differences

In attempting to distinguish quality from satisfaction, a number of differences have been previously drawn, as shown in Table 6.2.[23] These differences occur at rather fundamental levels pertaining to (1) whether the concept requires experience with the product or service, (2) the dimensions consumers use to form quality versus satisfaction judgments, (3) the nature of the expectations or standards used for these judgments, (4) the degree of cognitive versus affective content, (5) the existence of other conceptual antecedents that might impact each of the concepts, and (6) the primary temporal focus, an issue surrounded by some amount of controversy.

Experience Dependency

Because of an individual's ability to vicariously relate to other people's experience or to mere description of a product or service, quality perceptions do not require exposure to consump-

Table 6.2

Conceptual Differences Between Quality and Satisfaction

Comparison dimension	Quality	Satisfaction
Experience dependency	None required, can be externally or vicariously mediated	Required
Attributes and dimensions	Specific to characteristics defining quality for the product or service (e.g., the "four Cs" of a diamond)	Potentially all attributes or dimensions of the product or service (e.g., the setting of a diamond)
Expectations and standards	Ideals, "excellence"	Predictions, norms, needs, etc.
Cognition or affect	Primarily cognitive	Cognitive and affective
Conceptual antecedents	External cues (e.g., price, reputation, various communication sources)	Conceptual determinants (equity, regret, affect, dissonance, attribution, etc.)
Temporal focus (short-term versus long-term)	Primarily long-term (overall or summary)	Primarily short-term (transaction- or encounter-specific)

tion. Many establishments (e.g., five-star restaurants) are perceived as high quality by consumers who have never visited them. Satisfaction, in contrast, is purely experiential. How can consumers gauge whether they have been fulfilled unless they have experienced this sense of fulfillment?

Attributes and Dimensions

As stated in Table 6.2, the dimensions underlying quality judgments are rather specific, whether they are cues or attributes. For any given product or service, there will be some degree of consensus as to what the relevant quality dimensions are. For example, in grading the quality of diamonds, the defining quality characteristics or "four Cs" are cut, color, clarity, and carat weight. Other cues such as country of origin and vendor may or may not be important (as the movie *Blood Diamond* and the Tiffany brand attest). Similarly, in residential real estate, the three primary cues are "location, location, location." This example, used frequently in the realty industry, is meant to be both subtly humorous and partially true, as most other relevant aspects of housing, including price, style of house, and reputation of the school district, are generally correlated with location.

Satisfaction judgments, in contrast, can result from any dimension, quality-related or not. For example, a quality shopping mall would almost certainly include quality merchandisers, attractive ambience, and a varied set of amenities (e.g., child care, dining establishments). However, (dis) satisfaction could be influenced by congestion on the access roads, rowdy teenagers, and stockouts at individual outlets—none of which are necessarily under the control of the mall's management.

Expectations and Standards

In similar fashion, the standards used for quality judgments are based on ideals or excellence perceptions. In contrast, a large number of nonquality referents, including predictive expectations, needs, product category norms, and even expectations of quality (to be discussed), are used in satisfaction judgments.

Cognition or Affect?

Quality judgments, being largely attribute-based, are thought to be primarily cognitive.[24] Quality would appear to be a hard, performance-based judgment. In fact, researchers use performance ratings as indicators of quality expressions by the consumer. And even when quality is used in an overall fashion as in Ford's "Quality is Job 1," it is assumed that great attention has been paid to design, manufacturing, training, and inspection and that these elements of production and service are the best technically available. Interestingly, new theorizing and data (to be briefly discussed at the end of this chapter) suggest that there may be some affect in a quality judgment, particularly for services; the reasoning and evidence to date, however, lean heavily toward greater cognitive content.

Alternatively, satisfaction is now thought to be both a cognitive and an affective response. Recently, the parallel operation of cognition, e.g., expectancy disconfirmation, and affect, emotion, in the satisfaction response has been demonstrated in a number of settings.[25] The rationale for this parallel operation will be discussed in Chapters 12 and 13, where a model of joint cognitive and affective influences will be presented.

Conceptual Antecedents

Compared to satisfaction, quality has fewer conceptual antecedents, although personal and impersonal communications play a major role. Additionally, many different product cues are used to infer quality by consumers: advertising; brand name; price and its correlates, such as the cost of production and coupon values; guarantees; and a host of factors individually important to the consumer (Chapter 3).[26] In contrast, and as noted, satisfaction is known to be influenced by a number of cognitive and affective processes including equity, attribution, and emotion. Many of these have yet to be covered and will be discussed in the remaining chapters of this book. The consumption-processing model, introduced in Chapter 13, illustrates the complexity of the satisfaction process.

Short-Term or Long-Term Temporal Focus

Three views of the temporal relation between satisfaction and quality exist. All have merit. In the first, satisfaction is a short-term phenomenon, while quality persists over longer durations. For example, it is common for consumers to refer to a satisfying experience at a high-quality establishment. This example demonstrates that, in the parlance of these individuals, quality attaches to a product or service in a global sense whereas satisfaction is experience-specific. Thus, consumers purchase or patronize high-quality providers to experience satisfaction on a one-time and, perhaps, continuing basis. Each occurrence, however, generates a separate satisfaction episode.

Thus, there may exist general perceptions on the part of consumers that a product or service firm has a reputation for high quality (e.g., Lexus automobiles, Disneyworld) or low quality (e.g., municipal governments, third-world airlines, local drinking water in tropical countries). These examples illustrate how quality images are achieved over time and how, once achieved, they tend to persist. As noted, a global quality perception on the part of any one individual requires little, if any, personal experience. However, someone or some organization (such as Consumer's Union or J.D. Power & Associates) must have individually sampled or surveyed quality for these experiences to be compiled and disseminated more broadly.

Alternatively, according to the second view, quality can be sampled on each occurrence ("now *that* was a quality dining experience") and that these accumulate over time to result in long-term satisfaction. For example, consumers might say that they are satisfied with the consistent level of quality offered by a frequently patronized dry cleaner.

In yet a third interpretation, it is possible that quality and satisfaction coexist in both the short and long terms. Thus, consumers may be able to observe quality and be satisfied with quality concurrently in a single consumption episode. The reader may have noted that this scenario will require that consumers have expectations of quality. For now, the requirement that satisfaction have a referent in the short term, such as expectations, will be suspended. In the long term, the two concepts may coexist as overall impressions of quality and as summary states of individual satisfaction episodes. In the latter case, the consumer may proclaim that the aforementioned dry cleaner is very satisfying because its service has always been satisfactory. The long-term description is not a satisfaction response as much as it is a label for the dry cleaner's capacity to satisfy.

These differing viewpoints will vary across specific consumption events, specific market segments, and specific consumers. It will not be possible to provide an overall generalization. However, one study is illustrative of what one might find if this issue were researched in individual settings.[27] In this study, the authors content-analyzed the meanings of encounter satisfaction (denoting a single service episode at an establishment), overall satisfaction (reflecting all encounters with the establishment), and service quality (overall impressions of the superiority or inferiority of the provider). They found that consumers could not distinguish overall satisfaction from quality, but could distinguish both from encounter satisfaction. Moreover, when verbal content analysis was performed on the free-response comments, 95 percent of service encounter comments were event-specific, while the percentage dropped to 49 percent for overall satisfaction and to 40 percent for quality. In contrast, 36 percent of quality comments referred to global impressions, while only 20 percent of the overall satisfaction comments and a "measly" 0.4 percent of encounter satisfaction comments contained global references. Similar but less comprehensive results were found in a study comparing "quality of service" and "quality of experience."[28] While the elements of the two were similar (by design), the service dimension was more global, while the experience, not surprisingly, was more event-specific.

Distinguishing Short-Term and Long-Term Quality and Satisfaction Effects

The stage has been set to speculate on the relations between short-term (encounter) quality and satisfaction and long-term (global) quality and satisfaction. From the results of the preceding studies and other observations made in this chapter, a pattern is beginning to emerge. Specifically, it appears that encounter-specific and global judgments have both quality and satisfaction elements. There is some tendency, however, for encounter satisfaction to reflect encounter-specific quality judgments and for global quality to reflect cumulative satisfaction (see Figure 6.3).

Short- and Long-Term Quality Judgments

As previously discussed, encounter-specific quality judgments are thought to result from a comparison of performance to ideal or excellence standards. Although they are not shown in Figure 6.3, it is likely that these judgments also reflect prior beliefs about product or service quality in the same way that satisfaction is influenced by expectations of satisfaction (see Chapter 3). As these encounter episodes accumulate, they will provide the consumer with an impression of overall (global) quality. Figure 6.3 also shows influences of encounter satisfactions on global quality to suggest the possibility that satisfaction is incorporated into long-term quality judgments if con-

Figure 6.3 **Asymmetrical Reciprocal Influences Between Quality and Satisfaction at the Encounter and Global Levels**

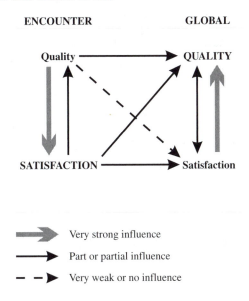

sumption is experienced. If global satisfaction has developed, a strong link to quality is shown. Here, it is assumed that long-term satisfactory individual experience can only enhance or reinforce overall perceptions of quality. Finally, as with short-term quality, not shown in Figure 6.3 are the effects of firm reputation, well-publicized information, and vicarious experience on perceptions of global quality.

Short- and Long-Term Satisfaction Judgments

As noted, customer satisfaction appears primarily (but not exclusively) as an encounter phenomenon. This includes satisfaction with the quality delivered and other forms of satisfaction influences such as equity and regret. In the short run, encounter-specific quality perceptions are one input to satisfaction. Over time, repeated satisfactions (or dissatisfactions) may build up into a more global satisfaction judgment. At this level, satisfaction remains as a personal, experiential judgment, whether encounter-specific or global.

Global satisfaction is conceptually similar to the approach taken in the quality-of-life area where quality of life and satisfaction with life are frequently used synonymously.[29] In this literature, life satisfaction is viewed as the cumulative result of satisfactions in various domains of life, including one's job, marriage, and residence. However, such life domains differ from most product and service experiences in that they are constantly experienced. That is, there are only limited intervals between samplings of performance, as in weekends for most jobs (see the Introduction). As a result, a single experience or encounter means little in the grander scheme of things for these categories, and it is, therefore, only meaningful to ask for a global satisfaction judgment in these instances.

In the product domain, homes, furniture, everyday appliances (e.g., refrigerators), and automobiles that are regularly driven may qualify for measurement at both the encounter-specific and global levels. Numerous other products tend to be consumed once, infrequently, irregularly, or in different use contexts (e.g., formal clothing) and, therefore, may only qualify for measurement at the encounter level. Services follow a similar scenario. Many services, such as pest control, medical care, and auto repair, are one-time, infrequent, or irregular events. Others such as mail delivery, refuse collection, and public utilities qualify for a global approach.

Thus, there appear to be asymmetric reciprocal influences between the quality and satisfaction concepts, as shown in Figure 6.3. At the encounter level, a strong influence from observations of quality to satisfaction with the quality encounter is hypothesized, but only a weaker influence in the reverse direction is shown, to acknowledge the possibility that some consumers will use their satisfaction to infer quality. Both encounter quality and encounter satisfaction judgments, however, act on their overall or global counterparts (in the case of satisfaction, only for products that are sampled sufficiently over time).

At this global level, one would speculate that quality is the more enduring concept, being somewhat akin to attitude and, therefore, also influenced by encounter satisfactions. Global satisfaction, if relevant for the particular product or service category, is hypothesized to be one (strong) influence on global quality, as are the accumulated individual experiences of quality. A reciprocal influence between global quality and global satisfaction is shown to allow for halo quality effects on perceptions of accumulated satisfaction experiences. Finally, a very limited or null diagonal effect is hypothesized from encounter quality to global satisfaction; encounter quality effects should be mostly mediated through encounter satisfaction.

Thus, under the current conceptualization, the two concepts of quality and satisfaction are entwined in an ongoing interplay of reciprocal effects, stronger in one direction than in another. At this point, it would be helpful to review the results of studies testing for directional or reciprocal effects. As the reader will find, however, the data suggest that the global quality relations are somewhat equivocal, suggesting alternative interpretations.

Tests of Frameworks Linking Quality and Satisfaction

Generally, studies testing quality and satisfaction have sought to determine the direction of causality between the two; earlier studies typically assumed that one or the other order dominated without consideration of short-term or long-term effects or reciprocity. In an "appropriate" test of this nature, one study applied structural equation modeling incorporating reciprocal paths between satisfaction and quality (i.e., satisfaction → quality and quality → satisfaction, or quality ↔ satisfaction) across four service industries.[30] Unfortunately, it is not clear whether the satisfaction and quality measures were encounter-specific or global. Of note, however, is the finding that, of the two reciprocal paths, only the quality → satisfaction path was significant. This result held for all industries. Additionally, only satisfaction was related to intention to repatronize. This set of findings is consistent with a quality → satisfaction → intention causal chain often found in the professional literature, suggesting that an encounter, rather than a global, perspective was taken by respondents, as in Figure 6.3.[31]

A similar approach was taken in a study of released hospital patients. Using a test of reciprocal paths identical to that of the previous study, the authors found that only the quality → satisfaction path was significant, in accord with the earlier findings. Moreover, satisfaction was more strongly related to intention to repatronize the hospital, should the need arise. In this study, the quality measures were clearly encounter-specific, as they pertained to elements of the particular stay patients had just completed at the hospital.[32]

Five additional studies have appeared since. All purport to test the temporal priority of quality and satisfaction in different configurations of encounter and global states. All strongly conclude that satisfaction is a function of quality or that satisfaction mediates the effects of quality on later perceptions of either intention or loyalty, in accord with the earlier findings. Details of the methodologies leave questions not easily resolved regarding whether the respondents (not the researchers) took an encounter or global stance. Respectively, the research venues consisted of fast-food outlets, publishing services, health care, chiropractic care, and seafood.[33] Given the varied nature of the studies, the weight of the evidence strongly suggests that satisfaction judgments are quality-based and not the reverse at some level of analysis.

Because the existing evidence points toward the encounter-specific model phase of Figure 6.3 where quality influences satisfaction, it might be instructive to formally propose how encounter judgments of quality are incorporated into encounter judgments of satisfaction. In so doing, the previous observation that not all product or service dimensions are related to quality will be elaborated more fully.

AN "ENCOUNTER QUALITY INFLUENCES SATISFACTION" MODEL

In proposing a "quality influences satisfaction" model, it is necessary to formally endorse the preceding perspective that satisfaction encompasses quality at the encounter-specific level—that quality is one of the key dimensions that are factored into the consumer's satisfaction judgment. This is consistent with at least one industry definition of quality, that of the International Organization for Standardization: "[Quality is the] totality of features and characteristics of a product or service that bear on its ability to satisfy stated and implied needs."[34] Thus, industry seems to agree that, in the short run, product or service features determine quality, which then satisfies consumer needs.

Satisfaction-Specific and Quality-Specific Attributes

Under the assumption that consumers can recognize quality as they have come to define it, they can also form expectations of quality; this premise was developed in Chapter 3. Perceived quality, then, can be compared to quality expectations, resulting in disconfirmations of quality that combine with other attribute or feature disconfirmations to influence satisfaction judgments, as detailed in Chapter 4. These satisfaction judgments, then, are partly due to a satisfaction-with-quality-attributes component and a satisfaction-with-other-attributes component.

One might reasonably question the diverse roles of these different performance dimensions. Do the same dimensions play a role in quality disconfirmations and nonquality disconfirmations? Are there nonquality disconfirmations? Finally, can the same performance dimensions be compared to one level of expectation for quality and yet another for satisfaction? The position taken here is that the answer to all three questions is yes.

The second question is addressed first. Are there nonquality performance dimensions that factor into nonquality disconfirmation? That is, are there dimensions of a product or service that are not part of a quality judgment? Reasoning presented earlier in this chapter (e.g., the four Cs of diamond quality versus nonquality dimensions) and in Chapter 5 would appear to support this possibility. Any dimension that is not critical for functional performance but does have the capacity to cause disagreement among consumers as to its appeal would qualify here. The style (but not the color) of a luxury automobile comes to mind, as does the elegance of chairs in a fashionable restaurant or the shape of the dinner plate in a set of fine china. In professional services provided by physicians, attorneys, and so on, the provider's gender or the building or location of the main office would be other examples. While these elements might be considered tangibles in the other quality frameworks, it should be reiterated that this perspective does not specify which tangibles pertain in any one encounter. Individuals will differ in their interpretation of quality and nonquality dimensions.

Likewise, other dimensions may impact both quality and nonquality judgments. Functional performance is one such example. A waitperson's lack of courtesy would probably influence satisfaction directly through a performance effect and would also decrease quality perceptions, negatively influencing satisfaction indirectly. Similarly, extraordinary service, such as personal sacrifice in an emergency, might have the same effect in a positive direction.

Finally, an argument is presented that quality judgments and satisfaction judgments may result from comparison to different expectations for the same attribute. It has been recognized for some time that expectations for the same feature may have different referents. The weather, outcomes of sporting events, and gift giving are all areas in which consumers might harbor ideals but would hold lower expectations as a practical matter. Moreover, expectation referents can also be based on norms, comparative brands, needs, and desires. Of note are investigations where empirical support was found for the simultaneous operation of ideal and predicted expectations and of desires and expectations, to cite two of many studies.[35]

This suggests the likelihood that, in product and service situations where quality judgments enter, at least two expectation referents may be operating. In accord with the SERVQUAL instrument, discussed in the present chapter and in Chapter 2, ideal or excellence-based expectations may be the reference for expectations of quality, while the more common predictive expectations may operate for direct influences on satisfaction. It now may be clear how consumers can be satisfied with low-quality expectation situations and dissatisfied with high-quality expectations—the two situations that diminish the correlation between quality and satisfaction.

Satisfaction With Low Quality

This situation can exist whenever a consumer's expectations in a given situation are low and performance is adequate to the task. Emergency situations fit this scenario well. It matters little if a mechanic uses duct tape and baling wire to fix a car that has broken down in "the middle of nowhere" if they make the car operational. Other scenarios fall into what this author calls satisfaction-as-relief (Chapter 13). This satisfaction mode is represented by negative reinforcement whereby a consumer is relieved of an aversive state. Over-the-counter medical preparations fit this description. Many have dubious ingredients, but may serve the consumer's goals quite well.

Dissatisfaction With High Quality

Similarly, the opposite situation can arise when some element of the product or service is not up to personal standards (i.e., when a consumer's predictive expectations are higher than those normally used to judge quality). Individual experiences at a five-star restaurant, for example, might be unsatisfactory on a given occasion because of a fluke event—a favorite waitperson is absent or the only available table is next to the food preparation area). The quality judgment, however, remains high despite this unique dissatisfying experience. This example illustrates the case where a nonquality element has decreased satisfaction but has not greatly impacted quality perceptions.

The Model

The framework proposed here, whereby encounter quality is antecedent to encounter satisfaction, is shown in Figure 6.4. This figure is essentially a continuation of Figure 6.1 in that it illustrates

Figure 6.4 **An Encounter-Specific Quality and Satisfaction Model**

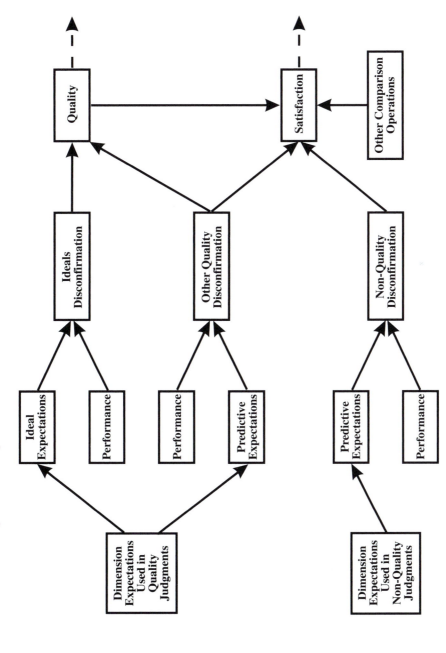

Source: Adapted from Richard L. Oliver, "A Conceptual Model of Service Quality and Service Satisfaction: Compatible Goals, Different Concepts," in *Advances in Services Marketing and Management,* vol. 2, ed. Teresa A. Swartz, David E. Bowen, and Stephen W. Brown (Greenwich, CT: JAI Press, 1993), 80, by permission of Elsevier.

the consumer's processing of the product or service provided by the firm. Also shown in the model are potential links to future global perceptions of quality and satisfaction. These links are meant to imply that each encounter experience reinforces (or serves to extinguish) previous encounter perceptions.[36]

The model details three categories of attributes: those that are unique to quality judgments (as framed by ideal expectations), those that may play dual roles as quality dimensions and satisfaction-with-quality dimensions (framed by predictive—not ideal—quality expectations), and those that are largely nonquality dimensions (framed by predictive nonquality expectations). Note that ideals are general standards that would pertain to all brands in a category, while predictive expectations are specific to a product or service provider and thus may be processed differently. Each of these expectation categories is potentially disconfirmed by the respective performance levels, resulting in three categories of disconfirmation. Ideals disconfirmation is shown to impact encounter quality directly, while predictive nonquality dimensions impact encounter satisfaction only.

Quality dimension disconfirmations, in contrast, may influence both quality and satisfaction. The link between quality disconfirmation and quality represents idiosyncratic quality influences not framed by ideal expectations. For example, an individual consumer might have a preference for a Tiffany diamond, despite the fact that a diamond purchased from other quality dealers may be identical in most respects to one in a Tiffany & Co. showroom. To this consumer, however, a non-Tiffany diamond lowers the quality judgment even though this diamond may be ideal in all other respects.

The second quality disconfirmation link to satisfaction represents satisfaction with quality. It is highly likely that this link, particularly when interpreted subjectively (not shown), is inherent in the meaning of a SERVQUAL score. This potential dual role of some product or service quality dimensions may account for the high correlations between quality and satisfaction judgments frequently found in the literature.

Last, a direct link between quality and satisfaction is hypothesized. This reflects the possibility of "raw quality" influences in the quality-satisfaction model. Also displayed are the influences of other comparative referents on satisfaction discussed in this section of the book. As shown in the figure, the model awaits testing.

The present discussion has not elaborated on detailed mechanisms of the global quality and satisfaction variables. The encounter-specific model is itself speculative, and forthcoming data would be instructive as to what form these mechanisms should take. In the next section of this chapter, a new dimension of quality, affective quality, is introduced. The previous discussion has assumed that only cognitive judgments (i.e., performance comparison ratings) were instrumental in defining quality for the consumer. Here, that assumption will be briefly relaxed.

Affective Quality: New Directions for Services

Researchers have explored the notion of affective quality, defined as the emotional content of a product and/or service experience. Based on earlier work in environmental psychology and retail personality and store image, writers have hypothesized that affect (see Chapter 12) would augment the prediction of quality above that obtained by using only cognitive measures.[37] Other researchers were able to demonstrate meaningful correlations between affective and cognitive measures and measures of overall quality, even including single-dimension surrogates such as affective reactions to waiting time.[38] This latter dimension of product or service quality, which appears in the literature from time to time, has shown promise and awaits further research. Current definitions of quality could conceivably be enriched, and purchase predictions based on quality may be enhanced, as affective quality components are incorporated within quality studies.

CONCLUSION

Despite the confusion existing between the conceptual boundaries of quality and satisfaction, these concepts have been shown to be distinct. They differ on a number of dimensions, most notably on experience-dependency and on the dominant temporal (short-term or long-term) referent. Generally, satisfaction is an immediate response to consumption, while quality exists prior to as well as subsequent to consumption as an enduring signal of product or service excellence.

The relationship between quality and satisfaction is complex due to the intricate interplay between performance dimensions used in quality judgments and those used in satisfaction judgments, and due to the differences between encounter-specific and global judgments. Based on both theory and data, performance-based quality has been framed as resulting from ideal expectations and from other idiosyncratic preferences of individual consumers. Similarly, satisfaction has been shown to respond to quality disconfirmation and to other performance dimension disconfirmations not related to quality.

In the next chapter, still another of the comparative operators that are known to influence satisfaction—*value*—is introduced. Like quality, the value mechanism is complex and shares many of the intricacies of quality as an antecedent of satisfaction. In fact, these concepts share many idiosyncrasies, and at times the distinction between the two will be obscure (and obscured).

NOTES

1. In order, these slogans are from Ford, Levi's, Zenith, Kent, and Motorola.
2. Griffin and Hauser, "Voice of the Customer"; Hauser and Clausing, "House of Quality"; Nagendra and Osborne, "Professional Services Marketing."
3. See, e.g., Balasubramanian, Mathur, and Thakur, "Impact of High-Quality Firm Achievements on Shareholder Value"; Ferguson, "Impact of the ISO 9000 Series Standards on Industrial Marketing"; Heller, "Superior Stock Market Performance of a TQM Portfolio"; Hendricks and Singhal, "Does Implementing an Effective TQM Program Actually Improve Operating Performance?"; Przasnyski and Tai, "Stock Market Reaction to Malcolm Baldrige National Quality Award Announcements." The evidence for stock market returns to satisfaction is much more positively robust; see Chapter 15.
4. Garvin, "What Does 'Product Quality' Really Mean?"; Steenkamp, "Conceptual Model of the Quality Perception Process."
5. See, e.g., Kordupleski, Rust, and Zahorik, "Why Improving Quality Doesn't Improve Quality"; Denove and Power, *Satisfaction.*
6. Ozment and Morash, "Augmented Service Offering for Perceived and Actual Service Quality."
7. Gummesson, "Quality Dimensions"; Mick and Fournier, "Paradoxes of Technology."
8. Mazumdar, Raj, and Sinha, "Reference Price Research"; Rao and Monroe, "Causes and Consequences of Price Premiums."
9. Steenkamp, *Product Quality.*
10. The word *fair* is particularly problematic in this regard. *Fair* can mean "better than poor, but less than good" to some respondents, and "good" or "excellent," as in fair or equitable treatment (Chapter 9), to others. See Devlin, Dong, and Brown, "Selecting a Scale for Measuring Quality."
11. Guaspari, *I Know It When I See It*; Holbrook and Corfman, "Quality and Value in the Consumption Experience"; Pirsig, *Zen and the Art of Motorcycle Maintenance.*
12. The terms are from various definitions in Garvin, "What Does 'Product Quality' Really Mean?"; Reeves and Bednar, "Defining Quality"; Steenkamp, "Conceptual Model of the Quality Perception Process"; and Zeithaml, "Consumer Perceptions of Price, Quality, and Value."
13. For interesting variations, see Johnson and Folkes, "How Consumers' Assessments of the Difficulty of Manufacturing a Product Influence Quality Perceptions"; and Sweeney and Lapp, "Critical Service Quality Encounters on the Web."
14. Zeithaml, Parasuraman, and Berry, *Delivering Quality Service*, p. 180. See also Parasuraman, Berry, and Zeithaml, "Refinement and Reassessment of the SERVQUAL Scale."

15. Teas, "Expectations, Performance Evaluation, and Consumers' Perceptions of Quality" and "Expectations as a Comparison Standard in Measuring Service Quality"; Parasuraman, Zeithaml, and Berry, "Reassessment of Expectations as a Comparison Standard in Measuring Service Quality."

16. See, e.g., Bitner and Hubbert, "Encounter Satisfaction versus Overall Satisfaction versus Quality"; Dabholkar, "Customer Satisfaction and Service Quality"; and Teas, "Expectations as a Comparison Standard in Measuring Service Quality," in which he refers to long-term quality as relationship quality in the context of services.

17. The pros and cons of single versus multiple item scales in general use (not necessarily quality) are discussed in Bergkvist and Rossiter, "Predictive Validity of Multiple-Item Versus Single-Item Measures of the Same Constructs." Readers must judge on an independent basis whether one item will provide the needed information. This author's preference is for multiple-item scales.

18. Oliver, "Conceptual Issues in the Structural Analysis of Consumption Emotion, Satisfaction, and Quality."

19. Bruner and Hensel, *Marketing Scales Handbook.*

20. See, e.g., Dagger, Sweeney, and Johnston, "Hierarchical Model of Health Service Quality"; and Parasuraman, Zeithaml, and Malhotra, "E-S-QUAL."

21. Dabholkar, "Convergence of Customer Satisfaction and Service Quality Evaluations with Increasing Customer Patronage."

22. Iacobucci, Grayson, and Ostrom, "Calculus of Service Quality and Customer Satisfaction."

23. This section and the model to follow are adapted and expanded from Oliver, "Conceptual Model of Service Quality and Service Satisfaction."

24. See Dabholkar, "Customer Satisfaction and Service Quality"; Iacobucci, Grayson, and Ostrom, "Calculus of Service Quality and Customer Satisfaction"; and Zeithaml, "Consumer Perceptions of Price, Quality, and Value."

25. Compeau, Grewal, and Monroe, "Role of Prior Affect and Sensory Cues on Consumers' Affective and Cognitive Responses and Overall Perceptions of Quality"; Mano and Oliver, "Assessing the Dimensionality and Structure of Consumption Experience"; Oliver, "Cognitive, Affective, and Attribute Bases of the Satisfaction Response" and "Conceptual Issues in the Structural Analysis of Consumption Emotion, Satisfaction, and Quality."

26. Excluding price as a direct signal, see, variously, Brucks, Zeithaml, and Naylor, "Price and Brand Name as Indicators of Quality Dimensions for Consumer Durables"; Chang and Wildt, "Impact of Product Information on the Use of Price as a Quality Cue"; Johnson and Folkes, "How Consumers' Assessments of the Difficulty of Manufacturing a Product Influence Quality Perceptions"; Moorthy and Srinivasan, "Signaling Quality with a Money-Back Guarantee"; Parker, "'Sweet Lemons'"; and Raghubir, "Coupon Value."

27. Bitner and Hubbert, "Encounter Satisfaction versus Overall Satisfaction versus Quality."

28. Otto and Ritchie, "Exploring the Quality of the Service Experience."

29. See, e.g., Lance, Mallard, and Michalos, "Tests of the Causal Directions of Global-Life Facet Satisfaction Relationships."

30. Cronin and Taylor, "Measuring Service Quality."

31. See, e.g., Heskett et al., "Putting the Service-Profit Chain to Work."

32. Gotlieb, Grewal, and Brown, "Consumer Satisfaction and Perceived Quality."

33. Brady and Robertson, "Searching For a Consensus on the Antecedent Role of Service Quality and Satisfaction"; Dabholkar, Shepherd, and Thorpe, "Comprehensive Framework for Service Quality"; Dagger, Sweeney, and Johnston, "Hierarchical Model of Health Service Quality"; de Ruyter, Bloemer, and Peeters, "Merging Service Quality and Service Satisfaction"; Olsen, "Comparative Evaluation and the Relationship Between Quality, Satisfaction, and Repurchase Loyalty."

34. Cited in Gummesson, "Quality Dimensions," p. 181.

35. Spreng, MacKenzie, and Olshavsky, "Reexamination of the Determinants of Consumer Satisfaction"; Tse and Wilton, "Models of Consumer Satisfaction Formation."

36. A complementary framework can be found in Silverman and Grover, "Forming Perceptions of Overall Quality in Consumer Goods," where quality and nonquality elements are separated into variations of the rings model (see Chapter 2).

37. Donovan and Rossiter, "Store Atmosphere"; Russell and Pratt, "Description of the Affective Quality Attributed to Environments"; Zimmer and Golden, "Impressions of Retail Stores."

38. Compeau, Grewal, and Monroe, "Role of Prior Affect and Sensory Cues on Consumers' Affective and Cognitive Responses and Overall Perceptions of Quality"; Dabholkar, "Consumer Evaluations of New

Technology-Based Self-Service Options"; Darden and Babin, "Exploring the Concept of Affective Quality"; Zhang and Li, "The Importance of Affective Quality."

BIBLIOGRAPHY

Balasubramanian, Siva K., Ike Mathur, and Ramendra Thakur. "The Impact of High-Quality Firm Achievements on Shareholder Value: Focus on Malcolm Baldrige and J.D. Power and Associates Awards." *Journal of the Academy of Marketing Science* 33, no. 4 (Fall 2005): 413–422.

Bergkvist, Lars, and John R. Rossiter. "The Predictive Validity of Multiple-Item Versus Single-Item Measures of the Same Constructs." *Journal of Marketing Research* 44 (May 2007): 175–184.

Bitner, Mary Jo, and Amy R. Hubbert. "Encounter Satisfaction versus Overall Satisfaction versus Quality: The Customer's Voice." In *Service Quality: New Directions in Theory and Practice*, ed. Roland T. Rust and Richard L. Oliver, 72–94. Thousand Oaks, CA: Sage, 1994.

Brady, Michael K., and Christopher J. Robertson. "Searching For a Consensus on the Antecedent Role of Service Quality and Satisfaction: An Exploratory Cross-National Study." *Journal of Business Research* 51, no. 1 (January 2001): 53–60.

Brucks, Merrie, Valarie A. Zeithaml, and Gillian Naylor. "Price and Brand Name as Indicators of Quality Dimensions for Consumer Durables." *Journal of the Academy of Marketing Science* 28, no. 3 (Summer 2000): 359–374.

Bruner, Gordon C., II, and Paul J. Hensel. *Marketing Scales Handbook: A Compilation of Multi-Item Measures*, vol. 2. Chicago: American Marketing Association, 1996.

Chang, Tung-Zong, and Albert R. Wildt. "Impact of Product Information on the Use of Price as a Quality Cue." *Psychology & Marketing* 13, no. 1 (January 1996): 55–75.

Compeau, Larry D., Dhruv Grewal, and Kent B. Monroe. "Role of Prior Affect and Sensory Cues on Consumers' Affective and Cognitive Responses and Overall Perceptions of Quality." *Journal of Business Research* 42, no. 3 (July 1998): 295–308.

Cronin, J. Joseph, Jr., and Steven A. Taylor. "Measuring Service Quality: A Reexamination and Extension." *Journal of Marketing* 56, no. 3 (July 1992): 55–68.

Dabholkar, Pratibha A. "Consumer Evaluations of New Technology-Based Self-Service Options: An Investigation of Alternative Models of Service Quality."*International Journal of Research in Marketing* 13, no. 1 (February 1996): 29–51.

———. "The Convergence of Customer Satisfaction and Service Quality Evaluations with Increasing Customer Patronage." *Journal of Consumer Satisfaction, Dissatisfaction and Complaining Behavior* 8 (1995): 32–43.

———. "Customer Satisfaction and Service Quality: Two Constructs or One?" In *Enhancing Knowledge Development in Marketing*, ed. David W. Cravens and Peter R. Dickson, 4:10–18. Chicago: American Marketing Association, 1993.

Dabholkar, Pratibha A., C. David Shepherd, and Dayle I. Thorpe. "A Comprehensive Framework for Service Quality: An Investigation of Critical Conceptual and Measurement Issues Through a Longitudinal Study." *Journal of Retailing* 76, no. 2 (Summer 2000): 139–173.

Dagger Tracey S., Jillian C. Sweeney, and Lester W. Johnston. "A Hierarchical Model of Health Service Quality: Scale Development and Investigation of an Integrated Model." *Journal of Service Research* 10, no. 2 (November 2007): 123–142.

Darden, William R., and Barry J. Babin. "Exploring the Concept of Affective Quality: Expanding the Concept of Retail Personality." *Journal of Business Research* 29, no. 2 (February 1994): 101–109.

Denove, Chris, and James D. Power IV. *Satisfaction: How Every Great Company Listens to the Voice of the Customer.* New York: Portfolio, 2006.

de Ruyter, Ko, José Bloemer, and Pascal Peeters. "Merging Service Quality and Service Satisfaction: An Empirical Test of an Integrative Model." *Journal of Economic Psychology* 18, no. 4 (June 1997): 387–406.

Devlin, Susan J., H.K. Dong, and Marbue Brown. "Selecting a Scale for Measuring Quality." *Marketing Research* 15, no. 3 (Fall 2003): 13–16.

Donovan, Robert J., and John R. Rossiter. "Store Atmosphere: An Environmental Psychology Approach." *Journal of Retailing* 58, no. 1 (Spring 1982): 34–57.

Ferguson, Wade. "Impact of the ISO 9000 Series Standards on Industrial Marketing." *Industrial Marketing Management* 25, no. 4 (July 1996): 305–310.

Garvin, David A. "What Does 'Product Quality' Really Mean?" *Sloan Management Review* 26, no. 1 (Fall 1984): 25–43.

Gotlieb, Jerry B., Dhruv Grewal, and Stephen W. Brown. "Consumer Satisfaction and Perceived Quality: Complementary or Divergent Constructs?" *Journal of Applied Psychology* 79, no. 6 (December 1994): 875–885.

Griffin, Abbie, and John R. Hauser. "The Voice of the Customer." *Marketing Science* 12, no. 1 (Winter 1993): 1–27.

Guaspari, John. *I Know It When I See It: A Modern Fable about Quality.* New York: AMACON, 1985.

Gummesson, Evert. "Quality Dimensions: What to Measure in Service Organizations." In *Advances in Services Marketing and Management: Research and Practice*, ed. Teresa A. Swartz, David E. Bowen, and Stephen W. Brown, 1:177–205. Greenwich, CT: JAI Press, 1992.

Hauser, John R., and Don Clausing. "The House of Quality." *Harvard Business Review* 66, no. 3 (May–June 1988): 63–73.

Heller, Thomas. "The Superior Stock Market Performance of a TQM Portfolio." *Center for Quality of Management Journal* 3, no. 1 (Winter 1994): 23–32.

Hendricks, Kevin B., and Vinod R. Singhal. "Does Implementing an Effective TQM Program Actually Improve Operating Performance? Empirical Evidence from Firms That Have Won Quality Awards." *Management Science* 43, no. 9 (September 1997): 1258–1274.

Heskett, James L., Thomas O. Jones, Gary W. Loveman, W. Earl Sasser Jr., and Leonard A. Schlesinger. "Putting the Service-Profit Chain to Work." *Harvard Business Review* 72, no. 2 (March–April 1994): 164–174.

Holbrook, Morris B., and Kim P. Corfman. "Quality and Value in the Consumption Experience: Phaedrus Rides Again." In *Perceived Quality: How Consumers View Stores and Merchandise,* ed. Jacob Jacoby and Jerry C. Olson, 31–57. Lexington, MA: Lexington Books/D.C. Heath, 1985.

Iacobucci, Dawn, Kent A. Grayson, and Amy L. Ostrom. "The Calculus of Service Quality and Customer Satisfaction: Theoretical and Empirical Differentiation and Integration." In *Advances in Services Marketing and Management: Research and Practice*, ed. Teresa A. Swartz, David E. Bowen, and Stephen W. Brown, 3:1–67. Greenwich, CT: JAI Press, 1994.

Johnson, Allison R., and Valerie S. Folkes. "How Consumers' Assessments of the Difficulty of Manufacturing a Product Influence Quality Perceptions." *Journal of the Academy of Marketing Science* 35, no. 3 (September 2007): 317–328.

Kordupleski, Raymond E., Roland T. Rust, and Anthony J. Zahorik. "Why Improving Quality Doesn't Improve Quality (or Whatever Happened to Marketing?)." *California Management Review* 35, no. 3 (Spring 1993): 82–95.

Lance, Charles E., Alison G. Mallard, and Alex C. Michalos. "Tests of the Causal Directions of Global-Life Facet Satisfaction Relationships." *Social Indicators Research* 34, no. 1 (January 1995): 69–92.

Mano, Haim, and Richard L. Oliver. "Assessing the Dimensionality and Structure of Consumption Experience: Evaluation, Feeling, and Satisfaction." *Journal of Consumer Research* 20 (December 1993): 451–466.

Mazumdar, Tridib, S.P. Raj, and Indrajit Sinha. "Reference Price Research: Review and Propositions." *Journal of Marketing* 69, no. 4 (October 2005): 84–102.

Mick, David Glen, and Susan Fournier. "Paradoxes of Technology: Consumer Cognizance, Emotions, and Coping Strategies. *Journal of Consumer Research* 25, no. 2 (September 1998): 123–143.

Moorthy, Sridhar, and Kannan Srinivasan. "Signaling Quality with a Money-Back Guarantee: The Role of Transaction Costs." *Marketing Science* 14, no. 4 (1995): 442–466.

Nagendra, Prashanth B., and Stephen W. Osborne. "Professional Services Marketing: A House of Quality Approach." *Journal of Professional Services Marketing* 21, no. 1 (2000): 23–43.

Oliver, Richard L. "Cognitive, Affective, and Attribute Bases of the Satisfaction Response." *Journal of Consumer Research* 20, (December 1993): 418–430.

———. "Conceptual Issues in the Structural Analysis of Consumption Emotion, Satisfaction, and Quality: Evidence in a Service Setting." In *Advances in Consumer Research*, ed. Chris T. Allen and Deborah Roedder John, 21:16–22. Provo, UT: Association for Consumer Research, 1994.

———. "A Conceptual Model of Service Quality and Service Satisfaction: Compatible Goals, Different Concepts." In *Advances in Services Marketing and Management: Research and Practice*, ed. Teresa A. Swartz, David E. Bowen, and Stephen W. Brown, 2:65–85. Greenwich, CT: JAI Press, 1993.

Olsen, Svein Ottar. "Comparative Evaluation and the Relationship Between Quality, Satisfaction, and Repurchase Loyalty." *Journal of Academy of Marketing Science* 30, no. 3 (Summer 2002): 240–249.

Otto, Julie E., and J.R. Brent Ritchie. "Exploring the Quality of the Service Experience: A Theoretical and Empirical Analysis." In *Advances in Services Marketing and Management*, ed. Teresa A. Swartz, David E. Bowen, and Stephen W. Brown, 4:37–61. Greenwich, CT: JAI Press, 1995.

Ozment, John, and Edward A. Morash. "The Augmented Service Offering for Perceived and Actual Service Quality." *Journal of the Academy of Marketing Science* 22, no. 4 (Fall 1994): 352–363.

Parasuraman, A., Leonard L. Berry, and Valarie A. Zeithaml. "Refinement and Reassessment of the SERVQUAL Scale." *Journal of Retailing* 67, no. 4 (Winter 1991): 420–450.

Parasuraman, A., Valarie A. Zeithaml, and Leonard L. Berry. "Reassessment of Expectations as a Comparison Standard in Measuring Service Quality: Implications for Further Research." *Journal of Marketing* 58, no. 1 (January 1994): 111–124.

Parasuraman, A., Valarie A. Zeithaml, and Arvind Malhotra. "E-S-QUAL: A Multiple-Item Scale for Assessing Electronic Service Quality." *Journal of Service Research* 7, no. 3 (February 2005): 213–233.

Parker, Philip M. "'Sweet Lemons': Illusory Quality, Self-Deceivers, Advertising, and Price." *Journal of Marketing Research* 32, no. 3 (August 1995): 291–307.

Pirsig, Robert M. *Zen and the Art of Motorcycle Maintenance: An Inquiry Into Values.* New York: Bantam Books, 1974.

Przasnyski, Zbigniew H., and Lawrence S. Tai. "Stock Market Reaction to Malcolm Baldrige National Quality Award Announcements: Does Quality Pay?" *Total Quality Management* 10, no. 3 (May 1999): 391–400.

Raghubir, Priya. "Coupon Value: A Signal for Price?" *Journal of Marketing Research* 35, no. 3 (August 1998): 316–324.

Rao, Akshay R., and Kent B. Monroe. "Causes and Consequences of Price Premiums." *Journal of Business* 69, no. 4 (October 1996): 511–535.

Reeves, Carol A., and David A. Bednar. "Defining Quality: Alternatives and Implications." *Academy of Management Review* 19, no. 3 (July 1994): 419–445.

Russell, James A., and Geraldine Pratt. "A Description of the Affective Quality Attributed to Environments." *Journal of Personality and Social Psychology* 38, no. 2 (February 1980): 311–322.

Silverman, Steven N., and Rajiv Grover. "Forming Perceptions of Overall Quality in Consumer Goods: A Process of Quality Element Integration." In *Research in Marketing*, ed. Jagdish N. Sheth and Atul Parvatiyar, 12:251–87. Greenwich, CT: JAI Press, 1995.

Spreng, Richard A., Scott B. MacKenzie, and Richard W. Olshavsky. "A Reexamination of the Determinants of Consumer Satisfaction." *Journal of Marketing* 60, no. 3 (July 1996): 15–32.

Steenkamp, Jan-Benedict E.M. "Conceptual Model of the Quality Perception Process." *Journal of Business Research* 21, no. 4 (December 1990): 309–333.

———. *Product Quality: An Investigation into the Concept and How It Is Perceived by Consumers.* Assen, Netherlands: Van Gorcum, 1989.

Sweeney, Jillian C., and Wade Lapp. "Critical Service Quality Encounters on the Web: An Exploratory Study." *Journal of Services Marketing* 18, no. 4 (2004): 276–289.

Teas, R. Kenneth. "Expectations as a Comparison Standard in Measuring Service Quality: An Assessment of a Reassessment." *Journal of Marketing* 58, no. 1 (January 1994): 132–139.

———. "Expectations, Performance Evaluation, and Consumers' Perceptions of Quality." *Journal of Marketing* 57, no. 4 (October 1993): 18–34.

Tse, David K., and Peter C. Wilton. "Models of Consumer Satisfaction Formation: An Extension." *Journal of Marketing Research* 25, no. 2 (May 1988): 204–212.

Zeithaml, Valarie A. "Consumer Perceptions of Price, Quality, and Value: A Means-End Model and Synthesis of Evidence." *Journal of Marketing* 52, no. 3 (July 1988): 2–22.

Zeithaml, Valarie A., A. Parasuraman, and Leonard L. Berry. *Delivering Quality Service: Balancing Customer Perceptions and Expectations.* New York: Free Press, 1990.

Zhang, Ping, and Na Li. "The Importance of Affective Quality." *Communications of the ACM* 48, no. 9 (September 2005): 105–108.

Zimmer, Mary R., and Linda L. Golden. "Impressions of Retail Stores: A Content Analysis of Consumer Images." *Journal of Retailing* 64, no. 3 (Fall 1988): 265–293.

CHAPTER 7

THE MANY VARIETIES OF VALUE IN THE CONSUMPTION EXPERIENCE

From the earliest eras of trade and commerce, buyers have been plied with exhortations of "great value" or the qualified "great value for the money." It does not matter what superlative adjectives precede the word *value*, nor does it matter if the qualifier is present in the phrase. Value means exactly what it implies . . . or does it? Just what is value in exchange and how does it relate to satisfaction?[1] The answer first appears obvious and then, upon reflection, becomes vaporous. In fact, promises of generic value have no legal meaning. Sellers are not required to deliver on value claims, which explains why such promises are so common.

The provision of value to consumers by marketers is implicit in the exchange contract. Yet *value* is a term fraught with so many interpretations that it is a wonder when consumers and marketers agree that such a contract exists. On the encouraging side, certain regularities will be found to appear, nonetheless. This is so because *value* as a generic term has taken on particular meanings in its many and varied uses. One purpose of this chapter is to take the reader through the many variants of value that imply a satisfactory provision to the consumer. A second purpose is to contrast and compare the concept of value with the two related concepts of quality and satisfaction.

Readers of the first edition will note that this is a new chapter. It is an outgrowth of a monograph requested by the editor of a collection of readings on value who asked that the topic of value-as-excellence be addressed.[2] This posed something of a conundrum for this author as I had already framed excellence in the context of quality. The real question, however, was whether the topic of value should be integrated with the quality chapter or introduced separately. After further study into value, it became clear that the topics were best discussed separately. The reader will be the ultimate judge of the appropriateness of this choice.

AXIOLOGY: THE STUDY OF VALUES

The study of values is referred to as axiology, which includes the study of value, values, valuing, valuation, evaluation, types of value(s), and systems of value(s). Fortunately or unfortunately, value is intertwined with (confused with?) other concepts of similar ilk, including utility, universal human values, public values (commonly accepted public policy), cultural truisms (beliefs that are widely shared and rarely questioned), hedonic experience, quality of life, and, as used in marketing, the List of Values (LOV).[3]

The task here is to define these judgments in the consumable and durable goods markets and the service market. The reader will recognize that judgments of this nature are pertinent to the hierarchies discussed in Chapter 2 in the context of means-end chains, where consumers are probed for the value-meanings of consumption, and in Chapter 5, where Maslow's need hierarchy was discussed.[4] It would now be of "value" to attempt to pin down the value-related issues that are more aligned with consumption outcome satisfaction, including the interplay with quality discussed in the preceding chapter.

This effort was addressed in the aforementioned collection of articles wherein likely consumer interpretations of value were categorized into an eight-cell scheme along three dimensions, based on prior work by the editor of the volume.[5] This framework, called the Typology of Consumer Value, was based on whether the value dimension was self- or other-oriented, active or reactive, and intrinsic or extrinsic. Two subsets of the eight cells are explained in greater detail next.

Self-Oriented Values

Active self-oriented values of an intrinsic nature were labeled as *play*. The prominent value experienced is fun or pleasurable self-satisfaction.[6] In contrast, reactive self-oriented values are defined by *aesthetics*. Here one enjoys the sense of beauty transmitted by external agents. The value received involves admiration of the artistic mastery conveyed by the object, performance, imagery, and so on.

In contrast, extrinsic forms of self-oriented value include *efficiency* and *excellence*. Efficiency, the active form of this value, includes pursuits that maximize outcomes (O) while minimizing inputs (I), an O/I calculation of sorts. Convenience is one prototype of this value as the act of acquisition may be obtained with minimal effort on the part of the consumer. The reactive form of excellence includes quality, as noted, whereby the same consumer responds to the outside provision of what is interpreted as excellence in design, construction, provision, and so on. This differs from the intrinsic value of aesthetics as, presumably, the same quality would be observed by others, whereas aesthetics are individually interpreted.

Other-Oriented Values

The remaining four value forms require that other individuals or beings provide the essence of the value inherent in the respective value-state. Beginning as before with the intrinsic categories, the active form of this value is labeled *ethics*. Here, one's behaviors, and the value received from them, require approval from a collective. Listed under this category are virtue, justice, and morality. Each of these systems is human-made in that the legal system, for example, can vary across collectives, as can definitions of morality and what is thought to be virtue.

The second of the other-oriented intrinsic values is *spirituality*. Here the external "observer" is a deity or a mystical icon or, curiously, even hallucinogenics. Prototypes of this value are faith, sacredness, magic, and ecstasy, the latter perhaps best interpreted as a state of mind. The last category of other-oriented extrinsic values is more straightforward. The active category is *status*, meaning that the prestige of accomplishment or success is ever-present in the mind of the beholder, while its reactive counterpart is *esteem*. Esteem requires the expressed admiration of others in the form of reputation or reactions to other symbols of position.

This discussion outlines the value typology as proposed in the eight-cell matrix. The matrix, which is difficult to refute in terms of its comprehensiveness, is useful as a guide for future study. As far as is known, there is no test of this framework; devising such a test would be a worthy undertaking to be sure. Attention now turns to more commonplace forms of value in consumption, some historical and some less so. Then the conundrum of valuing value will be addressed, followed by practical issues.

RENDITIONS OF VALUE AS PRE- AND POSTCONSUMPTION EVENTS

As with many of the anticipated concepts within consumption, value judgments of whatever nature may occur in two time frames. Value can be assessed or predicted prior to purchase and/or usage or after. For a single consumer, the same criteria may be used in both periods or the criteria may differ, since consumption itself can be a form of discovery, similar to the relevant attributes used in choice versus postpurchase evaluation discussed in Chapter 2.

Like satisfaction, value is a human comparator response. Individuals cannot know if some thing or event provides value unless a standard of valuation is available. Thus, consumption events provide value to the extent that they are judged as such, displaying value's tautological nature. This allows value to take on either a cognitive, affective, or combined definition. Unlike hard valuations that might exist in the financial equity markets, for example, value can exist without a cognitive component. That is not to say that value cannot be cognitively assessed, for it surely can be, but it suggests that cognition is not necessary for a judgment of value to come into being. Later, the issue of how consumption affect (e.g., delight, thrill) can be judged for its value will be entertained. For now, it is convenient to say that consumers are capable of doing so.

In a comprehensive thesis on how value takes on meaning in a consumer context, apart from its place in goal hierarchies, a perspective on value as couched in a web of consumption concepts is proposed.[7] In this exploratory work, four *themes* underlie the meaning of value as derived from consumers' experiences: (1) low price, (2) getting what is wanted, (3) quality compared to price, and (4) what is received for what is sacrificed.

Based on further analysis in this noteworthy article, value is modeled as a function of five *factors*. Specifically, value is hypothesized to be *positively* related to: (1) quality, (2) other extrinsic attributes such as functionality, (3) intrinsic attributes such as pleasure, and (4) "high-level abstractions" including personal values. Note the correspondence here with the eight-cell typology discussed previously. Additionally, value is posited to be a *negative* function of the fifth factor, (5) perceived sacrifice, defined in terms of both monetary outlays and nonmonetary costs such as time and effort. Based on these propositions, value appears to be a positive function of what is received and a negative function of what is sacrificed. This results in a value "equation," as follows:

$$Value = f\ (Receipts\,/\,Sacrifices) \qquad (7.1)$$

Merging this framework with that of the typology, it becomes evident that two overarching themes may describe how consumers perceive value in consumption. One addresses single-stimulus concepts, while the second considers two, such as the receipts/sacrifices term. The correspondence to quality in the preceding chapter is direct. Single-stimulus concepts require only one, perhaps integrated, megaperception and tend to be holistic. Two- or multiple-stimuli concepts ask the consumer to consider the components in a juxtaposed or comparative manner. A recent review is available that covers the field via a compilation of the literature. Both single and multiple perspectives are covered from a more mechanical approach inclining toward the industrial market and differing from that taken here, although overlap is inevitable.[8] These perspectives are elaborated next.

SINGLE-STIMULUS DEFINITIONS OF VALUE IN CONSUMPTION

Perhaps the easiest rendition of value in lay terms is the singular notion of *worth*. Price and quality, taken separately, would fit this category. Often, this is referred to as a "utility" definition, where the term *utility* is frequently used as a summary concept that permits discussion of consumer goals without the necessity of greater formal specification. Moreover, although utility is frequently represented in axiomatic terms, there exists no semantic definition of utility receiving widespread acceptance. For example, writings variously describe utility as usefulness, hedonic quality, "pleasure," and even satisfaction. While this fluid definition may prove to be satisfactory for the purposes addressed here, a group of authors have recently speculated as to why utility becomes problematic when used to describe consumer outcomes in the postchoice consumption period.[9]

Such single-stimulus definitions provide unambiguous evaluations of value and many utility investigators rely on their use. In fact, researchers have tested many measurement variations of value in the context of public goods and services. They conclude that consumers use the term pervasively, that its meaning is consistent, although vague, regardless of how it is measured, and that the closest semantic term to describe value is "worthwhileness." Moreover, evidence is presented to show that consumers can place positive and negative value on events not normally valued in monetary terms (e.g., conceiving twins, gum sticking to one's shoe).[10]

Thus, value is a "worthiness" number assigned to the concept under consideration. It permits comparisons to other valuations along a numeric continuum. Ignoring ideal points, an item's value is its point estimate in currency, utility, or exchange terms. It follows that interpretations of "excellent value" are defined by valuations on the high side of the continuum; items lacking demonstrable value are positioned at the low end. For the purpose of its use, it does not matter that the concept of value can be defined in a greater dimensionality; utility estimates take these additional dimensions into account by virtue of utility's holistic nature.

Many common events benefit from the singular notion of utility-as-worth, which can be defined in currency terms. For example, in its many variants, worth can mean the exchange terms required for acquisition (e.g., cost), the exchange value obtained at disposition (e.g., sale price), the estimated or imagined value of the item in ownership (e.g., appraisal), what one would be willing to pay if ownership were possible (e.g., the bid), and what one would require to give up the item (e.g., the asked). For the same item at the same time, each of these measures could vary, sometimes markedly.[11]

Worth has taken on specific evaluative forms in different areas. Interestingly, the discipline that has advanced this concept most usefully is securities analysis. It is now generally recognized that the worth of a firm is its value to shareholders, and firm valuation is now commonplace in financial circles; empirical valuation models are well developed and value estimates are now routinely made. This has prompted one set of authors to begin their book with the exploratory query, "Why value value?"[12] This question immediately sets the stage for further analysis as it implies that value can be elusive and requires valuation attempts beyond the simple act of pricing.

One main implication from the financial markets that seems to have eluded many is that price and value are not necessarily congruent even for hard assets. Consumers buy and rebuy toothpaste for a price, but have no easy means of estimating the value to their dental health provided by regular usage of this substance. In actuality, the value of a dentifrice may be many times its cumulative cost. Thus, as in securities investing, the value in this context is the (discounted) cumulative future return of the item. Other examples include education, wellness programs, and insurance.

Perhaps the most common example of a single-stimulus value judgment is in the realm of hedonic consumption, which is not clearly specified in the earlier typology (although "fun" might qualify). Here, the concepts of value, utility, and pleasure merge, as the foremost as well as some current interpretations of utility involve pleasure. In the earliest writings on utility, the concept was referred to as the hedonic quality of experience—attaining pleasure and avoiding pain.

The valuation of pleasure and its negative counterpart pain, actually the displeasure of pain, would at first appear to be a single-stimulus judgment. Individuals are known to exclaim that they are happy or sad, pleased or displeased, or mirthful or sorrowful as if it were a single judgment. The qualifier *very* added to any of these terms simply moves the judgment to one or the other extreme of a single continuum. Indeed, many one-item scales or rank scores of both extremes of the hedonic continuum exist and have been used for some time. Thus, it would seem that hedonic consumption could be easily valued by virtue of the pleasure it provides. It does not matter that variants of pleasure, such as delight, are attained in such consumption, for delight can be viewed as a high arousal form of pleasure (see Chapters 4 and 12).

This author sees pleasure-as-value or value-as-pleasure as an oversimplification. Taking the experience of hedonic pleasure as an ultimate outcome of life ignores the literature on subjective well being, which clearly shows that even pleasure is relative.[13] Individuals have both internal and external mechanisms by which to compare their current level of pleasure. An obvious example is the displeasure of pain, a negative sensation that clearly is compared to the human resting state. Individuals know that pain is unpleasant because their bodies have evolved to sense and display it (unlike insects, for example, which have no pain receptors). On a medical pain scale that uses this comparative notion to assess the severity of pain, the greatest extreme point is phrased as "as much as you can bear." This immediately begs the issue of degrees of pain at bearable and unbearable levels. Similarly, pleasure can be compared to its prior internally experienced levels. Delight, ecstasy, and thrill can all be compared to simple pleasure or happiness.

Use of external comparative referents to determine one's pleasure value is also common. Previously satisfied consumers may become disgruntled when they learn that other consumers acquired a similar item for less cost or obtained greater value. Marketers use this innate human comparative tendency to create dissatisfaction with older models of the same brand (leading, for example, to auto-design changes) or competitive offerings, as noted in Chapter 1. And, on the positive side of the situation, seemingly unhappy individuals can change their state of mind by shifting, perhaps subconsciously, the comparative referent to a lower standard, as in the "satisfied poor."[14]

Moreover, theories of worthy or ultimate life values, cited previously, do not list the sensation of pleasure; rather, virtuous traits (e.g., kindness, honesty) or enduring life situations (e.g., self-esteem, self-fulfillment) are overrepresented in these lists. Pleasure is simply too fleeting a sensation to be held out as an ultimate life experience (although happiness is not). Further, the satisfaction literature views pleasure as one component along with other affects and cognitions, as discussed at various locations in this book.

Nonetheless, hedonic consumption is pursued by consumers and one must assume that the resulting affects and more distinct emotions provide a sense of value to these individuals. Unfortunately, a generally agreed-upon metric for measuring or comparing hedonic utility to other types of value has not been forthcoming. Generally, researchers assume that, when given a list of mixed goods, services, and aesthetics, consumers can value them on a common scale. For example, one study measured the value to consumers of varied items, from cash to chocolate to bus trips to wine, on an eleven-point 0–10 scale bounded by "you think this item is completely useless or valueless to you" to "very great personal use or value" and used the results to provide numeric indices for each item. This is a very different question from the affect scales used for measuring pleasure or other positive affects and still more different from scales recommended for satisfaction.[15] Thus, hedonic value *can be* measured empirically, but the researcher takes much on faith in assuming that the as-yet-unknown psychophysics of valuing pleasure will be manifest in consumer ratings.

Another popular version of value has arisen in discussions of a loyal customer base. One road to loyalty, it is said, is to provide value to customers—thus value-based loyalty.[16] But this implies that the value behind the loyalty to one firm is greater than that of another, itself implying a comparison. This rendition of value demands that the specific nature of the comparator be known, for it immediately begs the question of "value compared to what?" Writers are quite clear on what this comparison is—value compared to that of competitive offerings. So what is it that is supposed to be compared? It is presumed that consumers should know—or the marketer will inform them. The present discussion is now in the realm of dual-stimulus definitions, to be pursued next.

Dual-Stimulus Definitions of Value in Consumption

Value in the context of two stimuli is by definition a comparative process. This is not the same as saying that value is defined by two dimensions, such as the ambience and the food served in a restaurant. Rather, the two stimuli do not have to be on the same conceptual plane, as might occur in the proverbial choice between what one has "in hand" and the total unknown behind a closed door.

There are two comparative processes that consumers can use in assessing value. The first is an intraproduct comparison such as when benefits are compared to costs; the second is an interproduct comparison that occurs when consumers compare the value of a product to its alternatives. The first comparison is actually a precursor to the second, but consumers do not necessarily process value comparisons in two stages. Both views are prominent in the literature, however. Most academics research the first comparison for an understanding of the underlying psychological process of value determination, while practitioners talk about the second comparison for its relation to loyalty, an interoffering judgment. Thus, consumers can judge the value of a monopolistic offering, or they can simply state that they find more value in a product than in its competition and thus will continue to rebuy it in the future. Discussion of each follows.

Intraproduct or Internal Value: Valuing Value

There is and continues to be a growing body of literature on the meaning of consumption value from the perspective of the consumer. Typically, authors define value as the customer's desire for specific consequences instrumental in accomplishing an intended goal, as in means-end analysis. Here, it is clear that value is a derivative of the consumer's goals in purchasing. In addition, it is not uncommon for writers to elaborate on this definition by distinguishing between *value in use* and *value in possession*.[17] Use value implies that the goal of purchasing is to obtain the functional consequences of the product or service. The product is simply a means to an end, such as when a disposable battery is used to power a toy. Possession value, in contrast, implies that the mere ownership of a product is its goal. Art, status symbols, and accomplishments such as mountain climbing qualify here.

In the first case, the value to customers is what they would pay for the functional consequences and not the product itself. Thus, the same long-life battery used for a pacemaker would have greater value than when used for a watch. The fact that the battery may cost the same for both uses again illustrates the divergence of value and price. In the second case, the value is purely psychological and may differ greatly across consumers. Clearly, the owner of a unique Van Gogh places a high value on possessing it and may not part with it for any price. Only when the owner desires to sell the painting at auction, perhaps, does some correspondence between value and price materialize.

These examples illustrate the intraproduct comparison process. Here the valuation is against a goal of consumption. In the case of value in use, the goal is the production of desired consequences. In the battery example, the battery's value is powering a toy. The value of the toy, in turn, is in providing enjoyment. Interestingly, the toy is typically valued more highly than the battery even though the toy would not function without the battery. The toy without the battery still retains value in possession; it contains enjoyment potential even though it is not powered. For example, the owner could put the toy on a shelf and admire it, whereas the same sort of appreciation would be unlikely in the case of a battery.

The conundrum here is that the toy's utility can also be judged against the activity that might be pursued in its stead, including the resting state. Thus, the enjoyment of playing with the toy can be compared to the imagined enjoyment of playing with another toy, watching TV, or doing nothing at all. In this framing, the battery and the toy should have the same value, since the enjoyment of play cannot take place without both. But, again, they do not.

This brings the discussion to comparisons of what is received to what is given, as in the definition of value as a function of rewards versus costs. Numerous examples of this type of value assessment are available. *Consumer Reports* frequently rates products as "best buys." This means that, within its criteria, the ratio of what is received to a consumable's price is the best value for the money. The publication typically finds that many medium- and even low-priced products are best buys. In the same way, mass storage devices can be rated on gigabytes per dollar, common household and grocery items are rated on volume of contents per dollar, and homes on the basis of dollars per square foot of living space. As long as the something per dollar is quantifiable or nearly so, this comparison is too tempting to ignore.

Thus, one can produce a hierarchical list of the degree to which cost is embedded in the internal valuation process. At the extreme upper level, cost may be irrelevant. The value of the outcome (i.e., its goal) is sought at any cost. Examples might be an infertile couple's desire to have children, a terminally ill patient's willingness to spend and risk all to recover, and an addict's craving for a drug. Bidders at auctions may engage in "bidding wars" over a desired object, and collectors may pay any price to complete a collection (or to start one). In a phrase, this type of value is "priceless."

Skipping to the extreme lower level of internal value, the consequences and, perhaps, goal-related outcomes are compared to price or cost more generally. Now cost is considered in the value equation and value can be both internal and external. This means that the item can be assessed in isolation from any other thing as long as a value rule is known. For example, a coin can be valued for its gold content using the current price of gold as a standard. It can also be given additional valuation based on its rarity, which is based on the original number of coins minted, those remaining in circulation, and so on. And the coin can further be valued on its condition, the degree of wear being determined by the level of detail that remains. Interestingly, this same single-object valuation now permits two objects, similarly judged, to be compared.

Elaboration on the middle level of cost consideration in value, reserved until now, necessarily takes the discussion to interobject comparisons. Thus, it provides a segue to the more formal material in the next section. At this middle level, cost is considered only in relation to a general category of similar pursuits. One way to look at this level is to assume a fixed cost for an item or activity and examine all alternatives that fulfill this criterion. A common example is travel or vacationing. Consumers who have saved many thousands of dollars earmarked for a vacation will instruct the travel agent to prepare alternatives that fall within this cost constraint. The cost is then considered foregone and is not entertained further. The alternatives, however, are still considered for their value. Generally, these will be qualitatively different alternatives that compete on that basis.

Still other examples are home buying, entertainment, education, and aesthetics. In the case of home buying, the upper limit as to cost is set by the buyer's income, which puts a cap on the range of homes under consideration. Since brokers and financial planners encourage buyers to "buy as much house as you can" because the mortgage payments may be fixed, whereas income is thought to rise, the homes under consideration will be in the same price range, but differ markedly in terms of architectural design, layout, location, and so on. Thus, for each residence under consideration, the constellation of home facets is judged for its (intrinsic) value. This value, then, becomes the criterion on which the houses are judged against one another—an interobject comparison as discussed in the following section. (Author's note: this was composed before the "meltdown" of 2008–09.)

It is important to note that business-to-business (B2B) markets are also frequently assessed using internal comparisons of the benefits versus costs/sacrifices form and, in the next evaluation phase, firm versus firm comparisons. Costs in B2B markets may be more easily quantifiable than are benefits due to the necessity of accounting for them. Items related to account establishment, maintenance, and even severance have been included in many value studies in this type of market.[18] Studies of consumers, in contrast, often take this basic notion on principle; it is not uncommon to see the phrase "good value for the money," often an untestable evaluation, and a number of studies are available to support this proposition in its many forms.[19]

Interobject Comparisons

This brings discussion to interobject comparisons where the value judgment is now more direct. As noted in the preceding discussion, a direct comparative referent is needed to form the prototype against which alternatives are compared. This may be an ideal object or, absent that, "best in class." Interobject comparisons permit an additional dimension not available to intraobject evaluations. Whereas intraobject valuations require some internal or external standard of measure, interobject comparisons do not. As long as consumers can indicate a preference between two of these, the evaluation standards do not require specification. Often, individuals cannot state why they prefer one alternative to another, although statistical procedures such as conjoint analysis are able to draw out preference dimensions.[20] This is particularly true in matters of aesthetics and just about all the intrinsic values in the value typology.

The desire on the part of researchers to understand the hidden criteria consumers use to decide whether one alternative has more value than another has provided the impetus for research on preference, such as preference mapping and study of the inner workings of the brain. Whereas science may eventually discover how individuals make preference judgments when they lack hard cognitive cues, such future discoveries do not apply to the present discussion. The preferences exist, nonetheless, and the preferred item is the one consumers value most.

Writers have searched for the best way to describe this hidden evaluation function. While many options, including scaling, conjoint analysis, and multiattribute attitude modeling, are available, it would be convenient if a single concept could be studied for insight into how the consumer views the concept of value. For now, readers must mentally interlace the previous chapter with the present, recalling the author's conundrum of whether quality and value belong in the same chapter or in separate chapters. What, then, is their relation?

PROPOSED AND ACTUAL MODEL TESTS CONTAINING QUALITY AND VALUE: WHAT CAN BE LEARNED?

It would be instructive to begin with a quality-value model now in widespread use and discussed in greater detail in prior and later chapters, the American Customer Satisfaction Index (ACSI).[21] This model, the statistical composition of which is proprietary, has been displayed in many publications and its conceptual properties are known. In particular, both quality and value are shown as distinct components, with quality antecedent to value. The logic behind this ordering is that quality is the numerator-input to the quality (receipts)-over-cost (sacrifices) version of value shown in Equation 7.1. In fact, this interpretation is the most common in the literature and appears in both theoretical and empirical renditions of models containing the two.[22] Theoretical proponents of this value form, in particular, find this interpretation attractive. One such proponent, however, distinguishes differences across the four stages of transaction, acquisition (possession), usage, and redemption—which is meant to imply that value accrues when accumulated "worth" is transferred to its end reward. The first two stages were tested and found to reflect the quality/cost model components. Close inspection of the scales reveals that acquisition is sacrifice-bound while transaction value is akin to shopping pleasure (affective quality as in the previous chapter).[23]

The empirical tests of models containing quality and value are uniformly persuasive in their findings. Value is found to be a function of quality and, when sacrifices (usually prices or costs) are also included, these contribute further to the value criterion. Many of these tests are noted here; others can be found in a cited earlier review.[24] One observation stands out, however; the tests are of the more easily measured concepts. More philosophical conceptual kin such as worth tend not to be tested, although they can be found in two value scales (to be discussed).

This notwithstanding, quality *is* one of the components of value in consumption. Consumers derive value from quality; it enhances their consumption experience and, in economic terms, gives them added utility. Thus, quality is a precursor to both value and satisfaction. This brings up the issue of how value relates to satisfaction.

VALUE AS A SATISFACTION-LIKE POSTPURCHASE COMPARISON

Elsewhere, this author has noted that satisfaction, an undisputed goal of consumption, does not appear in the eight-cell value typology, thereby raising a number of interesting questions.[25] Namely, (1) Is satisfaction value—are they the same concept? (2) Is satisfaction one of the values in the typology under a different rubric? (3) Is it an additional value defined by another dimension not considered? That is, is satisfaction a related, but conceptually distinct, concept within this broader dimension? (4) If so, is satisfaction an antecedent of value—do consumers receive value from satisfaction? (5) Alternatively, is it a consequent—do consumers receive satisfaction from value in consumption? And (6) Are satisfaction and value linked bidirectionally in a larger web of consumption constructs? A graphical depiction of each of these alternative representations is shown in Figure 7.1. But first a digression is in order to address the more philosophical issues raised at various points in this chapter. Discussion returns to this figure later.

What, Now, Is Value?

The six questions in the preceding paragraph are intriguing but cannot be pursued until there is some agreement over the definitions of satisfaction and value. By now, the many approaches taken here to pin down a definition of value point to three possibilities, corresponding to three interpretations of value and the role of sacrifice in each. The first is what the consumable gives the consumer regardless of cost. It is utility in its truest sense. It is how much the consumer would suffer—how much less whole the consumer would be—in its absence, in effect in a deficit, as depicted in Chapter 5. This includes items that can be assessed for their worth and those that cannot—the priceless item. When people claim that their life would be "worthless" without some entity, their very existence is the value of that entity to them.

The second definition is an assessment comparative to other alternatives whether qualitatively similar or not, the "inter" comparison. Here the phrase "more value than" (although the actual

Figure 7.1   **Six Representations of Satisfaction and Value**

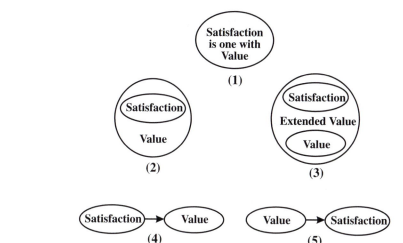

Source: Adapted from Richard L. Oliver, "Value as Excellence in the Consumption Experience," in *Consumer Value: A Framework for Analysis and Research*, ed. Morris B. Holbrook (London: Routledge, 1999), p. 54, by permission from Routledge.

valuation may not have been made) comes into play. This is an ordinal assessment that may be quantifiable. When individuals drop out of the workforce to pursue an MBA, they are making an implicit judgment that their future job prospects will have more value at the end of the program than if they had stayed in the labor market and worked for the length of the MBA program. Unfortunately, the true value of this comparison can never be known, but it is projected nonetheless. The cost of the interlude is often substantial, involving both tuition and forgone income. The individual makes the value determination regardless.

The third definition reflects the value equation of outcomes that may be compared to sacrifices, the "intra" comparison, and is characterized by the "best buy" moniker. Here the comparison is explicit in the definition. Which of these values is the real value? One way of answering this question is to look for commonalities among them.

What is apparent is that the numerator of the value equation is common to all. What the consumers have, will have, or believe they have or will have is the universal. Thus, like the notion of utility, value is the additional worth that an entity brings to one's life. Without the object, the consumer suffers a value decrement. Separately, it is the consumer's choice whether comparisons are made to internal or external standards, other alternatives, or to cost. If any of these comparisons are made, the value takes on other nuances, but still is value. Thus, value is what is added to the consumer's existence. This addition can be cast in terms of additional pleasure, monetary worth, or simple utility. Or it can be cast in terms of maintaining pleasure or ensuring against loss of pleasure (e.g., insurance). Or it can be cast in terms of restoring an individual to homeostasis, as in the case of a medicine restoring health. Of interest is the fact that these three perspectives on value correspond to what this author has called "satisfaction-as-pleasure," "satisfaction-as-contentment," and "satisfaction-as-relief," more fully discussed in Chapter 13. Thus, there must be some correspondence between value and satisfaction, as follows.

What, Now, Is the Role of Value in Satisfaction (or Vice Versa)?

Few would disagree that a comparison of performance outcomes (i.e., quality) to sacrifices (i.e., cost-based value) is, in all likelihood, one of the antecedents of satisfaction. That would make value one of the comparative operations in satisfaction formation that is listed in the Introduction, Figure 1.4. In this perspective, the "receipts compared to sacrifices" version of value is viewed as one among the other comparative operations in postpurchase judgments. In effect, it operates in parallel with the other comparators in the satisfaction response. This view is consistent with the position that a cost-based definition of value is one antecedent of satisfaction.

In fact, there is now a large body of evidence testing the causal order of the quality → value → satisfaction chain. The first link, quality preceding value, is found in a number of sources.[26] The second link, between value and satisfaction, is also found in various sources.[27] Occasionally, but not regularly, the links become reversed or may be bidirectional, but the bulk of the evidence favors the quality-value-satisfaction sequence. Given these occasional lapses and in a seemingly tautological perspective, it may also be the case that satisfaction is a precursor to value or, perhaps, another form of value. That is, some of the value derived from consumption could be satisfaction-based. This further begs the question of where satisfaction belongs in the value typology.

For satisfaction to be an input to the value one receives in consumption, it must provide one of the outcomes in the value typology or an outcome not accounted for in this framework. Close inspection of the eight cells, which cover efficiency, excellence, status, esteem, play, aesthetics, ethics, and spirituality, suggests that these outcomes, if attained, would provide a sense of satisfaction to the recipient. If satisfaction is still another component of value, then what is the missing dimension on which it is defined? One conclusion from this analysis is that satisfaction and value are related but different concepts and that satisfaction is not a variant of value. More will be said of this next.

It is now time to address the question of which of the frameworks in Figure 7.1 is most accurate given the logic and (somewhat convoluted) analysis presented here. It should be noted at the outset that the first representation, number (1) in the figure, can be dismissed. Satisfaction emerges as a distinct construct when compared to *any* of the definitions of value discussed here. To show this, it is only necessary to provide example cases where satisfaction can exist in the absence of value and where value can exist in the absence of satisfaction, an exercise useful in distinguishing satisfaction from quality, as suggested in the previous chapter. In what follows, two examples are given, one relating to the first perspective of value as having no bearing on cost, and a second in which receipts are compared to costs including the case of zero cost.

In an example of priceless value, a consumer may own an heirloom, passed down from ancestors, that is of immense value on the market. Yet this hypothetical consumer has no need for it, stores it in a safe, and derives no satisfaction from it. It is not fulfilling in any way and is a mere possession. Alternatively, a simple possession such as a common jigsaw puzzle may be very satisfying each time it is completed, but has no value beyond its ability to challenge and satisfy.

In another example involving sacrifices, the actual cost may have been sufficiently low and even zero, as in a free good. In this case, just about any level of reasonable receipts may provide immense value. The consumer, however, may find little satisfaction or even need fulfillment in this case. An unneeded or disliked gift of great value would provide yet another example. Alternatively, a needed item may become very dear (expensive), giving great satisfaction but little value in the receipts-over-cost sense. For example, a makeshift emergency automobile repair may be truly satisfying (i.e., satisfaction-as-relief; see Chapter 13) if it enables a motorist to reach the nearest service station. The road mechanic may charge an exorbitant price, thereby offering poor value for this service. The motorist's needs, however, were fulfilled nonetheless. Here, the value is of a higher order and must be explained without regard for cost.

These examples illustrate both the divergence and interplay between satisfaction and value. As noted previously, satisfaction exists as the consumer's fulfillment response. The value of this response is the end-state of the consumer after having been satisfied (fulfilled). Satisfaction provides value in what it leaves with the consumer—the satisfied state. It may also be the case that knowing that one has received value can be satisfying, as in the cost-based version; alternatively, satisfaction may provide a sense of *extended* value in that the consumer values (places a high utility on) being satisfied. This may explain the basis for the conundrum of the primacy of satisfaction or value. At the same time that consumption value enhances satisfaction, satisfaction may be a valued outcome for many consumers. The extent to which satisfaction provides extended value awaits further research.

These views are also suggested by the authors of a well-conceived book on the topic who explicitly distinguish between satisfaction and value.[28] In short, they define value as follows:

- A consumer desire
- Independent of usage or consumption timing
- Independent of either product or service category
- Providing strategic direction for an organization

In contrast, satisfaction is described as:

- A consumer reaction
- Dependent on usage experience
- Product- or service-specific
- Providing strategic feedback

These definitions bring the discussion back to Figure 7.1 and the question of which of the six representations is correct. Having previously dismissed representation (1), the preceding analysis would suggest that representation (2) is also problematic. The reason is clear from the difficulty noted earlier of positioning satisfaction in the value typology. Unless satisfaction is a *personal* value (sometimes referred to as *self-satisfaction*), a combination of topics that has not been sufficiently studied as yet in a consumer context, satisfaction rarely appears in and cannot be considered to be contained in a set of values, despite the fact that it may be valued.

Representation (3) goes beyond (2) to suggest that there is a conceptually higher plane of "extended value," alluded to previously. This would take discussion to a higher order of value in consumer consumption, approaching the issue of the quality of life. In essence, attaining and receiving elements of value as well as being satisfied would jointly contribute to the (extended) value of one's life. This, too, is an underresearched issue in consumption, in general, although not so in the quality of life or happiness fields. Perhaps there may be a convergence of extended value and happiness at some point.

In contrast to the first three of the six representations, there is merit to the remaining three perspectives in Figure 7.1, although it has already been stated that the data strongly suggest that (5) dominates (4) under the weight of the evidence *and* that researchers have made pointed distinctions between the two. But, for the sake of argument, when value is viewed as a desirable end state of consumption, satisfying consumption events may be of value to consumers. Thus, being satisfied gives value. Again, the state of satisfaction is separate from the end state of being satisfied, which is valued. Thus, there is merit to representation (4) despite the evidence to the contrary. Similarly, when value is viewed as receipts compared to costs, it becomes one of the satisfaction comparators detailed in the Introduction. In this case, value gives satisfaction as in representation (5) and may represent the efficiency cell in the eight-cell typology. Additionally, if any of the remaining values in the typology also provides satisfaction, the same argument applies. It appears at this point that extended value as satisfaction, terminal values in the means-end analyses, and quality of life may, in fact, have a convergent state.

It is now apparent that representation (6) may be a compromise of those entertained here. Value and satisfaction mutually influence each other as value transforms and modulates between calculated states and end states. Both have common antecedents in consumption events, such as product or service performance, and both have common consequences such as loyalty. Thus, both are embedded in a web of consumption constructs, as suggested earlier.

This latter perspective also suggests the role of quality in value. In agreement with the large body of literature attesting to the relationship, quality is an input to value. Value, then, becomes a superordinate concept subsuming quality. And, in accord with the previous chapter, quality is an input to satisfaction through the comparison of performance to excellence standards. Then, in a seemingly circular pattern, quality enhances satisfaction and value, thus providing additional satisfaction—satisfaction deriving first from quality and then from value.

It should not be overlooked that the value and satisfaction provided by quality derive from other desired purchase outcomes that, by their nature, define the essence of quality. As typically found in studies investigating the meaning of quality to consumers, quality brings reliability, durability, status, self-confidence, and ease of decision making. For these reasons, quality is value, thereby being a "valued quality" in consumption. But, at the same time, it is suggested that the value derived from consumption does not necessarily correspond to values desired by individuals in general, which reflect desirable end states in life sought by all individuals, as noted in the early parts of this chapter. For example, the list of Rokeach-based values includes accomplishment, belongingness, enjoyment, excitement, fulfillment, fun, security, self-respect, and warm relationships.[29] Note that some of these, such as enjoyment and security, can be obtained through consumption and indeed overlap with some of the values in the typology, while others, such as self-fulfillment, are not easily achieved in this manner.

Lest the reader grow weary, the relationships discussed in this section have been portrayed graphically in Figure 7.2. The figure depicts the web of consumption constructs (referred to as a nomological network) in which quality, cost-based value, satisfaction, and higher forms of consumption value are embedded. Thus, it is proposed that satisfaction-related value, or even value-related satisfaction, is not "one thing." Rather it is a constellation of consumption-based constructs that includes quality—an excellence-based consumer judgment. Note that, for purposes of discovery, extended value, as in representation (3), is included as an ultimate goal. One hopes that researchers will use this framework to corroborate the reasoning presented here.

Measuring Consumer Values

Yes. It is possible to measure consumer values (loosely defined). Two scales known to the author have been proposed.[30] Readers are encouraged to obtain and work with these from the original

Figure 7.2 **Nomological Net of Value Concepts in Consumption**

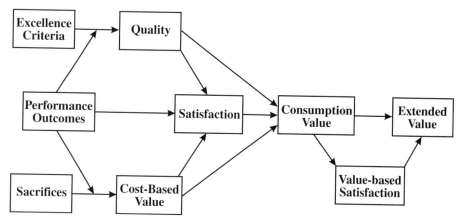

Source: Adapted from Richard L. Oliver, "Value as Excellence in the Consumption Experience," in *Consumer Value: A Framework for Analysis and Research,* ed. Morris B. Holbrook (London: Routledge, 1999), p. 59, by permission from Routledge.

sources because the approaches taken were similar and the scale dimensions that emerged through factor analyses shared commonalities. Readers will also recognize the concepts that were developed (five in the first case, four in the second), as many of them correspond to discussions throughout this chapter.

In both scales, the very first dimension was quality, defined largely in technical terms. The second, again in each case, was emotion, defined to a large extent in terms of pleasure. The third dimension in both was price. The items corresponded to fairness, value for the money, and economy, as in low price. In the first study, a second price dimension then emerged, referred to as "behavioral," which concerned how little difficulty or effort was required to acquire the product. At this point, readers will decide if these later dimensions tap value or other related concepts. The last dimension in the first study was reputation (of the firm's products). And the final dimension in the second study was "social," meaning prestige more so than status.

Two different validation techniques were employed. Overall value was used in the first study and willingness-to-buy and recommendations provided criteria in the second. Significant correlations were observed in all cases. Again, the studies must be perused for their usefulness in any given situation. While many of these observed dimensions are not "philosophical" in the sense of value as discussed here, they may certainly prove "of value" to those in the field.

What of Value in Marketing Strategy?

This topic is much easier to discuss than to implement, although "how-to" sources are too numerous to cite. While the intent of this chapter was not to focus on strategy, an effort was made to discuss the behavioral basis for consumer and, to a much lesser extent, B2B actions in the marketplace. In fact, the typical strategic value analysis takes the form of a matrix in which the stages of consumption or relationships in the B2B market, for example, form one dimension and numerous others such as "value proposition," "value assessment," "value-added," and "value change" are mapped against these stages.

Authors have proposed various sought-after values based on the phase of consumer contact. For example, some researchers have referred to this time-based analysis as a value "chain" whereby values are assessed as differing over acquisition, transaction or exchange, possession, use, and reacquisition of lost customers.[31] Others focus on the differing values and value importances for buyers and sellers, a point made earlier in this chapter, while still others continue to wrestle with the classic trade-offs between price and quality in the determination of value.[32]

And, in accord with current wisdom, a distinction can be made at the concrete and functional attribute product/service levels. At least in terms of consumer awareness and focus, satisfaction can dwell at the lower levels of the value hierarchy, while values tend, almost by definition, to reside at higher levels of goal attainment. However, in a departure from the writings on satisfaction and value, this author sees a convergence of the two, again if properly assessed. There is no reason to believe that the pursuit of higher-level goals cannot be satisfying (or dissatisfying). For example, altruistic giving is satisfying to many donors, accomplishments (e.g., attaining a degree or certification) are satisfying, and even peace of mind can be satisfying in the contentment or tranquility experienced. It has been said that, at some point, value attainment and self-satisfaction and even happiness become essentially indistinguishable from the lay consumer's point of view. Perhaps this is where studies in these fields are moving; further work will address this question.

CONCLUSION

To the reader, this chapter no doubt appears murky and rambling, unlike the previous chapter on the more concrete notion of quality, although even that topic had an ephemeral edge to it, as suggested in the popular book *Zen and the Art of Motorcycle Maintenance*.[33] It is apparent that value is not one thing. The earlier value typology contained eight variations, this author has explored others, and authors researching universal human values have proposed still others that were not detailed here in order to keep the focus on the topic of consumer satisfaction. Nonetheless, value as a satisfaction precursor or as a higher-order consequent will continue to play an important role in consumer responses to consumption events.

NOTES

1. Parts of this chapter are from Oliver, "Value as Excellence in the Consumption Experience," by permission of Routledge.

2. Holbrook, ed., *Consumer Value.*

3. Najder, *Values and Evaluations*; Kahneman and Varey, "Notes on the Psychology of Utility"; Schwartz and Bilsky, "Toward a Universal Psychological Structure of Human Values"; Rokeach, *Nature of Human Values*; Kahle, *Social Values and Social Change*; Baron and Spranca, "Protected Values"; Maio and Olson, "Values as Truisms"; Higgins, "Value from Hedonic Experience *and* Engagement"; Kahneman, Diener, and Schwarz, eds., *Well-Being*; Kamakura and Novak, "Value-System Segmentation."

4. Gutman, "Exploring the Nature of Linkages Between Consequences and Values" and "Means-End Chains as Goal Hierarchies."

5. Holbrook, *Consumer Value* and "The Nature of Customer Value."

6. See Burns, "Exploring Self (Dis)Satisfaction as an Outcome of Product Use Experiences."

7. Zeithaml, "Consumer Perceptions of Price, Quality, and Value."

8. See Sánchez-Fernández and Iniesta-Bonillo, "Consumer Perceptions of Value."

9. Huber et al., "Thinking about Values in Prospect and Retrospect."

10. Galanter, "Utility Functions for Nonmonetary Events"; Kemp, "Magnitude Estimation of the Utility of Public Goods"; Kemp, Lea, and Fussell, "Experiments on Rating the Utility of Consumer Goods"; Kemp and Willetts, "Rating the Value of Government-Funded Services."

11. See, e.g., Carmon and Ariely, "Focusing on the Forgone"; and Darke and Dahl, "Fairness and Discounts."

12. Copeland, Koller, and Murrin, *Valuation*, Chapter 1.

13. Crosby, "Model of Egoistical Relative Deprivation"; Parducci, "Relativism of Absolute Judgments."

14. Olson and Schober, "Satisfied Poor."

15. Kemp, Lea, and Fussell, "Experiments on Rating the Utility of Consumer Goods." An example of an affect scale appears in Watson, Clark, and Tellegen, "Development and Validation of Brief Measures of Positive and Negative Affect."

16. Fredericks and Salter, "Beyond Customer Satisfaction"; Johnson, Herrman, and Huber, "Evolution of Loyalty Intentions"; Lassar, Mittal, and Sharma, "Measuring Customer-Based Brand Equity"; Neal, "Satisfaction Is Nice, But Value Drives Loyalty."

17. Woodruff and Gardial, *Know Your Customer*. The value in use/possession distinction is made at p. 55. Also see Parasuraman, "Reflections on Gaining Competitive Advantage Through Customer Value"; Woodruff, "Customer Value"; and Woodruff and Flint, "Marketing's Service-Dominant Logic and Customer Value."

18. E.g., Eggert and Ulaga, "Customer Perceived Value"; A. Kumar and Grisaffe, "Effects of Extrinsic Attributes on Perceived Quality, Customer Value, and Behavioral Intentions in B2B Settings"; P. Kumar, "Impact of Performance, Cost, and Competitive Considerations on the Relationship Between Satisfaction and Repurchase Intent in Business Markets"; Lapierre, "Customer-Perceived Value in Industrial Contexts"; Lapierre, Filiatrault, and Chebat, "Value Strategy Rather than Quality Strategy"; Lindgreen and Wynstra, "Value in Business Markets"; Simpson, Siguaw, and Baker, "Model of Value Creation"; Spiteri and Dion, "Customer Value, Overall Satisfaction, End-User Loyalty, and Market Performance in Detail Intensive Industries"; Ulaga and Chacour, "Measuring Customer-Perceived Value in Business Markets."

19. E.g., Agarwal and Teas, "Perceived Value"; Agustin and Singh, "Curvilinear Effects of Consumer Loyalty Determinants in Relational Exchanges"; Blackwell et al., "Antecedents of Customer Loyalty"; Bolton, Kannan, and Bramlett, "Implications of Loyalty Program Membership and Service Experiences for Customer Retention and Value"; Chen and Dubinsky, "Conceptual Model of Perceived Customer Value in E-Commerce"; Cronin et al., "Cross-Sectional Test of the Effect and Conceptualization of Service Value"; Grewal et al., "Developing a Deeper Understanding of Post-Purchase Perceived Risk and Behavioral Intentions in a Service Setting"; Kerin, Jain, and Howard, "Store Shopping Experience and Consumer Price-Quality-Value Perceptions"; Sweeney, Soutar, and Johnson, "Role of Perceived Risk in the Quality-Value Relationship"; Varki and Colgate, "Role of Price Perceptions in an Integrated Model of Behavioral Intentions."

20. E.g., Zaltman, *How Consumers Think*. For an example of the use of conjoint analysis of value in the industrial market, see van der Haar, Kemp, and Omta, "Creating Value That Cannot Be Copied."

21. Fornell et al., "American Customer Satisfaction Index."

22. While empirical tests can be found in the next note, two papers are early representations of this view. See Dodds, "In Search of Value"; and Zeithaml, "Consumer Perceptions of Price, Quality, and Value." A more recent paper summarizes this framework: Salegna and Goodwin, "Consumer Loyalty to Service Providers."

23. Grewal, Monroe, and Krishnan, "Effects of Price-Comparison Advertising on Buyers' Perceptions of Acquisition Value, Transaction Value, and Behavioral Intentions"; Parasuraman and Grewal, "Impact of Technology on the Quality-Value-Loyalty Chain."

24. The cited review Sánchez-Fernández and Iniesta-Bonillo, "Consumer Perceptions of Value." The supportive studies include Andreassen and Lindestad, "Customer Loyalty and Complex Services"; Cronin et al., "Assessing the Effects of Quality, Value, and Customer Satisfaction on Consumer Behavioral Intentions in Service Environments"; Grewal et al., "Effect of Store Name, Brand Name and Price Discounts on Consumers' Evaluations and Purchase Intentions"; Ralston, "Effects of Customer Service, Branding, and Price on the Perceived Value of Local Telephone Service"; Teas and Agarwal, "Effects of Extrinsic Product Cues on Consumers' Perceptions of Quality, Sacrifice, and Value"; and Varki and Colgate, "Role of Price Perceptions in an Integrated Model of Behavioral Intentions."

25. Oliver, "Varieties of Value in the Consumption Satisfaction Response" and "Value as Excellence in the Consumption Experience."

26. Bolton and Drew, "Multistage Model of Customers' Assessments of Service Quality and Value"; Brady and Cronin, "Customer Orientation"; Chang and Wildt, "Price, Product Information, and Purchase Intention"; Cronin et al., "Cross-Sectional Test of the Effect and Conceptualization of Service Value"; Kerin et al., "Store Shopping Experience and Consumer Price-Quality-Value Perceptions"; A. Kumar and Grisaffe, "Effects of Extrinsic Attributes on Perceived Quality, Customer Value, and Behavioral Intentions in B2B Settings"; Lapierre, Filiatrault, and Chebat, "Value Strategy Rather than Quality Strategy"; Sweeney et al.,

"Role of Perceived Risk in the Quality-Value Relationship"; Tellis and Johnson, "Value of Quality"; Varki and Colgate, "Role of Price Perceptions in an Integrated Model of Behavioral Intentions"; Wakefield and Barnes, "Retailing Hedonic Consumption."

27. Lam et al., "Customer Value, Satisfaction, Loyalty, and Switching Costs"; Lapierre et al., "Value Strategy Rather than Quality Strategy"; Lee and Overby, "Creating Value for Online Shoppers"; Patterson and Spreng, "Modelling the Relationship Between Perceived Value, Satisfaction and Repurchase Intentions in a Business-to-Business, Services Context"; Varki and Colgate, "The Role of Price Perceptions in an Integrated Model of Behavioral Intentions"; Webb and Jagun, "Customer Care, Customer Satisfaction, Value, Loyalty and Complaining Behavior."

28. Woodruff and Gardial, *Know Your Customer,* p. 98.

29. Rokeach, *Nature of Human Values.*

30. Petrick, "Development of a Multi-Dimensional Scale for Measuring the Perceived Value of a Service"; Sweeney and Soutar, "Consumer Perceived Value."

31. E.g., Evans and Berman, "Conceptualizing and Operationalizing the Business-to-Business Value Chain"; Flint, Woodruff, and Gardial, "Customer Value Change in Industrial Marketing Relationships"; Grewal et al., "Internet and the Price-Value-Loyalty Chain"; Hogan, "Expected Relationship Value"; Parasuraman and Grewal, "Impact of Technology on the Quality-Value-Loyalty Chain"; Walter, Ritter, and Gemünden, "Value Creation in Buyer-Seller Relationships."

32. Carmon and Ariely, "Focusing on the Forgone"; Creyer and Ross, "Tradeoffs Between Price and Quality"; Hoyer, Herrmann, and Huber, "When Buyers Also Sell"; Oliver, "Co-Producers and Co-Participants in the Satisfaction Process."

33. Pirsig, *Zen and the Art of Motorcycle Maintenance.*

BIBLIOGRAPHY

Agarwal, Sanjeev, and R. Kenneth Teas. "Perceived Value: Mediating Role of Perceived Risk." *Journal of Marketing Theory and Practice* 9, no. 4 (Fall 2001): 1–14.

Agustin, Clara, and Jagdip Singh. "Curvilinear Effects of Consumer Loyalty Determinants in Relational Exchanges." *Journal of Marketing Research* 42, no. 1 (February 2005): 96–108.

Andreassen, Tor Wallin, and Bodil Lindestad. "Customer Loyalty and Complex Services: The Impact of Corporate Image on Quality, Customer Satisfaction and Loyalty for Customers with Varying Degrees of Service Expertise." *International Journal of Service Industry Management* 9, no. 1 (1998): 7–23.

Baron, Jonathan, and Mark Spranca. "Protected Values." *Organizational Behavior and Human Decision Processes* 70, no. 1 (April 1997): 1–16.

Blackwell, Steven A., Sheryl L. Szeinbach, James H. Barnes, Dewey W. Garner, and Victoria Bush. "The Antecedents of Customer Loyalty: An Empirical Investigation of the Role of Personal and Situational Aspects on Repurchase Decisions." *Journal of Service Research* 1, no. 4 (May 1999): 362–375.

Bolton, Ruth N., and James H. Drew. "A Multistage Model of Customers' Assessments of Service Quality and Value." *Journal of Consumer Research* 17, no. 4 (March 1991): 375–384.

Bolton, Ruth N., P.K. Kannan, and Matthew D. Bramlett. "Implications of Loyalty Program Membership and Service Experiences for Customer Retention and Value." *Journal of the Academy of Marketing Science* 28, no 1 (Winter 2000): 95–108.

Brady, Michael K., and J. Joseph Cronin Jr. "Customer Orientation: Effects on Customer Service Perceptions and Outcome Behaviors." *Journal of Service Research* 3, no. 3 (February 2001): 241–251.

Burns, Mary Jane. "Exploring Self (Dis)Satisfaction as an Outcome of Product Use Experiences." *Journal of Consumer Satisfaction, Dissatisfaction and Complaining Behavior* 7 (1994): 252–256.

Carmon, Ziv, and Dan Ariely. "Focusing on the Forgone: How Value Can Appear So Different to Buyers and Sellers." *Journal of Consumer Research* 27, no. 3 (December 2000): 360–370.

Chang, Tung-Zong, and Albert R. Wildt. "Price, Product Information, and Purchase Intention: An Empirical Study." *Journal of the Academy of Marketing Science* 22, no. 1 (Winter 1994): 16–27.

Chen, Zhan, and Alan J. Dubinsky. "A Conceptual Model of Perceived Customer Value in E-Commerce: A Preliminary Investigation." *Psychology & Marketing* 20, no. 4 (April 2003): 323–347.

Copeland, Tom, Tim Koller, and Jack Murrin. *Valuation: Measuring and Managing the Value of Companies.* 3rd ed. New York: John Wiley, 2000.

Creyer, Elizabeth H., and William T. Ross Jr. "Tradeoffs Between Price and Quality: How a Value Index Affects Preference Formation." *Journal of Consumer Affairs* 31, no. 2 (Winter 1997): 280–302.

Cronin, J. Joseph, Jr., Michael K. Brady, Richard R. Brand, Roscoe Hightower Jr., and Donald J. Shemwell. "A Cross-Sectional Test of the Effect and Conceptualization of Service Value." *Journal of Services Marketing* 11, no. 6 (1997): 375–391.

Cronin, J. Joseph, Jr., Michael K. Brady, and G. Tomas M. Hult. "Assessing the Effects of Quality, Value, and Customer Satisfaction on Consumer Behavioral Intentions in Service Environments." *Journal of Retailing* 76, no. 2 (Summer 2000): 193–218.

Crosby, Faye. "A Model of Egoistical Relative Deprivation." *Psychological Review* 83, no. 2 (March 1976): 85–113.

Darke, Peter R, and Darren W. Dahl. "Fairness and Discounts: The Subjective Value of a Bargain." *Journal of Consumer Psychology* 13, no. 3 (2003): 328-338.

Dodds, William B. "In Search of Value: How Price and Store Name Information Influence Buyers' Product Perceptions." *Journal of Services Marketing* 5, no. 3 (Summer 1991): 27–36.

Eggert, Andreas, and Wolfgang Ulaga. "Customer Perceived Value: A Substitute for Satisfaction in Business Markets?" *Journal of Business & Industrial Marketing* 17, nos. 2–3 (2002): 107–118.

Evans, Joel R., and Barry Berman. "Conceptualizing and Operationalizing the Business-to-Business Value Chain." *Industrial Marketing Management* 30, no. 2 (February 2001): 135–148.

Flint, Daniel J., Robert B. Woodruff, and Sarah Fisher Gardial. "Customer Value Change in Industrial Marketing Relationships: A Call for New Strategies and Research." *Industrial Marketing Management* 26, no. 3 (March 1997): 163–175.

Fornell, Claes, Michael D. Johnson, Eugene W. Anderson, Jaesung Cha, and Barbara Everitt Bryant. "The American Customer Satisfaction Index: Nature, Purpose, and Findings." *Journal of Marketing* 60, no. 4 (October 1996): 7–18.

Fredericks, Joan O., and James M. Salter II. "Beyond Customer Satisfaction." *Management Review* 84, no. 5 (May 1995): 29–32.

Galanter, Eugene. "Utility Functions for Nonmonetary Events." *American Journal of Psychology* 103, no. 4 (Winter 1990): 449–470.

Grewal, Dhruv, Gopalkrishnan R. Iyer, Jerry Gotlieb, and Michael Levy. "Developing a Deeper Understanding of Post-Purchase Perceived Risk and Behavioral Intentions in a Service Setting." *Journal of the Academy of Marketing Science* 35, no. 2 (June 2007): 250–258.

Grewal, Dhruv, Gopalkrishnan R. Iyer, R. Krishnan, and Arun Sharma. "The Internet and the Price-Value-Loyalty Chain." *Journal of Business Research* 56, no. 5 (May 2003): 391–398.

Grewal, Dhruv, R. Krishnan, Julie Baker, and Norm Borin. "The Effect of Store Name, Brand Name and Price Discounts on Consumers' Evaluations and Purchase Intentions." *Journal of Retailing* 74, no. 3 (Autumn 1998): 331–352.

Grewal, Dhruv, Kent B. Monroe, and R. Krishnan. "The Effects of Price-Comparison Advertising on Buyers' Perceptions of Acquisition Value, Transaction Value, and Behavioral Intentions." *Journal of Marketing* 62, no. 2 (April 1998): 46–59.

Gutman, Jonathan. "Exploring the Nature of Linkages Between Consequences and Values." *Journal of Business Research* 22, no. 2 (March 1991): 143–148.

———. "Means-End Chains as Goal Hierarchies." *Psychology & Marketing* 14, no. 6 (September 1997): 545–560.

Higgins, E. Tory. "Value from Hedonic Experience *and* Engagement." *Psychological Review* 113, no. 3 (July 2006): 439–460.

Hogan, John E. "Expected Relationship Value: A Construct, a Methodology for Measurement, and a Modeling Technique." *Industrial Marketing Management* 30, no. 4 (May 2001): 339–351.

Holbrook, Morris B. "The Nature of Customer Value: An Axiology of Services in the Consumption Experience." In *Service Quality: New Directions in Theory and Practice*, ed. Roland T. Rust and Richard L. Oliver, 21–71. Thousand Oaks, CA: Sage, 1994.

———, ed. *Consumer Value: A Framework for Analysis and Research*. London: Rutledge, 1999.

Hoyer, Wayne D., Andreas Herrmann, and Frank Huber. "When Buyers Also Sell: The Implications of Pricing Policies for Customer Satisfaction." *Psychology & Marketing* 19, no. 4 (April 2002): 329–355.

Huber, Joel, John Lynch, Kim Corfman, Jack Feldman, Morris B. Holbrook, Donald Lehmann, Bertrand Munier, David Schkade, and Itamar Simonson. "Thinking about Values in Prospect and Retrospect: Maximizing Experienced Utility." *Marketing Letters* 8, no. 3 (July 1997): 323–334.

Johnson, Michael D., Andreas Herrman, and Frank Huber. "The Evolution of Loyalty Intentions." *Journal of Marketing* 70, no. 2 (April 2006): 122–132.

Kahle, Lynn R. *Social Values and Social Change: Adaptation to Life in America.* New York: Praeger, 1983.

Kahneman, Daniel, Ed Diener, and Norbert Schwarz, eds. *Well-Being: The Foundations of Hedonic Psychology.* New York: Russell Sage Foundation, 1999.

Kahneman, Daniel, and Carol Varey. "Notes on the Psychology of Utility." In *Interpersonal Comparisons of Well-Being,* ed. Jon Elster and John E. Roemer, 127–159. Cambridge: Cambridge University Press, 1991.

Kamakura, Wagner A., and Thomas P. Novak. "Value-System Segmentation: Exploring the Meaning of LOV." *Journal of Consumer Research* 19, no. 1 (June 1992): 119–132.

Kemp, Simon. "Magnitude Estimation of the Utility of Public Goods." *Journal of Applied Psychology* 76, no. 4 (August 1991): 533–540.

Kemp, Simon, Stephen E.G. Lea, and Sharon Fussell. "Experiments on Rating the Utility of Consumer Goods: Evidence Supporting Microeconomic Theory." *Journal of Economic Psychology* 16, no. 4 (December 1995): 543–561.

Kemp, Simon, and Karyn Willetts. "Rating the Value of Government-Funded Services: Comparison of Methods." *Journal of Economic Psychology* 16, no. 1 (March 1995): 1–21.

Kerin, Roger A., Ambuj Jain, and Daniel J. Howard. "Store Shopping Experience and Consumer Price-Quality-Value Perceptions." *Journal of Retailing* 68, no. 4 (Winter 1992): 376–397.

Kumar, Anand, and Douglas B. Grisaffe. "Effects of Extrinsic Attributes on Perceived Quality, Customer Value, and Behavioral Intentions in B2B Settings: A Comparison Across Goods and Service Industries." *Journal of Business-to-Business Marketing* 11, no. 4 (2004): 43–74.

Kumar, Piyush. "The Impact of Performance, Cost, and Competitive Considerations on the Relationship Between Satisfaction and Repurchase Intent in Business Markets." *Journal of Service Research* 5, no. 1 (August 2002): 55–68.

Lam, Shun Yin, Venkatesh Shankar, M. Krishna Erramilli, and Bvsan Murthy. "Customer Value, Satisfaction, Loyalty, and Switching Costs: An Illustration from a Business-to-Business Service Context." *Journal of the Academy of Marketing Science* 32, no. 3 (Spring 2004): 293–311.

Lapierre, Jozée. "Customer-Perceived Value in Industrial Contexts." *Journal of Business & Industrial Marketing* 15, nos. 2–3 (2000): 122–140.

Lapierre, Jozée, Pierre Filiatrault, and Jean-Charles Chebat. "Value Strategy Rather than Quality Strategy: A Case of Business-to-Business Professional Services." *Journal of Business Research* 45, no. 2 (June 1999): 235–246.

Lassar, Walfried, Banwari Mittal, and Arun Sharma. "Measuring Customer-Based Brand Equity." *Journal of Consumer Marketing* 12, no. 4 (Fall 1995): 11–19.

Lee, Eun-Ju, and Jeffrey W. Overby. "Creating Value for Online Shoppers: Implications for Satisfaction and Loyalty." *Journal of Consumer Satisfaction, Dissatisfaction and Complaining Behavior* 17 (2004): 54–67.

Lindgreen, Adam, and Finn Wynstra. "Value in Business Markets: What Do We Know? Where Are We Going?" *Industrial Marketing Management* 34, no. 7 (October 2005): 732–748.

Maio, Gregory R., and James M. Olson. "Values as Truisms: Evidence and Implications." *Journal of Personality and Social Psychology* 74, no. 2 (February 1998): 294–311.

Najder, Z. *Values and Evaluations.* Oxford: Clarendon Press, 1975.

Neal, William D. "Satisfaction is Nice, But Value Drives Loyalty." *Marketing Research* 11, no. 1 (Spring 1999): 20–23.

Oliver, Richard L. "Co-Producers and Co-Participants in the Satisfaction Process: Mutually Satisfying Consumption." In *The Service-Dominant Logic of Marketing: Dialog, Debate, and Directions,* ed. Robert F. Lusch and Stephen L. Vargo, 118–127. Armonk, NY: M.E. Sharpe, 2006.

———. "Value as Excellence in the Consumption Experience." In *Consumer Value: A Framework for Analysis and Research,* ed. Morris B. Holbrook, 43–62. London: Routledge, 1999.

———. "Varieties of Value in the Consumption Satisfaction Response." In *Advances in Consumer Research,* ed. Kim P. Corfman and John G. Lynch Jr., 23:143–47. Provo, UT: Association for Consumer Research, 1996.

Olson, Geraldine I., and Brigitte I. Schober. "The Satisfied Poor: Development of an Intervention-Oriented Theoretical Framework to Explain Satisfaction with a Life in Poverty." *Social Indicators Research* 28, no. 2 (February 1993): 173–193.

Parasuraman, A. "Reflections on Gaining Competitive Advantage Through Customer Value." *Journal of the Academy of Marketing Science* 25, no. 2 (Spring 1997): 154–161.

Parasuraman, A., and Dhruv Grewal. "The Impact of Technology on the Quality-Value-Loyalty Chain: A Research Agenda." *Journal of the Academy of Marketing Science* 28, no. 1 (Winter 2000): 168–174.

Parducci, Allen. "The Relativism of Absolute Judgments." *Scientific American*, December 1968, pp. 84–90.

Patterson, Paul G., and Richard A. Spreng. "Modelling the Relationship Between Perceived Value, Satisfaction and Repurchase Intentions in a Business-to-Business, Services Context: An Empirical Examination. *International Journal of Service Industry Management* 8, no. 5 (1997): 414–434.

Petrick, James F. "Development of a Multi-Dimensional Scale for Measuring the Perceived Value of a Service." *Journal of Leisure Research* 34, no. 2 (2002): 119–134.

Pirsig, Robert M. *Zen and the Art of Motorcycle Maintenance: An Inquiry Into Values.* New York: Bantam Books, 1974.

Ralston, Roy W. "The Effects of Customer Service, Branding, and Price on the Perceived Value of Local Telephone Service." *Journal of Business Research* 56, no. 3 (March 2003): 201–213.

Rokeach, Milton. *The Nature of Human Values.* New York: Free Press, 1973.

Salegna, Gary J., and Stephen A. Goodwin. "Consumer Loyalty to Service Providers: An Integrated Conceptual Model." *Journal of Consumer Satisfaction, Dissatisfaction and Complaining Behavior* 18 (2005): 51–67.

Sánchez-Fernández, Raquel, and M. Ángeles Iniesta-Bonillo, "Consumer Perceptions of Value: Literature Review and a New Conceptual Framework." *Journal of Consumer Satisfaction, Dissatisfaction and Complaining Behavior* 19 (2006): 40–58.

Schwartz, Shalom H., and Wolfgang Bilsky. "Toward a Universal Psychological Structure of Human Values." *Journal of Personality and Social Psychology* 53, no. 3 (September 1987): 550–562.

Simpson, Penny M., Judy A. Siguaw, and Thomas L. Baker. "A Model of Value Creation: Supplier Behaviors and Their Impact on Reseller-Perceived Value." *Industrial Marketing Management* 30, no. 2 (February 2001): 119–134.

Spiteri, Joseph M., and Paul A. Dion. "Customer Value, Overall Satisfaction, End-User Loyalty, and Market Performance in Detail Intensive Industries." *Industrial Marketing Management* 33, no. 8 (November 2004): 675–687.

Sweeney, Jillian C., and Geoffrey N. Soutar. "Consumer Perceived Value: The Development of a Multiple Item Scale." *Journal of Retailing* 77, no. 2 (Summer 2001): 203–220.

Sweeney, Jillian C., Geoffrey N. Soutar, and Lester W. Johnson. "The Role of Perceived Risk in the Quality-Value Relationship: A Study in a Retail Environment." *Journal of Retailing* 75, no. 1 (Spring 1999): 77–105.

Teas, R. Kenneth, and Sanjeev Agarwal. "The Effects of Extrinsic Product Cues on Consumers' Perceptions of Quality, Sacrifice, and Value." *Journal of the Academy of Marketing Science* 28, no. 2 (Spring 2000): 278–290.

Tellis, Gerard J., and Joseph Johnson. "The Value of Quality." *Marketing Science* 26, no. 6 (November–December 2007): 758–773.

Ulaga, Wolfgang, and Samir Chacour. "Measuring Customer-Perceived Value in Business Markets: A Prerequisite for Marketing Strategy Development and Implementation." *Industrial Marketing Management* 30, no. 6 (August 2001): 525–540.

van der Haar, Jeanke W., Ron G.M. Kemp, and Onno (S.W.F.) Omta. "Creating Value That Cannot Be Copied." *Industrial Marketing Management* 30, no. 8 (November 2001): 627–636.

Varki, Sajeev, and Mark Colgate. "The Role of Price Perceptions in an Integrated Model of Behavioral Intentions." *Journal of Service Research* 3, no. 3 (February 2001): 232–240.

Wakefield, Kirk L., and James H. Barnes. "Retailing Hedonic Consumption: A Model of Sales Promotion of a Leisure Service." *Journal of Retailing* 72, no. 4 (Fall 1996): 409–427.

Walter, Achim, Thomas Ritter, and Hans Georg Gemünden. "Value Creation in Buyer-Seller Relationships: Theoretical Considerations and Empirical Results from a Supplier's Perspective." *Industrial Marketing Management* 30, no. 4 (May 2001): 365–377.

Watson, David, Lee Anna Clark, and Auke Tellegen. "Development and Validation of Brief Measures of Positive and Negative Affect: The PANAS Scales." *Journal of Personality and Social Psychology* 54, no. 6 (June 1988): 1063–1070.

Webb, Dave, and Abiodun Jagun. "Customer Care, Customer Satisfaction, Value, Loyalty and Complaining Behavior: Validation in a UK University Setting." *Journal of Consumer Satisfaction, Dissatisfaction and Complaining Behavior* 10 (1997): 139–151.

Woodruff, Robert B. "Customer Value: The Next Source for Competitive Advantage." *Journal of the Academy of Marketing Science* 25, no. 2 (Spring 1997): 139–153.

Woodruff, Robert B., and Daniel J. Flint. "Marketing's Service-Dominant Logic and Customer Value." In *The Service-Dominant Logic of Marketing: Dialog, Debate, and Directions*, ed. Robert F. Lusch and Stephen L. Vargo, 183–195. Armonk, NY: M.E. Sharpe, 2006.

Woodruff, Robert B., and Sarah Fisher Gardial. *Know Your Customer: New Approaches to Understanding Customer Value and Satisfaction.* Cambridge, MA: Blackwell, 1996.

Zaltman, Gerald. *How Consumers Think: Essential Insights into the Mind of the Market.* Boston: Harvard Business School Press, 2003.

Zeithaml, Valarie A. "Consumer Perceptions of Price, Quality, and Value: A Means-End Model and Synthesis of Evidence." *Journal of Marketing* 52, no. 3 (July 1988): 2–22.

CHAPTER 8

EQUITY

How Consumers Interpret Fairness

This chapter is about justice, justice in the marketplace where the consumer presides as judge and jury. The pursuit of justice implies that something has been found to be unjust. In the marketplace, a consumer's sense of injustice generally results from perceived unfairness in some dimension of purchasing and consumption, such as unfair prices, price gouging, and even illegal profits. During natural catastrophes, for example, victims may be charged outrageous prices for essential survival items such as batteries, bottled water, and fuel. Auto service centers may charge for unneeded repairs, securities firms may understate the risk (and loss) potential of complicated investment vehicles, and food stores may redate or recycle expired perishable products.

Most typically, however, little attention is paid to equitable treatment in consumption because the comparison standards used in fairness judgments are individualistic and less universal than expectations or other comparison standards. Moreover, fairness judgments involve idiosyncratic tangible and intangible elements, such as shopping effort, good faith bargaining, and a sense of value for price paid. In this context, price is but one of many possible factors in marketplace justice.

The equity concept is extremely important even though the comparison standards are nebulous. Inequity (and equity) is known to affect the satisfactions and dissatisfactions of those who are sensitive to this phenomenon. This claim is supported by the literatures in law, sociology, psychology, social psychology, and organizational psychology. Accordingly, it would be truly unusual if consumption activities were not influenced by equity considerations as well. Consider, for example, the feelings of a car buyer upon learning that a neighbor negotiated the purchase of an identical automobile from the same dealer at a price thousands of dollars less. Anecdotal evidence such as this and a growing body of evidence in the professional literature support the necessity of considering equity in efforts to account more fully for satisfaction and dissatisfaction judgments made by consumers.[1]

EQUITY: WHAT IT IS

In elementary terms, equity is a fairness, rightness, or deservingness comparison to other entities, whether real or imaginary, individual or collective, person or nonperson.[2] One can compare oneself to another individual, to a fictional prototypical character, to an average of a group of individuals, or to any entity with which one has dealings, such as a company, government, or societal organization.

The essence of equity is contained in a "rule of justice" stated by an early pioneer in the study of equity, George Homans: "[A person's] rewards in exchange with others should be proportional to his investments."[3] This prescriptive tenet brings out many characteristics of equity processes. First, this statement introduces the notion of exchange encounters with others. Interestingly, this aspect of the definition pertains more to the focus here, exchange in purchasing and consumption, than it does to other literatures. For example, a person can feel inequitably treated about life in general, as suggested in the common lament "Life ain't fair."[4] However, inequitable treatment in an actual exchange relationship makes the comparison much more personal, as the other party contributing to the feeling of inequity will generally be known to the consumer and will have benefited at the consumer's expense.

Another aspect of the preceding definition is proportionality. In effect, Homans states that one's rewards should be proportional to the costs and other inputs to the reward. In a consumer context, consumers might pay a dollar for a regular light bulb with an expected life of 2,000 hours. If consumers pay three times as much for a "long-life" bulb, they should expect to receive at least 6,000 hours of service.

This example makes the point that there is more to Homans's rule than the simple calculation of a proportion. All reward and cost combinations are proportional in some respect. If the light bulb consumer had only one option, that of the $1 bulb, the ratio of hours of service to dollars of cost would be 2,000 to 1. Is this fair? How would the consumer know? When a second, more expensive bulb is introduced, the 2,000-to-1 ratio can be used as a standard for judging whether the cost of the long-life bulb is fair in view of the expected level of service received. Thus, what the equity statement really means is that, for fairness to be sensed, the proportion of reward to investment must be similar to some other proportion against which it is compared.

In fact, it is possible to conceptualize inequity in two extreme cases—zero outcomes and zero inputs. In the first, where the reward is zero (or perhaps negative, as in the purchase of a fake artwork and the subsequent humiliation), the inequity is obvious; no reward was received for the inputs rendered. In the second case of costless rewards, the cost may be zero or nearly so (which makes the proportion infinite), but the consumer may still experience a sense of inequity. For example, two consumers receive free door prizes. One gets a coffee mug, and the other receives a prize of $1,000. Is this fair? To some people it is, and to others it is not.

A Mathematical Representation of Equity and Its Problems

Interpretations of Homans's prescription led a number of writers to propose the following familiar equity equation:[5]

$$(Os/Is) \sim (Oc/Ic) \tag{8.1}$$

where

O = outcomes
I = inputs or investments
s = self
c = comparison person, group, or entity
$\sim$ = proportional operator

Early research attempted to apply this equation to social situations in the strict mathematical sense, with only modest success. Critics of these efforts noted that the calculation of numeric outcome/input ratios should be limited to exchange situations in which outcomes and inputs are easily quantified and where the two self and other ratios (i.e., the O/I terms) are in the same units of measure.[6]

In addition to the unit of measure problem, other difficulties in operationalizing the equity equation arise because most comparisons involve multidimensional factors in both the input and outcome terms of the ratios. Whereas many of the empirical findings in the nonmarketing equity literature involve single inputs and single outcomes (e.g., hours of effort and dollars of pay), a parallel body of literature has begun to address multidimensional equity components, most notably in the domain of inputs: "Multidimensional input is characteristic of everyday equity judgments. Rarely are such judgments made on the basis of a single piece of information. Typically, they entail the use of different kinds or types of information."[7]

Consider, as is done later in this chapter, the typical negotiated purchase of an automobile—a prime example of the operation of equity principles. The consumer brings a number of inputs to the purchase: effort, information acquisition, a trade-in, cash, personal loan information, the willingness to take on debt, and the frustration of the bargaining process. While some of these inputs can be quantified (cash, debt), most cannot (effort, frustration). This immediately raises the question of how these can be combined.

The issue becomes complicated further by other interpretations of equity having social connotations that transcend any resemblance to a mathematical formula.[8] For example, equity assumes a proportionality operator where higher inputs beget higher outcomes. However, another interpretation of equitable distribution might presume equality of outcomes. An equality rule would do away with inputs entirely, so that an equal level of outcomes would result regardless of the level of inputs. This is the philosophy of collectivist societies where all receive similar life benefits regardless of their contribution to the society's wealth. In still another interpretation, the distribution of resources (rewards) would be based on needs only. According to this philosophy, inputs are replaced with needs (deficits) so that a lack of needs would actually decrease outcomes.

These latter examples illustrate the point that definitions of equity are socially determined and arise from interpersonal philosophies common to a culture or subculture. In this sense, many equity norms are held as passive expectations, as in fair play in sports and "handshake" agreements more generally. Thus, feelings of equity may not be processed unless these norms are violated or if a particular exchange relationship has a history of, or the potential for, untoward behavior on the part of one participant. For example, many telemarketing products sold in boiler room operations are notorious for such shady dealings and devious tactics.

This same line of reasoning may also explain why equity concerns do not appear in lists of product features or salient attributes collected before purchasing. If a particular industry or company is generally known for upright dealings, it does not occur to consumers that inequity may be perceived after purchase and consumption, when it would dramatically impact satisfaction. In an unfortunate example, many consumers become disenchanted with charities when they learn how little of their contribution actually goes to help the needy. This example suggests that no particular outcome/input ratio may be calculated in individual circumstances. Rather, consumers have the potential to recognize inequity when they see it.

In a worst-case example, a large philanthropic company was found to have engaged in a Ponzi scheme, whereby up-front donors were promised "matching gifts" for their contributions by anonymous donors.[9] In fact, later donations were used to "match" earlier donations, and no anonymous donors existed. Philanthropists taken in by this scheme were reported to have expressed amazement that such nefarious activity would take place within the philanthropic community. It was simply "beyond comprehension."

Thus, for all the reasons presented here, it is useful to relax the assumption of a strict mathematical interpretation of inequity for the same reason that researchers are able to successfully predict satisfaction without having to mathematically calculate expectation-performance discrepancy scores. The reason is that consumers have a sense of what is fair or right to them, based on how they interpret the situation. Some will make elementary attempts to estimate inequity, as when a customer compares the cost of a high-definition television to the price paid by another consumer buying an identical TV; still other consumers will simply "know" that they have been treated unfairly. In either case, they will hold onto their perceptions of inequity and act in the future accordingly. Management, of course, will need to know the sources of these perceptions. An approach used by this author to study this problem will be presented later.

"Positive" Inequity

Like the terms *discrepancy* and *disconfirmation*, the word *inequity* implies a negative deficit in lay terms. However, as is also the case with disconfirmation, it is possible for an individual to be overbenefited—that is, to obtain more outcomes than are deserved under the application of a "correct" equity formula. Thus, equity exists on a continuum bounded by negative inequity where outcomes are less than deserved, through equity where outcomes are justly deserved, to positive inequity where outcomes are greater than deserved.[10] This last possibility will be specifically entertained, as it is not so unusual as it may seem at first.

For example, test coaching consultants frequently promise that they can improve test performance, such as scores on the Scholastic Aptitude Test (SAT), by 100 points or so. Fees are typically in the hundreds of dollars. Three students of the same age who wish to improve their SAT scores attend the coaching program. One student increases her score by 100 points, as promised. The second student increases his score by only 10 points, while the third improves his score by 225 points. Who was overbenefited and who was underbenefited? Thus, like disconfirmation, inequity is a bipolar concept, as displayed below.

Equity: "correctly benefited"

Negative inequity: "underbenefited"				Positive inequity: "overbenefited"
1	2	3	4	5

This "under/over" benefiting scale has been used in studies by the author with interesting results, discussed later. In yet another rendition, the three equity states were inferred from experimental treatments with the intent of prompting respondents into one of the three conditions in the context of a Web vendor.[11] The findings were as predicted and will be discussed shortly as well.

The Effect of Differing Roles

The preceding discussion suggests that unless consumers are queried, management will be in a poor position to understand fully consumer feelings of inequity. This is so because the marketer-consumer relationship involves potentially opposing roles and aims in exchange. The consumer's goal is to improve the quality of life; any one specific purchase may be an infrequent event in this quest. The marketer, in contrast, must consummate this and other transactions to turn a profit and survive. Thus, exchange in consumption frequently involves a nonprofessional, perhaps a rational decision maker pitted against a professional businessperson or firm.

This phenomenon of differing roles makes the purchase and consumption aspect of inequity somewhat unique. Early work in social psychology frequently assumed a social exchange based on the notion of equal partners (e.g., spouses, coworkers). When roles are disparate, such as they are in marketing exchanges involving consumers, researchers must rely on theories of distributive justice or what has come to be known as expectation states theory.[12] This perspective requires only that each party have expectations of the role of the other; justice is interpreted in terms of the other's performance on the expected role dimensions.

For example, parents and teachers are involved in the "purchase" and provision of a complex product known as education. The purchase may be made with hard cash, as in the case of private school tuition, or with tax dollars for public school.[13] In both cases, parents expect that their children will be treated fairly vis-à-vis the other students—that is, given the same opportunities for expression, equal attention, and access to learning resources such as computers. However, the teacher has expectations of the parents' role as well. Namely, parents are expected to instill respect for and deference to the teacher, to facilitate and encourage homework, and to ensure that the children are punctual and alert in class. These two sets of expectations define equity in this particular exchange. They are related to each other, but not directly comparable because the roles of parent and teacher are disparate.

The expectation states framework is readily seen as much more useful in consumer-vendor exchanges. By definition, neither party is "equal." Buyer and seller exist at opposite sides of the exchange in roles that are not at all similar. Excluding time spent in the transaction, their inputs are rarely the same, because the parties have in common only that an exchange takes place and it is not clear that the buyer desires this in all cases. Nor are their outcomes similar, since the seller desires the product's profit margin while the buyer desires the product's utility.

THE ROLE OF EQUITY IN CONSUMER SATISFACTION

Person-to-Person Comparisons

Purchase and consumption activities provide a rich venue for the application of equity principles due to the potentially large number of referent persons and introduce a large body of literature on "social comparison."[14] The category of other persons could include an agent in a sales transaction, a service provider, another purchaser of the same product, or even owners of large corporations. In the last case, many consumers are outraged at the very large salaries of corporate chief executive officers (CEOs), particularly when a given CEO oversees providers of life's necessities, such as oil refiners. And, in another example, sports fans can compare themselves and the prices they pay for tickets to the players and their salaries. Generally, equity principles predict that consumers will compare their inputs and outcomes to those expected (or predicted) of the other referent. In the case of a negotiated sales transaction (e.g., automobiles, homes, flea market purchases), the purchase price and the seller's perceived profit would be likely elements in this comparison.

Although the cognitive mechanisms used by consumers will be elaborated later in this chapter, it is known that many consumers do have perceptions, however inaccurate, of the returns to others in sales transactions, including salesperson commissions and dealer profits.[15] This topic was the subject of a series of papers by this author and a colleague in which automobile buyers reported on their own inputs to and outcomes from service or sale, as well as those perceived of their salesperson.[16] The studies found that the consumers were sensitive to their outcomes and to the seller's inputs, more so than to their inputs and the salesperson's outcomes. This was so despite the fact that some referent outcomes (e.g., salespersons' perceived commissions) were correlated (negatively) with satisfaction.

In another study of simulated stock market trades,[17] participants with investing experience were given scenarios of likely outcomes for a hypothetical purchase. In half the scenarios, the investors made more than their broker (the combined broker and firm commission is specifically detailed on brokerage sales statements); in the other half, the broker made more than the investor. Although all the investors made money in all their trades, the manipulation of equity and inequity proved to be significant in the hypothesized manner. Namely, in those situations where subjects made less than their broker, satisfaction ratings were predictably lower. Since investors put their personal funds at risk, while the broker makes a commission regardless of whether investors make or lose money, the equity considerations in this situation are fairly straightforward. Not all subjects were sensitive to this manipulation, however. More will be said of this later. Nonetheless, this example and that of the auto buyers show that equity is a factor in consumer-salesperson interactions.

Comparisons can also be made to individuals having no relationship to the specific transaction that the consumer encounters. Other consumers known or unknown to the focal person, imaginary consumers, consumers in other geographic regions (e.g., adjacent states with lower sales taxes), and even prototypical consumers as described by the government (e.g., the consumer who really received full disclosure when buying an insurance policy) are candidate comparison referents for inequity judgments. This problem becomes particularly acute when prices charged fluctuate (dynamic pricing) due to variations in supply and demand across time, days, or business conditions. While these price differences appear perfectly justifiable in economic terms, consumers perceive these differences as "discriminatory."[18]

For example, studies have found that consumers are sensitive to the knowledge that other consumers had gotten better prices or better treatment from merchants.[19] In these studies, the "other consumers" were not known to the participants; rather they were hypothetical consumers or simply data on normative levels of what other consumers would have paid or received. These studies illustrate the point that equity comparisons can involve standards of comparison that exist only as imagined interpersonal norms. This concept of interpersonal inequity is, perhaps, one reason why automobile dealerships such as those of GM's Saturn Division (at the time of this writing) promote a one-price, no-haggling sales strategy.

In the aforementioned study of Web purchasing, this "unknown to others" perspective was tested directly.[20] Respondents were asked to participate in a simulated Web purchasing study without mention of the researchers' intent. Unbeknown to the randomly assigned respondents, some were asked to complete the purchase cycle without mention of the now ubiquitous "promotion code" field, which asks for a discount code if a consumer has one available. This code is similar to grocery coupons except that the Web variation almost always prompts would-be purchasers, while grocery stores may or may not. In the overbenefited case, respondents had their code fields completed, thereby receiving a discount. In contrast, those in the underbenefited case saw the code field with the prompt "Do you have a promotion code," but had no means in the experiment to search for one, assuming that they would be savvy enough to know how this is done. As predicted, the overbenefited group had greater satisfaction and were more likely to complete the purchase, while the underbenefited respondents had less satisfaction and were more likely to fail to complete the purchase (known as shopping cart abandonment) when compared to the control (the "correctly benefited" group) who saw no code field at all.

In yet another example of person-to- (unknown)-person comparisons, observers have related the response of software upgrade subscribers to the practices of Microsoft and Borland in the early 1990s.[21] These companies permitted users of other brands of software to switch to the Microsoft or Borland version at the same price as current users of the previous version (past patrons). Needless to say, the loyal patrons were outraged because the competitive-brand users had no investment in the upgrade version, yet were allowed to pay the same price.

Person-to-Merchant Comparisons

Consumers make two types of comparisons to the merchant or vendor. The first is purely individual-oriented whereby the consumers' interest is only in ensuring that they get what they paid for or what they deserved. Thus, the merchant's role is to provide the product selection and level of service commensurate with the consumer's effort and price paid. The latter issue of a fair price has dominated the literature in this domain, and details go much beyond the scope intended in the present volume. Readers are encouraged to peruse this literature for the insights into price equity (more generally known as price fairness) provided.[22]

This person-to-merchant comparison becomes especially relevant with regard to complaint resolution because a product or service shortcoming violates the equity exchange norm implicit in the purchase. Specifically, it reduces the consumer's outcomes to zero or to a deficit, particularly if other aspects of the consumer's life are affected. For example, a malfunctioning digital video recorder not only deprives the consumer of its use but also results in lost programming. Authors have investigated this phenomenon in depth, including the nature of the proper response by the firm to bring the consumer back to "equity."[23] Much more will be said of this topic in Chapter 14.

The second dimension of the merchant's role in equity is the merchant's return—what the company gets from the consumer's purchase. There is a subtle distinction here between the consumer's price per se, the merchant's cost, and the merchant's profit. When consumer prices track the costs of materials, as they supposedly do for gasoline, consumers accept this situation as a "pass-along." The point here, however, is the perceived difference between cost-of-goods and selling price to the consumer, regardless of the type and amount of middlemen. Clearly, most consumers understand that sellers make a profit on each sale. However, unconscionable profits (i.e., price gouging) are not well tolerated as consumers are in a position to infer motives of the seller's price increase.[24]

Other elements of purchases that benefit the merchant beyond profits are also candidates for consideration in equity judgments. In one of the author's equity-based car studies, automobile purchasers were asked about profit and other outcomes a dealer (as opposed to the salesperson) receives from consumers, including referrals to other potential customers; a well-maintained, easy-to-sell trade-in; and, of course, the sale of a high-price consumer durable in a relatively low-volume business.[25] When combined with dealer inputs and the consumer's inputs and outcomes, dealer outcomes were shown to play a role in equity perceptions separately from those concerning the salesperson.

Lastly, the type of merchant also sends profit signals to consumers. Mass retailers such as Wal-Mart (and its subsidiary, Sam's Club) are expected to have lower prices because consumers are aware of the mass volume discounts and purchasing power of these firms and the "warehouse" decor of their stores. In similar vein, online retailers are expected to have lower prices because they generally do not have stores to lease or own and manage; when they do, the online price should be lower than the equivalent store. In a twist of logic, it has been shown that competing stores selling equivalent goods, including high-end stores selling "product overlap" with lower-price merchants, can give the impression of fair pricing simply by matching the lower prices on some popularly purchased products.[26]

Consequences of Inequity

The consequences of equity comparisons, as found in the literature, are similar to those of satisfaction, including intention to rebuy, complaining, and both positive and negative word of mouth, discussed in greater detail in Chapter 14. Additionally, equity concepts are known to affect satisfaction directly or through indirect mediators such as the emotions, discussed in Chapter 12.[27] However, it may be more accurate to say that, first, equity considerations influence satisfaction and that it is satisfaction that affects intention, complaining, and word of mouth. This issue awaits further research.

The preceding discussion has laid the groundwork for consideration of how equity operates in consumer judgments. Specifically, a likely mechanism explaining how the equity judgment is processed and how it later influences satisfaction and dissatisfaction is now presented.

HISTORICAL VERSUS CONTEMPORARY INTERPRETATIONS OF EQUITY INFLUENCES

A number of perspectives link outcome and input combinations, such as the familiar equity formulation in Equation 8.1, to satisfaction. The first perspective, perhaps typified by the classical experimental paradigm whereby outcome/input ratios are manipulated, posits a direct path from the outcome/input combinations to satisfaction. Theoretically, this suggests that the inputs and outcomes have intrinsic equity interpretations that directly translate to satisfaction judgments (see Figure 8.1, panel A). In the second approach, specific interpretations or dimensions of equity, apart from the inputs and outcomes themselves, are posited to intervene between inputs and outcomes and satisfaction. Theoretically, this would imply that individuals perceive specific meaning to outcome/input comparisons that cannot be construed as satisfaction, but which affect satisfaction (see Figure 8.1, panel B).

Nonintervening Frameworks

Early writers on equity proposed a social psychological approach to nonintervening interpersonal strategies. In an elaboration of the outcome possibilities facing two parties to a transaction, these authors discuss various transformations the parties can apply to the outcome combinations so that these outcome (or payoff) solutions become mutually satisfactory.[28] In effect, the outcomes themselves describe the satisfactoriness of the situation.

These so-called transformations available to the parties are actually strategies that define paths to influence satisfaction within a relationship. An example is use of the hedonistic strategy of maximizing one's personal outcomes (and satisfaction), which has been called "max own." Other transformations include maximizing the other party's outcomes (altruism), maximizing both one's own and another's outcomes (max joint), maximizing one's own relative advantage or the difference between one's own and another's outcomes (max rel), and minimizing this difference (min diff).

These five strategies are suggested as capable of both influencing and explaining interpersonal satisfaction and dissatisfaction. For example, the altruism, max joint, and min diff strategies should enhance satisfaction, while max own and max rel may foster dissatisfaction on the part of the

Figure 8.1 **Two Representations of Inequity Influences**

A. Non-Intervening Approaches (Direct Links to Satisfaction)

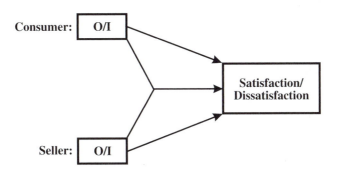

B. Intervening Approaches (Indirect Link to Satisfaction)

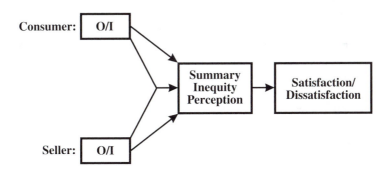

other person. As proposed, however, the success of the various strategies in influencing satisfaction may be unique to specific individuals within pairs and thus may be difficult to generalize to a firm's market.

There may be situations, however, in which consumers could agree on the degree to which a particular strategy would generate satisfaction. For example, under max own, satisfaction should increase linearly as one's outcomes increase, regardless of those of the other party. Gambling winnings in a casino provide one setting where a consensus on the success of a max own strategy might occur. Thus, some aspects of the "max/min" framework may be useful to the researcher because if any one of the proposed strategies is preferred by a majority of consumers, the meaning behind a consumer equity response may emerge.

To gain additional insight into the equity process, however, it would be helpful to know if consumers processed these strategies further. Using the casino example again, consumers may compare their outcomes (winnings) to the maximum amount that they intended to gamble. If so, this ratio may represent a sort of return to the consumer, and it may be that the return and not the amount won correlates most strongly with satisfaction. Thus, if the return ("doubled my money") is a cognition separate from the amount won, then the return could become the most immediate antecedent of satisfaction. This result would mean that the individual inputs and outcomes in the equity equation (the gambler's betting limit and the amount won) would not have to be known if the prediction of satisfaction is the researcher's sole goal. This possibility suggests that an intervening-variable framework may be somewhat better suited to the aggregate perspective needed for consumer analysis.

Intervening Approaches

The intervening-variable notion has been proposed, in part, to accommodate different interpretations (such as the transformations) of the meaning of equity and inequity. Although the traditional equity equation assumes that equity occurs when the ratio of outcomes to inputs is proportional for all parties, various other interpretations have been found in the literature. It appears that the most common of the competing interpretations are (1) fairness or "proportional" equity, as in the equity formula, and (2) preference or maximizing one's own outcome relative to that of the other—the equivalent of the max rel strategy. These two concepts have been discussed at length by their proponents and are reviewed shortly.[29]

More recent discussions of the difference between the fairness and preference interpretations have recast these phenomena in other terms, all indicative of a conceptual broadening. For example, the word *equality* may be used to refer to fairness while *self-interest* relates to preference. Work on the egocentric fairness bias (preference) finds that individuals believing in a "just world" find their behaviors "fairer" than those of others performing the same behaviors. Other work on the "fair process effect" has found that "unfair" outcomes favorable to the object person (a reversal of fair process) are due to internal competencies, whereas "fair" (equal) outcomes may be attributed to external constraints. And, in the arena of mental accounting, research shows that receiving amounts greater than fair market in a trade is fairer than fair market or less. Thus, the fairness of favorably prejudicial unfairness is not unknown in the realm of human justice.[30]

Fairness: The Equity Dimension of Equity

The notion of fairness is almost synonymous with equity in that it implies a form of distributive justice whereby individuals get what they deserve based on their inputs.[31] Thus, the fairness dimension of equity would reflect the inputs and outcomes of both parties to the transaction in a manner referred to as the weak proportional equity formula. Although stated mathematically in its original form, this equation can be conceptualized verbally. It requires only that the outcomes and inputs of both parties be in rough approximation to each other (hence weak proportionality). In essence, this is the more common interpretation whereby fairness increases as inequity (negative or positive) decreases.

Later, discussion will turn to a related concept known as the *fair process* effect whereby the methods of distributing input resources and outcomes are assessed for fairness.[32] This is also a "deservingness" phenomenon since individuals may know not the specific outcomes of others, but just that they got what they deserved. This effect will be more difficult to assess as measurement must rely on self-reports more so than required by the present topic.

Preference: The Inequity Dimension of Equity

To recap the previous discussion, the egoism, egocentric, or preference viewpoint states that one party to a transaction will feel less distress (and more fairness) than the other party when inequity is in the first party's favor. Theorists now view preference, as this view here, as any combination of outcomes that benefits the perceiver of the situation more so than the other party or parties, a situation best described as advantageous or prejudicially favorable inequity.[33] Unlike fairness, preference should increase as inequity becomes more positive or becomes overly beneficial.

While these two perspectives are intriguing, the degree to which fairness and/or preference plays a role in consumer satisfaction judgments is not known. Nor is it known whether these intervening constructs contribute to satisfaction beyond the level accounted for by the inputs and outcomes of both parties alone (the nonintervening approach). In fact, two issues appear relevant with regard to this perspective. First, are these intervening concepts needed? Second, do they completely mediate the effects of inputs and outcomes on satisfaction? Researchers in the area attempted to shed light on these issues with the following, seemingly cynical statement: "So long as individuals perceive they can maximize their outcomes [net of inputs] by behaving equitably, they will do so. Should they perceive that they can maximize their outcomes by behaving inequitably [to their advantage], they will do so."[34]

Thus individuals are thought to have dual motivations. At the same time as they would like to maximize their outcomes, they would like to think that this state of nature is perceived as fair. Given the checks and balances of many exchange systems, equity seeking in exchange may be the only legitimate or feasible means to this goal. Equity, then, will be pursued when that is the most likely route to goal maximization; otherwise, the preference route will be pursued. Satisfaction, in turn, would depend on the degree to which one or both were achieved in specific situations. The weighting scheme applied by consumers to these concepts, however, is an empirical question.

This competing framework was tested in previously noted articles by this author.[35] As discussed, automobile buyers were queried as to their inputs and outcomes regarding the purchase as well as those perceived for the salesperson and dealer. Summary scales of fairness and preference were also measured, as was satisfaction. Sample items from the measures used for inputs and outcomes and complete scales used for fairness and preference follow (scored on 1–7 agree/disagree scales; R = reverse score). A list of similar items substituted "dealer" for "salesperson."

Buyer inputs: In dealing with the salesperson, I put in a lot of time and effort.
Buyer outcomes: In dealing with the salesperson, I received a good deal on the car I bought.
Seller inputs: In dealing with me, the salesperson put in time away from other customers.
Seller outcomes: In dealing with me, the salesperson received a high commission on the sale.

Fairness (complete scale):
   I was treated fairly by the salesperson.
   I was *not* treated right by the salesperson. (R)
   The deal I agreed to with the salesperson was fair.

Preference (incomplete scale; the last item immediately follows the list):
   I think the salesperson got more out of the deal than I did. (R)
   I think I got more out of the deal than the salesperson.

The last preference item was a seven-point scale as follows:

I came out ahead		We both benefited equally			The salesperson came out ahead	
7	6	5	4	3	2	1

The results across both salesperson and dealer analyses were consistent. When satisfaction was regressed on fairness and preference, only fairness predicted satisfaction; the preference coefficient was not significant. At this point, it appears that the consumers in this study were very righteous in their dealings and feelings with the salesperson and dealer entities; they were more satisfied to the extent that they perceived fairness, not preference (where they would have gotten more) in the exchange.

This would be a correct, but misleading conclusion, however, because the consumers appeared to have dual motivations, as hypothesized. To understand what consumers actually meant by fairness and preference, each of these scales was regressed on combinations of the input and outcome variables. In doing so, the equity format in Equation 8.1 was not used. Despite the intuitive nature of this ratio, research shows that it gives unreliable results unless all terms are measured on true metric scales or with other restricting transformations. This line of research is, no doubt, one of the issues that will consume the interest of equity researchers for some time. Nonetheless, since the study required a formulaic decision, the subtractive form was selected. It is appealing on its face and does give results that have been defended against those with opposing views.[36]

This subtractive form of calculating equity combinations has been deemed permissible when the inputs and outcomes are collected on scales having only an arbitrary metric.[37] In the equation

$$(O_s - I_s) - (O_c - I_c), \tag{8.2}$$

the O and the I are as shown in Equation 8.1. The self (s) benefits as self outcomes increase, self inputs decrease, comparison other's (c) inputs increase, and other's outcomes decrease.

By using this basic formula, the input and outcome variables were combined in two ways, one reflecting equity and the other reflecting inequity—scored in the direction of positive inequity in favor of the consumer:

$$Consumer: (outcomes - inputs) - Seller: (outcomes - inputs) \tag{8.3}$$

$$100 - | [Consumer: (outcomes - inputs) - Seller: (outcomes - inputs)] | \tag{8.4}$$

Equation 8.3, which is the easier of the two to understand, is the preference version. Here, positive inequity in the consumer's favor increases as consumer outcomes increase and inputs decrease, and as the seller's outcomes decrease and inputs increase. Thus, under this formula, consumers desire that they reap maximum outcomes while investing minimal inputs and that the seller invest maximum inputs while receiving minimal outcomes.

Equation 8.4 appears essentially identical with two exceptions. First, the absolute value notation (also used in Chapter 6) means that any deviation from exact equality, whether in favor of the consumer or of the seller, will result in inequity and a positive score within the absolute value sign. Because it is desired that the equation be scored in a direction where higher scores represent fairness, the score is subtracted from an arbitrary constant, such as 100. As shown, this form of the equation represents equity. A score of 100 represents perfect equity (100 minus 0 is interpreted as *no in*equity).

When the overall fairness and preference scales were regressed on these two versions of the fairness and preference formulas in the two data sets used in the study, a strange result appeared. The most significant finding was a strong relation between the preference Equation 8.3 and the

Figure 8.2   **The Oliver and Swan Consumer Equity Findings**

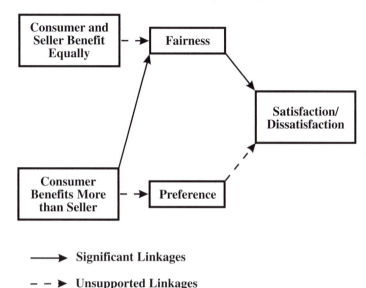

fairness dependent variable. That is, consumers appeared to be interpreting fairness as reflective of a preference score. Fairness to these consumers meant besting the seller (the same result appeared for both salesperson and dealer). So, whereas fairness predicted satisfaction, positive inequity—where the consumer came out ahead—predicted fairness. This framework is shown in Figure 8.2.

Similar results were found in a simulated study of responses to complaining.[38] Although details of the scenarios were not presented, subjects were randomly placed in four complaint-resolution conditions represented by high versus low outcomes and equitable versus inequitable outcome/input ratios. A combined equity/satisfaction scale was used as the dependent variable. Results showed that the most equitably satisfied subjects were in the high-outcome/low-input cell (advantageous inequity). In order of decreasing levels of satisfaction were the high/high subjects (high outcome equity), low/low subjects (low outcome equity), and low/high subjects (disadvantageous inequity). Once, again, advantageous inequity was seen as fair or, as in this study, equitable.

What accounts for these two sets of findings? One explanation pertains to individuals and how they evaluate fairness, and another pertains to the perceptions consumers have of businesspeople. The first explanation is somewhat telling of the human condition. Generally, individuals are thought to have an egocentric, self-serving bias, particularly in dealing with casual acquaintances. In fact, it has been shown that people associate fair behaviors to themselves and unfair behaviors to others more frequently than can be accounted for by chance.[39]

Regarding the second explanation, why is it that the nature of a buyer-seller exchange may promote a bias toward advantageous inequity? As the reader may have noticed from personal observation, automobile dealer advertising frequently claims that the dealer is "sacrificing" profits in order to sell inventory. Additionally, since automobile sales are usually negotiated, consumers may feel entitled to whatever advantage they are able to gain through bargaining; merchants, in turn, should be responsible for their own interests. In still another explanation, buyers may feel (correctly) that they purchase a car infrequently, perhaps once every four or five years, whereas the salesperson is in the business of selling cars every day for a living. Thus, for equity to occur, consumers may believe that their outcomes should equal in one purchase what the salesperson would make in ten or so. Although this example is extreme, it does make the point that consumers apparently desire an inequitable deal in their favor.

Thus, current interpretations of consumer equity do not conform to the view that equity is a proportionality or even an equality phenomenon. Rather equity is a particular psychological balance formed by consumers idiosyncratically. Unless researchers test various formulations against one another, the degree of objective inequity in a consumer's equity judgment will go undetected, and a fuller explanation of satisfaction differences across consumers will be compromised.

This observation brings up three related issues. First, are there still other dimensions of equity not accounted for by comparisons of inputs and outcomes? Second, can equity contribute to an understanding of the satisfaction response beyond the influence of disconfirmation? Third, do individuals differ in the degree to which they react to inequity in forming satisfaction judgments? These issues are addressed next.

ADDITIONAL TOPICS IN CONSUMER EQUITY

Distributive Versus Procedural and Interactional Fairness

The equity process described so far involves *distributive* justice, namely, how rewards or outcomes are partitioned among the participants in an exchange. Could it be that even when outcomes net of inputs are fairly distributed, or even inequitably distributed in the consumer's favor, perceptions of inequity remain? Apparently so, if there are yet other elements about the exchange that violate the consumer's sense of fairness. In an effort to explain what these other influences might be, writers both inside and outside the consumer psychology discipline have introduced two other fairness notions, *procedural* fairness and *interactional* fairness, to the consumer satisfaction literature. Taken together with distributive fairness, the sum total of these fairness dimensions is referred to as *systemic* justice or equity. Tests of all three have been performed simultaneously with the result that, at the minimum, two of the three fairness dimensions have been related to various criteria. Typically, distributive justice, to which we have been referring, is one of the two.[40]

Procedural Fairness

Procedural fairness, perhaps the second of the fairness concepts introduced to the general and consumer psychology literatures, explores the *manner* in which the outcomes were delivered.[41] Typically, three elements of arriving at the distribution of outcomes play a role. The first is the ability to participate in the distribution decision, including the chance to provide information; the second is the belief that this information is used in the decision; and the third is the feeling that one's participation influenced the outcome. The importance of procedural fairness is illustrated in a study of traffic offenders who had their case dismissed without a hearing. Despite this (most) favorable outcome, many became angry because they were denied the opportunity to have their side of the story heard.[42]

Other research followed. In the psychological literature, reviews of studies concluded that procedural fairness and distributive fairness might be compensatory in that when one is lacking or unattainable, individuals look to the other for means to achieving equity. And in a study of voters (consumers and participants of the political process), the very access and ability to vote is seen as a procedural fairness issue. In consumption, the great bulk of the literature covers the topics of complaining and service recovery (Chapter 14), where fairness or unfairness is rather easily sensed in both procedure and outcome and, interestingly, with regard to salespeople whose performance ratings are assessed for the manner in which performance goals are attained and in the results for the salesperson in terms of remuneration.[43]

Other research shows extensions to these basic findings and contexts. Work in the area of computer user satisfaction, for example, finds that distributional fairness (being provided the right equipment on a fair basis) and procedural fairness (fair establishment of priorities across user groups) add to the variance explained in user satisfaction over traditional measures.[44]

Interactional Fairness

Interactional fairness, in its own right, taps the manner in which the consumer is treated in terms of respect, politeness, and appreciation of others' thoughts, feelings, and efforts.[45] In this sense, the equity standards are those of common dignity, owed to all members of society. Interactional fairness differs from procedural fairness in pertaining to the person-to-person dealings that provide the process of justice.

Research both inside and outside marketing settings shows fairly conclusively that all forms of fairness add to the explanation of variance in satisfaction; interactional justice is one of these components that must be considered for a fuller accounting of fairness effects. Within marketing, early reports of results from qualitative analysis of critical incidents in service settings demonstrate that all three forms of fairness (fair distribution of outcomes, fair procedures, and fair interactions) are represented in consumer comments.[46] In a regression of overall satisfaction on scales measuring the three fairness dimensions, all were found to have made significant contributions to satisfaction. Distributional fairness (justice) yielded the largest effect; interactional fairness, although significant, the least—suggesting that this last dimension is sensitive to the amount of personal contact in the transaction. In support of this notion, early research on consumers has shown that two redress actions in a complaint setting, voice (allowing the consumer the opportunity to explain grievances) and an apology, enhanced satisfaction—the former being a procedural strategy and the latter an interactional strategy. The effects were diminished, however, if no remunerative allowance was made by the firm.[47]

Other studies followed including interactional fairness in tests of equity models, and mostly appeared with reference to complaining behavior. Generally, distributed justice continued to dominate the fairness dimensions. Of interest is the fact that interactional justice appears to have greater impact on the antecedents of satisfaction, including intention, commitment, word of mouth, and trust in the provider.[48] These studies and others cited suggest a curious interplay of fairness concepts expressed in the following quote: "when customers do not get the service outcome they want [distributive justice], they are less likely to recognize employee effort and hard work [procedural and interactional issues]."[49]

This and other new findings on procedural and interactional fairness suggest a modification to the conceptual representation of equity effects, as shown in Figure 8.3. The figure shows that the newly conceptualized justice dimensions enhance the ability to predict satisfaction by accounting for fairness in process and fairness (dignity) in interaction. It also shows potential feedback effects of the outcomes received (i.e., distributed) on all fairness dimensions. It is assumed here that all fairness measures are taken after outcomes are received, so that the consumer reports procedural and interactional fairness retroactively (as denoted by the backward-pointing arrows). Although this is not how the entire purchase or service use sequence unfolds, it is how consumers will perceive it when they decide to repurchase or repatronize (but see the following exception).

It has been stated earlier that there are times when others' outcomes are not visible or known to

Figure 8.3   **Equity Model Showing the Dimensions of Fairness**

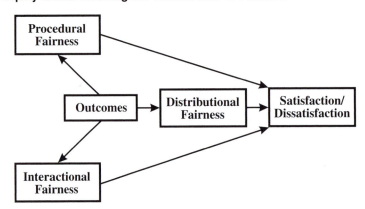

all. This could happen, for example, with regard to salespersons' earnings. In this case, the observer may use procedural justice to infer distributive justice, in which case the roles of the two in Figure 8.3 would be reversed. In an extension of this logic, interactional equity may become prominent and take the place of the distributive moderator.[50] Clearly, multiple dimensions of equity must be considered and their relative influence monitored to properly account for differential effects.

Does Equity Work in Parallel With Disconfirmation?

Is inequity simply another form of disconfirmation? While it is true that consumers can have expectations of equity in a transaction, which may be disconfirmed at a later time, it is argued here that equity is a distinct cognition involving different comparative referents. To see how this may be, it would be helpful to understand how consumers may process equity considerations and disconfirmation simultaneously. Can outcomes exceed expectations, but create inequity at the same time? Similarly, is equity possible if expectations are not attained?

An affirmative answer to these questions requires that the equity and disconfirmation processes be distinct. At first, they may appear similar, for they share many characteristics. For example, both are comparison processes, both involve prior standards used for the comparison, and both are known to affect satisfaction. There appear to be more differences, however, than similarities. In fact, a review of the concepts impacting consumer satisfaction found that equity and disconfirmation were the two foremost precursors of the satisfaction response affecting satisfaction separately.[51]

Figure 1.4 shows that equity and disconfirmation are conceptually distinct and can be considered as complementary influences on satisfaction, despite the fact that they share a comparative basis. It is argued that these constructs differ most fundamentally on (1) the standard for comparison, (2) the nature of this standard, (3) the attributes and dimensions used in the comparison, (4) the stages in the comparison process, and (5) the emotional reaction to the various states of the two concepts. Each is discussed in greater detail next (see Table 8.1).

Comparison Referents and Their Nature

As discussed, the referents that are used for the comparison process in equity judgments are out-comes and inputs of self and others. Once combined, either objectively (calculated) or subjectively

Table 8.1

Conceptual Differences Between Equity and Disconfirmation

Comparison dimension	Equity	Disconfirmation
Standard of comparison	Others' inputs and outcomes	Expectations, desires, norms
Nature of comparison standard(s)	Passive, interpersonal social norms	Generally actively processed performance predictions
Attributes and dimensions	Only those having fairness or preference implications (e.g., price paid)	Potentially all attributes or dimensions of the product or service
Stages in process	Two: inputs and outcomes of each party compared first; the two outcome/input ratios compared next	One: comparison of performance to expectations, desires, norms only
Emotional response	Negative: anger, distress, resentment, vindication	Negative: anger, disappointment
	Zero (equity): fairness, justice	Zero (confirmation): contentment
	Positive: guilt, glee (a sense of egocentric "justice")	Positive: delight

(sensed), they are compared to passive interpersonal norms that have been acquired through various forms of socialization. In consumer analysis, these can be viewed in the context of one's role partner (e.g., a salesperson) or in the context of institutional procedures and their fair application to all members (customers) generally.

In disconfirmation, the standards for comparison are expectations and other marketplace norms (e.g., best brand). Generally, these should be more actively processed than equity norms, because the product or service expectations have been instilled through promotion, because of word of mouth or previous experience, or because the customer pursues specific benefits in purchasing the product. Thus, consumers desire that certain benefits will occur in disconfirmation processes, while in contrast they may believe that fairness conditions prevail as normal in equity processes.

Attributes and Dimensions Used for Comparison

In equity comparisons, the relevant attributes must have fairness implications. Price is an obvious example, as are the service dimensions of personnel-intensive consumables, such as the ubiquitous marketing of automobiles; matters of personal taste (e.g., the color of an appliance) probably do not qualify as equity concerns. Nor should any dimension qualify that is shared by all consumers. Equity becomes an issue when perceived inequity exists, in the spirit of the social comparison literature. For example, cable TV typically provides more channels than any one viewer will desire. By overproviding channels, the cable company ensures that no one consumer in the cable area will feel inequitably treated. Only when subscribers compare themselves to viewers in other areas or compare cable service to other services with even greater access (e.g., satellite) do perceptions of inequity arise.

In contrast, any dimension of the product or service is a candidate for disconfirmation perceptions. In fact, even expectations of equity can be disconfirmed. In this sense, the equity versus disconfirmation model is similar to that of quality and disconfirmation in Chapter 6 (see Figure 6.4) and is not portrayed separately here.

Number of Stages in the Process

In another processing difference, equity and inequity judgments appear as a two-stage process in which each party's inputs and outcomes are compared first. Later, the results of this first stage are compared across parties. In the disconfirmation judgment, only one stage is required, that of comparing performance to expectations or norms. Thus, the equity judgment is necessarily more complex than that of disconfirmation.

Emotional Responses

Last, yet another characteristic distinguishing the two postpurchase phenomena is the accompanying emotional tone.[52] Although more extensive discussion is reserved for Chapter 12, it can be said here that the initial outcomes of the two processes are thought to differ on an emotional basis. For example, negative inequity has been described as resulting in distress, resentment, and vindication, while negative disconfirmation results in a range of negative emotions from the less extreme disappointment to the more extreme affects such as anger. While equity and disconfirmation may share strong negative affects, greater subtleties may be evident for the less extreme negative states.

On the positive sides of the equity and disconfirmation continua, positive inequity is thought to result in both guilt that one has been treated more fairly than others and, interestingly, the opposite emotion, reflective of an egocentric bias—that one deserved extra-fair treatment. Thus, in the case of a consumer besting a salesperson, glee or a sheepish sense of pleasure may ensue. In contrast, positive disconfirmation is hypothesized to result in delight or perhaps elation.

Finally, equity resulting from the absence of inequity should result in positive affects related to fairness, such as a sense of justice or fair play. In contrast, confirmation (zero disconfirmation) is expected to add little emotional content to the purchase decision, resulting in a general sense of contentment. Thus, on the basis of the antecedents, consequences, and actual processes, a number of conceptual distinctions can be drawn between equity and disconfirmation.

Tests of Joint Influence

There are now a number of tests of joint influence, some of which have been cited in the previous discussion. As tested in the early studies of auto purchasing that pitted buyers against salespeople and dealers, the two processes of equity and disconfirmation occurred jointly to influence satisfaction.[53] Disconfirmation apparently captured the expectational basis of performance while equity (fairness) captured the degree to which the consumer's outcomes and inputs exceeded those of both salesperson and dealer. Interestingly, the fairness effect (reflecting advantageous inequity) was stronger than that of disconfirmation as measured by standardized regression coefficients (0.51 versus 0.37 for the salesperson; 0.49 versus 0.14 for the dealer). But in accord with the meta-analytic review in note 51, many of the studies used in the analysis were conceptualized and executed in an equity/inequity context and may have overstated the equity effect more generally. At least two other studies have found quite the opposite results, however.[54]

These contrasting findings could be explained in terms of the difference between product satisfaction and satisfaction in interpersonal or institutional exchange. Consumers cannot feel inequitably treated by a product, but they can feel so by other persons or profit entities (including the manufacturer). It is noteworthy as well that when all three equity dimensions are compared to, say, a single disconfirmation scale, the equity variables taken as a whole do tend to exert considerably more influence, perhaps due to the overrepresentation of equity concepts. Nonetheless, these studies underscore the necessity of studying both processes when it is reasonable to assume that consumers make comparative outcome and input judgments as part of the purchase and consumption process.

Equity Sensitivity: Who and How Many Are Affected?

Many writers in the equity area assume that all individuals are affected in some way by equity and inequity considerations. Other researchers disagree, however, arguing that such an assumption is an overgeneralization. In fact, the author has heard comments from others in the field who, upon hearing discussion of equity in satisfaction processes, claim that they "don't think of that when asked a satisfaction question." Perhaps they do not. In fact, the field of information processing (prepurchase decision making) has been criticized for assuming complex decision heuristics that many, if not most, consumers do not bother to engage.

It can be safely presumed that not all consumers consciously use every concept known to affect satisfaction as covered in this book; this "processing perspective" will be formally presented in Chapter 13. Research on memory and choice shows that individuals cannot process large amounts of information at one time (but may over a period of time), with the amount diminishing as additional demands on information processing are made. Thus, a fairly new perspective in the study of equity in satisfaction has emerged, that of sensitivity (or lack thereof) to various elements of the equity process. It is a simple task to extend the sensitivity concept to other satisfaction influences in the purchase and consumption process, as has been done with disconfirmation sensitivity (see Chapter 4).

If a sensitivity analysis of equity processing in consumption were implemented, two issues become pertinent. First is the identification of individuals who consider equity judgments at all, particularly when other satisfaction influences are operating. The security trade study, detailed in Chapter 4 and elsewhere, specifically addressed this question (among others).[55] The results of the analysis showed that, when it was pitted against influences from expectations, performance, disconfirmation, and attribution—all designed to have theoretically approximate objective influences—(advantageous) inequity was a significant predictor of satisfaction at the aggregate level. However, in an individual-level analysis, only five subjects out of forty demonstrated primary equity influences. It cannot be said whether 12.5 percent of the sample is a representative estimate or not. However, this approach is offered as a way to determine the percentage of concept-sensitive consumers in individual applications.

A second issue relating to equity sensitivity has recently been raised. In this line of research, drawn from the organizational behavior literature, focus shifts to classifying individuals on the basis of whether they are sensitive to exact equity, as in the formula, or to underreward or overreward.[56] Individuals with preferences for underreward are referred to as *benevolents*, those preferring exact equity are *equity sensitives*, and those with preferences for overreward are labeled *entitleds*. In the context of consumer equity, the benevolents would probably be less sensitive to any equity consideration, while entitleds probably would respond favorably to advantageous inequity. Equity sensitives would be concerned with all aspects of the exchange, including both inputs and outcomes for themselves, the salesperson, and the dealer. This is a promising direction in equity research and needs further study in consumer satisfaction.

CONCLUSION

As more and more consumption activity involves a transaction component, either because the sales or order-taking function becomes more prominent or because the service sector of consumption takes on a greater role in consumers' lives, matters of equity and inequity will become more salient in satisfaction decisions. Generally, consumers will find as fair the particular combination of their and others' inputs and outcomes that is meaningful to them. Perhaps this fairness perception will exist only as a sense of injustice without more formal numeric analysis. However, consumers' reactions to inequity are likely to be similar regardless of the form of the inequity judgment.

Fair exchange, as defined by the consumer and whether it is to the consumer's advantage or not, is a desired value in society. If fair exchange is not attained, then fairness in redress or service recovery will offer the marketer a second chance to provide justice to the consumer. As a rather large number of studies cited in this chapter illustrate, the complaining process will generate fairness perceptions along the same line of analysis used for the initial purchase and consumption stages.

Thus, equity processes are, to a large degree, under the control of marketers and their agents. In this sense, equity is doled out to consumers. In contrast, what can be expected when consumers create their own disadvantage in consumption? The next chapter shows what happens when consumers perceive that "they could have done better."

NOTES

1. See, e.g., Oliver and Swan, "Consumer Perceptions of Interpersonal Equity and Satisfaction in Transactions."

2. As described in the Glossary (see the Introduction), this term is frequently confused with *brand equity*, a managerial concept represented by marketplace perceptions of loyalty, quality, and awareness or recognition. See Yee and Donthu, "Developing and Validating a Multidimensional Consumer-Based Brand Equity Scale."

3. Homans, *Social Behavior*, p. 235.

4. For a recent discussion of the different forms of "ain't fair" situations, see Finkel, *Not Fair!*

5. Perhaps the first is that of Adams, "Toward an Understanding of Inequity." Also see Walster, Walster, and Berscheid, *Equity*.

6. See, e.g., Harris, "Pinning down the Equity Formula."

7. Farkas and Anderson, "Multidimensional Input in Equity Theory," p. 892. For an exposition in the retailing sector, see Dorsch and Carlson, "Transaction Approach to Understanding and Managing Customer Equity."

8. Deutsch, "Equity, Equality, and Need."

9. See Stecklow, "Incredible Offer," and subsequent articles following up on this case.

10. See Weiss, Suckow, and Cropanzano, "Effects of Justice Conditions on Discrete Emotions."

11. Oliver, Shor, and Tidd, "Induced Over-Benefiting and Under-Benefiting on the Web."

12. A recent meta-analysis can be found in Kalkhoff and Thye, "Expectation States Theory and Research." An early exposition is that of Berger, Conner, and Fişek, *Expectation States Theory*.

13. An interesting inequity side-issue is raised here. Specifically, should the private school parent be "rebated" for that portion of public school tax dollars not being used?

14. See Mussweiler, "Comparison Processes in Social Judgment."

15. For an example in the used-car market, see Browne, *Used-Car Game*. Despite its date of publication, this book continues to sell well and can be found new on Amazon.com.

16. Oliver and Swan, "Consumer Perceptions of Interpersonal Equity and Satisfaction in Transactions" and "Equity and Disconfirmation Perceptions as Influences on Merchant and Product Satisfaction"; Swan and Oliver, "Applied Analysis of Buyer Equity Perceptions and Satisfaction with Automobile Salespeople"; Andaleeb and Basu, "Technical Complexity and Consumer Knowledge as Moderators of Service Quality Evaluation in the Automobile Service Industry."

17. Oliver and DeSarbo, "Response Determinants in Satisfaction Judgments."

18. Haws and Bearden, "Dynamic Pricing and Consumer Fairness Perceptions"; Kimes and Wirtz, "Has Revenue Management Become Acceptable?"; Maxwell, "Rule-Based Price Fairness and Its Effect on Willingness to Purchase."

19. Darke and Dahl, "Fairness and Discounts"; Feinberg, Krishna, and Zhang, "Do We Care What Oth-

ers Get?"; van den Bos, Lind, et al., "How Do I Judge My Outcomes When I Do Not Know the Outcomes of Others?"

20. See Oliver and Shor, "Digital Redemption of Coupons"; and Oliver, Shor, and Tidd, "Induced Over-Benefiting and Under-Benefiting on the Web."

21. Cited in Martins and Monroe, "Perceived Price Fairness," p. 76.

22. For an overview, see Xia, Monroe, and Cox, "Price Is Unfair!" Other sources include L. Bolton and Alba, "Price Fairness"; R. Bolton and Lemon, "Dynamic Model of Customers' Usage of Services"; Dorsch and Carlson, "Transaction Approach to Understanding and Managing Customer Equity"; Grewal, Hardesty, and Iyer, "Effects of Buyer Identification and Purchase Timing on Consumers' Perceptions of Trust, Price Fairness, and Repurchase Intentions"; Suter and Hardesty, "Maximizing Earnings and Price Fairness Perceptions in Online Consumer-to-Consumer Auctions"; and Vaidyanathan and Aggarwal, "Who Is the Fairest of Them All?"

23. See, e.g., Cho, Im, and Hiltz, "Impact of e-Services Failures and Customer Complaints on Electronic Commerce Customer Relationship Management"; Estelami, "Competitive and Procedural Determinants of Delight and Disappointment in Consumer Complaint Outcomes"; Goodwin and Ross, "Consumer Evaluations of Responses to Complaints"; Karande, Magnini, and Tam, "Recovery Voice and Satisfaction After Service Failure"; Mattila and Cranage, "Impact of Choice on Fairness in the Context of Service Recovery"; and McColl-Kennedy and Sparks, "Application of Fairness Theory to Service Failures and Service Recovery."

24. Bolton, Warlop, and Alba, "Consumer Perceptions of Price (Un)Fairness"; Campbell, "Perceptions of Price Unfairness"; Homburg, Hoyer, and Koschate, "Customers' Reactions to Price Increases."

25. Oliver and Swan, "Equity and Disconfirmation Perceptions as Influences on Merchant and Product Satisfaction."

26. See Gourville and Moon, "Managing Price Expectations Through Product Overlap"; and Huang, Chang, and Chen, "Perceived Fairness of Pricing on the Internet."

27. Weiss, Suckow, and Cropanzano, "Effects of Justice Conditions on Discrete Emotions."

28. See Homans, *Social Behavior*, especially Chapter 13; and Kelley and Thibaut, *Interpersonal Relations*, in Chapter 6.

29. Messick and Sentis, "Fairness and Preference" and "Fairness, Preference, and Fairness Biases."

30. Diekmann et al., "Self-Interest and Fairness in Problems of Resource Allocation"; Purohit, "Playing the Role of Buyer and Seller"; Tanaka, "Judgments of Fairness by Just World Believers"; van den Bos, Bruins, et al., "Sometimes Unfair Procedures Have Nice Aspects"; and van den Bos, Wilke, et al., "Evaluating Outcomes by Means of the Fair Process Effect."

31. Cook and Messick, "Psychological and Sociological Perspectives on Distributive Justice."

32. See van den Bos, Lind, et al., "How Do I Judge My Outcome When I Do Not Know the Outcome of Others?"

33. Weiss, Suckow, and Cropanzano, "Effects of Justice Conditions on Discrete Emotions."

34. Walster, Walster, and Berscheid, *Equity*, p. 16.

35. Oliver and Swan, "Consumer Perceptions of Interpersonal Equity and Satisfaction in Transactions" and "Equity and Disconfirmation Perceptions as Influences on Merchant and Product Satisfaction."

36. See the articles by Harris, "Pinning Down the Equity Formula"; Mellers and Hartka, "Test of a Subtractive Theory of 'Fair' Allocations"; Singh, "'Fair' Allocations of Pay and Workload" and "Subtractive Versus Ratio Model of 'Fair' Allocation."

37. In addition to Mellers and Hartka in the previous note, also see Alwin, "Distributive Justice and Satisfaction with Material Well-Being"; and Brockner and Adsit, "Moderating Impact of Sex on the Equity-Satisfaction Relationship."

38. Lapidus and Pinkerton, "Customer Complaint Situations."

39. Diekmann et al., "Self-Interest and Fairness in Problems of Resource Allocation"; Liebrand, Messick, and Wolters, "Why We Are Fairer Than Others"; Messick et al., "Why We Are Fairer Than Others"; Thompson and Loewenstein, "Egocentric Interpretations of Fairness and Interpersonal Conflict"; Vaidyanathan and Aggarwal, "Who Is the Fairest of Them All?"

40. See, variously, Beugré and Baron, "Perceptions of Systemic Justice"; Blodgett, Hill, and Tax, "Effects of Distributive, Procedural, and Interactional Justice on Postcomplaint Behavior"; Clemmer and Schneider, "Fair Service"; de Ruyter and Wetzels, "Customer Equity Considerations in Service Recovery"; Maxham and Netemeyer, "Firms Reap What They Sow"; and McColl-Kennedy and Sparks, "Application of Fairness Theory to Service Failures and Service Recovery," where the authors illustrate multi-item scales for measuring the three constructs.

41. Barrett-Howard and Tyler, "Procedural Justice as a Criterion in Allocation Decisions"; Goodwin and Ross, "Consumer Responses to Service Failures"; Thibaut and Walker, *Procedural Justice*.

42. Lind and Tyler, *Social Psychology of Procedural Justice*, p. 2.

43. Anand, "Procedural Fairness in Economic and Social Choice"; Brockner and Wiesenfeld, "Integrative Framework for Explaining Reactions to Decisions"; Huffman and Cain, "Adjustments in Performance Measures"; Karande, Magnini, and Tam, "Recovery Voice and Satisfaction After Service Failure"; Mattila and Cranage, "Impact of Choice on Fairness in the Context of Service Recovery"; Saxby, Tat, and Johansen, "Measuring Consumer Perceptions of Procedural Justice in a Complaint Context."

44. Johnson, Tsiros, and Lanconi, "Measuring Service Quality"; Joshi, "Investigation of Equity as a Determinant of User Information Satisfaction."

45. Bies and Moag, "Interactional Justice."

46. Clemmer, "Investigation into the Relationship of Fairness and Customer Satisfaction with Services"; Clemmer and Schneider, "Fair Service."

47. Goodwin and Ross, "Consumer Evaluations of Responses to Complaints."

48. See the following, some of which include measures of interactional and other fairness dimensions: Blodgett, Hill, and Tax, "Effects of Distributive, Procedural, and Interactional Justice on Postcomplaint Behavior"; de Ruyter and Wetzels, "Customer Equity Considerations in Service Recovery"; Tax, Brown, and Chandrashekaran, "Customer Evaluations of Service Experiences"; Weun, Beatty, and Jones, "Impact of Service Failure Severity on Service Recovery Evaluations and Post-Recovery Relationships."

49. Mohr and Bitner, "Role of Employee Effort in Satisfaction with Service Transactions," p. 239.

50. van den Bos, Lind, et al., "How Do I Judge My Outcome When I Do Not Know the Outcomes of Others?"; Blodgett, Hill, and Tax, "Effects of Distributive, Procedural, and Interactional Justice," where the interactional dimension had the largest impact on repurchase intention (but not satisfaction).

51. Szymanski and Henard, "Customer Satisfaction." See, also, Smith, Bolton, and Wagner, "Model of Customer Satisfaction with Service Encounters Involving Failure and Recovery"; Yim et al., "Justice-Based Service Recovery Expectations." Note that Szymanski and Henard found a greater equity "effect coefficient" over that of disconfirmation. This result could be explained by the small number of equity studies in their meta-analysis and the fact that these studies used equity as the focal concept under investigation.

52. This section draws from a number of studies using different methodologies (narrations, scenario presentations, scaled measures) and different foci (negative emotions only, combined positive and negative emotion "sets," emotion versus nonemotion); the conclusions here reflect an amalgam. See, e.g., Chebat and Slusarczyk, "How Emotions Mediate the Effects of Perceived Justice on Loyalty in Service Recovery Situations"; Hassebrauck, "Ratings of Distress as a Function of Degree and Kind of Inequity"; Mikula, Scherer, and Athenstaedt, "Role of Injustice in the Elicitation of Differential Emotional Reactions"; Schoefer and Ennew, "Impact of Perceived Justice on Consumers' Emotional Responses to Service Complaint Experiences"; and Smith and Bolton, "Effect of Customers' Emotional Responses to Service Failures on Their Recovery Effort Evaluations and Satisfaction Judgments." The latter reference contains a fairly comprehensive list of equity-related emotions at p. 12.

53. Oliver and Swan, "Equity and Disconfirmation Perceptions as Influences on Merchant and Product Satisfaction," p. 381.

54. E.g., Oliver and DeSarbo, "Response Determinants in Satisfaction Judgments"; and Patterson, Johnson, and Spreng, "Modeling the Determinants of Customer Satisfaction for Business-to-Business Professional Services."

55. Oliver and DeSarbo, "Response Determinants in Satisfaction Judgments."

56. For a review with measurement suggestions, see Sauley and Bedeian, "Equity Sensitivity."

BIBLIOGRAPHY

Adams, J. Stacy. "Toward an Understanding of Inequity." *Journal of Abnormal and Social Psychology* 67, no. 5 (November 1963): 422–436.

Alwin, Duane F. "Distributive Justice and Satisfaction with Material Well-Being." *American Sociological Review* 52, no. 1 (February 1987): 83–95.

Anand, Paul. "Procedural Fairness in Economic and Social Choice: Evidence from a Survey of Voters." *Journal of Economic Psychology* 22, no. 2 (April 2001): 247–270.

Andaleeb, Syed Saad, and Amiya J. Basu. "Technical Complexity and Consumer Knowledge as Moderators of Service Quality Evaluation in the Automobile Service Industry." *Journal of Retailing* 70, no. 4 (Winter 1994): 367–381.

Barrett-Howard, Edith, and Tom R. Tyler. "Procedural Justice as a Criterion in Allocation Decisions." *Journal of Personality and Social Psychology* 50, no. 2 (February 1986): 296–304.

Berger, Joseph, Thomas L. Conner, and M. Hamit Fişek. *Expectation States Theory: A Theoretical Research Program.* Cambridge, MA: Winthrop, 1974.

Beugré, Constance D., and Robert A. Baron. "Perceptions of Systemic Justice: Distributive, Procedural, and Interactional Justice." *Journal of Applied Social Psychology* 31, no. 2 (February 2001): 324–339.

Bies, Robert J., and Joseph S. Moag. "Interactional Justice: Communication Criteria of Fairness." In *Research on Negotiation in Organizations*, ed. R.J. Lewicki, B.H. Sheppard, and M.H. Bazerman, 1:43–55. Greenwich, CT: JAI Press, 1986.

Blodgett, Jeffrey G., Donna J. Hill, and Stephen S. Tax. "The Effects of Distributive, Procedural, and Interactional Justice on Postcomplaint Behavior." *Journal of Retailing* 73, no. 2 (Summer 1997): 185–210.

Bolton, Lisa E., and Joseph W. Alba. "Price Fairness: Good and Service Differences and the Role of Vendor Costs." *Journal of Consumer Research* 33, no. 2 (September 2006): 258–265.

Bolton, Lisa E., Luk Warlop, and Joseph W. Alba. "Consumer Perceptions of Price (Un)Fairness." *Journal of Consumer Research* 29, no. 4 (March 2003): 474–491.

Bolton, Ruth N., and Katherine N. Lemon. "A Dynamic Model of Customers' Usage of Services: Usage as an Antecedent and Consequence of Satisfaction." *Journal of Marketing Research* 36, no. 2 (May 1999): 171–186.

Brockner, Joel, and Laury Adsit. "The Moderating Impact of Sex on the Equity-Satisfaction Relationship: A Field Study." *Journal of Applied Psychology* 71, no. 4 (November 1986): 585–590.

Brockner, Joel, and Batia M. Wiesenfeld. "An Integrative Framework for Explaining Reactions to Decisions: Interactive Effects of Outcomes and Procedures." *Psychological Bulletin* 120, no. 2 (September 1996): 189–208.

Browne, Joy. *The Used-Car Game: A Sociology of the Bargain.* Lexington, MA: D.C. Heath, 1973.

Campbell, Margaret C. "Perceptions of Price Unfairness: Antecedents and Consequences." *Journal of Marketing Research* 36, no. 2 (May 1999): 187–199.

Chebat, Jean-Charles, and Witold Slusarczyk. "How Emotions Mediate the Effects of Perceived Justice on Loyalty in Service Recovery Situations: An Empirical Study." *Journal of Business Research* 58, no. 5 (May 2005): 664–673.

Cho, Yooncheong, Il Im, and Roxanne Hiltz. "The Impact of e-Services Failures and Customer Complaints on Electronic Commerce Customer Relationship Management." *Journal of Consumer Satisfaction, Dissatisfaction and Complaining Behavior* 16 (2003): 106–118.

Clemmer, Elizabeth C. "An Investigation into the Relationship of Fairness and Customer Satisfaction with Services." In *Justice in the Workplace: Approaching Fairness in Human Resource Management*, ed. Russell Cropanzano, 193–207. Hillsdale, NJ: Lawrence Erlbaum, 1993.

Clemmer, Elizabeth C., and Benjamin Schneider. "Fair Service." In *Advances in Services Marketing and Management*, ed. Teresa A, Swartz, David E. Bowen, and Stephen W. Brown, 5:109–126. Greenwich, CT, JAI Press, 1996.

Cook, Karen S., and David M. Messick. "Psychological and Sociological Perspectives on Distributive Justice: Convergent, Divergent, and Parallel Lines." In *Equity Theory: Psychological and Sociological Perspectives*, ed. David M. Messick and Karen S. Cook, 1–12. New York: Praeger, 1983.

Darke, Peter R., and Darren W. Dahl. "Fairness and Discounts: The Subjective Value of a Bargain." *Journal of Consumer Psychology* 13, no. 3 (2003): 328–338.

de Ruyter, Ko, and Martin Wetzels. "Customer Equity Considerations in Service Recovery: A Cross-Industry Perspective." *International Journal of Service Industry Management* 11, no. 1 (2000): 91–108.

Deutsch, Morton. "Equity, Equality, and Need: What Determines Which Value Will Be Used as the Basis of Distributive Justice?" *Journal of Social Issues* 31, no. 3 (Fall 1975): 137–149.

Diekmann, Kristina A., Steven M. Samuels, Lee Ross, and Max H. Bazerman. "Self-Interest and Fairness in Problems of Resource Allocation: Allocators Versus Recipients." *Journal of Personality and Social Psychology* 72, no. 5 (May 1997): 1061–1074.

Dorsch, Michael J., and Les Carlson. "A Transaction Approach to Understanding and Managing Customer Equity." *Journal of Business Research* 35, no. 3 (March 1996): 253–264.

Estelami, Hooman. "Competitive and Procedural Determinants of Delight and Disappointment in Consumer Complaint Outcomes." *Journal of Service Research* 2, no. 3 (February 2000): 285–300.

Farkas, Arthur J., and Norman H. Anderson. "Multidimensional Input in Equity Theory." *Journal of Personality and Social Psychology* 37, no. 12 (December 1979): 879–896.

Feinberg, Fred M., Aradhna Krishna, and Z. John Zhang. "Do We Care What Others Get? A Behaviorist Approach to Targeted Promotions." *Journal of Marketing Research* 39, no. 3 (August 2002): 277–291.

Finkel, Norman J. *Not Fair! The Typology of Commonsense Unfairness.* Washington, DC: American Psychological Association, 2001.

Goodwin, Cathy, and Ivan Ross. "Consumer Evaluations of Responses to Complaints: What's Fair and Why." *Journal of Consumer Marketing* 7, no. 2 (Spring 1990): 39–47.

———. "Consumer Responses to Service Failures: Influence of Procedural and Interactional Fairness Perceptions." *Journal of Business Research* 25, no. 2 (September 1992): 149–163.

Gourville, John T., and Youngme Moon. "Managing Price Expectations Through Product Overlap." *Journal of Retailing* 80, no. 1 (2004): 23–35.

Grewal, Dhruv, David M. Hardesty, and Gopalkrishnan R. Iyer. "The Effects of Buyer Identification and Purchase Timing on Consumers' Perceptions of Trust, Price Fairness, and Repurchase Intentions." *Journal of Interactive Marketing* 18, no. 4 (Autumn 2004): 87–100.

Harris, Richard J. "Pinning down the Equity Formula." In *Equity Theory: Psychological and Sociological Perspectives*, ed. David M. Messick and Karen S. Cook, 207–241. New York: Praeger, 1983.

Hassebrauck, Manfred. "Ratings of Distress as a Function of Degree and Kind of Inequity." *Journal of Social Psychology* 126, no. 2 (April 1986): 269–270.

Haws, Kelly L., and William O. Bearden. "Dynamic Pricing and Consumer Fairness Perceptions." *Journal of Consumer Research* 33, no. 3 (December 2006): 304–311.

Homans, George Caspar. *Social Behavior: Its Elementary Forms.* New York: Harcourt, Brace & World, 1961.

Homburg, Christian, Wayne D. Hoyer, and Nicole Koschate. "Customers' Reactions to Price Increases: Do Customer Satisfaction and Perceived Motive Fairness Matter?" *Journal of the Academy of Marketing Science* 33, no. 1 (Winter 2005): 36–49.

Huang, Jen-Hung, Ching-Te Chang, and Cathy Yi-Hsuan Chen. "Perceived Fairness of Pricing on the Internet." *Journal of Economic Psychology* 26, no. 3 (June 2005): 343–361.

Huffman, Cynthia, and Lisa B. Cain. "Adjustments in Performance Measures: Distributive and Procedural Justice Effects on Outcome Satisfaction." *Psychology & Marketing* 18, no. 6 (June 2001): 593–615.

Johnson, Rose L., Michael Tsiros, and Richard A. Lanconi. "Measuring Service Quality: A Systems Approach." *Journal of Services Marketing* 9, no. 5 (1995): 6–19.

Joshi, Kailash. "An Investigation of Equity as a Determinant of User Information Satisfaction." *Decision Sciences* 21, no. 4 (December 1990): 786–807.

Kalkhoff, Will, and Shane R. Thye. "Expectation States Theory and Research: New Observations from Meta-Analysis." *Sociological Methods and Research* 35, no. 2 (November 2006): 219–249.

Karande, Kiran, Vincent P. Magnini, and Leona Tam. "Recovery Voice and Satisfaction After Service Failure: An Experimental Investigation of Mediating and Moderating Factors." *Journal of Service Research* 10, no. 2 (November 2007): 187–203.

Kelley, Harold H., and John W. Thibaut. *Interpersonal Relations: A Theory of Interdependence.* New York: Wiley, 1978.

Kimes, Sheryl E., and Jochen Wirtz. "Has Revenue Management Become Acceptable? Findings from an International Study on the Perceived Fairness of Rate Fences." *Journal of Service Research* 6, no. 2 (November 2003): 125–135.

Lapidus, Richard S., and Lori Pinkerton. "Customer Complaint Situations: An Equity Theory Perspective." *Psychology & Marketing* 12, no. 2 (March 1995): 105–122.

Liebrand, Wim B.G., David M. Messick, and Fred J.M. Wolters. "Why We Are Fairer Than Others: A Cross-Cultural Replication and Extension." *Journal of Experimental Social Psychology* 22, no. 6 (November 1986): 590–604.

Lind, E. Allen, and Tom R. Tyler. *The Social Psychology of Procedural Justice.* New York: Plenum Press, 1988.

Martins, Marielza, and Kent B. Monroe. "Perceived Price Fairness: A New Look at an Old Concept." In *Advances in Consumer Research*, ed. Chris T. Allen and Deborah Roedder John, 21:75–78. Provo, UT: Association for Consumer Research, 1994.

Mattila, Anna S., and David Cranage. "The Impact of Choice on Fairness in the Context of Service Recovery." *Journal of Services Marketing* 19, no. 5 (2005): 271–279.

Maxham, James G., III, and Richard G. Netemeyer. "Firms Reap What They Sow: The Effects of Shared Values and Perceived Organizational Justice on Customers' Evaluations of Complaint Handling." *Journal of Marketing* 67, no. 1 (January 2003): 46–62.

Maxwell, Sarah. "Rule-Based Price Fairness and Its Effect on Willingness to Purchase." *Journal of Economic Psychology* 23, no. 2 (April 2002): 191–212.

McColl-Kennedy, Janet R., and Beverley A. Sparks. "Application of Fairness Theory to Service Failures and Service Recovery." *Journal of Service Research* 5, no. 3 (February 2003): 251–266.

Mellers, Barbara, and Elizabeth Hartka. "Test of a Subtractive Theory of 'Fair' Allocations." *Journal of Personality and Social Psychology* 56, no. 5 (May 1989): 691–697.

Messick, David M., Suzanne Bloom, Janet P. Boldizar, and Charles D. Samuelson. "Why We Are Fairer Than Others." *Journal of Experimental Social Psychology* 21, no. 5 (September 1985): 480–500.

Messick, David M., and Keith P. Sentis. "Fairness and Preference." *Journal of Experimental Social Psychology* 15, no. 4 (July 1979): 418–434.

———. "Fairness, Preference, and Fairness Biases." In *Equity Theory: Psychological and Sociological Perspectives*, ed. David M. Messick and Karen S. Cook, 61–94. New York: Praeger, 1983.

Mikula, Gerold, Klaus R. Scherer, and Ursula Athenstaedt. "The Role of Injustice in the Elicitation of Differential Emotional Reactions." *Personality and Social Psychology Bulletin* 24, no. 7 (July 1998): 769–783.

Mohr, Lois A., and Mary Jo Bitner. "The Role of Employee Effort in Satisfaction with Service Transactions." *Journal of Business Research* 32, no. 3 (March 1995): 239–252.

Mussweiler, Thomas. "Comparison Processes in Social Judgment: Mechanisms and Consequences." *Psychological Review* 110, no. 3 (July 2003): 472–489.

Oliver, Richard L., and Wayne S. DeSarbo. "Response Determinants in Satisfaction Judgments." *Journal of Consumer Research* 14, no. 4 (March 1988): 495–507.

Oliver, Richard L., and Mikhael Shor. "Digital Redemption of Coupons: Satisfying and Dissatisfying Effects of Promotion Codes." *Journal of Product & Brand Management* 12, no. 2 (2003): 121–134.

Oliver, Richard L., Mikhael Shor, and Simon T. Tidd. "Induced Over-Benefiting and Under-Benefiting on the Web: Inequity Effects on Feelings and Motivations with Implications for Consumption Behavior." *Motivation and Emotion* 28, no. 1 (March 2004): 85–106.

Oliver, Richard L., and John E. Swan. "Consumer Perceptions of Interpersonal Equity and Satisfaction in Transactions: A Field Survey Approach." *Journal of Marketing* 53, no. 2 (April 1989): 21–35.

———. "Equity and Disconfirmation Perceptions as Influences on Merchant and Product Satisfaction." *Journal of Consumer Research* 16, no. 3 (December 1989): 372–383.

Patterson, Paul G., Lester W. Johnson, and Richard A. Spreng. "Modeling the Determinants of Customer Satisfaction for Business-to-Business Professional Services." *Journal of the Academy of Marketing Science* 25, no 1 (Winter 1997): 4–17.

Purohit, Devavrat. "Playing the Role of Buyer and Seller: The Mental Accounting of Trade-Ins." *Marketing Letters* 6, no. 2 (March 1995): 101–110.

Sauley, Kerry S., and Arthur G. Bedeian. "Equity Sensitivity: Construction of a Measure and Examination of Its Psychometric Properties." *Journal of Management* 26, no. 5 (October 2000): 885–910.

Saxby, Carl L., Peter K. Tat, and Jane Thompson Johansen. "Measuring Consumer Perceptions of Procedural Justice in a Complaint Context." *Journal of Consumer Affairs* 34, no. 2 (Winter 2000): 204–216.

Schoefer, Klaus, and Christine Ennew. "The Impact of Perceived Justice on Consumers' Emotional Responses to Service Complaint Experiences." *Journal of Services Marketing* 19, no. 5 (2005): 261–270.

Singh, Ramadhar. "'Fair' Allocations of Pay and Workload: Tests of a Subtractive Model with Nonlinear Judgment Function." *Organizational Behavior and Human Decision Processes* 62, no. 1 (April 1995): 70–78.

———. "Subtractive Versus Ratio Model of 'Fair' Allocation: Can the Group Level Analyses Be Misleading?" *Organizational Behavior and Human Decision Processes* 68, no. 2 (November 1996): 123–144.

Smith, Amy K., and Ruth N. Bolton. "The Effect of Customers' Emotional Responses to Service Failures on Their Recovery Effort Evaluations and Satisfaction Judgments." *Journal of the Academy of Marketing Science* 30, no. 1 (Winter 2002): 5–23.

Smith, Amy K., Ruth N. Bolton, and Janet Wagner. "A Model of Customer Satisfaction with Service Encounters Involving Failure and Recovery." *Journal of Marketing Research* 36, no. 3 (August 1999): 356–372.

Stecklow, Steve. "Incredible Offer: A Big Charity Faces Tough New Questions about Its Financing." *Wall Street Journal*, May 15, 1995.

Suter, Tracy A., and David M. Hardesty. "Maximizing Earnings and Price Fairness Perceptions in Online Consumer-to-Consumer Auctions." *Journal of Retailing* 81, no. 4 (2005): 307–317.

Swan, John E., and Richard L. Oliver. "An Applied Analysis of Buyer Equity Perceptions and Satisfaction with Automobile Salespeople." *Journal of Personal Selling & Sales Management* 11, no. 2 (Spring 1991): 15–26.

Szymanski, David M., and David H. Henard. "Customer Satisfaction: A Meta-Analysis of the Empirical Evidence." *Journal of the Academy of Marketing Science* 29, no. 1 (Winter 2001): 16–35.

Tanaka, Ken'ichiro. "Judgments of Fairness by Just World Believers." *Journal of Social Psychology* 139, no. 5 (October 1999): 631–638.

Tax, Stephen S., Stephen W. Brown, and Murali Chandrashekaran. "Customer Evaluations of Service Experiences: Implications for Relationship Marketing." *Journal of Marketing* 62, no. 2 (April 1998): 60–76.

Thibaut, John, and Laurens Walker. *Procedural Justice: A Psychological Analysis.* Hillsdale, NJ: Lawrence Erlbaum, 1975.

Thompson, Leigh, and George Loewenstein. "Egocentric Interpretations of Fairness and Interpersonal Conflict." *Organizational Behavior and Human Decision Processes* 51, no. 2 (March 1992): 176–197.

Vaidyanathan, Rajiv, and Praveen Aggarwal. "Who Is the Fairest of Them All? An Attributional Approach to Price Fairness Perceptions." *Journal of Business Research* 56, no. 6 (June 2003): 453–463.

van den Bos, Kees, Jan Bruins, Henk A.M. Wilke, and Elske Dronkert. "Sometimes Unfair Procedures Have Nice Aspects: On the Psychology of the Fair Process Effect." *Journal of Personality and Social Psychology* 77, no. 2 (August 1999): 324–336.

van den Bos, Kees, E. Allan Lind, Riël Vermunt, and Henk A.M. Wilke. "How Do I Judge My Outcomes When I Do Not Know the Outcomes of Others? The Psychology of the Fair Process Effect." *Journal of Personality and Social Psychology* 72, no. 5 (May 1997): 1034–1046.

van den Bos, Kees, Henk A.M. Wilke, E. Allen Lind, and Riël Vermunt. "Evaluating Outcomes by Means of the Fair Process Effect: Evidence for Different Processes in Fairness and Satisfaction Judgments." *Journal of Personality and Social Psychology* 74, no. 6 (June 1998): 1493–1503.

Walster, Elaine G., William Walster, and Ellen Berscheid. *Equity: Theory and Research.* Boston, MA: Allyn & Bacon, 1978.

Weiss, Howard M., Kathleen Suckow, and Russell Cropanzano. "Effects of Justice Conditions on Discrete Emotions." *Journal of Applied Psychology* 84, no. 5 (October 1999): 786–794.

Weun, Seungoog, Sharon E. Beatty, and Michael A. Jones. "The Impact of Service Failure Severity on Service Recovery Evaluations and Post-Recovery Relationships." *Journal of Services Marketing* 18, no. 2 (2004): 133–146.

Xia, Lan, Kent B. Monroe, and Jennifer L. Cox. "The Price Is Unfair! A Conceptual Framework of Price Fairness Perceptions." *Journal of Marketing* 68, no. 4 (October 2004): 1–15.

Yee, Boonghee, and Naveen Donthu. "Developing and Validating a Multidimensional Consumer-Based Brand Equity Scale." *Journal of Business Research* 52, no. 1 (April 2001): 1–14.

Yim, Chi Kin (Bennett), Flora Fang Gu, Kimmy Wa Chan, and David K. Tse. "Justice-Based Service Recovery Expectations: Measurement and Antecedents." *Journal of Consumer Satisfaction, Dissatisfaction, and Complaining Behavior* 16 (2003): 36–52.

CHAPTER 9

REGRET AND HINDSIGHT

What Might Have Been and What I Knew Would Be

"I could've had a V8!"

What does this common lament about a well-known vegetable drink say to the consumer? It is meant to imply that the consumer in the advertisement, less than satisfied after trying an alternative beverage, is reflecting on what could have been done differently. This reflection brings to mind the V8 brand and thoughts of how much more satisfying it would have been. The feeling expressed in the advertisement is regret. The makers of V8 do not have a license on the concept of regret, and others have used similar appeals. For example, a very well-known ad for Waterman pens proclaimed that purchasing this brand is a decision that the consumer would never live to regret—as opposed to buying a forged painting or buying stocks "like they were going out of style" (at the time, it appeared that they were).

Although both these examples are regret prototypes, this chapter actually contains two related themes. The first part discusses the imagining or creation of a separate reality of what might have happened if things had been done otherwise. The later part of the chapter discusses the re-creation of a reality that made the outcome received a foregone conclusion. The former topic is regret, and the latter is referred to as hindsight bias. They share the perspective that the consumer had the capacity to know better. In the case of hindsight, the consumer did know better.

THE COMPARATIVE NATURE OF REGRET AND HINDSIGHT

Why are these phenomena comparison operations? Because the consumer is thought to compare outcomes received to others that could also have occurred. In the case of regret, the outcomes are those that might have happened or those that did happen to another consumer who made a different choice of product or service. In the V8 example, the consumer would say, "I can imagine how much better a V8 would have satisfied my taste and quenched my thirst." Alternatively, this same consumer may observe that a friend ordered a V8, which was much more satisfying than the first consumer's choice of carrot juice. In either case, the consumer now understands that something else would have been better than what was selected. Implied in this remorseful conclusion is the assumption that the consumer knew of the other choices and their likely outcomes: "I could have done better."

Figure 9.1 **Comparison Operations Under Regret and Hindsight**

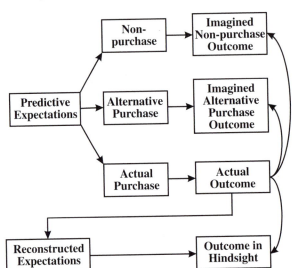

In the case of hindsight, the consumer makes a negative comparison to the same outcome predicted at an earlier time. In effect, the consumer says, "I knew this would happen! I knew my action would lead to this negative outcome, and I should have behaved differently and avoided it." This phenomenon is often referred to as "Monday morning quarterbacking."[1]

Figure 9.1 graphically displays these operations. Note that regret has many possible comparison referents including the case of inaction, while hindsight has only one—the reconstructed expectation formed through observation of the outcome. In Chapter 3, a similar concept was referred to as a retrospective expectation. These concepts differ in that retrospective expectations may be simple recollections subject to errors of memory. With hindsight bias, it is assumed that individuals have a motivation to distort recollections (to be discussed).

HINDSIGHT AND REGRET CATEGORIZED BY PERCEIVED RESPONSIBILITY

What are the limits of regret? That is, when does regret become more like hindsight and when does it become so diffuse that an individual feels free of regret despite the unfortunate consequences of a decision? Prior works and reasoning presented here suggest that a feeling of personal responsibility is one substantial moderating condition.[2] This seemingly obvious condition has been questioned on the basis of the unfortunateness of the outcome regardless of causal agency. In a series of exchanges, it has been established to this author's satisfaction that unfortunateness indeed does lead to unhappiness, but not to regret.[3] Of interest is the relation of responsibility to controllability, for people cannot be responsible for that over which they have no control (although they may choose to place themselves in uncontrollable situations).[4] For now, choice is assumed to be controllable by the purchaser; further discussion is reserved for Chapter 11.

Regret stems from a comparison to alternative outcomes that could have been likely or could have been foreseen *by the chooser* (or purchaser, or some agent involved in influencing the decision, or some individual or group personally identified with the decision—hence responsibility, even at a distance). However, not all alternative events are necessarily equally likely or foreseeable. Consider three possibilities: the desired event is extremely unlikely, the desired event is as likely as another alternative, and the desired event is certain, barring extremely unlikely freak occurrences of nature. The example used here is the personal computer (PC) industry in the early 1980s.

At that time, a number of competitors were beginning to sport their wares in the PC market. Among the products offered at the time were the 1981 Osborne 1 "transportable," the Apple Macintosh, the IBM PC, the Compaq PC, and the Digital Equipment Rainbow. Osborne was a small, upstart, innovative company, as were Apple and Compaq to some extent. In contrast, IBM and Digital were established.

Assume three consumers: A, B, and C. Consumer A takes a chance on the Osborne despite misgivings about the viability of the company and the competitiveness of its products. Consumer B buys a Macintosh, while consumer C opts for a Digital Rainbow because of the company's established status in the computer market. History shows that Osborne went out of business (in 1983); Apple, IBM, and Compaq continued in the PC market; and Digital abandoned its Rainbow, leaving owners stranded without product support. Which consumer feels regret, which consumer proclaims, "I knew this would happen!" and which consumer feels no responsibility for misfortune?

Consider consumer B first. The Macintosh survived, but the IBM and Compaq offerings, being DOS (disk operating system) machines, received much greater support in the software and hardware aftermarkets because of the willingness of IBM to open its code and architecture to secondary providers. Consumer B could have had an IBM! Consumer A, in contrast, took a chance on a small upstart company and now finds that the fears consumers have for the survival of obscure companies were justified. Consumer A "knew Osborne wouldn't make it" despite hoping that it would. Finally, consumer C is shocked and angry that Digital abandoned the Rainbow, but feels no personal responsibility: who could have known that a company as large as Digital Equipment would not stand by its product line?

Thus, the extent to which these consumers feel personal responsibility for their mishaps determines whether regret, hindsight, or a lack of guilt results. Hindsight occurs when consumers feel strongly, after the fact, that they knew a negative outcome would occur but hoped that it would not. Regret occurs when alternative outcomes were likely, but the degree to which one choice would be preferable to another could not have been known with certainty. For example, the carrot juice consumer may have thought that a carrot-based product was preferable to a mostly tomato-based product, but did not know for sure. Finally, neither regret nor hindsight occurs when the consumer feels that the outcome could not have been foreseen under any reasonable assumptions and, therefore, expresses only surprise, shock, and anger. This personal responsibility perspective is shown in Figure 9.2.

REGRET

Consider the following two choices in a free gamble:

1. A 25 percent chance of winning $80, a 50 percent chance of winning $50, and a 25 percent chance of winning $20
2. A 10 percent chance of winning $1,000 and a 90 percent chance of winning nothing

Under ordinary probability theory, option 2 has a higher expected payoff ($100 versus $50).[5] Moreover, it has a very attractive potential win of $1,000 if the 1-in-10 chance is realized. When offered a choice between these two gambles, many consumers may, in fact, choose option 2.

Figure 9.2 **Responsibility as a Moderator of Regret and Hindsight**

Retrospective Likelihood of Negative Consequences	Typical Consumer Retrospective Reaction	Retrospective Response
Certain (or almost so)	Knew It Would Happen! (But hoped it wouldn't)	Hindsight
High	Feared It Would	Strong Regret
	Thought It Might	
	Thought It Could	
Moderate	Just a Possibility	Moderate Regret
	One of Many Possibilities	
	Remote Chance	
	Shouldn't Have Happened	
Low	Never Thought It Would	Weak Regret
Impossible	Never Beyond My Wildest Dreams! (Did I expect this to happen)	Surprise, Shock (No Regret)

However, suppose a perfectly rational consumer chooses option 1. Studies investigating choices of this nature frequently find that many individuals will select the "sure thing" of winning something over the possibility of winning nothing. Why might they do so? The possibility that option 1 would be selected became known as a paradox because it appeared to violate rationality assumptions. After all, the expected value of the second gamble is twice that of the first. This argument, however, considered only economic or mathematical rationality and not psychological rationality. From a consumer's perspective, choice 2 contains a 90 percent probability of receiving nothing at all. If this highly likely outcome occurs, what thoughts might course through the consumer's mind?

If the individual had selected option 1, a gain was guaranteed. Moreover, the lowest amount of the win was $20, and there was a 50–50 chance of winning $50, and still another 1-in-4 chance of winning $80. In the face of these options, the choice of option 1 contained a psychological benefit not accounted for in standard probability theory. Namely, the consumer would be saved the embarrassment of forgoing a sure win if the highly likely zero return occurred under option 2. This is the phenomenon of regret—the possibility that something better would have happened if only the consumer had made a different choice. This regret is often referred to as *buyer's remorse*.

This example shows how consumers' anticipation of regret can influence their decision making. It also points to the anxieties consumers would experience if regret were realized. Thus, anticipatory regret is a prechoice phenomenon, introduced in Chapter 3, and is part of the dissonance process discussed further in Chapter 10. The present discussion centers on the realization of regret as it affects postpurchase satisfaction. The two are related, however, as anticipations frequently are based on prior realizations. In fact, lotteries and games of chance are often used as research vehicles for the study of anticipatory regret.[6]

Much of the early work in this area can be found in the behavioral decision theory literature. Work in behavioral decision theory began in an attempt to explain why seemingly educated, logical individuals frequently made decisions that violated economic principles. Researchers working in this field split into two camps: those interested in fallacious reasoning, including hindsight bias, which is discussed later, and those interested in reasoning that incorporated psychological "logic" not fully accounted for by economics or mathematics, such as regret.

Early explanations of regret generally explored aspects of this concept under other terms such as *postdecision surprise* and *counterfactual thinking*.[7] Fortunately, the articles noted previously; a compendium of works in an edited volume (now somewhat dated); and a number of new works in the consumer behavior area, to be discussed, are sufficiently compelling to establish this concept as a valid postpurchase response.[8] Future work is needed and will be forthcoming as the discipline matures. For now, a number of reasonable propositions from a number of sources concerning the appearance and consequences of consumer regret will be entertained.

Sources of Referents for the Occurrence of Regret

It has been said that satisfaction is a comparator response in that performance is meaningless unless it has a referent. Even at their most basic level, human needs (Chapter 5) and even goodness or badness, as used in the popular attitude models, provide this baseline for satisfaction. Earlier, the notion of eudaimonia versus hedonic enjoyment was entertained as a new, worldlier pursuit of satisfaction.[9] If one accepts this, the essence of "flow" or of self-realizations sought remains as comparators of interest. Regret is more definitive, for the comparators are the alternative outcomes one compares to performance. Much has been written on this topic; the real question is how these comparators are identified within consumption behaviors.[10]

Proactive Observation

The onset of regret is, almost by universal agreement, best captured by consideration of the cliché "what might have been." How do individuals know what might have been? In many circumstances, intentional direct observation is possible. For example, a choice between two stocks on the securities exchange provides a classic example of the regret phenomenon. Every day, the closing prices of public stocks are published in most major newspapers. All an investor needs do to experience regret (or its opposite, referred to as rejoicing) is to look up closing prices.[11] This can be done after any holding period desired by the investor (e.g., daily, monthly, semiannually). There is no room for ambiguity here, although, as has been noted, consumers have it in their power to choose to avoid encountering feedback.[12]

Vicarious Experience

In a second mode of selecting referents for regret, individuals can observe the outcomes of others people who have made alternative choices. For example, a consumer might compare his automobile purchase to that of his neighbor who had purchased another model of the same make, year, and price range. At a more aggregate level, he could look up the repair records of other cars that he might have considered in the *Consumer Reports* annual automobile issue. In both these instances, the likely outcomes of alternative purchases can be estimated. Unlike the example of the stock investor, however, these outcome estimates are likelihoods and not certainties.

Simulation

In a third mode of establishing a comparative referent, individuals can imagine what might have happened. Often this comparison is made to the alternative state of taking no action at all. In this latter case, any negative consequences of taking the action can be compared to the absence of the same negative states if inaction had been chosen.[13] For example, stomach distress caused by an ineffective pain reliever would cause the consumer to imagine a "better" situation with only the pain.

More typically, however, a consumer might construct a likely scenario of what would probably have happened if an alternative choice had been made. Such "counterfactual constructions" are referred to as simulations, or the creation of a "once-possible but unrealized world."[14] Regret is a specific example of counterfactual thinking in that what might have been is not what happened and, thus, is counter to the present facts.

Suppose, for example, that an undergraduate student decides to major in business administration and graduates at the beginning of a major recession. While struggling to find a job, she discovers that the demand for teachers is increasing rapidly. In this situation, it is easy to imagine how much better job prospects would be now if only she had decided to major in education instead. Of course, she cannot really know for certain whether the chances of finding an alternative job would have been better because of the preponderance of unknowns that would have appeared during four or more years of college. These unknowns include a different curriculum with different instructors and fellow students and maybe even a different university in a different geographic region. However, the very selective current knowledge of higher demand for employees in alternative occupations suggests to the student that her job chances would be better if only she had. . . .

At this point, it may appear that negative outcomes are required for regret to occur. This is not necessarily the case. Consider the following combinations of a consumer's outcome and an alternative outcome:

A. Negative actual outcome, given a positive alternative outcome
B. Negative actual outcome, given a less negative alternative outcome
C. Positive actual outcome, given a more positive alternative outcome

None of these scenarios is immune to regret. Example A is the most typical case for illustrating regret, such as when a chosen investment results in a loss and an equivalent unchosen investment gains. However, the remaining two scenarios could also foster ill feelings. In example B, a prospective homebuyer considers two houses in southern California. One house is built on a hill overlooking the ocean, and the other house is on the beach with essentially the same ocean view. The buyer opts for the house on the hill. Later, heavy rains wash the hillside house into the ocean, but only flood the house on the flat terrain. Surely this owner feels regret over the choice of location. The knowledge that the other choice would not have cost the loss of his home makes the actual loss worse. His home would still be intact "if only . . ." In example C, two bettors put money on a horse race. One bettor's horse comes in third, while the other's horse wins. Both bettors are "in the money," but the first bettor regrets not having bet on the winning horse. The knowledge that another horse came in first lessens her pleasure; because of her choice, she could have had more enjoyment, but did not. In short, comparisons to better outcomes appear to detract from the satisfaction (or add to the dissatisfaction) of one's outcomes in life.

An early study of the tribulations of college students shows this result rather dramatically.[15] The author gave student volunteers five scenarios as follows:

A. A very favorable event occurs.
B. A very favorable event almost occurs but does not.
C. A neutral event occurs.
D. A very unfavorable event almost occurs but does not.
E. A very unfavorable event occurs.

The ABCDE order seen here is based on actual outcomes. That is, favorable events should be preferred to missed favorable events (e.g., being a runner-up in a contest), then to neutral events, then to missed unfavorable events (e.g., a tumor is found to be benign), and last to unfavorable events (a tumor found to be malignant), in that order. What the author found, however, is that when subjects were asked to rate their satisfaction with these outcomes in a role-playing situation, the order appeared as ADCBE. Alternative B actually dropped from second to fourth place, flip-flopping with D. Why? The regret of just missing a very favorable outcome was viewed negatively, while the rejoicing at just missing a very unfavorable event was judged positively. In both cases, the comparison referents of what might have been (e.g., winning the contest; finding a malignant tumor) were strong counterfactuals that swayed the respondents' judgment.

When this scenario was recast as the winning of medals at the Olympics (gold, silver, bronze), the same result appeared: bronze medalists were happier than silver medalists. This result occurred because of downward comparisons (to be discussed) by the bronze winners (i.e., better to win bronze than no medal at all) and upward comparisons by the silver medalists (to the gold medalist), a result replicated in a second study of student grade contrasts.[16]

It has already been said that the status quo—that is, inaction—is a viable alternative and that negative outcomes of action can be contrasted to what would have happened in the absence of the action, which, in most cases, is nothing out of the ordinary. Now, is it possible for positive outcomes to result in regret when the only comparison alternative is the status quo? According to research, the answer is yes if the positive outcome came at the expense of, say, risk. For example, if a bettor risks his weekly earnings of $800 on a lottery and wins a secondary prize of $1,000, this positive outcome cannot be considered in the absence of the risk that was borne. The bettor can still regret the loss of peace of mind while waiting for the lottery results, particularly given the small return on this risk. It is not uncommon for investors to say, "I came out OK, but if I had it to do all over again, I probably wouldn't have put myself at risk."[17]

Positive Regret: Clarifying Rejoicing

The possibility that favorable outcomes can be compared to alternative negative outcomes, in effect the mirror image of regret, appears, although infrequently, in the literature under the term *rejoicing*, as noted. Although individuals do rejoice when very negative outcomes (e.g., natural calamities, possible cancer) are avoided (much of which is attributed to luck), there are reasons why less attention is paid to this phenomenon, at least in the more normal activities of consumption.[18] First, positive outcomes are desired in consumption and, when attained, effectively give the consumer what was expected. This resulting confirmation gives the consumer little motivation to process the outcome further. This result has been demonstrated in the context of experimental stock market outcomes.[19] For positive outcomes, exaggerated affect, such as delight, occurred only when a less attractive alternative (e.g., a lower return or loss) was made salient.

Second, despite the prior findings, the unattractiveness of an alternative (the chosen stock returned a gain, the unchosen a loss) frequently results in relief, not rejoicing: the consumer's reaction is "Whew, that could have happened to me!" In Chapter 5, relief was described as a negative reinforcement of a transitory nature. People do not like to dwell on missed misfortunes and near disasters. One extreme of this phenomenon is the classic notion of comic relief. In fact, one author specifically describes this positive outcome of regret as resulting from the anticipation of having a second chance to miss the misfortune: "I won't let this happen to me again."[20]

Third, in the situation of vicarious experience, theory would predict that rejoicing would occur when alternatives purchased by others result in losses. This is not a regret situation unless one has some stake in the decision, as noted earlier. Given this caveat, this situation frequently brings forth empathy, pity, and a sense of compassion over the other person's loss (with the unfortunate possibility of a *schadenfreude* response). Thus, for all three reasons, the reaction of rejoicing over a less fortunate purchase outcome is probably more rare than the more common regret. In fact, the very definition of regret is that it is a negative reaction to the belief that another decision would have been better.

Common Alternative Negative Correlates of Regret

Rejoicing aside, it appears that regret acts universally to detract from the enjoyment of a positive outcome or add to the misery of a negative outcome, with consequential effects on satisfaction. This is shown in Figure 9.3, where the actual outcome is shown as prompting comparisons to nonpurchase outcomes and to the outcomes of alternative purchases. The outcome itself could have positive or negative effects on satisfaction; the influences of the two regret alternatives are shown as detracting from satisfaction. The remaining influences in the figure are discussed later.

As with other satisfaction proxies (equity and disconfirmation differences—see Table 8.1—are yet another example), regret has many imitators. Generalized unhappiness has already been discussed. Other related emotions have been nicely described in a number of sources.[21] Although greater elaboration is presented in Chapters 12 and 13, some common associations with regret are shown in Table 9.1. Generally, these emotions will be consequences of regret and all are negatively valenced. The table gives only a brief description of each for the purposes intended here. Somewhat greater detail on regret and disconfirmation is forthcoming.

A Priori Consideration of Regret

A common criticism of the experience of regret and its effect on postdecision feelings is that if regret could have been anticipated as a likely outcome of choice, then why does it have an impact? In other words, if a bettor plays a lottery, then the loss of the entire amount risked is a likely outcome known from the onset of decision making. Thus, this outcome should have been absorbed into the predecision phase of purchasing so that it would have little additional effect if it occurred. Another way of viewing this situation is that if the possibility of a complete loss is considered a priori, there is no surprise when it occurs. There are two issues here. First, is regret limited only to surprising outcomes? Second, is the actual loss as experienced distinct from its anticipation?

In answer to the first, regret results from an unfavorable comparison to foregone outcomes, real or imagined. Whether the outcome is foreseen or not is only part of the issue. Clearly, if the

Figure 9.3 **Regret, Hindsight, and Associated Negative Effects on Satisfaction (with Disconfirmation)**

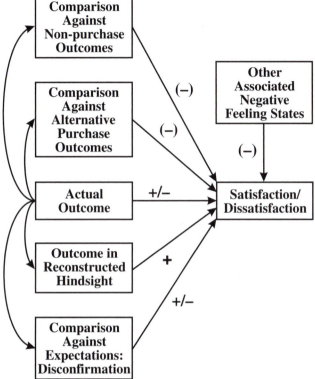

negative outcome is unforeseen, there is negative surprise. However, the consumer must also have and use a comparison outcome that was foregone for regret to occur. Otherwise, the consumer experiences only negative disconfirmation (or disappointment) and no regret! As noted, an unforeseen negative outcome may actually be less regretful than one that was foreseen, because the consumer could not have anticipated the first outcome and may feel less responsible (see Figure 9.2). However, unawareness in anticipation does not alter the impact of unforeseen outcomes once their presence is known.[22]

Thus, anticipated outcomes are regret-prone because the real issue is not so much the foreseeability of the outcome, but whether another choice, also available to the consumer a priori, would have resulted in a more favorable outcome. But there remains yet another issue, not considered by the critics. It is this author's contention that the realization of an outcome is frequently different from its imagination in anticipation. Outcomes can be "worse than I ever would have believed." Alternatively, they can be so good that they are "beyond my wildest dreams." This is why no predecision heuristic or decision rule can ever fully account for reactions to outcomes. As long as there is a random element to the life mechanisms that generate outcomes, and as long as there are unknown variables and processes in the outcome's determination, and as long as consumers attach affect (emotion) to the outcomes they experience, this experience cannot be completely and accurately forecast.

Table 9.1

Common Regret-Associated Negative Emotions and Their Different States

"True" regret	Sorrow over what might have been
Sadness (unhappiness)	A feeling of general unpleasantness (melancholy)
Disappointment	A lessened feeling of pleasure over what you wished had happened
Frustration	Heightened feelings of disappointment over repeated (often personal) failings
Self-blame	A sense of personal guilt or wrongdoing
Shame	A sense of personal embarrassment over having performed poorly against a standard
Guilt	A sense of having wronged someone or some standard
Remorse	Distress arising from continuing guilt over wrongs in the past
Envy	Discomfort from knowing of another person's more fortunate outcome or circumstances
Disconfirmation (negative)	A knowing that you received less than you expected or anticipated
Dissatisfaction	Unpleasant fulfillment (against a variety of comparators)

Joint Operation of Regret and Disconfirmation

To show that regret and disconfirmation can operate jointly, thereby establishing their separate identities, it is necessary to illustrate that both influences can occur in the same setting. Evidence for this possibility can now be found in a number of papers reporting on tests of the relative impacts of these two variables.[23] In the context of this research, disconfirmation was initially described as disappointment; the manipulations are clearly of disconfirmation, however. Recall that disappointment is a mild form of negative disconfirmation (Chapter 4). Figure 9.3 shows how actual outcomes can trigger both processes at the same time, as the comparative referents are distinct. (Realized) regret is a comparison against other outcomes, even imagined ones, while disconfirmation is an observed outcome comparison against expectations or norms. In fact, this difference allows researchers to test for separate effects.

In a typical study (there are other variations), respondents are given a choice between options that minimize regret (where the worst possible outcomes of the chosen option are better than the best of the unchosen) and options that minimize disappointment (defined as negative surprise—where the worst possible outcome of the chosen option provides the subject with a nonzero reward). In a second variation, the two are paired together without forced choice and parallel processes are hypothesized. Yet to be tested are studies using direct measures of each with input to equation modeling with measured satisfaction (not happiness) as the dependent variable. As with other concepts discussed in this book, definitive conclusions await further testing.[24]

Determinants of Regret

Based on the small amount of available conceptual and empirical work, some early insights to the determinants of regret can be offered. The initial focus is on the characteristics of the decision; later, focus briefly shifts to the characteristics of the individual.

Decision Difficulty: Outcome Complexity

Generally, the difficulty of choice, discussed more fully in the next chapter, appears to be a factor in regret. In an easy, mundane choice between, say, two nearly identical brands of dried peas, it is difficult to conceive of dried pea outcomes that would initiate a what-might-have-been search. Similarly, if one option dominates the other so that the worst-case scenario of the chosen is always better than the best case of the unchosen, little regret would be expected. The choice of accepting a free "mystery gift" versus turning it down would be one example. Excepting harmful gifts, little would be lost by accepting the gratuity.

Now, what of difficult decisions? Difficulty, here, can mean combinations of three aspects. It can mean that all the facts that can be known about the options are known and the decision is close. Deciding on one of two vacation destinations might be an example. In choosing either of the vacation options, one forgoes the unique advantages of the other option, and vice versa. Alternatively, difficulty can mean that a great deal of uncertainty surrounds each option. The choice between two experimental medical procedures might be an example of this case. In a third case, the possibility exists that a large number of options are available with varying degrees of uncertainty. Here, it is the vastness of choice that is central to regret (and to dissonance, discussed in the next chapter, as well).

It is not clear which of these cases would be more prone to regret. Even a good vacation outcome, regardless of which of the two close options was chosen, can still result in an imagined comparison to how it might have been had the other been chosen. A beach versus mountains choice is difficult because of the many mutually exclusive unique features of each, but there is no ambiguity surrounding the essential characteristics of a beach vacation versus those of a mountain vacation. Alternatively, a choice between two highly uncertain medical procedures can still cause the patient to wonder, "I wonder how it might have been, had I . . ."

The multiplexity of outcomes issue is a complexity of its own.[25] First, the number of outcomes increases the possibility of regret by increasing the favorability mix of alternatives. Second, it introduces the possibility of different sorts of comparisons, including comparisons to the outcomes of other people, introducing the emotion of envy (listed in Table 9.1). Third, it compounds the uncertainty of decision making because all outcomes have different probabilities of occurrences and, incidentally, of violations of these probabilities known only after the fact. This could occur when it becomes known that insiders had greater beforehand knowledge and could influence the outcome itself.

Decision Consequences

The negativity of the consequences influences regret directly. For example, automobile accidents are highly unpredictable and highly consequential in terms of personal injury, property damage, legal liability, traffic citations, and insurance (financial) implications.[26] Given the unpredictability of an individual accident, accident victims frequently lament that "this never would have happened" if only they had taken another route, left at a different time, or driven more slowly. Yet, in many cases, the different time of day, route, or speed would make no difference in the actual probability of an accident. If rush hour lasts from 4 to 6 p.m., a five-minute interval on either side of 5 p.m. makes no difference at all from a probability standpoint. Accidents at every minute in this interval are equally likely or unlikely. However, on this particular day, the totally unpredictable confluence of events leading up to this accident could have been avoided if departure had been delayed or hastened by a single minute. Knowing this, the lure of regret is unmistakable.

The idea that regret is fostered by negative consequences is so common in the literature that no supportive arguments beyond the obvious need be made and the reader is referred to the basic reviews in the field.[27] The unfortunate aspect of regret is that a seemingly positive outcome can be repositioned as negative simply by the contrast of alternatives after the fact. Thus, focusing on missed opportunities may be counterproductive in this regard, and the marketing literature, in particular, is replete with examples of competitive efforts to encourage dissatisfaction with current ownership for purposes of causing switching in the next purchase round. This notion was introduced early in this volume and will reappear in the last chapter.[28]

Decision Unfamiliarity

Based on norm theory, an early study in consumption discusses the likelihood that unfamiliar decisions, or decisions different from convention (the default option), may enhance regret.[29] Specifically, out-of-the-ordinary behavior resulting in negative consequences should beget more self-blame because of the inherent unfamiliarity of its consequences. In an early study in the consumer behavior field, subjects indicated that they would be more upset if they bought an off-brand product that turned out to be defective than if they had bought a defective name-brand product.[30] A second result from that study showed that passing up a sale in favor of a future, bigger sale that never occurred was more regret-inducing than buying at the first sale and finding lower prices in a later sale. Similarly, extending the accident example above, drivers who have an accident would most likely experience still greater regret if they had taken an alternate, rather than a familiar, route to the same destination, even if the accident rates on the two routes were identical. In all these examples, encountering failure by deviating from convention is more regretful than failure caused by following convention. This phenomenon is closely related to the practice of adhering to the status quo, as discussed next.

Action Versus Inaction

The regret associated with taking any action can be compared to the regret associated with taking no action, referred to as commission versus omission in the literature.[31] Taking no action typically maintains the status quo, but not necessarily, as, for example, when one discontinues a long-standing habit. In yet another example in the field of finance, an investor considers selling stock, does not, and finds that the stock should have been sold. The regret associated with this "sin of omission" may be compared to the reaction of a second investor who sells and finds that the stock should have been held. Predictably, this second "sin of commission" results in greater judged regret. The reason is that commission appears to be more deliberate, upsets the status quo, and assigns greater responsibility to the decision maker. In fact, it may be possible that omission is preferred to commission even when the negative results of omission are greater than those of commission.

Interestingly, the finding that commission results in greater regret than omission has been found to reverse itself if long-term recollections are involved. For example, it has been shown that life satisfaction is more adversely affected by actions not taken (e.g., not finishing college, not planning for retirement, a missed romantic opportunity). Generally, it had been thought that commission causes more regret in the short run and omission in the long run. In effect, the reason is that the omissions can no longer be ameliorated and that the long-term negative consequences are now known.[32]

In an example of omission-caused regret in a gambling context, it is thought that regret may occur when probabilities of wins are minuscule, but large amounts of winnings are involved. A frequent example is small-stake, large-prize gambles such as lotteries. Here, the consumer has the option of buying a ticket for $1 or not buying at all. Suppose the consumer bets $1 on the lottery and loses. Her maximum regret is $1, the cost that would have been avoided if she had not played the lottery. Now suppose that the consumer avoids the lottery and another bettor wins $10 million. Despite the extremely low odds, this knowledge can cause a sense of regret, and it has already been noted that lotteries capitalize on this emotion with the mental implant: "If only I had played, that might have been me!" It should now be clear why casinos celebrate jackpot wins with attention-grabbing displays and why at least one major national sweepstakes promoter has "prize patrols" on TV—all in an effort to create regret among those who chose to pass up the chance to win.

Reversals of this correspondence between omission and commission, short-term and long-term, have been observed, however, particularly in specific circumstances. In an interesting example in consumption, promotions proclaiming "now or never," "one-time chance," and "never again (at this price)" can result in inaction regret, while these same inactions can actually decrease over time, probably due to the availability of constantly occurring similar offers in the realm of commerce. This observation is buttressed by the "cheaper in the future" expectations of consumers in innovative environments. Alternatively, "dearer in the future" effects have also been found, and it is becoming clear that regret is a very manipulatable emotion when managed by professionals. In a related phenomenon, incompletion, whether by omission ("I forgot to do it") or commission ("I forgot to finish what I started"), enhances availability of the task and associated regret.[33]

Upward and Downward Comparisons

Upward and downward comparisons have already been mentioned in terms of Olympic medalists' desire to be first (to win the gold) or to be a medalist at all (to win the bronze). Typically, upward comparisons to athletes more fortunate foster regret even though the actual outcomes of the silver medalists are impressive indeed. In contrast, bronze medalists are quite content to have received a medal at all, often experiencing more satisfaction than those winning the silver. These results, frequently referred to as "neither the best nor worst of all possible worlds," are easily manipulated to cause regret regardless of the consumer's choice. The reader may have noted that regret research in both psychology and consumption increased around 1990, a fact documented in a recent review.[34] This has resulted in a plethora of reversals, mediations, mutations (a term also applied to how individuals formulate regret), and reconceptualizations; the upward-downward phenomenon is no exception.

As summarized and elaborated, individuals are capable of creating their own regret almost regardless of the circumstances.[35] More recent works have looked at the benefits of controlling or dealing with regret as a life-enhancing experience as if to say that regret is an evolutionary learning tool.[36] The point here is that, as writers have noted, the consumption applications are without bounds and that regret can be found to increase "with *both* downward and upward counterfactual thought."[37] Individual tendencies toward one or the other of these are briefly discussed next.

Individual Characteristics

On the surface, there are two possible traits that might predispose individuals to regret. The first is a chronic wish to have chosen differently, a philosophical desire to replay the past with different choices, an issue outside the scope of the present discussion. The second characteristic is an element of self-blame. In Chapter 11, this will be referred to as an internal attribution. Thus, with regret, a person internalizes the responsibility for the outcome and desires that it had turned out differently.

Reviewers have scoured the literature for such personality traits and the results are rather sparse. In one review, twelve personality traits were correlated first with the incidence of counterfactual thoughts in general and then with upward versus downward comparisons.[38] Of the twelve traits (optimism, self-esteem, desire for control, locus of control [internal versus external], need for cognition, rumination, belief in a just world, positive interpretation, acceptance, active coping, future coping, neuroticism), *none* were correlated with counterfactual thought in general. With regard to directional counterfactuals, seven of twenty-four were marginally significant $r \sim 0.2$, as follows.

Upward comparisons (known to be generally a negative contrast) were inversely correlated with optimism, self-esteem, acceptance, and positive interpretation, while downward comparisons were positively correlated with optimism, self-esteem, and belief in a just world. The self-esteem relations were in accord with prior findings while the optimism outcome was in accord with reviews, one in consumption.[39] Thus, it appears that regret is as mysterious and manipulatable as expressed here. As before, more definitive results await even the recent studies. The effect of regret on satisfaction, however, is not in dispute.

Evidence for the Consequences of Regret

Is there evidence for the influence of regret on satisfaction or satisfaction-like consequences? Generally, researchers have investigated the occurrence of regret, rather than its consequences. Fortunately, work in customer satisfaction has been more focused since the first edition of this book and almost all studies have been reported in various sections of this chapter. Survey work containing validated scales for use in equation modeling has lagged behind, however, and as a result, good contrastive and weighted findings against other satisfaction determinants have not appeared.

Based on the prior discussion, there are two phases of regret that should be sampled. *Anticipated* regret can be measured either before the fact or retrospectively (see Chapter 3). The following items, in agree-disagree format, are adapted from an early study on regret in consumption and are further divided into the timing of the decision (the first four statements) and the choice itself (the remaining statements):[40]

1. I would feel regret if I bought X now and found that the price was lowered later.
2. I would feel bad if I waited until later to buy X and found that the price was higher than it is now.
3. I would feel terrible if I bought X now and it went on sale in the near future.
4. It would cause regret if I passed on a sale now and needed to buy the same product later at the regular price.
5. I would be very upset if I bought X and found out later that Y would have been better.
6. I would feel regret if I bought X over identically priced Y and found that Y would have performed better.
7. I would feel terrible if I bought X and a new and improved version came out soon at the same price.
8. I would be upset if I bought X, thinking it was better than same-priced Y, and it was actually worse.

In a continued effort to stimulate *postpurchase* (realized) research on regret, a somewhat augmented regret scale from the first edition is offered here. Four new items have been added to the bottom of the list, two reflecting the difference between "hot" and "wistful" regret and two reflecting "rejoicing." The hot versus wistful distinction corresponds to committed actions in the short run compared to omitted actions in the long run.[41]

What are your feelings concerning your decision to buy _____?

Regrettable decision	1	2	3	4	5	Excellent decision
Many doubts about choice	1	2	3	4	5	No doubts about choice
Sorry I made the decision	1	2	3	4	5	I have no regrets
Will never buy again	1	2	3	4	5	Would buy again
I should have chosen another	1	2	3	4	5	My choice was correct
Do not want to do it again	1	2	3	4	5	Want to do it again
Choice was a *really bad* mistake	1	2	3	4	5	Choice was *one of my best*
Always thinking about missed choices I had	1	2	3	4	5	Never think about my past choices
Damn, that was a terrible choice I made	1	2	3	4	5	Wow, what a great choice I made!
This choice made my life terribly gloomy	1	2	3	4	5	I'm basking in the sun over my choice

As shown, the scale is constructed so that high scores reflect a lack of regret, which should therefore correlate positively with satisfaction. Hopefully, researchers will begin testing regret effects on customer satisfaction within simultaneous equation models so that this scale and improved versions will see more widespread use. Greater use will illuminate the intricacies of regret's influence on the satisfaction response as well as allow practitioners to study regret as a meaningful consequence of consumption.

Regret as an Initiator of Self-Protection

It has been noted that the apprehension of regret will cause consumers to protect themselves against it.[42] Using such a prepurchase, ego-protective mechanism of avoiding risk and regret, consumers may be able to avoid regret-prone decisions, as alluded to previously. This can be done by selecting an option that has no unfavorable consequences worse than the best consequences of the other alternatives in the consideration set. As a practical matter, however, it may be difficult to find such a bundle of alternatives. Realistically, regret is an inevitable result of consumption and of life in general. Therefore, as a defense mechanism, a consumer may claim, "I knew it all along." This perspective diffuses the surprise of the negative outcome, as if the consumer were prepared to accept it.

It has been noted in many literatures that the presence of other people will exacerbate this phenomenon.[43] As will be discussed in Chapter 11, it is common for individuals to attribute negative events that occur to someone else to faulty reasoning on the part of the other person. That is, to an observer, events appear more foreseeable in retrospect than they are in reality, a phenomenon known as hindsight bias. Thus, people whose outcomes are negative may be judged harshly by their peers for "not having known better." In recognition of this common response to the negative outcomes of others, the focal person is likely to create an ego-protective defense of agreeableness. This response is even more effective if it is used preemptively. Thus, when faced with negative outcomes observable to others, the about-to-be-accused responds, "I knew this would happen."

HINDSIGHT BIAS

This second section of the chapter turns to hindsight bias whereby regret is explained away. Consumers do this by claiming to have predicted that a comparatively unfavorable outcome or the actual outcome would occur. Known by many terms, including the *knew-it-all-along* effect, it can be described as a retrospective increase in the foresight odds that a particular event (or nonevent) will occur—after it is observed to have occurred.

Generally, the classic experiment displaying hindsight proceeds as follows: Two randomly selected groups are given a scenario that will eventually be resolved to a conclusion. A common example might be the results of a forthcoming election. The conclusion is whether one or the other candidate will win. One group provides odds estimates based on preelection polling of particular so-called bellwether states. The other group is given the conclusion—that a particular candidate won. Members of this second group are then asked to estimate what the odds would have been if they had not been told what had happened. The difference between the two group estimates is evidence for hindsight bias—the influence of outcome knowledge on remembrances of prior predictions. This, of course, implies that the second group reassesses the implications of these historical trends.

Evidence for this effect is substantial. Both discursive and statistical reviews show that outcome knowledge moves predecision retrospections in the direction of the outcome.[44] However, the more inclusive statistical review shows this effect to be modest, with an estimated range of correlations between outcome knowledge and change in probability assessments of 0.14 to 0.29, depending on assumptions regarding unreliability of measures.

Thus, the present discussion centers on what effect hindsight has, if any, on postpurchase judgments. A number of issues will be briefly discussed, including moderating conditions for hindsight bias, potential motivations for this bias, and evidence in a marketing context. The chapter concludes by summing up what is known about regret and hindsight and by linking these concepts to the satisfaction response.

Moderating Conditions and Causes

The aforementioned reviews conclude that two primary moderators are operative in accounts of hindsight bias. It appears that this bias is greater when individuals focus on the occurrence of an event rather than on its nonoccurrence and when subjects are unfamiliar with, as opposed to knowledgeable of, the context of the outcome, the latter moderator subsuming the surprisingness of the outcome. The researchers note that these are independent effects, so that high bias is evident with unfamiliar, but explainable, occurrences, such as when novice investors are asked to judge the probability of a realized stock market crash, given the events preceding it. These two conclusions would appear to be reasonable in light of other findings that unusual or unexpected event occurrences are more attention-getting than the status quo and that contextual knowledge (expertise) provides a logic structure for the interpretation of events and their likelihoods.[45]

Various speculations have been advanced for the reasons behind hindsight. Two are commonly accepted. First, individuals are thought to be motivated to save face by impressing others with their ability to have forecast the event with only the advantage of foresight. Second, individuals are thought to have an innate desire to understand the environment in which they live and to gain confidence in these understandings.[46] This argument is based on "creeping determinism," whereby individuals update their knowledge of a phenomenon with observations of perceived cause and effect.

The evidence for these two explanations is mixed; studies supporting one or the other view offer convincing arguments. However, the weight of the evidence leans toward cognitive explanations in those studies designed to discriminate between them. Reviews provide an integrative route, concluding that hindsight bias is an inextricable combination of the two factors, so much so that one factor can prime the other factor in the same decision. This is a reasonable conclusion in light of the evidence these authors present.[47]

A third, correlated reason for the occurrence of hindsight is surprise. Here, the effects are curvilinear. As one would expect, outcomes that are expected are assimilated and no hindsight, taken literally, is found—a mere expectation effect (see Chapter 3). Surprising outcomes that can be explained away produce classic hindsight effects in that "sense-making" operations are used and become believable to others. At the extreme, surprising outcomes that do not make sense in that they are incredible result in less hindsight, if any, and are attributed to irrational and unexplainable phenomena so that no one could have expected them.[48] Thus, in the realm of normal and explainable events, hindsight not only is plausible, but works to the advantage of all concerned.

Given these reasons, what is the effect of hindsight on satisfaction? It appears that hindsight permits individuals to save face, allows them to better explain (understand?) why events turned out differently from what they expected, and enhances self-esteem. Thus it appears that all effects are somewhat positive. Like regret, hindsight reflections are usually observed in unfavorable outcome situations.[49] As such, hindsight may mitigate the outcome or cause individuals to be more accepting of negative outcomes. Under this line of logic, the effect of hindsight on satisfaction in Figure 9.3 is shown as positive.

Evidence in a Marketing Context

Surprisingly, few studies on hindsight in consumption postpurchase studies have been performed. This is as true now as it was at the first writing of this book. Perhaps the most descriptive study in the satisfaction field, in that it is fully integrated with the expectancy disconfirmation model, is summarized here for its insight.[50] In this study, the authors manipulated pre-use expectations and the performance of personalized mailing envelopes in an actual choice situation. Subjects in the high-performance condition received laser-printed envelopes while those in the low-performance group received versions produced on a dot-matrix printer. All subjects were then asked to rate their expectations again on the same expectation scales used previously. Results showed the traditional hindsight effects whereby high-performance subjects overstated their prior expectations while low-performance subjects underrated their expectations. These effects were significant, as predicted. Additionally, the authors present evidence that when hindsight effects occur, hindsight expectations are used in place of foresight (i.e., retrospective) expectations when satisfaction judgments are formed. They also show that the effect on satisfaction is positive, as portrayed in Figure 9.3. However, the disconfirmation effect on satisfaction was more than twice as large as the hindsight effect.

This assimilation tendency of hindsight leads to the speculation that it will bolster satisfaction or decrease the level of dissatisfaction. In effect, the consumer would say, "This is an unfortunate outcome, but then I knew it would happen. Thus I feel better about it than if it were a complete surprise." Researchers would benefit from knowing more precisely how hindsight, when it occurs, impacts satisfaction. A simple measure, embedded in a satisfaction survey, would provide an early insight into hindsight influences. As phrased in agree/disagree format, the stem of the question would read: "I knew this would happen" or "I was afraid this would happen." Once hindsight comes into play, however, it has proven to be remarkably resistant to countering.[51] The implications of this finding may become more conclusive as further study emerges.

CONCLUSION

So that the central topic of this chapter, regret, is not forgotten, the chapter concludes by noting that regret remains as a potentially strong comparison referent in the what-might-have-been camp.

Regret, however, may have greater theoretical import than hindsight because regret is a learning heuristic. Consumers would generally wish to avoid regret or minimize its impact, either by making low-risk decisions or by bolstering immunity to regret.

In contrast, hindsight bias may be viewed as a threat to learning and growth, as it prohibits learning from experience. It may instill complacency by inhibiting the consideration of alternatives to choice, thereby redirecting thought to the processing of outcomes. Consumers may be motivated to view outcomes as unique events in postpurchase evaluation, thus reinforcing the sterile performance effect. If people knew all along about their bad decisions, then why did they make them?

An answer to this question may help managers use regret to their advantage and perhaps, also, to that of consumers. Generally, consumers seek to avoid regret, and anything management can do to minimize it will aid purchasing and soften the effects of negative purchase outcomes. Because regret is a comparison to other alternatives, managers can provide price and service guarantees that will obviate the need for consumers to make comparisons.

Interestingly, purchase outcome apprehension takes discussion directly to the topic of the next chapter, where the immediate pre to postpurchase process of cognitive dissonance is discussed. Dissonance will be discussed, not only as a pre-choice phenomenon, but also as the beginning of the postpurchase sequence and continuing into it, possibly setting the stage for cognitions such as regret avoidance and expectation formation. Unlike regret, however, dissonance is not an outcome comparison operation. Rather, it is a core process running through the consumption experience.

NOTES

1. See Roese and Maniar, "Perceptions of Purple."

2. The previous edition of this book used the word *responsibility* and this usage continues here, based, in part, on a seminal paper in consumer behavior, Simonson's "Influence of Anticipating Regret and Responsibility on Purchase Decisions," and, more recently, McConnell et al., "What If I Find It Cheaper Someplace Else?" Since the Simonson publication, at least four reviews have appeared, two of which are in marketing. The word *responsibility* is apparently out of vogue and the new moniker is *causal agency* or *controllability*, both of which are discussed in Chapter 11. Indeed, there now appears to be a consensus of converging theoretical correspondence across the three topics of regret, dissonance, and attribution that speaks well for the development of the field. This author may be faulted for being "old-school," but I continue to see these three topics as conceptually distinct with the inevitable overlap similar to that between expectancy and (expectancy) disconfirmation, for example. Readers will surely wish to review the following articles for their depth of insight and forward-leaning perspective: Gilovich and Medvec, "Experience of Regret"; Roese, "Counterfactual Thinking"; McGill, "Counterfactual Reasoning in Causal Judgments"; Zeelenberg and Pieters, "Theory of Regret Regulation 1.0." Fortunately, these articles cover the field so thoroughly that my efforts are both buttressed and diminished as a result.

3. See Connolly, Ordóñez, and Coughlan, "Regret and Responsibility in the Evaluation of Decision Outcomes"; Zeelenberg et al., "Experience of Regret and Disappointment"; Ordóñez and Connolly, "Regret and Responsibility"; and Zeelenberg, van Dijk, and Manstead, "Regret and Responsibility Resolved?"

4. Girotto, Legrenzi, and Rizzo, "Event Controllability in Counterfactual Thinking"; Mandel and Lehman, "Counterfactual Thinking and Ascriptions of Cause and Preventability"; Markman et al., "Impact of Perceived Control on the Imagination of Better and Worse Possible Worlds"; Roese and Olson, "Outcome Controllability and Counterfactual Thinking."

5. The calculations are as follows. Option 1: $(0.25 \times \$80) + (0.5 \times \$50) + (0.25 \times \$20) = \$50$. Option 2: $(0.1 \times \$1000) + (0.9 \times \$0) = \$100$.

6. Bar-Hillel and Neter, "Why Are People Reluctant to Exchange Lottery Tickets?"; Landman and Petty, "'It Could Have Been You'"; McMullen, Markham, and Gavanski, "Living in Neither the Best Nor Worst of All Possible Worlds."

7. Boninger, Gleicher, and Strathman, "Counterfactual Thinking"; Harrison and March, "Decision Mak-

ing and Postdecision Surprises"; Roese, "Functional Basis of Counterfactual Thinking"; Roese and Olson, "Structure of Counterfactual Thought."

8. Roese and Olson, eds., *What Might Have Been.*

9. Ryan and Deci, "On Happiness and Human Potentials"; Waterman, "Two Conceptions of Happiness."

10. Dröge, Halstead, and Mackoy, "The Role of Competitive Alternatives in the Postchoice Satisfaction Formation Process"; Tsiros, "Effect of Regret on Post-choice Valuation"; Windschitl and Wells, "Alternative-Outcomes Effect."

11. Use of the term *rejoicing* to reflect an emotion loosely described as "better than I feared" (see Chapter 12) has become common in the literature. Originally referred to as elation, it is sometimes operationalized as positive disconfirmation, which is not technically correct. As discussed in Chapter 4, positive disconfirmation can result in negative consequences if it is insufficient. See, however, Greenleaf, "Reserves, Regret, and Rejoicing in Open English Auctions"; Inman, Dyer, and Jia, "Generalized Utility Model of Disappointment and Regret Effects on Post-Choice Evaluation"; Landman, "Regret and Elation Following Action and Inaction."

12. Ritov and Baron, "Outcome Knowledge, Regret, and Omission Bias"; Zeelenberg, Beattie, et al., "Consequences of Regret Aversion"; and Zeelenberg and Beattie, "Consequences of Regret Aversion 2."

13. This topic will be covered later. For now, see Baron and Ritov, "Reference Points and Omission Bias"; and N'gbala and Branscombe, "When Does Action Elicit More Regret than Inaction and Is Counterfactual Mutation the Mediator of This Effect?"

14. Kahneman and Miller, "Norm Theory"; Sanna, Turley-Ames, and Meier, "Mood, Self-Esteem, and Simulated Alternatives."

15. Johnson, "Knowledge of What Might Have Been."

16. Medvec, Madey, and Gilovich, "When Less Is More"; Medvec and Savitsky, "When Doing Better Means Feeling Worse."

17. Samuelson, "Status Quo Bias in Decision Making." The example is from Tykocinski and Pittman, "Consequences of Doing Nothing."

18. Mellers, "Choice and the Relative Pleasure of Consequences"; Walchli and Landman, "Effects of Counterfactual Thought on Postpurchase Consumer Affect."

19. Gleicher et al., "Role of Counterfactual Thinking in Judgments of Affect."

20. Landman, "Through a Glass Darkly."

21. Davis et al., "Self-Blame Following a Traumatic Event"; Landman, *Regret*; Mellers, Schwartz, and Ritov, "Emotion-Based Choice"; Niedenthal, Tangney, and Gavanski, "'If Only I Weren't' Versus 'If Only I Hadn't'"; van Dijk, Zeelenberg, and van der Pligt, "Not Having What You Want Versus Having What You Do Not Want"; Zeelenberg and Pieters, "Theory of Regret Regulation."

22. Lin and Huang, "Influence of Unawareness Set and Order Effects in Consumer Regret"; McConnell et al., "What If I Find It Cheaper Someplace Else?"

23. Early studies are summarized in Loomes and Sugden, "Testing for Regret and Disappointment in Choice under Uncertainty." See also Sanna and Turley, "Antecedents to Spontaneous Counterfactual Thinking"; Tsiros, "Effect of Regret on Post-choice Valuation"; and Zeelenberg, van Dijk, et al., "On Bad Decisions and Disconfirmed Expectancies."

24. The following studies examine regret and outcomes only in a close approximation to expectancy disconfirmation: Creyer and Ross, "Development and Use of a Regret Experience Measure to Examine the Effects of Outcome Feedback on Regret and Subsequent Choice"; Taylor, "Regret Theory Approach to Assessing Consumer Satisfaction."

25. Boles and Messick, "Reverse Outcome Bias"; Sagi and Friedland, "Cost of Richness"; Windschitl and Wells, "Alternative-Outcomes Effect."

26. Williams, Lees-Haley, and Price, "Role of Counterfactual Thinking and Causal Attribution in Accident-Related Judgments."

27. Gilovich and Medvec, "Experience of Regret"; Roese, "Counterfactual Thinking"; Roese and Olson, "Counterfactual Thinking"; van Dijk, Zeelenberg, and van der Pligt, "Not Having What You Want Versus Having What You Do Not Want"; Zeelenberg and Pieters, "Theory of Regret Regulation."

28. Dröge, Halstead, and Mackoy, "Role of Competitive Alternatives in the Postchoice Satisfaction Formation Process"; Inman and Zeelenberg, "Regret in Repeat Purchase Versus Switching Decisions"; Tsiros and Mittal, "Regret"; Zeelenberg and Pieters, "Comparing Service Delivery to What Might Have Been."

29. Kahneman and Miller, "Norm Theory."

30. Simonson, "Influence of Anticipating Regret and Responsibility on Purchase Decisions."

31. Mannetti, Pierro, and Kruglanski, "Who Regrets More after Choosing a Non-Status-Quo Option?"; Schweitzer, "Disentangling Status Quo and Omission Effects"; Spranca, Minsk, and Baron, "Omission and Commission in Judgment and Choice."

32. Gilovich and Medvec, "Temporal Pattern to the Experience of Regret."

33. Respectively, Abendroth and Diehl, "Now or Never"; McConnell et al., "What If I Find It Cheaper Someplace Else?"; Arkes, Kung, and Hutzel, "Regret, Valuation, and Inaction Inertia"; Feldman, Miyamoto, and Loftus, "Are Actions Regretted More than Inactions?"; Savitsky, Medvec, and Gilovich, "Remembering and Regretting."

34. Zeelenberg and Pieters, "Theory of Regret Regulation," Figure 1.

35. McMullen, "Affective Contrast and Assimilation in Counterfactual Thinking"; McMullen, Markham, and Gavanski, "Living in Neither the Best Nor Worst of All Possible Worlds"; Tetlock, "Close-Call Counterfactuals and Belief-System Defenses."

36. Inman, "Regret Regulation"; King and Hicks, "Whatever Happened to 'What Might Have Been'?"; McMullen and Markman, "Downward Counterfactuals and Motivation"; Nasco and Marsh, "Gaining Control Through Counterfactual Thinking."

37. Walchli and Landman, "Effects of Counterfactual Thought on Postpurchase Consumer Affect."

38. Kasimatis and Wells, "Individual Differences in Counterfactual Thinking."

39. See, e.g., Sanna, "Self-Efficacy and Counterfactual Thinking"; Sanna, Turley-Ames, and Meier, "Mood, Self-Esteem, and Simulated Alternatives"; and Walchli and Landman, "Effects of Counterfactual Thought on Postpurchase Consumer Affect."

40. These items are variations of those used in Simonson, "Influence of Anticipating Regret and Responsibility on Purchase Decisions."

41. Kahneman, "Varieties of Counterfactual Thinking"; Gilovich, Medvec, and Kahneman, "Varieties of Regret."

42. Miller and Taylor, "Counterfactual Thought, Regret, and Superstition."

43. See Bernard Weiner, *Judgments of Responsibility*, Chapter 3.

44. Hawkins and Hastie, "Hindsight"; Christensen-Szalanski and Willham, "Hindsight Bias."

45. Mannetti, Pierro, and Kruglanski, "Who Regrets More After Choosing a Non-Status-Quo Option?"; Nario and Branscombe, "Comparison Processes in Hindsight and Causal Attribution."

46. See, e.g., Campbell and Tesser, "Motivational Interpretations of Hindsight Bias"; Roese and Olson, "Counterfactuals, Causal Attributions, and the Hindsight Bias."

47. See, e.g., Connolly and Bukszar, "Hindsight Bias"; Hell et al., "Hindsight Bias"; and Wasserman, Lempert, and Hastie, "Hindsight and Causality."

48. Ofir and Mazursky, "Does a Surprising Outcome Reinforce or Reverse the Hindsight Bias?"; Pezzo, "Surprise, Defence, or Making Sense"; Pieters, Koelemeijer, and Roest, "Assimilation Processes in Service Satisfaction Formation."

49. Haslam and Jayasinghe, "Negative Affect and Hindsight Bias"; Schkade and Kilbourne, "Expectation-Outcome Consistency and Hindsight Bias."

50. Zwick, Pieters, and Baumgartner, "On the Practical Significance of Hindsight Bias."

51. Hertwig, Gigerenzer, and Hoffrage, "Reiteration Effect in Hindsight Bias"; Pohl and Hell, "No Reduction in Hindsight Bias after Complete Information and Repeated Testing."

BIBLIOGRAPHY

Abendroth, Lisa J., and Kristin Diehl. "Now or Never: Effects of Limited Purchase Opportunities on Patterns of Regret over Time." *Journal of Consumer Research* 33, no. 3 (December 2006): 342–351.

Arkes, Hal R., Yi-Han Kung, and Laura Hutzel. "Regret, Valuation, and Inaction Inertia." *Organizational Behavior and Human Decision Processes* 87, no. 2 (March 2002): 371–385.

Bar-Hillel, Maya, and Efrat Neter. "Why Are People Reluctant to Exchange Lottery Tickets?" *Journal of Personality and Social Psychology* 70, no. 1 (January 1996): 17–27.

Baron, Jonathan, and Ilana Ritov. "Reference Points and Omission Bias." *Organizational Behavior and Human Decision Processes* 59, no. 3 (September 1994): 475–498.

Boles, Terry L., and David M. Messick. "A Reverse Outcome Bias: The Influence of Multiple Reference Points on the Evaluation of Outcomes and Decisions." *Organizational Behavior and Human Decision Processes* 61, no. 3 (March 1995): 262–275.

Boninger, David S., Faith Gleicher, and Alan Strathman. "Counterfactual Thinking: From What Might

Have Been to What May Be." *Journal of Personality and Social Psychology* 67, no. 2 (August 1994): 297–307.

Campbell, Jennifer D., and Abraham Tesser. "Motivational Interpretations of Hindsight Bias: An Individual Difference Analysis." *Journal of Personality* 51, no. 4 (December 1983): 605–620.

Christensen-Szalanski, Jay J.J., and Cynthia Fobian Willham. "The Hindsight Bias: A Meta-analysis." *Organizational Behavior and Human Decision Processes* 48, no. 1 (February 1991): 147–168.

Connolly, Terry, and Edward W. Bukszar. "Hindsight Bias: Self-Flattery or Cognitive Error?" *Journal of Behavioral Decision Making* 3, no. 3 (July–September 1990): 205–211.

Connolly, Terry, Lisa D. Ordóñez, and Richard Coughlan. "Regret and Responsibility in the Evaluation of Decision Outcomes." *Organizational Behavior and Human Decision Processes* 70, no. 1 (April 1997): 73–85.

Creyer, Elizabeth A., and William T. Ross Jr. "The Development and Use of a Regret Experience Measure to Examine the Effects of Outcome Feedback on Regret and Subsequent Choice." *Marketing Letters* 10, no. 4 (November 1999): 379–392.

Davis, Christopher G., Darrin R. Lehman, Roxane Cohen Silver, Camille B. Wortman, and John H. Ellard. "Self-Blame Following a Traumatic Event: The Role of Perceived Avoidability." *Personality and Social Psychology Bulletin* 22, no. 6 (June 1996): 557–567.

Dröge, Cornelia, Diane Halstead, and Robert D. Mackoy. "The Role of Competitive Alternatives in the Postchoice Satisfaction Formation Process." *Journal of the Academy of Marketing Science* 25, no. 1 (Winter 1997): 18–30.

Feldman, Julie, John Miyamoto, and Elizabeth F. Loftus. "Are Actions Regretted More than Inactions?" *Organizational Behavior and Human Decision Processes* 78, no. 3 (June 1999): 232–255.

Gilovich, Thomas, and Victoria Husted Medvec. "The Experience of Regret: What, When, and Why." *Psychological Review* 102, no. 2 (April 1995): 379–395.

———. "The Temporal Pattern to the Experience of Regret." *Journal of Personality and Social Psychology* 67, no. 3 (September 1994): 357–365.

Gilovich, Thomas, Victoria Husted Medvec, and Daniel Kahneman. "Varieties of Regret: A Debate and Partial Resolution." *Psychological Review* 105, no.3 (July 1998): 602–605.

Girotto, Vittorio, Paolo Legrenzi, and Antonio Rizzo. "Event Controllability in Counterfactual Thinking." *Acta Psychologica* 78, nos. 1–3 (December 1991): 111–133.

Gleicher, Faith, Kathryn A. Kost, Sara M. Baker, Alan J. Strathman, Steven A. Richman, and Steven J. Sherman. "The Role of Counterfactual Thinking in Judgments of Affect." *Personality and Social Psychology Bulletin* 16, no. 2 (June 1990): 284–295.

Greenleaf, Eric A. "Reserves, Regret, and Rejoicing in Open English Auctions." *Journal of Consumer Research* 31, no. 2 (September): 264–273.

Harrison, J. Richard, and James G. March. "Decision Making and Postdecision Surprises." *Administrative Science Quarterly* 29, no. 1 (March 1984): 26–42.

Haslam, Nick, and Nimali Jayasinghe. "Negative Affect and Hindsight Bias." *Journal of Behavioral Decision Making* 8, no. 2 (June 1995): 127–135.

Hawkins, Scott A., and Reid Hastie. "Hindsight: Biased Judgments of Past Events after the Outcomes Are Known." *Psychological Bulletin* 107, no. 3 (May 1990): 311–327.

Hell, Wolfgang, Gerd Gigerenzer, Siegfried Gauggel, Maria Mall, and Michael Müller. "Hindsight Bias: An Interaction of Automatic and Motivational Factors." *Memory & Cognition* 16, no. 6 (November 1988): 533–538.

Hertwig, Ralph, Gerd Gigerenzer, and Ulrich Hoffrage. "The Reiteration Effect in Hindsight Bias." *Psychological Review* 104, no. 1 (January 1997): 194–202.

Inman, J. Jeffrey. "Regret Regulation: Disentangling Self-Reproach from Learning." *Journal of Consumer Psychology* 17, no. 1 (2007): 19–24.

Inman, J. Jeffrey, James S. Dyer, and Jianmin Jia. "A Generalized Utility Model of Disappointment and Regret Effects on Post-Choice Evaluation." *Marketing Science* 16, no. 2 (1997): 97–111.

Inman, J. Jeffrey, and Marcel Zeelenberg. "Regret in Repeat Purchase Versus Switching Decisions: The Attenuating Role of Decision Justifiability." *Journal of Consumer Research* 29, no. 1 (June 2002): 116–128.

Johnson, Joel T. "The Knowledge of What Might Have Been: Affective and Attributional Consequences of Near Outcomes." *Personality and Social Psychology Bulletin* 12, no. 1 (March 1986): 51–62.

Kahneman, Daniel. "Varieties of Counterfactual Thinking." In *What Might Have Been: The Social Psychology of Counterfactual Thinking*, ed. Neal J. Roese and James M. Olson, 375–396. Mahwah, NJ: Lawrence Erlbaum, 1995.

Kahneman, Daniel, and Dale T. Miller. "Norm Theory: Comparing Reality to Its Alternatives." *Psychological Review* 93, no. 2 (April 1986): 136–153.

Kasimatis, Margaret, and Gary L. Wells. "Individual Differences in Counterfactual Thinking." In *What Might Have Been: The Social Psychology of Counterfactual Thinking*, ed. Neal J. Roese and James M. Olson, 81–101. Mahwah, NJ: Lawrence Erlbaum, 1995.

King, Laura A., and Joshua A. Hicks. "Whatever Happened to 'What Might Have Been'?" *American Psychologist* 62, no. 7 (October 2007): 625–636.

Landman, Janet. *Regret: The Persistence of the Possible.* New York: Oxford University Press, 1993.

———. "Regret and Elation Following Action and Inaction: Affective Responses to Positive and Negative Outcomes." *Personality and Social Psychology Bulletin* 13, no. 4 (December 1987): 524–536.

———. "Through a Glass Darkly: Worldviews, Counterfactual Thought, and Emotion." In *What Might Have Been: The Social Psychology of Counterfactual Thinking*, ed. Neal J. Roese and James M. Olson, 233–258. Mahwah, NJ: Lawrence Erlbaum, 1995.

Landman, Janet, and Ross Petty. "'It Could Have Been You': How States Exploit Counterfactual Thought to Market Lotteries." *Psychology & Marketing* 17, no. 4 (April 2000): 299–321.

Lin, Chien-Huang, and Wen-Hsien Huang. "The Influence of Unawareness Set and Order Effects in Consumer Regret." *Journal of Business and Psychology* 21, no. 2 (Winter 2006): 293–311.

Loomes, Graham, and Robert Sugden. "Testing for Regret and Disappointment in Choice under Uncertainty." *Economic Journal* 97 (Conference Supplement 1987): 118–129.

Mandel, David R., and Darrin R. Lehman. "Counterfactual Thinking and Ascriptions of Cause and Preventability." *Journal of Personality and Social Psychology* 71, no. 3 (September 1996): 450–463.

Mannetti, Lucia, Antonio Pierro, and Arie Kruglanski. "Who Regrets More after Choosing a Non-Status-Quo Option? Post Decisional Regret Under Need for Cognitive Closure." *Journal of Economic Psychology* 28, no. 2 (April 2007): 186–196.

Markman, Keith D., Igor Gavanski, Steven J. Sherman, and Matthew N. McMullen. "The Impact of Perceived Control on the Imagination of Better and Worse Possible Worlds." *Personality and Social Psychology Bulletin* 21, no. 6 (June 1995): 588–595.

McConnell, Allen R., Keith E. Niedermeier, Jill M. Leibold, Amani G. El-Alayli, Peggy P. Chin, and Nicole M. Kuiper. "What If I Find It Cheaper Someplace Else? Role of Prefactual Thinking and Anticipated Regret in Consumer Behavior." *Psychology & Marketing* 17, no. 4 (April 2000): 281–298.

McGill, Ann L. "Counterfactual Reasoning in Causal Judgments: Implications for Marketing." *Psychology & Marketing* 17, no. 4 (April 2000): 323–343.

McMullen, Matthew N. "Affective Contrast and Assimilation in Counterfactual Thinking." *Journal of Experimental Social Psychology* 33, no. 1 (January 1997): 77–100.

McMullen, Matthew N., and Keith D. Markman. "Downward Counterfactuals and Motivation: The Wake-Up Call and the Pangloss Effect." *Personality and Social Psychology Bulletin* 26, no. 5 (May 2000): 575–584.

McMullen, Matthew N., Keith D. Markman, and Igor Gavanski. "Living in Neither the Best Nor Worst of All Possible Worlds: Antecedents and Consequences of Upward and Downward Counterfactual Thinking." In *What Might Have Been: The Social Psychology of Counterfactual Thinking*, ed. Neal J. Roese and James M. Olson, 133–167. Mahwah, NJ: Lawrence Erlbaum, 1995.

Medvec, Victoria Husted, Scott F. Madey, and Thomas Gilovich. "When Less Is More: Counterfactual Thinking and Satisfaction Among Olympic Medalists." *Journal of Personality and Social Psychology* 69, no. 4 (October 1995): 603–610.

Medvec, Victoria Husted, and Kenneth Savitsky. "When Doing Better Means Feeling Worse: The Effects of Categorical Cutoff Points on Counterfactual Thinking and Satisfaction." *Journal of Personality and Social Psychology* 72, no. 6 (June 1997): 1284–1296.

Mellers, Barbara A. "Choice and the Relative Pleasure of Consequences." *Psychological Bulletin* 126, no. 6 (November 2000): 910–924.

Mellers, Barbara A., Alan Schwartz, and Ilana Ritov. "Emotion-Based Choice." *Journal of Experimental Psychology: General* 128, no. 3 (September 1999): 332–345.

Miller, Dale T., and Brian R. Taylor. "Counterfactual Thought, Regret, and Superstition: How to Avoid Kicking Yourself." In *What Might Have Been: The Social Psychology of Counterfactual Thinking*, ed. Neal J. Roese and James M. Olson, 305–331. Mahwah, NJ: Lawrence Erlbaum, 1995.

Nario, Michelle R., and Nyla R. Branscombe. "Comparison Processes in Hindsight and Causal Attribution." *Personality and Social Psychology Bulletin* 21, no. 12 (December 1995): 1244–1255.

Nasco, Suzanne Altobello, and Kerry L. Marsh. "Gaining Control Through Counterfactual Thinking." *Personality and Social Psychology Bulletin* 25, no. 5 (May 1999): 556–568.

N'gbala, Abhigni, and Nyla R. Branscombe. "When Does Action Elicit More Regret than Inaction and Is Counterfactual Mutation the Mediator of This Effect?" *Journal of Experimental Social Psychology* 33, no. 3 (May 1997): 324–343.

Niedenthal, Paula M., June Price Tangney, and Igor Gavanski. "'If Only I Weren't' Versus 'If Only I Hadn't': Distinguishing Shame and Guilt in Counterfactual Thinking." *Journal of Personality and Social Psychology* 67, no. 4 (October 1994): 585–595.

Ofir, Chezy, and David Mazursky. "Does a Surprising Outcome Reinforce or Reverse the Hindsight Bias?" *Organizational Behavior and Human Decision Processes* 69, no. 1 (January 1997): 51–57.

Ordóñez, Lisa D., and Terry Connolly. "Regret and Responsibility: A Reply to Zeelenberg et al. (1998)." *Organizational Behavior and Human Decision Processes* 81, no. 1 (January 2000): 132–142.

Pezzo, Mark V. "Surprise, Defence, or Making Sense: What Removes Hindsight Bias?" *Memory* 11, nos. 4–5 (July–September 2003): 421–441.

Pieters, Rik, Kitty Koelemeijer, and Henk Roest. "Assimilation Processes in Service Satisfaction Formation." *International Journal of Service Industry Management* 6, no. 3 (1995): 17–33.

Pohl, Rüdiger F., and Wolfgang Hell. "No Reduction in Hindsight Bias after Complete Information and Repeated Testing." *Organizational Behavior and Human Decision Processes* 67, no. 1 (July 1996): 49–58.

Ritov, Ilana, and Jonathan Baron. "Outcome Knowledge, Regret, and Omission Bias." *Organizational Behavior and Human Decision Processes* 64, no. 2 (November 1995): 119–127.

Roese, Neal J. "Counterfactual Thinking." *Psychological Bulletin* 121, no. 1 (January 1997): 133–148.

———. "The Functional Basis of Counterfactual Thinking." *Journal of Personality and Social Psychology* 66, no. 5 (May 1994): 805–818.

Roese, Neal J., and Sameep D. Maniar. "Perceptions of Purple: Counterfactual and Hindsight Judgments at Northwestern Wildcats Football Games." *Personality and Social Psychology Bulletin* 23, no. 12 (December 1997): 1245–1253.

Roese, Neal J., and James M. Olson. "Counterfactual Thinking: A Critical Overview." In *What Might Have Been: The Social Psychology of Counterfactual Thinking*, ed. Neal J. Roese and James M. Olson, 1–55. Mahwah, NJ: Lawrence Erlbaum, 1995.

———. "Counterfactuals, Causal Attributions, and the Hindsight Bias: A Conceptual Integration." *Journal of Experimental Social Psychology* 32, no. 3 (May 1996): 197–227.

———. "Outcome Controllability and Counterfactual Thinking." *Personality and Social Psychology Bulletin* 21, no. 5 (June 1995): 620–628.

———. "The Structure of Counterfactual Thought." *Personality and Social Psychology Bulletin* 19, no. 3 (June 1993): 312–319.

———, eds. *What Might Have Been: The Social Psychology of Counterfactual Thinking*. Mahwah, NJ: Lawrence Erlbaum, 1995.

Ryan, Richard M., and Edward L. Deci. "On Happiness and Human Potentials: A Review of Research on Hedonic and Eudaimonic Well-Being." *Annual Review of Psychology* 52, (2001): 141–166.

Sagi, Adi, and Nehemia Friedland. "The Cost of Richness: The Effect of the Size and Diversity of Decision Sets on Post-Decision Regret." *Journal of Personality and Social Psychology* 93, no. 4 (October 2007): 515–524.

Samuelson, William. "Status Quo Bias in Decision Making." *Journal of Risk and Uncertainty* 1, no. 1 (March 1988): 7–59.

Sanna, Lawrence J. "Self-Efficacy and Counterfactual Thinking: Up a Creek With and Without a Paddle." *Personality and Social Psychology Bulletin* 23, no. 6 (June 1997): 654–666.

Sanna, Lawrence J., and Kandi Jo Turley. "Antecedents to Spontaneous Counterfactual Thinking: Effects of Expectancy Violation and Outcome Valence." *Personality and Social Psychology Bulletin* 22, no. 9 (September 1996): 906–919.

Sanna, Lawrence J., Kandi Jo Turley-Ames, and Susanne Meier. "Mood, Self-Esteem, and Simulated Alternatives: Thought-Provoking Affective Influences on Counterfactual Direction." *Journal of Personality and Social Psychology* 76, no. 4 (April 1999): 543–558.

Savitsky, Kenneth, Victoria Husted Medvec, and Thomas Gilovich. "Remembering and Regretting: The Zeigarnik Effect and the Cognitive Availability of Regrettable Actions and Inactions." *Personality and Social Psychology Bulletin* 23, no. 3 (March 1997): 248–257.

Schkade, David A., and Lynda M. Kilbourne. "Expectation-Outcome Consistency and Hindsight Bias." *Organizational Behavior and Human Decision Processes* 49, no. 1 (June 1991): 105–123.

Schweitzer, Maurice. "Disentangling Status Quo and Omission Effects: An Experimental Analysis." *Organizational Behavior and Human Decision Processes* 58, no. 3 (June 1994): 457–476.

Simonson, Itamar. "The Influence of Anticipating Regret and Responsibility on Purchase Decisions." *Journal of Consumer Research* 19, no. 1 (June 1992): 105–118.

Spranca, Mark, Elisa Minsk, and Jonathan Baron. "Omission and Commission in Judgment and Choice." *Journal of Experimental Social Psychology* 27, no. 1 (January 1991): 76–105.

Taylor, Kimberly A. "A Regret Theory Approach to Assessing Consumer Satisfaction." *Marketing Letters* 8, no. 2 (April 1997): 229–238.

Tetlock, Philip E. "Close-Call Counterfactuals and Belief-System Defenses: I Was Not Almost Wrong But I Was Almost Right." *Journal of Personality and Social Psychology* 75, no. 3 (September 1998): 639–652.

Tsiros, Michael. "Effect of Regret on Post-choice Valuation: The Case of More Than Two Alternatives." *Organizational Behavior and Human Decision Processes* 76, no. 1 (October 1998): 48–69.

Tsiros, Michael, and Vikas Mittal. "Regret: A Model of Its Antecedents and Consequences in Consumer Decision Making." *Journal of Consumer Research* 26, no. 4 (March 2000): 401–417.

Tykocinski, Orit E., and Thane S. Pittman. "The Consequences of Doing Nothing: Inaction Inertia as Avoidance of Anticipated Counterfactual Regret." *Journal of Personality and Social Psychology* 75, no. 3 (September 1998): 607–616.

van Dijk, Wilco W., Marcel Zeelenberg, and Joop van der Pligt. "Not Having What You Want Versus Having What You Do Not Want: The Impact of Negative Outcome on the Experience of Disappointment and Related Emotions." *Cognition and Emotion* 13, no. 2 (March 1999): 129–148.

Walchli, Suzanne B., and Janet Landman. "Effects of Counterfactual Thought on Postpurchase Consumer Affect." *Psychology & Marketing* 20, no. 1 (January 2003): 23–46.

Wasserman, David, Richard O. Lempert, and Reid Hastie. "Hindsight and Causality." *Personality and Social Psychology Bulletin* 17, no. 1 (February 1991): 30–35.

Waterman, Alan S. "Two Conceptions of Happiness: Contrasts of Personal Expressiveness (Eudaimonia) and Hedonic Enjoyment." *Journal of Personality and Social Psychology* 64, no. 4 (April 1993): 678–691.

Weiner, Bernard. *Judgments of Responsibility: A Foundation for a Theory of Social Conduct.* New York: Guilford Press, 1995.

Williams, Christopher W., Paul R. Lees-Haley, and J. Randall Price. "The Role of Counterfactual Thinking and Causal Attribution in Accident-Related Judgments." *Journal of Applied Social Psychology* 26, no. 23 (December 1996): 2100–2112.

Windschitl, Paul D., and Gary L. Wells. "The Alternative-Outcomes Effect." *Journal of Personality and Social Psychology* 75, no. 6 (December 1998): 1411–1423.

Zeelenberg, Marcel, and Jane Beattie. "Consequences of Regret Aversion 2: Additional Evidence for Effects of Feedback on Decision Making." *Organizational Behavior and Human Decision Processes* 72, no. 1 (October 1997): 63–78.

Zeelenberg, Marcel, Jane Beattie, Joop van der Pligt, and Nanne K. de Vries. "Consequences of Regret Aversion: Effects of Expected Feedback on Risky Decision Making." *Organizational Behavior and Human Decision Processes* 65, no. 2 (February 1996): 148–158.

Zeelenberg, Marcel, and Rik Pieters. "Comparing Service Delivery to What Might Have Been: Behavioral Responses to Regret and Disappointment." *Journal of Service Research* 2, no. 1 (August 1999): 86–97.

———. "A Theory of Regret Regulation 1.0." *Journal of Consumer Psychology* 17, no. 1 (2007): 3–18.

Zeelenberg, Marcel, Wilco W. van Dijk, and Antony S.R. Manstead. "Regret and Responsibility Resolved? Evaluating Ordóñez and Connolly's (2000) Conclusions." *Organizational Behavior and Human Decision Processes* 81, no. 1 (January 2000): 143–154.

Zeelenberg, Marcel, Wilco W. van Dijk, Antony S.R. Manstead, and Joop van der Pligt. "The Experience of Regret and Disappointment." *Cognition and Emotion* 12, no. 2 (March 1998): 221–230.

———. "On Bad Decisions and Disconfirmed Expectancies: The Psychology of Regret and Disappointment." *Cognition and Emotion* 14, no. 4 (July 2000): 521–541.

Zwick, Rami, Rik Pieters, and Hans Baumgartner. "On the Practical Significance of Hindsight Bias: The Case of the Expectancy-Disconfirmation Model of Consumer Satisfaction." *Organizational Behavior and Human Decision Processes* 64, no. 1 (October 1995): 103–117.

PART III

SATISFACTION PROCESSES AND MECHANISMS

Part II detailed a number of complementary comparison operations to the expectancy disconfirmation response. In order of coverage, these were need fulfillment, quality or excellence, value, equity/inequity, and regret. In making these comparisons, consumers were described as, first, observing performance and, second, comparing performance to expectations, needs, excellence, worth, fairness standards, and "what might have been." In describing these comparisons, one must be careful to acknowledge that no one consumer makes all of these comparisons and, in fact, some may *only* observe performance, as noted in Chapter 2. There, the possibility that some consumers make no judgments whatsoever, comparative or otherwise, was briefly entertained. However likely or unlikely this possibility may be, there exist some "natural" human responses that are not postpurchase processes, per se, but occur nonetheless in response to occurrences in life. Sometimes referred to as "outcome dependent" reactions, they set the stage for other forms of processing.

Part III details those that are pertinent to consumption. The first concerns what may actually be referred to as a *prepurchase* response. It is manifested by the apprehensions and fears (anticipations of the negative) that consumers may have going into a purchase and results because of the foresight that the purchase may not turn out as desired or expected. More specifically, the consumer may be concerned that the purchase outcomes will turn out much worse than expected, or even more dreadful, worse than feared. Interestingly, this apprehension continues after purchase and before usage, possibly remaining even into usage. Because of its influence throughout the purchase process, individuals are thought to defend against it and to minimize its impact.

Known in the literature as "cognitive dissonance," this concept has been acknowledged for quite some time. Since the 1970s, however, consumer researchers have not been forthcoming with new insight on this very common phenomenon. Thus the purpose of Chapter 10, the first chapter in this section, is to rekindle interest in this important, but neglected, concept in postpurchase studies.

Chapter 11 covers attribution, the natural tendency of individuals to search for causality or meaningful relationships within the events that affect their lives. In effect, they desire to find order in their environment by discovering explanations for events and attributing these happenings to specific causes or causal agents. As applied to consumption, this process assumes, of course, that the outcomes (of purchasing) have already been observed, or, similarly, that non-appearing expected outcomes have been noted. Once attribution has been made, consumers are in a position to decide what further action they will take. In discussing this phenomenon, the different types of causal explanations will be defined in terms of what entity is responsible for the outcome and whether the outcome could have been foreseen and prevented by those responsible. Additionally, the end of Chapter 11 will examine a main consequence of attribution: consumer affect.

As discussed in Chapter 12, consumer affect encompasses the range of emotional responses consumers might display when responding to consumption outcomes. For example, anger over a product breakdown or service failure is common in consumption settings. In actuality, a number of emotional responses naturally occur in the marketplace from the very negative, including anger and rage, to the very positive including elation and delight. Parallel with the positivity-negativity of affective response is the accompanying level of heightened arousal. Negative affect can be displayed in either a high or low arousal manner as typified by the difference between anger and resentment. Similarly, positive affect can be partitioned into the high and low arousal states of delight and contentment. Many of these combinations of affect and arousal will be explored in an effort to describe the complexity of consumers' emotional responses in consumption.

Also discussed in Chapter 12 are the various roles emotions take in consumption. Emotions can be the subjects of anticipations, they can momentarily exist as transient states during consumption, and can vary markedly over time for extended encounters such as would occur in a hospital stay. Moreover, emotions may be further prompted by satisfaction itself in the manner of a patron saying that he/she was delighted over the satisfaction received. This borders on the possibility that satisfaction may be a form of cognitive instigator and, indeed, the chapter concludes with the role of cognitive judgment or *appraisal* in both satisfaction and emotion. In a final closing comment, the author gives an only somewhat revised answer to the question: Is satisfaction an emotion?

The first three chapters in this section set the stage for this author's "consumption processing model" in Chapter 13. The consumption processing model is an analog to the prepurchase phenomenon of information processing whereby the many and varied details of how consumers process prior information about products are used in forming a decision to buy or not to buy. Consumption processing describes postpurchase phenomena in the same way, but using conceptually different components. Consumption generates outcomes that are largely known with certainty. Because of this certainty, consumers can act on their experiences with some degree of confidence about what happened.

Chapter 13 in this section essentially links Part I of this book—where the disconfirmation model is discussed—to Part III. For simplicity, the other comparative operators in Part II are assumed to function in a manner similar to that of the disconfirmation response and are not considered separately. In the resulting abbreviated model, expectations, performance, and disconfirmation are proposed as causal agents for the attribution and affect responses. These latter reactions are shown as embedded in a sequence of reactions that combine in very particular ways. Depending on the nature and levels of disconfirmation, attribution, and affect, certain categories of "consumption responding" are hypothesized to occur. These are, respectively, contentment, pleasure, delight, and relief. Additionally, an early empirical test of this model is described; the results generally support its structure. The chapter concludes with recent suggestions for other consumption responding categories such as love and resignation. Validation of these categories awaits further work.

Thus, Part III attempts to show how the mediating, intervening roles of purchase apprehension, attribution, and affect play a role in enhancing, suppressing, or otherwise modifying the initial postpurchase responses of observing performance and making performance comparisons to a standard. This discussion will be taken as far as is appropriate, given the amount of theorizing and empirical evidence available to date. Hopefully, future research will provide extensions to this line of thought.

CHAPTER 10

COGNITIVE DISSONANCE

Fears of What the Future Will Bring (and a Few Hopes)

Homeowners often desire to enlarge the living space of their residences. For example, assume that homeowners without the means to buy a larger house decide, instead, to build an addition. Because there is no room on the lot to add space laterally, the family decides to add a second story. Plans are drawn, the contract is let, and construction begins. The first step in the process is to remove the roof. This is done. What happens now if the homeowners begin to have misgivings about their decision? Why might they?

This example illustrates the notion of purchase apprehension stemming from the commitment many consumers make to irrevocable decisions. Of course, many decisions can be undone, but some involve great difficulty. In the case of these homeowners, it may be possible to replace the roof and restore the home to near-original condition, but the general contractor and subcontractors would undoubtedly invoke a demanding penalty clause in the contract. This explains the consequences of "back-out" behavior, but does not explain why the family began to have misgivings.

In short, the homeowners became apprehensive about the uncertainty of their decision. It may not have fully occurred to them that major residential construction is filled with potential problems. The many independent subcontractors may or may not actually fulfill their separate obligations on time and with the level of quality promised. The architectural details of the new addition may or may not suit the rest of the house or the lot or the neighborhood as intended. The problems include the possibility of cost overruns, the necessity of unexpected modifications, and the timely availability of building materials. Also included is the potential for future problems, such as leaks in the roof or plumbing, heating, and electrical problems, both during the warranty period and after.

Most importantly, the potential problems include the possibility that the family may not like the final result. Unfortunately, at this point it is too late. The construction is now under way, and the homeowners must adapt to the changes upon completion or reside in a home that reminds them of their misgivings daily. What is this phenomenon of purchase apprehension and second thoughts, and what can consumers do about it? More importantly, how will it affect their ultimate satisfaction or dissatisfaction with the purchase? And, given the finality of their decision, might they rationalize the outcome as being, at least, better than they had hoped? The intent of this chapter is to provide some answers to these questions.

At a broader level, this chapter begins the task of looking more deeply into the comparative decisions discussed in the first two parts of this book. This exercise is initiated by reviewing an early topic in consumer behavior, one with an even longer history in psychology. The topic is known as cognitive dissonance, originally proposed by Leon Festinger in his book *A Theory of Cognitive Dissonance*, published over fifty years ago.[1] Many scholars have predicted the demise, death, rebirth, and relapse of this theory; some argued that it is impervious to extinction while others argued that it was a pseudotheory from the beginning. At least one writer labeled it one of social psychology's grandest theories and yet another opined that there was nothing to be gained by "further research" in the area.[2] Here, the dissonance perspective will be put under continued scrutiny, focusing on what is useful to postpurchase processes, in order to achieve additional insight into the satisfaction process. As the reader will note, this topic is a logical bridge between the previous chapter on regret and the following chapter on attribution.

DECISION-MAKING STAGES

While the central theme of this book concerns postpurchase processes, certain of the mechanisms generating the satisfaction response rely on prepurchase phenomena, most notably expectations and their more time-dependent cousins, anticipations (see Chapter 3). It is also highly likely that other feelings of a less cognitive and more emotive nature may be carried into consumption and later evaluation. Thus, it would be helpful to briefly examine the act of purchasing to see how these prepurchase concepts persist and change through a number of purchasing stages.

Four Phases of Consumption

Consider four consumers, Alpha, Beta, Gamma, and Delta. Alpha is in the later stages of choosing a very much-needed laptop for use at college and has narrowed down the selection to three brands. Each has desirable features in common and, additionally, has one or two unique features that are not duplicated by the other brands. Generally, the mutual exclusivity of the desirable unique features will create a form of decision conflict, similar to the difficulty involved in solving complex problems.[3] At this stage, however, Alpha has made no decision and has no decision-related second thoughts, since he remains engrossed in the process of forming preferences for one brand over the other. Interestingly, there may be some decision-related tension evident here because this consumer has actually made a specific type of decision, namely, to commit to making a decision! This necessarily results in satisfaction with both the decision process (difficulty versus ease) *and* satisfaction with the decision outcome, as discussed next.

Now consider Beta. Beta has undertaken considerable search and information acquisition and is ready to select a brand. The previous tension over making a decision may now take the form of an apprehension, because the choice of one brand over others will create a sense of anticipated loss over the forgone (desirable) unique features of the unchosen alternatives. The apprehension over these unattainable features makes the decision uncomfortable to the consumer because the choice, once made, locks in the forgone opportunities. Nonetheless, she commits to a particular brand, informs friends and others of the selection—thereby forming a sense of obligation—and begins the purchase process. She does not feel excessive strain, however, because the commitment to the brand exists only at the psychological level and not at the level of the actual transaction, which is yet another satisfaction entity and not discussed separately here, as it was partially covered in the preceding chapter.

Now consider Gamma. Gamma has encountered a situation where his individual laptop needs surpass the features of the models normally stocked in retail outlets. The special computer configuration needed by Gamma is available, but will have to be special-ordered. Because of the special nature of his needs and the low likelihood that this computer will be easily sold if Gamma changes his mind, the dealer requires a substantial down payment on the order. Gamma makes this payment, thereby committing to take delivery on the computer.

At this juncture, the uncertainties facing this consumer involve not only forgone opportunities, but also the uncertainty of delivery times, new information that might become available on the ordered or unchosen brands during the wait for delivery, a change in needs or preferences during this same time, and an apprehension about the costs of backing out of the purchase, including ill will from the dealer. Note that neither Alpha nor Beta faced these postpurchase uncertainties.

Gamma later finds himself in still another situation. The laptop arrives, but without the necessary key software installed. Gamma now owns the computer but is not in a position to fully use it. Anticipating that it will be fully operational sometime, Gamma is content to play PC solitaire when time is available. However, he still does not know if the additional software will run without problems, if the disk space, internal memory, and battery capacity are sufficient, if the laptop will prove to be reliable, if he will be pleased with its performance, or how long it will be suitable to the tasks that Gamma might require in the future.

The fourth consumer, Delta, has weathered all these uncertainties and is now considered a power user. Having experienced months of use, she now knows both the strong and weak points of the selected brand. The computer has had problems with insufficient memory and unpredictable freeze-ups in the middle of software runs. To make matters worse, the support program offered by the manufacturer has proved to be totally unreliable with unanswered phone calls, hang-ups, inordinately long waits, and less-than-knowledgeable staff. At this point, the only details not known to Delta are how long the computer will operate before crashing and how long the manufacturer will support this particular model.

None of these four consumers is free of concerns, although all are in different phases of the purchase process. Each of these phases, named for the four hypothetical consumers, is examined in detail, as shown in Table 10.1. The four stages are marked by distinct boundaries, which may be collapsed in many purchases where consumption is immediate (e.g., snacks). The alpha or predecision phase ends at the decision or choice; the beta phase ends at possession; the gamma phase ends prior to use. Because usage may entail extended consumption, the last phase cannot be detailed further until more is known. This four-phase sequence would appear to model many consumption events. Consider something as simple as a daily newspaper purchased at a newsstand. Decision conflict may arise if more than one well-regarded paper is available in a given location. If the purchase takes place during rush hour, the consumer may have to stand in line prior to purchase (possession). Finally, a trip home and/or immediate home responsibilities may intervene between possession and actual perusal.

Although the newspaper example is mundane, this sequence extends through more complicated products and services. At the risk of formally analyzing what many agree is a romantic process, consider the concept of marriage, which involves an intricate process of acquisition of a spouse, a process varying widely over cultures. Each of the decision phases and their boundary states are formally recognized. The alpha phase is courtship with a boundary marker of an accepted proposal. The beta phase is engagement with a boundary marker of the marriage ceremony. The gamma phase is the honeymoon with a preset boundary determined by the marital partners. Finally, the delta phase is the remainder of the marriage itself. The courtship literature is replete with numerous examples, anecdotal and otherwise, of the apprehensions that build up before a marriage and the incidences of back-out behavior up to and including the ceremony. This problem is also observed in the context of home purchasing, where buyers have put a deposit (earnest money) down on

Table 10.1

Purchase Decision Phases and Corresponding Elements of Uncertainty

Phase	Description	Focus of uncertainty	Psychological response
Alpha	Predecision	Desirability of alternatives	Decision conflict
Beta	Postdecision, prepurchase	Desirability of chosen versus forgone alternatives	Apprehension
Gamma	Postpurchase, prepossession and postpossession, preusage	Desirability of forgone alternatives Performance adequacy of chosen alternative	Apprehension, performance adequacy, self-doubt
Delta	Usage, postusage	Consequences of performance, future performance	Regret, guilt, resignation, (dis)satisfaction

their house and then wish to back out of the contract; other examples are probably familiar to the reader. Why does back-out behavior occur? What can be done about it? To answer these questions, the types of tensions that may lead to back-out and other behaviors can be accurately described by examining the stresses facing the consumer at each stage.

Purchase Phase Stresses

The first phase, alpha, consists of a difficult choice between close alternatives, resulting in predecision conflict. Note that little beyond decision difficulty is evident here. No purchase commitment has been made, and any predecision commitment is easily reversed. However, two phenomena occur in this phase with implications for satisfaction with the decision and later with the choice. Noted earlier is the obvious conclusion that easy decisions are more pleasant (satisfying) than difficult decisions. Forced (induced) decisions (for example, when a home buyer *must* make a choice between two houses with limited and unattractive options) are less pleasant than those with freedom of choice. Paradoxically, research shows that the lower satisfaction of a forced choice results in greater subsequent satisfaction with the decision outcome and vice versa.[4] Presumably, free choice allows room for regret while induced choice limits responsibility for the decision and permits greater focus on the positive aspects of the outcome.

As noted, the next, beta phase introduces purchase consideration of forgone alternatives on the part of the consumer. The postpurchase comparisons to these referents, resulting in regret and/or hindsight, have been discussed in Chapter 9. The purpose of this chapter is to describe the developmental processes leading up to these comparisons. In the beta phase, the consumer realizes, perhaps for the first time, that the purchase decision will allow the unchosen alternatives to remain as a reminder that another purchase outcome could have been realized. This state of anticipated regret leads to a general feeling of apprehension on the part of the consumer.

In the gamma phase, regardless of whether possession has occurred, an exchange has taken place and purchase or ownership is now a reality. This extra level of commitment brings with it the realization that the forgone alternatives are truly forgone, that the selected product may not perform as anticipated, and that an error of choice may have been made. In addition to apprehension, consumers may now experience performance anxiety (worry or concern that the product may not perform as expected) and self-doubt (the degree to which their decision-making

Figure 10.1   **Future Apprehensions During Consumption**

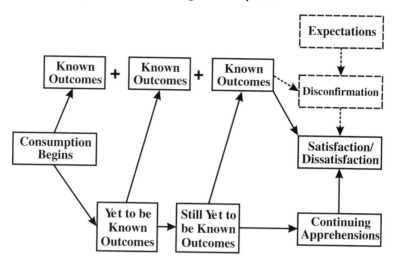

skills will prove to be wanting). Note that, as in the beta phase, actual performance has not yet been observed.

Finally, in the delta phase, the performance characteristics of the product are known, as are the consequences of this performance (e.g., a new window air-conditioning unit is not large enough to cool the entire second floor, so the consumer will now have to buy another or suffer through a miserable summer). Here, the consumer feels regret due to comparisons to what might have been, as well as disconfirmation and the resulting satisfaction or dissatisfaction with the purchase. Additionally, the consumer may consider issues of need satisfaction, equity concerns, and quality, when relevant. For many products and services, however, the story does not end here. If the product or service involves continuing consumption (automobiles, appliances), apprehension over future performance cannot be ignored. Thus, concerns over the future continue along with current observations of performance.

This latter mechanism is shown in Figure 10.1. In the case of consumption over long periods, each episode of outcomes generates with it immediate satisfaction or dissatisfaction and pleasant anticipations or unpleasant apprehensions of future outcomes. As these outcomes materialize, the process repeats itself until the remaining consumption potential is exhausted or the product or service is recycled, disposed of, or discontinued. In this sense, consumption apprehension, which will now be referred to as dissonance, may never disappear despite the appearance of purchase outcomes leading to satisfaction and dissatisfaction judgments. Just what is this potentially pervasive dissonance phenomenon that has captured the fancies of researchers both in and beyond the field of consumer behavior?

DISSONANCE: THE CONCEPT

In an attempt to describe the nature of dissonance, one must distinguish how dissonance is manifested and what causal agents are operative.[5] The second aspect is addressed first.

Causes

The causes referred to are, in a phrase, inconsistent cognitions. Specifically, two (or more) thoughts that should have the property of "X and Y" or "X, then Y" have instead the property of "X and not

Figure 10.2   **Consonance and Dissonance Structures**

Panel A: Consonance

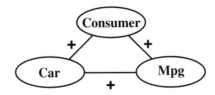

Panel B: Two Dissonant Structures

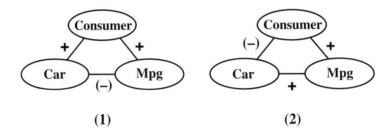

Y" or "X, then not Y." As an example, assume that a consumer prefers to purchase products made in the United States for patriotic or other reasons. This belief in buying domestic products can be considered the X in the "X and Y" relation. Now, this consumer, given this expressed belief, would be expected to own a U.S.-made car—the Y in the "X and Y" relationship. If so, then X and Y are *consonant*. However, if this consumer owns a foreign car instead, then the relations are *dissonant*. There may also be *irrelevant* relations involved—those that have no bearing on each other. For example, the fact that this consumer may own a foreign-made HDTV does not present a problem, as currently virtually all HDTVs are made overseas.

The generality of the properties of consonant/dissonant relations also extends to the prescriptions of balance theory, congruity theory, and consistency theory, where more elaborate relations are proposed.[6] Generally, these perspectives explicitly make the consumer part of the equation. They differ from dissonance theory only in the sense that dissonance results from a personal decision or action, while consistency theories require, at the minimum, only observations of inconsistencies in objects or others.

To show how consonant and dissonant relations would apply to a consumer decision, consider the hypothetical consumer in Figure 10.2 who is considering the purchase of a smallish, fuel-efficient hybrid car. Three relations are involved; that between the consumer and the attribute of fuel efficiency (high miles per gallon, or mileage), that between the car and fuel efficiency, and that between the consumer and the car. Panel A shows a consonant structure as the consumer likes (+) a car that has (+) a desired (+) attribute (fuel efficiency). Panels B1 and B2 show two dissonant structures, one where the liked (+) car does not possess (−) desirable (+) fuel efficiency (e.g., a sports car such as a Corvette) and one where a car possessing (+) desirable (+) fuel economy is disliked (−) (e.g., for other reasons, such as safety, to be discussed next).

Figure 10.3 **Consonance/Dissonance Structures for Complex Products**

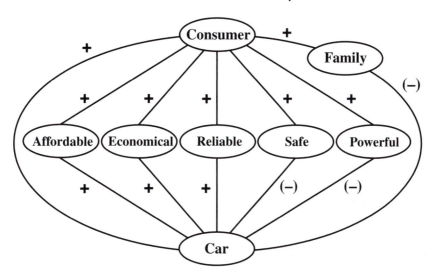

In consumer buying, the actual consistency/inconsistency structures are much more compli-cated than shown in Figure 10.2. In fact, the two dissonant structures are easily explained via the consideration of omitted determinant attributes. In panel B1, other features of the Corvette more than compensate for the poor fuel economy, and in panel B2, the excellent fuel economy does not compensate for perceived safety and power problems (e.g., acceleration, towing). More ap-propriately, consumer decisions for complex products appear as in Figure 10.3.

Here, the operation of five separate automobile features is illustrated, as opposed to the one previously. It is assumed that all five attributes—affordability, economical operation, reliability, safety, and power—are desirable to the consumer, who likes the car. This latter relation is repre-sented by the positive linkage at the far left in the figure. Moreover, the car scores favorably on the first three of the five attributes. These relations are consonant with the overall liking for the car. Unfortunately, the car falls short on two of the five, safety and power. Given the overall liking relation, these two elements of the purchase are dissonant and create a sense of tension for the consumer, particularly when driving situations require a sense of security, more power, or both (such as might occur on the highway).

This example can be made more dissonant, however, by including the sentiments of the con-sumer's family. Assume that the family dislikes the car for reasons that are outside the configu-ration shown here (such as capacity, age, style). If one also assumes a harmonious relationship between family sentiments and the consumer, then the family's reservations about the car provide yet another source of dissonance. There will thus be tension in this decision regardless of whether the consumer is considering the car for purchase (alpha phase), has decided that this is the car to buy (beta phase), has agreed to take delivery of the car (gamma phase), or is already driving the car (delta phase). This is the nature of dissonance, and the example provides a sense of the extremity it can attain.

In an effort to quantify the amount of dissonance in a decision, elementary formulas based on the number of consonant and dissonant elements under consideration are common. The following ratio is based on dissonance as a percentage of all cognitions:[7]

$$Dissonance = \Sigma D_i / (\Sigma D_i + \Sigma C_j) \tag{10.1}$$

The intent here is straightforward. Assume unit weights for all determinant attributes. The D_i values are the individual elements of the decision that are dissonant with an overall criterion (e.g., product liking or disliking). Similarly, the C_j values are the individual consonant elements. As the sum of the dissonant elements increases relative to the sum of all elements, consonant or otherwise, dissonance increases. As the sum of the consonant elements increases, dissonance decreases. As the ΣD_i value approaches zero, dissonance disappears and the decision becomes tension-free. Later, discussion will turn to how resolution such as this may occur.

What Dissonance Is

As now frequently understood, dissonance is a psychologically uncomfortable state of tension. Various writers have described it as a negative-toned motivational affective state or undifferentiated arousal experienced as a negative (unpleasant) state attributed to the arousal of attitude-discrepant behavior.[8] A number of authors use the general term *anxiety*, which would seem to encompass both negative affect and arousal due to any discrepant states that can be learned in response to cultural standards, which differ widely across the globe, most notably between Eastern and Western societies.[9]

Perhaps the more general phrase, *inconsistency-induced psychological discomfort,* is most appropriate for the present context because the tack taken here is that dissonance begins as simple apprehension and escalates over the decision cycle to later purchase phases. At the extreme, some authors have used the phrase *torn and conflicted* to refer to the ambivalence of dissonant states. More to the point, it is an apprehension over events yet to come and is closely tied to a well-known psychological construct labeled *consideration of future consequences.*[10] This distinguishes dissonance from disconfirmation and other comparative processes in which the purchase outcomes are known. It also allows for the parallel operation of dissonance and disconfirmation (as in Figure 10.1, where outcomes are observed for the more specific comparison to expectations) in instances where some purchase outcomes are known while others are yet to be known.

Thus, dissonance involves uncertainty over the occurrence of valenced outcomes. In consumption, the valence has been historically interpreted as negative in tone, such as when a consumer likes a product that is thought to have undesired features or consequences. At one extreme, the consumer might display uneasiness over this knowledge, followed by apprehension, anxiousness, worry, and, at the far extreme, fear and dread. As noted, positive outcomes can also involve future uncertainty and, similarly, are thought to generate arousal. For the marketer, these are less worrisome in consumption, however, as many products are pursued, not avoided, for the positive apprehensions involved, including hopes, wishes, and longings. It is up to the purveyor of uncertain positive outcomes to gauge whether the apprehensions of failure in the pursuit of pleasure aversely affect outcome satisfaction.

How Can Consumers Stand It?

Because of the generally negative nature of dissonant cognitions, one might wonder why consumers would pursue consumption activities with high levels of attendant dissonance. This is not as much of a problem as it first appears, however, for researchers have empirically shown that a common response to dissonance is psychological effort to reduce dissonance. After all, consumers do engage in risky consumption, including innovations of all varieties, extreme sports with potentially dangerous risks, securities purchases, and homes with mortgages that tax the homeowners' incomes. The reason, perhaps, that so many dissonance-causing purchases are made is that the dissonance-reducing mechanisms employed by consumers and aided by manufacturers are very effective. Generally, the increasing dissonance hypothesized over the purchase period is compensated for by commensurately strong efforts to reduce it. When this effort is insufficient, dissonance-induced outcomes, such as back-out behaviors, occur.

If this is so, the implications for management and for satisfaction research are rich, although complex. Assuming, as suggested in the previous chapter, that dissonance is intertwined with regret and that regret detracts from satisfaction, then actions to decrease dissonance prior to purchase will be beneficial. Moreover, decreasing dissonance should make consumers more confident of their purchase decisions, causing them to hold their presumably high expectations more strongly. High (not ideal) expectations, as has been shown, seem to elevate satisfaction ratings, ceteris paribus. Thus, it would be helpful to review the practical applications of the theory to determine if dissonance reduction strategies are sufficient for management's purposes.

DISSONANCE: THE EVIDENCE

The previous edition of this book reviewed the evidence at the time and concluded that it was more than ample. Reviews appearing at regular intervals generally reaffirmed the importance of dissonance theory as a research focus, but noted that dissonance theory had both branched out and been modified. One oft-cited review, however, concluded that these modifications are "inconsequential."[11] This conclusion is consistent with the numerous practical applications of dissonance theory. Before continuing, however, it may be of interest to delineate those aspects of dissonance theory that are pertinent to the behavior of consumers and those that are not.

Reviewers generally agree that there are four main research streams attributed to dissonance.[12] The first is referred to as free choice and has been discussed under the topic of predecision conflict. More precisely, the effects described are known as "spreading alternatives" in that the attractiveness of the to-be-selected option is elevated beyond its original position.[13] The second involves requiring subjects, as a condition of the experiment, to engage in attitude-discrepant behavior. For example, subjects may be asked to give a speech, advocating an issue to which they are opposed, in front of an audience. Dissonance theory predicts that this behavior would cause a shift in the subjects' position on the issue in the direction of the counterattitudinal speech. This is what has been found. The question for management is whether this type of experiment has an analogy in consumption. A likely answer is that this situation is atypical. Consumers are rarely forced to buy products and patronize services. They may be persuaded, perhaps, but are not likely to be coerced.

A third stream is effort justification. Here, individuals are asked to engage in difficult, unpleasant, or prolonged decisions. Regardless of the decision context, data show that this effort is justified with higher evaluations of the outcome. This finding, which is now widely accepted, explains the phenomena of ritualistic initiation rites (Greek-system hazing) and paying one's dues. Researchers have recently demonstrated this effect in the context of frequency reward (e.g., loyalty) programs whereby luxury rewards are preferred as point levels become more difficult to achieve.[14]

The fourth paradigm perhaps offers the greatest promise for marketers. Here postdecision, even including postoutcome, changes in alternative evaluation as a result of having made the purchase decision are examined. In a manner overlapping in substance with forced compliance (because the choices are now assumed to be common and part of normal consumption environments), participants in this set of conditions are given alternatives that are closely valued and asked to choose between them. Dissonance theory predicts and research has shown that, by spreading alternatives, individuals will elevate the desirability of the chosen alternative and reduce the desirability of the unchosen alternatives before the outcomes of choice are known. As stated previously, a choice does not necessarily involve consequences and often can be reversed. Hence, it fits into the beta phase of consumption. Even if the choice cannot be reversed, however, the conditions surrounding the purchase will generally apply to voluntary behaviors and thus will entail personal responsibility for the decision. An often-cited study, discussed next, provides an example of this mechanism.

In an early paper, essentially replicated in full some forty years later, independent groups of racetrack bettors ("consumers" in every sense of the word) were interviewed while standing in line to place a bet (group 1) and after they had made the bet (group 2).[15] Key questions concerned the bettors' estimates of the chance to win on the horse they were about to select, and their confidence in the bet. Results showed that postbet racetrack patrons made higher win and confidence estimates than did the prebet patrons by a statistically significant amount. Note that this is a classic gamma versus beta phase study, since all prebet interviews were performed before purchase and all postbet interviews were performed after purchasing and before the race outcomes were known. As the other horses in the race were the only alternatives available, increasing the chances to win of one horse implies that the chances of at least some of the other horses declined in the bettors' minds. This is the type of postdecision reevaluation predicted by dissonance theory. As the reader will note, postusage applications become muddled with a plethora of affective and cognitive responses yet to be discussed. To the extent possible, these will be entertained as lingering vestiges of dissonance apprehensions as usage outcomes unfold.

Up to this point, discussion has not been directed to two very important aspects of dissonance in customer satisfaction, namely, what causes it and what consumers and marketers can do to reduce it. In effect, it is time to specify the antecedents that drive the two opposing responses of dissonance induction and dissonance reduction.

Dissonance-Inducing Factors

Do all purchase decisions result in dissonance? Clearly not, or else life would be difficult to navigate in the current consumption climate. Consumers do not ruminate over trivial decisions (e.g., postage stamps), decisions without immediate, clearly visible outcomes (e.g., multivitamin supplements), or inconsequential decisions. Rather, it is now known that a set of antecedent conditions can be reliable indicators of dissonance-prone decisions and that these conditions encompass certain product categories and not others.

Although most basic references on dissonance detail the conditions under which dissonance is most likely to be aroused, those conditions specific to consumption situations would be most helpful at this point. In this regard, a very early review in consumer behavior, the conclusions of which remain valid, noted that three essential overriding conditions are operative: the importance of the decision, personal volition or responsibility, and irrevocability.[16] Generally, all these will exist as a matter of degree, as decisions can vary in importance, level of responsibility, and degree of difficulty involved in their revocation. For a more detailed analysis, a somewhat longer list of conditions will be presented along with some examples of their applicability.

Threshold Effects

Consumers are thought to possess differential thresholds for dissonance in the same way as they possess different levels of tolerance for anxiety. Whereas some consumers may be able to tolerate the two or three dissonant cognitions in Figure 10.3, others may not—for them, two would be above threshold. Still other consumers may not experience dissonance until four or five linkages among many are dissonant. Interestingly, research shows that the effect may also be curvilinear, with exceedingly large levels of dissonance causing a complete rethinking of the merits of the prior decision.[17] The rethinking could cause decision reversal or a change in decision evaluation from positive to negative. This conclusion may pertain more to dissatisfaction than to dissonance, however, as the findings were obtained under postoutcome conditions (delta phase) and not in the postdecision (beta) or preoutcome (gamma) phase.

Irrevocable Decisions

It has been suggested that the postdecision phase of choice is not so dissonance-arousing if the decision can be reversed, as in the examples of back-out behavior. However, many decisions cannot be changed, once made, without inordinate legal maneuvering: for example, the purchase of a house, the purchase of a new car once the title has transferred (the car becomes legally "used"), and stock market transactions, barring fraud. In each case, the decision is now history, and the consequences, good and bad, are inevitable. For this reason, many automobile dealers allow customers to take home a test-drive vehicle for more than an overnight period. Similarly, Apple Computer offered consumers a free, overnight trial of its new Macintosh computer, using the 1984 slogan "Test-drive a Macintosh." Interestingly, changeable (revocable) decisions are less dissonance arousing, but result in less satisfaction after the fact.[18]

Commitment to and Importance of the Decision

Although not perfectly correlated, it will be assumed that decisions that are important in the consumer's life entail commitment, once made.[19] Thus, decisions involving a great amount of capital relative to a family's resources, decisions having deep psychological significance (such as the choice of a college or place of worship), and decisions that are potentially ego-threatening qualify as dissonance-inducing. Marketers of children's educational tools (e.g., learning software, test preparation courses) frequently use this justification since children's developmental stages cannot be retraced.

A Large Number of Desirable Alternatives (High Cognitive Overlap)

For reasons already discussed, a choice between close alternatives is potentially dissonance inducing. Close alternatives with similar features are described as having "high cognitive overlap." If many desirable alternatives are available, still greater dissonance will ensue. The threat of regret now looms larger because the greater number of other possible alternatives to compare against suggests that at least one alternative would have provided a better outcome. Houses, schools, spousal suitors, and vacation locations all qualify here.

Desired Alternatives With Mutually Exclusive Features

In an apparent irony, low similarity (low cognitive overlap) may also be dissonance inducing. This is so because choice guarantees that something desirable about another alternative cannot be had, thereby providing an object for regret. The choice of a college is a good example of this, if for no other reason than geography. Schools in very different locations will have unique geographical or regional cultural differences that the prospective student may never have the chance to experience again.

Qualitatively Dissimilar Alternatives

In an extension of the previous situation, a choice between products or services that are not at all similar decreases the cognitive overlap to an extreme level and heightens the sense of impending regret. A choice between alternative vehicles (a car versus an SUV, a conventionally powered car versus a hybrid) or diverse careers, including the decision to stay employed versus dropping out of the labor market to continue an education, apply here.

Volition and Personal Responsibility

A central tenet in the long history of dissonance research is that consumers cannot experience dissonance unless they feel (perceive) that the decision was made of their own volition. This condition has now been relaxed, but remains a factor in dissonance induction. For example, in the context of omission versus commission, researchers were able to show dissonance induction in a game show context.[20] Each subject chose one of three unopened boxes with prizes inside. One box purportedly contained a "grand prize," while the remaining two contained "modest prizes." After the subject had chosen a box, the experimenter opened one of the remaining boxes and displayed a modest prize. Supposedly, the grand prize was in either the subject's box or the last remaining box. The subject was then given a chance to "trade." Whether the subjects decided to trade (commission) or stay (omission), all found that they received the modest, as opposed to the grand, prize.

Using a procedure of dissonance induction-reduction, the researchers then asked the subjects to place dollar values on their modest prizes. As predicted, those who had switched attached significantly higher value to their prize, compared to those who stayed. Commission with unfortunate results (the switching subjects thought they had traded the grand prize away) normally leads to greater dissonance and, therefore, greater dissonance reduction behaviors in the form of valuing the received prize more highly.

Thus, personal responsibility is undoubtedly a major impetus to dissonance; the self is intimately involved in dissonance arousal.[21] While little evidence in consumer research is available on this next issue, it may be that joint decisions or independently made decisions by others can have aversive consequences for an individual. Because dissonance has been framed in the affective context of apprehension, any decision, even by others, involving the individual or having potentially reflective (i.e., vicarious) consequences for a consumer may be dissonance-inducing.[22] Thus, the condition of personal responsibility may be less important under certain circumstances.

It should be clear that major purchase decisions, including those of long duration, most reliably possess the conditions for dissonance and much more so if consumer involvement plays a role. Major life decisions, many of which require services (e.g., education, retirement planning), fall into this category. In contrast, mundane items and transitory consumables even when generally of a high-involvement nature, such as nonrenewable time-share vacation homes, do not provoke dissonance to the same degree, if at all.[23] Now, how do consumers tolerate purchases and decisions of a highly dissonant nature? The answer is that consumers are thought to engage in one or more dissonance-reducing strategies, as discussed next.

Dissonance Reduction Strategies

Although consumers may use various dissonance-reducing strategies without assistance, managers who understand the dissonance process in the context of their product can aid the consumer, particularly with the provision of appropriate information. Numerous advertising campaigns are

Figure 10.4 **Operation of Dissonance Reduction Techniques**

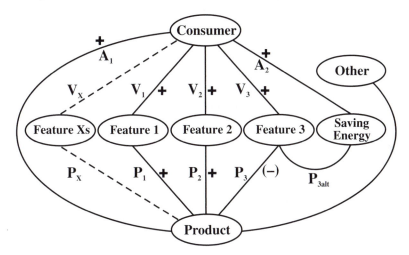

aimed at assuaging dissonance, such as Carlton's mid-1980s campaign, "If you smoke, please try Carlton." This message has both induction effects ("If you smoke"—implying another brand, of course) and reduction effects ("please try Carlton"—a very low-tar cigarette). Slogans and messages such as this are very common, and space will not permit their listing here.

Many of the dissonance reduction techniques can be discussed with reference to a modified graphic of Figure 10.3, which is provided in Figure 10.4. Assume that a particular product or service has three desirable determinant attributes, labeled feature 1, feature 2, and feature 3. The V_1 values in Figure 10.4 represent the feature valences, and in the example all are positive. The product-feature performance linkages, referred to as *instrumentalities*, are designated as P_i. Unfortunately, one of the desired features (P_3) is lacking (negative) in the example. This is the dissonant element, assuming that the consumer's overall evaluation of (affect toward) the product (A_1) is positive. What is the consumer to do?

Eliminating Dissonant Elements

This strategy is most easily accomplished by reinterpreting the valence of feature 3. If the consumer now finds that this feature is no longer a positively *valued* element (that is, $V_3 = 0$), then the dissonant linkage disappears. In the context of the car example in Figure 10.3, the consumer might now feel that power is no longer important. Perhaps a salesperson has reminded this consumer that a car's ability to reach 150 miles per hour is not a benefit in a region of the country with maximum speed limits of 70 miles per hour. This technique directly addresses changes in the attractiveness of outcomes and shares some elements with the psychological concept of disidentification.[24]

Denying the Truth of the Instrumentality (Denial)

An alternative mechanism to accomplish the same purpose is to mentally reconfigure the dissonant P_3 element from a minus to a plus sign. For example, if feature 3 were safety and the consumer's dissonance resulted from reading the results of the government's crash tests, the consumer might deny that the car was unsafe because, after all, the tests were performed on crash test dummies and not real people. In some sense, this technique is central to all attitude change, but bears specific reference to changing beliefs (instrumentalities), which can be accomplished using many mechanisms.[25] This strategy can also involve derogation of the source of the message as unreliable, unknowledgeable, and so on, whether the source is a spokesperson, advertisement, or corporate pronouncement.[26]

Making Beliefs Situation-Specific (Differentiation or Insulation)

In this mode of dissonance reduction, a consumer mentally entertains two maps of Figure 10.4, one for normal use and one for special situations. Thus, the dissonant element in Figure 10.4 can be taken out of an everyday structure and placed in the alternative structure reserved for unique occasions. For example, if feature 3 is the worn, tattered condition of a favorite pair of sneakers, their owner might argue that the shoes are kept specifically for yard work. In one example of numerous alternative maps, a Jewish couple's decision to buy an "ethnically inappropriate" German-made car is described using storytelling techniques.[27]

Making the Dissonant Element Part of a Larger Issue Where It Is Consonant (Transcendence)

Assume, as before, that feature 3 is the acceleration or power of a car and that the negatively valued P_3 reflects an underpowered, but fuel-efficient engine. It is possible to recast the underpowered engine within the framework of energy conservation, which the consumer supports (for example, A_2 is positive). Now V_3 reflects the desirability of the fuel efficiency provided by low-powered engines that conserve fuel. The previously dissonant element is now consonant within the new framework. That is, the role of power in accelerating the car has been transcended and is no longer an issue for this consumer. This requires, of course, that P_{3alt} be positive and that the old P_3 be eliminated from the original configuration (P_3, $V_3 = 0$). Transcendence processes are common in the literature.[28]

Adding Consonant Elements (Bolstering or Finding a Silver Lining)

Alternatively, consumers might find and add new consonant elements to the structure until the dissonance ratio in Equation 10.1 is reduced below threshold: for example, by discovering desirable features (Xs) in the product and adding them to the configuration in the left portion of Figure 10.4. This assumes that all V_X and all P_X are positive. It is also possible to discover undesirable features lacking in the focal product but present in the competition. In this case, all V_X and all P_X are negative, and the same result obtains. In yet another example of bolstering, consumers can elevate the desirability of features. This strategy was demonstrated in the game show example presented earlier, where subjects exaggerated the value of the modest prize they received after supposedly trading away the grand prize. In lieu of discovering new elements, consumers may selectively remember dominating consonant elements that had been left previously unattended.[29]

Denying Responsibility for the Decision

One very easy way to eliminate numerous sources of dissonance shown in Figure 10.4 is to void the "Consumer" and attribute the purchase to another. This tactic is common among partners in joint decisions (e.g., spouses) who are able to blame their counterpart for a decision that previously was, in fact, joint. Denial of responsibility is one of the most effective dissonance reduction (almost to elimination) techniques available to individuals. Of interest is that deference to a group, as alluded to previously, is another manner of deflecting responsibility. Both individual and group variations are easily measured.[30]

Minimizing the Importance of the Decision (Trivialization)

In this example, the entire consonance/dissonance configuration would disappear either by reducing the liking (A_1) to a level below threshold or by eliminating the conscious processing of the product category features and their performance.[31] In the second case, liking for the product or service may remain strong despite the fact that its characteristics are not heavily processed. Most mundane, everyday products probably maintain their consumer loyalty franchise by existing below the consumer's willingness to process performance (e.g., the daily newspaper).

Selective Forgetting

Selective forgetting is more a property of a clinical setting; individuals are known to block out memories and current perceptions of truly discomforting information. Travelers who fly after well-publicized air crashes must have some means of being at ease on their flights or else their trip will be psychologically unpleasant. These consumers may use selective forgetting or the alternative strategy of differentiation—that was a different plane, route, and so on. Interestingly, the opposite of forgetting, selective remembering, may alleviate dissonance as well by bringing to the fore more dominating, consonant elements, as in the strategy of bolstering, discussed previously.

Selective Exposure

This strategy, whereby individuals are believed to selectively seek out confirming information and to avoid disconfirming information, appears intuitive and is referred to as confirmation bias in the behavioral literature.[32] Although the sheer weight of the evidence suggests that consumers prefer decision-confirming to nonconfirming information, consumers cannot be consistently observed to engage in these complementary strategies despite their seemingly ego-protective nature. The reason is due to simple competition whereby comparative advertising abounds and, in many cases, two-sided communications are prevalent. The consumer, however, is not prevented from discounting this barrage of countervailing information.

Behavior Change (Undoing)

In this final strategy, consumers committed to a purchase that is creating dissonance may change their behavior, if possible, by undoing the decision. This is the mechanism behind back-out behavior and other forms of decision reversal. Alternatively, they may engage in a behavior that provides justification for the dissonant cognition, such as when a dieting consumer engages in excessive exercising to burn off the extra calories consumed in a very rich meal. In fact, one "new" perspective on dissonance theory, which the authors describe as a "return to its roots," is based on the strong notion that action-attitude inconsistency is more dissonance arousing than preaction cognition consistency. The implications for the purposes here, however, remain unchanged.[33]

Examples of Consumer Dissonance Induction and Reduction

Disconcertingly, but also in accord with the psychological literature, relatively few studies of dissonance have appeared over the past years in the consumer behavior literature. This is in contrast to the many new works on regret that may have taken precedence, as dissonance and regret are closely linked. Conclusions from early studies in the first edition of this book will be briefly reviewed and the small number of studies since that time will be noted. From a strategic standpoint, however, the implications of this "grand theory" remain as strong as ever.

In one of the earliest studies, refrigerator buyers were intercepted by a "retail spokesperson" (actually the study's designer) and later by a "market researcher" in the interim period between purchase and delivery and, by implication, consumption.[34] Because refrigerators are rarely transported home by the buyer, the delivery period provided a natural gamma phase in which purchase commitment had been made but use could not be observed by the purchaser. Three randomly selected groups of consumers were tested. Two received reassurance communications, one by letter and one by telephone. A third group, which received no communication, served as the control.

When compared to the control, the letter group had significantly less dissonance and significantly greater intention to shop at the retailer in the future. The findings were reversed for the telephone group, showing that communications can have opposing impacts depending on the message modality. Apparently, a letter served to soothe and reassure postpurchase doubts while the annoying nature of a telephone call planted greater doubts in the consumers' minds. In two other studies of communication-induced dissonance reduction, the successful side of this strategy has been replicated using automobile buyers and consumers of mail-order products.[35]

The prior discussion concerned the pre- and postdecision phases of consumption and not the potential interplay between dissonance and satisfaction. In an early delta phase experiment, researchers tested for postpurchase interactions between inferred dissonance and the two criteria of satisfaction and intention.[36] This example is reported to provide insight into the continued operation of dissonance in the usage period. In an appealing argument that dissonance would have residual effects on satisfaction ratings, but would not influence intention, the authors proposed that high effort coupled with low reward (i.e., outcome) would create dissonance and an attempt to justify the high effort. Under the assumption that low reward would be manifested in perceived negative disconfirmation, the authors hypothesized that individuals who experienced negative disconfirmation would publicly report high satisfaction (to justify the high effort), but low intention to purchase (to reflect the negative disconfirmation). Using patrons of guided tours, the results supported the hypothesis in that the greatest divergence between (favorable) satisfaction and (unfavorable) intention occurred for the negative disconfirmation group.

These two research paradigms were reported to illustrate the differential operation of dissonance in the pre- and postusage phases—postdecision in the first case. Although dissonance does play a role in purchase decisions including satisfaction with the decision, the focus of this book remains on the post-"anything" phase where the "anything" can be any and all of the variants of consumption. This is the reason why the alpha to gamma sequence was broken down into separate stages for analysis. Gamma is actually a transition phase because, in very short order, all the more specific satisfaction influences will exert their effects over whatever dissonance remains.

The woefully few recent studies will now be briefly described. Because of the small number of such studies, conclusions regarding the robustness of the findings are not justified. These will await further analysis along the lines of a meta-analysis.

In these recent works, the difference between cognitive and affective dissonance is distinguished and explored.[37] In the first, health risk was used to induce fear regarding failure to use birth control. When confronted with high fear information and queried as to their intentions to use or not, those with lower intentions and, therefore, less dissonance used affect-based dissonance reduction such as forgetting (selective recall), while those with high intentions used counterarguing or belief refutation, in accord with theory. In a second study with cross-cultural implications, the researchers found that dissonance could be tolerated (i.e., exist below threshold) in the face of ads inducing both happiness and sadness concurrently. This tolerance, referred to as duality, was more prevalent in Eastern world cultures than in Western culture; Americans apparently require greater resolution of their mixed feelings.

Of three other recent studies also displaying dissonance reduction phenomena, one has already been cited in the context of shifting schemas in country-of-origin issues in car purchasing wherein consumers used search heuristics to find a context where seemingly dissonant elements are consonant. In the second study, the authors illustrated more general dissonance reduction with the passage of time in a student life adjustment period. In this study, the researchers found that the passing of time was instrumental in selective forgetting; greater forgetting and longer-term tolerance was discovered for tangible elements as opposed to interpersonal elements of service (education) delivery. And, in the third study, the specific process of expectation revision (distortion) after the fact (see Chapter 3) was tested in restaurant settings and found to be one very likely mechanism available to consumers for dissonance reductions.[38]

While these latter studies provide intriguing results, they leave many questions unanswered about the role of dissonance in the usage period; little else is available to provide greater insight save the student adjustment study and one other very preliminary study suggesting that low levels of satisfaction do little to assuage dissonance, permitting it to endure.[39] Generally, the forced-choice and postchoice outcome studies in the social psychology literature cannot be viewed in the context of product consumption, where monetary costs and commitment to the outcome are necessary. Because of this, a series of speculative observations is proposed about the role of dissonance in customer satisfaction.

PROPOSED RELATIONS BETWEEN DISSONANCE AND SATISFACTION

On the basis of evidence presented in this chapter, it can be presumed that processes of dissonance induction and dissonance reduction are valid preconsumption concepts, especially (or only) for those products and services that meet the many and varied conditions for likely dissonance effects. Although future evidence may amend this assumption, all the suppositions in consumption behaviors point strongly to the appearance of dissonance effects in the more usual choice-between-alternatives tradition in purchasing. If so, then what can be gleaned from what we know?

Beta and Gamma Phase Effects

Because performance has not yet been observed, effects at the beta and gamma phases can operate only by influencing one of the antecedents of satisfaction, namely, expectations. However, rather than focusing solely on expectations, this concept should be broadened to include all comparison referents and, of course, regret, as discussed in the previous chapter.

If dissonance induction is stronger than dissonance reduction, the situation is ripe for the operation of regret. Dissonance should maintain focus on the unchosen alternatives or options, including nonaction. Thus, a main antecedent of regret is dissonance (and arguments could be made to reverse the order of this and the prior chapter). This is not a new observation; rather it is

Figure 10.5   **Operation of Dissonance in the Expectancy Disconfirmation Process**

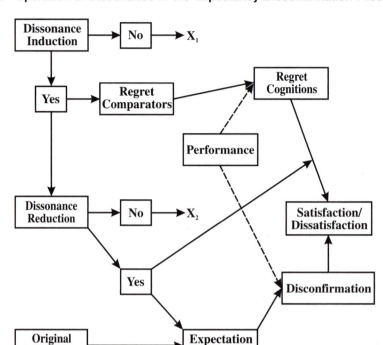

fundamental to the very essence of dissonance, where the earliest research in the field has shown that regret decreases as dissonance-induced dissonance reduction increases.[40] Alternatively, if dissonance reduction is stronger than dissonance induction, emphasis shifts to the effects of expectations generally. Thus, dissonance reduction should increase confidence in one's expectations with all the attendant effects, including the distortion of performance through assimilation. The effects on disconfirmation follow from this. Perhaps disconfirmation is similarly distorted through expectation effects made stronger through dissonance reduction.

Figure 10.5 shows the present perspective of how dissonance would impact the expectancy disconfirmation model as proposed here. The model in the figure assumes that the antecedents of dissonance are operative. This requires that at least some of the conditions for dissonance be present. If dissonance is not triggered in a particular purchase situation, no further influences need be traced and the process stops at X_1. If dissonance is triggered, two events occur. First, a set of regret comparators is brought into play; second, the process of dissonance reduction begins.

If dissonance reduction is lacking or ineffective, stopping at X_2, then nothing further happens and the regret comparators operate as before. If reduction is substantial, this may have the effect of bolstering the original expectation set, resulting in greater expectation effects than would have occurred under other conditions. Stronger expectation effects may have further influences when combined with performance to form disconfirmation perceptions, as noted previously. No predictions are made about a reduction of the regret comparators, as they may remain in place, with diminished emphasis. To reflect this property, the influence of dissonance reduction is shown as affecting the influence (i.e., the causal arrow) of the regret cognitions on satisfaction.

If the regret comparators remain salient, then performance will have two referents: purchase expectations and regret comparators (outcomes that might have been). The result of both comparisons, regret cognitions and disconfirmation, will now be operative in the prediction of satisfaction. Evidence for this prediction can be found in the quality-of-life literature, where regret has been shown to augment goal-based (outcome) predictions of life satisfaction.[41]

Delta Phase Effects

When dissonance continues into the performance period, it can result only from apprehensions of future performance, continued performance, or performance aspects that have not yet appeared. A family using a professional mover to relocate from one geographic area to another would experience these sensations. In sequence, the phases of a move are the bid, packing, loading (onto the van), transportation, timely arrival, unloading, unpacking, and damage inspection. Each one of these stages introduces its own internal set of apprehensions (e.g., the packing of fine china versus ordinary household items), as well as future apprehensions stemming from stages of the move that have yet to occur (e.g., timely arrival at the destination).

The gamma phase of consumption is best modeled by the graphic in Figure 10.1. At any one stage, the separate outcome influences become cumulative. Until the final stages of consumption are reached, continued apprehensions can serve only to decrease satisfaction unless dissonance reduction strategies are operating strongly. Although it is intuitively appealing, the effect of dissonance across consumption stages as discussed here has not been tested sequentially in one comprehensive study. Future research on this topic would be most welcome.

Measuring Dissonance in the Satisfaction Process

Historically, dissonance has been an elusive construct to measure. Most researchers have either inferred the existence of dissonance through appearances of induced stress in experimental manipulations or examined the consequences of the same manipulations. Of these consequences, attitude change has been the most commonly used dependent variable. Unfortunately, neither of these possibilities is practical in consumer research as they do not tap the psychological state of dissonance itself, namely anxiety or the state of being "torn and conflicted," noted previously. One measure showing some promise, with a final solution of four dimensions, did tap two predecision states, vigilance and procrastination, and two postdecision coping styles, buck-passing and "hypervigilance" (stressing).[42] All showed adequate reliabilities in the 0.7 to 0.8 range.

In an effort to provide a valid dissonance measure for use in consumer behavior, researchers have developed a ten-item scale with a reliability of 0.84.[43] As reported in this article, the scale represents the four dissonance dimensions of expected (dis)satisfaction, anxiety, decision uncertainty, and a tendency to seek decision support. As such, the last dimension taps dissonance reduction and not induction. Ancillary items, not in the dissonance scale, measured the number of alternative brands considered, stores visited, purchase frequency, expectations, product importance, self-confidence, persuadability, and product cost. Readers may wish to consult this study for its available insights.

Of more recent vintage is a programmatic research stream of dissonance scale construction and usage in hypothesis testing.[44] Here, the authors began with eighty-one emotional and cognitive descriptors of dissonance at all phases. This list was later culled down statistically to twenty-eight items and then to twenty-two after applying it to separate samples of furniture and car stereo buyers after purchase but before extensive usage. The final scale contained fifteen emotional and seven cognitive items, the latter on two subscales of "purchase wisdom" (e.g., "I wonder if I did the right thing") and "deal concern" (e.g., "I wondered if there was something wrong with the deal"). Reliabilities were in the 0.8 range. The small number of cognitive items per scale (four and three) resulted from overlap over the interim solutions. Although not reported, a single cognitive scale may have been sufficient if the two subscales were combined.

The authors then went on to cluster respondents based on their scale scores. Three clusters emerged, consisting of high- and low-dissonance consumers and a middle group of those "concerned" over the purchase. Tests across the three groups over the same two product categories showed that, as dissonance increased, satisfaction and value declined while switching propensity increased—all in accord with predictions of what consumers would feel if they had committed to the purchase and still harbored second thoughts. Although, beyond these findings, no causal or model tests were performed, this program of study shows great promise and should stimulate even more work in the future.

Given this promise, a complementary attempt is provided here to prime additional future research by suggesting short scales based on the antecedent-dissonance-consequence sequence. Ideally, the causes, consequences, and actual state of dissonance would have distinctive markers, but that condition is not likely since some overlap is unavoidable on a semantic basis. For example, the two scale development studies reviewed here do not report findings that clearly and unambiguously demarcate stages. A template follows, nonetheless.

Antecedent Items

A scale based on antecedents can be constructed from the *causes* of dissonance discussed previously. Each word set is represented by the more dissonance-provoking state on the left and consonance on the right. If these were to be converted to survey scales from 1 to 5, low scores would imply greater dissonance so that the untransformed scales would correlate positively with anticipated (but not necessarily realized) satisfaction.

Regarding my decision to buy this product (patronize this service):

Difficult decision	1	2	3	4	5	Easy decision
Important decision	1	2	3	4	5	Unimportant decision
Irrevocable decision	1	2	3	4	5	Reversible decision
Personally committed to decision	1	2	3	4	5	Not committed to decision
Many alternatives available	1	2	3	4	5	Few alternatives available
Personally responsible for decision	1	2	3	4	5	Not responsible for decision

Dissonance Items

The state of dissonance itself, one of psychological tension, has been measured in the psychological literature with a three-item scale intended to reflect *discomfort*.[45] Low scores, again, reflect dissonance.

As a result of my decision, I am feeling:

Uncomfortable	1	2	3	4	5	Comfortable
Uneasy	1	2	3	4	5	Not uneasy
Bothered	1	2	3	4	5	Not bothered

To these, the following items may be added. The resulting scale maintains the tenor of the original while more than doubling its length, thereby improving its reliability:

As a result of my decision, I am feeling:

Anxious	1	2	3	4	5	Calm
Tense	1	2	3	4	5	Relaxed
Apprehensive	1	2	3	4	5	Not apprehensive
Conflicted	1	2	3	4	5	Serene

Suggestions for Measuring Consequences

Finally, the consequences of dissonance would be measured in a number of ways. Since regret is one of these known consequences, the regret scale proposed in Chapter 9 would qualify as a consequence measure. Other consequences, including anger, disgust, annoyance, embarrassment, and shame, pertain to the affect state of the individual after the fact (postpurchase). To these guilt should be added, as the courses of action to reduce guilt are similar to those of dissonance, namely self-absolution.[46] Another set of consequences—specific efforts to resolve dissonance— awaits further measurement development. The list of dissonance-reduction techniques presented earlier can be used to generate ideas, but attempts would be considered speculative at this point since dissonance reduction may be idiosyncratic to persons or product categories. As expressed in the first edition of this book, it is hoped that the construction, validation, and dissemination of comprehensive dissonance scales will be undertaken to augment those noted here.

CONCLUSION

Dissonance is an intriguing aspect of what uncertainties of the future will bring. As it pertains to consumption, dissonance is integral to decision making and to ongoing or staged consumption. Because of the associated stress, dissonance coping strategies used by individuals and, more specifically, by consumers appear to be well known. Despite this conventional wisdom, little work on the occurrence and reduction of dissonance in consumption is currently available, and managers are generally unable to determine the extent of dissonance experienced by their customers or the degree of influence of dissonance on satisfaction. Interestingly, this inability has not deterred them from designing advertising with dissonance-assuaging messages (e.g., "please try Carlton"). One purpose of this chapter is to suggest paths for innovative future work on this topic. To this end, both a framework and measurement suggestions for the dissonance process are proposed to stimulate such much-needed research.

By the convention adopted here, discussion has been largely restricted to dissonant elements caused by pre- and postdecision conflict. Note, however, that there exists work, not covered here, on dissonance caused by outcomes inconsistent with the amount of effort expended (as in forced compliance). Because much of this research was performed in nonconsumption settings, it is of only marginal relevance to the present focus. Additionally, it was performed before or without reference to theories of reaction to discrepancy of which expectancy disconfirmation is one.

One aspect of this research on effort-outcome inconsistency that is directly relevant to consumption, however, is the attribution of responsibility. If an outcome is in conflict with other cognitions, to what do consumers assign causes and what else do they do? In fact, recent theorists have argued that a discrepancy is no longer needed for dissonance; rather, it is sufficient that individuals feel responsible for aversive consequences. However, consumers often find the aversive outcome at odds with their self-concept.[47] The point here is that the blame for aversive consequences or, for that matter, the praise for a task well done will be placed somewhere. The location of this target sets in motion a series of further cognitions and, as will be seen, affects. Assigning blame and praise, or attribution, as it is more commonly known, is the focus of the next chapter.

NOTES

1. Festinger, *Theory of Cognitive Dissonance.* This was originally an unpublished paper titled "Social Communication and Cognition: A Very Preliminary and Highly Tentative Draft" presented at a graduate seminar at the University of Minnesota in 1954; there was no separate journal article. Two early follow-up sources on dissonance are Abelson et al., *Theories of Cognitive Consistency*; and Wicklund and Brehm, *Perspectives on Cognitive Dissonance.*

2. See E. Aronson, "Theory of Cognitive Dissonance" and "Return of the Repressed"; E. Jones, "Major Developments in Social Psychology During the Past Five Decades"; and sixteen commentaries by various scholars that follow this article. For a more current set of reviews, see Harmon-Jones and Mills, *Cognitive Dissonance.*

3. Houston, Sherman, and Baker, "Feature Matching, Unique Features, and the Dynamics of the Choice Process"; Sanbonmatsu et al., "Contextual Influences on Judgment Based on Limited Information"; Zhang and Fitzsimons, "Choice-Process Satisfaction."

4. Botti and Iyengar, "Psychological Pleasure and Pain of Choosing"; Houston, Sherman, and Baker, "Feature Matching, Unique Features, and the Dynamics of the Choice Process"; Iyengar and Lepper, "When Choice Is Demotivating"; Zhang and Fitzsimons, "Choice-Process Satisfaction."

5. In the many sections that follow, the very obvious references to Festinger's seminal work in note 1 will be only sparingly cited to save the reader from numerous short endnotes.

6. See Abelson et al., *Theories of Cognitive Consistency.*

7. For more advanced treatments, see Shultz and Lepper, "Cognitive Dissonance Reduction as Constraint Satisfaction"; and Sakai, "Multiplicative Power-Function Model of Cognitive Dissonance."

8. See, for example, Beauvois and Joule, *Radical Dissonance Theory*; Elliot and Devine, "On the Motivational Nature of Cognitive Dissonance"; Gawronski and Strack, "On the Propositional Nature of Cognitive Consistency"; and Joule and Azdia, "Cognitive Dissonance, Double Forced Compliance, and Commitment."

9. Choi and Nisbett, "Cultural Psychology of Surprise"; Cooper, "Unlearning Cognitive Dissonance"; Heine and Lehman, "Culture, Dissonance, and Self-Affirmation"; Hoshino-Browne et al., "On the Cultural Guises of Cognitive Dissonance"; Kitayama et al., "Is There Any 'Free' Choice?"; Murphy and Miller, "Postdecisional Dissonance and the Commodified Self-Concept"; Williams and Aaker, "Can Mixed Emotions Peacefully Coexist?"

10. The phrase *torn and conflicted* is cited by McGregor, Newby-Clark, and Zanna, "'Remembering' Dissonance," p. 329. See, also, Strathman et al., "Consideration of Future Consequences."

11. Cooper and Fazio, "New Look at Dissonance Theory."

12. Harmon-Jones and Mills, "Introduction to Cognitive Dissonance Theory and an Overview of Current Perspectives on the Theory."

13. Shultz, Léveillé, and Lepper, "Free Choice and Cognitive Dissonance Revisited"; Stone, "What Exactly Have I Done?"

14. Kivetz and Simonson, "Earning the Right to Indulge."

15. Knox and Inkster, "Postdecision Dissonance at Post Time"; Brownstein, Read, and Simon, "Bias at the Racetrack."

16. Cummings and Venkatesan, "Cognitive Dissonance and Consumer Behavior."

17. Wilson et al., "Introspecting About Reasons Can Reduce Post-Choice Satisfaction."

18. Gilbert and Ebert, "Decisions and Revisions."

19. Beauvois and Joule, "Radical Point of View on Dissonance Theory."

20. Gilovich, Medvec, and Chen, "Commission, Omission, and Dissonance Reduction." The example used is, in fact, a variant of the Monty Hall problem.

21. Stone and Cooper, "Self-Standards Model of Cognitive Dissonance."

22. Matz and Wood, "Cognitive Dissonance in Groups"; Monin et al., "Reacting to an Assumed Situation vs. Conforming to an Assumed Reaction"; Norton et al., "Vicarious Dissonance."

23. Durgee and O'Connor, "Exploration into Renting as Consumption Behavior."

24. J. Aronson, Blanton, and Cooper, "From Dissonance to Disidentification"; Stone and Cooper, "Effect of Self-Attribute Relevance on How Self-Esteem Moderates Attitude Change in Dissonance Processes"; Svenson and Benthorn, "Consolidation Processes in Decision Making."

25. See, for example, Gibbons, Eggleston, and Benthin, "Cognitive Reactions to Smoking Relapse"; and Stone et al., "When Exemplification Fails."

26. Keller and Block, "Effect of Affect-Based Dissonance Versus Cognition-Based Dissonance on Motivated Reasoning and Health-Related Persuasion."

27. Woodside and Chebat, "Updating Heider's Balance Theory in Consumer Behavior."

28. Burris, Harmon-Jones, and Tarpley, "'By Faith Alone'"; Stalder and Baron, "Attributional Complexity as a Moderator of Dissonance-Produced Attitude Change."

29. For an apparent reversal of this technique, see McGregor, Newby-Clark, and Zanna, "'Remembering' Dissonance."

30. Gosling, Denizeau, and Oberlé, "Denial of Responsibility"; Mann et al., "Melbourne Decision Making Questionnaire"; McKimmie et al., "I'm a Hypocrite, But So Is Everyone Else."

31. Simon, Greenberg, and Brehm, "Trivialization."

32. Frey, "Recent Research on Selective Exposure to Information"; Jonas et al., "Confirmation Bias in Sequential Information Search After Preliminary Decisions"; M. Jones and Sugden, "Positive Confirmation Bias in the Acquisition of Information."

33. Axsom and Lawless, "Subsequent Behavior Can Erase Evidence of Dissonance-Induced Attitude Change." The main source for the "radical theory" is Beauvois and Joule, *Radical Dissonance Theory*.

34. Hunt, "Post-Transaction Communications and Dissonance Reduction."

35. Donnelly and Ivancevich, "Post-Purchase Reinforcement and Back-Out Behavior"; Milliman and Decker, "Use of Post-Purchase Communication to Reduce Dissonance and Improve Direct Marketing Effectiveness."

36. Geva and Goldman, "Duality in Consumer Post-Purchase Attitude."

37. Keller and Block, "Effect of Affect-Based Dissonance Versus Cognition-Based Dissonance on Motivated Reasoning and Health-Related Persuasion"; Williams and Aaker, "Can Mixed Emotions Peacefully Coexist?"

38. Respectively, Woodside and Chebat, "Updating Heider's Balance Theory in Consumer Behavior"; O'Neill and Palmer, "Cognitive Dissonance and the Stability of Service Quality Perceptions"; Clow, Kurtz, and Ozment, "Longitudinal Study of the Stability of Consumer Expectations of Services."

39. Sweeney, Soutar, and Johnson, "Are Satisfaction and Dissonance the Same Construct?"

40. Brehm and Wicklund, "Regret and Dissonance Reduction as a Function of Postdecision Salience of Dissonant Information."

41. Lecci, Okun, and Karoly, "Life Regrets and Current Goals as Predictors of Psychological Adjustment."

42. Mann et al., "Melbourne Decision Making Questionnaire."

43. Montgomery and Barnes, "POSTDIS."

44. Hausknecht et al., "'After I Had Made the Decision, I . . .'"; Sweeney, Hausknecht, and Soutar, "Cognitive Dissonance after Purchase"; Soutar and Sweeney, "Are There Cognitive Dissonance Segments?"

45. Elliot and Devine, "On the Motivational Nature of Cognitive Dissonance," p. 386.

46. Burnett and Lunsford, "Conceptualizing Guilt in the Consumer Decision-Making Process."

47. Harmon-Jones, "Toward an Understanding of the Motivation Underlying Dissonance Effects"; Scher and Cooper, "Motivational Basis of Dissonance"; Thibodeau and Aronson, "Taking a Closer Look."

BIBLIOGRAPHY

Abelson, Robert P., Elliot Aronson, William J. McGuire, Theodore M. Newcomb, Milton J. Rosenberg, and Percy H. Tannenbaum, eds. *Theories of Cognitive Consistency: A Sourcebook*. Chicago: Rand McNally, 1968.

Aronson, Elliot. "The Return of the Repressed: Dissonance Theory Makes a Comeback." *Psychological Inquiry* 3, no. 4 (1992): 303–311.

———. "The Theory of Cognitive Dissonance: A Current Perspective." In *Advances in Experimental Social Psychology*, ed. Leonard Berkowitz, 4:1–34. New York: Academic Press, 1969.

Aronson, Joshua, Hart Blanton, and Joel Cooper. "From Dissonance to Disidentification: Selectivity in the Self-Affirmation Process." *Journal of Personality and Social Psychology* 68, no. 6 (June 1995): 986–996.

Axsom, Danny, and William F. Lawless. "Subsequent Behavior Can Erase Evidence of Dissonance-Induced Attitude Change." *Journal of Experimental Social Psychology* 28, no. 4 (July 1992): 387–400.

Beauvois, Jean-Léon, and Robert-Vincent Joule. *A Radical Dissonance Theory*. Bristol, PA: Taylor & Francis, 1996.

———. "A Radical Point of View on Dissonance Theory." In *Cognitive Dissonance: Progress on a Pivotal Theory in Social Psychology*, ed. Eddie Harmon-Jones and Judson Mills, 43–70. Washington, DC: American Psychological Association, 1999.

Botti, Simona, and Sheena S. Iyengar. "The Psychological Pleasure and Pain of Choosing: When People Prefer Choosing at the Cost of Subsequent Outcome Satisfaction." *Journal of Personality and Social Psychology* 87, no. 3 (September 2004): 312–326.

Brehm, Jack W., and Robert A. Wicklund. "Regret and Dissonance Reduction as a Function of Postdecision Salience of Dissonant Information." *Journal of Personality and Social Psychology* 14, no. 1 (January 1970): 1–7.

Brownstein, Aaron L., Stephen J. Read, and Dan Simon. "Bias at the Racetrack: Effects of Individual Expertise and Task Importance on Predecision Reevaluation of Alternatives." *Personality and Social Psychology Bulletin* 30, no. 7 (July 2004): 891–904.

Burnett, Melissa S., and Dale A. Lunsford. "Conceptualizing Guilt in the Consumer Decision-Making Process." *Journal of Consumer Marketing* 11, no. 3 (1994): 33–43.

Burris, Christopher T., Eddie Harmon-Jones, and W. Ryan Tarpley. "'By Faith Alone': Religious Agitation and Cognitive Dissonance." *Basic and Applied Social Psychology* 19, no. 1 (1997): 17–31.

Choi, Incheol, and Richard E. Nisbett. "Cultural Psychology of Surprise: Holistic Theories and Recognition of Contradiction." *Journal of Personality and Social Psychology* 79, no. 6 (December 2000): 890–905.

Clow, Kenneth E., David L. Kurtz, and John Ozment. "A Longitudinal Study of the Stability of Consumer Expectations of Services." *Journal of Business Research* 42, no. 1 (May 1998): 63–73.

Cooper, Joel. "Unlearning Cognitive Dissonance: Toward an Understanding of the Development of Dissonance." *Journal of Experimental Social Psychology* 34, no. 6 (November 1998): 562–575.

Cooper, Joel, and Russell H. Fazio. "A New Look at Dissonance Theory." In *Advances in Experimental Social Psychology*, ed. Leonard Berkowitz, 17:229–266. Orlando, FL: Academic Press, 1984.

Cummings, William H., and M. Venkatesan. "Cognitive Dissonance and Consumer Behavior: A Review of the Evidence." *Journal of Marketing Research* 13, no. 3 (August 1976): 303–308.

Donnelly, James H., Jr., and John M. Ivancevich. "Post-Purchase Reinforcement and Back-Out Behavior." *Journal of Marketing Research* 7, no. 3 (August 1970): 399–400.

Durgee, Jeffrey F., and Gina Colarelli O'Connor. "An Exploration into Renting as Consumption Behavior." *Psychology & Marketing* 12, no. 2 (March 1995): 89–104.

Elliot, Andrew J., and Patricia G. Devine. "On the Motivational Nature of Cognitive Dissonance: Dissonance as Psychological Discomfort." *Journal of Personality and Social Psychology* 67, no. 3 (September 1994): 382–394.

Festinger, Leon. "Social Communication and Cognition: A Very Preliminary and Highly Tentative Draft." Reprinted in *Cognitive Dissonance: Progress on a Pivotal Theory in Social Psychology*, ed. Eddie Harmon-Jones and Judson Mills, 355–379. Washington, DC: American Psychological Association, 1999.

———. *A Theory of Cognitive Dissonance*. New York: Row, Peterson, 1957. Reprint, Stanford, CA: Stanford University Press, 1957.

Frey, Dieter. "Recent Research on Selective Exposure to Information." In *Advances in Experimental Social Psychology*, ed. Leonard Berkowitz, 19:41–80. Orlando, FL: Academic Press, 1986.

Gawronski, Bertram, and Fritz Strack. "On the Propositional Nature of Cognitive Consistency: Dissonance Changes Explicit, But Not Implicit Attitudes." *Journal of Experimental Social Psychology* 40, no. 4 (July 2004): 535–542.

Geva, Aviva, and Arieh Goldman. "Duality in Consumer Post-Purchase Attitude." *Journal of Economic Psychology* 12, no. 1 (March 1991): 141–164.

Gibbons, Frederick X., Tami J. Eggleston, and Alida C. Benthin. "Cognitive Reactions to Smoking Relapse: The Reciprocal Relation Between Dissonance and Self-Esteem." *Journal of Personality and Social Psychology* 72, no. 1 (January 1997): 184–195.

Gilbert, Daniel T., and Jane E.J. Ebert. "Decisions and Revisions: The Affective Forecasting of Changeable Outcomes." *Journal of Personality and Social Psychology* 82, no. 4 (April 2002): 503–514.

Gilovich, Thomas, Victoria Husted Medvec, and Serena Chen. "Commission, Omission, and Dissonance Reduction: Coping with Regret in the 'Monty Hall' Problem." *Personality and Social Psychology Bulletin* 21, no. 2 (February 1995): 182–190.

Gosling, Patrick, Maxime Denizeau, and Dominique Oberlé. "Denial of Responsibility: A New Mode of Dissonance Reduction." *Journal of Personality and Social Psychology* 90, no. 5 (May 2006): 722–733.

Harmon-Jones, Eddie. "Toward an Understanding of the Motivation Underlying Dissonance Effects: Is the Production of Aversive Consequences Necessary?" In *Cognitive Dissonance: Progress on a Pivotal Theory in Social Psychology*, ed. Eddie Harmon-Jones and Judson Mills, 71–99. Washington, DC: American Psychological Association, 1999.

Harmon-Jones, Eddie, and Judson Mills. "An Introduction to Cognitive Dissonance Theory and an Overview of Current Perspectives on the Theory." In *Cognitive Dissonance: Progress on a Pivotal Theory in Social Psychology*, ed. Eddie Harmon-Jones and Judson Mills, 3–21. Washington, DC: American Psychological Association, 1999.

———, eds. *Cognitive Dissonance: Progress on a Pivotal Theory in Social Psychology*. Washington, DC: American Psychological Association, 1999.

Hausknecht, Douglas R., Jillian C. Sweeney, Geoffrey N. Soutar, and Lester W. Johnson. "'After I Had Made the Decision, I . . .'; Toward a Scale to Measure Cognitive Dissonance." *Journal of Consumer Satisfaction, Dissatisfaction and Complaining Behavior* 11 (1998): 119–127.

Heine, Steven J., and Darrin R. Lehman. "Culture, Dissonance, and Self-Affirmation." *Personality and Social Psychology Bulletin* 23, no. 4 (April 1997): 389–400.

Hoshino-Browne, Etsuko, Adam S. Zanna, Steven J. Spencer, Mark P. Zanna, Shinobu Kitayama, and Sandra Lackenbauer. "On the Cultural Guises of Cognitive Dissonance: The Case of Easterners and Westerners." *Journal of Personality and Social Psychology* 89, no. 3 (September 2005): 294–310.

Houston, David A., Steven J. Sherman, and Sara M. Baker. "Feature Matching, Unique Features, and the Dynamics of the Choice Process: Predecision Conflict and Postdecision Satisfaction." *Journal of Experimental Social Psychology* 27, no. 5 (1991): 411–430.

Hunt, Shelby D. "Post-Transaction Communications and Dissonance Reduction." *Journal of Marketing* 34, no. 3 (July 1970): 46–51.

Iyengar, Sheena S., and Mark R. Lepper. "When Choice Is Demotivating: Can One Desire Too Much of a Good Thing?" *Journal of Personality and Social Psychology* 79, no. 6 (December 2000): 995–1006.

Jonas, Eva, Stefan Schulz-Hardt, Dieter Frey, and Norman Thelen. "Confirmation Bias in Sequential Information Search After Preliminary Decisions: An Expansion of Dissonance Theoretical Research on Selective Exposure to Information." *Journal of Personality and Social Psychology* 80, no. 4 (April 2001): 557–571.

Jones, Edward E. "Major Developments in Social Psychology During the Past Five Decades." In *Handbook of Social Psychology*, 3rd ed., 1:47–107. New York: Random House, 1985.

Jones, Martin, and Robert Sugden. "Positive Confirmation Bias in the Acquisition of Information." *Theory and Decision* 50, no. 1 (February 2001): 59–99.

Joule, Robert-Vincent, and Touati Azdia. "Cognitive Dissonance, Double Forced Compliance, and Commitment." *European Journal of Social Psychology* 33, no. 4 (July–August 2003): 565–571.

Keller, Punan Anand, and Lauren Goldberg Block. "The Effect of Affect-Based Dissonance Versus Cognition-Based Dissonance on Motivated Reasoning and Health-Related Persuasion." *Journal of Experimental Psychology: Applied* 5, no. 3 (September 1999): 302–313.

Kitayama, Shinobu, Alana Conner Snibbe, Hazel Rose Markus, and Tomoko Suzuki. "Is There Any 'Free' Choice? Self and Dissonance in Two Cultures." *Psychological Science* 15, no. 8 (August 2004): 527–533.

Kivetz, Ran, and Itamar Simonson. "Earning the Right to Indulge: Effort as a Determinant of Customer Preferences Toward Frequency Program Rewards." *Journal of Marketing Research* 39, no. 2 (May 2002): 155–170.

Knox, Robert E., and James A. Inkster. "Postdecision Dissonance at Post Time." *Journal of Personality and Social Psychology* 8, no. 4 (April 1968): 319–323.

Lecci, Len, Morris A. Okun, and Paul Karoly. "Life Regrets and Current Goals as Predictors of Psychological Adjustment." *Journal of Personality and Social Psychology* 66, no. 4 (April 1994): 731–741.

Mann, Leon, Paul Burnett, Mark Radford, and Steve Ford. "The Melbourne Decision Making Questionnaire: An Instrument for Measuring Patterns for Coping with Decisional Conflict." *Journal of Behavioral Decision Making* 10, no. 1 (March 1997): 1–19.

Matz, David C., and Wendy Wood. "Cognitive Dissonance in Groups: The Consequences of Disagreement." *Journal of Personality and Social Psychology* 88, no. 1 (January 2005): 22–37.

McGregor, Ian, Ian R. Newby-Clark, and Mark P. Zanna. "'Remembering' Dissonance: Simultaneous Accessibility of Inconsistent Cognitive Elements Moderates Epistemic Discomfort." In *Cognitive Dissonance:*

Progress on a Pivotal Theory in Social Psychology, ed. Eddie Harmon-Jones and Judson Mills, 325–353. Washington, DC: American Psychological Association, 1999.

McKimmie, Blake M., Deborah G. Terry, Michael A. Hogg, Antony S.R. Manstead, Russell Spears, and Bertjan Doosje. "I'm a Hypocrite, But So Is Everyone Else: Group Support and the Reduction of Cognitive Dissonance." *Group Dynamics: Theory, Research, and Practice* 7, no. 3 (September 2003): 214–224.

Milliman, Ronald E., and Phillip J. Decker. "The Use of Post-Purchase Communication to Reduce Dissonance and Improve Direct Marketing Effectiveness." *Journal of Business Communication* 27, no. 2 (Spring 1990): 159–170.

Monin, Benoît, Michael I. Norton, Joel Cooper, and Michael A. Hogg. "Reacting to an Assumed Situation vs. Conforming to an Assumed Reaction: The Role of Perceived Speaker Attitude in Vicarious Dissonance." *Group Processes & Intergroup Relations* 7, no. 3 (July 2004): 207–220.

Montgomery, Cameron, and James H. Barnes. "POSTDIS: A Short Rating Scale for Measuring Post Purchase Dissonance." *Journal of Consumer Satisfaction, Dissatisfaction and Complaining Behavior* 6 (1993): 204–216.

Murphy, Patricia L., and Carol T. Miller. "Postdecisional Dissonance and the Commodified Self-Concept: A Cross-Cultural Examination." *Personality and Social Psychology Bulletin* 23, no. 1 (January 1997): 50–62.

Norton, Michael I., Benoît Monin, Joel Cooper, and Michael A. Hogg. "Vicarious Dissonance: Attitude Change from the Inconsistency of Others." *Journal of Personality and Social Psychology* 85, no. 1 (July 2003): 47–62.

O'Neill, Martin, and Adrian Palmer. "Cognitive Dissonance and the Stability of Service Quality Perceptions." *Journal of Services Marketing* 18, no. 6 (2004): 433–449.

Sakai, Haruki. "A Multiplicative Power-Function Model of Cognitive Dissonance: Toward an Integrated Theory of Cognition, Emotion, and Behavior After Leon Festinger." In *Cognitive Dissonance: Progress on a Pivotal Theory in Social Psychology*, ed. Eddie Harmon-Jones and Judson Mills, 267–294. Washington, DC: American Psychological Association, 1999.

Sanbonmatsu, David M., Frank R. Kardes, Steven S. Posavac, and David C. Houghton. "Contextual Influences on Judgment Based on Limited Information." *Organizational Behavior and Human Performance* 69, no. 3 (March 1997): 251–264.

Scher, Steven J., and Joel Cooper. "Motivational Basis of Dissonance: The Singular Role of Behavioral Consequences." *Journal of Personality and Social Psychology* 56, no. 6 (June 1989): 899–906.

Shultz, Thomas R., and Mark R. Lepper. "Cognitive Dissonance as Constraint Satisfaction." *Psychological Review* 103, no. 2 (April 1996): 219–240.

Shultz, Thomas R., Eléne Léveillé, and Mark R. Lepper. "Free Choice and Cognitive Dissonance Revisited: Choosing 'Lesser Evils' Versus 'Greater Goods.'" *Personality and Social Psychology Bulletin* 25, no. 1 (January 1999): 40–48.

Simon, Linda, Jeff Greenberg, and Jack Brehm. "Trivialization: The Forgotten Mode of Dissonance Reduction." *Journal of Personality and Social Psychology* 68, no. 2 (February 1995): 247–260.

Soutar, Geoffrey N., and Jillian C. Sweeney. "Are There Coginitve Dissonance Segments?" *Australian Journal of Management* 28, no. 3 (December 2003): 227–249.

Stalder, Daniel R., and Robert S. Baron. "Attributional Complexity as a Moderator of Dissonance-Produced Attitude Change." *Journal of Personality and Social Psychology* 75, no. 2 (August 1998): 449–455.

Stone, Jeff. "What Exactly Have I Done? The Role of Self-Attribute Accessibility in Dissonance." In *Cognitive Dissonance: Progress on a Pivotal Theory in Social Psychology*, ed. Eddie Harmon-Jones and Judson Mills, 175–200. Washington, DC: American Psychological Association, 1999.

Stone, Jeff, and Joel Cooper. "The Effect of Self-Attribute Relevance on How Self-Esteem Moderates Attitude Change in Dissonance Processes." *Journal of Experimental Social Psychology* 39, no. 5 (September 2003): 508–515.

———. "A Self-Standards Model of Cognitive Dissonance." *Journal of Experimental Social Psychology* 37, no. 3 (May 2001): 228–243.

Stone, Jeff, Andrew W. Wiegand, Joel Cooper, and Elliot Aronson. "When Exemplification Fails: Hypocrisy and the Motive for Self-Integrity." *Journal of Personality and Social Psychology* 72, no. 1 (January 1997): 54–65.

Strathman, Alan, Faith Gleicher, David S. Boninger, and C. Scott Edwards. "The Consideration of Future Consequences: Weighing Immediate and Distant Outcomes of Behavior." *Journal of Personality and Social Psychology* 66, no. 4 (April 1994): 742–752.

Svenson, Ola, and Lars J. Benthorn. "Consolidation Processes in Decision Making: Post-decision Changes in Attractiveness of Alternatives." *Journal of Economic Psychology* 13, no. 2 (June 1992): 315–327.

Sweeney, Jillian C., Douglas R. Hausknecht, and Geoffrey N. Soutar. "Cognitive Dissonance after Purchase: A Multidimensional Scale." *Psychology & Marketing* 17, no. 5 (May 2000): 369–385.

Sweeney, Jillian C., Geoffrey N. Soutar, and Lester W. Johnson. "Are Satisfaction and Dissonance the Same Construct? A Preliminary Analysis." *Journal of Consumer Satisfaction, Dissatisfaction and Complaining Behavior* 9 (1996): 138–143.

Thibodeau, Ruth, and Elliot Aronson. "Taking a Closer Look: Reasserting the Role of the Self-Concept in Dissonance Theory." *Personality and Social Psychology Bulletin* 18, no. 5 (October 1992): 591–602.

Wicklund, Robert A., and Jack W. Brehm. *Perspectives on Cognitive Dissonance.* Hillsdale, NJ: Lawrence Erlbaum, 1976.

Williams, Patti, and Jennifer L. Aaker. "Can Mixed Emotions Peacefully Coexist?" *Journal of Consumer Research* 28, no. 4 (March 2002): 636–649.

Wilson, Timothy D., Douglas J. Lisle, Jonathan W. Schooler, Sara D. Hodges, Kristen J. Klaaren, and Suzanne J. LaFleur. "Introspecting About Reasons Can Reduce Post-Choice Satisfaction." *Personality and Social Psychology Bulletin* 19, no. 3 (June 1993): 331–339.

Woodside, Arch G., and Jean-Charles Chebat. "Updating Heider's Balance Theory in Consumer Behavior: A Jewish Couple Buys a German Car and Additional Buying-Consuming Transformation Stories." *Psychology & Marketing* 18, no. 5 (May 2001): 475–495.

Zhang, Shi, and Gavan J. Fitzsimons. "Choice-Process Satisfaction: The Influence of Attribute Alignability and Option Limitation." *Organizational Behavior and Human Decision Processes* 77, no. 3 (March 1999): 192–214.

CHAPTER 11

ATTRIBUTION IN THE SATISFACTION RESPONSE

WHY DID IT HAPPEN?

Why did the Ford Edsel fail? Ask any number of consumers who remember the events of 1957 to 1959 in the automotive industry, and they may have an answer. Perhaps they will remember the Edsel's vertical grille, which evoked comparisons to a horse collar or a car sucking on a lemon. They will remember the name (Edsel was the name of Henry Ford's only child), which connoted little of interest to automobile consumers and certainly nothing characteristic of speed, power, and agility. To many critics, the Edsel was an ugly car with a strange name. These and other answers focusing on obvious features of the car represent common responses to the question "Why?" In this example, respondents are asked to perform the role of *observers* of history in the sense that each individual can provide a detached and seemingly logical analysis of what went wrong—that is, why car buyers of that era shunned the Edsel.[1]

In fact, the Edsel failed because of a confluence of managerial and economic factors that few consumers understood. The Edsel was designed as a mid-priced, large, powerful car to compete with equivalent models produced by GM's Pontiac, Buick, and Oldsmobile divisions. It was rushed on the market in an effort to buttress Ford's only entry in this size range, Mercury. Similar to GM's five car lines, Ford wanted to make Edsel a separate division with separate dealerships. This haste resulted in frequent mechanical failures, ill-trained dealerships, and consumer discontent right at the beginning of the small-car craze. Incidentally, the stock market began a scary decline in 1957, an economic shakeout that sensitized consumers toward the benefits of small, fuel-efficient cars. These events, then, are the causes of the demise of the Edsel, which was phased out in 1959.

These *causes* clearly differ from the consumers' *reasons* why the Edsel might have failed. Reasons are intuitive explanations for events from the perspective of the observer. Unfortunately, these explanations can be no more sophisticated than permitted by the facts and reasoning available to the individual. For example, despite consumers' misgivings about the name Edsel, many automobile makes do quite well with uninteresting and otherwise nondescript names. The name Datsun (the predecessor of Nissan) was selected because it had the "sound" of an American name. Toyota contains the syllable *toy*. Moreover, many current models have numeric or alphanumeric names that mean little to consumers (e.g., the Porsche 900 series) until they take on a meaning of their own among owners and aficionados. Even the second likely reason given by consumers, the vertical grille, would not necessarily doom a car to failure. Most cars in the 1920s and 1930s had vertical grilles (owing to their inline and upright engine configurations).

Now, what if some of these hypothetical consumers actually purchased an Edsel? In this situation, the reasons for the demise of the Edsel take on a different cast because the consumers are in the position of explaining the car's lack of success with the knowledge that they had made the decision to purchase this make of car. Explanations like "ugly" and "strange name" are no longer attractive because they reflect poorly on the consumer's judgment. External reasons like poor workmanship, incompetent dealer servicing, and rising gas prices now make more sense, as they are elements that rational consumers would have considered. Perhaps this latter consumer would explain the Edsel's demise with reference to the increasing number of small, cheap, foreign cars in the marketplace. Such a reason provides a healthy degree of ego preservation and exonerates the consumer entirely.

In this second scenario, the consumer is no longer an observer, but is now an *actor* (a player in a drama). Thus, the reasons shift from detached explanations to those that serve to protect the consumer's good judgment. Instead of reflecting on buyers of such cars, consumers—as *persons*—now point to reasons in the environment or *situation*, such as managerial incompetence and world competitiveness. This shift illustrates the nature of *attribution*. To what do consumers attribute consumption outcomes? Another way of stating this question is, what are the perceived causes of negative (and positive) purchase outcomes as stated by the consumer?

THE ORIGINS OF ATTRIBUTION THEORY

The concept of causal explanation (as distinct from more "scientific" causes) is thought to have been first proposed in a comprehensive manner by Fritz Heider in his book *The Psychology of Interpersonal Relations*.[2] Although his goal was to explain individuals' reactions to other people, he was among the first to distinguish between reasons attributed to the person (self or other), such as effort and intent, and reasons attributed to the situation or environment, such as weather or economic conditions. Viewing causal explanatory attempts by individuals as reflective of a "naive science," Heider proposed the notion of commonsense explanation. This theory recognizes that even individuals who have no necessary expertise or competence in understanding psychology or science nonetheless formulate logical and even well-reasoned accounts of events that they wish to understand.

Perhaps due to the proliferation of psychology at the time, attribution and dissonance (see Chapter 10) vied briefly for attention as explanations of human perception. This later resulted in two major perspectives, those of Kelley and Weiner, which have spawned a large number of studies of the attribution process.[3] Although Weiner's work has achieved greater acceptance in consumption research, Kelley's work, as well as that of others, has proved valuable in other fields. Readers are referred to two substantive reviews of the attribution phenomenon and an attempt at a synthesis.[4]

Previously, three major distinctions in attribution theory were introduced as italicized terms: (1) the actor versus the observer, (2) causes versus reasons, and (3) explanations attributed to the person versus those attributed to the situation. The following sections offer a formal discussion of these topics.[5]

Actors and Observers

As generally understood, the actor is the focal individual, the person whose behavior or outcome is targeted for explanation. The observer is any other person who is able to view the actor from afar. In legal terms, the defendant is the actor while the witnesses and jury are observers. One conclusion from this analogy is that explanations of the same event will differ depending on whether the actor or the observer is asked to provide the explanation, a frequent legal conundrum. One obvious reason for this difference is that the observer presumably can be detached from the actor's outcomes whereas the actor cannot. Other obvious reasons abound.

For the present purpose, concern is primarily with the actor in the role of consumer, who is in the most immediate position to repeat or refrain from future consumption. Thus, the actor's explanations for product successes and failures are those that most immediately affect the satisfaction response. There are, however, two closely related circumstances in which the explanations of the consumer as observer are important. The first occurs when consumers' observations of someone else in the consumption experience have the potential to influence their own satisfaction—for example, when the consumer observes the performance of another, such as a service provider. Here, the consumer's satisfaction will be affected by the service provider's "acting."[6] The second occurs when the actor is engaged with another party to the consumption experience and hence can be, simultaneously, both actor and observer. This situation is best exemplified by a customer-salesperson transaction.

Causes and Reasons

Having roots in philosophy, the distinction between causes and reasons is a core concept in scientific explanation and the focus of epistemology, or the study of knowledge acquisition. The primary concern here is with lay epistemology, or the knowledge processing of the nonexpert. Causes are agents that are capable of bringing about an event or outcome. Their impact can be direct or indirect and even imperceptible to the receiver. An example would be the effect of fluoride on reduction in tooth decay through binding effects on tooth enamel, a process not sensed by the consumer. Unaware of this influence, consumers may therefore attribute their healthy teeth to other explanations that are consistent with their existing knowledge. A favorable dental checkup may be attributed to a particular toothbrush or to specific dietary habits (e.g., vegetarianism) having little to do with decay prevention.

Compared to causes, reasons are explanatory accounts by the consumer at the level of the consumer's understanding. They may correspond correctly to causes if the consumer is sophisticated in the knowledge category or has otherwise gained direct knowledge of what caused a particular event. Alternatively, reasons may have little basis in scientific fact, but will make perfect sense to the individual. An example might be of the "lucky hat" variety, whereby casino gamblers who experience good fortune while wearing a particular hat come to believe that the hat brought on the good fortune and refuse to gamble without it in the future. It does not matter that the bettor cannot construct the sequence of causality between the hat and the good fortune, for the charmed hat is the explanatory "science" as the bettor understands it.

A related concept is rationalization or justification, whereby consumers may or may not know a reason for their behavior, but give a socially acceptable account of the behavior nonetheless. The import of this is that current justifications have the potential to become tomorrow's reasons. For example, a dieter may explain eating an outrageously sweet dessert with reference to a fleeting sense of "low blood sugar." From then on, the subjective sense of low blood sugar becomes the reason for eating outrageous desserts in the future.

For the purposes of this chapter, the focus is on reasons and justifications that motivate the satisfaction response and later behaviors. This will require identification of consumers' reasoning—their attributions, whether right or wrong—for the consumption outcomes that have occurred. Firms may wish to correct or manage attributions through communication, but that is not a concern at this point. Corrected attributions remain as attributions, are analyzed in the same manner, and have similar predictable effects on later thoughts, satisfaction, and behavior.

Attributions to the Person or Situation

The distinction between person and situation is one of the main tenets of attribution theory. For example, assume that the consumer is an observer watching a TV documentary on consumer fraud. The commentator explains how a typical couple was cheated in a pyramid sales scheme whereby the couple joins a merchandising organization by paying a sponsor. The couple then becomes a sponsor and is encouraged to recruit others into the plan. These new recruits pay initiation fees similar to that paid by the original couple. Such schemes require the acquisition of a substantial inventory of merchandise. Selling merchandise, however, is not the main source of profit; recruiting other participants is. The original couple does not break even until the individuals it recruits also succeed in recruiting others. When the pyramid breaks down, all "investors" are left with unsold inventory and unrecoupable sponsor fees.[7]

Who is responsible for the couple's misfortune? The hypothetical consumer watching the documentary may proclaim that, although the originators of the scheme were less than forthcoming with success rates and other relevant information, the hapless couple featured in the documentary is guilty for being naive and greedy. Clearly the blame has been aimed at the person (the couple) and not the situation (an illegal pyramid sales scheme).

Reversing the situation, now assume that it was the TV viewer who was defrauded and is asked to assign blame in this instance. In all likelihood, the consumer would reverse the attribution in order to generate self-sympathy and would focus external blame on the mean-spirited perpetrators of the pyramid scheme. The viewer thus now concludes that it was the situation and not the person that should be blamed. This phenomenon—attributing negative outcomes of others to themselves while attributing negative outcomes happening to oneself to the situation—is rather pervasive, as shall be seen. Would the reverse have occurred if the outcomes had been positive (e.g., winning a lottery)? To answer this question and to gain insight into how consumers view consumption outcomes, research on the fundamental attribution error and other attribution biases is examined.

Biases and "Errors of Judgment" in Attribution

The fundamental attribution error is one of the biases that individuals bring to bear on judgments. These biases exist for numerous reasons, but one compelling argument is that consumers, like individuals in other pursuits in life, are "cognitive misers." That is, individuals are prone to accept orderly, preconceived explanations for events that do not greatly conflict with the facts of the events, rather than to entertain rival hypotheses that must be tested one against the other.[8] For example, if a mighty oak tree on a homeowner's property dies, it is easier to accept the explanation of old age than to entertain the possibilities of disease, insect infestation, or ground pollution as reasons.

Alternatively, if a cake mix fails to produce the moist, rich dessert featured on the packaging, it is easier for the cook to blame the food processor for a poor product, the merchant for improper storage, errors in the directions, or the homeowner's oven than it is to admit that the cook was at fault for not following directions or setting the oven at the wrong temperature. In both examples, the consumer used biased reasoning. Discussion now turns to how these biases might operate in the case of attributions to stable characteristics of people (herewith called dispositions) and of attributions to environmental events (situations).

Table 11.1 has been constructed to illustrate how individuals might view responsibility for

Table 11.1

Biased Attributions to Self and Other Under Different Outcome Conditions

Row	Outcome	Self	Other
1	Outcomes generally	Dispositional	Dispositional
2	To self versus to other	Situational	Dispositional
3	Positive to self/other	Dispositional	Situational
4	Negative to self/other	Situational	Dispositional

outcomes of decisions. The notion of perceptions of one's own outcomes (self) versus those of others has been adopted to relate to the pyramid scheme example provided here. Table 11.1 shows four types of analysis. The first row examines whether individuals view life outcomes generally as emanating from situational (environmental) factors or dispositional (individual) factors. This is a ceteris paribus analysis; the specifics of the decision are not considered. In the second row, the focus shifts to self-outcomes and others' outcomes analyzed separately. That is, do consumers generally view the causes of their outcomes versus those of others as resulting from situational or dispositional factors? In rows 3 and 4, the effect of the valence of the outcome is examined. Row 3 analyzes the effect of positive outcomes to self and others, while row 4 analyzes the effect of negative outcomes. The conclusions are drawn from a large number of studies.[9]

The conclusions in the first row show that individuals generally believe that people are largely responsible for their own destiny. There is an overriding tendency for individuals to attribute outcomes in life as reflective of characteristic dispositions. This conclusion changes, however, when self-outcomes are specifically targeted and contrasted with the outcomes of others.

From the earliest investigations to the present, research shows that attributions for the same outcome are differentially assigned depending on whether the outcome is to self or to others. Self-outcomes tend to be situationally attributed (allocentric) while other outcomes tend to be dispositionally attributed (idiocentric).[10] This phenomenon, known as the *fundamental attribution error*, was variously proposed by a number of theorists. For example, there is a pervasive tendency for actors [the self] to attribute their actions to situational requirements, whereas observers [of others] tend to attribute the same actions to stable personal dispositions."[11] The apparent reason for this conclusion is that the perceiver's attention is differentially directed when focus is on self or on other. Some individuals perceive their environment and do not focus on themselves. Other individuals are sufficiently unique, however, that attention is focused on the person, not the environment; the environment provides a measure of information overload in this context. In Heider's terms, others' behavior may "engulf the total field."[12]

Now, what happens when the outcome of self or other is positive as opposed to negative? Generally, positive outcomes to self are interpreted according to an egocentric bias and result in self-serving attributions.[13] Individuals are prone to take credit for their own accomplishments, but unfortunately are not so charitable with others. Others' successes are may be viewed with a sense of envy, resulting in a larger component of situational attribution than the perceivers would attribute to themselves.

The situation reverses when explanations for negative events are required. In an ego-protective manner, individuals are prone to ascribe their own failings to situational reasons and to ascribe others' failings to characteristics of the individual. This is seen in the example of the TV viewer and the victims of a pyramid scheme. In fact, the general tendency to take credit for success and blame others for failure has been found in numerous contexts, including sports outcomes and annual company reports. In sports, the media (as observers) speak of winning teams and losing coaches. In the corporate world, chief executive officers (as actors) speak of superb leadership in profitable times and unfortunate economic climates in leaner years. And, in the aggregate where no specific person can be targeted, the media "find" favorable economic news to explain increases in stock prices and the inevitable unfavorable happenings in commerce for stock declines.[14]

Why are these occurrences so regularly observed, particularly for attributions to self? As noted, individuals have subconscious strivings to maintain their self-esteem. Two of these motivations have been proposed in the literature: self-enhancement, which is used after positive outcomes to bolster one's ego, and self-protection, which is used after negative outcomes to ward off self-criticism and, perhaps, the criticism of others. These dual processes have been referred to in the context of self-regulating one's emotional state, thereby maintaining a general sense of well being. Unfortunately, motivational explanations for attributions to the fate of others tend to dwell on their personal failings, an occurrence outside the present discussion but widely observable nonetheless.[15]

It is important to note that the conclusions in Table 11.1 are tendencies, not absolute descriptions. That is, individuals tend to make external or situational attributions for their failures, for example, more than dispositional attributions. A 60/40 ratio of situational to dispositional attributions in this case would satisfy the conclusion drawn, despite the 40 percent of cases that violate the generalization. In fact, some researchers have questioned the generality of the conclusions and have proposed moderating conditions, while others have shown differences in attributional style for the same outcome.[16]

Although the differential attributions to self and other, as described here, are interesting and illustrative of the inherent biases in human judgment, the focus in this book is directed toward the individual consumer's reaction to consumption outcomes. At this point, the attribution process with reference to the actor and not the observer is explored further. In doing so, a more elaborate scheme of attributional processing that incorporates a different perspective on the attribution dimensions is described.

THE WEINER FRAMEWORK

Of the scholars who elaborated on Heider's original theorizing, Weiner has been one of the most influential in fostering research extensions and application to diverse areas. As most fully expressed in its book-length versions, his work differs from other frameworks in that it focuses on the intrinsic dimensions of attribution and not on the distinction between actors and observers.[17]

The Three Dimensions

As described in the earliest of accounts, analyses of attribution data focused primarily on an internal (to the individual) versus an external distinction. This dimension, referred to as the locus (as in location) of causality, is similar to the dispositional/situational difference in Table 11.1 where outcomes are attributed either to something within the person or to some outside agent.

Weiner provided additional insight on the phenomenon of attribution, basing his approach on responses of subjects to episodes of success and failure in academic achievement. When students' success and failure responses were subjected to content analysis, first one and then later two and three dimensions were discovered. This finding occurred regardless of whether the accounts dealt

Table 11.2

The Weiner Attribution Framework

	Internal locus		External locus	
	Stable	Unstable	Stable	Unstable
Uncontrollable	Aptitude	Mood	Task difficulty	Luck
Controllable	Motivation	Effort	Task assignment	Assistance

with success or failure. In agreement with other early works, the first dimension was clearly the internal/external locus distinction.

Further analysis showed that a second dimension was needed because some internal causes could be considered stable and predictable (e.g., scholastic aptitude or skill) while others were highly variable (event-specific study effort expended for a designated test). Likewise, some external causes were stable (e.g., the difficulty of a particular subject matter) while others were variable (the instructor or a particular examination). Thus, stability was found to further distinguish the nature of attributions made by Weiner's subjects.

In still further analysis, a third dimension—controllability—was added to account for variables that could be modified by the actor or an external agent. For example, effort is controllable while aptitude is not. Similarly, the time spent on any one examination question is controllable, while the scholastic abilities of the other students are not. This dimension was found to be largely independent of the first two, so that it makes an additional, unique contribution to explaining attributions of success and failure. In fact, this third dimension has been expanded or subsumed under a number of other theoretical perspectives that are expounded on at length in related disciplines.[18]

This three-component dimensionality has been subjected to testing and found to be reliably replicated. Other results have suggested additional dimensions, including globality (whether the cause is universal across situations as opposed to unique to the situation at hand), changeability (whether the actor can change the forces affecting the outcome), and intentionality (whether the actor intended the outcome to occur).[19] These same findings, however, also showed that change-ability and intentionality were highly related to the original controllability dimension and could be considered similar in effect. Only globality appeared distinct. This dimension, however, is not particularly relevant for consumption situations in which focus is directed to specific products and services.

If each of Weiner's three dimensions is viewed as dichotomous, such that it can be categorized as present or absent, then Table 11.2 results. This representation is common and can be found in many sources. The cell entries reflect the academic context of Weiner's work.

Consumer Interpretations

As applied to consumer contexts, the Weiner framework nicely describes the main attribution mechanisms consumers may use to describe purchase outcomes. For example, the internal/external dimension is easily interpreted in terms of the consumer and others involved in purchasing and consumption, including merchants, salespeople, and other consumers. The controllability dimension reflects the power available to consumers and merchants, including the price the consumer is willing to pay and the price asked by the retailer.[20] Finally, stability reflects the inherent uncertainty faced by both parties to the transaction, including the consistency of product and service quality and the availability of merchandise.

To show how adaptable the Weiner framework is to consumption experiences, the attributions in the eight cells of Table 11.2 can be shown to pertain without modification to the purchase of a complex product. For example, full-size bicycles for adults can range in price from a mere $100 to literally thousands of dollars. Imagine two consumers, one having a good experience selecting a bike and one having a bad experience. For ease of discussion, assume that the pleased consumer attributes the good outcome to internal reasons and that the unhappy consumer attributes the unfortunate outcome to external causes. The pleased consumer reports the reasons for finding a great bike as follows (specific attributions are shown in parentheses):

> I've always been a biker and have acquired a great deal of experience (aptitude). This was to be the best bike that I've ever owned, and I wanted to do everything right (motivation). I did a lot of reading and shopped a lot of stores (effort). Finally, I found what I thought would be a good buy, and it just felt right (mood). Just as I knew I would be, I am delighted with my purchase.

The second consumer, having suffered through a much more negative experience, reports the following:

> My friends convinced me to buy a bike even though I didn't know too much about bicycles. As a result, I knew that this would be a risky decision (task difficulty). To make matters worse, the only stores I knew that sold bikes were the big discount stores (task assignment). I didn't receive much help from the salespeople, who didn't seem to know much about bikes anyway (assistance). As luck would have it, they didn't have my size, but I went ahead and bought a bike anyway, thinking I'd get used to it (luck). I haven't, and I wish I hadn't made this purchase.

These two examples illustrate the economy of the Weiner classification system. In the example of the fortunate consumer, all attributions were internal and were paired with all specific combinations of stability and controllability. This was also true for the second example except that the attributions were external. This second consumer seemed to be buffeted by other forces such as unhelpful friends, unfamiliarity with specialty bike stores, poor sales help, and (bad) luck. Although the eight cells in Table 11.2 describe most types of attributions, in actuality there are many more that consumers can generate if greater detail is desired at the cost of information overload.[21] The primary benefit of Weiner's classification system is that larger sets of attributions can be conveniently framed within a smaller number of meaningful and actionable categories.

At this point, a review and new sampling of studies in consumer behavior that have examined attribution effects in postpurchase contexts are presented. Later, the primary situation giving rise to attributional processing will be detailed to provide insight as to when attributions will affect postpurchase judgments. But first note that there is an embedded fourth dimension in the Weiner matrix, that of success/failure, as in the bicycle consumer examples. Theoretically, this success/failure dichotomy could be added as a fourth level of analysis, but is not a dimension per se. Such a modification would not change the basic three dimensions, but would add to the list of consequences of the attributions. This point is noted here because much of attribution work in marketing has examined product failure where the attributions differ markedly from those of success.

POSTPURCHASE MARKETING EXAMPLES

In 1988, much of the consumer-related research on attribution was reviewed.[22] This paper remains the definitive work on the topic, although studies continue to be generated, albeit at a rate not indicative of its relevance to the field. Much of this attribution work in consumer behavior has examined the effect of attribution on a number of mixed consequences. Some studies examine the focus of the consumer's reaction, usually whether blame is directed at the merchant or the self. Others look at future consequences of attribution, such as whether the consumer intends to rebuy the product. Still others examine the redress preferences of consumers. Occasionally, satisfaction has been investigated, but not typically as a primary dependent variable.

The following discussion of these mixed investigations is broken down by attribution dimension. Comments on the consequences of attributions appear within each section. After these studies are reviewed, a framework describing how attribution may operate within the expectancy disconfirmation model of satisfaction will be presented, as this will formally link attribution to the satisfaction response.

Locus of Causality

The greatest amount of work and most consistent findings stem from analysis of the locus attribution dimension, particularly as defined by the internal/external dichotomy. Locus is now generally subsumed under assignment of responsibility. This has implications for, among other things, expectations for the assumption of redress. For example, in an intriguing example of the actor-observer distinction, researchers asked four groups of people to assign causality to failure situations described in prepared scenarios.[23] The four groups—consisting of ordinary automobile drivers, automobile mechanics, clothing shoppers, and clothing salespeople—were asked to identify the most likely explanation for the general failure categories of automobile breakdowns after repair and defective clothing (broken seams). The modal category assignments for responsibility are summarized as follows:

Individuals were prone to blame the service or marketing entity unless they identified with that entity or its representative. Even employees (mechanics and salespeople) blamed the nonconsumer *if* the problem occurred in the alternative profession. Consider, now, the potential for conflict in complaint situations that these results pose. If consumers are prone to blame the marketer, and the marketer's representative (customer service representative) is prone to blame the consumer, then a necessarily inharmonious encounter will ensue. Astute companies are sensitive to this problem and train their representatives accordingly. A variation of this type of training is the familiar policy that "the customer is always right." Further elaboration on redress options appears in Chapter 14.

Because the locus dimension targets assignment of responsibility for failure (and success), it should not be surprising that the internal/external dimension is strongly related to a number of postpurchase responses, particularly those having implications for blame assessments, including those of self and other. In this regard, consumers willing to shoulder blame (and credit) for their purchasing mishaps do redirect negative affect away from the vendor.[24] These affects, mostly involving anger, result in the usual responses, complaining and negative word of mouth, which are part of the redress and/or cathartic process. A number of studies find that the greater the degree of external attribution, the more redress is expected from external agents—including retailers, manufacturers, and third parties—and the more consumers communicate to firms and other consumers. In contrast, it has been found that as a greater number of self-attributions are generated, the more likely it is that consumers will remain reticent when dissatisfied.[25]

Controllability

Controllability is discussed before stability because research shows that this attribution dimension and its consequences frequently interact with locus and, as noted, have become one of the more applied of the attribution dimensions. Within consumption, however, it may be that controllability is more closely intertwined with locus than it is generally, because consumers are unlikely to have great control over external agents (manufacturers, retailers), while these marketing entities are just as unlikely to be able to control the activities of consumers. Thus, research frequently finds this locus-controllability interaction. In fact, controllability would appear to be undefined unless attributional locus has been assigned. Uncontrollability, however, need not have a definite locus since events without known causes are, by implication, not under the actor's control. The available studies in marketing, mostly with regard to the consequences of controllability, provide consumers with real or hypothetical external agents as part of the methodology.

When failures are viewed as controllable, blame is targeted to the perceived agent who had control. In marketing, the agent is typically the consumer (as self) or a marketing entity, such as a merchant. Obviously, if the merchant is deemed responsible and, additionally, is perceived as acting with intent (e.g., fraud) or negligence (e.g., a restaurant serving improperly cooked food), then strong emotional reactions are generated beyond what would occur if the same outcome were unintentional (e.g., undetectable contamination in food delivered to a grocery). In the latter case, external locus of causality would be evident, but controllability would not. Studies show that controllability is related to complaining and even retribution toward the firm.[26]

Waiting or delay is a maddening aspect of most services, retail stores, and even mail (or e-mail) order. An interesting early study of airline travelers with delayed flights demonstrates that the control dimension is related to emotional response, in this case anger. If the travelers felt that the airline could have foreseen and avoided the departure delay (as opposed to weather-related delays, for example), they directed their frustration toward the airline. This, of course, applies to all waiting scenarios, and an entire literature on queuing theory has emerged as a result.[27]

Finally, one researcher shows direct effects of controllability of still another sort in a failure context on consumer dissatisfaction.[28] Using travel agencies as a research context, the author found that "messy" and unorganized agencies that failed to find the lowest fare for a flight were held more accountable than agencies with an orderly, neat appearance. Presumably, subjects attributed the disorganization as the reason for the pricing errors.

Stability

The stability of the causal agent is important to the consumer because it signals whether the same problem (or success) can be expected in the future or whether the event was a fluke and, thus, unlikely to be repeated. This is an important dimension because stability affects both the antecedents and the consequences of postpurchase reactions. Because stability and uncertainty are related, the consumer's future expectations will be affected. Observations of stable performance on the part of product or service or the firm will create greater confidence in the future level of expected performance. Similarly, unstable performance reduces confidence, expands the range of performance, and brings lower and negative performance outcomes into consideration.

This creates a ripple effect in that consumers will try to protect themselves against future loss. Not only will their future intentions be affected but so will redress preferences. For example, if consumers attribute product failure to unstable causes, they are likely to accept an exchange and try the product again. However, if the attribution is to a stable cause, refunds will be preferred.

Additionally, negative word of mouth in the form of warnings is prompted by attributions of stable failure. And it does not need to be emphasized that satisfaction is unlikely—even if the outcome is positive—when the outcome is viewed as a fluke, as in the weather-related air-travel example.[29]

Many of the previous studies have been in the context of product failure. Generally, successes serve to increase consumers' confidence in their own behavior, even if they know that it is due to circumstance or luck.[30] Perhaps this is the reason that rare positive events such as those eliciting delight do not warrant the level of attributional focus seen here. At the other extreme, evidence is accumulating for the emotion of attribution-induced anger and its related consequence of blame.[31] In postpurchase research, the piecemeal nature of this evidence is unfortunate, because attributions are natural reactions of individuals' efforts to understand the reasons for consumption outcomes and are important for the consequences of further consumption processing. Thus, the attribution process (including the special case of a lack of attributional processing) is a mediating phenomenon between observations of performance outcomes and a number of postpurchase behaviors of immediate consequence to marketers.

To stimulate further investigation of this process and to provide a framework for what future investigations may show, discussion continues in more general terms, using as a guide the social psychology literature, as was done in the first part of this chapter. Two questions are explored in greater detail. The first concerns conditions that foster attribution processing and when it should not occur. The second discusses the consequences, particularly the affective consequences, of attributions. This will bring discussion closer to the nature of the satisfaction/dissatisfaction response and the focus of the next chapter.

THE CAUSAL BASIS FOR ATTRIBUTIONS

In the spirit of studying causal ascription, or the whys of outcomes, a fair question is this: Why do attributions occur—what is their cause? The first part of the answer is that attributions occur whenever consumers are primed to reflect on the origins of an outcome. Once they are primed, the question of why they should pursue attribution reasoning becomes relevant. In this context, it has already been noted that successes may not generate attributional processing because they are, in most instances, foregone conclusions in the minds of consumers. Of further interest is the fact that failures may not be processed if (1) the failure was not significant to the consumer (e.g., a fireplace starter does not light, prompting the consumer to use a match), or (2) the failure was expected (e.g., not winning a lottery).

These examples illustrate the point that attribution requires a motivating stimulus, and a fair amount of literature now suggests that anything unusual that stimulates people's attention to the outcome will bring on causal search. This phenomenon is exacerbated by involvement (in the usual sense) and even personality predispositions that may bring about excessive search (overattribution).[32] Although individual differences, particularly culture, are known to greatly affect the incidence of attribution, this topic is much beyond what is offered here. Suffice it to say that the evidence conclusively shows that Western cultures, as opposed to Eastern (more collectivist) societies, are more sensitive and willing to form external attributions.[33]

The Role of Disconfirmation

As is generally accepted in the literature, the most prominent causal agent for the onset of attribution is disconfirmation of expectations; this observation pertains whether the disconfirming evidence is thought to be discrepant or "familiar"; sharing some characteristics with regret.[34] The disconfirmation process described in this agency literature is identical to the way it is discussed in the satisfaction literature, thereby providing a strong rationale for the study of attribution in the context of consumer satisfaction and dissatisfaction.[35]

This disconfirmation-to-attribution finding has taken a number of forms, as noted. In its most general mode, events that do not conform to expectations are thought to produce attributional processing and, in the absence of information regarding causality, further search for an explanation of the event. In an effort to elaborate on the many variations of nonconforming events, writers have explored the nature of unexpectedness, and a number of conclusions can be drawn. Weiner has previously reviewed this literature and has summarized the findings.[36] Generally, three major categories of causes exist, with a number of variations:

Category A: Unexpectedness

1. Positive surprise
2. Negative surprise
3. Novelty
4. "Unexplainable" (difficult to interpret) events
5. Unexplained internal arousal (including stress)

Category B: Unattained or frustrated goals (including negative outcomes)

1. Failure generally
2. Unfulfilled achievements
3. Unfulfilled desires
4. Rejection (e.g., social)
5. Losses (e.g., games, gambles)
6. Inequity

Category C: Other

1. Unusual successes
2. Outcomes of great importance

It should be immediately clear that all forms of unexpectedness instigate attributional search. More generally, this tendency can be viewed as an attempt to understand the reasons behind the unexpected so that the event becomes more predictable in the future and the element of negative surprise, in particular, can be avoided.

The desire to understand and, in the future, avoid unattained goals—the second major category—stems from the more universal desire to pursue pleasure and avoid pain. Of interest is the observation that implicit goals, such as the pursuit of fairness and equity, have also been shown to instigate attributional processing when frustrated.[37] Note that negativity is a central feature of unattainment, but is not necessarily a feature of unexpectedness. The assumption of negativity is embedded in the concept of unattained goals and desires, but is less perfectly correlated with unexpectedness. Some unexpected events are negative (negative surprises, unexplained arousal such as anxiety), but this is not a universal assumption. This point is noted here because some accounts of the causes of attributions cite negativity as one of the central dimensions. It is true, however, that negative and unexpected events are extremely provocative of attributional processing, including, again, unexpected goal frustration—a central theme in the personal control literature.[38] The effects appear to be interactive in the sense that a great amount of processing occurs for this combination of unpleasant surprise.

The third category in the list allows for successes and important outcomes. Success may instigate attributional processing, but at a much less likely level when compared to failure. More typically, these types of attributions are accompanied by success, where success attributions tend to be more internal, stable, and controllable. There are many examples from the educational attainment and sports psychology literature. When external attributions are made, gratitude or thankfulness is expressed.[39] In general, the more expected and everyday the outcome, the less likely it is to instigate causal search, if at all.

The Model

Based on the results of the studies noted here and other sources, Weiner proposed a general model of the attribution process whereby individually experienced outcomes elicit evaluations with two components.[40] In this scheme, an initial reaction is proposed wherein the general emotional tone of an event (e.g., happiness over success or sadness over failure) is established, a stage referred to as outcome-dependent, attribution-independent. The first part of this stage is referred to as a primary evaluation (e.g., good for me, bad for me). This primary evaluation results in a primary affective reaction. Generally, this will be a state of pleasure or displeasure in response to the goodness or badness of the event.

This first-stage sequence is accompanied by a secondary appraisal involving attributions. As noted, the attributions are categorized by their dimensionality—namely, locus (internal/external), stability, and controllability. It is not clear how closely the primary and secondary evaluations appear in a time sequence, for this aspect of the Weiner model has not been vetted. The evaluations may appear concurrently, differing only in level of abstraction, or the primary stage may, indeed, precede the secondary appraisal. For now, it will be assumed that they are nearly parallel processes occurring, perhaps, "spontaneously."

To show how this initial sequence fits into a disconfirmation-based satisfaction framework, the attribution model discussed so far can be wedded to the expectancy disconfirmation framework. This combined model constitutes the first part of this author's consumption processing conceptualization, which is more fully discussed in Chapter 13.[41] The combined disconfirmation-attribution model is shown in Figure 11.1.

Note that disconfirmation is a function of expectations (or some other normative standard to fit the wider range of unexpectedness found in attribution), used as comparative referents for the relevant outcome set. Here, disconfirmation, the basic comparative process, is expanded to include the two primary disconfirmation dimensions revealed in the attribution literature, unexpectedness and goal frustration. This begins the two-appraisal model as introduced.

Elaborated more fully here, the primary reaction to the outcome is an outcome-dependent, attribution-independent evaluation, so called because it does not involve the attribution process. In a sense, this reflects an "outcomes-only" assessment similar to the performance-only model of satisfaction in Chapter 2. In the present context, individuals observe the outcome and respond with a good (for me) or bad (for me) reaction. Generally, the overall tenor of these reactions will be of the happy/sad or pleasant/unpleasant variety. The secondary reaction is generated by the disconfirmation response, which begins the attribution process. It is necessary to sequence the attribution process from the primary appraisal assessment in order to reflect the nature of the outcome—whether it was a success or failure. As noted, both theory and empirics show major differences between attribu-

Figure 11.1 **The Disconfirmation-Attribution Affect Sequence**

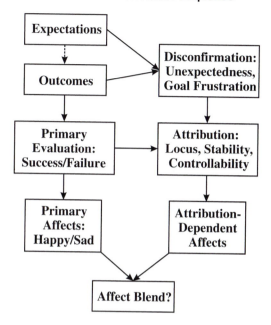

tions for success and failure. The final affective response is referred to as a blend, because it is not possible to determine without reference to a specific situation whether the primary and secondary affects will be congruent (happy, pride; angry, blame) or incongruent, referred to earlier as "mixed" (happy, guilty—as in positive inequity, discussed in Chapter 8). More detail is presented next.

Attribution-Dependent Affect

Although emotion (affect) is the topic of the next chapter, it has been introduced here to complete the attribution sequence. For simplicity, discussion of the attribution dimensions is restricted to one, locus, maintaining as before the success or failure distinction. This will limit discussion of possible affective responses to four situations: attributions of success and failure to both internal and external causes. Weiner adopts the "first cognitive, then affective" sequence in the context of attributional processing. The primacy of affect or cognition in this sequence is not fully resolved in psychology, but is less controversial here since attributions are outcome-dependent. That is, events must be perceived by a person's sensory systems and processed cognitively before attributions are assigned,[42] an assumption that is relaxed in the next chapter.

Weiner observes that his framework is intended to be perfectly general and not limited to specific contexts. However, much of the original research took place in achievement (academic) settings, and the resulting affects are characteristic of that context; typical results appear in Table 11.3. As shown, these are a condensation of the results of early studies in the field and continue to be reported as representative.[43] Note, again, that analysis is restricted to locus attributions under success and failure settings. The next chapter expands this list of affects markedly.

Note that these attributions are consistent with the attribution dimensionality argument. Successes attributed to oneself should result in pride and a sense of personal competence. When success

Table 11.3

Typical Locus Attributions Under Success and Failure

	Success	Failure
Internal attribution	Pride	Guilt
	Competence	Regret
External attribution	Gratitude	Anger
	Thankfulness	Blame

is attributed to others (as in assistance) or to unexpected outside interventions (such as a tip from a stranger on a horse race), both gratitude and thankfulness (reflecting the less personal nature of "free advice") should result. Failure attributions operate in the same way. A loss or failure caused by others is shown to result in anger and blame. Finally, internally attributed failure results in guilt and regret (over forgone alternatives).

Incidentally, satisfaction (actually, personal satisfaction) is a frequently mentioned affect in the Weiner paradigm, particularly for success. This provides early evidence of the influence of attribution in the satisfaction process, and the marketing evidence, already discussed, has also shown this to be the case. The satisfaction concept as described in this book, however, is a more complex phenomenon than that represented by success in academic contexts, which is more akin to accomplishment. Nonetheless, it does show that satisfaction is a consequence of attributional processing, although the pattern of influence may be indirect.

ATTRIBUTION MEASUREMENT

This chapter concludes with suggestions for measuring attribution in the satisfaction process. Although attribution measurement is rarely performed in satisfaction surveys, discussion of the attribution phenomenon and the conclusions from prior research presented in this chapter strongly suggest that management would benefit from knowing what attributions its consumers assign for satisfactory and unsatisfactory product or service performance. The reason should be clear. Because the attributional perceptions of the actor and observer are frequently at variance, the consumer as actor is very likely to draw different attributional conclusions from the manager as observer.

This situation can take many forms. The example of the complainant and customer service response has been noted in the context of assignment of responsibility (blame). Other examples include interactions between customer and salesperson and between customer and service provider. Perhaps the most important difference in attributional perceptions, however, exists between the firm's management and its customer base. Research shows, for example, that successful performance will be differentially attributed to the customer by the customer and to the firm by the firm's management. Failure, however, will tend to be attributed to the firm by the customer and to some other entity (e.g., suppliers, but also including the customer) by the firm. This would suggest, perhaps, that both the consumer's perspective and management's perspective should be sampled.

Qualitative Measures

Unfortunately, the measures that have been developed appear in the external literatures where the focus is on nonconsumer topics. In these external areas, when feasible, a widely used form of measure is the coding of verbal protocols.[44] Here, participants are asked to write down why they believe an outcome occurred; the researcher then interprets the respondents' transcriptions and codes the answers as to the degree of internality, stability, and controllability. This is obviously not practical in the typical satisfaction survey employing large sample sizes and parsimonious survey lengths. Rather, a standard format is needed for scales that can be easily understood by the average consumer and the results of which can be easily understood by management.

The marketing and consumer behavior literatures have not developed attribution measurement to this level, unfortunately. The attribution measures that have been used in consumer behavior, admittedly dated, lack standardization and have generally minimal psychometric properties. Readers will find only manipulations, single-item scales, or lists of blame assignments with specific entities identified. Of the most recent, the three items used focus primarily on merchant locus and measured responsibility, fault, and blame. While these capture the essence of assignability, further development is needed.[45]

Standard Scales

Although other formats have been proposed, the causal dimension scale has been well received in the psychological literature. Validity and reliability data are available, and a revised version, in which the control dimension has been expanded to separately measure personal versus external control, has been published.[46]

The following is this author's attempt at a version of this scale more adaptable for use in consumption. As shown, the items are grouped by dimension and are all worded in the same direction. Here, low scores represent greater internal locus, greater stability, and greater controllability. To modify this scale to make it more consumer-friendly, the dimension labels in parentheses would be omitted, the items in each dimension would be interspersed, and certain of the items would be reversed. Despite the developmental properties of this scale, it remains awkwardly worded from a consumer standpoint and situation-specific refinement is necessary.

Instructions: Think about the reasons why your product or service experience turned out as it did.

Who or what do you think is responsible for this outcome? The outcome could have occurred because of something you did; something the manufacturer, service provider, merchant, salesperson, advertiser, etc., did; or something in the environment, such as the weather.

Write your answer here: _____

The following items reflect feelings you might have about why the purchase outcome turned out as it did. Circle the number that best reflects your feelings about this outcome.

The outcome:

(Locus dimension)

Reflects an aspect of my behavior	1	2	3	4	5 Reflects an aspect of other persons or things
Occurred because of something I did	1	2	3	4	5 Occurred because of something others did
Was caused by something about me	1	2	3	4	5 Was caused by something else

(Stability dimension)

Outcome will always occur this way	1	2	3	4	5	Unsure the outcome will reoccur this way
Outcome will be the same over time	1	2	3	4	5	Outcome will vary over time
Reason for the outcome will never change	1	2	3	4	5	Reason for the outcome will always differ

(Controllability dimension)

Outcome was controlled by me or others	1	2	3	4	5	Outcome was uncontrolled by me or others
Outcome was intended by me or others	1	2	3	4	5	Outcome was not intended by me or others
Someone is responsible for the outcome	1	2	3	4	5	No one is responsible for the outcome

This rendition focuses the emphasis somewhat from targeting the cause to targeting the outcome and its cause. This shift in emphasis presumes that the cause and its effect (the outcome) are closely linked. Generally, consumers should be able to relate more to outcomes as having causes than to causes per se. As of this writing, this is a speculation, and further conclusions await testing.

At times and on certain topics, the issue of consumer sensitivity to a concept has been of interest. For example, in Chapter 4, disconfirmation sensitivity was discussed in terms of identifying those who are more attuned to processing disconfirmation as opposed to those who accept outcomes without further reference to expectations or other comparative referents. This is also the case with attribution, as evidence on the effect of attributional complexity has shown. To this end, an attributional complexity scale has been formulated and may be of use to firms wishing to explore the substrata of their detractors or complimenters.[47] The authors of the scale refer to these segments as "attributional simpletons or experts." I leave the readers with this information to do with as they choose.

CONCLUSION

This chapter has demonstrated that attribution is a common phenomenon in reactions to events, including consumption experiences. Once initiated, the attribution process results in some predictable patterns of blame (failure) or gratitude (success) assessment. Generally, these patterns will fall within the structure of the locus, stability, and controllability framework. For consumers, these should be predictive of a number of thoughts and actions, most notably the pursuit of redress.

Research has expanded markedly on the topic since the first edition of this book, particularly within consumption scenarios. To an extent, this rebirth largely supports earlier work although in the new context of e-commerce. The principles remain invariant, however, and even Weiner's retrospective, "Attributional Thoughts about Consumer Behavior," bears this out. What is lacking, however, is a measure, easily interpretable by the consumer, for use in surveys with uncomplicated formats. Web surveys, in particular, will require this property, and researchers are encouraged to streamline the somewhat awkward Causal Dimension Scale, essentially unchanged since the 1980s.

Discussion now turns to the affective consequences of attributional conclusions. As shown in a number of works, both within and outside of consumption studies, consumers experience various emotions when they assign attributions. The more severe the outcome, whether it be success or failure, the greater the likelihood of attributional processing and the greater the degree of felt emotion. This allows for an examination of the outcome → disconfirmation → attribution → affect sequence as it plays into the final satisfaction judgment. This last phase of the sequence—affect—is the topic of the next chapter.

NOTES

1. Bonsall, *Disaster in Dearborn*. As of this writing, it is more than fifty years since this marketing effort. As a testimony to its timelessness, Edsel automobile collector clubs are well established.

2. Heider, *Psychology of Interpersonal Relations*. At least one writer traces attribution' origins to the late 1800s. See Van Overwalle, "Test of the Joint Model of Causal Attribution."

3. See Bem, "Self-Perception"; Kelley, "Attribution in Social Interaction"; and Weiner et al., "Perceiving the Causes of Success and Failure."

4. Weiner, "Attributional Thoughts about Consumer Behavior"; Harvey and Weary, "Current Issues in Attribution Theory and Research"; Kelley and Michela, "Attribution Theory and Research," Martinko and Thomson, "Synthesis and Extension of the Weiner and Kelley Attribution Models"; and Weary, Stanley, and Harvey, *Attribution*.

5. Since the first edition of this book, much of what is to follow has become generally accepted as fundamental to attribution theory. Readers desiring to explore the early writings in the field may wish to consult the citations provided in the first edition as well as the additional sources noted here.

6. See Adelman, Ahuvia, and Goodwin, "Beyond Smiling"; Chung-Herrera, Goldschmidt, and Hoffman, "Customer and Employee Views of Critical Service Incidents"; Cowley, "Views from Consumers Next in Line"; Deighton, "Consumption of Performance"; Harris, Mohr, and Bernhardt, "Online Service Failure, Consumer Attributions and Expectations"; and Van Raaij and Pruyn, "Customer Control and Evaluation of Service Validity and Reliability."

7. This is an example of the well-known Ponzi scheme, which has numerous variations. See Zuckoff, *Ponzi's Scheme*.

8. Hansen, "Commonsense Attribution."

9. See, for example, Fiske and Taylor, *Social Cognition*.

10. See Cowley, "Views from Consumers Next in Line"; and Duff and Newman, "Individual Differences in the Spontaneous Construal of Behavior."

11. Jones and Nisbett, "Actor and Observer," p. 80. For a historical perspective on what the authors refer to as "correspondence bias," see Gilbert and Malone, "Correspondence Bias."

12. Heider, *Psychology of Interpersonal Relations*, p. 54.

13. See, for example, Ross and Sicoly, "Egocentric Biases in Availability and Attribution"; and Weary, "Examination of Affect and Egotism as Mediators of Bias in Causal Attributions."

14. Andreassen, "On the Social Psychology of the Stock Market"; Bettman and Weitz, "Attributions in the Board Room"; Biddle and Hill, "Causal Attributions and Emotional Reactions to Outcome in a Sporting Contest"; Lau and Russell, "Attributions in the Sports Pages"; Roesch and Amirkhan, "Boundary Conditions for Self-Serving Attributions"; Wann and Schrader, "Controllability and Stability in the Self-Serving Attributions of Sport Spectators."

15. For a thorough treatment of the assignment of blame, whether to self or others, see Alicke, "Culpable Control and the Psychology of Blame."

16. See, for example, Anderson, "Motivational and Performance Deficits in Interpersonal Settings"; and Block and Funder, "Social Roles and Social Perception."

17. Weiner, *Attributional Theory of Motivation and Emotion* and *Judgments of Responsibility*.

18. See, for example, Kofta, Weary, and Sedek, *Personal Control in Action*; and Weary, Gleicher, and Marsh, *Control Motivation and Social Cognition*.

19. See the summary of studies and conclusions of de Jong, Koomen, and Mellenbergh, "Structure of Causes for Success and Failure."

20. Burton et al., "Role of Attributions in Consumer Perceptions of Retail Advertisements Promoting Price Discounts"; Vaidyanathan and Aggarwal, "Who Is the Fairest of Them All?"

21. See an example using sixty-three causal dimensions in Anderson, "Causal Structure of Situations."

22. Folkes, "Recent Attribution Research in Consumer Behavior."

23. Folkes and Kotsos, "Buyers' and Sellers' Explanations for Product Failure."

24. Boshoff and Leong, "Empowerment, Attribution and Apologising as Dimensions of Service Recovery";

Botti and McGill, "When Choosing Is Not Deciding"; Dubé and Menon, "Multiple Roles of Consumption Emotions in Post-Purchase Satisfaction with Extended Service Transactions"; Harris, Mohr, and Bernhardt, "Online Service Failure, Consumer Attributions and Expectations"; Kaltcheva and Weitz, "Effects of Brand-Consumer Relationships Upon Consumers' Attributions and Reactions"; Maxham and Netemeyer, "Longitudinal Study of Complaining Customers' Evaluations of Multiple Service Failures and Recovery Efforts"; McGill, "Predicting Consumers' Reactions to Product Failure"; Tsiros, Mittal, and Ross, "Role of Attributions in Customer Satisfaction."

25. Curren and Folkes, "Attributional Influences on Consumers' Desires to Communicate about Products"; Folkes, "Consumer Reactions to Product Failure"; Laczniak, DeCarlo, and Ramaswami, "Consumers' Response to Negative Word-of-Mouth Communication"; Machleit and Mantel, "Emotional Response and Shopping Satisfaction"; Richins, "Negative Word-of-Mouth by Dissatisfied Consumers"; Smith, Bolton, and Wagner, "Model of Customer Satisfaction with Service Encounters Involving Failure and Recovery"; Taylor, "Role of Affective States and Locus of Attribution in Evaluations of Service."

26. Burton, Sheather, and Roberts, "Reality or Perception?"; Folkes, "Consumer Reactions to Product Failure"; Hui and Toffoli, "Perceived Control and Consumer Attribution for the Service Encounter"; Van Raaij and Pruyn, "Customer Control and Evaluation of Service Validity and Reliability"; Wann and Schrader, "Controllability and Stability in the Self-Serving Attributions of Sport Spectators."

27. Selected examples in the field of consumer behavior include Folkes, Koletsky, and Graham, "Field Study of Causal Inferences and Consumer Reaction"; Houston, Bettencourt, and Wenger, "Relationship Between Waiting in a Service Queue and Evaluation of Service Quality"; and Taylor, "Waiting for Service."

28. Bitner, "Evaluating Service Encounters."

29. Houston, Bettencourt, and Wenger, "Relationship Between Waiting in a Service Queue and Evaluation of Service Quality"; Hui and Toffoli, "Perceived Control and Consumer Attribution for the Service Encounter"; Tsiros, Mittal, and Ross, "Role of Attributions in Customer Satisfaction"; Wann and Schrader, "Controllability and Stability in the Self-Serving Attributions of Sport Spectators."

30. Darke and Freedman, "Lucky Events and Belief in Luck"; Oliver and DeSarbo, "Response Determinants in Satisfaction Judgments."

31. Alicke, "Culpable Control and the Psychology of Blame"; Creyer and Gürhan, "Who's to Blame?"; Miller and Gunasegaram, "Temporal Order and the Perceived Mutability of Events"; Quigley and Tedeschi, "Mediating Effects of Blame Attributions on Feelings of Anger."

32. León and Hernândez, "Testing the Role of Attribution and Appraisal in Predicting Own and Other's Emotions"; Leyens, Yzerbyt, and Corneille, "Role of Applicability in the Emergence of the Overattribution Bias"; Sanbonmatsu, Akimoto, and Biggs, "Overestimating Causality."

33. Choi, Nisbett, and Norenzayan, "Causal Attribution Across Cultures"; Lee, Hallahan, and Herzog, "Explaining Real-Life Events"; Mattila and Patterson, "Impact of Culture on Consumers' Perceptions of Service Recovery Efforts"; Maxwell, "Biased Attributions of a Price Increase"; and Ybarra and Stephan, "Attributional Orientations and the Prediction of Behavior."

34. Hastie, "Causes and Effects of Causal Attribution"; Johnson, Boyd, and Magnani, "Causal Reasoning in the Attribution of Rare and Common Events"; Lipe, "Counterfactual Reasoning as a Framework for Attribution Theories"; Pyszczynski and Greenberg, "Role of Disconfirmed Expectancies in the Instigation of Attributional Processing"; Pyszczynski, Greenberg, and LaPrelle, "Social Comparison after Success and Failure"; Whittlesea and Williams, "Discrepancy-Attribution Hypothesis: I" and "Discrepancy-Attribution Hypothesis: II"; and Wong and Weiner, "When People Ask 'Why' Questions, and the Heuristics of Attributional Search."

35. Creyer and Gürhan, "Who's to Blame?"; Griffin, Babin, and Attaway, "Anticipation of Injurious Consumption Outcomes and Its Impact on Consumer Attributions of Blame"; Houston, Bettencourt, and Wenger, "The Relationship Between Waiting in a Service Queue and Evaluation of Service Quality"; Stiensmeier-Pelster, Martini, and Reisenzein, "Role of Surprise in the Attribution Process"; Tsiros, Mittal, and Ross, "Role of Attributions in Customer Satisfaction."

36. Weiner, "'Spontaneous' Causal Thinking." Since the Weiner review, an interesting additional facet has been found. The more difficult the attribution *process* (not task difficulty) is, the more attributional effort is expended. See Hamilton et al., "Attribution Difficulty and Memory for Attribution-Relevant Information"; and Stalder and Baron, "Attributional Complexity as a Moderator of Dissonance-Produced Attitude Change."

37. Hegtvedt, Thompson, and Cook, "Power and Equity."

38. See Kofta, Weary, and Sedek, *Personal Control in Action*; and Mizerski, "Attribution Explanation of the Disproportionate Influence of Unfavorable Information."

39. See, for example, Dweck, *Mindset*; and Emmons and McCullough, *Psychology of Gratitude*.

40. Weiner, *Attributional Theory of Motivation and Emotion* and *Judgments of Responsibility*. See, also, Weary, Stanley, and Harvey, *Attribution*.

41. Oliver, "Processing of the Satisfaction Response in Consumption."

42. Anderson and Slusher, "Relocating Motivational Effects."

43. Russell and McAuley, "Causal Attributions, Causal Dimensions, and Affective Reactions to Success and Failure." See, also, Brehm and Brummett, "Emotional Control of Behavior."

44. See Benson, "Attributional Measurement Techniques"; Howard, "Conceptualization and Measurement of Attributions"; and Siegert and Ward, "Factor-Analytic Examination of the Attributional Dimension Scale."

45. See, e.g., Bitner, "Evaluating Service Encounters"; Burton et al., "Role of Attributions in Consumer Perceptions of Retail Advertisements Promoting Price Discounts"; Folkes, "Consumer Reactions to Product Failure"; Folkes and Kotsos, "Buyers' and Sellers' Explanations for Product Failure"; and Maxham and Netemeyer, "Longitudinal Study of Complaining Customers' Evaluations of Multiple Service Failures and Recovery Efforts."

46. Russell, "Causal Dimension Scale"; Russell, McAuley, and Tarico, "Measuring Causal Attributions for Success and Failure"; McAuley, Duncan, and Russell, "Measuring Causal Attributions"; Vallerand and Richer, "On the Use of the Causal Dimension Scale in a Field Setting." The adaptation that follows is from Russell, p. 1143.

47. See Fletcher et al., "Attributional Complexity."

BIBLIOGRAPHY

Adelman, Mara B., Aaron Ahuvia, and Cathy Goodwin. "Beyond Smiling: Social Support and Service Quality." In *Service Quality: New Directions in Theory and Practice*, ed. Roland T. Rust and Richard L. Oliver, 139–171. Thousand Oaks, CA: Sage, 1994.

Alicke, Mark D. "Culpable Control and the Psychology of Blame." *Psychological Bulletin* 126, no. 4 (July 2000): 556–574.

Anderson, Craig A. "The Causal Structure of Situations: The Generation of Plausible Causal Attributions as a Function of Type of Event Situation." *Journal of Experimental Social Psychology* 19, no. 2 (March 1983): 185–203.

———. "Motivational and Performance Deficits in Interpersonal Settings: The Effect of Attributional Style." *Journal of Personality and Social Psychology* 45, no. 5 (November 1983): 1136–1147.

Anderson, Craig A., and Morgan P. Slusher. "Relocating Motivational Effects: A Synthesis of Cognitive and Motivational Effects on Attributions for Success and Failure." *Social Cognition* 4, no. 3 (1986): 270–292.

Andreassen, Paul B. "On the Social Psychology of the Stock Market: Aggregate Attributional Effects and the Regressiveness of Prediction." *Journal of Personality and Social Psychology* 53, no. 3 (September 1987): 490–496.

Bem, Daryl J. "Self-Perception: An Alternative Interpretation of Cognitive Dissonance Phenomena." *Psychological Review* 74, no. 3 (May 1967): 183–200.

Benson, Mark J. "Attributional Measurement Techniques: Classification and Comparison of Approaches for Measuring Causal Dimensions." *Journal of Social Psychology* 129, no. 3 (June 1989): 307–323.

Bettman, James R., and Barton A. Weitz. "Attributions in the Board Room: Causal Reasoning in Corporate Annual Reports." *Administrative Science Quarterly* 28, no. 2 (June 1983): 165–183.

Biddle, Stuart J.H., and Andrew B. Hill. "Causal Attributions and Emotional Reactions to Outcome in a Sporting Contest." *Personality and Individual Differences* 9, no. 2 (1988): 213–223.

Bitner, Mary Jo. "Evaluating Service Encounters: The Effects of Physical Surroundings and Employee Responses." *Journal of Marketing* 54, no. 2 (April 1990): 69–82.

Block, Jack, and David C. Funder. "Social Roles and Social Perception: Individual Differences in Attribution and Error." *Journal of Personality and Social Psychology* 51, no. 6 (December 1986): 1200–1207.

Bonsall, Thomas E. *Disaster in Dearborn: The Story of the Edsel*. Stanford, CA: Stanford University Press, 2002.

Boshoff, Christo, and Jason Leong. "Empowerment, Attribution and Apologising as Dimensions of Service Recovery: An Experimental Study." *International Journal of Service Industry Management* 9, no. 1 (1998): 24–47.

Botti, Simona, and Ann L. McGill. "When Choosing Is Not Deciding: The Effect of Perceived Responsibility on Satisfaction." *Journal of Consumer Research* 33, no. 2 (September 2006): 211–219.

Brehm, Jack W., and Beverly H. Brummett. "The Emotional Control of Behavior." In *Personal Control in Action: Cognitive and Motivational Mechanisms*, ed. Miroslaw Kofta, Gifford Weary, and Grzegorz Sedek, 133–154. New York: Plenum, 1998.

Burton, Scot, Donald R. Lichtenstein, Abhijit Biswas, and Katherine Fraccastoro. "The Role of Attributions in Consumer Perceptions of Retail Advertisements Promoting Price Discounts." *Marketing Letters* 5, no. 2 (April 1994): 131–140.

Burton, Suzan, Simon Sheather, and John Roberts. "Reality or Perception? The Effect of Actual and Perceived Performance on Satisfaction and Behavioral Intention." *Journal of Service Research* 5, no. 4 (May 2003): 292–302.

Choi, Incheol, Richard E. Nisbett, and Ara Norenzayan. "Causal Attribution Across Cultures: Variation and Universality." *Psychological Bulletin* 125, no. 1 (January 1999): 47–63.

Chung-Herrera, Beth G., Nadav Goldschmidt, and K. Doug Hoffman. "Customer and Employee Views of Critical Service Incidents." *Journal of Services Marketing* 18, no. 4 (2004): 241–254.

Cowley, Elizabeth. "Views from Consumers Next in Line: The Fundamental Attribution Error in a Service Setting." *Journal of the Academy of Marketing Science* 33, no. 2 (Spring 2005): 139–152.

Creyer, Elizabeth H., and Zeynep Gürhan. "Who's to Blame? Counterfactual Reasoning and the Assignment of Blame." *Psychology & Marketing* 14, no. 3 (May 1997): 209–222.

Curren, Mary T., and Valerie S. Folkes. "Attributional Influences on Consumers' Desires to Communicate about Products." *Psychology & Marketing* 4, no. 1 (Spring 1987): 31–45.

Darke, Peter R., and Jonathan L. Freedman. "Lucky Events and Belief in Luck: Paradoxical Effects on Confidence and Risk-Taking." *Personality and Social Psychology Bulletin* 23, no. 4 (April 1997): 378–388.

Deighton, John. "The Consumption of Performance." *Journal of Consumer Research* 19, no. 3 (December 1992): 362–372.

de Jong, Peter F., Willem Koomen, and Gideon J. Mellenbergh. "Structure of Causes for Success and Failure: A Multidimensional Scaling Analysis of Preference Judgments." *Journal of Personality and Social Psychology* 55, no. 5 (November 1988): 718–725.

Dubé, Laurette, and Kalyani Menon. "Multiple Roles of Consumption Emotions in Post-Purchase Satisfaction with Extended Service Transactions." *International Journal of Service Industry Management* 11, no. 3 (2000): 287–304.

Duff, Kimberly J., and Leonard S. Newman. "Individual Differences in the Spontaneous Construal of Behavior: Idiocentrism and the Automatization of the Trait Inference Process." *Social Cognition* 15, no. 3 (Fall 1997): 217–241.

Dweck, Carol S. *Mindset: The New Psychology of Success*. New York: Random House, 2006.

Emmons, Robert A., and Michael E. McCullough. *The Psychology of Gratitude*. New York: Oxford University Press, 2004.

Fiske, Susan T., and Shelley E. Taylor. *Social Cognition*. 2nd ed. New York: McGraw-Hill, 1991.

Fletcher, Garth J.O., Paula Danilovics, Guadalupe Fernandez, Dena Peterson, and Glenn D. Reeder. "Attributional Complexity: An Individual Differences Measure." *Journal of Personality and Social Psychology* 51, no. 4 (October 1986): 875–884.

Folkes, Valerie S. "Consumer Reactions to Product Failure: An Attributional Approach." *Journal of Consumer Research* 10, no. 4 (March 1984): 398–409.

———. "Recent Attribution Research in Consumer Behavior: A Review and New Directions." *Journal of Consumer Research* 14, no. 4 (March 1988): 548–565.

Folkes, Valerie S., Susan Koletsky, and John L. Graham. "A Field Study of Causal Inferences and Consumer Reaction: The View from the Airport." *Journal of Consumer Research* 13, no. 4 (March 1987): 534–539.

Folkes, Valerie S., and Barbara Kotsos. "Buyers' and Sellers' Explanations for Product Failure: Who Done It?" *Journal of Marketing* 50, no. 2 (April 1986): 74–80.

Gilbert, Daniel T., and Patrick S. Malone. "The Correspondence Bias." *Psychological Bulletin* 117, no. 1 (January 1995): 21–38.

Griffin, Mitch, Barry J. Babin, and Jill S. Attaway. "Anticipation of Injurious Consumption Outcomes and Its Impact on Consumer Attributions of Blame." *Journal of the Academy of Marketing Science* 24, no. 4 (Fall 1996): 314–327.

Hamilton, David L., Paul D. Grubb, Deborah A. Acorn, Tina K. Trolier, and Sandra Carpenter. "Attribution Difficulty and Memory for Attribution-Relevant Information." *Journal of Personality and Social Psychology* 59, no. 5 (November 1990): 891–898.

Hansen, Ranald. "Commonsense Attribution." *Journal of Personality and Social Psychology* 39, no. 12 (December 1980): 996–1009.

Harris, Katherine E., Lois A. Mohr, and Kenneth L. Bernhardt. "Online Service Failure, Consumer Attributions and Expectations." *Journal of Services Marketing* 20, no. 7 (2006): 453–458.

Harvey, John H., and Gifford Weary. "Current Issues in Attribution Theory and Research." *Annual Review of Psychology* 35 (1984): 427–459.

Hastie, Reid. "Causes and Effects of Causal Attribution." *Journal of Personality and Social Psychology* 46, no. 1 (January 1984): 44–56.

Hegtvedt, Karen A., Elaine A. Thompson, and Karen S. Cook. "Power and Equity: What Counts in Attributions for Exchange Outcomes?" *Social Psychology Quarterly* 56, no. 2 (June 1993): 100–119.

Heider, Fritz. *The Psychology of Interpersonal Relations.* New York: Wiley, 1958.

Houston, Mark B., Lance A. Bettencourt, and Sutha Wenger. "The Relationship Between Waiting in a Service Queue and Evaluation of Service Quality: A Field Theory Perspective." *Psychology & Marketing* 15, no. 8 (December 1998): 735–753.

Howard, Judith A. "The Conceptualization and Measurement of Attributions." *Journal of Experimental Social Psychology* 23, no. 1 (January 1987): 32–58.

Hui, Michael K., and Roy Toffoli. "Perceived Control and Consumer Attribution for the Service Encounter." *Journal of Applied Social Psychology* 32, no. 9 (September 2002): 1825–1844.

Johnson, Joel T., Kenneth R. Boyd, and Phyllis S. Magnani. "Causal Reasoning in the Attribution of Rare and Common Events." *Journal of Personality and Social Psychology* 66, no. 2 (February 1994): 229–242.

Jones, Edward E., and Richard E. Nisbett. "The Actor and Observer: Divergent Perceptions of the Causes of Behavior." In *Attribution: Perceiving the Causes of Behavior*, ed. Edward E. Jones, David E. Kanouse, Harold H. Kelley, Richard E. Nisbett, Stuart Valins, and Bernard Weiner, 79–94. Morristown, NJ: General Learning Press, 1972.

Kaltcheva, Velitchka, and Barton Weitz. "The Effects of Brand-Consumer Relationships Upon Consumers' Attributions and Reactions." In *Advances in Consumer Research*, ed. Eric J. Arnould and Linda H. Scott, 26:455–462. Provo, UT: Association for Consumer Research, 1999.

Kelley, Harold H. "Attribution in Social Interaction." In *Attribution: Perceiving the Causes of Behavior*, ed. Edward E. Jones, David E. Kanouse, Harold H. Kelley, Richard E. Nisbett, Stuart Valins, and Bernard Weiner, 1–26. Morristown, NJ: General Learning Press, 1972.

Kelley, Harold H., and John L. Michela. "Attribution Theory and Research." *Annual Review of Psychology* 31 (1980): 457–501.

Kofta, Miroslaw, Gifford Weary, and Grzegorz Sedek, eds. *Personal Control in Action: Cognitive and Motivational Mechanisms.* New York: Plenum, 1998.

Laczniak, Russell N., Thomas E. DeCarlo, and Sridhar N. Ramaswami. "Consumers' Response to Negative Word-of-Mouth Communication: An Attribution Theory Perspective." *Journal of Consumer Psychology* 11, no. 1 (2001): 57–73.

Lau, Richard R., and Dan Russell. "Attributions in the Sports Pages." *Journal of Personality and Social Psychology* 39, no. 1 (July 1980): 29–38.

Lee, Fiona, Mark Hallahan, and Thaddeus Herzog. "Explaining Real-Life Events: How Culture and Domain Shape Attributions." *Personality and Social Psychology Bulletin* 22, no. 7 (July 1996): 732–741.

León, Inmaculada, and Juan A. Hernândez. "Testing the Role of Attribution and Appraisal in Predicting Own and Other's Emotions." *Cognition and Emotion* 12, no. 1 (January 1998): 27–43.

Leyens, Jacques-Philippe, Vincent Yzerbyt, and Olivier Corneille. "The Role of Applicability in the Emergence of the Overattribution Bias." *Journal of Personality and Social Psychology* 70, no. 2 (February 1996): 219–229.

Lipe, Marlys Gascho. "Counterfactual Reasoning as a Framework for Attribution Theories." *Psychological Bulletin* 109, no. 3 (May 1991): 456–471.

Machleit, Karen A., and Susan Powell Mantel. "Emotional Response and Shopping Satisfaction: Moderating Effects of Shopper Attributions." *Journal of Business Research* 54, no. 2 (November 2001): 97–106.

Martinko, Mark J., and Neal F. Thomson. "A Synthesis and Extension of the Weiner and Kelley Attribution Models." *Basic and Applied Social Psychology* 20, no. 4 (December 1998): 271–284.

Mattila, Anna S., and Paul G. Patterson. "The Impact of Culture on Consumers' Perceptions of Service Recovery Efforts." *Journal of Retailing* 80, no. 3 (2004): 196–206.

Maxham, James G., III, and Richard G. Netemeyer. "A Longitudinal Study of Complaining Customers' Evaluations of Multiple Service Failures and Recovery Efforts." *Journal of Marketing* 66, no. 4 (October 2002): 57–71.

Maxwell, Sarah. "Biased Attributions of a Price Increase: Effects of Culture and Gender." *Journal of Consumer Marketing* 16, no. 1 (1999): 9–23.

McAuley, Edward, Terry E. Duncan, and Daniel W. Russell. "Measuring Causal Attributions: The Revised Causal Dimension Scale (CDSII)." *Personality and Social Psychology Bulletin* 18, no. 5 (October 1992): 566–573.

McGill, Ann L. "Predicting Consumers' Reactions to Product Failure: Do Responsibility Judgments Follow from Consumers' Causal Explanations?" *Marketing Letters* 2, no. 1 (January 1991): 59–70.

Miller, Dale T., and Saku Gunasegaram. "Temporal Order and the Perceived Mutability of Events: Implications for Blame Assignment." *Journal of Personality and Social Psychology* 59, no. 6 (December 1990): 1111–1118.

Mizerski, Richard W. "An Attribution Explanation of the Disproportionate Influence of Unfavorable Information." *Journal of Consumer Research* 9, no. 3 (December 1982): 301–310.

Oliver, Richard L. "Processing of the Satisfaction Response in Consumption: A Suggested Framework and Research Propositions." *Journal of Consumer Satisfaction, Dissatisfaction and Complaining Behavior* 2 (1989): 1–16.

Oliver, Richard L., and Wayne S. DeSarbo. "Response Determinants in Satisfaction Judgments." *Journal of Consumer Research* 14, no. 4 (March 1988): 495–507.

Pyszczynski, Thomas A., and Jeff Greenberg. "Role of Disconfirmed Expectancies in the Instigation of Attributional Processing." *Journal of Personality and Social Psychology* 40, no. 1 (January 1981): 31–38.

Pyszczynski, Thomas A., Jeff Greenberg, and John LaPrelle. "Social Comparison after Success and Failure: Biased Search for Information Consistent with a Self-Serving Conclusion." *Journal of Experimental Social Psychology* 21, no. 2 (March 1985): 195–211.

Quigley, Brian M., and James T. Tedeschi. "Mediating Effects of Blame Attributions on Feelings of Anger." *Personality and Social Psychology Bulletin* 22, no. 12 (December 1996): 1280–1288.

Richins, Marsha L. "Negative Word-of-Mouth by Dissatisfied Consumers: A Pilot Study." *Journal of Marketing* 47, no. 1 (Winter 1983): 68–78.

Roesch, Scott C., and James H. Amirkhan. "Boundary Conditions for Self-Serving Attributions: Another Look at the Sport Pages." *Journal of Applied Social Psychology* 27, no. 3 (February 1997): 245–261.

Ross, Michael, and Fiore Sicoly. "Egocentric Biases in Availability and Attribution." *Journal of Personality and Social Psychology* 37, no. 3 (March 1979): 322–336.

Russell, Dan "The Causal Dimension Scale: A Measure of How Individuals Perceive Causes." *Journal of Personality and Social Psychology* 42, no. 6 (June 1982): 1137–1145.

Russell, Daniel W., and Edward McAuley. "Causal Attributions, Causal Dimensions, and Affective Reactions to Success and Failure." *Journal of Personality and Social Psychology* 50, no. 6 (June 1986): 1174–1185.

Russell, Daniel W., Edward McAuley, and Valerie Tarico. "Measuring Causal Attributions for Success and Failure: A Comparison of Methodologies for Assessing Causal Dimensions." *Journal of Personality and Social Psychology* 52, no. 6 (June 1987): 1248–1257.

Sanbonmatsu, David M., Sharon A. Akimoto, and Earlene Biggs. "Overestimating Causality: Attributional Effects of Confirmatory Processing." *Journal of Personality and Social Psychology* 65, no. 5 (November 1993): 892–903.

Siegert, Richard J., and Tony Ward. "A Factor-Analytic Examination of the Attributional Dimension Scale." *Australian Journal of Psychology* 47, no. 3 (December 1995): 141–146.

Smith, Amy K., Ruth N. Bolton, and Janet Wagner. "A Model of Customer Satisfaction with Service Encounters Involving Failure and Recovery." *Journal of Marketing Research* 36, no. 3 (August 1999): 356–372.

Stalder, Daniel R., and Robert S. Baron. "Attributional Complexity as a Moderator of Dissonance-Produced Attitude Change." *Journal of Personality and Social Psychology* 75, no. 2 (August 1998): 449–455.

Stiensmeier-Pelster, Joachim, Alice Martini, and Rainer Reisenzein. "The Role of Surprise in the Attribution Process." *Cognition and Emotion* 9, no. 1 (January 1995): 5–31.

Taylor, Shirley. "The Role of Affective States and Locus of Attribution in Evaluations of Service." *Canadian Journal of Administration Sciences* 13, no. 3 (September 1996): 216–225.

———. "Waiting for Service: The Relationship Between Delays and Evaluations of Service." *Journal of Marketing* 58, no. 2 (April 1994): 56–69.

Tsiros, Michael, Vikas Mittal, and William T. Ross Jr. "The Role of Attributions in Customer Satisfaction: A Reexamination." *Journal of Consumer Research* 31, no. 2 (September 2004): 476–483.

Vaidyanathan, Rajiv, and Praveen Aggarwal. "Who Is the Fairest of Them All? An Attributional Approach to Price Fairness Perceptions." *Journal of Business Research* 56, no. 6 (June 2003): 453–463.

Vallerand, Robert J., and François Richer. "On the Use of the Causal Dimension Scale in a Field Setting: A Test with Confirmatory Factor Analysis in Success and Failure Situations." *Journal of Personality and Social Psychology* 54, no. 4 (April 1988): 704–712.

Van Overwalle, Frank. "A Test of the Joint Model of Causal Attribution." *European Journal of Social Psychology* 27, no. 2 (March-April 1997): 221–236.

Van Raaij, W. Fred, and Ad Th.H. Pruyn. "Customer Control and Evaluation of Service Validity and Reliability." *Psychology & Marketing* 15, no. 8 (December 1998): 811–832.

Wann, Daniel L., and Michael P. Schrader. "Controllability and Stability in the Self-Serving Attributions of Sport Spectators." *Journal of Sport Psychology* 140, no. 2 (April 2000): 160–168.

Weary, Gifford. "Examination of Affect and Egotism as Mediators of Bias in Causal Attributions." *Journal of Personality and Social Psychology* 38, no. 2 (February 1980): 348–357.

Weary, Gifford, Faith Gleicher, and Kerry L. Marsh, eds. *Control Motivation and Social Cognition.* New York: Springer-Verlag, 1993.

Weiner, Bernard. *An Attributional Theory of Motivation and Emotion.* New York: Springer-Verlag, 1986.

———. "Attributional Thoughts about Consumer Behavior." *Journal of Consumer Research* 27, no. 3 (December 2000): 382–887.

———. *Judgments of Responsibility: A Foundation for a Theory of Social Conduct.* New York: Guilford, 1995.

———. "'Spontaneous' Causal Thinking." *Psychological Bulletin* 97, no. 1 (January 1985): 74–84.

Weiner, Bernard, Irene Frieze, Andy Kukla, Linda Reed, Stanley Rest, and Robert M. Rosenbaum. "Perceiving the Causes of Success and Failure." In *Attribution: Perceiving the Causes of Behavior*, ed. Edward E. Jones, David E. Kanouse, Harold H. Kelley, Richard E. Nisbett, Stuart Valins, and Bernard Weiner, 95–120. Morristown, NJ: General Learning Press, 1972.

Whittlesea, Bruce W.A., and Lisa D. Williams. "The Discrepancy-Attribution Hypothesis: I. The Heuristic Basis of Feelings of Familiarity." *Journal of Experimental Psychology: Learning, Memory, and Cognition* 27, no. 1 (January 2001): 3–13.

———. "The Discrepancy-Attribution Hypothesis: II. Expectation, Uncertainty, Surprise, and Feelings of Familiarity." *Journal of Experimental Psychology: Learning, Memory, and Cognition* 27, no. 1 (January 2001): 14–33.

Wong, Paul T.P., and Bernard Weiner. "When People Ask 'Why' Questions, and the Heuristics of Attributional Search." *Journal of Personality and Social Psychology* 40, no. 4 (April 1981): 650–663.

Ybarra, Oscar, and Walter G. Stephan. "Attributional Orientations and the Prediction of Behavior: The Attribution-Prediction Bias." *Journal of Personality and Social Psychology* 76, no. 5 (May 1999): 718–727.

Zuckoff, Mitchell. *Ponzi's Scheme: The True Story of a Financial Legend.* New York: Random House, 2005.

CHAPTER 12

EMOTIONAL EXPRESSION IN THE SATISFACTION RESPONSE

From "America's love affair with the car" to the "passion for collecting" to the disdain and indifference people afford items of disposable trash, emotions of various sorts are found among consumers.[1] From the opera aficionado and sports fanatic to the anxious first-time home buyer and reluctant child in the dentist's chair, consumers seek and avoid, long for and fear, and enjoy and regret outcomes of purchasing and consumption. Consumption evokes elements of approach-avoidance, the anticipation of positive and negative outcomes, and the realization of these outcomes. Emotions become part of this realization.

As testament to the "passion" in the realization of driving, for example, an ad for the Chevrolet Camaro SS (Super Sport) likened its six-speed shift transmission to an "escalation" of emotions: (1) anticipation, (2) acceleration, (3) stimulation, (4) exhilaration, (5) jubilation, and (6) rejuvenation. The ad made no mention of any cognitive elements and it is unlikely that Chevrolet conducted advertising research to determine the descriptors best characterizing the emotional meaning of transmission ratios. What explains this? Perhaps nothing more than the copywriter's "feelings."

Some background is necessary at this point. As opposed to its history in general psychology, emotion continues to be a fairly underresearched topic (in an academic sense) in consumer behavior. A reasonable question is: Why did the study of emotion languish for so long before being pursued by consumer researchers? The answer is steeped in the evolution of consumer behavior topics. Emotive consumer research had its roots in the postwar era of the 1950s and 1960s. Lacking a solid scientific base, researchers of the time relied heavily on Freudian principles for explanations of what motivated purchasing and consumption.[2]

This era of "motivation research" persisted into the mid-1960s, when consumer researchers became disenchanted with motivation research explanations, which frequently incorporated sexual fantasy. This disenchantment was the impetus for a number of authors to propose more logical flowchart and decision process models that embraced information-processing themes. There was little room for "softer" explanations for the pursuit of consumption such as joy, ecstasy, aesthetics, and even sensual pleasure, as these themes recalled the earlier motivation research writings.

The pendulum has begun to retrace its path. Led by calls for a paradigm shift and research on emotional themes in advertising, study of the role of emotion is now becoming central to understanding the consumption experience.[3] Why would advertisers emphasize the emotional outcomes of purchasing if consumers could not relate to emotional experiences in consumption? Even the most mundane product (e.g., a safety pin), which by itself connotes no emotional response, can

314

be promoted as having been "Made in America," thereby inducing pride—an emotion—that in all probability could be a deciding factor in choice.

Thus, and as noted in Chapter 3, anticipated emotion can be an effective input to the purchasing decision.[4] It follows, then, that the realization of one or more emotions will be a potent outcome for the consumer's postdecision response. More importantly, emotion has been shown to be linked to the consumer's satisfaction response and, indirectly, to repurchase intent. Discussion of this important topic begins by attempting a definition of emotion and then by tracing the origin of the concept. The applicability of emotion to the satisfaction response is described next, and research findings linking emotion to satisfaction are explained. The chapter concludes with current interpretations of emotion and thoughts on whether satisfaction itself is an emotion.

EMOTION AND ITS ORIGIN

What is emotion, and how does it differ from or coincide with other familiar states such as affect and mood? It might be helpful to begin with what one author and emotion researcher has proposed as the "laws of emotion."[5] These are as follows (with interpretation by this author): Emotions arise when an event is interpreted as having some implication for an individual, a process known as *appraisal*. This event must be perceived as "real" or imagined as so (e.g., suspension of disbelief in movies). The resulting feelings and implications are projected to the future, which may be advantageously or adversely affected, thereby intensifying or diminishing the emotion. Adaptation to these events may be possible, thereby establishing a new baseline for interpretation via extinction or habituation. The onset or implications of the events provide motivation for controllable impulses before or after event manifestation via approach (event seeking), avoidance, or various self-strategies (e.g., coping).

If the above sounds overly cognitive, it is. In contrast, a number of writers had previously distinguished neural or physiologically based emotions as well as emotions consisting of pure affect without the necessity of appraisal.[6] At the initial or biological level, sensorimotor stimuli such as smell, taste, sound, sight, and "derivative" inputs such as facial expression and posture can all bring on emotions (facial expression and posture are also manifestations of specific emotions— e.g., smiling or high fives).[7] With regard to affect- or emotion-instigated emotion, it is frequently observed that emotions can "cascade" into other emotional expressions on the basis of intensity (sadness inducing anger), lateral complementarity (affection inducing pleasure; the absence of affection inducing longing) , or a combination of the two (affection inducing the pleasure of admiration). Figure 12.1 portrays an interpretation of these "law-like" perspectives.

As shown, emotion involves evoking stimuli (events); internal reactions; observable manifestations, including motivation states and behavioral characteristics; and consequences that have adaptive (e.g., coping) or disruptive effects. The internal reactions include core concepts central to emotional response, such as neural and physiological arousal; affective states, including excitement and pleasure or displeasure; and the cognitive processes of appraisal and labeling (to be more fully discussed). Substituting habituation and innovation for adaptation and disruption moves the model one step closer to the satisfaction response.

How can such a wide disparity of interpretation surround such a basic topic as emotion? One possible answer lies in an explanation of the developmental stages of the human brain and its evolutionary basis. While the following presentation falls short of a definitive treatment of these matters, a number of very readable authorities trace discussion to Darwin's and then James's early observations of emotion's origins.[8]

Figure 12.1   **Graphical Portrayal of Emotion Substrates and Substages**

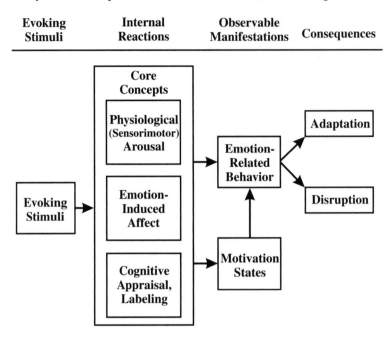

The Brain and Emotion

Essentially, the human brain developed adaptively, with substructures appearing sequentially atop the brain stem and forward of the cerebellum (see Figure 12.2). Before the more advanced development of the cerebrum, the large, folded surface area of the human brain known as gray matter, these primitive substructures were sufficient to ensure the sensations of hunger and thirst and the tendencies toward procreation and preservation, resulting in the pursuit of food, water, and a mate and the fight-or-flight response. These substructures, collectively referred to as the limbic system, contain the pituitary, amygdala, and hypothalamus glands, among others.[9]

Of concern to the present discussion is the recognition that the most primitive emotional responses are governed by the limbic system. These responses include pleasure and displeasure, aggression, fear, and arousal mechanisms, including vigilance. While there is disagreement on the following point, responses generally under control of limbic activity are referred to as basic because they are thought to be universal among mammalian species, susceptible to neuronal and hormonal influence, and not easily subject to cognitive control.

With the growth and enhancement of the cerebrum, which enabled humans to process information cognitively, and the corresponding linkages to the limbic system, these basic responses came under cognitive influence. More precisely, they became subject to cognitive interpretation. This permitted the basic emotions to become more complex and to provide a greater latitude of expression. For example, arousal brought on by the presence of a predator could be channeled from fear to courage, and sadness brought on by someone's demise could be interpreted as personal grief or as compassion for others, or both.

Interestingly, the developmental stages of an infant proceed in essentially the same manner. The newborn infant, with its premature and still developing brain, can first express only distress

Figure 12.2   **Illustration of Brain Structures**

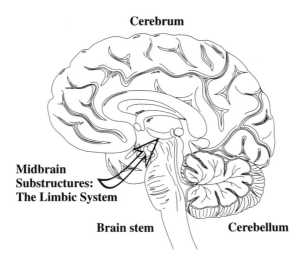

and delight. Later, as the child's cognitive facilities develop, these primitive negative and positive responses begin to bifurcate, becoming cognitively differentiated. Generalized distress later contains fear and anger, and delight later encompasses joy and affection. Each of these emotions will further differentiate throughout the developmental stages of human maturation up to the cognitive integration abilities of the individual.[10]

Problems of definition may now be understood in terms of where "pure" emotion begins to be a prime for, or be integrated with or within, cognition. The greater the amount of cognitive interpretation required, the more cognitive the "emotion" becomes—for example, a sense of achievement. Perhaps this is why disagreement exists in the literature. Other difficulties in the definition of emotion have to do with the closely related concepts of affect and mood.

Emotion, Affect, and Mood

The terms *affect*, *emotion*, and *mood* are frequently used interchangeably, but these concepts are differentiated in many and diverse sources.[11] Affect refers to the feeling side of consciousness, as opposed to thinking, which taps the cognitive domain. Feeling includes pleasure and displeasure, happiness and sadness, liking and disliking, and the psychological and visceral sensations, such as ecstasy, brought on by the neural and hormonal bodily systems.

Emotion includes some level of energization—most researchers refer to this as arousal, various forms of affective labeling, and cognitive interpretations of affect that may be given a single description. An example of this interpretation, mentioned earlier, is pride—a feeling of pleasure resulting from the knowledge of accomplishment in self or others, such as one's family members or, perhaps, a sport team. Thus, emotion is more cognitively involved than elementary forms of affect. Unfortunately, common use in the study of psychology now would include pride, an emotion, within a list of affects—because pride is an affective response to a cognition. Thus, distinctions between the terms *emotion* and *affect* have become muddled. There will be no remission from this dilemma; lists of affects often include emotions, and lists of emotions contain what some researchers would prefer to call affects.

Last, moods can be distinguished on the basis of their duration and low levels of intensity.[12] As generally described in the literature, mood is a temporary state of pleasant or unpleasant disposition with or without easily identified causes, although it, too, has many variations; for example, melancholy is a mood that can take the form of irritability or grouchiness. Generally, relevant mood states will be freely referred to as affects, as the distinction will not impede discussion.

THE STRUCTURE OF "UNIVERSAL" EMOTIONS

In the present effort to relate the concept of emotion to customer satisfaction, it would be instructive to see how a broader arrangement of emotions derives or contains the basic emotions alluded to previously and, perhaps, to examine satisfaction in these contexts. Later, an attempt will be made to formally categorize satisfaction within an emotion framework. An immediate goal is to explore the commonalities among the various emotions in consumption and to show how they can be categorized into similar and dissimilar sets.

Emotions as Discrete Affects

The Izard approach to emotion derives from the evolutionary and biological arguments for basic emotions, as described previously.[13] The author proposes ten discrete emotions that coexist as separate responses available to individuals (i.e., they are unipolar). Since it is unlikely that all, or even a subset, would be manifest at one time (an exception will be noted), they are posited as conceptually independent. Thus, there are no "emotion sets" in this framework except that it does distinguish the positive from the negative affects.

Izard's ten basic emotions, each of which is believed to reflect a unique pattern of subjective experience, physiological response, and expressive behavior, are listed here as pairs of words that reflect differences in intensity from low to high: (1) interest-excitement, (2) joy-elation, (3) surprise-astonishment, (4) sadness-grief, (5) anger-rage, (6) disgust-revulsion, (7) fear-terror, (8) contempt-scorn, (9) shame-shyness, and (10) guilt-remorse. The first two emotions are the positive affects; the third—surprise—is affect-neutral in that it can be positive or negative; and emotions 4 through 10 are the negative affects. As noted, these basic emotions may be experienced individually or in combination, such as anger, disgust, and contempt (referred to as the hostility triad).

Affect as a Two-Dimensional Construct

In contrast to the discrete approach, an emerging body of theory and evidence suggests that emotions can be described in terms of two primary dimensions that define a circular configuration, shown in Figure 12.3, commonly referred to as a *circumplex*. Based on several analyses of different samples, Russell suggests that pleasantness/unpleasantness and arousal/quietude are affect's two primary dimensions.[14] Moreover, he concludes that multiple dimensions (i.e., a dimensionality greater than two), although commonly found, tend to be unstable across samples and situations. In this context, the dimensionality of emotion "space" and its content (the dimension identifications) are referred to as the structure of emotion. The specific two-dimensional structure of pleasantness and arousal shares commonalities with the Pleasure-Arousal Theory (PAT), which is discussed in the consumer behavior literature.[15]

This configuration is conceptually richer than the earlier discussion of basic emotions in that low-arousal affects are given equal representation. It now appears that the basic emotions are high-arousal responses to evoking stimuli and that researchers have not been prone to consider

Figure 12.3 **The Affect Circumplex**

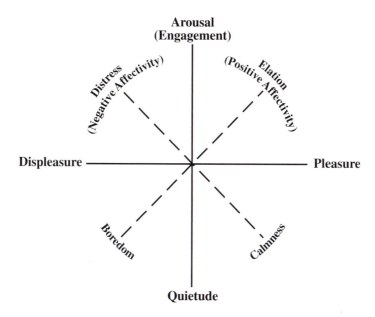

the possibility that low-arousal states (e.g., calmness—and perhaps serenity) are also basic. This structure also allows for a greater range of positive emotions (along the right periphery), while the unidimensional scheme contains only joy and interest as positive emotions.

In an interpretation conceptually similar to Russell's, other researchers rotate the circumplex in Figure 12.3 by forty-five degrees and suggest that positive affectivity (PA) and negative affectivity (NA) are the two primary independent dimensions of the circumplex.[16] This new dimensionality is represented by the dashed axes in the figure. Positively correlated with these two axes is engagement (i.e., arousal or activation, as defined by Russell), positioned at forty-five degrees between them. In this manner, strongly engaged positive affectivity (e.g., elation), negative affectivity (e.g., distress), and neutral or nondescript affect (e.g., surprise) are all likely affective outcomes. The same would be true of low-arousal affect (e.g., sleepy, relaxed, and quiet).[17] In the Russell interpretation, the highest and lowest levels of arousal are affect-neutral.

This rotation of the primary axes does not change the configuration of the affects; it merely redefines the dimensions on which they are described. Thus, pleasure is moderately aroused positive affect while displeasure is moderately aroused negative affect. The locations of the two pleasure extremes on the circumplex are such that pleasure and displeasure are negatively correlated, whereas positive and negative affectivity are orthogonal (independent). This is a potentially important distinction because it explains why some studies find negatively correlated affect extremes while others find uncorrelated extremes.

Data attesting to the replicability of this two-dimensional view are widely supportive of its structure, with minor inconsistencies noted when details are pursued in efforts to find situational variations. When three dimensions appear, the second and third tend to be components of arousal, such as frequency and intensity. Moreover, findings of the independence of positive and negative affect, as originally suggested, appear fairly robust across many and diverse contexts. This consistency provides some confidence that positive and negative affect, when combined with high and low arousal, underlie many of the affects experienced in day-to-day events, including consumption.[18] Later, this two-dimensional characterization will be found to be useful in understanding the affective basis for the satisfaction response.

Emotion as a Blend of Affects

In yet a third circumplex model, Plutchik juxtaposes eight basic emotions (joy, acceptance, fear, surprise, sadness, disgust, anger, and anticipation) in a circle (shown in tabular form in Table 12.1) so that the combination of adjacent, once-removed, and twice-removed emotions produces still other emotions.[19] The table shows the basic emotions, their high- and low-intensity counterparts, and the once- and twice-removed combinations; interpretations by this author, as needed or revised from the original source, are designated with asterisks. As examples of combinatorial pairs, the adjacent categories of joy and acceptance produce love (in the familial sense), the once-removed categories of joy and fear produce guilt, and the twice-removed categories of joy and surprise produce delight. Intensity or arousal is relegated to a depth dimension, producing emotions above and below the basic eight (e.g., high fear = terror; low fear = apprehension). Evidence for this framework appears in Plutchik's books and elsewhere.[20]

These models illustrate how complex emotions originate. From the Izard and other basic schemes, it can be concluded that some emotions, such as anger, are biologically primitive. The two-dimensional circumplex models show that the infant's calls of distress and delight are early manifestations of displeasure and pleasure, respectively, which can also be viewed as moderately or highly aroused levels of negative and positive affect. Moreover, the level of arousal modifies the expression of these happy and sad affects, so that negative affect can range from boredom to rage and positive affect from serenity to ecstasy. Plutchik's framework shows how more complex affects result if two (or more) affects are blended, regardless of arousal. Table 12.1 shows, for example, that a surprised state of sadness could be interpreted as disappointment while the anticipation of joy would yield optimism. A surprised state of happiness would be interpreted as elation or delight, while the anticipation of sadness would result in pessimism, fear, or terror—depending on how extreme sadness was manifested.

EVIDENCE FOR SATISFACTION IN EMOTION FRAMEWORKS

The emotional basis for the satisfaction response is not well documented in the literature. This may be so because lay synonyms for the word *satisfaction* are normally considered as being equivalent. For example, *happy* and *pleased* are frequently used to tap satisfaction feelings, as in the delighted/ terrible scale where all three terms are used for descriptor anchors in the same one-item scale.[21] In fact, satisfaction had been appearing in a number of the emotional typologies discussed here when the first edition of this book was composed (and little else since).

What follows is a synthesis of studies reviewed in the first edition of this book and displayed in Figure 12.4. In all cases, the words *satisfied*, *satisfying*, and *satisfactory* are assumed to be representative of the satisfaction state. Its negative counterpart, dissatisfaction, is shown with those affects most closely corresponding when tested in the same framework. This author has stylized the solutions for both satisfaction and dissatisfaction for purposes of conclusion and discussion. What is not in dispute is that there are multiple positionings of satisfaction depending on the research context (life satisfaction, product satisfaction), scaling idiosyncrasies, and encapsulated time frames (postpurchase, postusage, on multiple occasions, over extended periods of usage, etc.).

Table 12.1

The Plutchik Circumplex

Basic emotions with high/low intensity	Adjacent combinations	Once-removed combinations	Twice-removed combinations
Anticipation: vigilance/interest	Anticipation and joy: optimism	Anticipation and acceptance: fatalism	Anticipation and fear: anxiety
Joy: ecstasy/serenity	Joy and acceptance: love	Joy and fear: guilt	Joy and surprise: delight
Acceptance: adoration/acknowledgement[a]	Acceptance and fear: submission	Acceptance and surprise: curiosity	Acceptance and sadness: resignation
Fear: terror/apprehension	Fear and surprise: awe	Fear and sadness: despair	Fear and disgust: revulsion[a]
Surprise: amazement/distraction	Surprise and sadness: disappointment	Surprise and disgust: repulsion[a]	Surprise and anger: outrage
Sadness: grief/pensiveness	Sadness and disgust: remorse	Sadness and anger: revengefulness[a]	Sadness and anticipation: pessimism
Disgust: loathing/boredom	Disgust and anger: contempt	Disgust and anticipation: cynicism	Disgust and joy: repugnance[a]
Anger: rage/annoyance	Anger and anticipation: aggressiveness	Anger and joy: gloating[a]	Anger and acceptance: dominance

[a] Interpretation by RLO.

Figure 12.4   **Synthesis of Affect Circumplex Models Containing Satisfaction and Dissatisfaction**

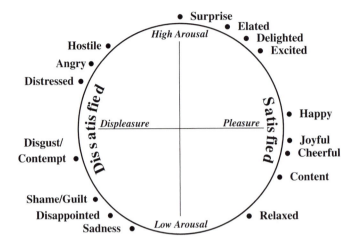

In the examples reviewed, extrapolating the findings to the consumer domain allows a number of insights to emerge, particularly with respect to the arousal dimension. One reasonable conclusion is that positive product experiences, represented by reports of satisfaction, can be pleasurable, approach excitement or delight, or tend toward contentment or relaxation—thus differing only on the degree of arousal. Thus, depending on study context, satisfaction appears to float around happiness and pleasure and between low-arousal positive affects such as relaxation and high-arousal affects such as excitement or delight, as discussed in Chapter 4.[22] In a similar manner, dissatisfying experiences might be perceived as unpleasant, disappointing, or angering (see Chapter 14). Thus, satisfaction as a response category on a survey may be an incomplete descriptor in that it may mask the underlying degree of arousal, as well as the cognitive interpretation underlying the emotions, inherent in the satisfaction response.

In attempting to synthesize the perspectives discussed here, the purpose is not to argue for one individual solution over another. Rather, the insights gained from the findings suggest a number of issues for the emotional content of the satisfaction response. One is that pleasure, delight, and contentment may represent alternative emotional meanings of satisfaction. Another issue, following from the first, is that arousal appears to draw out two other elements that are found in satisfaction-related works.

First, it appears that emotional extremes, including delight, excitement, and distress, are naturally occurring emotions in satisfaction and dissatisfaction. Second, high-arousal affective states have easily identifiable and widely acknowledged descriptors such as ecstasy, anger, and rage. As arousal declines, so does the affect level, decaying initially into generally pleasant and/or unpleasant states and then into complacency and perhaps melancholy. This correlated arousal dimension will be used in the response mode framework to be suggested in the next chapter, along with a proposed distinction between contentment, pleasure, and other satisfaction states.

Thus, the literature on emotion typologies creates more ambiguity than it resolves on the meaning of satisfaction from an emotional standpoint. If consumers respond that they are satisfied, does it mean that they are in a state of contentment, or of pleasure, or of delight? The word *satisfied* is not capable of distinguishing these different levels of arousal. Being merely contented is not as satisfying as being happy or delighted, or is it? The existing consumer literature on emotion and satisfaction will be examined shortly to see if this issue can be resolved. But first the methods of evaluating emotion in satisfaction studies are discussed.

MEASURING AFFECT IN SATISFACTION CONTEXTS

A number of affect measures have been employed in various disciplines representing each of the theories and perspectives discussed here. Perhaps the greatest amount of work done in consumer behavior prior to 1990 dealt with emotional responses to advertising.[23] Of more recent note is the copyrighted pictorial representation of the Pleasure-Arousal-Dominance (PAD) theory, where cross-cultural "manikins" are used to form scales representing the three dimensions of pleasure (smiling/frowning faces), arousal (increasing gut activity represented by cartoon-like explosions), and dominance (represented by the relative size of the manikin).[24] This literature may prove helpful, but it must be remembered that advertising is primarily intended as a prepurchase strategy and, as such, cannot be expected to generate the levels of involvement found in postpurchase reactions. Additionally, much of this work examines emotional reactions to the advertisement itself, not to the product, although there are exceptions to this generalization.

While many methods have been used to measure emotion and affect, by far the most common is the self-rating scale. Here, respondents are asked to gauge the degree to which they have experienced various emotions in a particular setting. The emotions are presented in list form, and either an intensity (how much) or frequency (how often) scale is used to assess the degree to which the emotion has been felt. Because of the ubiquity of contexts in which this scale has been used, discussion is restricted to those helpful in satisfaction analyses. The following discussion presents specific measures that have been used as well as those that show promise. To more fully appreciate these measures, two measurement issues require elaboration.

Identifying Consumption Emotions

Although many consumption studies now include brief emotion scales, these typically are selected form the shorter lists of positive/negative affect items derived from the diverse sources and methods discussed to this point. The approach is easily defended because the emotion clusters (or single items at the extreme) generally demonstrate high reliabilities and have, at the least, face validity. This is not to say that all are constructed with care, since often the emotion scales are culled from study items designed for another purpose. For example, some literature contains three-item scales representing "positive affect" having the following components: positive word of mouth, "satisfaction," and repurchase intention. These choices are clearly not appropriate for emotion scales because the items are not affects—which, for example, would include pleasure and delight—but are consequences of affect, even including the "satisfaction" item. For a discussion of the application of the various psychological theories discussed here and elsewhere, readers are referred to the comprehensive review, cited earlier.[25]

Perhaps the most comprehensive investigation of the emotions displayed in consumption settings appeared in 1997 and has not been updated since that time.[26] The study examined responses across six purchase scenarios (the consumer's favorite possession, a recent important purchase, and purchases of clothing, food, durables, and services). The time frames included purchase consideration, actual purchase, and usage. Both positive and negative feelings were solicited. The

Figure 12.5   **Affects in Richins's CES Superimposed on the Affect Circumplex**

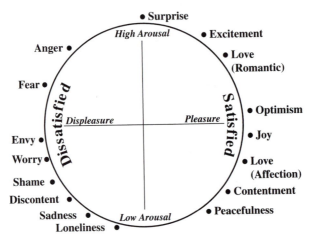

initial list of 175 descriptors was reduced to a smaller set on the basis of familiarity of the term. On separate samples, terms were culled on the basis of actual usage in describing consumption events and whether these emotion terms were experienced or not. The combined sets of culled questions were then submitted to another sample responding to usage for an important purchase, an unsatisfactory purchase, a special possession, and a future purchase. Two further studies and statistical analysis resulted in sixteen scales corresponding to the affect circumplex in Figure 12.4 and now portrayed as Figure 12.5. The sixteen scales constitute what the author referred to as the Consumption Emotions Set (CES).

Descriptor differences across Figures 12.4 and 12.5 are found to be disparate on a number of dimensions. The similarities are discussed first. In this regard, it is clear that the two dimensions of affectivity and arousal are represented. The terms *excited/excitement, joy/joyful, content/contentment, relaxed/peacefulness, shame, sadness, angry,* and of course *surprise* are congruent. In contrast, differences exist as follows: The original circumplex also contains *elation/delight, cheerful, disappointed, distressed,* and *hostile.* These are, for the most part, more extreme arousal terms. The CES, in contrast, contains *optimism, love* (romantic and affectionate), *loneliness, worry, envy,* and *fear.*[27] There are two themes to these nuances in the CES. The first theme appears to be a forward orientation as represented by optimism and worry for the future; the second is social in nature, including the love terms, loneliness (in the absence of social contact), and envy and fear (of others, perhaps). No scale in the CES contains satisfaction despite the comprehensiveness of the techniques used.

Thus, the CES taps what might be referred to as social satisfaction with products and is aligned with the fabric of social comparison satisfaction, a central theme in other areas of the satisfaction literature. Nonetheless, it is clear that many products and, particularly, services involve other persons in the consumption space. Researchers are encouraged to blend both frameworks, the traditional and the social, into studies where such influences operate. As will be shown, however, the appraisal basis for responses to consumption events, discussed briefly earlier in this chapter, necessarily brings in the high arousal affects originally proposed in the initial circumplex representations of emotion.

Bipolar Versus Unipolar Scales in Emotion Measurement

The issue of bipolar versus unipolar scales is controversial. Consider the emotion of pleasure. In bipolar format, this item would appear on a survey as follows:

Displeased	1	2	3	4	5	Pleased
			Neither			

This scale assumes that pleasure and displeasure are bipolar opposites, that they are mutually exclusive. Generally, this assumption underlies any theoretical structure having the emotion of interest (here, pleasure) as a dimension, as in the pleasure-arousal theory.[28]

Unfortunately, whenever the respondent has both pleasant and unpleasant experiences with the same object, either because it has multiple features that can give rise to pleasant and unpleasant experiences separately (e.g., any multifaceted product such as a residence) or because the object has been used over time and each experience is different (e.g., restaurant dining), this scale will be inappropriate. Respondents having equally frequent pleasant and unpleasant experiences will probably respond at the midpoint "Neither." This, however, is not what "Neither" represents. As this scale is constructed, "Neither" is meant to imply the lack of either positive or negative affect, not mixed experience.

Alternative unipolar scales would appear as follows:

Pleased:	1	2	3	4	5
	Not at all	A little	Moderately	Quite a bit	Extremely

Displeased:	1	2	3	4	5
	Not at all	A little	Moderately	Quite a bit	Extremely

Note that these scales are more true to the discrete emotions approach. Here, respondents can report that they were both pleased and displeased, pleased and not displeased, and so on. Unfortunately, however, problems remain even with this approach.

One such problem is that some consumers will sum their experiences, decide whether the consumable was mostly pleasing or mostly displeasing, and give mirror-image responses. That is, the scale scores will appear as 5 and 1, 1 and 5, 2 and 4, and so on. If all consumers respond in this fashion, then the scales become redundant and only one is needed. A greater problem, however, is that when they are used in multifaceted or multiple-occasion settings, the scales confound the measurement properties of intensity and frequency.[29]

Intensity Versus Frequency

The second important issue in measuring emotion or affect within any theoretical framework is the degree of the emotion response. Two options are available to the researcher. The first scale, duplicating the Pleased scale above, gauges the actual intensity of felt emotion:

Pleased:	1	2	3	4	5
	Not at all	A little	Moderately	Quite a bit	Extremely

An obvious shortcoming of an intensity scale is that it is unique to the most aroused encounter that the respondent has had with an emotion. What if a restaurant patron were extremely pleased on one occasion and only moderately pleased on all others? Some respondents in this situation would report their most extreme visit, rating the restaurant as a 5; others would rate it as a 3, for the number of moderately pleasing visits dominates the one extreme exception; and still others would average in the one extremely pleasing visit and rate the restaurant as a 4. This problem will create noise in the data and lower validity.

A second option is to use frequency scales, appearing as follows:

1. Pleased:	1	2	3	4	5
	Never or almost never	Seldom	Occasionally	Often	Very often

2. Pleased:	1	2	3	4	5
	With nothing	With a few things	With about half	With most things	With everything

These scales appear much better suited for multiple-occasion (scale 1) or multifaceted (scale 2) product or service encounters. Admittedly, the scales do not tap the intensity dimension. It would be assumed that the multiple occurrences included events of all intensity levels, but this, of course, is a speculative assumption. A potential problem would exist if the sample consisted mainly of persons who had seldom or infrequently patronized a service, for they would be sensitive to the intensity of their limited experiences.

Thus, as a general rule, intensity should be used for single encounters with one-dimensional or nearly one-dimensional performance characteristics. Alternatively, frequency should be used whenever the experience can be considered multifaceted, such as a household move and/or home-buying experience, or when consumption experiences are measured over a time period, such as years of college attendance. In the last case, the intensity dimension is not lost if the researcher uses affects of different intensity reflecting the same basic emotion. For example, anger might be represented by three descriptors: upset, angry, and enraged. The intensity of felt anger could be viewed as the sum of the three scales.

An interesting result, known as the "peak-end" or "duration neglect" phenomenon, has been observed for consumption periods of long duration, such as the aforementioned education, hospital stays, political terms, community life, family life, durable ownership, and long-term service arrangements. When queried at the culmination of such consumption "mega-episodes," respondents tend to focus on the most extreme (either high or low) encounter as well as on the most recent.[30] The prominence of the most recent event is easily explained by the recency effect; apparently the most extreme encounter relies on its memorability or its unusualness, particularly if "out of range." The breadth of this phenomenon has yet to be thrashed out and caution is required if memory effects are to be fully explored. For example, trend has been found to be yet another influence.[31]

Lists of items representing all frameworks discussed in this chapter are available from the respective sources and are not reproduced here. Generally, a minimum of three items is used to represent each of the discrete emotions in the Izard and Plutchik models and each of the four to eight sectors of the PAT model. Items representing this latter model can be found in the original source, as are other variations, including a short form and a graphic version.[32] Generally, these items were constructed for more clinical applications and are not well-suited for consumer applications or are too abstract (the graphic version). In an attempt to model consumption responses more accurately, representative items selected by this author from adaptations of the PAT, referred to generically as the self-report affect circumplex, appear in Table 12.2. In practice, all would be used as stems for an intensity or frequency scale.

Note that the very high and very low activation emotions are valence-neutral. That is, they tend to be unlabeled states of nature. This may be truer for the very low categories, however. Very high activation states do tend to have valences. Examples would include startlement and shock as unpleasant experiences and thrill and ecstasy as pleasant experiences. Others, such as surprise, do require a label, as in "pleasant surprise."

STUDIES OF CONSUMER EMOTION

Origins of Consumer Emotion

Insights into the operation of emotion within consumer experiences began with research, previously cited, that showed that distinct primary affect dimensions are prominent in advertisement evaluations. Using the earliest of the emotion typologies, researchers demonstrated the existence of positive and negative affect in response to advertising exposure. Other studies showing a variety of emotions elicited by consumption fall short of specifying linkages to other pre- and postconsumption variables, including satisfaction.[33] In contrast, distinct attribution-dependent emotions (Chapter 11) such as anger, gratitude, and guilt have been identified in the context of product and service reactions. However, even these research efforts fail to show how emotion relates to satisfaction as it has been defined here—a feeling that the product or service has fulfilled or exceeded its intended function. To understand this relationship, studies that measure emotion and satisfaction are needed in order to assess the correspondence between the two.

Emotion and Satisfaction in Consumption

The study of the operation of emotions in satisfaction decisions is now much more developed than it was at the time of the first edition of this book. In fact, some of this new work, on anticipation, surprise, and value, has already been incorporated into earlier chapters of this volume. Still other topics yet to be discussed include the role of emotion in dissatisfaction and recovery and with regard to loyalty in consumption. By necessity, the current coverage can only be suggestive and hopefully comprehensive in its brevity. As this is written, researchers no doubt are testing satisfaction frameworks that include emotion as central to the satisfaction decision.

Selected references to reviews of emotion in consumer behavior have been provided here and within the contexts of advertising (where much of the work began) and in consumption more generally. Outside of marketing and within the psychological community, the study of emotion has reached a "plateau" of sorts since the applied field appears to have been unable to absorb all the recent advances at the theoretical level, with the possible exception of the quality of life literature. Methodological advances now make use of equipment-performing techniques such as functional magnetic resonance imaging (fMRI), making many studies cost-prohibitive. In spite of this difficulty, consumer behavior provides almost a limitless vehicle for research and it is expected that research will continue unabated.

In assessing the role of emotion in satisfaction judgments, researchers must be careful to distinguish preexisting emotions (e.g., mood, life satisfaction) from those deriving from the consumption experience itself. Research both in consumer satisfaction and in psychology shows that positive and negative affective orientations color later affective judgments of every variety.[34] Researchers may wish to consider a consumer's preexisting personal disposition in order to fully account for

Table 12.2

Selected Items From the Self-Report Affect Circumplex With a Focus on Consumption

Activation level	Valence		
	Pleasant	Neutral	Unpleasant
Very high		**Surprised**, astonished, amazed	
High	**Delighted**, elated, excited		**Angry**, enraged, furious
Moderately high	**Enthusiastic**, joyful, cheerful		**Annoyed**, distressed, irritated
Moderate	**Pleased**, happy, gratified		**Sad**, frustrated, gloomy
Moderately low	**Content**, fulfilled, warm/serene		**Resigned**, worried, tense
Low	**Relaxed**, calm, peaceful		**Bored**, distanced, depressed
Very low		**Unemotional**, quiet, taciturn	

Note: Anchor terms are in bold.

satisfaction responses, but it must be realized that this is not a controllable influence from the standpoint of marketing strategy. Discussion turns now to a growing number of studies in which satisfaction and emotion were jointly investigated.

Three stages of consumption will provide focus. In the first, preexisting emotions will be discussed with reference to their impact on satisfaction decisions. These effects are additional to the effect of anticipatory emotions discussed in Chapter 3, for the interest here is not on choice per se but on the carryover effects to postconsumption processes. Then, emotion within or during consumption, including long-duration consumption, will be discussed. Finally, allusion will be made to postconsumption emotions, although this topic will be largely deferred until Chapter 14.

Preconsumption Emotion Effects

Aside from anticipations as proxies for expectations, still another distinction recognizes the more direct impact of preemotions on postemotions. This would appear similar to the effect of expectations on satisfaction (assimilation), but it has already been acknowledged that much of this expectation effect is subject to revision during the consumption episode. Here, the emphasis is on risk and fear (of consequences), purely affective purchasing, and reflective judgments—not totally unlike disconfirmation but with greater focus.

Perceived risk, one of the earliest topics in consumer behavior, retains its role in consumption. Risk is an apprehension (see Chapter 10), a fear, and a stimulus for negative affect. In this regard, studies have shown that risk can have both a confirmatory effect on outcomes, as in the common "I knew it would happen" effect (see Chapter 9), as well as enhance decision outcomes, as consumers will be motivated to pursue decisions that minimize the potential "worst outcome." This latter approach is known as "mood management."[35]

When decisions are governed by purely affective considerations and judged as such within the Positive Affect/Negative Affect with arousal framework (often abbreviated PA/NA), decision outcomes are known to follow this pattern as well. In a sense, this is closely tied into the distinction between utilitarian and hedonic products, the latter being much more affective in nature. Generally, affective expectations for hedonic products result in consistent product evaluations (satisfaction). When utilitarian products are evaluated or when hedonic outcomes must be analyzed for their inconsistency with expectations (in effect, introducing cognition), the utilitarian elements have greater impact.[36]

For example, this author and a colleague examined a full circumplex of emotions along with measures of utilitarian and hedonic value, representing abstractions of functional and aesthetic outcomes of consumption (see Chapter 3).[37] Of interest is the fact that subjects in this study were allowed to select their focal product, with only broad choice restrictions based on involvement. The great divergence of products, some representing high involvement and others low, ensured the external generalizability of the results. A number of significant findings emerged.

First, the affect circumplex was fully supported in the context of consumption satisfaction. In two dimensions, pleasantness/unpleasantness and arousal emerged as predicted. In three dimensions, the utilitarian/hedonic variables provided the content of the additional dimension, suggesting that the nature of the product features (utilitarian versus hedonic) provides some of the structure of the satisfaction response.

A second finding provided evidence for the joint operation of product influences and emotion on satisfaction. When put into a causal framework, satisfaction was found to be a significant function of positive affect, negative affect, and utilitarian (functional) influence. Hedonic influences operated through positive affect while utilitarian influences had no PA/NA impacts except through

Figure 12.6   **The Mano and Oliver Hedonic Versus Utilitarian Framework**

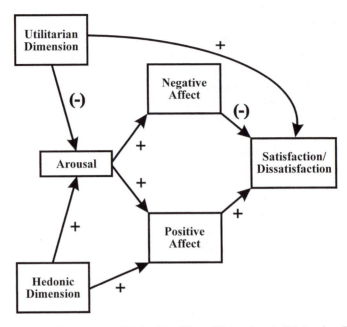

Source: Adapted from Haim Mano and Richard L. Oliver, "Assessing the Dimensionality and Structure of Consumption Experience: Evaluation, Feeling, and Satisfaction," *Journal of Consumer Research* 20, no. 3 (December 1993): 451–66, by permission of the *Journal of Consumer Research*, Inc.

arousal, where they served to diminish arousal in the construction of emotion. The summary model is shown in Figure 12.6 with the signs of the coefficients indicated.

Lastly, the mechanism by which the experience of outcomes causes the consumer to consciously (as if instructed) "reflect back" on expectations has been examined. Whether internal-locus or "chance" oriented, consumers will assimilate their expectations levels in outcome judgments. Only those who externally attribute outcomes tend to not use expectations, particularly if they are affective.[38] This topic will be discussed further where the consumption experience itself is evaluated in an ongoing or immediate post-judgment sense. This will require further understanding of the cognitive basis for emotions, referred to as *appraisal*.

Affects During Transient and Extended Consumption

Transient Responses

As used here, transient response refers not to the brevity of the actual consumption event, but to the nature of the consumer's report of prior experiences. This is a difficult "call" because, although the consumer's ownership of a car is an extended event, surveys typically reflect a snapshot of feelings at one point in time as opposed to asking the respondent to reflect back on the duration of experience, as they might for an extended stay at a vacation resort. The reader is asked to bear this subtle distinction in mind as this section unfolds.

In previous research, the effects of experience with "bundles" of attributes (including the summated score over all attributes) on overall satisfaction have been shown to relate directly to

Figure 12.7 **The Attribute Satisfaction Model**

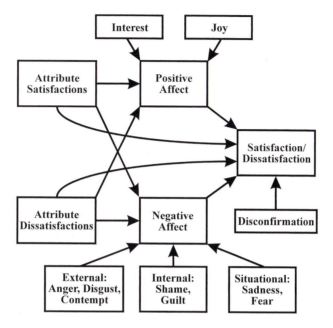

Source: Adapted from Richard L. Oliver, "Cognitive, Affective, and Attribute Bases of the Satisfaction Response," *Journal of Consumer Research* 20, no. 3 (December 1993): 418–30, by permission of the *Journal of Consumer Research*, Inc.

satisfaction and intention. Examples might be attributes performing positively versus those performing negatively or physical attributes versus information on those attributes.[39] This approach is noteworthy in that actual attribute *states* can be examined, as contrasted to general descriptions of overall performance or of functional or hedonic value. Moreover, these investigations extend to individual attribute (bundle) disconfirmations as well as to information content regarding the products and services per se. Emotion, however, was not the focus of either referenced study.

In a variation of this theme, a study by this author examined satisfaction influences at the attribute level for a product and a service and related these through the emotions to satisfaction.[40] Summary scores of product feature satisfactions and dissatisfactions were formed and related to Izard's positive-affect scales of interest and joy and to three negative-affect subsets. Based on attribution theory, these were the external attributions (anger, disgust, contempt), the internal attributions (shame, guilt), and situational attributions (sadness, fear). The model, shown in Figure 12.7, posited that the attribute satisfactions and dissatisfactions were the sources of the affects, that the affects would partially mediate the attribute influences on overall satisfaction, and that the attributes would also have direct effects on satisfaction.

Essentially, all hypothesized relations were supported. Positive affect and negative affect were a function of attribute satisfaction and dissatisfaction, respectively, and satisfaction was found to be a function of the affects and attribute satisfaction. Two other findings from this study are noteworthy. First, interest and joy yielded different results in the automobile sample; of these, only joy was related to satisfaction. Second, disconfirmation made independent contributions to the prediction of satisfaction beyond that of the affect sequence. This latter finding supports the separate influences of affective and cognitive influences on satisfaction.

If the researcher bypasses the attribute influences and simply looks at consumption emotions as causes of satisfaction, results can be stated in terms of specific emotional states and their effect; it then behooves the researcher to infer the attribute causes of these emotions after the fact. For example, in one early study, the positive affects from the Izard scheme (interest and joy) along with the hostility triad of anger, disgust, and contempt were related to a number of satisfaction measures.[41] Using two different product categories (automobiles and cable TV), the results showed that the positive and negative affect categories contributed independently and significantly to satisfaction judgments beyond the effects of expectancy disconfirmation variables. This was an important finding in satisfaction research at the time, as it opened the possibility that satisfaction is neither purely cognitive nor purely affective in content.

This study was followed by an effort to extend the prior findings through an examination of the affective structure of satisfaction.[42] That is, attention was focused on the dimensionality of emotions in satisfaction in the same way that emotion researchers have examined the dimensionality of emotion in more general contexts. Again using the Izard scale, the authors found dimensions of hostility (generalized negative affect), pleasant surprise, and interest among a sample of automobile owners. Moreover, all were significantly related to various satisfaction measures in a regression format, indicating statistically independent effects.

Although specific affects arising from brief product or service encounters are of interest, extended consumption episodes provide a greater venue for emotion to emerge in its various forms. At this point in the study of affect, the existence of PA and NA is almost a foregone conclusion in the consumption of most consumables with "personality"; very mundane products may be simply too functional or utilitarian to provide depth of processing and, hence, emotional manifestations. Alternatively, extended encounters have elements of both functional and hedonic response. For example, frequently consumed categories of entertainment, recreation, and both spectator and participative sports would show both. This "applied" literature is now commonplace and brief mention is made here. Movies, nature, and sporting events are examples where researchers would be remiss if they did not include emotion sampling in their investigation.[43] Of note are studies that show that the experience of negative emotions can be satisfying if negative emotions were desired (e.g., the movie *Schindler's List* which focused on treatment of minorities by the Nazis in World War II), demonstrating again the case of positive disconfirmation of negative emotion expectations).[44] And, as will be discussed in Chapter 14, the disproportionate influence of negative emotions can be ameliorated if responded to in a correct manner by the firm.[45]

Extended Encounters

The previous discussion largely involved what is known as core affect in that it is always present in those consumption (and other) situations in which emotion can be expected to be manifest. This section broaches what is known as a "prototypical emotional episode," described as "a complex process that unfolds over time," involving "causally connected subevents (antecedent[s]; appraisal; physiological, affective, and cognitive changes; [and] behavioral response").[46]

In a comprehensive examination of the extended consumption of banks, restaurants, airlines, and hospital services, researchers investigated the various delineated stages for their potential to elicit emotions and behaviors.[47] Each of the following emotions was identified and analyzed further for identification of specific markers: the positive emotions of happiness and delight, the negative emotions of anxiety and fear, the other-attributed emotions of anger and frustration, and the self-attributed emotions of guilt and shame. For these eight emotions, the researchers determined the stages of (1) antecedents, (2) experiential, expressive, cognitive, and behavioral manifestations, and (3) self-control efforts resulting from appraisals. This study, an early report of later detailed analyses, was an important first step in demonstrating emotional unfolding in episodic consumption.

This line of investigation is now repeatedly applied in services, in particular, because of their required interplay of consumer and service provider. When performed against criteria of satisfaction as in the critical incidents approach (see Chapter 2), explanatory conclusions are permitted. For example, it has been found that the intensity and valence of the general emotional tone affect satisfaction in the expected direction. Of interest, however, is that the product component of services (e.g., the flight in air travel) most typically affects the negative dimension while the service personnel are more likely to be associated with positive aspects; similarly, in an examination of tourist attractions where other customers were a factor, the ambiance (a physical characteristic) of the site tended to have negative influences while the other patrons tended to be a positive influence (but not by much).[48]

Aside from the events that occur over the episode, the nature of the "unfolding" is also important. It has already been stated that "peak-end" values and trend (positive or negative) are important. Further research suggests that the trend is more effective if each step follows a "just perceivable increment," which, in prior literatures, was referred to as a "just noticeable difference." Moreover, the arousal dimension appears to have an additional effect (as it should under the circumplex model). It appears that increasing arousal levels serve to maintain satisfaction, but only up to a point referred to as "target."[49] At this point, satiation or adaptation begins to set in, as described in many previous sections of this book, particularly with regard to delight (see Chapter 4).

Emotions as Satisfaction Outcomes

Interestingly, there are two paths to take at this juncture. If satisfaction is an emotion (this conundrum will be addressed at the end of this chapter), then satisfaction, like any other emotion, should have antecedent conditions and consequences. If the reader has followed this discourse this far, there is no need to consider the possibility of antecedents; answers were available long before the term *satisfaction* had been formally described. It derives from the fifteenth-century Latin *satisfacere* (make enough) and no doubt was used many years before that. Of greater interest, however, is the question of other *emotions* that are primed by satisfaction. This is not to say there are consequences of satisfaction, for the last section of this book (Chapters 14 and 15) addresses that issue. Loyalty, the topic of the last chapter, will prove to be especially problematic to pin down. Rhetorically, is loyalty an emotion?

What is known is that the consequences of satisfaction, including repurchase intentions, complaining or complimenting, word of mouth, switching, and (again) loyalty, are more behavioral than emotional.[50] Can satisfaction, defined as pleasurable or unpleasurable fulfillment, result in further emotional responding? This author would agree that this is entirely plausible. Unfortunately, little has been written on this topic and a different approach (to be pursued shortly) may be helpful (but will turn out not to be). But first, a short recapitulation.

To summarize the work that has been done to date on the emotional underpinnings of satisfaction, it can be concluded with some degree of certainty that there is unique emotional content to the satisfaction response. The affect literature, reviewed earlier, suggests that satisfaction changes form based on the level of arousal in the response. Could it be that the separate influence of cognition, as suggested, is one of the reasons for the differing levels of arousal? This possibility is explored further in the following discussion, which considers approaches, including appraisal, alluded to previously.

COGNITIVE DETERMINANTS OF EMOTION

How do emotions arise in consumption? Early insights into the answer to this question were provided in the previous chapter on attribution processes. A more accurate response to the question is that some explanations are more elementary and others are more complex than those based on attribution reasoning alone. Emotions have many sources, some of which are not consciously processed. For the purpose of studying postpurchase consumption, however, a more immediate concern is understanding conscious reactions to product experience.

Cognitive Appraisal Revisited

The act of appraisal means evaluating the significance or worth of an event. When people evaluate or appraise events in life, two elements of cognition come into play. The first is perceived knowledge, what is believed to be fact. The second is a judgment of what this knowledge means from the standpoint of one's personal well-being.[51] Thus, facts are evaluated on the basis of their significance for goals and aspirations, and it is this appraisal that gives events emotional significance. In essence, knowledge (a cognition) is compared to goals (another cognition), and emotion results. Note that a perceived lack of knowledge (a knowing of what one does not know) is also knowledge in this context. Hence, uncertainty and unexpectedness also fit nicely into this analysis.

For example, anger results when a (consumption) goal is frustrated by someone or something, such as when a new recipe does not turn out well when used for the first time with guests one wishes to please or impress. As noted in the last chapter, this example assumes that the chef externally attributes the poor dinner outcome to errors in the recipe. In addition to anger, embarrassment may also result. Embarrassment is felt when a personal failing is likely to be known or is observed by others.[52] This example illustrates the point (to be discussed shortly) that further appraisals may ensue after the initial reaction. To take an example of a favorable consumption outcome, an automobile owner may be delighted when a new brand of automobile polish leaves the car's finish exceptionally deep and glossy. Further appraisal may result in a sense of personal accomplishment and pride of ownership.

A critical element of appraisal is that knowledge will do nothing if it has no personal relevance. Lack of personal relevance, itself an appraisal, ensures that further appraisal mechanisms will not be brought into play. Thus, "vitamin-enhanced," a recent nuance in bottled waters, may mean little to an entrenched beer drinker. This issue will prove to be important when an attempt to assess the satisfaction potential of uninvolved consumers is made in the next chapter.

Appraisal is not a new concept in the study of emotion, but a number of issues are yet to be resolved. For example, do all appraisals have to begin with cognition? Apparently not, for people can appraise the relevance of their emotions for their well-being, such as when the culinary consumer assesses the consequences of expressing disappointment in the presence of guests. In fact, a back-and-forth interplay of emotion and cognition over time is not unusual. This same consumer, for example, may reassess the reasons for the unsatisfactory recipe outcome and modify the initial anger into alternative emotions, such as guilt for not having recognized the mistake in the directions.

Despite the possibility of emotion-cognition-emotion sequencing, where emotion can appear before cognition, discussion will concentrate on the cognitive aspects of appraisal with particular emphasis on what appraisal "causes." In all probability, the more basic "cognition first, emotion second" sequence encompasses a large number of consumption situations. Moreover, the cross-cultural universality of cognitive appraisal has more or less been resolved.[53] As one would expect, the basic emotions have universal appraisal patterns; deviations are more likely for more complex appraisals such as those involving attribution.

Two-Appraisal Models

A potentially important variation on the appraisal theme is parallel appraisals of the same event, as introduced by Weiner and alluded to in the previous chapter. Other researchers have suggested similar processes under different names. For example, one writer refers to automatic and extended appraisal, where the automatic process occurs spontaneously and generally consists of the basic emotions, including distress and happiness. The extended process consists of a cognitive reflection on the event giving rise to appraisal. This is similar to another explanation of automatic, nonvolitional and deliberate volitional appraisal. Still another refers to separate appraisals of the emotion generated by the outcome and appraisal of the outcome itself; the terms *syncratic* and *analytical* are used to describe essentially the same processes. Other researchers have proposed multiple forms of cognitive appraisal, such as coping strategy and action necessity.[54] Generally, these and other higher-order processes go beyond this initial level of discussion. For the purposes intended here, the two-appraisal model will allow for the discussion of the dual roles of affect and cognition in satisfaction formation; brief mention will be made of the action tendency or possible third dimension.

The two-appraisal model (with an extension to a third behavioral stage) is shown graphically in Figure 12.8.[55] For ease of discussion, the convention is adopted of assuming that the first appraisal, based on *goal relevance* and, if so, a *goal-relevant* (purchase) success or failure, evokes the basic and perhaps automatic response of positive or negative outcomes at a certain level of arousal. In other words, was this "good for me" or "bad for me"? This process was referred to in the previous chapter as primary affect. Figure 12.8 shows subsequent sequences of events, all of which are initiated by this first order of processing.

The second appraisal step, corresponding to more cognitive interpretation, evokes various forms of reasoning. For simplicity, these are referred to collectively as judgments of the appraisal dimensions and may be viewed as secondary to the initial cognitive appraisal. As shown in Figure 12.8, these appraisals evoke separate outcomes and sequences of events initiated by the conclusions of the consumer's reasoning process. It is highly likely that these outcomes will be affective (emotional) in nature, as discussed next. Lastly, decisions involving action tendencies are shown. While mentioned only briefly in the present discussion, they will get more attention in the next chapter.

Affects Resulting From Cognitive Appraisal

As noted, appraisal is an analysis of the relevance of an event to a person's life. A more immediate issue, however, is the determination of the specific appraisals made in consumption. In this way, consumption-specific appraisal affects can be more precisely identified. One way to begin the identification process is to examine appraisal taxonomies and/or structures and select those dimensions that are most likely in consumption. This literature continues to develop, and a number of authoritative works are available in psychology.[56] This author's attempt to synthesize these works, shown in Table 12.3, is based on a summary view of a large number of studies in which emotions were either caused by appraisal dimensions or associated with them. In addition, some personal interpretation is introduced, and certain dimensions appearing rarely in consumption have been omitted.

It is apparent from the table that cognitively based emotions are linked to the relevance of events and to the impact of these outcomes on the person's life. These impacts, in the first column of Table 12.3, are referred to as appraisal dimensions. In large part, the resulting emotions

Figure 12.8 **An Extended Two- or Three-Appraisal Model**

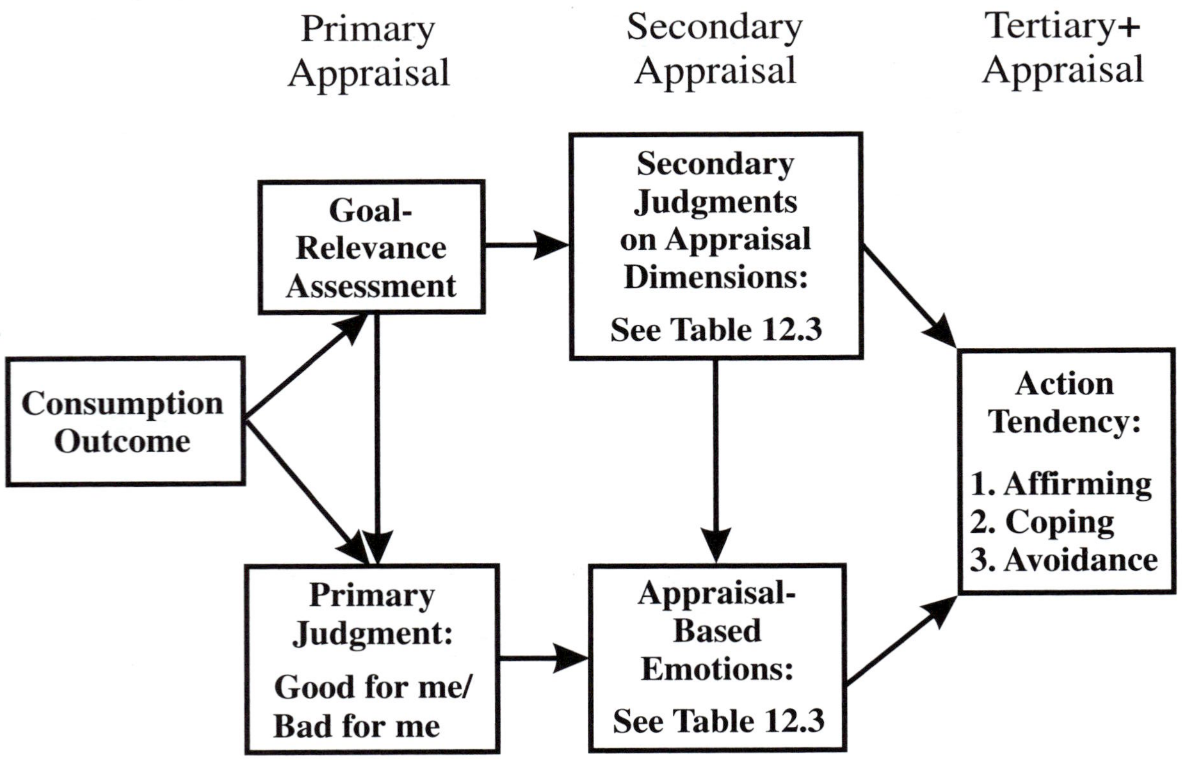

Primary Appraisal	Secondary Appraisal	Tertiary+ Appraisal

```
                                    ┌──────────────────┐
                                    │  Secondary       │
                                    │  Judgments       │──────────────┐
                                    │  on Appraisal    │              │
                                    │  Dimensions:     │              ▼
             ┌──────────────┐       │  See Table 12.3  │       ┌──────────────┐
             │  Goal-       │──────▶└──────────────────┘       │  Action      │
             │  Relevance   │                                  │  Tendency:   │
             │  Assessment  │                                  │              │
             └──────────────┘                                  │  1. Affirming│
                    ▲  │                                        │  2. Coping   │
                    │  │                                        │  3. Avoidance│
            ┌───────────────┐                                  └──────────────┘
            │  Consumption  │                                         ▲
            │  Outcome      │                                         │
            └───────────────┘       ┌──────────────────┐             │
                    │               │  Primary         │      ┌──────────────┐
                    └──────────────▶│  Judgment:       │─────▶│  Appraisal-  │
                                    │  Good for me/    │      │  Based       │
                                    │  Bad for me      │      │  Emotions:   │
                                    └──────────────────┘      │  See Table   │
                                                              │  12.3        │
                                                              └──────────────┘
```

Table 12.3

Selected Appraisal Dimensions and Emotional Labels

Appraisal dimension	Typical emotion or emotion-state labels	
	Positive	Negative
Goal relevance	Attention, interest	Disinterest, indifference
Motivational state: maximum reward/minimum punishment	Approach orientation: e.g., affiliation	Avoidance orientation: e.g., disassociation, withdrawal
Motive or desire: congruency/incongruency	Affects loading on the positive side of the circumplex models	Affects loading on the negative side of the circumplex models
Goal attainment/failure	Feelings of success: achievement	Feelings of failure: loss, inadequacy
Anticipated effort	Challenge, interest, pride	Boredom
Unexpectedness: certainty/uncertainty	Anticipation, hope	Anxiety, apprehension, fear
Unexpectedness: novelty	Joy	Disappointment
Unexpectedness: suddenness	Relief, surprise	Shock, startlement, surprise
Controllability: self	Gratification, pride	Guilt, regret, remorse, shame
Controllability: other	Gratitude	Anger, annoyance, contempt, scorn, disappointment, distrust
Controllability: situation	Happiness, luck	Frustration, despair, sadness
Legitimacy/fairness/unfairness	Happiness, pride	Anger, annoyance, contempt, distrust, guilt, rage

are dimension-specific. The positive and negative emotions in the second and third columns are those covered in this book and in the external literature. Observe the correspondence to the circumplex models, in particular Figures 12.4 and 12.5, and to the emotions in Tables 12.1 and 12.2. It is clear that there is remarkable convergence of investigative technique and emotion identification throughout the various fields in which emotion is studied. Consumption is no exception.

Notably, satisfaction rarely appears in lists of appraisal emotions (and does not here). Rather, more precise labels, such as achievement, are used to describe appraised events, such as goal attainment. This raises two questions. First, can this appraisal analysis prove useful to consumer researchers in the study of satisfaction, a topic to be broached shortly, and second, where does satisfaction belong?

Where Is Satisfaction?

One interesting question stemming from the summaries in Table 12.3 is the location of satisfaction. Why does it not appear prominently in appraisal lists? As it turns out, of the reviewed frameworks used in the summary, only two categorize satisfaction as an appraised emotion.[57] The first conceptualization, which is not empirically based, puts satisfaction in the category of "confirmed prospects." Interestingly, dissatisfaction is not categorized, for this work refers to disconfirmed prospects as disappointment. According to earlier discussion in Chapter 4, however, satisfaction is more than a simple confirmation of expected outcomes or prospects, and disappointment is a special case of a (slight) negative disconfirmation. In the second conceptualization, satisfaction appears as realizing an expected change in events, experiencing a pleasant event that helps one to reach goals, or receiving an event that furthers one's plans (goals). These suppositions are not tested in the framework, however, and appear somewhat disjoint. And, in the previous chapter's discussion on attribution, satisfaction would appear to be a discriminating affect perhaps for ability attributions under the case of success, while dissatisfaction might appear for cases of situational failure.

Inductive Approaches

A second line of inquiry into identifying the location of satisfaction among appraisal affects has investigated emotions, including satisfaction, within a scaling or cluster categorization framework. These techniques are more data-driven than theory-driven, but provide insight nonetheless. For example, using a decision tree approach, researchers (specific studies are discussed next) have placed satisfaction in the reached-own-goal or satisfied need category, along with contentment. In these same studies, dissatisfaction falls into the perceived injustice category along with bitterness.

When a cluster analysis was used on data, one set of writers found that satisfaction fell into a large subcluster of emotions that can be referred to as "cheerfulness," which also includes amusement, bliss, gaiety, glee, jolliness, joviality, joy, delight, enjoyment, gladness, happiness, jubilation, elation, ecstasy, and euphoria.[58] Unfortunately, finer positive affect discriminations fade in this "constellation of cheer." Contentment, on the other hand, loads with pleasure and few other affects. With regard to dissatisfaction, which was not measured, its close relative, disappointment, appears with dismay and displeasure.

Again using clustering, a stream of research found that satisfaction exists within a macrocluster of "positive terms without interpersonal reference," which can generally be labeled as good or pleasant.[59] Within this cluster are three subclusters that can loosely be described as contentment, happiness, and pride. Within the happiness subcluster are six sub-subclusters: gladness, amusement, hopefulness, cheerfulness, blissfulness, and elation. Satisfaction exists within the gladness cluster along with delight, glee, gratification, pleasure, reassurance, release, relief, and playfulness. Note that satisfaction's arousal-related variants of delight, pleasure, and contentment are mentioned as close relatives.

Dissatisfaction in this second solution exists within a macrocluster of terms relating to anger, hatred, and disgust, and in the anger subcluster specifically. Other anger subclusters include annoyance and indignation. Terms coexisting in the dissatisfaction sub-subcluster include crossness, crankiness, discontent, grouchiness, and grumpiness. Of interest is the observation that unsatisfiedness and disappointment exist in a separate macrocluster of shame, sadness, and pain, and within these, in the sadness subcluster.

In somewhat different approach, another research program had subjects rate hundreds of words on the basis of whether they were "feeling" words or "being" words in order to classify them according to their affective (feeling) orientation or cognitive (being) orientation.[60] The results showed that the word *satisfaction* was classified as cognitive while *self-satisfaction* (being at ease with one's position in life, akin to well-being) was affective. A further irony occurred in that *dissatisfied* was classified as affective. These findings actually support the combined cognitive-affective satisfaction model since, apparently, some facets of satisfaction are cognitive (outcomes) and others are affective (one's feeling about outcomes). Finally, the clustering-based CES described earlier in this chapter does not contain either satisfaction or dissatisfaction, although it does contain the words *pleased* and *discontented*.[61]

INSIGHTS IN THE POSTPURCHASE LITERATURE

A final approach to identifying appraisal-related emotions elicited during consumption involves identifying the emotional consequences of postpurchase processes that have been discovered in the consumer satisfaction tradition. Essentially, this is what has been done in this book up to now.

Although not discussed as appraisal dimensions, the central theme of each chapter from Chapter 2 through 11 addresses a dimension used by consumers to determine their satisfaction. Chapters 2, 5, 6, and 7 discuss the salience of particular product or service dimensions—namely, performance, needs, ideals (quality), and value. Here, these can be more broadly viewed as consumption goals, and the salience of each can be described as goal relevance. Chapter 3 covers the subject of expectations, including the certainty or uncertainty of attaining consumption goals. In Chapter 10, discussion returns to a different sort of uncertainty, cognitive dissonance. Chapter 4 elaborates on congruency and incongruency, framed as performance comparisons to a standard. Chapter 8, on equity and inequity, addresses the concept of legitimacy from the perspective of deservedness and fairness. Chapters 9 and 11, on regret and attribution, discuss, among other topics, the controllability of consumption outcomes. Finally, this chapter discusses attainment and failure in the context of consumption. The topical words in this paragraph were selected to reflect the terminology used in the various appraisal literatures noted in Table 12.3.

Appraisal-Based Consumption Emotions

In pursuing appraisal emotions in the consumption literature, it is unfortunate that the subject of appraisal, although recommended as one of many starting points, has not been more thoroughly fleshed out since the initial publication of this book. Of the dimensions appearing in appraisal works, only attribution (self versus other control—as discussed in the previous chapter) and fairness (legitimacy) have been investigated. A few studies appearing in consumer behavior and in the applied sector of psychology are reported here. Again, readers wishing to see satisfaction emerge from these investigations will be disappointed. Of note, however, is that only a very few studies take the analysis to the consequences of appraisal-related affect, thereby providing a lead-in to the next chapter.

The first study used a critical incident technique with gift giving as the focus to identify situations in which emotions were experienced as a result of appraisals.[62] Both emotions (satisfaction was not measured) and appraisals were investigated. Scales for the latter (reported in the appendix of the study) included pleasantness, effort, activity, certainty, other, self, and situational agency, fairness, and obstacle. The lengthy results are not reported here except to say that pleasantness and control were two major (discriminant) functions. The particular combination of appraisals and resulting emotions were reported but not explored for their implications.

Another study examined three emotions (anger, sadness, and joy—two satisfaction items were embedded in the latter scale) and three appraisals (goal relevance, goal congruence, and coping potential). In a computer usage analysis, limited support was obtained for high relevance coupled with low goal congruence in the propensity to complain. In a similar study of lost luggage during air travel, emotional and "semi" emotional responses (anger, resignation, worry, and "good humor") were compared to appraisal judgments of unexpectedness, goal obstructiveness, coping ability, and norm incompatibility. The results showed that a complexity of "emotional blends" predicted fliers' ability to cope with the unexpected and goal-obstructive nature of lost luggage; "good humor" was one such mechanism.[63]

In another study of voters' disappointment over a favored political candidate leaving the race, the three emotions of sadness, anger, and hope were investigated. Results showed temporal effects of initial anger, sadness, and hope for the candidate's future return to politics, suggesting a descriptive role of appraisal analysis more than a strategy role, although planning for the future was stressed as a behavioral outcome. In a similar study of temporal events using vignettes of restaurant service encounters, nine emotions (surprise, peacefulness, excitement, joy, contentment, relief, anger, discontent, and worry—and no satisfaction) were compared to the appraisal dimensions of typicality, unexpectedness, controllability, self-other-situational agency, motive consistency, and coping potential. The fairly straightforward relations between frustration on the dimensions and the emotions were supported. Motive consistency and coping potential stood out as primary appraisal dimensions on importance.[64]

The Tertiary Phase: Action Tendencies

The third phase of the appraisal model in Figure 12.8 has been addressed in two studies. Both used the context of complaining and how a consumer would respond as a result. The figure shows three options: affirmation or acceptance; coping or engaging specific behavioral postures resulting from the emotion state; and avoidance, either consciously or subconsciously, in the present or future. All are valid "styles" and only brief mention of these studies and their findings can be presented here.

In these studies (both are similar, the second following from the first), in-depth interviews were conducted to assess the emotions and coping behaviors of individuals reporting dissatisfying marketplace experiences.[65] Expressions of anger, disgust, contempt, sadness, fear, shame, and guilt (all negative and all lacking representations of satisfaction or dissatisfaction) were compared to expressed blame attributions of external, internal, and situational control. Although based on narratives, the three coping strategies described as problem-focused (direct action to solve the problem), emotion-focused (inward mental orientation, such as self-blame, to ameliorate the problem), and avoidance (forgetting) were detailed and the nature of the cause (internal, external, situational) was related to the emotion experienced.

Specific action tendencies were identified in the second study. In the affirmation category, accepting responsibility (accommodation) was most common. In the coping area, confrontation and social support–seeking were likely to be engaged. And for avoidance strategies, mental distancing and devaluation (not unlike trivialization in dissonance reduction) were found. Readers are invited to investigate the original sources as the methodologies used described idiosyncratic results of individual consumers. Nonetheless, these studies, which tap the entire appraisal model shown in Figure 12.8, are prototypes of future studies yet to be performed.

CONCLUSION

The lengthy reviews of the emotion literature in the first part of this chapter and the appraisal literature in the later part were conducted to discover the emotional role of satisfaction in consumption. It may be helpful at this point to review this author's opinion on this topic in the first edition of this book:

> Generally, no conclusions can be drawn. The appearance of satisfaction in various frameworks has been elusive and spotty. Sometimes satisfaction appears, other times it does not. Its position in the circumplex models was highly variant; its association with other emotions in the lists in which it was examined was inconsistent; and the appearance of satisfaction among appraised emotions was haphazard.[66]

A more guarded conclusion is warranted at this time. Researchers now recognize that emotional responding is part and parcel of satisfaction construction. Consumers are emotional creatures and have been since before the creation of the spoken word. Emotions exist even in the absence of the consideration of a purchase, as when individuals reflect on how they would feel about consumables external to their own life (e.g., the exhilaration of commercial space flight—now a reality for the wealthy at about $200,000 a reservation). They can respond emotionally in anticipation of a purchase, in anticipation of usage (e.g., having reservations for a concert or vacation), during usage, after usage, in anticipation of repeated future usage, and even vicariously for others' usage (e.g., a friend's wedding). The only unknown for inclusion of emotion in responding is when it will occur in the research context.

Moreover, there is now great consensus on the constellation of emotions consumers can express. Although there are cultural variations, particularly for complex emotions or blends of emotions, emotions exist as primitives and as derivations of these primitives, each of which has evoking conditions. They prime reactions to consumption events, sometimes are the events themselves, and are the results of events. While scholars can perform consumer research without regard for emotion responding (as they had for many years), it would be unusual and inefficient to do so now. Without the inclusion of emotion, emotion clusters cannot be identified, the percent of dependent construct variance cannot be fully accounted for, and research conclusions would be sterile by today's standards. Indeed, data have now shown that stock market valuation estimates can be improved by taking into account the relative satisfaction levels within firms and industries (see Chapter 15).

However, the question of whether satisfaction is an emotion still has not been answered. Indirect evidence for the relationship between the two concepts has been provided in the models shown in Figures 12.6 and 12.7. The latest work on appraisal in consumption incorporates affect within cognitive perspectives, although greater explanation of this phenomenon has yet to congeal. Excluding pure emotion contexts, emotion can be found to reside along with or in causal juxtaposition with cognition, both of which precede an ultimate satisfaction response, at least at the time of a query to the consumer. This puts satisfaction within the "nomological consumption net," but distinguishable nonetheless. If one insists on referring to satisfaction as an emotion, then it must be concluded that it is a hybrid cognition-emotion not well described in the psychological literature.

In the Introduction to this volume, *satisfaction* was defined as the consumer's fulfillment response. No data or theory encountered by this author is at odds with this definition. If consumers desire hedonic fulfillment (e.g., the thrill of fast driving), anhedonic fulfillment (e.g., owning a car that goes 150 miles per hour), or mixed cognitive and affective fulfillment (e.g., "I love knowing that I can drive that fast"), then fulfillment of these simple or compound wishes is satisfying.

Alternatively, individual consumers can emphasize the affective or cognitive components of their purchase outcomes, one over the other. For example, consumers can emphasize the degree of delight experienced in consuming a cognitively fulfilling product (e.g., completing a demanding jigsaw puzzle). Thus satisfaction will be correlated with delight, the affective component. Alternatively, they can emphasize the knowledge of possessing a pleasing product, expressing the pride of ownership. This satisfaction is more cognitively oriented. Finally, as yet another alternative, consumers can feel satisfied about fact, anhedonic cognition, as in the knowledge of consumption: "Been there, done that."

This summary readies discussion for the next chapter, which describes different forms (referred to as prototypes) of satisfaction. Each is based on what the consumer finds fulfilling about consumption. From unemotional consumption to consumption events charged with emotion, all are described as satisfying (or dissatisfying) by consumers of varying perspectives. Moreover, through the use of this perspective, researchers will be able to determine which consumers reside as various prototypes by applying the concepts discussed to this point and techniques to be provided later.

NOTES

1. See, Marsh and Collett, "Driving Passion"; Muensterberger, *Collecting*; and Rathje and Murphy; *Rubbish!* For a fairly recent discourse on the psychological background on emotion and its use and potential application in marketing, see O'Shaughnessy and O'Shaughnessy, *Marketing Power of Emotion.*

2. See, e.g., Dichter, *Handbook of Consumer Motivations*; and Martineau, *Motivation in Advertising.*

3. Aaker, Stayman, and Vezina, "Identifying Feelings Elicited by Advertising"; Hirschman and Holbrook, "Hedonic Consumption"; Holbrook and Hirschman, "Experiential Aspects of Consumption."

4. Darke, Chattopadhyay, and Ashworth, "Importance and Functional Significance of Affective Cues in Consumer Choice"; Wood and Bettman, "Predicting Happiness."

5. Frijda, "Laws of Emotion."

6. For more clinical treatments of emotion's origins, see Buck, "Biological Affects"; and Izard, "Four Systems for Emotion Activation." For a very recent exposition of the neurobiological bases of emotion, including results of functional magnetic resonance imaging (fMRI) scanning, see Barrett et al., "Experience of Emotion."

7. Schnall and Laird, "Keep Smiling"; Sundaram and Webster, "Role of Nonverbal Communications in Service Encounters."

8. Darwin, *Expression of Emotion in Man and Animals*; James, *Principles of Psychology,* Chapter 25. For more current renditions of the main theses of these original sources, see Buck, *Communication of Emotion*; and Izard, *Psychology of Emotions.*

9. Joseph, "Limbic System."

10. Discussion of this phenomenon, where distress and delight are described as manifestations of aversive

and appetitive systems, can be found in Lang, "Emotion Probe." See, also, Doost et al., "Development of a Corpus of Emotional Words Produced by Children and Adolescents," in which the developmental stages are explored, and Oatley and Johnson-Laird, "Toward a Cognitive Theory of Emotions."

11. See the comprehensive work of Bagozzi, Gopinath, and Nyer, "Role of Emotions in Marketing." Although satisfaction is addressed, the writers note, as this author does here, that "satisfaction is neither a basic emotion nor a central emotional category in leading theories of emotions," p. 201. In another recent review by Laros and Steenkamp, "Emotions in Consumer Behavior," the authors essentially reproduce the results of others with regard to positive and negative affect, the first-order basic emotions, and related descriptors, but do not find satisfaction. This volume (and the first edition) explain why this is so and why satisfaction requires separate study.

12. Gardner, "Mood States and Consumer Behavior."

13. Izard, *Patterns of Emotions* and *Human Emotions.* The most recent source is Carroll E. Izard, *The Psychology of Emotions.*

14. Russell, "Affective Space Is Bipolar" and "Circumplex Model of Affect."

15. See Reisenzein, "Pleasure-Arousal Theory and the Intensity of Emotions." Interestingly, PAT is an outgrowth of pleasure-arousal-dominance (PAD) theory, which was based on three, not two, dimensions. Russell was one of the early proponents of this earlier framework, later reduced to PAT because of the instability found in scaling solutions. Nonetheless, PAD remains useful in the study of consumer behavior, appearing in the advertising evaluation literature and retail environment literatures. See Foxall and Greenley, "Consumers' Emotional Responses to Service Environments"; Morris, "SAM"; and Russell and Mehrabian, "Evidence for a Three-Factor Theory of Emotions."

16. Watson and Tellegen, "Toward a Consensual Structure of Mood."

17. Larsen and Diener note a problem with this rotation solution and the resulting interpretation. It appears that the positive and negative low-arousal affects are mislocated. Calmness is actually a low-arousal positive affect and should be located opposite high-arousal positive affect. A similar argument can be made for boredom. See Larsen and Diener, "Promises and Problems with the Circumplex Model of Emotion." In defense of Watson and Tellegen's interpretation, calmness can be viewed as the low-arousal absence of negative affect, and similarly for boredom.

18. Actually, the data are rather conclusive in this regard; the available analyses are complementary to the point of being an anomaly in psychology. For a review, see Yik, Russell, and Barrett, "Structure of Self-Reported Current Affect." Other references include Chamberlain, "On the Structure of Subjective Well-Being"; Diener and Emmons, "Independence of Positive and Negative Affect"; Diener and Iran-Nejad, "Relationship in Experience between Various Types of Affect"; Larson, "On the Independence of Positive and Negative Affect within Hour-to-Hour Experience"; Meyer and Shack, "Structural Convergence of Mood and Personality"; and Storm and Storm, "Taxonomic Study of the Vocabulary of Emotions." Post-1990 references include Feldman, "Valence Focus and Arousal Focus"; Goldstein and Strube, "Independence Revisited"; Green, Salovey, and Truax, "Static, Dynamic, and Causative Bipolarity of Affect"; Mano, "Structure and Intensity of Emotional Experiences"; Remington, Fabrigar, and Visser, "Reexaming the Circumplex Model of Affect"; and Watson et al., "Two General Activation Systems of Affect."

19. Plutchik, *Emotion* and *Emotions and Life.* Plutchik's graphics along with an application to brand personality can be found in Sweeney and Brandon, "Brand Personality," pp. 647–649.

20. See the chapters in Plutchik and Conte, *Circumplex Models of Personality and Emotions*; Havlena, Holbrook, and Lehmann, "Assessing the Validity of Emotional Typologies"; Holbrook and Westwood, "Role of Emotion in Advertising Revisited"; and Zeitlin and Westwood, "Measuring Emotional Response," where a number of other complex blends are displayed at p. 38.

21. Andrews and Withey, "Developing Measures of Perceived Life Quality." This author's note: the scale itself is "terrible." The seven descriptors are not unidimensional as the poles (delight—an emotion, and terrible—a descriptor state) attest.

22. Finn, "Reassessing the Foundations of Customer Delight"; Oliver, Rust, and Varki, "Customer Delight."

23. See Aaker, Stayman, and Vezina, "Identifying Feelings Elicited by Advertising"; Batra and Holbrook, "Developing a Typology of Affective Responses to Advertising"; Derbaix, "Impact of Affective Reactions on Attitudes Toward the Advertisement and the Brand"; Edell and Burke, "Power of Feelings in Understanding Advertising Effects"; Olney, Holbrook, and Batra, "Consumer Responses to Advertising"; and Wiles and Cornwell, "Review of Methods Utilized in Measuring Affect, Feelings, and Emotion in Advertising."

24. Morris, "SAM."

25. Bagozzi, Gopinath, and Nyer, "Role of Emotions in Marketing."

26. Richins, "Measuring Emotions in the Consumption Experience."

27. The concept of "product love" has been previously introduced. See Ahuvia, "Beyond the Extended Self." Also see Brown, Doherty, and Clarke, *Romancing the Market.*

28. Reisenzein, "Pleasure-Arousal Theory and the Intensity of Emotions."

29. The following section draws from a number of sources. For a theoretical and empirical discussion of the correspondence between these concepts, see Diener et al., "Intensity and Frequency"; Schimmack and Diener, "Affect Intensity"; Thomas and Diener, "Memory Accuracy in the Recall of Emotions"; and Winkielman, Knäuper, and Schwarz, "Looking Back at Anger."

30. Dalakas, "Importance of a Good Ending in a Service Encounter"; Fredrickson, "Extracting Meaning from Past Affective Experiences"; Fredrickson and Kahneman, "Duration Neglect in Retrospective Evaluations of Affective Episodes."

31. Ariely and Carmon, "Gestalt Characteristics of Experiences"; Ariely and Zauberman, "On the Making of an Experience."

32. Larsen and Diener, "Promises and Problems with the Circumplex Model of Emotion"; Mackinnon et al., "Short Form of the Positive and Negative Affect Schedule"; Russell, Weiss, and Mendelsohn, "Affect Grid"; Watson, Clark, and Tellegen, "Development and Validation of Brief Measures of Positive and Negative Affect."

33. See Derbaix and Pham, "Affective Reactions to Consumption Situations"; and O'Shaughnessy and O'Shaughnessy, *Marketing Power of Emotion.*

34. Babin and Darden, "Good and Bad Shopping Vibes"; Clark and Watson, "Mood and the Mundane"; Gardner, "Mood States and Consumer Behavior"; Luong, "Affective Service Display and Customer Mood"; Seidlitz and Diener, "Memory for Positive versus Negative Life Events"; Wright and Bower, "Mood Effects on Subjective Probability Assessment."

35. Chaudhuri, "Consumption Emotion and Perceived Risk"; Mayer et al., "Broader Conception of Mood Experience"; Mellers, "Choice and the Relative Pleasure of Consequences"; Mellers et al., "Decision Affect Theory."

36. Chitturi, Raghunathan, and Mahajan, "Form Versus Function"; Darke, Chattopadhyay, and Ashworth, "Importance and Functional Significance of Affective Cues in Consumer Choice"; Jiang and Wang, "Impact of Affect on Service Quality and Satisfaction"; Mattila and Wirtz, "Role of Preconsumption Affect in Postpurchase Evaluation of Services"; Phillips and Baumgartner, "Role of Consumption Emotions in the Satisfaction Response"; Wilson et al., "Preferences as Expectation-Driven Inferences"; Yeung and Wyer, "Affect, Appraisal, and Consumer Judgment."

37. Mano and Oliver, "Assessing the Dimensionality and Structure of Consumption Experience."

38. Cowley, Farrell, and Edwardson, "Role of Affective Expectations in Memory for a Service Encounter."

39. Mittal, Ross, and Baldasare, "Asymmetric Impact of Negative and Positive Attribute-Level Performance on Overall Satisfaction and Repurchase Intentions"; Spreng, MacKenzie, and Olshavsky, "Reexamination of the Determinants of Consumer Satisfaction."

40. Oliver, "Cognitive, Affective, and Attribute Bases of the Satisfaction Response."

41. Westbrook, "Product/Consumption-Based Affective Responses and Postpurchase Processes."

42. Westbrook and Oliver, "Dimensionality of Consumption Emotion Patterns and Consumer Satisfaction."

43. Evrard and Aurier, "Influence of Emotions on Satisfaction with Movie Consumption"; Liljander and Strandvik, "Emotions in Service Satisfaction"; Machleit and Eroglu, "Describing and Measuring Emotional Response to Shopping Experience"; Madrigal, "Cognitive and Affective Determinants of Fan Satisfaction with Sporting Event Attendance"; Price, Arnould, and Deibler, "Consumers' Emotional Responses to Service Encounters"; Price, Arnould, and Tierney, "Going to Extremes"; Wakefield, Blodgett, and Sloan, "Measurement and Management of the Sportscape."

44. Andrade and Cohen, "On the Consumption of Negative Feelings"; Krishnan and Olshavsky, "Dual Role of Emotions in Consumer Satisfaction/Dissatisfaction."

45. Dubé and Menon, "Why Would Certain Types of In-Process Negative Emotions Increase Post-Purchase Consumer Satisfaction with Services?"; A. Smith and Bolton, "Effect of Customers' Emotional Responses to Service Failures on Their Recovery Effort Evaluations and Satisfaction Judgments."

46. Russell and Barrett, "Core Affect, Prototypical Emotional Episodes, and Other Things Called *Emotion*," p. 805.

47. Menon and Dubé, "Scripting Consumer Emotions in Extended Service Transactions."

48. Grove and Fisk, "Impact of Other Customers on Service Experiences"; van Dolen et al., "Affective Consumer Responses in Service Encounters."

49. Diener, Lucas, and Scollon, "Beyond the Hedonic Treadmill"; Dubé and Morgan, "Capturing the Dynamics of In-Process Consumption Emotions and Satisfaction in Extended Service Transactions"; Holbrook and Gardner, "Approach to Investigating the Emotional Determinants of Consumption Durations"; Ng, "Happiness Surveys"; Wirtz, Mattila, and Tan, "Moderating Role of Target-Arousal on the Impact of Affect on Satisfaction."

50. One of many studies is Dubé and Maute, "Antecedents of Brand Switching, Brand Loyalty, and Verbal Responses to Service Failure."

51. Discussions of appraisal can be found in Frijda, "Place of Appraisal in Emotion"; Frijda, Kuipers, and ter Schure, "Relations among Emotion, Appraisal, and Emotional Action Readiness"; Johnson-Laird and Oatley, "Language of Emotions" and "Basic Emotions, Rationality, and Folk Theory"; Lazarus, "Cognition and Motivation in Emotion"; and the relevant chapters in Scherer, Schorr, and Johnstone, *Appraisal Processes in Emotion.*

52. Grace, "How Embarrassing!"

53. Mauro, Sato, and Tucker, "Role of Appraisal in Human Emotions"; Mesquita and Ellsworth, "Role of Culture in Appraisal"; Scherer, "Profiles of Emotion-Antecedent Appraisal." But see Wierzbicka, "Talking About Emotions."

54. Buck, "Prime Theory"; Ekman, "Argument for Basic Emotions"; Frijda, "Place of Appraisal in Emotion"; Frijda, Kuipers, and ter Schure, "Relations among Emotion, Appraisal, and Emotional Action Readiness"; Lazarus, "Cognition and Motivation in Emotion"; Weiner, "Attributional Theory of Achievement Motivation and Emotion."

55. This section, derived from Lazarus, "Relational Meaning and Discrete Emotions," deviates in some respects from Weiner's sequence in the previous chapter and contains this author's modifications to conform to consumption situations.

56. In addition to the works previously cited, also see Ortony, Clore, and Collins, *Cognitive Structure of Emotions*; Roseman, "Appraisal Determinants of Discrete Emotions" and "Model of Appraisal in the Emotion System"; Roseman, Antoniou, and Jose, "Appraisal Determinants of Emotions"; Roseman, Spindel, and Jose, "Appraisals of Emotion-Eliciting Events"; and C. Smith and Lazarus, "Appraisal Components, Core Relational Themes, and the Emotions."

57. Ortony, Clore, and Collins, *Cognitive Structure of Emotions*; Scherer, "Criteria for Emotion-Antecedent Appraisal."

58. Shaver et al., "Emotion Knowledge."

59. Storm and Storm, "Taxonomic Study of the Vocabulary of Emotions."

60. Clore, Ortony, and Foss, "The Psychological Foundations of the Affective Lexicon."

61. Richins, "Measuring Emotions in the Consumption Experience."

62. Ruth, Brunel, and Otnes, "Linking Thoughts to Feelings."

63. Nyer, "Study of the Relationships Between Cognitive Appraisals and Consumption Emotions"; Scherer and Ceschi, "Lost Luggage."

64. Dalakas, "Effect of Cognitive Appraisals on Emotional Responses During Service Encounters"; Levine, "Anatomy of Disappointment."

65. Godwin, Patterson, and Johnson, "Consumer Coping Strategies with Dissatisfactory Service Encounters"; Stephens and Gwinner, "Why Don't Some People Complain?"

66. Oliver, *Satisfaction*, p. 318.

BIBLIOGRAPHY

Aaker, David A., Douglas M. Stayman, and Richard Vezina. "Identifying Feelings Elicited by Advertising." *Psychology & Marketing* 5, no. 1 (Spring 1988): 1–16.

Ahuvia, Aaron C. "Beyond the Extended Self: Loved Objects and Consumers' Identity Narratives." *Journal of Consumer Research* 32, no. 1 (June 2005): 171–184.

Andrade, Eduardo B., and Joel B. Cohen. "On the Consumption of Negative Feelings." *Journal of Consumer Research* 34, no. 3 (October 2007): 283–300.

Andrews, Frank M., and Stephen B. Withey. "Developing Measures of Perceived Life Quality: Results from Several National Surveys." *Social Indicators Research* 1, no. 1 (May 1974): 1–26.

Ariely, Dan, and Ziv Carmon. "Gestalt Characteristics of Experiences: The Defining Features of Summarized Events." *Journal of Behavioral Decision Making* 13, no. 2 (April–June 2000): 191–201.

Ariely, Dan, and Gal Zauberman. "On the Making of an Experience: The Effects of Breaking and Combining Experiences on Their Overall Evaluation." *Journal of Behavioral Decision Making* 13, no. 2 (April–June 2000): 219–232.

Babin, Barry J., and William R. Darden. "Good and Bad Shopping Vibes: Spending and Patronage Satisfaction." *Journal of Business Research* 35, no. 3 (March 1996): 201–206.

Bagozzi, Richard P., Mahesh Gopinath, and Prashanth U. Nyer. "The Role of Emotions in Marketing." *Journal of the Academy of Marketing Science* 27, no. 2 (Spring 1999): 184–206.

Barrett, Lisa Feldman, Batja Mesquita, Kevin N. Ochsner, and James J. Gross. "The Experience of Emotion." *Annual Review of Psychology* 58 (2007): 373–403.

Batra, Rajeev, and Morris B. Holbrook. "Developing a Typology of Affective Responses to Advertising." *Psychology & Marketing* 7, no. 1 (Spring 1990): 11–25.

Brown, Stephen, Anne Marie Doherty, and Bill Clarke, eds. *Romancing the Market.* London: Routledge, 1998.

Buck, Ross. "The Biological Affects: A Typology." *Psychological Bulletin* 106, no. 2 (April 1999): 301–336.

———. *The Communication of Emotion.* New York: Guilford Press, 1984.

———. "Prime Theory: An Integrated View of Motivation and Emotion." *Psychological Review* 92, no. 3 (July 1985): 389–413.

Chamberlain, Kerry. "On the Structure of Subjective Well-Being." *Social Indicators Research* 20, no. 6 (December 1988): 581–604.

Chaudhuri, Arjun. "Consumption Emotion and Perceived Risk: A Macro-Analytic Approach." *Journal of Business Research* 39, no. 2 (June 1997): 81–92.

Chitturi, Ravindra, Rajagopal Raghunathan, and Vijay Mahajan. "Form Versus Function: How the Intensities of Specific Emotions Evoked in Functional Versus Hedonic Trade-Offs Mediate Product Preferences." *Journal of Marketing Research* 44, no. 4 (November 2007): 702–714.

Clark, Lee Anna, and David Watson. "Mood and the Mundane: Relations Between Daily Life Events and Self-Reported Mood." *Journal of Personality and Social Psychology* 54, no. 2 (February 1988): 296–308.

Clore, Gerald L., Andrew Ortony, and Mark A. Foss. "The Psychological Foundations of the Affective Lexicon." *Journal of Personality and Social Psychology* 53, no. 4 (October 1987): 751–766.

Cowley, Elizabeth, Colin Farrell, and Michael Edwardson. "The Role of Affective Expectations in Memory for a Service Encounter." *Journal of Business Research* 58, no. 10 (October 2005): 1419–1425.

Dalakas, Vassilis. "The Effect of Cognitive Appraisals on Emotional Responses During Service Encounters." *Services Marketing Quarterly* 27, no. 1 (2005): 23–41.

———. "The Importance of a Good Ending in a Service Encounter." *Services Marketing Quarterly* 28, no. 1 (2006): 35–53.

Darke, Peter R., Amitava Chattopadhyay, and Laurence Ashworth. "The Importance and Functional Significance of Affective Cues in Consumer Choice." *Journal of Consumer Research* 33, no. 3 (December 2006): 322–328.

Darwin, Charles. *The Expression of Emotion in Man and Animals.* New York: D. Appleton, 1899.

Derbaix, Christian M. "The Impact of Affective Reactions on Attitudes Toward the Advertisement and the Brand: A Step Toward Ecological Validity." *Journal of Marketing Research* 32, no. 4 (November 1995): 470–479.

Derbaix, Christian M., and Michel T. Pham. "Affective Reactions to Consumption Situations: A Pilot Investigation." *Journal of Economic Psychology* 12, no, 2 (June 1991): 325–355.

Dichter, Ernest. *Handbook of Consumer Motivations.* New York: McGraw-Hill, 1964.

Diener, Ed, and Robert A. Emmons. "The Independence of Positive and Negative Affect." *Journal of Personality and Social Psychology* 47, no. 5 (November 1984): 1105–1117.

Diener, Ed, and Ashgar Iran-Nejad. "The Relationship in Experience between Various Types of Affect." *Journal of Personality and Social Psychology* 50, no. 5 (May 1986): 1031–1038.

Diener, Ed, Randy J. Larsen, Steven Levine, and Robert A. Emmons. "Intensity and Frequency: Dimensions Underlying Positive and Negative Affect." *Journal of Personality and Social Psychology* 48, no. 5 (May 1985): 1253–1265.

Diener, Ed, Richard E. Lucas, and Christie Napa Scollon. "Beyond the Hedonic Treadmill: Revising the Adaptation Theory of Well-Being." *American Psychologist* 61, no. 4 (May–June 2006): 305–314.

Doost, Hamid T. Neshat, Ali R. Moradi, Mohammad R. Taghavi, William Yule, and Tim Dalgleish. "The

Development of a Corpus of Emotional Words Produced by Children and Adolescents." *Personality and Individual Differences* 27, no. 3 (September 1999): 433–451.

Dubé, Laurette, and Manfred Maute. "The Antecedents of Brand Switching, Brand Loyalty, and Verbal Responses to Service Failure." In *Advances in Services Marketing and Management*, ed. Teresa A. Swartz, David E. Bowen, and Stephen W. Brown, 5:127–151. Greenwich, CT: JAI Press, 1996.

Dubé, Laurette, and Kalyani Menon. "Why Would Certain Types of In-Process Negative Emotions Increase Post-Purchase Consumer Satisfaction with Services? Insights from an Interpersonal View of Emotions." In *Advances in Services Marketing and Management*, ed. Teresa A. Swartz, David E. Bowen, and Stephen W. Brown, 7:131–158. Greenwich, CT: JAI Press, 1998.

Dubé, Laurette, and Michael S. Morgan. "Capturing the Dynamics of In-Process Consumption Emotions and Satisfaction in Extended Service Transactions." *International Journal of Research in Marketing* 15, no. 4 (October 1998): 309–320.

Edell, Julie A., and Marian Chapman Burke. "The Power of Feelings in Understanding Advertising Effects." *Journal of Consumer Research* 14, no. 3 (December 1987): 421–433.

Ekman, Paul. "An Argument for Basic Emotions." *Cognition and Emotion* 6, nos. 3–4 (May–July 1992): 169–200.

Evrard, Yves, and Philippe Aurier. "The Influence of Emotions on Satisfaction with Movie Consumption." *Journal of Consumer Satisfaction, Dissatisfaction and Complaining Behavior* 7 (1994): 119–125.

Feldman, Lisa A. "Valence Focus and Arousal Focus: Individual Differences in the Structure of Affective Experience." *Journal of Personality and Social Psychology* 69, no. 1 (July 1995): 153–166.

Finn, Adam. "Reassessing the Foundations of Customer Delight." *Journal of Service Research* 8, no. 2 (November 2005): 103–116.

Foxall, Gordon R., and Gordon E. Greenley. "Consumers' Emotional Responses to Service Environments." *Journal of Business Research* 46, no. 2 (October 1999): 149–158.

Fredrickson, Barbara L. "Extracting Meaning from Past Affective Experiences: The Importance of Peaks, Ends, and Specific Emotions." *Cognition and Emotion* 14, no. 4 (July 2000): 577–606.

Fredrickson, Barbara L., and Daniel Kahneman. "Duration Neglect in Retrospective Evaluations of Affective Episodes." *Journal of Personality and Social Psychology* 65, no. 1 (July 1993): 45–55.

Frijda, Nico H. "The Laws of Emotion." *American Psychologist* 43, no. 5 (May 1988): 349–358.

———. "The Place of Appraisal in Emotion." *Cognition and Emotion* 7, nos. 3–4 (May–July 1993): 357–387.

Frijda, Nico H., Peter Kuipers, and Elisabeth ter Schure. "Relations among Emotion, Appraisal, and Emotional Action Readiness." *Journal of Personality and Social Psychology* 57, no. 2 (August 1989): 212–228.

Gardner, Meryl Paula. "Mood States and Consumer Behavior: A Critical Review." *Journal of Consumer Research* 12, no. 3 (December 1985): 281–300.

Godwin, Beth F., Paul G. Patterson, and Lester W. Johnson. "Consumer Coping Strategies with Dissatisfactory Service Encounters: A Preliminary Investigation." *Journal of Consumer Satisfaction, Dissatisfaction and Complaining Behavior* 12 (1999): 145–154.

Goldstein, Miriam D., and Michael J. Strube. "Independence Revisited: The Relation between Positive and Negative Affect in a Naturalistic Setting." *Personality and Social Psychology Bulletin* 20, no. 1 (February 1994): 57–64.

Grace, Debra. "How Embarrassing! An Exploratory Study of Critical Incidents Including Affective Reactions." *Journal of Service Research* 9, no. 3 (February 2007): 271–284.

Green, Donald P., Peter Salovey, and Kathryn M. Truax. "Static, Dynamic, and Causative Bipolarity of Affect." *Journal of Personality and Social Psychology* 76, no. 5 (May 1999): 856–867.

Grove, Stephen J., and Raymond P. Fisk. "The Impact of Other Customers on Service Experiences: A Critical Incident Examination of 'Getting Along.'" *Journal of Retailing* 73, no. 1 (Spring 1997): 63–85.

Havlena, William J., Morris B. Holbrook, and Donald R. Lehmann. "Assessing the Validity of Emotional Typologies." *Psychology & Marketing* 6, no. 2 (Summer 1989): 97–112.

Hirschman, Elizabeth C., and Morris B. Holbrook. "Hedonic Consumption: Emerging Concepts, Methods and Propositions." *Journal of Marketing* 46, no. 3 (Summer 1982): 92–101.

Holbrook, Morris B., and Meryl P. Gardner. "An Approach to Investigating the Emotional Determinants of Consumption Durations: Why Do People Consume What They Consume for as Long as They Consume It?" *Journal of Consumer Psychology* 2, no. 2 (1993): 123–142.

Holbrook, Morris B., and Elizabeth C. Hirschman. "The Experiential Aspects of Consumption: Consumer Fantasies, Feelings, and Fun." *Journal of Consumer Research* 9, no. 2 (September 1982): 132–140.

Holbrook, Morris B., and Richard A. Westwood. "The Role of Emotion in Advertising Revisited: Testing a Typology of Emotional Responses." In *Cognitive and Affective Responses to Advertising*, ed. Patricia Cafferata and Alice M. Tybout, 353–371. Lexington, MA: Lexington Books, 1989.

Izard, Carroll E. "Four Systems for Emotion Activation: Cognitive and Noncognitive Processes." *Psychological Review* 100, no. 1 (January 1993): 68–90.

———. *Human Emotions.* New York: Plenum Press, 1977 .

———. *Patterns of Emotions.* New York: Academic Press, 1972.

———. *The Psychology of Emotions.* New York: Plenum Press, 1991.

James, William. *The Principles of Psychology*, vol. 2. 1890. New York: Dover, 1950.

Jiang, Ying, and Cheng Lu Wang. "The Impact of Affect on Service Quality and Satisfaction: The Moderation of Service Contexts." *Journal of Services Marketing* 20, no. 4 (2006): 211–218.

Johnson-Laird, P.N., and Keith Oatley. "Basic Emotions, Rationality, and Folk Theory." *Cognition and Emotion.* 6, nos. 3–4 (May–June 1992): 201–223.

———. "The Language of Emotions: An Analysis of a Semantic Field." *Cognition and Emotion* 3, no. 2 (March 1989): 81–123.

Joseph, R. "The Limbic System: Emotion, Laterality, and Unconscious Mind." *Psychoanalytic Review* 79, no. 3 (Fall 1992): 405–456.

Krishnan, H. Shanker, and Richard W. Olshavsky. "The Dual Role of Emotions in Consumer Satisfaction/Dissatisfaction." In *Advances in Consumer Research*, ed. Frank R. Kardes and Mita Sujan, 22:454–460. Provo, UT: Association for Consumer Research, 1995.

Lang, Peter J. "The Emotion Probe: Studies of Motivation and Attention." *American Psychologist* 50, no. 5 (May 1995): 372–385.

Laros, Fleur J.M., and Jan-Benedict E.M. Steenkamp. "Emotions in Consumer Behavior: A Hierarchical Approach." *Journal of Business Research* 58, no. 10 (October 2005): 1437–1445.

Larsen, Randy J., and Ed Diener. "Promises and Problems with the Circumplex Model of Emotion." In *Review of Personality and Social Psychology*, ed. Margaret S. Clark, 13:25–59. Newbury Park, CA: Sage, 1992.

Larson, Reed W. "On the Independence of Positive and Negative Affect within Hour-to-Hour Experience." *Motivation and Emotion* 11, no. 2 (June 1987): 145–156.

Lazarus, Richard S. "Cognition and Motivation in Emotion." *American Psychologist* 46, no. 4 (April 1991): 352–367.

———. "Relational Meaning and Discrete Emotions." In *Appraisal Processes in Emotion: Theory, Methods, Research*, ed. Klaus R. Scherer, Angela Schorr, and Tom Johnstone, 37–67. New York: Oxford University Press, 2001.

Levine, Linda J. "The Anatomy of Disappointment: A Naturalistic Test of Appraisal Models of Sadness, Anger, and Hope." *Cognition and Emotion* 10, no. 4 (July 1996): 337–359.

Liljander, Veronica, and Tore Strandvik. "Emotions in Service Satisfaction." *International Journal of Service Industry Management* 8, no. 2 (1997): 148–169.

Luong, Alexandra. "Affective Service Display and Customer Mood." *Journal of Service Research* 8, no. 2 (November 2005): 117–130.

Machleit, Karen A., and Sevgin A. Eroglu. "Describing and Measuring Emotional Response to Shopping Experience." *Journal of Business Research* 49, no. 2 (August 2000): 101–111.

Mackinnon, Andrew, Anthony F. Jorm, Helen Christensen, Ailsa E. Korten, Patricia A. Jacomb, and Bryan Rodgers. "A Short Form of the Positive and Negative Affect Schedule: Evaluation of Factorial Validity and Invariance Across Demographic Variables in a Community Sample." *Personality and Individual Differences* 27, no. 3 (September 1999): 405–416.

Madrigal, Robert. "Cognitive and Affective Determinants of Fan Satisfaction with Sporting Event Attendance." *Journal of Leisure Research* 27, no. 3 (1995): 205–227.

Mano, Haim. "The Structure and Intensity of Emotional Experiences: Method and Context Convergence." *Multivariate Behavioral Research* 26, no. 3 (1991): 389–411.

Mano, Haim, and Richard L. Oliver. "Assessing the Dimensionality and Structure of Consumption Experience: Evaluation, Feeling, and Satisfaction." *Journal of Consumer Research* 20, no. 3 (December 1993): 451–466.

Marsh, Peter, and Peter Collett. "Driving Passion." *Psychology Today* 21 (June 1987): 16–24.

Martineau, Pierre. *Motivation in Advertising.* New York: McGraw-Hill, 1957.

Mattila, Anna, and Jochen Wirtz. "The Role of Preconsumption Affect in Postpurchase Evaluation of Services." *Psychology & Marketing* 17, no. 7 (July 2000): 587–605.

Mauro, Robert, Kaori Sato, and John Tucker. "The Role of Appraisal in Human Emotions: A Cross-Cultural Study." *Journal of Personality and Social Psychology* 62, no. 2 (February 1992): 301–317.

Mayer, John D., Peter Salovey, Susan Gomberg-Kaufman, and Kathleen Blainey. "A Broader Conception of Mood Experience." *Journal of Personality and Social Psychology* 60, no. 1 (January 1991): 100–111.

Mellers, Barbara A. "Choice and the Relative Pleasure of Consequences." *Psychological Bulletin* 126, no. 6 (November 2000): 910–924.

Mellers, Barbara A., Alan Schwartz, Katty Ho, and Ilana Ritov. "Decision Affect Theory: Emotional Reactions to the Outcomes of Risky Options." *Psychological Science* 8, no. 6 (November 1997): 423–429.

Menon, Kalyani, and Laurette Dubé. "Scripting Consumer Emotions in Extended Service Transactions: A Prerequisite for Successful Adaptation in Provider Performance." In *Advances in Consumer Research*, ed. Eric J. Anould and Linda H. Scott, 26:18–24. Provo, UT: Association for Consumer Research, 1999.

Mesquita, Batja, and Phoebe C. Ellsworth. "The Role of Culture in Appraisal." In *Appraisal Processes in Emotion: Theory, Methods, Research*, ed. Klaus R. Scherer, Angela Schorr, and Tom Johnstone, 233–248. New York: Oxford University Press, 2001.

Meyer, Gregory J., and John R. Shack. "Structural Convergence of Mood and Personality: Evidence for Old and New Directions." *Journal of Personality and Social Psychology* 57, no. 4 (October 1989): 691–706.

Mittal, Vikas, William T. Ross Jr., and Patrick M. Baldasare. "The Asymmetric Impact of Negative and Positive Attribute-Level Performance on Overall Satisfaction and Repurchase Intentions." *Journal of Marketing* 62, no. 1 (January 1998): 33–47.

Morris, Jon D. "SAM: The Self-Assessment Manikin; An Efficient Cross-Cultural Measurement of Emotional Response." *Journal of Advertising Research* 35, no. 6 (November–December 1995): 63–68.

Muensterberger, Werner. *Collecting: An Unruly Passion.* Princeton, NJ: Princeton University Press, 1994.

Ng, Yew-Kwang. "Happiness Surveys: Some Comparability Issues and an Exploratory Survey Based in Just Perceivable Increments." *Social Indicators Research* 38, no. 1 (May 1996): 1–27.

Nyer, Prashanth U. "A Study of the Relationships Between Cognitive Appraisals and Consumption Emotions" *Journal of the Academy of Marketing Science* 25, no. 4 (Fall 1997): 296–304.

Oatley, Keith, and P.N. Johnson-Laird. "Toward a Cognitive Theory of Emotions." *Cognition and Emotion* 1, no. 2 (March 1987): 29–50.

Oliver, Richard L. "Cognitive, Affective, and Attribute Bases of the Satisfaction Response." *Journal of Consumer Research* 20, no. 3 (December 1993): 418–430.

———. *Satisfaction: A Behavioral Perspective on the Consumer.* New York: Irwin/McGraw-Hill, 1997.

Oliver, Richard L., Roland T. Rust, and Sajeev Varki. "Customer Delight: Foundations, Findings, and Managerial Insight." *Journal of Retailing* 73, no. 3 (Autumn 1997): 311–336.

Olney, Thomas J., Morris B. Holbrook, and Rajeev Batra. "Consumer Responses to Advertising: The Effects of Ad Content, Emotions, and Attitude Toward the Ad on Viewing Time." *Journal of Consumer Research* 17, no. 1 (March 1991): 440–453.

Ortony, Andrew, Gerald L. Clore, and Allan Collins. *The Cognitive Structure of Emotions.* Cambridge, UK: Cambridge University Press, 1988.

O'Shaughnessy, John, and Nicholas Jackson O'Shaughnessy. *The Marketing Power of Emotion.* New York: Oxford University Press, 2003.

Phillips, Diane M., and Hans Baumgartner. "The Role of Consumption Emotions in the Satisfaction Response." *Journal of Consumer Psychology* 12, no. 3 (2002): 243–252.

Plutchik, Robert. *Emotion: A Psychoevolutionary Synthesis.* New York: Harper & Row, 1980.

———. *Emotions and Life: Perspectives from Psychology, Biology, and Evolution.* Washington, DC: American Psychological Association, 2003.

Plutchik, Robert, and Hope R. Conte, eds. *Circumplex Models of Personality and Emotions.* Washington, DC: American Psychological Association, 1997.

Price, Linda L., Eric J. Arnould, and Sheila L. Deibler. "Consumers' Emotional Responses to Service Encounters: The Influence of the Service Provider." *International Journal of Service Industry Management* 6, no. 3 (1995): 34–63.

Price, Linda L., Eric J. Arnould, and Patrick Tierney. "Going to Extremes: Managing Service Encounters and Assessing Provider Performance." *Journal of Marketing* 59, no. 2 (April 1995): 83–97.

Rathje, William, and Cullen Murphy. *Rubbish! The Archaeology of Garbage.* New York: HarperCollins, 1992.

Reisenzein, Rainer. "Pleasure-Arousal Theory and the Intensity of Emotions." *Journal of Personality and Social Psychology* 67, no. 3 (September 1994): 525–539.

Remington, Nancy A., Leandre R. Fabrigar, and Penny S. Visser. "Reexaming the Circumplex Model of Affect." *Journal of Personality and Social Psychology* 79, no. 2 (August 2000): 286–300.

Richins, Marsha L. "Measuring Emotions in the Consumption Experience." *Journal of Consumer Research* 24, no. 2 (September 1997): 127–146.

Roseman, Ira J. "Appraisal Determinants of Discrete Emotions." *Cognition and Emotion* 5, no. 3 (May 1991): 161–200.

———. "A Model of Appraisal in the Emotion System: Integrating Theory, Research, and Applications." In *Appraisal Processes in Emotion: Theory, Methods, Research*, ed. Klaus R. Scherer, Angela Schorr, and Tom Johnstone, 68–91. New York: Oxford University Press, 2001.

Roseman, Ira J., Ann Aliki Antoniou, and Paul E. Jose. "Appraisal Determinants of Emotions: Constructing a More Accurate and Comprehensive Theory." *Cognition and Emotion* 10, no. 3 (May 1996): 241–277.

Roseman, Ira J., Martin S. Spindel, and Paul E. Jose. "Appraisals of Emotion-Eliciting Events: Testing a Theory of Discrete Emotions." *Journal of Personality and Social Psychology* 59, no. 5 (November 1990): 899–915.

Russell, James A. "Affective Space Is Bipolar." *Journal of Personality and Social Psychology* 37, no. 3 (March 1979): 345–356.

———. "A Circumplex Model of Affect." *Journal of Personality and Social Psychology* 39, no. 6 (December 1980): 1161–1178.

Russell, James A., and Lisa Feldman Barrett. "Core Affect, Prototypical Emotional Episodes, and Other Things Called *Emotion:* Dissecting the Elephant." *Journal of Personality and Social Psychology* 76, no. 5 (May 1999): 805–819.

Russell, James A., and Albert Mehrabian. "Evidence for a Three-Factor Theory of Emotions." *Journal of Research in Personality* 11, no. 3 (September 1977): 273–294.

Russell, James A., Anna Weiss, and Gerald A. Mendelsohn. "Affect Grid: A Single-Item Scale of Pleasure and Arousal." *Journal of Personality and Social Psychology* 57, no. 3 (September 1989): 493–502.

Ruth, Julie A., Frédéric F. Brunel, and Cele C. Otnes. "Linking Thoughts to Feelings: Investigating Cognitive Appraisals and Consumption Emotions in a Mixed-Emotions Context." *Journal of the Academy of Marketing Science* 30, no. 1 (Winter 2002): 44–58.

Scherer, Klaus R. "Criteria for Emotion-Antecedent Appraisal: A Review." In *Cognitive Perspectives on Emotion and Motivation,* ed. V. Hamilton, Gordon H. Bower, and Nico H. Frijda, 89–126. Norwell, MA: Kluwer Academic, 1988.

———. "Profiles of Emotion-Antecedent Appraisal: Testing Theoretical Predictions Across Cultures." *Cognition and Emotion* 11, no. 2 (March 1997): 113–150.

Scherer, Klaus R., and Grazia Ceschi. "Lost Luggage: A Field Study of Emotion-Antecedent Appraisal." *Motivation and Emotion* 21, no. 3 (September 1997): 211–235.

Scherer, Klaus R., Angela Schorr, and Tom Johnstone, eds. *Appraisal Processes in Emotion: Theory, Methods, Research.* New York: Oxford University Press, 2001.

Schimmack, Ulrich, and Ed Diener. "Affect Intensity: Separating Intensity and Frequency in Repeatedly Measured Affect." *Journal of Personality and Social Psychology* 73, no. 6 (December 1997): 1313–1329.

Schnall, Simone, and James D. Laird. "Keep Smiling: Enduring Effects of Facial Expressions and Postures on Emotional Experience and Memory." *Cognition and Emotion* 17, no. 5 (September 2003): 787–797.

Seidlitz, Larry, and Ed Diener. "Memory for Positive versus Negative Life Events: Theories for the Differences between Happy and Unhappy Persons." *Journal of Personality and Social Psychology* 64, no. 4 (April 1993): 654–664.

Shaver, Phillip, Judith Schwartz, Donald Kirson, and Cary O'Connor. "Emotion Knowledge: Further Exploration of a Prototype Approach." *Journal of Personality and Social Psychology* 52, no. 6 (June 1987): 1061–1086.

Smith, Amy K., and Ruth N. Bolton. "The Effect of Customers' Emotional Responses to Service Failures on Their Recovery Effort Evaluations and Satisfaction Judgments." *Journal of the Academy of Marketing Science* 30, no. 1 (Winter 2002): 5–23.

Smith, Craig A., and Richard S. Lazarus. "Appraisal Components, Core Relational Themes, and the Emotions." *Cognition and Emotion* 7, nos. 3–4 (May–July 1993): 233–269.

Spreng, Richard A., Scott B. MacKenzie, and Richard W. Olshavsky. "A Reexamination of the Determinants of Consumer Satisfaction." *Journal of Marketing* 60, no. 3 (July 1996): 15–32.

Stephens, Nancy, and Kevin P. Gwinner. "Why Don't Some People Complain? A Cognitive-Emotive Process Model of Consumer Complaint Behavior." *Journal of the Academy of Marketing Science* 26, no. 3 (Summer 1998): 172–189.

Storm, Christine, and Tom Storm. "A Taxonomic Study of the Vocabulary of Emotions." *Journal of Personality and Social Psychology* 53, no. 4 (October 1987): 805–816.

Sundaram, D.S., and Cynthia Webster. "The Role of Nonverbal Communications in Service Encounters." *Journal of Services Marketing* 14, no. 5 (2000): 378–391.

Sweeney, Jillian C., and Carol Brandon. "Brand Personality: Exploring the Potential to Move from Factor Analytical to Circumplex Models." *Psychology & Marketing* 23, no. 8 (August 2006): 639–663.

Thomas, David L., and Ed Diener. "Memory Accuracy in the Recall of Emotions." *Journal of Personality and Social Psychology* 59, no. 2 (August 1990): 291–297.

van Dolen, Willemijn, Jos Lemmink, Jan Mattsson, and Ingrid Rhoen. "Affective Consumer Responses in Service Encounters: The Emotional Content in Narratives of Critical Incidents." *Journal of Economic Psychology* 22, no. 3 (June 2001): 359–376.

Wakefield, Kirk L., Jeffrey G. Blodgett, and Hugh J. Sloan. "Measurement and Management of the Sportscape." *Journal of Sport Management* 10, no. 1 (January 1996): 15–31.

Watson, David, Lee Anna Clark, and Auke Tellegen. "Development and Validation of Brief Measures of Positive and Negative Affect: The PANAS Scales." *Journal of Personality and Social Psychology* 54, no. 6 (June 1988): 1063–1070.

Watson, David, and Auke Tellegen. "Toward a Consensual Structure of Mood." *Psychological Bulletin* 98, no. 2 (September 1985): 219–235.

Watson, David, David Wiese, Jatin Vaidya, and Auke Tellegen. "The Two General Activation Systems of Affect: Structural Findings, Evolutionary Considerations, and Psychobiological Evidence." *Journal of Personality and Social Psychology* 76, no. 5 (May 1999): 820–838.

Weiner, Bernard. "An Attributional Theory of Achievement Motivation and Emotion." *Psychological Review* 92, no. 4 (October 1985): 548–573.

Westbrook, Robert A. "Product/Consumption-Based Affective Responses and Postpurchase Processes." *Journal of Marketing Research* 24, no. 3 (August 1987): 258–270.

Westbrook, Robert A., and Richard L. Oliver. "The Dimensionality of Consumption Emotion Patterns and Consumer Satisfaction." *Journal of Consumer Research* 18, no. 1 (June 1991): 84–91.

Wierzbicka, Anna. "Talking About Emotions: Semantics, Culture, and Cognition." *Cognition and Emotion* 6, nos. 3–4 (May–July 1992): 285–319.

Wiles, Judith A., and T. Bettina Cornwell. "A Review of Methods Utilized in Measuring Affect, Feelings, and Emotion in Advertising." *Current Issues and Research in Advertising* 13, no. 2 (1990): 241–275.

Wilson, Timothy D., Douglas J. Lisle, Dolores Kraft, and Christopher G. Wetzel. "Preferences as Expectation-Driven Inferences: Effects of Affective Expectations on Affective Experience." *Journal of Personality and Social Psychology* 56, no. 4 (April 1989): 519–530.

Winkielman, Piotr, Bärbel Knäuper, and Norbert Schwarz. "Looking Back at Anger: Reference Periods Change the Interpretation of Emotion Frequency Questions." *Journal of Personality and Social Psychology* 75, no. 3 (September 1998): 719–728.

Wirtz, Jochen, Anna S. Mattila, and Rachel L.P. Tan. "The Moderating Role of Target-Arousal on the Impact of Affect on Satisfaction: An Examination in the Context of Service Experience." *Journal of Retailing* 76, no. 3 (Fall 2000): 347–365.

Wood, Stacy L., and James R. Bettman. "Predicting Happiness: How Normative Feeling Rules Influence (and Even Reverse) Durability Bias." *Journal of Consumer Psychology* 17, no. 3 (2007): 188–201.

Wright, William F., and Gordon H. Bower. "Mood Effects on Subjective Probability Assessment." *Organizational Behavior and Human Decision Processes* 52, no. 2 (July 1992): 276–291.

Yeung, Catherine W.M., and Robert S. Wyer Jr. "Affect, Appraisal, and Consumer Judgment." *Journal of Consumer Research* 31, no. 2 (September 2004): 412–424.

Yik, Michelle S.M., James A. Russell, and Lisa Feldman Barrett. "Structure of Self-Reported Current Affect: Integration and Beyond." *Journal of Personality and Social Psychology* 77, no. 3 (September 1999): 600–619.

Zeitlin, David M., and Richard A. Westwood. "Measuring Emotional Response." *Journal of Advertising Research* 26, no. 5 (October–November 1986): 34–44.

CHAPTER 13

THE PROCESSING OF CONSUMPTION

Do consumers consciously process their consumption activities? Like the adage of the glass being half empty or half full, the answer is both yes and no, depending on one's perspective. Consumers are aware of their consumption outcomes, and, when prompted, can relate their experiences to others. This is apparent from the numerous customer surveys collected in virtually all corners of society. But are consumption outcomes routinely processed in everyday life? A safe answer to this question is that some are and others are not. Still another answer is that some consumers process consumption outcomes and others do not. And yet another answer is that consumers harbor *latent* satisfactions, which may be subconscious in a psychoanalytic sense.[1] To fully understand this processing versus nonprocessing phenomenon, one must examine consumption reactions in an integrated perspective.

The purpose of this chapter is to combine the concepts in previous chapters and show how they interrelate. It will thus become apparent that a new model of the consumer is needed to accommodate different consumption processing styles. Perhaps it would be more accurate to say that some of the assumptions regarding typical consumer responses to consumption events require modification. In particular, assumptions regarding the degree to which each of the main concepts in this book operates in specific situations need to be examined in greater detail.

To illustrate, the operation of the expectancy disconfirmation model was discussed in Chapter 4. It was argued that in some circumstances only the expectation component of the model might operate to affect satisfaction. Alternatively, in other situations, disconfirmation may dominate satisfaction judgments. Later in that chapter, a study was discussed showing that different consumers may use different parts of the model selectively for the same purchase scenario.[2] In this chapter, this segmentation approach is extended to a greater variety of satisfaction's antecedents, including attribution and affective responses.

A RESPONSE MODE APPROACH TO CONSUMPTION

The perspective that guides this chapter is the variety of human experience. This implies that individuals may mean different things when they claim to be satisfied and that there may be a number of adaptive states for a satisfaction response.[3] The possibility that the term *satisfied* is imprecise in both content and meaning is evident from the litany of contexts in which the word is used, such as in the circumplex models and the scaling results reviewed in Chapter 12. This imprecision results from the fact that consumer responses to product experiences are unique along a number of dimensions.

First, different consumers are known to react to the same situation differently due to either temperament or mood.[4] Second, the same consumer's reaction to a product may change over time as the newness of the product gives way to the routine of using it daily. Third, products themselves have different meanings to consumers, ranging from the level of involvement in the product category to the very "meaning" of the product to a person's life.[5]

Thus, it is argued that consumers have different orientations toward products, and it is this orientation that determines the satisfaction response that will be evoked. For example, a consumer may own an automobile for the simple function of transportation, in which case little emotion is likely to be expressed, or for the driving pleasure it gives. Likewise, a toy may present interesting experiences when new, but generate only simple enjoyment or perhaps even boredom as a child becomes accustomed to it. And a product that once provided pleasure may become unreliable over time (e.g., an aging lawn mower; breaking drive belts on a vacuum cleaner), so that the owner expresses relief when it does not break down under use. The examples in this paragraph are representative of the different response modes that will be more fully developed shortly.

The Dilemma for Management

The introduction to this book suggested that *satisfaction* was one of those overextended terms in the English language that have come to mean different things to different people. Unfortunately, this presents a problem for the marketing manager or researcher who has in mind only the satisfaction most closely linked to loyalty, profits, and brand share (share of wallet). Because many customer surveys typically use only a single-item scale to measure satisfaction, one consumer's satisfaction "apple" becomes indistinguishable from another's satisfaction "orange."[6] Consider two refrigerator owners, one who has just upgraded to a fancy model with an ice cube and ice water control panel and another with the identical unit that is now four years old. Both are asked to report how satisfied they are on the following scale:

Dissatisfied   1   2   3   4   5   Satisfied

The first consumer is ecstatic, savoring the novelty of crushed ice on demand. Which scale value will be used by this consumer? Category 5, no doubt. The second consumer does not think much about the refrigerator, but when confronted with the query, rates it 5, reasoning that the unit is performing as it should—keeping the food cold. It is true that the researcher could make the scale more challenging by labeling all categories with more discriminating qualifiers (e.g., very satisfied), but this is not the point. Both consumers are satisfied; where they differ is that they are not at the same location in the satisfaction-emotion space. Simply put, the scale does not access the arousal or engagement dimension of the consumers' responses. A second scale or some other indicator is needed to augment the "How satisfied are you?" question.

To clarify what this means, the results of studies that place satisfaction in the context of closely related emotions (bearing in mind that satisfaction, itself, is not a pure emotion), previously discussed in Chapter 12, are reexamined here. In the previous edition of this book, the findings of all emotion studies that include the word *satisfied* or *satisfaction* had been categorized. Studies since that time record no change in the nature of the responses. Dissatisfaction, which occurred less frequently, was also examined. Abbreviated conclusions are presented here so that other peripheral studies can be included in the present summary.

Satisfaction in a Classification Context

Based on the results of circumplex analyses, word classification studies, and clusterings of individual respondents, summaries of which were presented in the previous chapter, the results for satisfaction are clear. Three themes are prominent. The two most frequently observed are satisfaction as contentment and/or happiness, and pleasure. Delight or elation is the third, appearing less frequently. Dissatisfaction was not as easy to pin down. By far, the largest theme involved negative mood states such as disappointment and sadness. Others include anger and hostility, annoyance and frustration, and fear. This set of diverse dissatisfaction findings probably results from the greater latitude of negative affect states and a tendency of individuals to describe negative life states in general as dissatisfactory.

Given only these results, a reasonable conclusion is that satisfaction takes on different meanings in different contexts and respondent populations. A second conclusion is that a number of different product experiences are summed up under the rubric of satisfaction and that these experiences can be viewed as representing response orientations to satisfaction. Based on the preceding analysis, it appears that contentment, pleasure, and delight are three such states. It is known from the affect circumplex models that these differ on the arousal or engagement dimension of affect: contentment is low-arousal positive affect, pleasure is moderately aroused positive affect, and delight is high-arousal positive affect. The corresponding negative terms are boredom and tedium, displeasure, and distress, which can take on many forms depending on the attributions individuals may make.

These conclusions are not sufficient for the purpose of this chapter, however, because they do not account for the antecedent (causal) conditions for the emotions. More particularly, the cognitive appraisals giving rise to each of the response states are not specified. In this regard, the appraisal literature introduced in Chapter 12 will prove helpful in determining the crucial appraisals involved in satisfaction-related judgments.

Satisfaction in an Appraisal Context Revisited

Recall from Chapter 12 that various appraisal themes contained satisfaction "of sorts." Commonalities included two categories identified as goal attainment and need satisfaction or fulfillment. Presumably because effort is generally required to achieve a goal, two of these need satisfaction states could be labeled "satisfaction" (the quotes are important) and relaxation (as in the relaxing of a tension state). This categorization does not reflect much of consumption as expressed in the marketplace, however. An additional analysis, the Weiner approach (Chapter 11), resulting from analysis of postoutcome protocols, showed that individuals reported "satisfaction" as resulting from specific combinations of attributional processing. This method, however, is an ex post facto analysis and is not causal. Only a tree-like appraisal approach has the potential to address satisfaction and dissatisfaction directly. A framework based on discussion here and elsewhere is shown in Figure 13.1.[7]

Figure 13.1 illustrates that satisfaction occurs when events have consequences for an individual in the immediate present or in the future. Present events can lead to positive feelings (joy, pleasure) or any one of the negative emotions, including distress. Not shown are irrelevant events, including reflections on the past, musings about the future, and even current events lacking immediate implications. Of the relevant prospects for the future are hopes (positive expectations) and fears (expectations of the negative). Confirmed hopes should lead to satisfaction; disconfirmed hopes will most probably result in disappointment. In contrast, confirmed fears will result in some variation of distress, while disconfirmed fears will, in all probability, lead to relief.

This framework is a worthy start, but does not adequately address all the nuances of satisfaction in consumption. Nonetheless, the appraisal literature and the analyses in the preceding chapters will be drawn upon to provide a more complete representation of the processes leading up to

Figure 13.1 **A Typical Appraisal Sequence for Satisfaction**

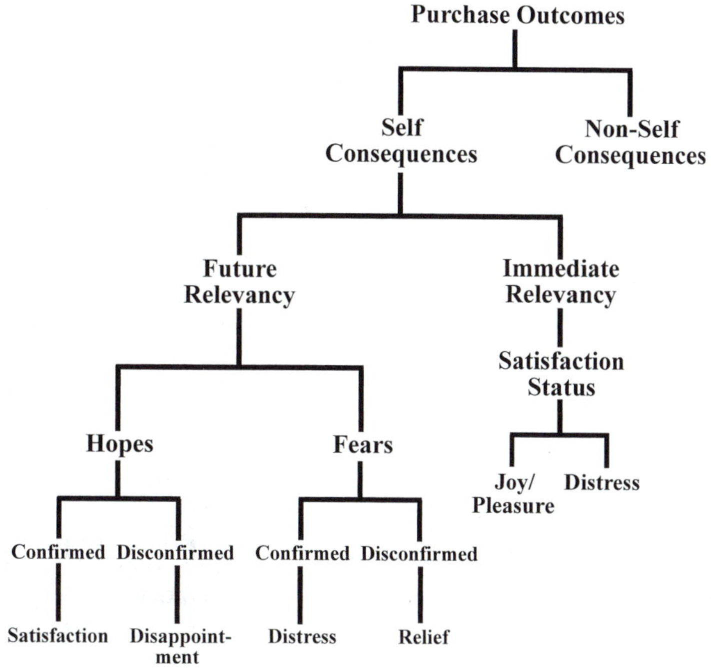

Source: Adapted from Andrew Ortony, Gerald L. Clore, and Allan Collins, *The Cognitive Structure of Emotions* (Cambridge, England: Cambridge University Press, 1988), p. 19, by permission of Cambridge University Press.

satisfaction and dissatisfaction. Some satisfaction influences, primarily attribution and equity, are not easily integrated into the main framework. Instead, these influences, using attribution as an example, will be treated as overlays on the framework. In a sense, they will be parallel appraisals coexisting with more central appraisals within the satisfaction response.

A FORMAL APPRAISAL MODEL FOR THE SATISFACTION RESPONSE

In Chapter 4, the expectancy disconfirmation model of the satisfaction sequence begins with expectations and the subsequent comparison of performance to expectations. The model therefore relies heavily on the three states of positive disconfirmation (performance better than expected), negative disconfirmation (worse than expected), and confirmation (as expected). To these, it would be instructive to add two alternative states of nonoccurring performance. The first portrays a situation in which performance has not yet occurred but is still anticipated, while the second is a realization that performance has failed to occur. The difference between the two states is that performance remains likely in the first case (a newly planted fruit tree that has yet to bear fruit) and is assumed not to be forthcoming in the second (a deadline, such as the fruit-bearing season, has passed).

Figure 13.2 displays the general appraisal framework developed for this chapter to explain the emotional content of the satisfaction response. As noted, this particular display shows only expectation-related influences for clarity and presumes three states of nature. The first (and middle path in the figure) addresses the case of expected favorable outcomes; the second, to its right, ad-

Figure 13.2 **General Framework of the Appraisal Model With the Favorable Expectation Emotion Sequence**

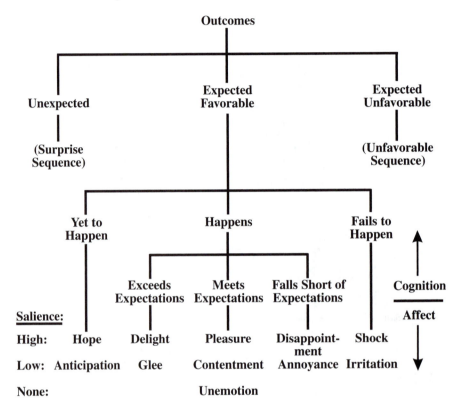

dresses expected negative outcomes; and the leftmost path is reserved for unexpected outcomes. Embedded within this overall framework is the complete favorable expectation sequence. This is the most common reason for purchasing—to fulfill the consumer's desires, which, presumably, revolve around favorable life outcomes.

The Favorable Outcome Sequence

As stated previously, five states of nature generally result from holding expectations. Beginning with the yet-to-happen non-occurrence branch in the frame, one can see that the expected event is not precluded from happening in the short to intermediate term. This situation is described in Chapter 10 as representing the gamma stage, where the purchase has been made but hoped-for outcomes have yet to be observed.

In the second state of nonoccurrence (and at the right in Figure 13.2 in the favorable outcome sequence), the consumer may assume that the event will not happen or is indeterminant. That is, the time frame is such that the reasonable likelihood of the favorable event is no longer operable. This could occur when the purchase has time limitations. For example, certain securities options give the buyer a right to buy or sell stock at a profitable price within a certain time frame. If market conditions do not permit this price to occur, then the option expires and is worthless, and the entire purchase price, including commissions, is lost. Many real estate and rental contracts are worded in this manner. Another example is the promises of home or landscape contractors to finish a project by a certain date. Often they do not fulfill this promise, and the homeowner is abandoned without the work having been completed. Failed promises of product redress or service recovery also fit this situation.

Last, Figure 13.2 shows the core of the expectancy disconfirmation model. Here, an outcome labeled as favorable exceeds, meets, or falls short of the expected level, and the high-involvement reactions of delight, pleasure, and disappointment are shown, as identified in Chapter 12. Note that contentment is described as a less aroused manifestation of pleasure. A still more unaroused manifestation is apathy or unemotion, where the expected is so commonplace as to go virtually unnoticed.

This brings up the necessity of distinguishing high-involvement from low-involvement reactions, referred to as salience in Figure 13.2. As one might surmise, involvement enhances the arousal inherent in all emotions, particularly those that are satisfaction-related.[8] Thus, each of the emotional responses will differ in terms of the consumer's involvement level, but only as a matter of degree, a widely recognized phenomenon.[9] For example, the delight response under high involvement probably decays to mere glee under low involvement. Moreover, disappointment under failed expectations may fall to simple annoyance under low involvement; the shock of expected favorable outcome nonoccurrence may fall to the more common state of irritation; and hope for outcomes yet to come may become ordinary anticipation.

The Unfavorable Outcome Sequence

Attention now turns to the case of expected unfavorable outcomes, shown in Figure 13.3. Readers might wonder why the unfavorable sequence is even discussed since consumers should not knowingly venture into a product experience if unfavorable outcomes are expected. Unfortunately, all consumers encounter the necessity of pursuing consumption activities with likely unpleasant outcomes. Complaining, an obvious example, is discussed Chapter 14. Other examples include unavoidable consumption, such as dealing with local utilities and government agencies; required phases of consumption, such as bargaining over an automobile purchase; and unpleasant but necessary consumption, such as surgery, legal proceedings, and dental work.

As shown in Figure 13.3, yet-to-happen unfavorable outcomes promote, at the extreme level of salience, fear or perhaps dread over the possibility of their occurrence. This reduces to the more common state of anxiety when the expected outcomes are less salient. If these outcomes never occur, then rejoicing is experienced for truly salient events and relief occurs for those less salient. As will be argued later in this chapter, this state of relief may be interpreted as satisfaction, since it fulfills a wish not to encounter unfavorable outcomes. The insurance industry must indeed be grateful for this phenomenon.

As before, this brings discussion to the expectancy disconfirmation portion of the model. Here, met expectations of an unfavorable event can result in generalized distress in the case of high salience and in mere tolerance (of the unfavorable outcome) in the case of low salience. When outcomes are less severe than anticipated, the consumer experience is that of a feeling of being relieved (a lessening of the negative stimulus, as opposed to the finality of relief—a summary state) under high salience, as the outcome was not as bad as feared. If involvement is low, some amusement may be observed, for the consumer may chuckle, "It wasn't as bad as I thought." Finally, in the worst-case scenario of outcomes lower than the level of low expectations, despair may be felt, as if there were no hope. Under low salience, this situation may manifest itself as dismay or resignation to the bad state of fairly unimportant affairs.

Figure 13.3   **The Appraisal Model With the Unfavorable Expectation Emotion Sequence**

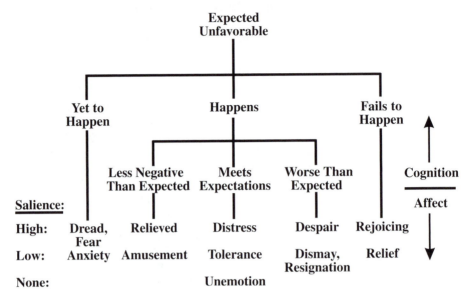

The Unexpected Outcome Sequence

One other eventuality must be considered—the occurrence of truly unexpected events, shown in Figure 13.4. Many purchase outcomes involve unanticipated benefits (extra features in a software program) and problems (obscure exclusions in insurance policies). Here, the first reaction is surprise, an affectively neutral response.[10] The situation is then appraised for its valence, which is categorized in Figure 13.4 as favorable, unfavorable, or neutral. Surprising events without implications may generate curiosity, but little else. Curiosity serves the purpose of further evaluation of future potential; a lower-involvement reflection of this is mere interest, which, interestingly, has an appraisal structure of its own.[11]

Goal-relevant pleasant surprises may result in amazement, as in amazingly good, or in elation, which shares components of delight. Less relevant outcomes may be viewed as novel and generate little additional interest. Important negative surprises may result in shock, feelings of horror, or simply fright for events of very low salience. Less goal-relevant negative outcomes of a surprising nature may only result in alarm, while low-involvement negative events may entail unease or disquietude.

This completes the expectancy disconfirmation-based appraisal mechanism for emotion in the satisfaction response. Note that other comparative themes of satisfaction as discussed in this book (e.g., needs, quality, and value) have not yet been incorporated. These are subsumed as outcomes to be judged along expectancy disconfirmation lines and may be viewed as goals or desires of purchasing. As such, they are evaluated as outcomes compared to preexisting need levels and quality and/or value desires. Two additional topics—attribution and equity—are important appraisal sequences, although less involved. Both operate along with expectancy disconfirmation, as prior research has shown.

Little appraisal work has appeared on equity perceptions. That is, as far as this author is aware, the appraisal dimensions of equity have not been formally specified. However, the relation between equity and attribution has received a small amount of attention, and it appears that the attribution

Figure 13.4 **The Appraisal Model With the Unexpected Outcome Sequence**

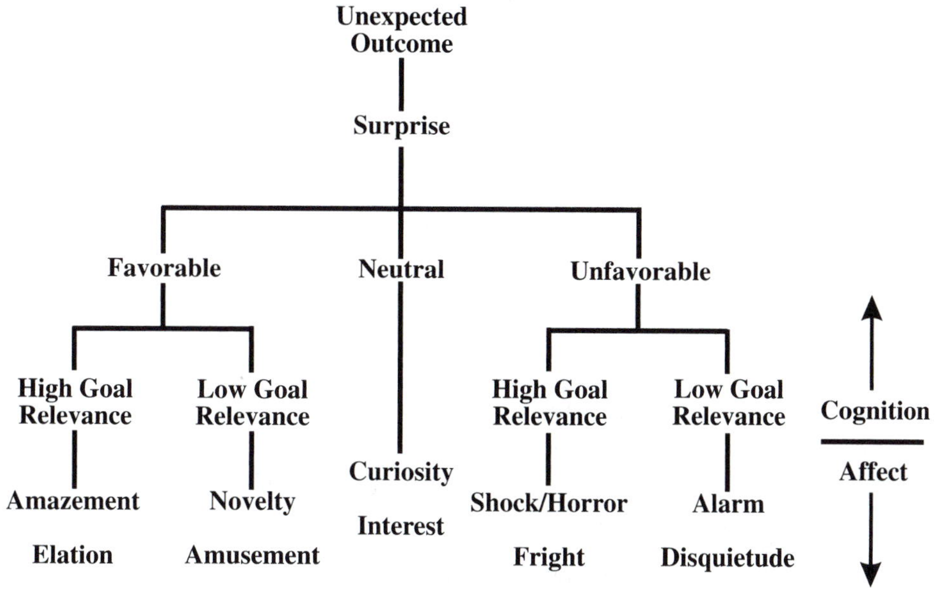

processes for success and failure and for equity and inequity follow similar attribution logic.[12] For example, gratitude may exist when outcomes are perceived as fair, and anger may result when events are viewed as inequitable. Thus, discussion will focus on only one overlay to the appraisal process, that of attributions of responsibility for success and failure.

The Success and Failure Attribution Sequences

This analysis is straightforward. From Chapter 12, it is known that a small number of emotional responses summarize attributions for success and failure.[13]

For *success,* the following generalizations hold:

- Internal locus: pride (that I did it)
- External locus: gratitude (that others did it for me)
- Stable cause: confidence, anticipation (that it will happen again)
- Unstable cause: lack of confidence; luck, relief when it occurs
- Controllable: competence (in my controllable abilities) or confidence (that others are in control)
- Uncontrollable: relief, luck

For *failure,* the following hold:

- Internal locus: guilt and shame (that I was not able to prevent it)
- External locus: anger (that I was victimized by others)
- Stable cause: frustration, resignation, and acceptance of failure; despair
- Unstable cause: frustration, unpleasant surprise

- Controllable: anger (that failure was not prevented)
- Uncontrollable: surprise, frustration (that it happened to me)

These predictions are summarized in Figures 13.5 and 13.6. In producing these figures, an assumption was made that the locus predictions dominate for both success and failure. Individuals should be proud when they make successful purchases and thankful (grateful) when acknowledging that other people are responsible. Failure, when internally attributed, results in guilt when volition is involved and shame when failure is due to an innate failing.[14] Stability has the effect of instilling certainty (i.e., confidence in success or frustration in failure) in oneself or others; and controllability involves one's own or other people's competencies.

Adding the Appraisal Framework to the Expectancy Disconfirmation Model

The consumption processing framework consistent with this discussion, shown in Figure 13.7, is a modification of the expectancy disconfirmation framework and the author's original consumption processing model.[15] The disconfirmation model variables appear in unshaded boxes; the variable additions appear in shaded boxes. The reader will note similarities to the less complete models presented in Chapters 11 and 12.

The shaded sequence above the outcomes → satisfaction/dissatisfaction link shows the nonprocessing phase of consumption whereby consumers react to consumption outcomes with more or less spontaneous affect. This mirrors the primary appraisal sequence resulting from a general observation that the product outcome was "good for me" or "bad for me," resulting in a primary affect. In contrast, the lower remainder of Figure 13.7 shows the cognitive processing sequence, which begins with the expectancy disconfirmation model as augmented by other appraisals such as equity, links these appraisals to attribution processing, and connects both to appraisal-related emotions. Both the nonprocessing and processing sequences then affect satisfaction and dissatisfaction, along with other cognitive influences. These other influences include anhedonic (sterile, performance-only) cognition, as represented by the direct link between outcomes and satisfaction. In its entirety, this framework will be used to elaborate the satisfaction prototypes described next.

SATISFACTION PROTOTYPES

Earlier in this chapter, it was suggested that consumers do not necessarily have the same sort of satisfaction in mind when they claim that they are satisfied. Why is this? One answer is that they are responding from different motivational orientations. Chapter 5 described the different types of reinforcement, reproduced here as Figure 13.8 with some modifications.

Figure 13.8 assumes a consumer in a state of homeostasis, shown as hedonic neutrality. If consumption results in outcomes that maintain neutrality over time, the consumer will experience a general state of contentment. Alternatively, if consumption results in an increment in positively valenced utility, the consumer will derive greater pleasure. Moreover, the resulting increment in pleasure may contain an element of the unexpected, hence surprising additional pleasure, resulting in the emotion previously referred to as delight. Consumers below neutrality and not resigned to a negatively valenced state can seek to obtain relief and return to neutrality. Relief may also contain unexpected surprising pleasure, a rebound referred to in the literature as the operation of an "opponent process," which is not shown for simplicity.

These four states represent the basic satisfaction prototypes suggested in this book. They deviate from the author's previous attempt in that surprise and novelty are now wrapped into the delight

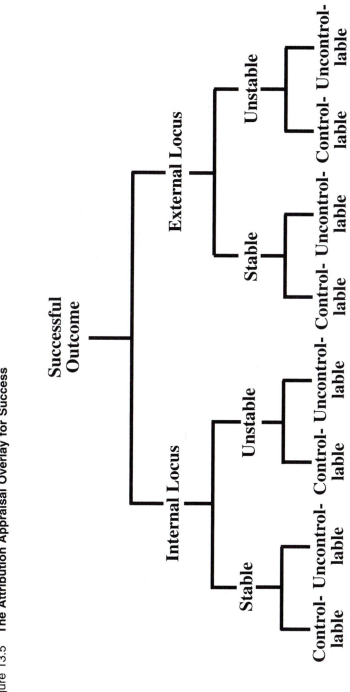

Figure 13.5   The Attribution Appraisal Overlay for Success

Figure 13.6 **The Attribution Appraisal Overlay for Failure**

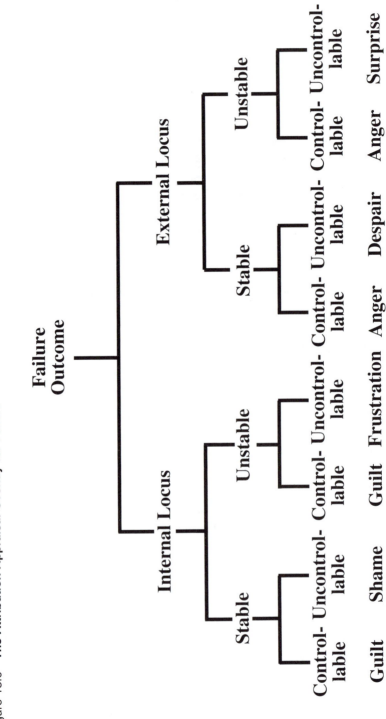

Figure 13.7   **The General Consumption Processing Model**

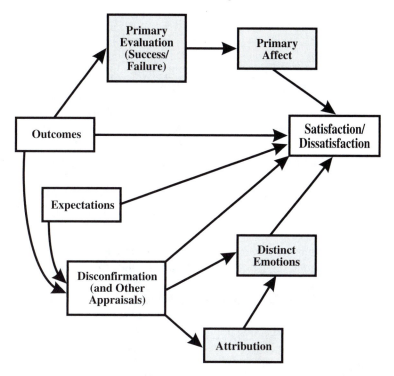

Figure 13.8   **The Consumption Processing Reinforcements**

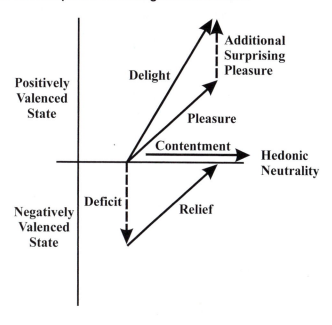

Table 13.1

Characteristics of the Proposed Response Modes

Response mode	Expectation processing	Performance processing	Disconfirmation processing	Primary affect	Attribution processing
Contentment	None or passive	Passive	None	Contentment, acceptance, tolerance	None
Pleasure	Active	Active	Moderately active	Pleasure, happiness, joy	Moderately active
Delight	Active (but may be latent)	Active	Acutely active	Delight, elation, ecstasy	Active
Relief	Anxiously active	Very active	Active	Relief, restoration, resignation	Active

prototype, which is consistent with the discussion of delight in Chapter 4. Note that this framework focuses on the positive (satisfying) prototypes and excludes the negative states of dissatisfaction, which will be profiled in Chapter 14.

Each satisfaction response mode can be distinguished from the others by the nature of the cognitions, attributions, and emotions operating across the stages of consumption (from left to right in Figure 13.7). With the exception of product or service (attribute) performance, the nature and operation of each of the processing variables may be very different. In particular, the distinct emotions resulting from attribution and other processing, if present, are posited to be more frequently observed in certain satisfaction modes and, therefore, may be diagnostic of the role of the product to the consumer, as shown in Table 13.1.

Each of these proposed consumption response states is discussed with regard to operation of the major variables in the substages of the consumption-processing framework. A test, not published elsewhere, is then performed to provide validation support for the model's predictions.

Proposed Categories of Consumption Response Orientation

Response orientations are characteristic tendencies to behave in a specific manner when confronted with common stimuli. When referring to prechoice phenomena, the phrase *motivational typologies* is used to describe an analogous categorization of consumers.[16] Essentially, segments of consumers that share common response tendencies are identified. The response orientations for the consumption-processing model follow.

Contentment (Maintenance)

As the prior review indicated, a common meaning of satisfaction appears to be contentment, or what will be described here as *satisfaction-as-contentment*. Contentment is a passive response that results when pleasant homeostatic states are maintained or prolonged. This type of satisfaction is a reaction to the continued operation of ongoing (consumption) processes, either in the case of a long-lasting consumer durable or in terms of continuous repeat buying. Contentment satisfaction is characterized by low levels of arousal and may entail disinterest. In this state, a reasonable assumption is that expectations have become passive and are not actively processed, typically because they have become permanently coded into the consumer's schema (e.g., the expectation that a reliable watch will keep correct time). Alternatively, contentment has been described as a comparison of "life as it is" to "life as it should be" (i.e., normalcy).[17]

In the same manner, performance processing may have become passive in that consumers have adapted to a static or usual level of performance that they have experienced over time. Because performance remains well within acceptable levels in these situations, disconfirmation perceptions should not appear. As a result, the primary evaluation (see Figure 13.7) is acceptance or tolerance, which, as the latter term implies, can have negative overtones. Finally, because disconfirmation is absent (i.e., confirmation prevails), little arousal should exist and no attribution processing would be expected. The upper sequence of Figure 13.7 summarizes this state nicely.

This one satisfaction state alone may explain why reports of satisfaction levels in surveys are inordinately high, approaching 90 percent.[18] If a survey focuses on an ongoing-use situation, such as the watch example used here, most subjects will respond from a satisfaction-as-contentment perspective and the remaining satisfaction states will be mixed in at varying levels of satisfaction or dissatisfaction. Although the data would clearly include consumers responding from the perspective of other response states, these individuals may be small in number compared to those whose watches have been operating accurately in contentment mode. Thus, one should not expect to find high levels of reported dissatisfaction.

No attribution processing would take place in this consumption mode, primarily because of low levels of arousal. However, it must be acknowledged that low-level attribution processing may occur. For example, performance evaluation in this scenario of continued purchasing and/or use might be attributed by the consumer to stable effort and, if attribution processing did occur, to those emotions generated by stable effort attribution. These are likely to be low-intensity emotions (e.g., serenity, calmness), consistent with the primary affects of contentment and tolerance suggested earlier.

It is also possible that the potential disinterest expressed in this mode could indicate a general unemotional response to the product category. This would represent an extreme of low-arousal (or no-arousal) postpurchase response where satisfaction may mean the absence of dissatisfaction, as found in early clustering solutions where some consumers express little, if any, affect toward a consumable.[19] Until further work on nonemotion consumption emerges, this state will be subsumed within the contentment category.

Thus, given the ongoing consumption of a contentment mode product, disconfirmation (and subsequent attribution processing) should not be present. In this event, the primary affect state, based on performance or expectations in situations where performance is not processed (e.g., insurance in the absence of claims), will be the central emotion expressed in this response mode.

Note that this proposition does not necessarily imply low involvement, although low-involvement responses would certainly fit this processing state. High-involvement products could also fit this mode as long as the consumer had acclimated to the usual form of product functioning. Stable performance from a family automobile or home illustrates this possibility.

Pleasure

Satisfaction-as-pleasure is one of two consumption response modes representing what might be called the reinforcement satisfactions. This phrase is intended to reflect the difference between positive reinforcement (inducing or increasing a pleasurable state) and negative reinforcement (reducing or eliminating an unpleasant state)—see Chapter 5. The case of positive reinforcement or pleasure mode is discussed at this point, for it appears to be intermediate to the preceding state of contentment and the following state of delight.

Pleasure is thought to occur when a product, such as entertainment, makes consumers happy in the classic operation of positive reinforcement. It also occurs in unappraised affective responses such as aesthetic appreciation and purely sensory experiences such as music (see Chapter 7). Satisfaction-as-pleasure may involve moderate to high arousal, moderate to high interest, and other easily identifiable emotional states. For this processing state, expectations are probably processed, as are outcomes and disconfirmation. This will bring into play the disconfirmation emotions of Figure 13.2. The primary affects, however, would operate independently; examples are happiness and sadness.[20]

Because disconfirmation-induced attributional processing is likely, other parallel emotions of an attributional nature, such as appreciation and gratitude, may operate as well. Thus, the basic pleasure response of happiness or sadness may be augmented with other positive affects of an appraised nature. The pleasure response can also be reduced by appraisals of a slightly negative nature, such as when insects detract from the full enjoyment of a picnic. Although not all aspects of the consumption processing model may be fully accessed, or accessed at moderate levels of arousal, satisfaction-as-pleasure is best modeled by both the nonprocessing (primary affect) and processing stages in Figure 13.7.

In the special case of confirmation of a pleasure state, disconfirmation effects would be absent. Consumers expecting a particular brand of humor from their favorite comedian and receiving exactly that should only express the level of pleasure that they know this comedian can deliver. Thus, attribution and related emotion responses would not occur; the primary affect would remain as the only variable capable of influencing satisfaction. This case differs, however, from the contentment response mode because expectations are active and the arousal level underlying the primary evaluation is much higher. As a result, the primary affect experienced by the consumer in a confirming pleasure state should be more descriptive and more easily retrieved than that for a confirming contentment state.

Delight

As noted in Chapters 3 and 11, consumer delight has only recently been a research focus in consumption; practitioner interest, however, is evident.[21] Delight is occasionally found in the affect lists used in the psychology literature, and it emerges, when tested, in the highly aroused section of positive affect in circumplex models. Perhaps this is so because, as a number of authors note, delight is a second-order emotion that results specifically from a combination of joy and surprise. Thus, delight, as discussed here and elsewhere, is a heightened affect state in which performance in the form of pleasure is accompanied by surprise. For example, critical incident studies frequently report that exceptionally favorable service incidents that were particularly memorable to consumers lead to delight. For example, a restaurant customer might note that a waitperson "treated me like royalty."

For the consumer to experience *satisfaction-as-delight*, expectation processing must occur after the fact—in a retrospective sense, because the consumer must have at least a latent baseline against which to judge the surprisingness of the outcome (see the previous discussion of surprise in Chapter 4). In the restaurant example, the typical courtesy normally afforded by waitpersons provided this baseline. Additionally, the delight phenomenon ensures that disconfirmation processing will be present since both expectation and performance assessments will be activated. This will result in a very intense primary affective response of pleasant surprise, or delight. Hence, it appears that the processing model in Figure 13.7 would be fully accessed for this satisfaction state. That is, all model variables would be operative and not passive, as they might be for the confirmation state of the pleasure response mode.

Relief

The fourth consumption response is *satisfaction-as-relief*, occurring when a product or event eliminates an aversive state in the manner of negative reinforcement. A gas station on a lonely road, most medications, a successful legal defense, and the satisfaction that consumers get, if any, from complaining are examples of this satisfaction response mode. A distinction is made between this and the state of satisfaction-as-pleasure because individuals are thought to have a hedonic bias for seeking out pleasure and avoiding pain. Thus, pleasure is pursued, savored, and pursued further, whereas the removal of an aversive state is pursued but not necessarily savored because the act of savoring recalls the negative life event. It is this distinction that suggests that the relief of negative reinforcement is less enduring than the pleasure of positive reinforcement and results in return to simple normalcy, as shown in Figure 13.8.[22]

Because of the nagging presence of the aversive state, higher arousal and heightened interest with more rapid decay are expected to mark this consumption mode. Although expectations may take the form of a generalized apprehension, they most probably are actively processed. Almost by definition, satisfaction-as-relief requires that performance be processed. Moreover, this satisfaction state is likely to decay rapidly as if the aversive state were best forgotten, despite the likelihood that disconfirmation and attributions will be evident. The primary affect relates to relief, restoration, or resignation if full relief is not accomplished.

Summary of the Model

Based on research demonstrating the appearance of satisfaction in both cognitive (e.g., appraisal) and affective (e.g., circumplex) investigations, a combined framework for analyzing buyer reactions to product outcomes is presented. As shown in Figure 13.7, the model begins with outcome-induced evaluation and disconfirmation. The primary evaluation of success or failure results in a primary positive or negative affect, setting the general affective tone of the consumption experience.

The second sequence in the model relies on the expectancy disconfirmation paradigm and assumes that comparative operations are the key to further processing. These operations, known as appraisals, include disconfirmation judgments and other comparisons, such as equity or inequity, discussed in Part II of this book. If disconfirmation or another appraisal is acknowledged and is sufficiently arousing, the attribution phase of the model is invoked. If not, generally positive or negative affects deriving from performance or expectations will determine the consumer's overall response to the product or service experience. If appraisal does evoke the attribution process, the consumer's product response is more complex, consisting of the primary affect plus specific types of distinct emotions resulting from the consumer's analysis of the product outcome.

A TEST OF THE MODEL

Since the original publication of the author's consumption processing model, data were collected conforming to its presumptions. In addition to the traditional expectation, disconfirmation, emotion, and satisfaction variables measured in prior studies, the model required that two additional measurement sections be included in the survey. The first was designed to tap consumption response orientations—how the consumer views the product. Specifically, survey items reflecting consumer-generated expressions of delight, pleasure, contentment, and relief were constructed and tested. Second, indications of the types of processing engaged in by consumers were required; that is, did consumers process expectations, performance, disconfirmation, and attribution as

Figure 13.9   **Outline of the Consumption Mode Framework**

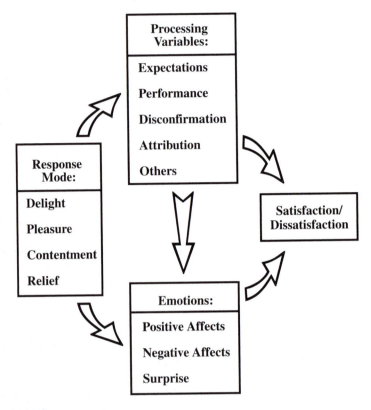

proposed? Last, a traditional set of emotion questions was required to determine if the expected types of emotions were observed corresponding to predictions about each consumption mode. In effect, the framework tested was as shown in Figure 13.9.

Shown are the four proposed response modes that differentially elicit processing of key variables in satisfaction responding (expectations, performance, disconfirmation, and attribution—others are acknowledged, but were not tested). These processing variables, in turn, are proposed to elicit emotions in addition to the primary affect engendered by the outcome of success versus failure. Additionally, the processing states may produce certain anhedonic cognitions (e.g., performance alone) affecting satisfaction directly and bypassing the affect sequence. The focus, at this point, is on the four major elements of Figure 13.9: the response modes, processing variables, emotions, and satisfaction or dissatisfaction.

The Study

Because previous research frequently has used the automobile as a focal product because of the high variability in consumer expressions of involvement for this product category, 115 automobile owners were asked to respond to a survey about their experiences with their cars. Along with other data, they were asked to complete a section on "Feelings about Your Car," designed to determine the way they viewed automobile ownership (delight, pleasure, contentment, or relief) and the kinds

Table 13.2

Factor Analysis Findings for the Response Modes

Items		\multicolumn{4}{c}{Factor and loadings}
		I	II	III	IV
1	I get a great deal of pleasure from driving my car.	.80			
2	My car offers me relaxation and fun.	.78			
3	Driving my car is one of the most enjoyable things I do.	.68			
4	I am sentimentally attached to my car.	.66			
5	I have a great deal of interest in my car.	.65			
6	I view my car just as a means of transportation.		.86		
7	When I bought this car, all I wanted it to do was get me around.		.81		
8	I expect very little out of my car except that it gets me where I want to go.		.64		
9	Generally, I am pretty unemotional about my car.		.56		
10	My car can do things I never expected.			.79	
11	What my car does exceeds my wildest expectations.			.76	
12	My car frequently performs beyond my expectations.			.74	
13	I am constantly surprised by the things my car can do.			.64	
14	My expectations for my car are more like hopes that it will not break down.				.79
15	Sometimes I hope that my car will just get me where I want to go.				.77
16	I am relieved when I get to where I am going.				.69
17	I worry about my car's performance constantly.				.65

of thoughts they frequently had when driving their cars (i.e., what they processed—expectations, performance, disconfirmation, and attribution). These responses, based on items determined from pretest subjects not used for the main study, were factor-analyzed. Ambiguous items were deleted by using conventional procedures until a nonoverlapping factor solution was achieved. The final item lists, one each for the response modes and the processing modes, contained only items loading above 0.5 and no double-loading items (i.e., above 0.5 on two or more factors). The results for the satisfaction response modes appear in Table 13.2.

This factor solution contains four meaningful factors that can be interpreted as pleasure, unemotion (as opposed to contentment), delight, and relief. Relief, as used here, is interpreted not as curative, as in a pain medication, but as an expression of relief (thankfulness) when the car does not malfunction or break down (unrealized fears—the second form of relief to be discussed). This is the context of relief for this product category. As will be seen, the individuals who responded to this mode viewed satisfactory performance as an absence of problems, a somewhat unique interpretation offered first in the earlier edition of this book.

Interestingly, the contentment mode did not materialize as proposed at this stage of the analysis.

Table 13.3

Cluster Z-Score Means on the Response Mode Scales

Cluster number	Response mode				Summary description	n
	Pleasure	Delight	Relief	Unemotion		
1	1.42	1.20	−.63	−1.11	Delighted	13
2	.44	−.20	−.56	−.63	Pleased	31
3	.21	−.11	.45	.96	Contented	19
4	.18	1.27	.23	−.70	Surprised	15
5	−.86	−.39	1.91	.95	Relieved	13
6	−1.15	−.89	−.47	.58	Tolerant	24

Rather, the items constituting the second factor reflected a general level of apathy toward automobile consumption. Traditionally, factor analysis identifies groups of correlated survey items and does not cluster individual respondents. Further analysis, to be presented, will reveal the presence of contented consumers as a market segment.

Response Mode Profiles

The four factors from the previous analysis were converted to scales by adding the items, as is common in this type of research, so that each respondent received a pleasure score, an unemotion score, and so on. Each scale score was then converted to z scores (standardized scores) for use in cluster analysis. Interestingly, a four-cluster solution, which would conceivably have duplicated the four response modes, left interpretation ambiguities. In contrast, an acceptably interpretable cluster solution was obtained with six clusters, as shown in Table 13.3, ranked by the average pleasure score of members in each cluster.

This solution is of general interest, because it reveals more response modes than originally proposed and demands consideration of some of the assumptions about what consumers mean when they refer to unexpectedness and performing beyond expectations. Each cluster is discussed in turn.

Cluster 1 exhibits strong evidence of a delight response orientation. These individuals ($n = 13$; see Table 13.3 for cluster sizes), a mere 11 percent of the sample, score very high on both pleasure and delight (which will be subject to some reinterpretation shortly). Additionally, they are low on relief and, especially, unemotion (i.e., they *are* emotional about their cars).

Cluster 2, in contrast, is the pleasure group. These individuals score moderately high on pleasure and below average on delight, relief, and unemotion. Delight is not well represented in this group because the pleasure experienced by its members is most probably expected, not unexpected.

Also in accord with the predicted consumption processing modes, cluster 3 appears to be the contented group. These individuals are essentially average on pleasure and delight, somewhat above the mean on relief, but very high on unemotion. This is a dispassionate group, not likely to be highly involved with their cars.

Cluster 4, described here as surprised, presents some surprises of its own. This group scored very high on delight, but only average on pleasure and relief, and below average on unemotion (i.e., high on emotion). Now it is apparent that the delight items, originally intended to capture exceeding expectations in a positively extreme manner (e.g., "wildest expectations"), were actually capturing any deviation from expectations, positive or negative. For example, the other three descriptors for this factor in Table 13.2 included such phrases as "things I never expected," "performs beyond my expectations," and "surprised by the things my car can do." Interestingly, satisfaction-as-surprise was originally proposed as a consumption mode, but was abandoned because it did not fit into the reinforcement theme.[23]

Paradoxically, and as noted in Chapter 4, surprise in consumption is central to much of experiential marketing. A small number of studies have begun to address surprise in specific contexts (e.g., unexpected coupons in packaging), and measurement issues have been addressed.[24] Although surprise is part of the delight response, there may be sufficient background to pursue surprise as an independent consumption goal (or, alternatively, a goal to be avoided). The northern European festival of Halloween, also celebrated in the United States, involves fright as a central concept and, in the context of automobiles, the negative surprise of a breakdown or unexpected repair would detract from the pride of ownership—thereby lowering the pleasure score. Nonetheless, surprise does fit into the appraisal scheme shown in Figure 13.4, and the findings here suggest that it may be a fifth response orientation.

Cluster 5 exhibits the characteristics of the relief group. Individuals in this cluster score very high on relief, low on pleasure and delight, and high on unemotion. This "expression" of unemotion probably derives from resignation, a trait proposed in Table 13.1 for this state. Last, cluster 6 is a very displeased group, low on delight and relief, and moderately high on unemotion. Because of the high unemotion score, these consumers would be characterized as tolerant, in that they appear to be tolerating their cars for lack of means to acquire another.

Notably, all the groups are of adequate size as a percentage of the sample, with the largest groups being pleased and tolerant toward their cars. At this point, further validation of the meaningfulness of these groups will be performed with additional analysis of their processing profiles, emotional profiles, and satisfaction levels.

Processing Profiles

In accord with the framework in Figure 13.9, the next step in the analysis is to determine the processing tendencies of the clusters. Specifically, do the higher-arousal groups engage in greater amounts of satisfaction processing, as predicted, and do the less involved groups omit consideration of some of or all the variables in the figure? To answer these questions, an analysis of the processing styles, similar to that performed to determine response styles, is needed. Accordingly, a list of statements reflective of individuals' motivation to assess expectations, performance, disconfirmation, and attribution was drawn from pretest findings. This list was factor-analyzed and reduced in length, as before, until a suitable set of independent factors was obtained. The final list of statements is shown in Table 13.4.

One immediate observation from the results is that no pure expectation items appeared as a distinct factor in the solution. Rather, it appears that the processing of expectations was absorbed by the disconfirmation statements, a result to consider in future research.

The content of the first factor suggests that it relates to the processing of performance, since all items reflect observations or reactions to the car's performance characteristics. The second factor, with five items, is indicative of attribution processing, while the third concerns the formation of disconfirmation perceptions. The fourth factor relates to a general lack of interest in all aspects of the car, which seems descriptive of nonprocessing. Although it would appear that this last factor has the reverse meaning of the performance-processing factor, the factor analysis results imply that there is some degree of independence between the two concepts. Thus, both will be included in the analyses that follow.

Table 13.4

Factor Analysis Findings for the Processing Modes

Items		Factor and loadings			
		I	II	III	IV
1	I react strongly to things about my car.	.67			
2	I keep thinking about my car's performance.	.64			
3	I like to forget about my car as soon as I leave it. (reverse)	.63			
4	I am always monitoring how well my car is performing.	.60			
5	When something unexpected happens to my car, I want to get to the bottom of it.		.73		
6	When my car surprises me, I want to figure out why.		.71		
7	I do not understand some of the things my car does, so I do not think about them. (reverse)		.68		
8	When things happen to my car, I want to know the reasons why.		.53		
9	The reasons for my car's performance do not interest me.		.50		
10	I find myself frequently comparing my car to what I wanted.			.83	
11	I had many expectations about my car, and now I match them to what I am getting.			.81	
12	I keep asking myself if I should have expected my car to perform this way.			.56	
13	My car's performance has caused me to reflect on the reasons I bought it.			.55	
14	I never think or worry about my car.				.69
15	If someone asked me how well my car was running, I would not have much to say.				.68
16	When my car runs better or worse than usual, I never give it a second thought.				.60
17	I get bored talking to others about cars.				.53

Table 13.5 contains the response cluster means on the four processing variables identified in the factor analysis. These data were constructed by creating processing variable scales from the items in Table 13.4 and converting the scale scores to z scores. The cell entries are average scores for the respondents in each of the six clusters determined earlier.

These data conform to the expected characteristics of the response profiles. The delighted group scores very high on performance processing, high on attribution processing, moderately high on disconfirmation processing, and very low on nonprocessing. The pleased group is moderate on all dimensions and somewhat low on disconfirmation, perhaps because these respondents received what they pursued (pleasure). The contented group is very low on attribution, as one would expect from its similarly high score on nonprocessing, but is found to do some disconfirmation processing. The surprised group is high on performance monitoring and very high on disconfirmation, but low on attribution. Perhaps this finding results because the respondents in this group do not know to whom or to what to attribute the outcomes.[25]

Table 13.5

Cluster Means on the Processing Scales

Response cluster	Processing scales			
	Performance	Attribution	Disconfirmation	Nonprocessing
Delighted	1.34	.73	.37	−.80
Pleased	.07	.22	−.36	−.14
Contented	−.08	−.49	.32	.41
Surprised	.43	−.21	.67	−.36
Relieved	−.54	−.21	.08	.25
Tolerant	−.74	−.05	−.46	.38

Finally, the relieved and tolerant groups do very little processing. This finding agrees with their proposed resignation orientation toward their automobile situation. Additionally, they have very similar profiles with the exception that the tolerant group is very low on disconfirmation processing as if to say they are aware of the expected low level of their car's performance. To find a means of more finely discriminating these two groups and to further confirm the consumption orientations of the six clusters (see Figure 13.9), analysis proceeds to the emotion responses.

Emotional Linkages

Discrete (unipolar) emotions scaling was used as the emotion inventory in the present study because of its prior use in consumer satisfaction research.[26] Cluster means of the remaining nine standardized emotion scores are reported in Table 13.6, along with satisfaction and disconfirmation (to be discussed).

The data in Table 13.6 illustrate the additional satisfaction insights that researchers can ascertain by adopting the response mode approach over traditional methods. Examination of the specific emotional profiles provides further understanding of what drives the satisfaction response. Table 13.6 is arranged so that the positive affects in Izard's scheme (joy and interest) appear in the first two columns, followed by surprise, which can be positive or negative, in the third column. The negative affects appear next, beginning with the externally attributed affects of anger and disgust. Within this negative affect block, the situational affects of sadness and fear appear next, followed by the internally attributed affects of shame and guilt. Finally, satisfaction/dissatisfaction and disconfirmation means are reported in the two rightmost columns to show how they reflect the sentiments of the emotion profiles.

The data show that the delighted group is high on both joy and interest and still higher on surprise. This reinforces the identification of this cluster as delighted, for it is composed of individuals displaying the key delight dimensions of pleasure and surprise. Note that all negative affect scores are below the mean. Similarly, the pleasure group is universally below the mean on the negative affects, as well as below the mean on surprise. This distinguishes it from the delight group since satisfaction-as-pleasure seekers should not be surprised with their outcomes. Additionally, the positive affects are above the mean, but not as high as might be expected for this group.

The contentment group, which is predicted to have a relatively unemotional orientation, is slightly above and below the mean for all variables, as expected. In contrast, the surprise group

Table 13.6

Cluster Means on the Emotion and Satisfaction Measures

Response cluster	Emotion and satisfaction variables										
	Joy	Interest	Surprise	Anger	Disgust	Sadness	Fear	Shame	Guilt	Satisfaction	Disconfirmation
Delighted	.97	.88	1.07	-.40	-.27	-.32	-.30	-.43	-.37	.59	.64
Pleased	.10	.11	-.36	-.23	-.24	-.18	-.25	-.33	-.31	.30	.02
Contented	-.11	-.30	.03	-.15	.11	-.05	.10	.45	.07	.04	.13
Surprised	.51	.50	.47	.66	-.06	.06	.44	.52	.28	-.43	.06
Relieved	-.87	-.37	-.06	.48	.80	.96	.76	.60	.91	-1.08	-.57
Tolerant	-.41	-.50	-.40	-.04	-.03	-.11	-.30	-.34	-.13	.12	-.21

shows mixed emotions, scoring second highest on surprise (after the delight group). Interestingly, the surprise group displays high scores on the positive affects of joy and interest *and* on the negative affects, particularly anger, fear, and shame. This is consistent with the commonly accepted perspective on surprise as a bivalent affect and supports the interpretation of this group as containing both pleasantly surprised and unpleasantly surprised consumers, a subject of speculation for the low pleasure score for this group (see Table 13.3).

The last two groups, despite being similar on the processing variables, have very different emotion profiles. The relief group is very angry, scoring low on the positive affects and universally high on all the negative affects. Relief in this context is akin to relieved, as in "I'm relieved that my car didn't break down on the interstate." Apparently, this group is resigned to its automobile ownership situation, but still harbors very negative feelings. The tolerant group, in contrast, is low on positive affect, but either average or modestly low on the negative affects. This group's resignation displays itself in a more reserved manner not characteristic of the hostility generated by the relief group.

Finally, analysis of the satisfaction scores integrates all information in Tables 13.3, 13.5, and 13.6. In order from most satisfied to most dissatisfied, the groups align themselves as follows: delighted, pleased, tolerant, contented, surprised, and relieved. The difference between the tolerant and contented groups is very small (0.08), and it is probably not meaningful to draw conclusions from this finding. Normally, satisfaction levels for the contented group would be predicted to be higher than those for the tolerant group, in accord with the disconfirmation findings (to be discussed).

The results also show that the relief group is most dissatisfied by some margin, as would be predicted by knowledge of the information in the other tables. Finally, the surprised group appears composed of more individuals experiencing negative than positive surprise, as the satisfaction levels are second only to the relief group in terms of dissatisfaction.

The disconfirmation data provide further support for interpretations of the response modes. Recall that disconfirmation measures are based on the positiveness of disconfirmation, not on the extent of processing disconfirmation. It is therefore expected that disconfirmation will track satisfaction levels to some extent. Thus, it is not surprising to find that the delighted group is most positive and the relief group is most negative. The pleased and contented groups are closely aligned, while the tolerant group shows moderately low levels of positive disconfirmation. Finally, the surprised group is near the average since, again, this group is comprised of both positively surprised (i.e., disconfirmed) and negatively surprised consumers.

Interestingly, a near replication of this study appeared after the first edition of this book was published.[27] Using a very similar methodology in the context of visits to a government employment office (a service), three positive respondent clusters were found (happy, hopeful, and positively surprised) and four negative (angry, depressed, guilty, humiliated). These were reduced via further analysis to four "megaclusters" of delighted, angry but content, angry and humiliated, and emotionless. Because a government employment office is not technically a product or purchased service, some of the findings are socially interactive in nature (e.g., angry but humiliated), displaying "mixed emotions," discussed in the next section. Nonetheless, this study attests to the universal and complex nature of the satisfaction response.

This takes the consumption-processing model as far as the author is able, given current data. Other researchers have more recently pursued this line of analysis into the determinants of customer satisfaction (to be discussed) by investigating satisfaction prototypes, treating each consumer *individually*, rather than considering a homogeneous market consisting of identical consumers with varying product experiences. Consumers appear to demonstrate not only different consumption perspectives (i.e., the response modes), but also varying degrees of processing consumption events and of responding to their nuances.

OTHER PROPOSED SATISFACTION STATES

Since the author's consumption processing states were first proposed, other researchers have attempted to extend the consumption satisfaction response to other likely expression modes. The first is interesting in that it addresses what may be interpreted as a confused state of postpurchase responding whereby the consumer has mixed feelings, some of which are satisfying and some dissatisfying. Based on earlier work on "ambivalence" in consumption, this construct has recently been embedded in a limited satisfaction network.[28] The ambivalence phenomenon could be the result of three or more causes, namely indifference, which has already been discussed under the rubric of unemotion; nonprocessing, which is conceptually similar in terms of its consequences, or true mixed feelings representing a mix of good and bad attribute "satisfactions." This latter case argues, once again, for a multi-item satisfaction instrument incorporating either multiple feeling constructs (contentment, pleasure, delight) or multiple attribute items reflecting each attribute satisfaction separately.

Of note is the finding that ambivalence in ratings of restaurant seafood *decreased* both satisfaction and loyalty independently.[29] Two possibilities explain this result. First, ambivalence—may represent a confused state whereby the uncertainty and lack of an ability to express judgment—may be a negatively valent state for consumers. Second, methodologically, ambivalent consumers may use the scale midpoint to judge the consumable, while other consumers find the product or service generally satisfying so that the midpoint represents a low, hence negative, rating (see Chapter 2, Figure 2.9). In either case, this satisfaction state may be distanced from the unemotion state discussed here.

Another, anthropological investigation of narratives about innovations in electronic technology found that *individual* consumers may display feelings of seven different "satisfactions," two of which are variants of those proposed in this author's previous writings cited here; the remaining five can be viewed as interesting extensions in the sense that they *are* couched in a satisfaction network of responses.[30] In the first two, novelty satisfaction is reframed, not as a response to the unexpected but as the discovery of new, unanticipated benefits, as when a computer user finds that the device can provide more novel applications than were present in previous versions. In the second, satisfaction-as-relief is described as the finding that anticipated failings "failed" to materialize, as opposed to relief of an aversive state (negative reinforcement). The reader will note the resemblance of this reaction to unrealized fears in Figure 13.3 and to the interpretation of relief in the context of the automobile ownership study.

The remaining five are satisfaction-as-awe; satisfaction-as-trust; its reverse image, *dis*satisfaction-as-helplessness; satisfaction-as-resignation; and satisfaction-as-love. Awe is a sense of bewildering wonderment not fully comprehended, an incomplete satisfaction in this author's opinion in that the cognitive aspect of fulfillment is only vaguely understood. Helplessness and resignation (Figure 13.3) are similarly constructed, but refer to different time frames. Helplessness is described as being unable to prevent or accommodate the ongoing march of technological innovation and requisite new skill sets so that the consumer feels "left behind," while resignation is recognition that a negative dissatisfying situation will not change, thereby requiring coping strategies.[31] Trust would appear to be a valid satisfaction, especially when social relationships are involved.[32] It appears prominently in the relationship literature, which is vast. Finally, love is now recognized as a strong attachment to a consumable, as in "I just *love* my car." It has been found in taxonomy studies of product and service response and has recently been empirically tested.[33]

Another narrative study takes this latter notion of satisfaction-as-love to another dimension.[34] Using the term *deep soulful satisfaction*, the author bridges the gap between satisfaction and spirituality, first discussed in Chapter 7 as one of the inherent meanings of value. A number of examples are provided in the context of everyday consumables (e.g., makeup, coffee, pets, motorcycles) whereby consumers find spiritual meaning beyond satisfaction in their daily lives, thereby enhancing their quality of life. At this point, the discussion of consumption processing must end so as not to encroach on a higher-order belief system more properly posed elsewhere. Other researchers are encouraged to take this discussion to the next level.

In an attempt to provide a wider range of descriptors for a multi-point or multi-item satisfaction scale, a number of satisfaction-like terms were rated on their direction and strength.[35] The intent of this study was not to reveal satisfaction modalities but to find terms that represented the continuum of satisfaction responses. Nevertheless, some of the terms are of interest for further exploration while others have been in the satisfaction lexicon for some time (e.g., *delighted*). Terms worthy of further study as modalities include positives such as *exhilarated*, *euphoric*, and *enthralled* (not studied were the synonyms *charming* and *spellbound* in the latter case), and negatives including *appalling* and *terrible* (*repulsive* would seem to fit here as well). This is to say that any unique state of a hybrid emotion (having a cognitive and affective profile) would be candidates for satisfaction modalities yet to be investigated. On a final note, two of the descriptors tested in this study (*over the moon* and *in seventh heaven*) may broach the spirituality dimension in the previous paragraph.

These developments notwithstanding, the author's original Consumption Satisfaction Scale (CSS) is reproduced here in Table 13.7.[36] Originally intended to show how many of the concepts in this book could assist in the construction of a satisfaction measure, the CSS has proved valid over time; many requests have been fielded for its content. Consistent reliability estimates in the 0.9 range have been reported. Note the correspondence of the items with those used in the model test in Table 13.2.

Also note how each scale item taps varied dimensions of satisfaction discussed here. In addition to the satisfaction anchor, which *must* be present, there are two overall performance or purchase evaluation items, including one that can be viewed as a proxy for quality, three attribution items, two affect items, a need fulfillment item, a dissonance item, a regret item, and a negative disconfirmation item. Missing are items representing expectations, value, and equity. No expectation item is included because it would not be clear what level it would represent (predicted, ideal), so the scoring would be ambiguous. Equity and inequity in the form of "I received a fair deal" or other statements representing fairness or preference (see Chapter 8) could be included, if desired for the particular context at hand, as could value.

Disconfirmation, particularly positive disconfirmation, appears underrepresented in the scale. This is intentional as disconfirmation is a distinctly separate (but related) concept. If disconfirmation is to be measured separately, then researchers are advised to omit disconfirmation from the satisfaction scale. If not, disconfirmation should be included in the satisfaction scale to more fully represent satisfaction's many antecedents. A positively worded disconfirmation scale would appear, for example, as "This car exceeded my highest expectations."

To shorten the scale, any item but the satisfaction anchor can be considered for deletion. A pretest reliability analysis may be helpful in specific situations to determine which items contribute the least to the scale's reliability. To augment the scale, tailor-made items can be added as long as they are in the domain of satisfaction. The domain of satisfaction is that set of concepts that gives satisfaction its fundamental meaning. Thus, statements reflecting antecedents, such as need fulfillment, or statements reflecting satisfaction's multiple meanings, such as delight, are

Table 13.7

The Consumption Satisfaction Scale (CSS)

Scale tem	Conceptual basis
This is one of the best ____ I could have bought.	Overall performance and quality
This ____ is exactly what I need.	Need fulfillment
This ____ has not worked out as well as I thought it would. (reverse)	Failed expectations
I am satisfied with ____ (my decision to buy ____).	Satisfaction "anchor"
Sometimes I have mixed feelings about having purchased ____. (reverse)	Cognitive dissonance
My choice to buy this ____ was a wise one.	Success attribution
If I could do it over again, I would buy a different ____. (reverse)	Regret
I have truly enjoyed this ____.	Positive affect
I feel bad (guilty) about my decision to buy this ____. (reverse)	Failure attribution (remorse)
I am not happy that I bought this ____. (reverse)	Negative affect
Owning this ____ has been a good experience.	Purchase evaluation
I am sure it was the right thing to buy this ____.	Success attribution

possibilities. In fact, the four response modes of delight, pleasure, contentment, and relief would provide four alternative means of increasing the item list. For example,

- This product gives me a great deal of delight.
- I am pleased with this product's performance.
- Using this product is a source of contentment for me.
- This product gives me relief from _____.

CONCLUSION

A straightforward conclusion drawn from this chapter is that the overly simplified question—Are you satisfied?—does not tap into the complexity of the satisfaction response. Because satisfaction can mean a variety of complex consumption-responding states, researchers are advised to determine the cognitive (processing) and affective (emotional) substrata of the satisfaction response. Research on the differential consequences of the many forms of satisfaction has yet to be undertaken. Such future research would initiate an entirely new phase of postpurchase investigation, advancing further refinements in the consumption-processing model and in an understanding of what drives the model.

Now that satisfaction has been taken to its limits, discussion turns to what occurs after consumers experience satisfaction or dissatisfaction. Specifically, focus shifts in the next chapter to the immediate consequences of being satisfied or dissatisfied. Finally, the last chapter explores what happens to satisfaction as episodes are repeated and time progresses. What long-term effects does satisfaction have on the firm's customers and on the firm itself, including its profits?

NOTES

1. *Latent* satisfaction has been defined as a lack of awareness of one's state of satisfaction. See Bloemer and Kasper, "Complex Relationship Between Consumer Satisfaction and Brand Loyalty."

2. Oliver and DeSarbo, "Response Determinants in Satisfaction Judgments."

3. Major sections of this chapter borrow from the author's consumption processing model, originally proposed in Oliver, "Processing of the Satisfaction Response in Consumption," reproduced under a blanket permission from the publisher, Consumer Satisfaction, Dissatisfaction and Complaining Behavior Inc. Substantial revision and updating to this paper have been made, and the present discussion is now developed further.

4. E.g., Knowles, Grove, and Pickett, "Mood Versus Quality Effects on Customers' Responses to Service Organizations and Service Encounters"; Meyer and Shack, "Structural Convergence of Mood and Personality."

5. Bennett, Härtel, and McColl-Kennedy, "Experience as a Moderator of Involvement and Satisfaction on Brand Loyalty in a Business-to-Business Setting"; Gabbott and Hogg, "Consumer Involvement in Services."

6. The drawbacks (and some benefits) of single-item scales are discussed in Bergkvist and Rossiter, "Predictive Validity of Multiple-Item Versus Single-Item Measures."

7. These examples are culled from Ortony, Clore, and Collins, *Cognitive Structure of Emotions*, p. 19; Scherer, "Criteria for Emotion-Antecedent Appraisal"; Weiner, *Attributional Theory of Motivation and Emotion*; and Oliver, *Satisfaction*, Chapter 12.

8. Mano and Oliver, "Assessing the Dimensionality and Structure of Consumption Experience."

9. See, e.g., Daly, Lancee, and Polivy, "Conical Model for the Taxonomy of Emotional Experience"; and Plutchik, *Emotions and Life*.

10. See Meyer and Niepel, "Surprise."

11. Kashdan, "Curiosity"; Loewenstein, "Psychology of Curiosity"; Silvia, "What Is Interesting?"

12. Hegtvedt, Thompson, and Cook, "Power and Equity"; Kaplan, Reckers, and Reynolds, "Application of Attribution and Equity Theories to Tax Evasion Behavior."

13. A small number of attribution-dependent affects appeared in Table 11.3 and the associated text.

14. A discussion of gratitude can be found in McCullough at al., "Is Gratitude a Moral Affect?" Guilt (and shame) are discussed in Burnett and Lunsford, "Conceptualizing Guilt in the Consumer Decision-Making Process"; and Niedenthal, Tangney, and Gavanski, "'If Only I Weren't' Versus 'If Only I Hadn't.'"

15. Oliver, "Processing of the Satisfaction Response in Consumption."

16. Westbrook and Black, "A Motivation-Based Shopper Typology."

17. Veenhoven, "Is Happiness Relative?"

18. Peterson and Wilson, "Measuring Customer Satisfaction."

19. Neo and Murrell, "Valenced Emotions in Satisfaction"; Oliver and Westbrook, "Profiles of Consumer Emotions and Satisfaction in Ownership and Usage"; Westbrook and Oliver, "Dimensionality of Consumption Emotion Patterns and Consumer Satisfaction."

20. In an interesting study of two sports, one "new" at the time (skateboarding) and one "usual" (baseball), the authors infer greater pleasure and positive disconfirmation among skateboarders. See Francis and Browne, "Effect of User Orientation on Disconfirmation Processing."

21. See, e.g., Keiningham and Vavra, *Customer Delight Principle.*

22. A second interpretation of relief, whereby consumers express relief that an anticipated fear did not materialize, as shown in Figure 13.3, will be noted in a later section of this chapter.

23. Oliver, "Processing of the Satisfaction Response in Consumption," p. 10.

24. Vanhamme, "Link Between Surprise and Satisfaction"; Vanhamme and Snelders, "Role of Surprise in Satisfaction Judgements"; Heilman, Nakamoto, and Rao, "Pleasant Surprises."

25. This finding contrasts with the more general observation in the literature that disconfirmation is a cause of attributional processing. The joint appearance of above-average disconfirmation and attribution processing was found in the delight group. Apparently disconfirmation *in this sample* is a necessary, but not sufficient, cause for attribution as both the surprised and contented groups displayed above-average disconfirmation and below-average attribution.

26. See Izard, *Psychology of Emotions*, p. 104, for the discrete emotion scale. The emotion of contempt (scorn) was not investigated because of its ill fit in the present context. Studies that have tested this scale include Oliver, "Cognitive, Affective, and Attribute Bases of the Satisfaction Response" and "Investigation

of the Attribute Basis of Emotion and Related Affects in Consumption"; Oliver and Westbrook, "Profiles of Consumer Emotions and Satisfaction in Ownership and Usage"; and Westbrook and Oliver, "Dimensionality of Consumption Emotion Patterns and Consumer Satisfaction."

27. Liljander and Strandvik, "Emotions in Service Satisfaction."

28. Olsen, Wilcox, and Olsson, "Consequences of Ambivalence on Satisfaction and Loyalty"; Otnes, Lowrey, and Shrum, "Toward an Understanding of Consumer Ambivalence"; Ruth, Brunel, and Otnes, "Linking Thoughts to Feelings."

29. Olsen, Wilcox, and Olsson, "Consequences of Ambivalence on Satisfaction and Loyalty."

30. Fournier and Mick, "Rediscovering Satisfaction."

31. See Stauss and Neuhaus, "Qualitative Satisfaction Model"; and Chapter 12, Figure 12.3, and the accompanying text of this book.

32. E.g., Harris and Goode, "Four Levels of Loyalty and the Pivotal Role of Trust." See, also, Hardin, *Trust and Trustworthiness.*

33. Ahuvia, "Beyond the Extended Self"; Richins, "Measuring Emotions in the Consumption Experience."

34. Durgee, "Deep Soulful Satisfaction."

35. Ganglmair and Lawson, "Measuring *Affective Response to Consumption* Using Rasch Modeling."

36. Oliver, *Satisfaction*, p. 343.

BIBLIOGRAPHY

Ahuvia, Aaron C. "Beyond the Extended Self: Loved Objects and Consumers' Identity Narratives." *Journal of Consumer Research* 32, no. 1 (June 2005): 171–184.

Bennett, Rebekah, Charmine E.J. Härtel, and Janet R. McColl-Kennedy. "Experience as a Moderator of Involvement and Satisfaction on Brand Loyalty in a Business-to-Business Setting." *Industrial Marketing Management* 34, no. 1 (January 2005): 97–107.

Bergkvist, Lars, and John R. Rossiter. "The Predictive Validity of Multiple-Item Versus Single-Item Measures of the Same Constructs." *Journal of Marketing Research* 44, no. 2 (May 2007): 175–184.

Bloemer, José, and Hans Kasper. "The Complex Relationship Between Consumer Satisfaction and Brand Loyalty." *Journal of Economic Psychology* 16, no. 2 (July 1995): 311–329.

Burnett, Melissa S., and Dale A. Lunsford. "Conceptualizing Guilt in the Consumer Decision-Making Process." *Journal of Consumer Marketing* 11, no. 3 (1994): 33–43.

Daly, Eleanor M., William J. Lancee, and Janet Polivy. "A Conical Model for the Taxonomy of Emotional Experience." *Journal of Personality and Social Psychology* 45 (August 1983): 443–457.

Durgee, Jeffrey F. "Deep, Soulful Satisfaction." *Journal of Consumer Satisfaction, Dissatisfaction and Complaining Behavior* 12 (1999): 53–63.

Fournier, Susan, and David Glen Mick. "Rediscovering Satisfaction." *Journal of Marketing* 63, no. 4 (October 1999): 5–23.

Francis, Sally K., and Beverly Browne. "Effect of User Orientation on Disconfirmation Processing." *Journal of Consumer Satisfaction, Dissatisfaction and Complaining Behavior* 4 (1991): 139–143.

Gabbott, Mark, and Gillian Hogg. "Consumer Involvement in Services: A Replication and Extension." *Journal of Business Research* 46, no. 2 (October 1999): 159–166.

Ganglmair, Alexandra, and Rob Lawson. "Measuring *Affective Response to Consumption* Using Rasch Modeling." *Journal of Consumer Satisfaction, Dissatisfaction and Complaining Behavior* 16 (2003): 198–210.

Hardin, Russell. *Trust and Trustworthiness.* New York: Russell Sage Foundation, 2002.

Harris, Lloyd C., and Mark M.H. Goode. "The Four Levels of Loyalty and the Pivotal Role of Trust: A Study of Online Service Dynamics." *Journal of Retailing* 80, no. 2 (1980): 139–158.

Hegtvedt, Karen A., Elaine A. Thompson, and Karen S. Cook. "Power and Equity: What Counts in Attributions for Exchange Outcomes?" *Social Psychology Quarterly* 56 (June 1993): 100–119.

Heilman, Carrie M., Kent Nakamoto, and Ambar G. Rao. "Pleasant Surprises: Consumer Response to Unexpected In-Store Coupons." *Journal of Marketing Research* 39, no. 2 (May 2002): 242–252.

Izard, Carroll E. *The Psychology of Emotions.* New York: Plenum Press, 1991.

Kaplan, Steven E., Philip M.J. Reckers, and Kim D. Reynolds. "An Application of Attribution and Equity Theories to Tax Evasion Behavior." *Journal of Economic Psychology* 7 (December 1986): 461–476.

Kashdan, Todd B. "Curiosity." In *Character Strengths and Virtues: A Handbook and Classification*, ed.

Christopher Peterson and Martin E.P. Seligman, 125–141. Washington, DC: American Psychological Association, 2004.

Keiningham, Timothy, and Terry Vavra. *The Customer Delight Principle: Exceeding Customers' Expectations for Bottom-Line Success.* Chicago: McGraw-Hill, 2001.

Knowles, Patricia A., Stephen J. Grove, and Gregory M. Pickett. "Mood Versus Quality Effects on Customers' Responses to Service Organizations and Service Encounters." *Journal of Service Research* 2, no. 2 (November 1999): 187–199.

Liljander, Veronica, and Tore Strandvik. "Emotions in Service Satisfaction." *International Journal of Service Industry Management* 8, no. 2 (1997): 148–169.

Loewenstein, George. "The Psychology of Curiosity: A Review and Reinterpretation." *Psychological Bulletin* 116, no. 1 (July 1994): 75–98.

Mano, Haim, and Richard L. Oliver. "Assessing the Dimensionality and Structure of Consumption Experience: Evaluation, Feeling, and Satisfaction." *Journal of Consumer Research* 20 (December 1993): 451–466.

McCullough, Michael E., Shelley D. Kilpatrick, Robert A. Emmons, and David B. Larson. "Is Gratitude a Moral Affect?" *Psychological Bulletin* 127, no. 2 (March 2001): 249–266.

Meyer, Gregory J., and John R. Shack. "Structural Convergence of Mood and Personality: Evidence for Old and New Directions." *Journal of Personality and Social Psychology* 57, no. 10 (October 1989): 691–706.

Meyer, Wulf-Uwe, and Michael Niepel. "Surprise." In *Encyclopedia of Human Behavior*, ed. V.S. Ramachandran, 4:353–358. San Diego, CA: Academic Press, 1994.

Neo, Mai, and Audrey J. Murrell. "Valenced Emotions in Satisfaction: A Look at Affect in Shopping." In *Advances in Consumer Research*, ed. Leigh McAlister and Michael L. Rothschild, 20:667–672. Provo, UT: Association for Consumer Research, 1993.

Niedenthal, Paula M., June Price Tangney, and Igor Gavanski. "'If Only I Weren't' Versus 'If Only I Hadn't': Distinguishing Shame and Guilt in Counterfactual Thinking." *Journal of Personality and Social Psychology* 67, no. 4 (October 1994): 585–595.

Oliver, Richard L. "Cognitive, Affective, and Attribute Bases of the Satisfaction Response." *Journal of Consumer Research* 20, no. 2 (December 1993): 418–430.

———. "An Investigation of the Attribute Basis of Emotion and Related Affects in Consumption: Suggestions for a Stage-Specific Satisfaction Framework." In *Advances in Consumer Research*, ed. John F. Sherry Jr. and Brian Sternthal, 19:237–244. Provo, UT: Association for Consumer Research, 1992.

———. "Processing of the Satisfaction Response in Consumption: A Suggested Framework and Research Propositions." *Journal of Consumer Satisfaction, Dissatisfaction and Complaining Behavior* 2 (1989): 1–16.

———. *Satisfaction: A Behavioral Perspective on the Consumer.* New York: Irwin/McGraw-Hill, 1997.

Oliver, Richard L., and Wayne S. DeSarbo. "Response Determinants in Satisfaction Judgments." *Journal of Consumer Research* 14, no. 4 (March 1988): 495–507.

Oliver, Richard L., and Robert A. Westbrook. "Profiles of Consumer Emotions and Satisfaction in Ownership and Usage." *Journal of Consumer Satisfaction, Dissatisfaction and Complaining Behavior* 6 (1993): 12–27.

Olsen, Svein Ottar, James Wilcox, and Ulf Olsson. "Consequences of Ambivalence on Satisfaction and Loyalty." *Psychology & Marketing* 22, no. 3 (March 2005): 247–269.

Ortony, Andrew, Gerald L. Clore, and Allan Collins. *The Cognitive Structure of Emotions.* Cambridge, UK: Cambridge University Press, 1988.

Otnes, Cele, Tina M. Lowrey, and L.J. Shrum. "Toward an Understanding of Consumer Ambivalence." *Journal of Consumer Research* 24, no. 1 (June 1997): 80–93.

Peterson, Robert A., and William R. Wilson. "Measuring Customer Satisfaction: Fact and Artifact." *Journal of the Academy of Marketing Science* 20, no. 2 (Winter 1992): 61–71.

Plutchik, Robert. *Emotions and Life: Perspectives from Psychology, Biology, and Evolution.* Washington, DC: American Psychological Association, 2003.

Richins, Marsha L. "Measuring Emotions in the Consumption Experience." *Journal of Consumer Research* 24, no. 2 (September 1997): 127–146.

Ruth, Julie A., Frédéric F. Brunel, and Cele C. Otnes. "Linking Thoughts to Feelings: Investigating Cognitive Appraisals and Consumption Emotions in a Mixed-Emotions Context." *Journal of the Academy of Marketing Science* 30, no. 1 (Winter 2002): 44–58.

Scherer, Klaus R. "Criteria for Emotion-Antecedent Appraisal: A Review." In *Cognitive Perspectives on Emotion and Motivation*, ed. V. Hamilton, Gordon H. Bower, and Nico H. Frijda, 89–126. Norwell, MA: Kluwer Academic, 1988.

Silvia, Paul J. "What Is Interesting? Exploring the Appraisal Structure of Interest." *Emotion* 5, no. 1 (March 2005): 89–102.

Stauss, Bernd, and Patricia Neuhaus. "The Qualitative Satisfaction Model." *International Journal of Service Industry Management* 8, no. 3 (September 1997): 236–249.

Vanhamme, Joëlle. "The Link Between Surprise and Satisfaction: An Exploratory Research on how best to Measure Surprise." *Journal of Marketing Management* 16, no. 6 (July 2000): 565–582.

Vanhamme, Joëlle, and Dirk Snelders. "The Role of Surprise in Satisfaction Judgements." *Journal of Consumer Satisfaction, Dissatisfaction and Complaining Behavior* 14 (2001): 27–45.

Veenhoven, Ruut. "Is Happiness Relative?" *Social Indicators Research* 24, no. 1 (February 1991): 1–34.

Weiner, Bernard. *An Attributional Theory of Motivation and Emotion.* New York: Springer-Verlag, 1986.

Westbrook, Robert A., and William C. Black. "A Motivation-Based Shopper Typology." *Journal of Retailing* 61, no. 1 (Spring 1985): 78–103.

Westbrook, Robert A., and Richard L. Oliver. "The Dimensionality of Consumption Emotion Patterns and Consumer Satisfaction." *Journal of Consumer Research* 18, no. 1 (June 1991): 84–91.

SATISFACTION'S CONSEQUENCES: WHAT HAPPENS NEXT?

In the previous chapters, the antecedents of satisfaction or, more specifically, the causes of the satisfaction response were examined. In the final part of this book, focus shifts to what satisfaction causes—its consequences. After all, this latter topic is the raison d'être for studying satisfaction in the first place. If there were no positive or negative consequences to successes or failures in the marketplace, satisfaction would exist only as a curiosity.

Part IV of the book consists of two chapters. The first examines the immediate consequences of satisfaction in the short run. Here, the topic of complaining (as well as complimenting) is discussed, and a complaint-handling model, based on expectancy disconfirmation, is provided. Interestingly, firms are also advised to "handle" compliments as well as complaints, and reasons for a response in this latter case are provided. Additional topics in this chapter include consumer responses to dissatisfaction and how these responses group together into consumer profiles. These profiles will show that, generally, consumers use either public complaining or private complaining (word of mouth), but not necessarily both. Also discussed quite early in the chapter is the most frequent response of all to consumption, at least from the perspective of the firm: that of *doing nothing*. Most consumers do not report either their successes or their failures to the firm, which may therefore have to take steps to obtain this information.

New to this chapter are two topics. The first integrates the conceptual and empirical literature on attribution, equity, and appraisal with the traditional complaining discussion. Like much of the satisfaction response, the expectancy disconfirmation model of complaining is responsive to these influences as well. The second topic is a much-extended treatment of word of mouth. With the advent and accelerated proliferation of website purchasing and the resulting dissemination of purchasing outcomes via the Internet, word of mouth or "buzz" is becoming a major venue for complaining (and complimenting) responses worldwide. The chapter would not be complete without coverage of the important development of viral marketing, which enhances the effect of word of mouth.

In the last section of this chapter, a current index of word of mouth, promoted as a "one-number" satisfaction indicator, is discussed in light of the controversy surrounding it. In accord with a number of critiques, it is found to be wanting. In its stead, a number of other measures of complaining and complimenting, word of mouth, and recommending are proposed. These, of course, will need to be augmented with antecedents, largely discussed in the previous chapters, in order to ascertain the actionable causes of these critical postpurchase variables.

In Chapter 15, the most extensively revised and augmented chapter, discussion of consumer satisfaction and loyalty is extended to cover currently available research at the time of this writing. This last chapter addresses the long-term effects of satisfaction in both behavioral and, of necessity, monetary terms. Here, the notion of consumer loyalty is elaborated, and "true" loyalty, as opposed to "happenstance" loyalty, is explained. Other effects, including repurchase intention and the more easily observable behavior of repeat purchasing—both as proxies for "true" loyalty—are opened to scrutiny. At this point, a four-stage model of loyalty progression is proposed in which each stage represents a successively growing allegiance to the focal brand. Tests of this model are beginning to find expression in the literature, although much more work needs to be done before its validity is established. Next, the now ubiquitous growth of loyalty programs is discussed so that the repeat purchasing generated by these managerial efforts can be assessed for its ability to represent the development of "true" loyalty. In particular, the chapter investigates where these programs operate within the proposed staged loyalty framework.

Then, a two-dimensional model of loyalty formation based on the author's "Whence " article, referenced in the chapter, is presented. This model assumes that, in addition to the consumer's fervent desire to identify with the brand based on the experiential progression through the aforementioned stages, a social community supportive of the brand, if feasible, also can be instrumental in this next higher order of loyalty formation. This "consumption community" is described as melding with the individual's strongly held brand preference (fortitude) to cement a doubly supportive bond referred to as "fully immersed" loyalty.

Last, the available evidence on the linkage between satisfaction, loyalty, and profitability is discussed. This discourse is also new to this edition in the sense that much of the empirical data has only recently emerged. As the reader will see, customer satisfaction *is* related to a firm's profits through a number of mechanisms, as prior intuition had suggested. This relationship is not perfect, though, since many companies that routinely dissatisfy consumers do survive, and many "good" companies do not last. In the main, however, data from the recently implemented Customer Satisfaction Index program, now becoming globally adopted, shows conclusively that satisfied (and presumably loyal) consumers do contribute to shareholder wealth. Satisfaction is one ingredient of this success formula for most firms and a speculative transitioning process is proposed for the transformation of satisfaction into loyalty. This point, once established, will provide a fitting close to the chapter and the book.

CHAPTER 14

AFTER SATISFACTION

The Short-Run Consequences

Answer: To do nothing, absolutely nothing.

Question: What is the most frequent consumer response to both satisfying and dissatisfying consumption outcomes?

This fact, posed in the format of a Jeopardy game show question, may appear at first to be incredulous or unbelievable, but upon reflection is immediately logical. Consumers do not do anything, in the main, in response to consumption. They just consume and, perhaps, think and feel. Doing, or expressing themselves via behavior, requires an extra effort that hardly seems justifiable. This observation takes on even more import with the realization that it is true for both successful and unsuccessful purchases.

Because of consumers' reluctance to share their sentiments with firms, management typically relies on sales data and sales trends to gauge consumer response. Unfortunately, sales data do not reveal the number of individuals who are repurchasing, buying the product for the first (or last) time, or stockpiling for future consumption. When sales (and stock price) inevitably decline for those firms that do not measure up to consumer expectations, it is often too late for the firm to remedy the cause of slacking sales. To put this observation in hypothetical perspective, assume that the average firm loses 20 percent of its customers in a given year due to dissatisfaction. Consider what this figure might be for firms with greater levels of dissatisfaction, coupled with other inevitable forms of customer loss, such as disinterest in the product category and attrition.

More enlightened companies routinely gauge consumer response through market research. This is not a panacea, however, because market research can fail to provide management with valid feedback for numerous methodological reasons. Putting methodology aside, an early study showed that even when customer feedback is available from consumer affairs departments, management may shield itself from the onus of complaint data.[1] The authors provide evidence that firms with a high proportional number of complaints may actually inhibit communication of this information from consumer affairs when making customer policy decisions. This practice, in turn, leads to more inattention to the consumer and to increases in the number of complaints.

Additionally, customer feedback about poor service delivery may be subject to tinkering. Distorted feedback may occur if those most adversely affected by poor results can intervene in the data collection or reporting process. This could happen if, for example, salespeople fill out survey forms for consumers or browbeat them into providing favorable data. Similarly, if surveys are returned directly to the business unit responsible for the problem, such as a franchised food outlet, higher-level management may be unaware that problems exist.

This chapter will examine common consumer responses to consumption, specifically those that appear shortly after consumption outcomes are known. It will be instructive to analyze likely company responses to these activities, especially responses that have the capacity to satisfy previously dissatisfied consumers. Unfortunately, some common firm responses may be responsible for causing even greater dissatisfaction among customers; discussion will center on how to avoid this possibility.

WHAT DO CONSUMERS DO?

As stated earlier, most consumers do little in response to consumption outcomes. This section will attempt to explain why this is so and what events will make consumers correspond with the firm. Obviously, all consumer responses to be discussed here result from either a successful or an unsuccessful product or service experience. Because a nonresponse following successful purchasing is more understandable, it will be analyzed first.

Nonresponse Following Successful Consumption

It should be clear from the discussion of expectations within the expectancy disconfirmation model that expectations are a key aspect of the answer to the nonresponse phenomenon. Simply meeting expectations does little to arouse further interest on the part of the consumer. If what was expected or promised was received, then no loss of function (i.e., performance) was sustained, no attributional processing was instigated, no heightened affect beyond what was anticipated resulted. In short, the consumer is very likely to be in contentment mode, where everything is as it should be. When this is coupled with normal daily demands of home and job, consumers simply do not have time to communicate that consumption events occurred as promised. Fortunately, most product and service offerings are adequately designed and rendered so that the lack of consumer response indicates that all is well.

The percentage of ordinary successful consumption events that fall into this do-nothing category is not known, except that it is probably a large proportion, perhaps approaching 100 percent. Simple inspection of one's own purchasing habits would appear to bear this out. Alternatively, *surprisingly* successful consumption often does engender response—primarily positive word of mouth and complimenting to the firm or provider, although the incidence of such responses is not well known. These surprisingly successful events that prompt favorable commentary will be discussed in greater detail later.

Nonresponse Following Unsuccessful Consumption

In contrast to the prior situation, estimates of do-nothing responses to unsuccessful purchases were more available when the first edition of this book was published. Since that time, studies of this nature have remained proprietary and are generally not released in the public domain. The Internet is partly responsible for this as blogs and other venues provide a sense of catharsis for those wishing to vent. The representativeness of the resulting numbers cannot be verified, however (and is easily falsified with multiple same-source postings), so that no reliable figures are worthy of note. Thus, one can only rely on the earlier estimates that prompted this author to conclude at the time, with the exception of durables, more consumers would rather do nothing than complain when dissatisfied. Even though complaining was found to be highest for durables, as noted, which tend to have a higher dollar loss at stake, and lowest for services, where the complaint typically involves the failings of an individual service provider, the rate of doing nothing was relatively constant at 40 percent.

Other estimates vary. Those cited here were compiled by TARP (formerly the Technical Assistance Research Program) and reported over the years with summary updates until recently.[2] Generally, up to 50 percent of dissatisfied consumers and 75 percent of business-to-business customers will complain to a front-line employee. Less than 5 percent of these consumers will escalate the complaint to corporate management. For large-ticket items, the complaint rate to management is higher, at 5 to 10 percent. An 800 phone number will double the number of complaints going to corporate headquarters, but less than 1 percent will be addressed to a senior executive.[3] In all cases, the numbers are anecdotal or large-sample reflections and span indeterminate time frames. These examples are representative and illustrate what is now commonly referred to as the "tip-of-the-iceberg" problem (approximately 15 percent above the water line), and at least one study in Denmark shows that complaint rates have remained steady for more than twenty-five years (with a slight ten-year increase in third-party complaints).[4] In other words, many if not all of a firm's dissatisfied customers are not identifiable to top management.

Why are consumers reluctant to complain? Researchers have hypothesized that personality plays some role in this aversion, and scales measuring the propensity to seek redress have been constructed.[5] These are couched in general terms, however, and the concepts of psychological willingness will be discussed shortly. Generally, the noncomplaining literature emerged in two waves. The first focused on product characteristics, product function and quantifiable issues such as cost and convenience, the second on behavioral impediments unique to consumers. These are discussed in turn.

The Economic Model

Clearly, the cost of the item and its significance to the consumer play a factor, as does the cost of complaining, including time and effort. Generally, these economic factors assume a rational analysis of cost, benefit, and the probability of a successful complaint encounter on the part of the consumer. A number of descriptions and models of this process are summarized in Figure 14.1.[6] Not shown is the mirror-image response of noncomplaining since the reasons are simply inversive of those stated here.[7]

As the figure shows, the influences on perceived costs involve (1) direct monetary outlays in the form of the purchase price or indirect losses due to overcharging or finding a cheaper price elsewhere, (2) ancillary damages resulting from product failure, (3) the time and (4) the effort of making and following up on a complaint, and (5) the importance to the consumer of having a functioning product. Perceived benefits include (1) monetary reimbursement or (2) product replacement or service re-rendering redress, (3) additional compensation for the trouble encountered, (4) correction of the problem leading to failure, (5) an acknowledgment of the firm's responsibility in the form of an apology, and (6) the opportunity to vent frustration over the incident, commonly called catharsis. Finally, the perceived probability of success appears as a function of (1) the reputation of the firm in responding to complaints, (2) sanctions (or threats) the consumer may use to force compliance with the complaint request, and (3) the consumer's experience or efficacy in the complaining process.

Figure 14.1   **The Complaining Decision: Economic Model**

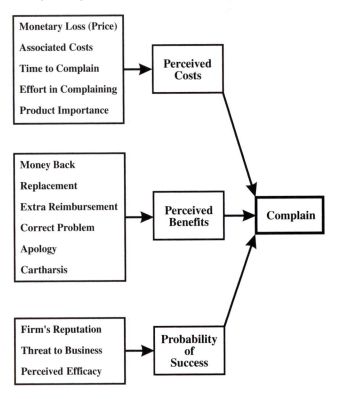

The Behavioral Model

As shown in Figure 14.2, a consumer's reluctance to complain can also involve psychological factors related to the consumer's ability and motivation to complain.[8] In this context, ability refers to formal institutions, such as the Better Business Bureau, that facilitate complaining activity; knowledge of such complaint channels and procedures; access to channels; and communication fluency—a potential problem for those with English as a second language. Class action settlements are a particularly good example of this situation. While some involve small subsets of consumers with large dollar claims, many others typically involve a large number of potential litigants with only minor dollar claims that are easily "written off" as insignificant and not worthy of further action. In this latter case, when individual consumers cannot be identified, defendants are required to provide public notice. But these notices of the availability of such redress are frequently found in obscure sections of the print media in very small print. Claim forms may be difficult to navigate and require documentation not usually retained by the consumer, such as sales receipts, repair receipts, and dates. Many consumers therefore never file a claim because they are not aware of the avenues of redress or become disillusioned after seeing the effort required.

   Motivation to complain takes many forms. First, complaining must be culturally mandated or institutionalized. Some cultures, particularly those with a passively fatalistic philosophy, put the onus of product failure on the predetermined destiny of the consumer. Researchers have suggested that collectivist cultures also dissuade recovery appeals, although recent interpretations

Figure 14.2   **The Complaining Decision: Behavioral Model**

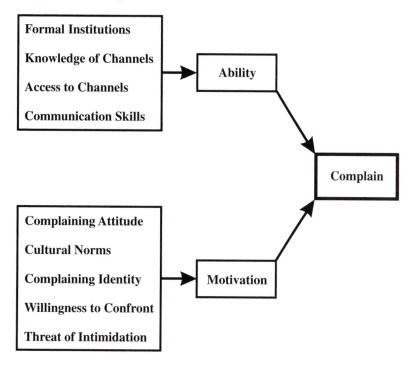

suggest that economic development may also play a role.[9] With the rapid development of the southern and eastern Asian populations, this latter possibility may be tested. Second, in regard to the propensity to seek redress mentioned earlier, consumers differ in their attitude toward or likelihood of complaining depending on numerous circumstances playing into the complaint scenario.[10] In a sense, this is consistent with attitude models generally whereby a reasoned approach to behavior is taken and rationality prevails. Third, the consumer must be willing to be identified as a complainer, a label many find distasteful—so much so that the label "chronic complainer" is one to be avoided.[11] Last, many people view the act of complaining as confrontational and wish to avoid this situation, which can be particularly threatening if the firm attempts to intimidate or berate the consumer.[12] Thus, these psychological costs may be too onerous for many dissatisfied consumers, creating the feeling that complaining is "just not worth it."

In summary, a model of complaining, or not complaining, would include both economics and behavior and, within these categories, costs, benefits, probabilities of success, abilities, and motivations. This framework leads to grander models of complaining that have been proposed.[13] Readers may find these overly general, perhaps, in that they give a "big picture" but little actionable direction, although some models incorporate concepts, such as fairness, that have been covered in previous chapters. The discussion that follows is an attempt to provide greater specificity to these efforts.

A COMPLAINT PROCESS MODEL

To understand how complaints might operate in the consumer's psyche, an expansion of the complaining process along operational lines would be beneficial. As noted, the models discussed

Figure 14.3 **Graphical Representation of a Consumer's Dissatisfaction Deficit, Redress Expectations, and Effect of the Firm's Response on Redress Deficit**

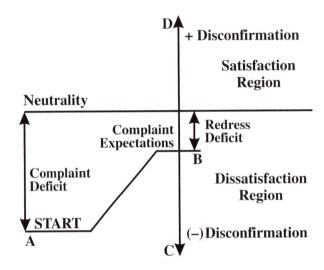

previously identify sets of predetermining conditions. The present discussion extends these models, beginning with the presumption that the consumer, having considered both costs and benefits and also motivation and ability, has decided to complain.

As shown in Figure 14.3, the dissatisfied consumer begins in a deficit situation. The deficit exists as the sum of monetary outlays; associated costs such as transportation and assembly; psychological costs such as frustration, anxiety, and stress; and loss of product function or intended service outcomes. Thus, the dissatisfied consumer initially resides at point A in the figure.

The consumer's emotional response to dissatisfaction may hinge on the expectation of redress, depending particularly on the locus of causality attribution (see Chapter 11). If consumers attribute the failure to the manufacturer or marketer rather than to themselves, expectations of redress will probably be stronger. In any event, most consumers will have expectations of complaining, as shown in Figure 14.3.[14] An assumption of this model is that the level of expected redress is not fully satisfactory to the consumer, a level labeled as point B in the figure. This situation would be particularly true for the traditional money-back and guaranteed-replacement warranties, which only restore the loss of monetary outlay in the first case and product function in the second.[15] To show how the consumer may view these guarantees, the details of three warranties are examined in Table 14.1. Also shown are effects of the (relatively) new price-matching guarantee, whereby consumers need only provide evidence that another outlet is currently selling the same exact product at a lower price in order to receive a refund of the difference (and sometimes more) between what they paid and what the rival outlet charges.[16] Later, the characteristics of a correct firm response to dissatisfaction will be suggested.

The table illustrates the inadequacies of these strategies. Assume that a parent has purchased an electromechanical toy for a child's birthday; the toy is labeled "some assembly required." Upon opening the present, the child appears delighted with the gift and eagerly waits for the toy to be put together. After a lengthy assembly of the mechanical components, the electronics fail.

Assume, now, three separate responses to this same set of circumstances. In one case, the con-

Table 14.1

Costs and Redress Returns for Three Common Warranties

Consumer's cost	Redress received under guarantees of		
	Money-back	Price-matching	Replacement[a]
Shopping effort	No	No	N/A
Shopping time	No	No	N/A
Delivery time	No	N/A	N/A
Monetary cost	Yes	Yes (partial)	N/A
Shipping and handling	No	N/A	N/A
Unpacking and set-up time	No	N/A	No
Loss of product function	No	N/A	No
Consumption time	No	N/A	No
Ancillary loss	No	N/A	No
Return (repack/ship/re-render)	No	N/A	No
Return time	No	No (partial)	No
Complaint contact costs	No	No	No
Future trouble	Yes	Unknown	No

[a] Includes service guarantees (where the service is re-rendered).

sumer disassembles the toy for repackaging, returns it, and asks for the promised "money-back" refund. This consumer loses the obvious elements of time and effort (transaction costs) as well as the joy of seeing the child appreciate this particular toy. In addition to these psychological costs, the parent must now find a second gift which cannot be given on the child's birthday, now past. Additionally, it must be of equal or better "delight" value to the child.

Price-matching guarantees provide intermediary redress. Here, the consumer must find an exact replacement (including model number) at a different outlet and at a lower price. Now, the consumer must confront the retailer with this adverse information and rely on the merchant's goodwill to honor this promise. This is not "time-free" redress since, typically, the original merchant must contact the second to confirm the lower price (advertisements assist in this step) and also verify that the model number is exact. Much to the chagrin of the consumer, it often is not, since model numbers for the same product are frequently retailer-specific.

The third, "replacement-warranty" consumer, in contrast, asks for and receives an identical item from the merchant. After the parent assembles the toy, now for the second time, everything appears restored, but it is not. The parent and child have lost the joint pleasure of relishing the toy on the child's birthday. Additionally, both parent and child may be apprehensive of future problems with the toy's electronics. In an economist's terms, the replacement toy contains less utility because it has cost more than anticipated and brings less joy. This consumer remains at point B in Figure 14.3.

Interestingly, these examples would be considered illustrative of the likely responses of "good" firms by current standards in that none of the consumers apparently encountered resistance from the merchant or a reluctance to honor the warranty. If these additional problems had occurred, the list of costs would have been much longer.

In this regard, it is unfortunate that, despite numerous articles on how businesses do and should respond to complaints, truly unenlightened marketers still succeed in frustrating the complaining process by discouraging complaints, making the process burdensome, or underdelivering on their warranties.[17] Many merchants, for example, still charge restocking fees, offer an exchanges-only

Figure 14.4   **The Expectancy Disconfirmation Model as Applied to Complaint Handling**

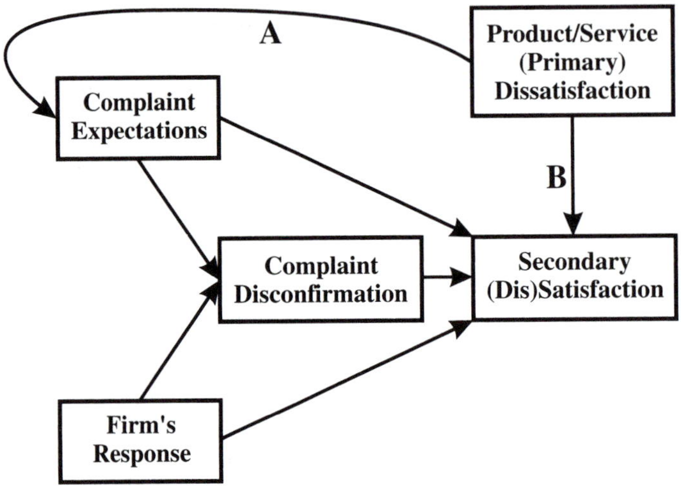

policy, limit refunds to a thirty-day period, or require excessive documentation of product claims. These practices have been referred to as failure escalation; the low level of customer retention when such strategies are used is well documented.[18] More will be said of the effects of such escalation or "double dissatisfaction" strategies (and of recovery strategies) shortly.

Complaint Handling Within the Expectancy Disconfirmation Model

In the expectancy disconfirmation model, the psychological dynamics of complaint handling appear as shown in Figure 14.4. The figure shows that the process of complaint satisfaction or dissatisfaction follows the same pattern found for initial dissatisfaction with the product or service, referred to here as primary dissatisfaction.

In this process, it is assumed that consumers will generally have (1) expectations of the outcomes of complaining (including the possibility of no outcome), (2) observations of the firm's response—the firm's "performance," (3) the willingness to compare this response to their expectations (complaint disconfirmation), and (4) the motivation to form judgments of secondary satisfaction or dissatisfaction—that is, satisfaction or dissatisfaction with the firm's response or lack of response. The model presumes that primary dissatisfaction is the motivating influence for the complaining process to occur. This influence is represented by curved arrow "A" and is not to be confused with influence "B," which will be discussed shortly.

Aside from the obvious influence of complaint disconfirmation, Figure 14.4 shows three other direct influences on complaint satisfaction. As in the basic expectancy disconfirmation model discussed in Chapter 4, expectations should serve to color complaint satisfaction perceptions; firms with reputations of poor complaint-handling practices create biased consumer perceptions of how the firms will respond.[19] Similarly, a direct firm-response influence may appear, such as when an aggressively antagonistic reply from a firm angers consumers without the necessity of a comparison to expectations. Last is the direct effect of primary dissatisfaction, as represented by arrow "B." Given that it takes an initial episode of dissatisfaction to prime a complaint, it is not surprising that the extent of primary dissatisfaction may influence later satisfaction or dissatisfaction with the firm's response, thereby acting as a secondary expectation influence on secondary (postcomplaining) satisfaction. In effect, primary dissatisfaction is a need deficit as shown in Figure 5.1, whereas complaint redress, if successfully accomplished, is the negative reinforcement.

Indirect Evidence for the Complaining Framework

Since the first edition of this book, numerous studies on complaining resolution have been conducted. Generally, no study tests the framework in its entirety, however, for a number of reasons. First, expectations of complaining responses are rarely obtained, nor are they manipulated in experiments. Either consumers are sampled after the fact of their complaining activities (including the null set) or are given manipulations of likely firm responses and asked to comment and judge satisfaction, intent, word of mouth, and so on. Nonetheless, partial tests have been performed; those known to the author are referenced here.[20] More data exists on the degree to which successful complaint resolution can override or even surmount satisfaction levels of noncomplainers, some of whom may have been inconvenienced and others not so.

Based on the proposed model, the influence of the firm's response when compared to complaining expectations appears to be key in determining how consumers will react to their complaining efforts. Unenlightened firms will negatively disconfirm even low expectations (i.e., failure escalation), driving the consumer to point C in Figure 14.3. In fact, it is estimated that, in the context of services, "more than half" of efforts to respond to service failure actually reinforce negative reactions.[21] Unfortunately, research trends since these earlier reports do not allow for similar descriptive statistics, and the introduction of experimental methods used to research recovery cannot be used to obtain estimates of larger populations.

In this vein, the reader may remember Intel Corporation's many responses to consumers after a flaw had been discovered in its Pentium processor. The firm's reaction escalated from denial, to "not our fault," to "good enough for the average user," to a replacement policy only if users could prove that the nature of their work would be affected, and finally to a begrudging recall program. All these responses were demonstrated by the company that had used the phrase "Intel Inside" as a mark of quality. This historical anecdote will not be forgotten since many instructors continue to use the Harvard Business School case, *Intel's Pentium: When the Chips are Down.*[22]

Reactions such as Intel's have been known to spur a state of consumer "warfare" against the offending firm, including the pursuit of legal redress, letter-writing campaigns, retaliation, and even destruction of the firm's products, an extreme example of grudge holding and other unusual responses to the firm.[23] In Intel's case, users ravaged the Internet with Pentium jokes. This phenomenon was also picked up by the media, thereby prolonging the ill effects of the initial problem.

In contrast, enlightened marketers will attempt to exceed the consumer's complaint expectations, even to the point of overdelivering on their warranties. This strategy has been given much press in the literature.[24] Empirical data on this phenomenon are noteworthy. In one study, for example, researchers had individual students send complaint letters to companies whose products the students had found unsatisfactory.[25] After the letters were sent, students' expectations of complaint satisfaction were measured on a satisfaction scale ranging from 0 to 100. The authors judged as exceptionally good those responses that were received in a short time (less than 30 days versus more than 30 days) and that included a "free good." Other firm actions used in the analysis included receipt of a letter only and the lack of any response at all in the investigated time frame. This analysis created six response categories that permitted evaluation of the students' satisfaction with different company reactions on the same 0 to 100 scale used for the expectations measure. The results are shown in Table 14.2.

Table 14.2

Satisfaction Scores in the Complaining Letter Study

	Response time frame	
Firm's "response"	Early (<30 days)	Late (>30 days)
No response	39.2 (30 days)	25.4 (60 days)
Letter only	69.2	67.0
"Free good"	82.9	81.6

Of relevance to the data in Table 14.2 is the fact that the expected satisfaction score over all letter writers was 62.3. As theory would predict, a nonresponse from the firm, particularly as the time since the complaint increases, results in a large decrement in satisfaction. Receiving nothing but a letter improves satisfaction above expected levels only marginally, with smaller increments for late responses. However, a free good (defined as a product replacement, cents-off coupon, free-good coupon, or refund check) improves satisfaction greatly. Moreover, the impact of this response seems to maintain even if the time frame is increased. Interestingly, very similar results were obtained in a study of responses to e-mail complaints.[26] Here the authors found much greater postcomplaint satisfaction for responding firms (as would be expected), those responding quickly, and those with personalization (a signature). Firms that "passed the buck" by rerouting the complaint to other departments (burying the complaint) resulted in significantly lower satisfaction scores.

These studies presented early evidence of the impact of positively disconfirming complainants' expectations to achieve (or restore) satisfaction. Graphically, the "exceed complainants' expectation" strategy appears at point D in Figure 14.3. Given a sufficiently "delighting" positive disconfirmation, the consumer can be brought across neutrality into the satisfaction region despite the initially dissatisfying incident.

At first, these data would appear to argue for two sure strategies to placate dissatisfied *and* complaining customers. The first is timeliness and the second is unanticipated overdelivering. Unfortunately, the data since the time of this study are only partially supportive. The effects of timeliness appear to have remained unchanged except that it has now been shown that not only the number of consumer requests but also the complainant's frustration increases with the time delay.[27] Consumers do appreciate prompt (favorable) replies, perhaps due to the apparent immediacy of being wronged; they have not yet had time for their resentment to "simmer." This outcome, of course, assumes that all other factors, including the nature of the redress and certain intangibles, such as courtesy, are constant. This author was unable to find any study suggesting that later redress yielded more favorable responses than earlier redress.[28]

Evidence on overdelivering, however, is fraught with controversy. Some evidence suggests that consumers may feel more satisfied after successful recovery than if they had not complained or had no issue requiring redress in the first place. Researchers have referred to this phenomenon as the service recovery paradox (SRP) because it seems contradictory that failure recovery could be advantageous to the seller. Actually, the consumer's gratification may explain the apparent paradox.

Researchers have performed a meta-analytic review (e.g., a summary of studies) of research on this effect, defined as one in which "postfailure satisfaction exceeds prefailure satisfaction."[29] Twenty-four separate findings from twenty-one papers were compiled and the SRP was found *tested* in nineteen and repeat purchase intention in another twelve. Other events were also studied, but the number of studies was too small to elaborate. Of note is that a net positive SRP effect was found to be significant ($p = 0.017$), referred to as a "small to medium" level, over all studies, although there were instances of non-effects and negative effects across the individual findings. The intention effect was negative ($p = 0.068$), missing the .05 cutoff by a small margin, suggesting that favorable repeat behaviors may be unlikely even though recovery was a satisfying event.

Why is the SRP effect not stronger if successful recovery is such a panacea, which it arguably is not? One paper suggests that a number of moderating conditions are required and that they may not exist in all situations.[30] These include failures that are not considered "severe," no prior failure with the firm, unstable causes, and the firm's lack of control (see Chapter 11 for the latter two conditions). When these conditions prevail, customers appear to be in a "more forgiving" mode.

In another answer to this query, a small number of studies examined firms that overdelivered on their redress.[31] This included "free goods" and other forms of overcompensation, a logical extension of the exceeding-expectations paradigm. However, rarely are such expectations measured, so that these studies reported on a test of compensation that exceeded another level of compensation in the study. If both compensation levels were below expectations (one cannot know this), then the fact that the higher of the two did not generate greater end-feeling states says nothing about supporting or refuting the paradigm. Here is what was found.

The literature is about equally divided on both the reasons for ambivalent findings and the results. Studies finding positive or mixed results versus those finding negative consequences of overgenerosity are careful to note the extenuating reasons for the results. Overgenerosity works for the very reasons it should—exceeding expectations. However, when it does not, consumers appear skeptical for a number of reasons. Either the firm should have "gotten it right the first time" or the offer is "too much too late" or the firm seems to be trying to "buy me off" so the consumer will not spread the negative news. Overdelivery, therefore, must be carefully planned so that it does not appear contrived. Moreover, a host of parallel factors such as empathy, courtesy, and a genuine sense of contrition may be required. If this sounds contrary to the "exceeding-expectations" mantra used throughout this book, it should not, as complexity is embedded in any strategy based on well-grounded theory.

It should be noted that there is another side to the paradox, literally. The worst-case scenario is not necessarily nondelivery or underdelivery. It is repeated episodes of redress failure. One wonders how firms can permit this catastrophe to prevail, yet they do. There is no need to cite literature on this failure when it is discovered (or uncovered); researchers can reproduce the consequences of the double or multiple failure scenario in the laboratory or simply document real-world events.[32]

More Problems of Overgenerosity

In an apparent exacerbation of the perils of overgenerosity, many businesses believe that a generous complaint response policy will stimulate illegitimate requests for redress from nonpurchasers or from individuals who have abused the product, causing it to fail. This phenomenon, known as fraudulent complaining, is a legitimate concern to management.[33] As an opportunistic criminal act, complaint fraud is common to both product and service firms. What can be done about it while still maintaining a level of generosity sufficient to generate good faith, redress fairness (to be discussed), or some degree of overdelivery on requests for redress?

Because the overgenerous marketer is concerned about rewarding fraud with free goods, thereby driving up costs, it is important to have an estimate of the likelihood that any given complaint is fraudulent. This will require an investigatory period in which all redress claims are verified. Here,

Table 14.3

Complaint Settlement Breakeven Values

Complaint investigation cost ($)	Expected percentage fraudulent estimate				
	10	20	30	40	50
20	200	100	67	50	40
40	400	200	133	100	80
60	600	300	200	150	120
80	800	400	267	200	160
100	1,000	500	333	250	200

the researcher's goal is to determine the general percentage of claims that will prove to be bogus. Once a sufficient sample size has been achieved to ensure the accuracy of the estimate, the cost of investigating one complaint can be determined. This figure can be calculated by summing up the total labor, communication, and travel expenses of the complaint investigation and dividing by the number of complaints. Once the percentage of fraudulent claims and the costs of investigation have been estimated, it is possible to calculate the amount of requested redress that can be paid out automatically without investigation. Representative figures are given as breakeven amounts in Table 14.3.

These amounts are determined by the formula

Maximum payout = (complaint investigation cost) ÷ (percentage fraudulent)

and result from a simple breakeven calculation, the logic of which follows. Assume that the estimated percentage of fraudulent claims is 10 percent and that the cost of investigation is $20. From the preceding formula, the maximum payout is $200. This number reflects the fact that it would take ten investigations at $20 each, or $200, on average, to find one fraudulent claim. Thus, a claim of $150 should not be investigated while a $250 claim should.

Objections to this approach come from company managers who have philosophical qualms about paying out any claim that is fraudulent. In the end, each manager must make a personal or policy decision whether to pursue the formula approach—which is a managerial strategy—or go with one's sense of philosophical purpose. Whichever approach is used, management should not lose sight of the firm's overriding goal—to ensure that the legitimate complaining consumer receives a favorable disconfirmation of complaint expectations. At this point, two issues come to mind. First, what are the consumer's complaint expectations? And second, what is favorable? Is it mere positive disconfirmation?

The Case of Unknown Complaint Expectations

Consumers often complain without stating what they believe the firm should do in response. Sometimes, the consumer does not know what expectations to have. For example, in an account of a problem more common before the development of digital cameras, a student provided a letter from a photograph finisher indicating that the student's pictures could not be developed because the negatives had been destroyed in the course of processing. The firm sent a free roll of film to make up for the student's loss. This response is a classic example of unenlightened business practice, but is common in this industry. What should the firm have done?

This example illustrates a particularly poignant problem because the developer could not know what pictures were destroyed, never to be retrieved. Irreplaceable pictures of a child's first birthday party, a graduation, a wedding, or a trip to a one-time event such as the Olympics might have been on that lost roll of film. One new roll of film, or for that matter a thousand new rolls of film, cannot replace the lost memories of these events. Moreover, no two consumers will have identical photographs with identical meaning. Here, it is not possible for the company to deal with expectations; it must, instead, deal with satisfactions.

The query "What will it take to satisfy you?" or "How can we satisfy you?" will, after an initial period of surprise and introspection, generate responses from consumers.[34] Some responses, such as another trip for a family of four to Hawaii, will not be feasible. Others will be reasonable, such as a family photographic session at a local studio. Over time, the firm will compile a list of reasonable requests to compensate for similar losses, which it can then suggest to those consumers who do not have specific requests. Again, the firm's concern should be to respond favorably to the consumer's wishes.

Other Consumer Responses

The number of consumer responses to dissatisfaction that generally go undetected by the manufacturing or retailing firm have been described as a "hidden agenda." These undetected actions include (1) boycotting the product class, (2) boycotting the offending brand, (3) boycotting the seller (retailer), (4) complaining privately (negative word of mouth), (5) pursuing redress directly from the seller, (6) seeking third-party redress (e.g., from the Better Business Bureau or the courts), and (7) complaining publicly (writing letters to the editor, staging public boycotts such as picketing). In addition, recent years have seen the skyrocketing advent of online purchasing, purchase failures, and nuances in hidden agenda complaining.[35] The findings here are surprising, at least with regard to two elements.[36]

For those consumers who did take action, the reasons are identical to those for purchasing generally. For consumers not taking action, results similar to those purchasing offline were also found—the vast majority saying that complaining was "too much trouble" or "hopeless." The first surprise was that, compared to other consumers, online consumers tend to blame themselves, apparently because of the more intensive search and involvement by the consumer in selecting a website and ordering. The second unusual outcome was that the focal failure carried over to online purchasing in general; almost 5 percent of online purchasers said that they would "never shop online again." This reaction underlines the inherent risk in selecting a purchasing channel with new and unknown dimensions. It appears that this may be an industry-wide phenomenon that will not be resolved until the parameters of the online venue, with known risks and rewards, are established.

Later, an attempt will be made to categorize some of these responses in terms of consumer profiles—known consumer types that are prone to one or another or combinations of these actions. For now, discussion focuses on why firms may prefer to channel these hidden-agenda activities into complaints rather than have them occur randomly and rampantly without the firm's knowledge.

FIRM STRATEGIES: PROMOTING COMPLAINTS AND ENCOURAGING COMPLIMENTS

Encouraging Complaints

Most firms would prefer to know about consumer dissatisfaction at the individual level rather than wait for sales to fall or negative mass publicity to build up. The reason is straightforward.

Firms are in a position to remedy product failure or redress loss if they are aware of it. As a result, firms will be able to stave off the deleterious effects of the hidden-agenda activities. Additionally, analysis has shown that market share gains can be expected, as can decreased costs of attracting customers through advertising, if firms maximize their attempts to encourage consumers' complaints (subject to cost constraints).[37]

Once a passive complaining situation is discovered, this proactive strategy will prime the consumer for the nature of the response received from the firm. In this sense, stimulating attention to redress can entail risks to the firm as the consumer is now awakened to any activities available as a result. As might be expected, a firm's unsatisfactory responses to complaints initiated by the firm directly affect secondary satisfaction or dissatisfaction, which might not have been observed otherwise. Imagine the wrath of a consumer, previously content to absorb the loss incurred if the promises of unsolicited redress on the part of the firm are unfulfilled!

Ordinarily, however, firms encouraging complaining will be prepared for satisfactory redress; research shows that it is those firms in competitive industries that can benefit most since the very act of competition stimulates proactive strategy. In contrast, firms with easy access to new customers have little incentive.[38] It is also the case that the very act of direct solicitation can have direct effects on the consumer's satisfaction through other proposed mechanisms. For example, the consumer is likely to experience reduced complaint contact costs, faster problem resolution, and greater individual attention, not to mention a higher likelihood of successful resolution from proactive firms that have already thought through the potentially large number of complaint scenarios as well as the likely redress options that will assuage the consumer in each.

In efforts to encourage complaining and ferret out consumers who would otherwise engage in hidden-agenda activities, a number of suggestions are available in the literature, all of which should be considered as part of a "quality information system."[39] Solicited consumer comments, whether of a positive or negative nature, will draw out dissatisfied consumers through two mechanisms. One is obvious: the dissatisfied consumer is now identified and encouraged to vent. The other reason is less obvious. Individuals are known to search for answers when queried. Many of these consumers will say, "Oh yeah, now that you mention it . . . ," which will frequently result in a "wish I hadn't asked" response on the part of the firm.

Two well-known strategies are discussed here. The first involves the use of "costless" (to the consumer) communication channels such as 800 numbers and postage-paid, short feedback cards. A modern variant is web-based electronic passive or active solicitation. In this case, a link or menu to the complaint resolution department is provided. These common complaint facilitators, however, still require that the consumer voluntarily offer comment. Furthermore, although consumers can be assured that these complaints (and some compliments) are forwarded, consumers cannot ascertain whether the firm will take action. Even when consumers receive an electronic receipt, they will not know about any resulting actions until some later time.

A second frequent practice is the callback.[40] With this technique, customers are contacted directly and asked pointedly if their product or service experience was satisfactory. In this manner, problems can be pinpointed, and additional diagnostic queries can be introduced. One drawback, however, is that the person-to-person approach removes the anonymity of a survey and may encourage yea saying and/or a reluctance to be overly critical. A second problem concerns the immediacy of the callback. If the callback is made too soon or at the time of service completion, problems that arise later will be missed. Finally, a third problem for users of this approach, in the form of a caveat, is that these callbacks should not be used as sales tools. If the interview ends in a sales pitch, the consumer may attribute the entire call to this one motive, and whatever goodwill was previously generated will likely be lost.

The degree to which complaint solicitations should be pursued is a function of the philosophy of the consumer affairs departments in companies as well as that of corporate management. It is commonly accepted that the complaint solicitation process will be fruitless and frustrating to the consumer if no action results from this practice. Generally, consumers should be thanked for providing consumption experience feedback, perhaps through an acknowledgment letter, no matter how negative the feedback appears. The skill of grace in the face of criticism is not inherent, but it is necessary if complaint solicitations are to be effective instruments of satisfaction.

What About Compliments

Compliments occur when the firm's product or service provides surprisingly exceptional performance, at least in the minds of some consumers. This performance could range from one particular consumption incident, such as the frequently found example of attendants providing exceptional service—typically due to employee empowerment—to consistently delivered professional service over a long period, such as the reliability of one's postal carrier despite "rain, sleet, or dark of night." In this latter case, it does not occur to the consumer how exceptional the carrier's performance is until individual events are accumulated and the consistency of performance is noted.[41]

Interestingly, research shows that a second reason for compliments is not so sanguine.[42] Many consumers who are only tepid in their praise correspond with firms as if to say, "Your service is good; keep up the good work. Here are some suggestions to improve further . . ." Thus, these consumers are, in effect, prodding the firm to do better, perhaps because they believe the firm has the capability to do so. Distinguishing these two complimenting consumers is the responsibility of the firm; lumping them together as equally favorable obscures the "contribution" of the second.

Whatever their nature, compliments are frequently received, and studies have been performed to analyze the proper firm response.[43] These studies conclude that firms should acknowledge compliments, although many do not. Examination of compliment acknowledgment letters provided by the same firms, however, revealed that responses to praise are often nonspecific, standardized, and less personal than the responses to complaints. In fact, impersonal formats were found to occur roughly three times as often when compared to complaint correspondence. Thus, a reasonable conclusion for management is that the consumer's attempt to compliment the firm should be reinforced with a similar effort by the firm, addressing the good points made in the consumer's letter. In some sense, this reinforcement can be considered a positive disconfirmation of sorts, as many consumers probably do not expect to hear further from the firm.

INTEGRATED PSYCHOLOGICAL PROCESSES: ATTRIBUTION, EQUITY, AND APPRAISAL

These three concepts, attribution, equity, and appraisal, are related to the complaining response in the same manner that they are related to satisfaction and dissatisfaction in general. Whether favorable or unfavorable, consumers may ask what the cause of the experience was, whether it was stable and controllable, and, if so, by whom. In the case of dissatisfaction, this sequence begins with the source of the problem. It has already been mentioned that online purchasers may blame themselves in that they may feel that they pursued the marketer. More frequently, they may attribute product and service failure to the firm or provider. The implications here are as before. Controllable failures that can be attributed to the firm result not only in anger, but also in strong sentiments that the firm should redress the wrong.

Beginning with the perceived causes of air transport delays and canceled flights, the research findings are consistent. If firms could have anticipated, avoided, or prevented a problem, consumers' anger results in dissatisfaction and feelings of requisite redress.[44] This response is somewhat moderated if the failure is, at least in part, due to uncontrollable causes such as weather, and further moderation is possible if the firm provides emotional support such as empathy. This rather ordinary process leads to the next step—is the redress offered by the firm fair? In fact, attribution (to the provider) for failure was found to be the most important dimension, before empowerment and an apology, in a study of service recovery.[45]

As noted in Chapter 8, the notion of fairness (and unfairness) permeates much of life, yet it is one of the most difficult of concepts to pin down; the common phrase "life ain't fair" does not specify fair to whom, by whom, by what standard, how, and so on. This is why formulaic or policy manuals are of only marginal help in truly satisfying complainants. In fact, at least one set of authors has suggested that such mechanistic formulas be supplemented with "organic" policies.[46] As used by these authors, *organic* means a justice-friendly internal corporate environment; what is needed here is something more akin to "touchy-feely." The "what can we do to resolve this" approach to complaint expectations is one exemplar of what can be done.

The literature on fairness in complaint handling is both large and nebulous, and only some brief, well-worn generalities can be cited here. First, it is clear that consumers do harbor expectations of complaining outcomes. Although they may not know exactly what they expect, they do expect something to be done. When expectations are more concrete, they are likely to involve the magnitude of the failure, alternative options including switching costs, and the length of the consumer's relationship with the provider. It is also clear that consumers expect any statements by the firm (e.g., "satisfaction guaranteed") to be honored. Alternatively, disclaimers beginning with the phrase "We are not responsible for . . ." are sure to reduce expectations of redress and, in all probability, purchase as well.[47]

As noted, studies testing equity concepts in complaint resolution are numerous, and only those testing the three components of distributive, procedural, and interactive justice concurrently are noted here.[48] When tested, the three concepts are almost universally described in the text or in the measurement appendixes as containing the following components:

- Distributive justice: replacement, money-back, or other compensation, either "high" or matching the nature of the loss; compensation relative to expectations (better or equal to, but never less); "fair" or "deserved" compensation.
- Procedural justice: speed (immediacy is best); control over the process; flexibility (adapting to individual circumstances); accessibility and ease—the where of complaining; the complaint handler's authority level—the "to whom" of complaining; voice and explanation—the "hearing me out" of complaining.
- Interactional justice: employee behaviors (effort, empathy, understanding, courtesy, honesty, rapport); an apology—which is found to work in the absence of anything tangible.

Additionally, a number of important equity-related complaint consequences have been observed. In addition to satisfaction, the most obvious of these is the consumer's intention to rebuy or repatronize.[49] It should come as no surprise that complaint resolution is an essential ingredient in the consumer's willingness to interact further with the marketer (or even to use the channel medium again, as data on online buying would attest).

At the psychological level, two consequences of interest are noted. First is the important issue of trust, which, admittedly, has not been given adequate coverage so far. Trust is a topic as vast as satisfaction and is outside what could be tackled in this one book. Nonetheless, it is inherent in all future volitional behaviors and often appears with satisfaction (which may or may not involve trust) in studies of consumption experiences.[50]

Last, and not so curiously, consumers have been found to appraise complaint situations and develop or recruit coping behaviors of various sorts that allow them to respond to failure, sometimes in a manner favorable to the firm and sometimes not.[51] These behaviors could involve accepting blame, taking the loss good-naturedly, or engaging in many hidden forms of retribution against the firm, including resentment-fueled negative word of mouth. The coping behaviors identified are instructive and may help management to tailor redress to particular complainant styles. This practice may be more operational at the individual-employee level, however, as the data show that wronged consumers are a varied lot. In fact, one study explores coping from the perspective of the customer service employee, who must respond to all manner of customer responses on a minute-by-minute basis.[52]

Two studies are of particular note in that they propose a more broad-based coping paradigm for consumers. The first study probes "embodied cultural models" consisting of social relationship dynamics.[53] Consumers wishing to maintain social bonds with the provider are hypothesized to cope via toleration, forgiveness, or absolution. Others desiring more cognitive resolution are prone to use a compensation- or compensatory-based approach as discussed in this chapter. A third category of consumers employed emotionally driven responses such as anger and antagonism.

The second paradigm overlaps with the first on the dimensions of emotional and utilitarian styles, but includes avoidance strategies as a third.[54] Here, avoidance includes ignoring the problem in the present, avoiding future contact with the firm (and perhaps with the channel, as in online purchasing), and possibly avoiding any future activities that would reflect back on the unfortunate incident, including word-of-mouth communication and perhaps, in extreme cases, usage of the product category. At this point, these approaches merely suggest what firms could do in responding to each of the coping modes, discussed in greater detail in the next section of this chapter.

At this time, it may be instructive to graphically sum up the postsatisfaction process in perspective. Figure 14.5 shows, first, that all postsatisfaction processes are closely intertwined. Primary satisfaction and its appraisal components, most notably equity or inequity and attribution, have been shown to be linked to complaining and word of mouth. Once a complaint is registered, the initial dissatisfying incident will prime the consumer for the nature of the response received from the firm. As might be expected, unsatisfactory responses to complaints directly affect secondary satisfaction or dissatisfaction through the mechanisms of both the redress received and the manner in which the complaint is handled (process).

The extent and nature of word of mouth are similarly affected and, additionally, are affected by secondary satisfaction, which may reflect failure recovery or, in the worst-case scenario, "double" dissatisfaction. Thus, unsatisfactory redress has both a direct and an indirect effect on word of mouth, the latter through the mediating mechanism of secondary satisfaction, shown as a double-headed arrow in Figure 14.5. Interestingly, the acts of complaining and *concurrent* negative word of mouth can have direct effects on the positiveness of satisfaction through other mechanisms. For example, the very act of complaining may enhance secondary satisfaction, not only through its ability to initiate redress but also through the cathartic effect of allowing the consumer to "get it off my chest." In contrast, the acts of private complaining and negative word of mouth also can affect dissatisfaction directly through the mechanism of reinforcing the communicator's ill feelings.[55] Typically, listeners, who are generally selected as sympathetic by the communicator, will agree with the content of the word of mouth, thus adding to the reinforcing effect of voicing one's troubles. Finally, the effect of secondary satisfaction on repurchase or repatronage intentions has been shown in a number of studies. This effect is similar to the effects of satisfaction on intention generally and should not be surprising in this context.

Figure 14.5 **Postsatisfaction Processes**

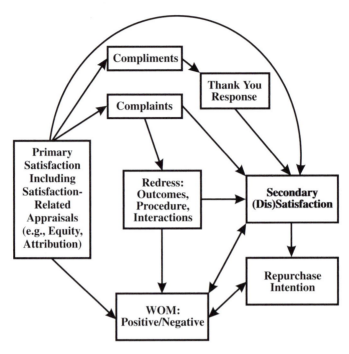

CONSUMER DISSATISFACTION PROFILES

As opposed to the appraisal-based typology in the previous discussion, early research on complaining behavior presumed the existence of a prototypical complaint-prone consumer. At the time, the pursuit of this profile appeared worthy, for it was thought that businesses could identify individuals with this proclivity and steer them away from their establishments. Generally these efforts were unsuccessful, in part, because researchers had not distinguished between dissatisfaction, complaint-proneness, and consumerism, a movement to improve marketing practices. Clearly, not all dissatisfied individuals complain, and not all complainers are consumer activists. Thus, this early literature provided inconsistent and often contradictory findings.

In a second wave of interest, studies took a different approach. Using part theoretical and part methodological tools, researchers attempted to define postpurchase consumer segments more scientifically. Some of these research efforts began with known behaviors that consumers exhibited following consumption, while others used theoretical frameworks, mostly based on Hirschman's work (to be discussed), to guide their conceptualization.[56]

Nontheoretic Frameworks

Nontheoretic frameworks have typically examined available data for patterns of similar responses. These data are now somewhat dated and it is not clear that the patterns, identified between ten and twenty years ago, remain current since some reflected social movement patterns of the time. *Reported* research of this nature has declined dramatically and what follows is historical by nature. What has not declined is word of mouth, which has taken new forms with the advent of the Internet.

At the most basic level, groups of consumers were described as upset or not upset over a purchase. The upset group could be broken down further into those who took some form of redress action versus those who did not. The action group proved to be younger, more educated, and more upscale demographically than the no-action group. The action group could be further subdivided according to three dissatisfaction responses of complaining, word of mouth, and brand switching. Generally, complaining correlated with the severity of the product problem and the degree of external attribution of blame to the retailer or manufacturer. As one would expect, switching correlated with these same variables and with the extent of difficulty involved in seeking redress. In contrast, word of mouth tended to be associated with severity, external blame, and high levels of social activity.

Later, responses to dissatisfaction were characterized as voice (complaining to the provider or firm), private action (word of mouth), and third-party action (mostly public complaining to third-party institutions such as the Better Business Bureau). Further analysis of consumers' scores on these dimensions yielded four groups of consumers: (1) passives, having low scores on all dissatisfaction activity dimensions; (2) voicers, scoring high on the complaining dimension and low on the others; (3) irates, scoring very high on word of mouth; and (4) activists, scoring high on complaining and particularly high on third-party actions.[57] Later work tended to capitalize on the correspondence of these findings with a model of discontent that predated these efforts, as described next.

The Hirschman "Exit, Voice, and Loyalty" Theoretical Framework

In 1970, Hirschman, as cited previously, proposed that individuals in institutional or commercial exchange relationships have essentially two response options to deteriorating performance: leave the relationship (exit), or communicate their displeasure to the institution (voice). Depending on the perceived responsiveness of the institution, these individuals may choose to communicate before deciding to exit or to simply exit if communication is deemed futile. In the later chapters in his book, Hirschman developed the concept of loyalty as a third response. Loyalty takes on two roles in this framework. First, it can be an outcome itself whereby individuals choose loyalty (staying) rather than exit or voice. In this sense, loyalty is the opposite of exit and is not necessarily a deep commitment to the provider (see Chapter 15). Alternatively, loyalty can be a moderating variable whereby high-loyalty individuals forgo exit until all efforts at voice have failed. Individuals with less loyalty will presumably bail out before exhausting all voice options.

Complaint researchers became intrigued by this conceptualization, although they were less interested in the loyalty option than in exit and voice. This may have been so because consumers were believed to have viable market alternatives and little vested interest in their exchange relation with a particular manufacturer or retailer. This assumption was probably more accurate for products—the focus of much of the early complaining research—than for services or relationship marketing, which were in their early developmental stages at the time.

Researchers in other areas have also capitalized on the exit-voice-loyalty framework. Hirschman himself reviewed some of the early efforts a few years after publication of his book.[58] Since that time, his framework has been applied to many different venues of dissatisfaction (political, marital, job) where a fourth outcome, neglect, has been added. Neglect is a dispassionate, psychological withdrawal response whereby the individual becomes apathetic to the relationship and is not willing to communicate the level of displeasure. Since psychological withdrawal, as opposed to physical withdrawal, is more hidden, this response was not well represented in the complaint literature. This lack was unfortunate, because neglect would appear to be the first phase of consumer alienation. Neglect did add a fourth dimension to dissatisfaction, however, permitting two-by-two analyses. In particular, exit and voice were considered *active* responses; loyalty and neglect were considered *passive*. And, in another cut of the framework, voice and loyalty were conceptualized as *constructive* responses, while exit and neglect were considered *destructive*.[59]

Consumer Dissatisfaction Studies Using the Hirschman Framework

A number of studies in the 1990s framed their findings around the Hirschman model, using various combinations of exit-voice-loyalty-neglect and the active/passive dichotomy.[60] More so than in earlier studies, the nature of the industry was also examined, primarily with regard to a competitive versus monopolistic dichotomy. For example, it was found that higher levels of dissatisfaction would increase exit and voice and would decrease loyalty (not at all surprising); that the existence of exit barriers would decrease exit, increase voice, and decrease loyalty (all supported); and that the attractiveness of alternative options would increase exit and voice and would decrease loyalty (all generally supported). Also identified was a "wait and squawk" approach whereby consumers would remain silent, hoping for performance to improve, until their patience was tested, resulting in a loud squawk to third parties, for example. These research approaches were refreshing in the sense that loyalty was tested and found to respond in accordance with theory.

Lastly, two studies of note used the Hirschman responses of exit, voice, and loyalty plus the concepts of neglect and opportunism (a self-serving exploitation of the relationship).[61] The researcher found direct relations between dissatisfaction and exit and between dissatisfaction and neglect, and an inverse relation between dissatisfaction and voice. Thus, more satisfied customers were more willing to voice concerns to the supplier. This latter, seemingly contradictory finding can be explained in two ways. First, because the research context involved relationship marketing, it is in the best interests of satisfied clients to voice concerns when problems arise so that the problems do not occur in the future, thus maintaining the satisfactory relationship. Second, the author distinguished between a single episode of problem occurrence and its role within the longer-term relationship. That is, a single, momentarily dissatisfying event can occur within a basically satisfying relationship and not upset the balance of positive encounters, a topic to be discussed in the next chapter. Unfortunately, the relations between dissatisfaction and loyalty and between dissatisfaction and opportunism were not supported.

In conclusion, these tests of Hirschman's propositions are interesting but fail to exploit the richness of his theory, and more current work has not been forthcoming. For example, Hirschman proposed that exit does not take place uniformly, but is initiated by those individuals who are most sensitive to decrements in quality. As a result, dissatisfying firms will find that their market has become concentrated on consumers having lower and lower standards and, perhaps, ability to pay. At some point, the firm will make rebound attempts to regain its previous clientele, or it will fold. This and other nuances of Hirschman's work will require further testing.

WORD OF MOUTH: CURRENT INTERPRETATIONS

It is more than likely that "word of mouth" predates even the spoken word in that facial expressions (e.g., frowns, smiles) and gestures are very primitive. For example, pointing and then giving a thumbs-up or thumbs-down (the popular signal of a gladiator's fate in the Roman Colosseum) are almost (but not quite) universal. The point is, of course, that verbal recommendations are a "primitive" in commercial dealings. In fact, Ernest Dichter, an early and famed motivation researcher, published a *Harvard Business Review* article on the same topic within two years of his seminal *Handbook*.[62]

But, more basically, why talk? A popular book sums this question up nicely.[63] An elementary answer is that communication occurs in the earliest life forms and is essential to survival of the species. Talk (communication) spreads knowledge of food, shelter, danger, and the availability of procreation. Communication allows species members to connect and form communities; communities allow for shared interests, common goals, assistance to reach those goals, and mutual protection against danger. Shared interests facilitate shared knowledge of skills, benefits, and risks. Shared knowledge of benefits and risks results in known economies of engagement and, later, commerce. And, at a level of well being, talk permits relief, catharsis, help seeking, and the staving off of boredom. This short list is neither complete nor universally generalizable, but it does drive home the point that society would not be where it is today (for good or bad) were it not for communication.

Determinants

In this section, the factors giving rise to word of mouth, henceforth WOM, will be broken down into performance determinants, sender motivations, receiver motivations, and firm-caused correspondence, recovery efforts, and their effects. Performance determinants are discussed first as these relate to the preceding content of Parts I to III of this book.

General Reactions to Performance

It does not have to be said that good and poor performance results are communicated to others under most normal circumstances. There are situations where good words are disproportionately sent, giving rise to the phrase "if you can't say anything good . . . "; others where negative comments proliferate, as in political campaigns and propaganda; and still others where balance is expected, as in unbiased, authoritative reviews. In the main, these situations fall within the realm of normal conversations and are not exceptional in any way. What, then, causes more engaged communications?

True to earlier discussions, surprisingly good or bad performance evokes a desire to spread the word. However, *surprisingly* good or bad news is not required; bad news in general is disproportionately conveyed compared to good. But when the emotional context is introduced, the goodness or badness of context draws out one or the other news item disproportionately.[64] As noted in Chapter 4, surprising events occur when an expected schema (normal performance deviation) is violated or when events occur that had no schema in that they were not processed in the context in which they occurred. Individuals experiencing this phenomenon within consumption are expected to respond similarly. Conceptual factors facilitating word of mouth have been noted to include expectancy disconfirmation and inequity; the prevalence of extremes of these events, both positive and negative, in stimulating WOM in consumption has been demonstrated.[65]

When the causal differences across positive and negative WOM are examined, the results are as expected. Negative WOM is associated with poor performance, as noted, usually linked to the utilitarian or functional features of the product. Complaining appears to enhance negative communications of all sorts, perhaps because both complaining and other forms of voice are assertive behaviors. Interestingly, complaining has been observed to continue even after switching has occurred and the consumer is no longer affiliated with the product. This may be a vestige of grudge holding, noted earlier, or a prolonged desire to further damage the image of the initial provider, consumable, or its producer.[66]

Alternatively, positive WOM is associated with delighting purchase experiences as well as exceptional service recovery. As opposed to the negative case, positive WOM is more often found with hedonic purchases or where affect is a component of delivery or usage. In this regard, customer participation is helpful, when appropriate, as individuals are less likely to derogate their own performance.[67]

Sender Characteristics

Aside from performance experience, characteristics of the transmitter play a role in the diffusion of WOM. Here, the distinction between the sending of negative versus positive WOM is subordinated to the broader nature of the consumer. Dichter was among the first to elaborate on these motives. His seminal paper defined the four "involvements" which we would now refer to as commitments and consider self-explanatory: product, self, other (receiver), and message or messenger, such as an advertisement or an endorser or detractor. Later, other researchers using a critical incidents technique with personal interviews augmented and refined these categories to include the three dimensions of altruism (helping others, warning others, helping the company), harming the company (vengeance), and helping oneself (self-enhancement, anxiety or dissonance reduction, and advice seeking).[68] A more recent study further elaborated on these dimensions in a venue not readily available until recently, as follows.

Using the Internet as a research vehicle (which, as noted, allows for almost unlimited WOM access), researchers expanded on previous works to include Internet communication via a research forum also known as a platform.[69] Using the prior studies to form a theoretical framework and a research instrument to survey web users contacted through web sources exclusively, five "utilities" of web usage were hypothesized: focus or adding value, consumption or obtaining value, approval or receiving compliments, moderating (acting as a go-between consumer, platform, and company), and homeostatic value, which is a form of therapeutic expression. The results confirmed the existence of self-interest, altruism, a more cognitive form of advocacy, and mixed motive segments. Surprisingly (or not so), this Internet study produced results consistent with the findings in offline environments, suggesting that the online technology broadens method and scope, but confirms the basic human nature of communication.

Of interest is that a type of source or sender person known as a "market maven" has penetrated the Internet as well. As originally proposed, mavens were considered "marketplace experts" and "fashion consultants" in that they were adept at spotting trends; the current moniker for this phenomenon is "recommendation agents," which can be purely mechanical or algorithmic.[70] Today, it is known that there is a constellation of traits that constitute this "personality profile" and that it manifests itself both in generalists and those with specific interests in the product category.[71] Again, Internet diffusion follows well-established patterns of innovation and its life cycle.

Community and Receiver Effects

Receiver effects are easily contained within a discussion of the Internet community. As tradition has it, most community members are receivers; fewer are both receivers and senders. Communities, of course, existed long before the Internet, but more research has been done on this medium due to its ease of access and breadth. Here we refer to communication communities as opposed to communities of loyal or like-minded consumers (see Chapter 15), although the two may very well share substantial overlap.[72]

There are a number of commonalities evident in this discussion. The first is that use of the aforementioned recommendation sources varies by the nature of the ties one has with the recommending community—which at the limit is an individual person or a source medium. Strong ties exist when an individual has physical or psychological closeness to a source such as a family member, friend, supervisor, or confidant in general. Weak ties include more impersonal sources, including acquaintances, screen personalities, and inanimate media such as writings, broadcasts, and other electronic sources. Strong tie sources can be expected to be biased; weak tie information is assumed to be nonpersonal, but may be biased as well. Somewhat obviously, strong tie sources are accessed first unless an individual chooses otherwise; weak ties, unlike traditional environments, may be much more effective for dissemination of bad news due to the wide swath of the Internet. Perceived expertise, experience, and knowledge are valued—but may not be used.[73]

Thus far, the attractiveness of a website community or its functions have been briefly discussed. But unlike social, face-to-face communities, websites have no barriers to exit; consumers can just drop out or cease communicating with total anonymity. The value of an online community to satisfaction, then, is its ability to produce for the client. This includes the fostering of satisfaction for friendly sites or the festering of dissatisfaction for less friendly (hostile) sites. Firms wishing to defuse hostile sites have undertaken "anti-domain" actions by constructing their own websites (forums) with domain names suggestive of those of their antagonists.[74] Proactive firms, however, will use websites and the attendant WOM to their advantage.

Company WOM Responses and Strategies

Aside from using the data gathered on the valence and extent of WOM, a number of strategies are available when consumers converse directly or indirectly with a firm. The first, referred to as consumer-initiated communications, follows the pattern of complaining and praising directly. In a study of a large number of individuals corresponding with firms about either inquiries or complaints, researchers contacted each respondent, asking questions designed to ferret out best response strategies from the firm.[75] The results were encouraging. First, simple inquiries resulted in the highest satisfaction levels when responses were punctual and personal. Since two-thirds of the contacts were inquiries, the firm's ability to handle inquiries appropriately may now be seen as an important way to induce favorable WOM and enable loyalty.

Findings regarding complaints from the same study reinforced what has already been proposed in this book. Equity's three dimensions (distributive, procedural, and interactional justice) were found to be powerful agents of postcomplaint satisfaction and loyalty. This effect—indeed, all positive effects—was more pronounced for heavy users of the category (as they have more purchase and performance trials) and for those already expressing high levels of loyalty. Also, a suggested U-shaped relationship between problem and complaining intensity was upheld. The greatest incidences of WOM activity were found for low- and high-level problems. These effects are not new, but are found repeatedly as businesses move from offline to online environments.[76]

It would be helpful to assess WOM as an ultimate criterion for business benchmarking and strategy. Referring back to Figure 14.5, it can be seen that WOM is a penultimate, if not one of the ultimate, takeaways of purchasing. This has prompted at least one observer to assess a WOM derivative measure as "the one number you need to grow."[77] As defined, it is constructed as a response to the single question, "How likely is it that you would recommend us to a friend or colleague?" Measured on an eleven-point scale from 0 to 10, the scores are interpreted as follows: Nine or 10 scorers are "promoters"; 7 or 8 scorers are "passives"; and those in the 0 to 6 range are "detractors." The firm's "promoter score" is the net of the percentage categorized as promoters minus the percentage categorized as detractors (passives are ignored). This difference has been shown to be highly correlated with a company's growth rate. Currently, the growth rates used in the analysis tend to be financial in nature, such as revenues or profits, and less likely to be marketing-related, such as share of customers. For the intended purpose, it matters little because all these criteria are correlated. Increasing satisfaction increases the positivity of WOM, which then reinforces and augments satisfaction's effects.[78]

Despite this finding, researchers have been quick to question the broad-based, seemingly definitive predictive conclusion of the original version of the promoter index.[79] Based on exhaustive analyses, these critics correctly note that any number of macroindices (they were not able to speak to microlevel data) do well in the prediction of the various measures of growth, including a number of different "renditions" of satisfaction-related concepts (entire scales, net scales—as in the promoter score, and "top-two box" scores discussed in Chapter 2). Taken together, these studies looked at thousands of consumer data points aggregated over company and financial periods from companies both within and across industries. These data included customer satisfaction indices from both the United States and abroad. The common conclusion was that the promoter score is no better than any other satisfaction or satisfaction-related scale, including those of brand commitment and purchase likelihood. The upshot is that behavioral data have a good, if not great, track record of predicting growth, share, or any other financially based metric.

This brings discussion to the wisdom of using only one measure to gauge the psychological impact of a firm's efforts, whether it be net promoter or satisfaction or other related concepts. With the exception of "one-off" studies used in video street interviews or the briefest of telephone polls performed during elections, for example, there is no scientifically compelling reason not to collect related (and particularly antecedent) data. The logic behind this broad-brushed statement is obvious. What explains the results of a one-variable study? What possible diagnostic value could be revealed by a "would you recommend" query? While the lay logic of using this information over less insightful concepts is commendable, how does one justifiably quantify the reasons behind this number? More importantly, what strategic recommendations can be put to management so that the number can be improved? Clearly, additional diagnostic information is required.

MEASURING THE SHORT-TERM CONSEQUENCES

The "one number" issue notwithstanding, this last section of the chapter provides additional tools needed to measure self-reported complaining and complimenting and the extent of positive and negative word of mouth. A scale measuring satisfaction with recovery will be provided. Authors working on exit-voice-loyalty issues have provided measures of the Hirschman concepts.[80] This section takes the next step. Discussed first are those variables most immediately affected by the consumer's primary satisfaction response (complaints and compliments, as in Figure 14.5).

Primary Postpurchase Variables

The following complaining and complimenting and word-of-mouth scales were used in a study by this author and colleague and may prove useful to researchers.[81] The context of the study was automobile purchasing and the two major dimensions were the car itself and, due to the sales-intensive nature of the purchase, the salesperson.

Complaining and Complimenting

	No	Yes	If Yes, how many times?				
I complained to the dealership about the car.	N	Y	1	2	3	4	5+
I praised the car to the dealership.	N	Y	1	2	3	4	5+
I complained to the salesperson about the way I was treated.	N	Y	1	2	3	4	5+
I complimented the salesperson on the fair treatment I received.	N	Y	1	2	3	4	5+

Word of Mouth

About how many people have you talked to concerning the good things or bad things about your

Car _____   Salesperson _____

Did you tell these people mostly positive or mostly negative things about the

	Mostly negative			Half and half			Mostly positive
Car	1	2	3	4	5	6	7
Salesperson	1	2	3	4	5	6	7

Recommendations

Did you recommend that these people

Not buy the car	1	2	3	4	5	6	7	Buy the car
Not buy from the salesperson	1	2	3	4	5	6	7	Buy from the salesperson

As expected, primary satisfaction was correlated with all these measures in the hypothesized direction; the extent of complaining correlated negatively, complimenting correlated positively, the positivity of word of mouth correlated positively, and the favorableness of recommendations correlated positively. All these relations were significant, and some were substantial. Researchers would be well served if items similar to these were included in satisfaction surveys, as suggested in the word-of-mouth discussion.

Secondary Satisfaction

This discussion of secondary satisfaction is facilitated by the publication of a service recovery satisfaction instrument; the concepts are perfectly general, however, and the scale's substance should be easily converted to product purchasing, especially if sales personnel (including telemarketers) or even online avatars are involved.[82] Through widely accepted scale development techniques, six recovery dimensions were identified that will be familiar to readers of this chapter. They are, in order of importance (variance explained) in the final solution, communication (a megadimension reflecting aspects of both procedural and interactional justice), empowerment, feedback, atonement, explanation, and "tangibles" such as the representative's apparel.

This is a dimensional scale (see Chapter 2) rather than a conceptual scale, which would consist of antecedents including expectations and disconfirmation, for example. Nevertheless, it is a tested and unique measure of postrecovery satisfaction having greater breadth of coverage than a one-item scale or question.

CONCLUSION

In the short run, consumers will have little to say regarding their outcomes of purchasing. Unfortunately, this does not necessarily mean that they are satisfied. Although data from corroborating sources are just beginning to appear, the consumption mode study presented in Chapter 13 suggests that, along with the unemotional user, even consumers in contentment mode will have little reason, emotional or otherwise, to communicate their contentment or disappointment to the manufacturer or service provider. Nor will delighted consumers necessarily find the motivation and opportunity to contact the firm.

More problematic are those dissatisfied consumers who choose the invisible options of doing nothing, pursuing negative word of mouth, switching, or sulking under an unbearable product experience that they know must be repeated. The availability of suitable alternatives will determine which of these invisible responses is pursued. Thus, unless the firm makes an effort to uncover this hidden discontent, the natural process of market share erosion will persist. This argues for aggressive measures to discover the extent of consumers' hidden-agenda activities.

Also discussed were typologies of dissatisfaction response styles with a special emphasis on word of mouth. Word of mouth is becoming a major tool of marketers, particularly on the Internet, where buzz and viral marketing dominate. Study of the process itself and those firms who use the Internet to communicate with consumers is progressing rapidly, and firms are encouraged to pursue this phenomenon for its effect on growth and profitability.

The next chapter details the long-term effects of both satisfaction and dissatisfaction. In a sense, the dissatisfaction consequences have already been discussed, as consumers are not likely to tolerate repeated dissatisfying episodes over the long term. It will be instructive, nonetheless, to treat dissatisfaction as a low level of satisfaction, thereby permitting greater focus on the effect of varying levels of satisfaction on consumer loyalty and on firm profitability.

NOTES

1. Fornell and Westbrook, "Vicious Circle of Consumer Complaints."

2. Goodman, "Basic Facts on Customer Complaint Behavior and the Impact of Service on the Bottom Line"; Goodman, Brien, and Segal, "Turning CFOs into Quality Champions"; Goodman, Maszal, and Segal, "Creating a Customer Relationship Feedback System That Has Maximum Bottom Line Impact."

3. See Morrow and Tankersley, "Exploratory Study of Consumer Usage and Satisfaction with 800 and 900 Numbers."

4. Juhl, Thøgersen, and Poulson, "Is the Propensity to Complain Increasing Over Time?"

5. Chebat, Davidow, and Codjovi, "Silent Voices"; Richins, "An Analysis of Consumer Interaction Styles in the Marketplace."

6. E.g., Bennett, "Anger, Catharsis, and Purchasing Behavior Following Aggressive Customer Complaints"; Chebat, Davidow, and Codjovi, "Silent Voices"; Estelami, "Sources, Characteristics, and Dynamics of Postpurchase Price Complaints"; Grønhaug and Gilly, "Transaction Cost Approach to Consumer Dissatisfaction and Complaint Actions"; Hansen, Swan, and Powers, "Encouraging 'Friendly' Complaint Behavior

in Industrial Markets"; Hogarth et al., "Problems with Credit Cards"; Homburg, Hoyer, and Koschate, "Customers' Reactions to Price Increases"; Huppertz, "Firms' Complaint Handling Policies and Consumer Complaint Voicing"; Johnston, "Linking Complaint Management to Profit"; Kolodinsky, "Usefulness of Economics in Explaining Consumer Complaints"; McColl, Mattsson, and Morley, "Effects of Service Guarantees on Service Evaluations During Voiced Complaint and Service Recovery"; Menon and Dubé, "Service Provider Responses to Anxious and Angry Customers"; Nyer, "Cathartic Complaining as a Means of Reducing Consumer Dissatisfaction"; Singh, "Exploring the Effects of Consumers' Dissatisfaction Level on Complaint Behaviors"; Webster and Sundaram, "Service Consumption Criticality in Failure Recovery"; Wirtz, Kum, and Lee, "Should a Firm with a Reputation for Outstanding Service Quality Offer a Service Guarantee?"; and Ursic, "Model of the Consumer Decision to Seek Legal Redress," where support for much of the economic model can be found.

7. Voorhees, Brady, and Horowitz, "Voice from the Silent Masses."

8. Ross and Oliver, "Accuracy of Unsolicited Consumer Communications as Indicators of 'True' Consumer Satisfaction/Dissatisfaction." Other articles of relevance to this section are Cornwell, Bligh, and Babakus, "Complaint Behavior of Mexican-American Consumers to a Third Party Agency"; McAlister and Erffmeyer, "Content Analysis of Outcomes and Responsibilities for Consumer Complaints to Third-Party Organizations"; Owens and Hausknecht, "Effect of Simplifying the Complaint Process"; and Peyrot and Van Doren, "Effect of a Class Action Suit on Consumer Repurchase Intentions."

9. Blodgett, Hill, and Bakir, "Cross-Cultural Complaining Behavior?"; Hernandez et al., "A Cross-Cultural Study of Consumer Complaining Behavior"; Patterson, Cowley, and Prasongsukarn, "Service Failure Recovery"; Ringberg, Odekerken-Schröder, and Christensen, "Cultural Models Approach to Service Recovery"; Voss et al., "Tale of Two Countries' Conservatism, Service Quality, and Feedback on Customer Satisfaction"; Watkins and Liu, "Collectivism, Individualism and In-Group Membership."

10. See Bodey and Grace, "Segmenting Service 'Complainers' and 'Non-Complainers' on the Basis of Consumer Characteristics"; East, "Complaining as Planned Behavior"; Kim et al., "Effect of Attitude and Perception on Consumer Complaint Intentions"; and Singh and Wilkes, "When Consumers Complain."

11. Goodwin and Spiggle, "Consumer Complaining."

12. Mattila and Wirtz, "Consumer Complaining to Firms."

13. Blodgett, Wakefield, and Barnes, "Effects of Customer Service on Consumer Complaining Behavior"; Boote, "Towards a Comprehensive Taxonomy and Model of Consumer Complaining Behaviour"; Buttle and Burton, "Does Service Failure Influence Customer Loyalty?"; Kowalski, "Complaints and Complaining"; Wright and Larsen, "Complaining about the Alliance."

14. Dawar and Pillutla, "Impact of Product-Harm Crises on Brand Equity"; Johnston and Fern, "Service Recovery Strategies for Single and Double Deviation Scenarios"; Kelley and Davis, "Antecedents to Customer Expectations for Service Recovery"; Singh and Widing, "What Occurs Once Consumers Complain?"; Yim et al., "Justice-Based Service Recovery Expectations."

15. See Davis, Gerstner, and Hagerty, "Money Back Guarantees in Retailing"; Fruchter and Gerstner, "Selling with 'Satisfaction Guaranteed'"; Moorthy and Srinivasan, "Signaling Quality with a Money-Back Guarantee"; Ostrom and Iacobucci, "Effect of Guarantees on Consumers' Evaluation of Services"; Schmidt and Kernan, "Many Meanings (and Implications) of 'Satisfaction Guaranteed'"; Tucci and Talaga, "Service Guarantees and Consumers' Evaluation of Services"; and Wirtz and Kum, "Designing Service Guarantees."

16. Articles addressing "low price guarantees" whereby retailers offer to match any lower price found after an item is purchased include Dutta and Biswas, "Effects of Low Price Guarantees on Consumer Post-Purchase Search Intention"; Estelami and Bergstein, "Impact of Market Price Volatility on Consumer Satisfaction with Lowest Price Refunds"; Estelami, Grewal, and Roggeveen, "Negative Effect of Policy Restrictions on Consumers' Post-Purchase Reactions to Price-Matching Guarantees"; Kukar-Kinney and Grewal, "Comparison of Consumer Reactions to Price-Matching Guarantees in Internet and Bricks-and-Mortar Retail Environments"; McConnell et al., "What If I Find It Cheaper Someplace Else?"; and McWilliams and Gerstner, "Offering Low Price Guarantees to Improve Customer Retention." Note that these claims are not redeemed as often as one might suppose since retailers frequently stock nearly identical merchandise from the same manufacturer under different model numbers, thereby negating the same-item, lower-price rule.

17. See Barlow and Møller, *Complaint Is a Gift*; Stauss and Seidel, *Complaint Management*; and Zemke and Woods, *Best Practices in Customer Service.*

18. Kelley, Hoffman, and Davis, "Typology of Retail Failures and Recoveries"; Maxham, "Service Recovery's Influence on Consumer Satisfaction, Positive Word-of-Mouth, and Purchase Intentions."

19. See Baer and Hill, "Excuse Making."

20. Andreassen, "Antecedents to Satisfaction with Service Recovery" and "What Drives Customer Loyalty with Complaint Resolution?"; Boshoff, "Experimental Study of Service Recovery Options"; S. Brown, Cowles, and Tuten, "Service Recovery"; Halstead, Dröge, and Cooper, "Product Warranties and Post-Purchase Service"; Maxham and Netemeyer, "Longitudinal Study of Complaining Customers' Evaluations of Multiple Service Failures and Recovery Efforts"; Oliver, "Investigation of the Interrelationship between Consumer (Dis)Satisfaction and Complaint Reports"; A. Smith, Bolton, and Wagner, "Model of Customer Satisfaction with Service Encounters Involving Failure and Recovery."

21. Hart, Heskett, and Sasser, "Profitable Art of Service Recovery," p. 150.

22. See D. Clark, "Intel Finds Pumped-Up Image Offers a Juicy Target in Pentium Brouhaha"; and numerous related articles. Also see Harvard Business School, *Intel's Pentium.*

23. Aron et al., "Consumer Grudgeholding"; Huefner and Hunt, "Extending the Hirschman Model" and "Consumer Retaliation as a Response to Dissatisfaction"; and Huefner et al., "Consumer Retaliation."

24. Bitner, Booms, and Tetreault, "Service Encounter"; Bowen and Lawler, "Empowerment of Service Workers"; Ford, McNair, and Perry, *Exceptional Customer Service*; Hart, "Power of Unconditional Service Guarantees."

25. G. Clark, Kaminski, and Rink, "Consumer Complaints." See, also, Baer and Hill, "Excuse Making."

26. Strauss and Hill, "Consumer Complaints by E-Mail."

27. Timeliness effects have recently been affirmed in Roehm and Brady, "Consumer Responses to Performance Failures by High-Equity Brands"; request effects are shown in Davidow and Leigh, "Effects of Organizational Complaint Responses on Consumer Satisfaction, Word of Mouth Activity and Repurchase Intentions."

28. Boshoff, "Experimental Study of Service Recovery Options"; S. Brown, Cowles, and Tuten, "Service Recovery"; Conlon and Murray, "Customer Perceptions of Corporate Responses to Product Complaints"; Feinberg et al., "Operational Determinants of Caller Satisfaction in the Call Center"; Naylor, "Complaining Customer."

29. de Matos, Henrique, and Rossi, "Service Recovery Paradox." See the original source for specific references to the studies used in the meta-analysis. A typical study showing a pattern of positive results, not cited in this review due to its recency, is Voorhees, Brady, and Horowitz, "Voice from the Silent Masses."

30. Magnini et al., "Service Recovery Paradox?"

31. Andreassen, "From Disgust to Delight"; Conlon and Murray, "Customer Perceptions of Corporate Responses to Product Complaints"; Estelami and De Maeyer, "Customer Reactions to Service Provider Overgenerosity"; Forbes, Kelley, and Hoffman, "Typologies of e-Commerce Retail Failures and Recovery Strategies"; Garrett, "Effectiveness of Compensation Given to Complaining Consumers"; Johnston and Fern, "Service Recovery Strategies for Single and Double Deviation Scenarios"; Kelley, Hoffman, and Davis, "Typology of Retail Failures and Recoveries"; Maxham, "Service Recovery's Influence on Consumer Satisfaction, Positive Word-of-Mouth, and Purchase Intentions"; A. Smith and Bolton, "Experimental Investigation of Customer Reactions to Service Failure and Recovery Encounters."

32. Gaeth et al., "Consumers' Attitude Change across Sequences of Successful and Unsuccessful Product Usage"; Maxham and Netemeyer, "Longitudinal Study of Complaining Customers' Evaluations of Multiple Service Failures and Recovery Efforts."

33. Chu, Gerstner, and Hess, "Managing Dissatisfaction"; and Reynolds and Harris, "When Service Failure Is Not Service Failure"; Wilkes, "Fraudulent Behavior by Consumers."

34. Karande, Magnini, and Tam, "Recovery Voice and Satisfaction After Service Failure."

35. Cho, Im, and Hiltz, "Impact of e-Services Failures and Customer Complaints on Electronic Commerce Customer Relationship Management"; Forbes, Kelley, and Hoffman, "Typologies of e-Commerce Retail Failures and Recovery Strategies"; Holloway, Wang, and Parish, "Role of Cumulative Online Purchasing Experience in Service Recovery Management."

36. Holloway and Beatty, "Service Failure in Online Retailing"; Harris, Mohr, and Bernhardt, "Online Service Failure, Consumer Attributions and Expectations."

37. Fornell and Wernerfelt, "Model for Customer Complaint Management." See, also, Worsfold, Worsfold, and Bradley, "Interactive Effects of Proactive and Reactive Service Recovery Strategies."

38. Estelami, "Competitive and Procedural Determinants of Delight and Disappointment in Consumer Complaint Outcomes" and "Profit Impact of Consumer Complaint Solicitation across Market Conditions."

39. See Berry and Parasuraman, "Listening to the Customer"; Sampson, "Ramifications of Monitoring Service Quality Through Passively Solicited Customer Feedback"; and Stauss and Seidel, *Complaint Management*, Chapter 5.

40. E.g., Gengler and Leszczyc, "Using Customer Satisfaction Research for Relationship Marketing"; Gombeski et al., "Patient Callback Program."

41. Boshoff and Leong, "Empowerment, Attribution and Apologising as Dimensions of Service Recovery"; Friman and Edvardsson, "Content Analysis of Complaints and Compliments"; Hocutt and Stone, "Impact of Employee Empowerment on the Quality of a Service Recovery Effort"; Payne et al., "Consumer Complimenting Behavior"; Sparks, Bradley, and Callan, "Impact of Staff Empowerment and Communication Style on Customer Evaluations."

42. Otto et al., "Complimenting Behavior."

43. Erickson and Eckrich, "Consumer Affairs Responses to Unsolicited Customer Compliments"; Kraft and Martin, "Customer Compliments as More than Complementary Feedback"; Martin and Smart, "Relationship Correspondence."

44. Folkes, Koletsky, and Graham, "Field Study of Causal Inferences and Consumer Reaction"; Griffin, Babin, and Attaway, "Anticipation of Injurious Consumption Outcomes and Its Impact on Consumer Attributions of Blame"; Hess, Ganesan, and Klein, "Service Failure and Recovery"; McColl-Kennedy and Sparks, "Application of Fairness Theory to Service Failures and Service Recovery"; Menon and Dubé, "Service Provider Responses to Anxious and Angry Customers"; Singh and Wilkes, "When Consumers Complain"; Taylor, "Waiting for Service"; and Vaidyanathan and Aggarwal, "Who Is the Fairest of Them All?"

45. Boshoff and Leong, "Empowerment, Attribution and Apologising as Dimensions of Service Recovery." See, also, Menon and Dubé, "Effect of Emotional Provider Support on Angry Versus Anxious Consumers."

46. Homburg and Fürst, "How Organizational Complaint Handling Drives Customer Loyalty."

47. McCollough, Berry, and Yadav, "Empirical Investigation of Customer Satisfaction after Service Recovery and Failure"; Yim et al., "Justice-Based Service Recovery Expectations."

48. Blodgett, Hill, and Tax, "Effects of Distributive, Procedural, and Interactional Justice on Postcomplaint Behavior"; Bowman and Narayandas, "Managing Customer-Initiated Contacts with Manufacturers"; Cho, Im, and Hiltz, "Impact of e-Services Failures and Customer Complaints on Electronic Commerce Customer Relationship Management"; de Ruyter and Wetzels, "Customer Equity Considerations in Service Recovery"; Homburg and Fürst, "How Organizational Complaint Handling Drives Customer Loyalty"; Kau and Loh, "Effects of Service Recovery on Consumer Satisfaction"; Mattila and Cranage, "Impact of Choice on Fairness in the Context of Service Recovery"; Maxham and Netemeyer, "Modeling Customer Perceptions of Complaint Handling Over Time"; A. Smith, Bolton, and Wagner, "Model of Customer Satisfaction with Service Encounters Involving Failure and Recovery"; Sparks and McColl-Kennedy, "Justice Strategy Options for Increased Customer Satisfaction in a Services Recovery Setting"; Tax, Brown, and Chandrashekaran, "Customer Evaluations of Service Experiences"; Voorhees and Brady, "Service Perspective on the Drivers of Complaint Intentions."

49. Examples, again, are numerous and include Blodgett, Granbois, and Walters, "Effects of Perceived Justice on Complainants' Negative Word-of-Mouth Behavior and Repatronage Intentions"; Halstead and Page, "Effects of Satisfaction and Complaining Behavior on Consumer Repurchase Intentions"; Holloway, Wang, and Parish, "Role of Cumulative Online Purchasing Experience in Service Recovery Management"; Lapidus and Pinkerton, "Customer Complaint Situations"; Maxham, "Service Recovery's Influence on Consumer Satisfaction, Positive Word-of-Mouth, and Purchase Intentions"; Peyrot and Van Doren, "Effect of a Class Action Suit on Consumer Repurchase Intentions"; Spreng, Harrell, and Mackoy, "Service Recovery"; and Voorhees and Brady, "Service Perspective on the Drivers of Complaint Intentions."

50. de Ruyter and Wetzels, "Impact of Perceived Listening Behavior in Voice-to-Voice Service Encounters"; Kau and Loh, "Effects of Service Recovery on Consumer Satisfaction"; Maxham, "Service Recovery's Influence on Consumer Satisfaction, Positive Word-of-Mouth, and Purchase Intentions"; Tax, Brown, and Chandrashekaran, "Customer Evaluations of Service Experiences"; Weun, Beatty, and Jones, "Impact of Service Failure Severity on Service Recovery Evaluations and Post-Recovery Relationships."

51. Chebat, Davidow, and Codjovi, "Silent Voices"; Godwin, Patterson, and Johnson, "Consumer Coping Strategies with Dissatisfactory Service Encounters"; McColl-Kennedy and Sparks, "Application of Fairness Theory to Service Failures and Service Recovery"; Mick and Fournier, "Paradoxes of Technology."

52. Bell and Luddington, "Coping with Customer Complaints."

53. Ringberg, Odekerken-Schröder, and Christensen, "Cultural Models Approach to Service Recovery."

54. Stephens and Gwinner, "Why Don't Some People Complain?"

55. Halstead, "Negative Word of Mouth."

56. Hirschman, *Exit, Voice, and Loyalty*.

57. Singh, "Typology of Consumer Dissatisfaction Response Styles"; Dart and Freeman, "Dissatisfaction Response Styles among Clients of Professional Accounting Firms." The latter study amusingly refers to the three responses of exit, word of mouth, and complaining as "walk, talk, and squawk," p. 75.

58. Hirschman, "'Exit, Voice, and Loyalty.'"

59. Dowding et al., "Exit, Voice and Loyalty." Readers will note that this is a review from a sociopolitical perspective and offers little to the consumer behavior literature.

60. Dart and Freeman, "Dissatisfaction Response Styles among Clients of Professional Accounting Firms"; Hansen, Swan, and Powers, "Vendor Relationships as Predictors of Organizational Buyer Complaint Response Styles"; Levesque and McDougall, "Customer Dissatisfaction"; Maute and Forrester, "Structure and Determinants of Consumer Complaint Intentions and Behavior"; Singh, "Typology of Consumer Dissatisfaction Response Styles."

61. Ping, "Effects of Satisfaction and Structural Constraints on Retailer Exiting, Voice, Loyalty, Opportunism, and Neglect" and "Unexplored Antecedents of Exiting in a Marketing Channel."

62. See Dichter, "How Word-of-Mouth Advertising Works" and *Handbook of Consumer Motivations*.

63. Rosen, *Anatomy of Buzz*.

64. Heath, "Do People Prefer to Pass Along Good or Bad News?"; Schützwohl, "Surprise and Schema Strength"; Schützwohl and Borgstedt, "Processing of Affectively Valenced Stimuli."

65. Blodgett, Granbois, and Walters, "Effects of Perceived Justice on Complainants' Negative Word-of-Mouth Behavior and Repatronage Intentions"; Bone, "Determinants of Word-Of-Mouth Communications During Product Consumption" and "Word-of-Mouth Effects on Short-term and Long-term Product Judgments"; Derbaix and Vanhamme, "Inducing Word-of-Mouth by Eliciting Surprise"; Dubé and Maute, "Antecedents of Brand Switching, Brand Loyalty, and Verbal Responses to Service Failure"; Samson, "Understanding the Buzz That Matters"; Anderson, "Customer Satisfaction and Word of Mouth." Note that Anderson did not find the incidence of negative word of mouth to be disproportionately large.

66. Halstead, "Negative Word of Mouth"; Naylor, "Why Do They Whine?"; Wangenheim, "Postswitching Negative Word of Mouth"; Harrison-Walker, "E-Complaining."

67. Arnold et al., "Customer Delight in a Retail Context"; T. Brown et al., "Spreading the Word"; File, Judd, and Prince, "Interactive Marketing"; Harrison-Walker, "Measurement of Word-of-Mouth Communication and an Investigation of Service Quality and Customer Commitment as Potential Antecedents"; Maxham, "Service Recovery's Influence on Consumer Satisfaction, Positive Word-of-Mouth, and Purchase Intentions."

68. Dichter, "How Word-of-Mouth Advertising Works"; Sundaram, Mitra, and Webster, "Word-of-Mouth Communications."

69. Hennig-Thurau et al., "Electronic Word-of-Mouth via Consumer-Opinion Platforms." See, also, Harrison-Walker, "E-Complaining."

70. Feick and Price, "Market Maven"; Iacobucci, Arabie, and Bodapati, "Recommendation Agents on the Internet"; D. Smith, Menon, and Sivakumar, "Online Peer and Editorial Recommendations, Trust, and Choice in Virtual Markets."

71. Allsop, Bassett, and Hoskins, "Word-of-Mouth Research"; Bansal and Voyer, "Word-of-Mouth Processes within a Services Purchase Decision Context"; Bone, "Word-of-Mouth Effects"; T. Brown et al., "Spreading the Word"; Harrison-Walker, "Measurement of Word-of-Mouth Communication."

72. Hung and Li, "Influence of eWOM on Virtual Consumer Communities."

73. An early, authoritative work on this topic is J. Brown and Reingen, "Social Ties and Word-of-Mouth Referral Behavior." See, also, Duhan et al., "Influences on Consumer Use of Word-of-Mouth Recommendation Sources"; and Goldenberg et al., "NPV of Bad News."

74. Dwyer, "Measuring the Value of Electronic Word of Mouth and Its Impact in Consumer Communities"; Goldenberg, Libai, and Muller, "Talk of the Network"; Harrison-Walker, "E-Complaining."

75. Bowman and Narayandas, "Managing Customer-Initiated Contacts with Manufacturers."

76. Anderson, "Customer Satisfaction and Word of Mouth"; Bansal et al., "Relating e-Satisfaction to Behavioral Outcomes."

77. Reichheld, "One Number You Need to Grow" and "Microeconomics of Customer Relationships."

78. Biyalogorsky, Gerstner, and Libai, "Customer Referral Management"; Kumar, Petersen, and Leone, "How Valuable Is Word of Mouth?"; Wangenheim and Bayón, "Chain from Customer Satisfaction via Word-of-Mouth Referrals to New Customer Acquisition" and "Effect of Word of Mouth on Services Switching."

79. Keiningham et al., "Longitudinal Examination of Net Promoter and Firm Revenue Growth"; Keiningham et al., "Value of Different Customer Satisfaction and Loyalty Metrics in Predicting Customer Retention,

Recommendation, and Share-of-Wallet"; Morgan and Rego, "Value of Different Customer Satisfaction and Loyalty Metrics in Predicting Business Performance"; Pingitore et al., "Single-Question Trap."

80. Ping, "Effects of Satisfaction and Structural Constraints on Retailer Exiting, Voice, Loyalty, Opportunism, and Neglect"; Singh, "Typology of Consumer Dissatisfaction Response Styles."

81. Swan and Oliver, "Postpurchase Communications by Consumers."

82. Bolshoff, "RECOVSAT."

BIBLIOGRAPHY

Allsop, Dee T., Bryce R. Bassett, and James A. Hoskins. "Word-of-Mouth Research: Principles and Applications." *Journal of Advertising Research* 47, no. 4 (December 2007): 398–411.

Anderson, Eugene W. "Customer Satisfaction and Word of Mouth." *Journal of Service Research* 1, no. 1 (August 1998): 5–17.

Andreassen, Tor Wallin. "Antecedents to Satisfaction with Service Recovery." *European Journal of Marketing* 34, nos. 1–2 (2000): 156–175.

———. "From Disgust to Delight: Do Customers Hold a Grudge?" *Journal of Service Research* 4, no. 1 (August 2001): 39–49.

———. "What Drives Customer Loyalty with Complaint Resolution?" *Journal of Service Research* 1, no. 4 (May 1999): 324–332.

Arnold, Mark J., Kristy E. Reynolds, Nicole Ponder, and Jason E. Lueg. "Customer Delight in a Retail Context: Investigating Delightful and Terrible Shopping Experiences." *Journal of Business Research* 58, no. 8 (August 2005): 1132–1145.

Aron, David, Kimberly Judson, Timothy Aurant, and Geoffrey Gordon. "Consumer Grudgeholding: An Ounce of Prevention Is Worth a Pound of Cure." *Marketing Management Journal* 16, no. 1 (Spring 2006): 158–173.

Baer, Robert, and Donna J. Hill. "Excuse Making: A Prevalent Company Response to Complaints?" *Journal of Consumer Satisfaction, Dissatisfaction and Complaining Behavior* 7 (1994): 143–151.

Bansal, Harvir S., Gordon H.G. McDougall, Shane S. Dikolli, and Karen L. Sedatole. "Relating e-Satisfaction to Behavioral Outcomes: An Empirical Study." *Journal of Services Marketing* 18, no. 4 (2004): 290–302.

Bansal, Harvir S., and Peter A. Voyer. "Word-of-Mouth Processes within a Services Purchase Decision Context." *Journal of Service Research* 3, no. 2 (November 2000): 166–177.

Barlow, Janelle, and Claus Møller. *A Complaint Is a Gift.* 2nd ed. San Francisco: Berrett-Koehler, 2008.

Bell, Simon J., and James A. Luddington. "Coping with Customer Complaints." *Journal of Service Research* 8, no. 3 (February 2006): 221–233.

Bennett, Roger. "Anger, Catharsis, and Purchasing Behavior Following Aggressive Customer Complaints." *Journal of Consumer Marketing* 14, no. 2 (1997): 156–172.

Berry, Leonard L., and A. Parasuraman. "Listening to the Customer: The Concept of a Service-Quality Information System." *Sloan Management Review* 38, no. 3 (Spring 1997): 65–76.

Bitner, Mary Jo, Bernard H. Booms, and Mary Stanfield Tetreault. "The Service Encounter: Diagnosing Favorable and Unfavorable Incidents." *Journal of Marketing* 54, no. 1 (January 1990): 71–84.

Biyalogorsky, Eyal, Eitan Gerstner, and Barak Libai. "Customer Referral Management: Optimal Reward Programs." *Marketing Science* 20, no. 1 (Winter 2001): 82–95.

Blodgett, Jeffrey G., Donald H. Granbois, and Rockney G. Walters. "The Effects of Perceived Justice on Complainants' Negative Word-of-Mouth Behavior and Repatronage Intentions." *Journal of Retailing* 69, no. 4 (Winter 1993): 399–428.

Blodgett, Jeffrey G., Donna Hill, and Aysen Bakir. "Cross-Cultural Complaining Behavior? An Alternative Explanation." *Journal of Consumer Satisfaction, Dissatisfaction and Complaining Behavior* 19 (2006): 103–117.

Blodgett, Jeffrey G., Donna Hill, and Stephen S. Tax. "The Effects of Distributive, Procedural, and Interactional Justice on Postcomplaint Behavior." *Journal of Retailing* 73, no. 2 (Summer 1997): 185–210.

Blodgett, Jeffrey G., Kirk L. Wakefield, and James H. Barnes. "The Effects of Customer Service on Consumer Complaining Behavior." *Journal of Services Marketing* 9, no. 4 (1995): 31–42.

Bodey, Kelli, and Debra Grace. "Segmenting Service 'Complainers' and 'Non-Complainers' on the Basis of Consumer Characteristics." *Journal of Services Marketing* 20, no. 3 (2006): 178–187.

Bone, Paula Fitzgerald. "Determinants of Word-Of-Mouth Communications During Product Consumption." In *Advances in Consumer Research*, ed. John F. Sherry Jr. and Brian Sternthal, 19:579–583. Provo, UT: Association for Consumer Research, 1992.

————. "Word-of-Mouth Effects on Short-term and Long-term Product Judgments." *Journal of Business Research* 32, no. 3 (March 1995): 213–223.

Boote, Jonathan. "Towards a Comprehensive Taxonomy and Model of Consumer Complaining Behaviour." *Journal of Consumer Satisfaction, Dissatisfaction and Complaining Behavior* 11 (1998): 140–151.

Boshoff, Christo. "An Experimental Study of Service Recovery Options." *International Journal of Service Industry Management* 8, no. 2 (1997): 110–130.

————. "RECOVSAT: An Instrument to Measure Satisfaction with Transaction-Specific Service Recovery." *Journal of Service Research* 1, no. 3 (February 1999): 236–249.

Boshoff, Christo, and Jason Leong. "Empowerment, Attribution and Apologising as Dimensions of Service Recovery: An Experimental Study." *International Journal of Service Industry Management* 9, no. 1 (1998): 24–47.

Bowen, David E., and Edward E. Lawler III. "The Empowerment of Service Workers: What, Why, How, and When." *Sloan Management Review* 33, no. 3 (Spring 1992): 31–39.

Bowman, Douglas, and Das Narayandas. "Managing Customer-Initiated Contacts with Manufacturers: The Impact of Share of Category Requirements and Word-of-Mouth Behavior." *Journal of Marketing Research* 38, no. 3 (August 2001): 281–297.

Brown, Jacqueline Johnson, and Peter H. Reingen. "Social Ties and Word-of-Mouth Referral Behavior." *Journal of Consumer Research* 14, no. 3 (December 1987): 350–362.

Brown, Stephen W., Deborah L. Cowles, and Tracy L. Tuten. "Service Recovery: Its Value and Limitations as a Retail Strategy." *International Journal of Service Industry Management* 7, no. 5 (1996): 32–46.

Brown, Tom J., Thomas E. Barry, Peter A. Dacin, and Richard F. Gunst. "Spreading the Word: Investigating Antecedents of Consumers' Positive Word-of-Mouth Intentions and Behaviors in a Retailing Context." *Journal of the Academy of Marketing Science* 33, no. 2 (Spring 2005): 123–138.

Buttle, Francis, and Jamie Burton. "Does Service Failure Influence Customer Loyalty?" *Journal of Consumer Behaviour* 1, no. 3 (2001): 217–227.

Chebat, Jean-Charles, Moshe Davidow, and Isabelle Codjovi. "Silent Voices: Why Some Dissatisfied Consumers Fail to Complain." *Journal of Service Research* 7, no. 4 (May 2005): 328–342.

Cho, Yooncheong, Il Im, and Roxanne Hiltz. "The Impact of e-Services Failures and Customer Complaints on Electronic Commerce Customer Relationship Management." *Journal of Consumer Satisfaction, Dissatisfaction and Complaining Behavior* 16 (2003): 106–118.

Chu, Wujin, Eitan Gerstner, and James D. Hess. "Managing Dissatisfaction: How to Decrease Customer Opportunism by Partial Refunds." *Journal of Service Research* 1, no. 2 (November 1998): 140–155.

Clark, Don. "Intel Finds Pumped-Up Image Offers a Juicy Target in Pentium Brouhaha." *Wall Street Journal*, December 5, 1994.

Clark, Gary L., Peter F. Kaminski, and David R. Rink. "Consumer Complaints: Advice on How Companies Should Respond Based on an Empirical Study." *Journal of Services Marketing* 6, no. 1 (Winter 1992): 41–50.

Conlon, Donald E., and Noel M. Murray. "Customer Perceptions of Corporate Responses to Product Complaints: The Role of Explanations." *Academy of Management Journal* 39, no. 4 (August 1996): 1040–1056.

Cornwell, T. Bettina, Alan David Bligh, and Emin Babakus. "Complaint Behavior of Mexican-American Consumers to a Third Party Agency." *Journal of Consumer Affairs* 25, no. 1 (Summer 1991): 1–18.

Dart, Jack, and Kim Freeman. "Dissatisfaction Response Styles among Clients of Professional Accounting Firms." *Journal of Business Research* 29, no. 1 (January 1994): 75–81.

Davidow, Moshe, and James H. Leigh. "The Effects of Organizational Complaint Responses on Consumer Satisfaction, Word of Mouth Activity and Repurchase Intentions." *Journal of Consumer Satisfaction, Dissatisfaction and Complaining Behavior* 11 (1998): 91–102.

Davis, Scott, Eitan Gerstner, and Michael Hagerty. "Money Back Guarantees in Retailing: Matching Products to Consumer Tastes." *Journal of Retailing* 71, no. 1 (Spring 1995): 7–22.

Dawar, Niraj, and Madan M. Pillutla. "Impact of Product-Harm Crises on Brand Equity: The Moderating Role of Consumer Expectations." *Journal of Marketing Research* 37, no. 2 (May 2000): 215–226.

de Matos, Celso Augusto, Jorge Luiz Henrique, and Carlos Alberto Vargas Rossi. "Service Recovery Paradox: A Meta-Analysis," *Journal of Service Research* 10, no. 1 (August 2007): 60–77.

Derbaix, Christian, and Joëlle Vanhamme. "Inducing Word-of-Mouth by Eliciting Surprise: A Pilot Investigation." *Journal of Economic Psychology* 24, no. 1 (February 2003): 99–116.

de Ruyter, Ko, and Martin Wetzels. "Customer Equity Considerations in Service Recovery: A Cross-Industry

Perspective." *International Journal of Service Industry Management* 11, no. 1 (2000): 91–108.

———. "The Impact of Perceived Listening Behavior in Voice-to-Voice Service Encounters." *Journal of Service Research* 2, no. 3 (February 2000): 276–284.

Dichter, Ernest. *Handbook of Consumer Motivations: The Psychology of the World of Objects.* New York: McGraw-Hill, 1964.

———. "How Word-of-Mouth Advertising Works." *Harvard Business Review* 44, no. 6 (November–December 1966): 147–166.

Dowding, Keith, Peter John, Thanos Mergoupis, and Mark Van Vugt. "Exit, Voice and Loyalty: Analytic and Empirical Developments." *European Journal of Political Research* 37, no. 4 (June 2000): 469–495.

Dubé Laurette, and Manfred Maute. "The Antecedents of Brand Switching, Brand Loyalty, and Verbal Responses to Service Failure." In *Advances in Services Marketing and Management*, eds. Teresa A Swartz, David E. Bowen, and Stephen W. Brown, 5:127-151. Greenwich, CT: JAI Press, 1996.

Duhan, Dale F., Scott D. Johnson, James B. Wilcox, and Gilbert D. Harrell. "Influences on Consumer Use of Word-of-Mouth Recommendation Sources." *Journal of the Academy of Marketing Science* 25, no. 4 (Fall 1997): 283–295.

Dutta, Sujay, and Abhijit Biswas. "Effects of Low Price Guarantees on Consumer Post-Purchase Search Intention: The Moderating Roles of Value Consciousness and Penalty Level." *Journal of Retailing* 81, no. 4 (2005): 283–291.

Dwyer, Paul. "Measuring the Value of Electronic Word of Mouth and Its Impact in Consumer Communities." *Journal of Interactive Marketing* 21, no. 2 (Spring 2007): 63–79.

East, Robert. "Complaining as Planned Behavior." *Psychology & Marketing* 17, no. 12 (December 2000): 1077–1095.

Erickson, G. Scott, and Donald W. Eckrich. "Consumer Affairs Responses to Unsolicited Customer Compliments." *Journal of Marketing Management* 17, nos. 3–4 (2001): 321–340.

Estelami, Hooman. "Competitive and Procedural Determinants of Delight and Disappointment in Consumer Complaint Outcomes." *Journal of Service Research* 2, no. 3 (February 2000): 285–300.

———. "The Profit Impact of Consumer Complaint Solicitation across Market Conditions." *Journal of Professional Services Marketing* 20, no. 1 (1999): 165–195.

———. "Sources, Characteristics, and Dynamics of Postpurchase Price Complaints." *Journal of Business Research* 56, no. 5 (May 2003): 411–419.

Estelami, Hooman, and Heather Bergstein. "The Impact of Market Price Volatility on Consumer Satisfaction with Lowest Price Refunds." *Journal of Services Marketing* 20, no. 3 (2006): 169–177.

Estelami, Hooman, and Peter De Maeyer. "Customer Reactions to Service Provider Overgenerosity." *Journal of Service Research* 4, no. 3 (February 2002): 205–216.

Estelami, Hooman, Dhruv Grewal, and Anne L. Roggeveen. "The Negative Effect of Policy Restrictions on Consumers' Post-Purchase Reactions to Price-Matching Guarantees." *Journal of the Academy of Marketing Science* 35, no. 2 (June 2007): 208–219.

Feick, Lawrence F., and Linda L. Price. "The Market Maven: A Diffuser of Marketplace Information." *Journal of Marketing* 51, no. 1 (January 1987): 83–97.

Feinberg, Richard A., Ik-Suk Kim, Leigh Hokama, Ko de Ruyter, and Cherie Keen. "Operational Determinants of Caller Satisfaction in the Call Center." *International Journal of Service Industry Management,* 11, no. 2 (2000): 131–141.

File, Karen Maru, Ben B. Judd, and Russ Alan Prince. "Interactive Marketing: The Influence of Participation on Positive Word-of-Mouth and Referrals." *Journal of Services Marketing* 6, no. 4 (Fall 1992): 5–14.

Folkes, Valerie S., Susan Koletsky, and John L. Graham, "A Field Study of Causal Inferences and Consumer Reaction: The View from the Airport." *Journal of Consumer Research* 13, no. 4 (March 1987): 534-539.

Forbes, Lukas P., Scott W. Kelley, and K. Douglas Hoffman. "Typologies of e-Commerce Retail Failures and Recovery Strategies." *Journal of Services Marketing* 19, no. 5 (2005): 280–292.

Ford, Lisa, David McNair, and Bill Perry. *Exceptional Customer Service: Going Beyond Your Good Service to Exceed the Customer's Expectation.* Holbrook, MA: Adams Media, 2001.

Fornell, Claes, and Birger Wernerfelt. "A Model for Customer Complaint Management." *Marketing Science* 7, no. 3 (Summer 1988): 287–298.

Fornell, Claes, and Robert A. Westbrook. "The Vicious Circle of Consumer Complaints." *Journal of Marketing* 48, no. 3 (Summer 1984): 68–78.

Friman, Margareta, and Bo Edvardsson. "A Content Analysis of Complaints and Compliments." *Managing Service Quality* 13, no. 1 (2003): 20–26.

Fruchter, Gila E., and Eitan Gerstner. "Selling with 'Satisfaction Guaranteed.'" *Journal of Service Research* 1, no. 4 (May 1999): 313–323.

Gaeth, Gary J., Irwin P. Levin, Shailesh Sood, Chifei Juang, and Jennifer Castellucci. "Consumers' Attitude Change across Sequences of Successful and Unsuccessful Product Usage." *Marketing Letters* 8, no. 1 (January 1997): 41–53.

Garrett, Dennis E. "The Effectiveness of Compensation Given to Complaining Consumers: Is More Better?" *Journal of Consumer Satisfaction, Dissatisfaction and Complaining Behavior* 12 (1999): 26–34.

Gengler, Charles E., and Peter T.L. Popkowski Leszczyc. "Using Customer Satisfaction Research for Relationship Marketing: A Direct Marketing Approach." *Journal of Direct Marketing* 11, no. 4 (Fall 1997): 36–42.

Godwin, Beth F., Paul G. Patterson, and Lester W. Johnson. "Consumer Coping Strategies with Dissatisfactory Service Encounters: A Preliminary Investigation." *Journal of Consumer Satisfaction, Dissatisfaction and Complaining Behavior* 12 (1999): 145–154.

Goldenberg, Jacob, Barak Libai, Sarit Moldovan, and Eitan Muller. "The NPV of Bad News." *International Journal of Research in Marketing* 24, no. 3 (September 2007): 186–200.

Goldenberg, Jacob, Barak Libai, and Eitan Muller. "Talk of the Network: A Complex Systems Look at the Underlying Process of Word-of-Mouth." *Marketing Letters* 12, no. 3 (August 2001): 211–223.

Gombeski, William R., Jr., Peter J. Miller, Joseph H. Hahn, Cheryl M. Gillette, Jerome L. Belinson, Laurel N. Bravo, and Patrick S. Curry. "Patient Callback Program: A Quality Improvement, Customer Service, and Marketing Tool." *Journal of Health Care Marketing* 13, no. 3 (Fall 1993): 60–65.

Goodman, John. "Basic Facts on Customer Complaint Behavior and the Impact of Service on the Bottom Line." *Competitive Advantage* 8, no. 1 (June 1999): 1–5.

Goodman, John, Jeff Maszal, and Eden Segal. "Creating a Customer Relationship Feedback System That Has Maximum Bottom Line Impact." *Journal of Customer Relationship Management,* no. 2 (March–April 2000): 289–296.

Goodman, John, Pat O'Brien, and Eden Segal. "Turning CFOs into Quality Champions." *Quality Progress* 33, no. 3 (March 2000): 47–54.

Goodwin, Cathy, and Susan Spiggle. "Consumer Complaining: Attributions and Identities." In *Advances in Consumer Research*, ed. Thomas K. Srull, 16:17–22. Provo, UT: Association for Consumer Research, 1989.

Griffin, Mitch, Barry J. Babin, and Jill S. Attaway. "Anticipation of Injurious Consumption Outcomes and Its Impact on Consumer Attributions of Blame." *Journal of the Academy of Marketing Science* 24, no. 4 (Fall 1996): 314–327.

Grønhaug, Kjell, and Mary C. Gilly. "A Transaction Cost Approach to Consumer Dissatisfaction and Complaint Actions." *Journal of Economic Psychology* 12, no. 1 (March 1991): 165–183.

Halstead, Diane. "Negative Word of Mouth: Substitute for or Supplement to Consumer Complaints?" *Journal of Consumer Satisfaction, Dissatisfaction and Complaining Behavior* 15 (2002): 1–12.

Halstead, Diane, Cornelia Dröge, and M. Bixby Cooper. "Product Warranties and Post-Purchase Service." *Journal of Services Marketing* 7, no. 1 (1993): 33–40.

Halstead, Diane, and Thomas J. Page Jr. "The Effects of Satisfaction and Complaining Behavior on Consumer Repurchase Intentions." *Journal of Consumer Satisfaction, Dissatisfaction and Complaining Behavior* 5 (1992): 1–11.

Hansen, Scott W., John E. Swan, and Thomas L. Powers. "Encouraging 'Friendly' Complaint Behavior in Industrial Markets: Preventing a Loss of Customers and Reputation." *Industrial Marketing Management* 25, no. 4 (July 1996): 271–281.

———. "Vendor Relationships as Predictors of Organizational Buyer Complaint Response Styles." *Journal of Business Research* 40, no. 1 (September 1997): 65–77.

Harris, Katherine E., Lois A. Mohr, and Kenneth L. Bernhardt. "Online Service Failure, Consumer Attributions and Expectations." *Journal of Services Marketing* 20, no. 7 (2006): 453–458.

Harrison-Walker, L. Jean. "E-Complaining: A Content Analysis of an Internet Complaint Forum." *Journal of Services Marketing* 15, no. 5 (2001): 397–412.

———. "The Measurement of Word-of-Mouth Communication and an Investigation of Service Quality and Customer Commitment as Potential Antecedents." *Journal of Service Research* 4, no. 1 (August 2001): 60–75.

Hart, Christopher W.L. "The Power of Unconditional Service Guarantees." *Harvard Business Review* 66, no. 4 (July–August 1988): 54–62.

Hart, Christopher W.L., James L. Heskett, and W. Earl Sasser Jr. "The Profitable Art of Service Recovery." *Harvard Business Review* 68, no. 4 (July–August 1990): 148–156.

Harvard Business School. *Intel's Pentium: When the Chips Are Down*. Case No. 9–595–058. Boston: Harvard Business School Publishing, 1994.

Heath, Chip. "Do People Prefer to Pass Along Good or Bad News? Valence and Relevance of News as Predictors of Transmission Probability." *Organizational Behavior and Human Decision Processes* 68, no. 2 (November 1996): 79–94.

Hennig-Thurau, Thorsten, Kevin P. Gwinner, Gianfranco Walsh, and Dwayne D. Gremler. "Electronic Word-of-Mouth via Consumer-Opinion Platforms: What Motivates Consumers to Articulate Themselves on the Internet?" *Journal of Interactive Marketing* 18, no. 1 (2004): 38–52.

Hernandez, Sigfredo A., William Strahle, Hector L. Garcia, and Robert C. Sorensen. "A Cross-Cultural Study of Consumer Complaining Behavior: VCR Owners in the U.S. and Puerto Rico." *Journal of Consumer Policy* 14, no. 1 (1991): 35–62.

Hess, Ronald L., Jr., Shankar Ganesan, and Noreen M. Klein. "Service Failure and Recovery: The Impact of Relationship Factors on Customer Satisfaction." *Journal of the Academy of Marketing Science* 31, no. 2 (Spring 2003): 127–145.

Hirschman, Albert O. "'Exit, Voice, and Loyalty': Further Reflections and a Survey of Recent Contributions." *Social Science Information* 13, no. 1 (February 1974): 7–26.

———. *Exit, Voice, and Loyalty: Responses to Decline in Firms, Organizations, and States*. Cambridge, MA: Harvard University Press, 1970.

Hocutt, Mary Ann, and Thomas H. Stone. "The Impact of Employee Empowerment on the Quality of a Service Recovery Effort." *Journal of Quality Management* 3, no. 1 (1998): 117–132.

Hogarth, Jeanne M., Marianne A. Hilgert, Jane M. Kolodinsky, and Jinkook Lee. "Problems with Credit Cards: An Exploration of Consumer Complaining Behaviors." *Journal of Consumer Satisfaction, Dissatisfaction and Complaining Behavior* 14 (2001): 88–107.

Holloway, Betsy B., and Sharon E. Beatty. "Service Failure in Online Retailing: A Recovery Opportunity." *Journal of Service Research* 6, no. 1 (August 2003): 92–105.

Holloway, Betsy B., Sijun Wang, and Janet Turner Parish. "The Role of Cumulative Online Purchasing Experience in Service Recovery Management." *Journal of Interactive Marketing* 19, no. 3 (Summer 2005): 54–66.

Homburg, Christian, and Andreas Fürst. "How Organizational Complaint Handling Drives Customer Loyalty: An Analysis of the Mechanistic and the Organic Approach." *Journal of Marketing* 69, no. 2 (July 2005): 95–114.

Homburg, Christian, Wayne D. Hoyer, and Nicole Koschate. "Customers' Reactions to Price Increases: Do Customer Satisfaction and Perceived Motive Fairness Matter?" *Journal of the Academy of Marketing Science* 33, no. 1 (Winter 2005): 36–49.

Huefner, Jonathan C., and H. Keith Hunt. "Consumer Retaliation as a Response to Dissatisfaction." *Journal of Consumer Satisfaction, Dissatisfaction and Complaining Behavior* 13 (2000): 61–82.

———. "Extending the Hirschman Model: When Voice and Exit Don't Tell the Whole Story." *Journal of Consumer Satisfaction, Dissatisfaction and Complaining Behavior* 7 (1994): 267–270.

Huefner, Jonathan C., Brian L. Parry, Collin R. Payne, Sean D. Otto, Steven C. Huff, Michael J. Swenson, and H. Keith Hunt. "Consumer Retaliation: Confirmation and Extension." *Journal of Consumer Satisfaction, Dissatisfaction and Complaining Behavior* 15 (2002): 114–127.

Hung, Kineta H., and Stella Yiyan Li. "The Influence of eWOM on Virtual Consumer Communities: Social Capital, Consumer Learning, and Behavioral Outcomes." *Journal of Advertising Research* 47, no. 4 (December 2007): 485–495.

Huppertz, John W. "Firms' Complaint Handling Policies and Consumer Complaint Voicing." *Journal of Consumer Marketing* 24, no. 7 (2007): 428–437.

Iacobucci, Dawn, Phipps Arabie, and Anand Bodapati. "Recommendation Agents on the Internet." *Journal of Interactive Marketing* 14, no. 3 (Summer 2000): 2–11.

Johnston, Robert. "Linking Complaint Management to Profit." *International Journal of Service Industry Management* 12, no. 1 (2001): 60–69.

Johnston, Robert, and Adrian Fern. "Service Recovery Strategies for Single and Double Deviation Scenarios." *Service Industries Journal* 19, no. 2 (April 1999): 69–82.

Juhl, Hans Jørn, John Thøgersen, and Carsten Stig Poulson. "Is the Propensity to Complain Increasing Over Time?" *Journal of Consumer Satisfaction, Dissatisfaction and Complaining Behavior* 19 (2006): 118–127.

Karande, Kiran, Vincent P. Magnini, and Leona Tam. "Recovery Voice and Satisfaction After Service Failure:

An Experimental Investigation of Mediating and Moderating Factors." *Journal of Service Research* 10, no. 2 (November 2007): 187–203.

Kau, Ah-Keng, and Elizabeth Wan-Yiun Loh. "The Effects of Service Recovery on Consumer Satisfaction: A Comparison Between Complainants and Non-Complainants." *Journal of Services Marketing* 20, no. 2 (2006): 101–111.

Keiningham, Timothy L., Bruce Cooil, Lerzan Aksoy, Tor Wallin Andreassen, and Jay Weiner. "The Value of Different Customer Satisfaction and Loyalty Metrics in Predicting Customer Retention, Recommendation, and Share-of-Wallet." *Managing Service Quality* 17, no. 4 (2007): 361–384.

Keiningham, Timothy L., Bruce Cooil, Tor Wallin Andreassen, and Lerzan Aksoy. "A Longitudinal Examination of Net Promoter and Firm Revenue Growth." *Journal of Marketing* 71, no. 3 (July 2007): 39–51.

Kelley, Scott W., and Mark A. Davis. "Antecedents to Customer Expectations for Service Recovery." *Journal of the Academy of Marketing Science* 22, no. 1 (Winter 1994): 52–61.

Kelley, Scott W., K. Douglas Hoffman, and Mark A. Davis. "A Typology of Retail Failures and Recoveries." *Journal of Retailing* 69, no. 4 (Winter 1993): 429–452.

Kim, Chulmin, Sounghie Kim, Subin Im, and Changhoon Shin. "The Effect of Attitude and Perception on Consumer Complaint Intentions." *Journal of Consumer Marketing* 20, no. 4 (2003): 352–371.

Kolodinsky, Jane. "Usefulness of Economics in Explaining Consumer Complaints." *Journal of Consumer Affairs* 29, no. 1 (Summer 1995): 29–54.

Kowalski, Robin M. "Complaints and Complaining: Functions, Antecedents, and Consequences." *Psychological Bulletin* 119, no. 2 (March 1996): 179–196.

Kraft, Frederic B., and Charles L. Martin. "Customer Compliments as More than Complementary Feedback." *Journal of Consumer Satisfaction, Dissatisfaction and Complaining Behavior* 14 (2001): 1–13.

Kukar-Kinney, Monika, and Dhruv Grewal. "Comparison of Consumer Reactions to Price-Matching Guarantees in Internet and Bricks-and-Mortar Retail Environments." *Journal of the Academy of Marketing Science* 35, no. 2 (June 2007): 197–207.

Kumar, V., J. Andrew Petersen, and Robert P. Leone. "How Valuable Is Word of Mouth?" *Harvard Business Review* 85, no. 10 (October 2007): 139–146.

Lapidus, Richard S., and Lori Pinkerton. "Customer Complaint Situations: An Equity Theory Perspective." *Psychology & Marketing* 12, no. 2 (March 1995): 105–122.

Levesque, Terrence J., and Gordon H.G. McDougall. "Customer Dissatisfaction: The Relationship Between Types of Problems and Customer Response." *Canadian Journal of Administrative Sciences* 13, no. 3 (September 1996): 264–276.

Magnini, Vincent P., John B. Ford, Edward P. Markowski, and Earl D. Honeycutt Jr. "The Service Recovery Paradox: Justifiable Theory or Smoldering Myth?" *Journal of Services Marketing* 21, no. 3 (2007): 231–225.

Martin, Charles L., and Denise T. Smart. "Relationship Correspondence: Similarities and Differences in Business Response to Complimentary versus Complaining Customers." *Journal of Business Research* 17, no. 1 (September 1988): 155–173.

Mattila, Anna S., and David Cranage. "The Impact of Choice on Fairness in the Context of Service Recovery." *Journal of Services Marketing* 19, no. 5 (2005): 271–279.

Mattila, Anna S., and Jochen Wirtz. "Consumer Complaining to Firms: The Determinants of Channel Choice." *Journal of Services Marketing* 18, no. 2 (2004): 147–155.

Maute, Manfred F., and William R. Forrester Jr. "The Structure and Determinants of Consumer Complaint Intentions and Behavior." *Journal of Economic Psychology* 14, no. 2 (June 1993): 219–247.

Maxham, James G., III. "Service Recovery's Influence on Consumer Satisfaction, Positive Word-of-Mouth, and Purchase Intentions." *Journal of Business Research* 54, no. 1 (October 2001): 11–24.

Maxham, James G., III, and Richard G. Netemeyer. "A Longitudinal Study of Complaining Customers' Evaluations of Multiple Service Failures and Recovery Efforts." *Journal of Marketing* 66, no. 4 (October 2002): 57–71.

———. "Modeling Customer Perceptions of Complaint Handling Over Time: The Effects of Perceived Justice on Satisfaction and Intent." *Journal of Retailing* 78, no. 4 (Winter 2002): 239–252.

McAlister, Debbie Thorne, and Robert C. Erffmeyer. "A Content Analysis of Outcomes and Responsibilities for Consumer Complaints to Third-Party Organizations." *Journal of Business Research* 56, no. 4 (April 2003): 341–351.

McColl, Rod, Jan Mattsson, and Clive Morley. "The Effects of Service Guarantees on Service Evaluations During Voiced Complaint and Service Recovery." *Journal of Consumer Satisfaction, Dissatisfaction and Complaining Behavior* 18 (2005): 32–50.

McColl-Kennedy, Jane, and Beverley A. Sparks. "Application of Fairness Theory to Service Failures and Service Recovery." *Journal of Service Research* 5, no. 3 (February 2003): 251–266.

McCollough, Michael A., Leonard L Berry, and Manjit S. Yadav. "An Empirical Investigation of Customer Satisfaction after Service Recovery and Failure." *Journal of Service Research* 3, no. 2 (November 2000): 121–137.

McConnell, Allen R., Keith E. Niedermeier, Jill M. Leibold, Amani G. El-Alayli, Peggy P. Chin, and Nicole M. Kuiper. "What If I Find It Cheaper Someplace Else? Role of Prefactual Thinking and Anticipated Regret in Consumer Behavior." *Psychology & Marketing* 17, no. 4 (April 2000): 281–298.

McWilliams, Bruce, and Eitan Gerstner. "Offering Low Price Guarantees to Improve Customer Retention." *Journal of Retailing* 82, no. 2 (2006): 105–113.

Menon, Kalyani, and Laurette Dubé. "The Effect of Emotional Provider Support on Angry Versus Anxious Consumers." *International Journal of Research in Marketing* 24, no. 3 (September 2007): 268–275.

———. "Service Provider Responses to Anxious and Angry Customers: Different Challenges, Different Payoffs." *Journal of Retailing* 80, no. 3 (2004): 229–237.

Mick, David Glen, and Susan Fournier. "Paradoxes of Technology: Consumer Cognizance, Emotions, and Coping Strategies." *Journal of Consumer Research* 25, no. 2 (September 1998): 123–143.

Moorthy, Sridhar, and Kannan Srinivasan. "Signaling Quality with a Money-Back Guarantee: The Role of Transaction Costs." *Marketing Science* 14, no. 4 (1995): 442–466.

Morgan, Neil A., and Lopo Leotte Rego. "The Value of Different Customer Satisfaction and Loyalty Metrics in Predicting Business Performance." *Marketing Science* 25, no. 5 (September–October 2006): 426–439.

Morrow, Kathleen, and Clint B. Tankersley. "An Exploratory Study of Consumer Usage and Satisfaction with 800 and 900 Numbers." *Journal of Direct Marketing* 8, no. 4 (Autumn 1994): 51–58.

Naylor, Gillian. "The Complaining Customer: A Service Provider's Best Friend?" *Journal of Consumer Satisfaction, Dissatisfaction and Complaining Behavior* 16 (2003): 241–248.

———. "Why Do They Whine? An Examination into the Determinants of Negative and Positive Word-of-Mouth." *Journal of Consumer Satisfaction, Dissatisfaction and Complaining Behavior* 12 (1999): 162–169.

Nyer, Prashanth U. "Cathartic Complaining as a Means of Reducing Consumer Dissatisfaction." *Journal of Consumer Satisfaction, Dissatisfaction and Complaining Behavior* 12 (1999): 15–25.

Oliver, Richard L. "An Investigation of the Interrelationship between Consumer (Dis)Satisfaction and Complaint Reports." In *Advances in Consumer Research*, ed. Melanie Wallendorf and Paul Anderson, 14:218–222. Provo, UT: Association for Consumer Research, 1987.

Ostrom, Amy L., and Dawn Iacobucci. "The Effect of Guarantees on Consumers' Evaluation of Services." *Journal of Services Marketing* 12, no. 5 (1998): 362–378.

Otto, Sean D., Collin R. Payne, Brian L. Parry, and H. Keith Hunt. "Complimenting Behavior: The Complimenter's Perspective." *Journal of Consumer Satisfaction, Dissatisfaction and Complaining Behavior* 18 (2005): 1–31.

Owens, Deborah L., and Douglas R. Hausknecht. "The Effect of Simplifying the Complaint Process: A Field Experiment with the Better Business Bureau." *Journal of Consumer Satisfaction, Dissatisfaction and Complaining Behavior* 12 (1999): 35–43.

Patterson, Paul G., Elizabeth Cowley, and Kriengsin Prasongsukarn. "Service Failure Recovery: The Moderating Impact of Individual-Level Cultural Value Orientation on Perceptions of Justice." *International Journal of Research in Marketing* 23, no. 3 (September 2006): 263–277.

Payne, Collin R., Brian L. Parry, Steven C. Huff, Sean D. Otto, and H. Keith Hunt. "Consumer Complimenting Behavior: Exploration and Elaboration." *Journal of Consumer Satisfaction, Dissatisfaction and Complaining Behavior* 15 (2002): 128–147.

Peyrot, Mark, and Doris Van Doren. "Effect of a Class Action Suit on Consumer Repurchase Intentions." *Journal of Consumer Affairs* 28, no. 2 (Winter 1994): 361–379.

Ping, Robert A., Jr. "The Effects of Satisfaction and Structural Constraints on Retailer Exiting, Voice, Loyalty, Opportunism, and Neglect." *Journal of Retailing* 69, no. 3 (Fall 1993): 320–352.

———. "Unexplored Antecedents of Exiting in a Marketing Channel." *Journal of Retailing* 75, no. 2 (Summer 1999): 218–241.

Pingitore, Gina, Neil A. Morgan, Lopo L. Rego, Adriana Gigliotti, and Jay Meyers. "The Single-Question Trap." *Marketing Research* 19, no. 2 (Summer 2007): 9–13.

Reichheld, Frederick F. "The Microeconomics of Customer Relationships." *MIT Sloan Management Review* 47, no. 2 (Winter 2006): 73–78.

————. "The One Number You Need to Grow." *Harvard Business Review* 81, no. 12 (December 2003): 46–54.

Reynolds, Kate L., and Lloyd C. Harris. "When Service Failure Is Not Service Failure: An Exploration of the Forms and Motives of 'Illegitimate' Customer Complaining." *Journal of Services Marketing* 19, no. 5 (2005): 321–335.

Richins, Marsha L. "An Analysis of Consumer Interaction Styles in the Marketplace." *Journal of Consumer Research* 10, no. 1 (June 1983): 73–82.

Ringberg, Torsten, Gaby Odekerken-Schröder, and Glenn L. Christensen. "A Cultural Models Approach to Service Recovery." *Journal of Marketing* 71, no. 3 (July 2007): 194–214.

Roehm, Michelle L., and Michael K. Brady. "Consumer Responses to Performance Failures by High-Equity Brands." *Journal of Consumer Research* 34, no. 3 (December 2007): 537–545.

Rosen, Emanuel. *The Anatomy of Buzz: How to Create Word-of-Mouth Marketing.* New York: Currency (Doubleday), 2000.

Ross, Ivan, and Richard L. Oliver. "The Accuracy of Unsolicited Consumer Communications as Indicators of 'True' Consumer Satisfaction/Dissatisfaction." In *Advances in Consumer Research*, ed. Thomas C. Kinnear, 11:504–508. Provo, UT: Association for Consumer Research, 1984.

Sampson, Scott E. "Ramifications of Monitoring Service Quality Through Passively Solicited Customer Feedback." *Decision Sciences* 27, no. 4 (Fall 1996): 601–622.

Samson, Alain. "Understanding the Buzz That Matters: Negative vs Positive Word of Mouth." *International Journal of Marketing Research* 48, no. 6 (2006): 647–657.

Schmidt, Sandra L., and Jerome B. Kernan. "The Many Meanings (and Implications) of 'Satisfaction Guaranteed.'" *Journal of Retailing* 61, no. 4 (Winter 1985): 89–108.

Schützwohl, Achim. "Surprise and Schema Strength." *Journal of Experimental Psychology: Learning, Memory, and Cognition* 24, no. 5 (September 1998): 1182–1199.

Schützwohl, Achim, and Kirsten Borgstedt. "The Processing of Affectively Valenced Stimuli: The Role of Surprise." *Cognition and Emotion* 19, no. 4 (June 2005): 583–600.

Singh, Jagdip. "Exploring the Effects of Consumers' Dissatisfaction Level on Complaint Behaviors." *European Journal of Marketing* 25, no. 9 (1991): 7–21.

————. "A Typology of Consumer Dissatisfaction Response Styles." *Journal of Retailing* 66, no. 1 (Spring 1990): 57–99.

Singh, Jagdip, and Robert E. Widing II. "What Occurs Once Consumers Complain? A Theoretical Model for Understanding Satisfaction/Dissatisfaction Outcomes of Complaint Responses." *European Journal of Marketing* 25, no. 5 (1991): 30–46.

Singh, Jagdip, and Robert E. Wilkes. "When Consumers Complain: A Path Analysis of the Key Antecedents of Consumer Complaint Response Estimates." *Journal of the Academy of Marketing Science* 24, no. 4 (Fall 1996): 350–365.

Smith, Amy K., and Ruth N. Bolton. "An Experimental Investigation of Customer Reactions to Service Failure and Recovery Encounters: Paradox or Peril?" *Journal of Service Research* 1, no. 1 (August 1998): 65–81.

Smith, Amy K., Ruth N. Bolton, and Janet Wagner. "A Model of Customer Satisfaction with Service Encounters Involving Failure and Recovery." *Journal of Marketing Research* 36, no. 3 (August 1999): 356–372.

Smith, Donnavieve, Satya Menon, and K. Sivakumar. "Online Peer and Editorial Recommendations, Trust, and Choice in Virtual Markets." *Journal of Interactive Marketing* 19, no. 3 (Summer 2005): 15–37.

Sparks, Beverley A., Graham L. Bradley, and Victor J. Callan. "The Impact of Staff Empowerment and Communication Style on Customer Evaluations: The Special Case of Service Failure." *Psychology & Marketing* 14, no. 5 (August 1997): 475–493.

Sparks, Beverley A., and Janet R. McColl-Kennedy. "Justice Strategy Options for Increased Customer Satisfaction in a Services Recovery Setting." *Journal of Business Research* 54, no. 3 (December 2001): 209–118.

Spreng, Richard A., Gilbert D. Harrell, and Robert D. Mackoy. "Service Recovery: Impact on Satisfaction and Intentions." *Journal of Services Marketing* 9, no. 1 (1995): 15–23.

Stauss Bernd, and Wolfgang Seidel. *Complaint Management: The Heart of CRM.* Mason, OH: TEXERE (Thomson), 2004.

Stephens, Nancy, and Kevin P. Gwinner. "Why Don't Some People Complain? A Cognitive-Emotive Process Model of Consumer Complaint Behavior." *Journal of the Academy of Marketing Science* 26, no. 3 (Summer 1998): 172–189.

Strauss, Judy, and Donna J. Hill. "Consumer Complaints by E-Mail: An Exploratory Investigation of Corporate

Responses and Customer Reactions." *Journal of Interactive Marketing* 15, no. 1 (Winter 2001): 63–73.

Sundaram, D.S., Kaushik Mitra, and Cynthia Webster. "Word-of-Mouth Communications: A Motivational Analysis." In *Advances in Consumer Research*, ed. Joseph W. Alba and J. Wesley Hutchinson, 25:527–531. Provo, UT: Association for Consumer Research, 1998.

Swan, John E., and Richard L. Oliver. "Postpurchase Communications by Consumers." *Journal of Retailing* 65, no. 4 (Winter 1989): 516–533.

Tax, Stephen S., Stephen W. Brown, and Murali Chandrashekaran. "Customer Evaluations of Service Experiences: Implications for Relationship Marketing." *Journal of Marketing* 62, no. 2 (April 1998): 60–76.

Taylor, Shirley. "Waiting for Service: The Relationship Between Delays and Evaluations of Service." *Journal of Marketing* 58, no. 2 (April 1994): 56–69.

Tucci, Louis A., and James Talaga. "Service Guarantees and Consumers' Evaluation of Services." *Journal of Services Marketing* 11, no. 1 (1997): 10–18.

Ursic, Michael L. "A Model of the Consumer Decision to Seek Legal Redress." *Journal of Consumer Affairs* 19, no. 1 (Summer 1985): 20–36.

Vaidyanathan, Rajiv, and Praveen Aggarwal. "Who Is the Fairest of Them All? An Attributional Approach to Price Fairness Perceptions." *Journal of Business Research* 56, no. 6 (June 2003): 453–463.

Voorhees, Clay M., and Michael K. Brady. "A Service Perspective on the Drivers of Complaint Intentions." *Journal of Service Research* 8, no. 2 (November 2005): 192–204.

Voorhees, Clay M., Michael K. Brady, and David M. Horowitz. "A Voice from the Silent Masses: An Exploratory and Comparative Analysis of Noncomplainers." *Journal of the Academy of Marketing Science* 34, no. 4 (October 2006): 514–527.

Voss, Christopher A., Aleda V. Roth, Eve D. Rosenzweig, Kate Blackmon, and Richard B. Chase. "A Tale of Two Countries' Conservatism, Service Quality, and Feedback on Customer Satisfaction." *Journal of Service Research* 6, no. 3 (February 2004): 212–230.

Wangenheim, Florian V. "Postswitching Negative Word of Mouth." *Journal of Service Research* 8, no. 1 (August 2005): 67–78.

Wangenheim, Florian V., and Tomás Bayón. "The Chain from Customer Satisfaction via Word-of-Mouth Referrals to New Customer Acquisition." *Journal of the Academy of Marketing Science* 35, no. 2 (June 2007): 233–249.

———. "The Effect of Word of Mouth on Services Switching: Measurement and Moderating Variables." *European Journal of Marketing* 38, nos. 9–10 (2004): 1173–1185.

Watkins, Harry S., and Raymond Liu. "Collectivism, Individualism and In-Group Membership: Implications for Consumer Complaining Behaviors in Multicultural Contexts." *Journal of International Consumer Marketing* 8, nos. 3–4 (1996): 69–96.

Webster, Cynthia, and D.S. Sundaram. "Service Consumption Criticality in Failure Recovery." *Journal of Business Research* 41, no. 2 (February 1998): 153–159.

Weun, Seungoog, Sharon E. Beatty, and Michael A. Jones. "The Impact of Service Failure Severity on Service Recovery Evaluations and Post-Recovery Relationships." *Journal of Services Marketing* 18, no. 2 (2004): 133–146.

Wilkes, Robert E. "Fraudulent Behavior by Consumers." *Journal of Marketing* 78, no. 4 (October 1978): 67–75.

Wirtz, Jochen, and Doreen Kum. "Designing Service Guarantees: Is Full Satisfaction the Best You Can Guarantee?" *Journal of Services Marketing* 15, no. 4 (2001): 282–299.

Wirtz, Jochen, Doreen Kum, and Khai Sheang Lee. "Should a Firm with a Reputation for Outstanding Service Quality Offer a Service Guarantee?" *Journal of Services Marketing* 14, no. 6 (2000): 502–512.

Worsfold, Kate, Jennifer Worsfold, and Graham Bradley. "Interactive Effects of Proactive and Reactive Service Recovery Strategies: The Case of Rapport and Compensation." *Journal of Applied Social Psychology* 37, no. 11 (November 2007): 2496–2517.

Wright, Newell D., and Val Larsen. "Complaining about the Alliance: Extending Kowalski's Theory of Complaining through a Hermeneutical Analysis of Online Complaining Data." *Journal of Consumer Satisfaction, Dissatisfaction and Complaining Data* 10, (1997): 170–184.

Yim, Chi Kin (Bennett), Flora Fang Gu, Kimmy Wa Chan, and David K. Tse. "Justice-Based Service Recovery Expectations: Measurement and Antecedents." *Journal of Consumer Satisfaction, Dissatisfaction and Complaining Behavior* 16 (2003): 36–52.

Zemke, Ron, and John A. Woods, eds. *Best Practices in Customer Service.* New York: HRD Press (AMACON), 1998.

CHAPTER 15

LOYALTY AND FINANCIAL IMPACT

Long-Term Effects of Satisfaction

Deadheads, Parrot Heads, Trekkies, punks, Harley owners, and loyal fans of all varieties—what explains their extreme commitment to a particular product, service, or entertainment? Why do devoted Deadheads attend every concert by the Grateful Dead, and devoted Parrotheads show equal loyalty to singer Jimmy Buffett? Why do many sports fans attend every home game played in a season, Trekkies memorize the storyline of every *Star Trek* episode, diners patronize a favorite restaurant repeatedly, voters routinely vote for candidates of the same party, and automobile buyers continually repurchase the same make of car? And why do individuals adopt a lifestyle based on a common consumption theme such as the punk rocker generation or the motorcycle subculture of Harley-Davidson (formalized by membership in local Harley Owners Group—H.O.G.®—chapters)? One answer is that all these loyal consumers have developed a deeply held preference for particular consumables in the marketplace and are willing to support their favorite brands with purchasing dollars.[1]

Up to now, this book largely has taken a transaction-specific approach, viewing satisfaction as a short-term phenomenon following a specific consumption situation. The stage is set to discuss more enduring effects, such as those central to longer-term experiences analogous to satisfaction in one's job, marriage, or everyday life.

But first, two clarifications are needed. First, maintaining loyalty or enduring preferences for products and services generally requires that consumers be able and willing to continue interaction with the brand in some way, usually by repetitive purchasing. For other consumers, this interaction could involve continued support; for example, a consumer might outgrow membership in Boy Scouts or Girl Scouts, but cherish the memories nonetheless and wish to continue promoting the consumable with nonpurchase behaviors, such as donating money to the parent organization or becoming a troop leader.

The second clarification addresses situations in which long-term participation is not likely. As a result, the potential for loyalty is minimal or irrelevant. One-time consumption events such as emergency surgery or a once-in-a-lifetime dream vacation are examples. These situations may entail high levels of satisfaction (or dissatisfaction), but the low likelihood or willingness to engage in them again renders loyalty issues moot. Thus, loyalty implies continued purposeful interaction, however infrequent, with a product or service.

Also entertained are those relationships fostered by a supporting firm largely to ensure future purchases when it is unlikely that a psychological bond could be established. Here, "points" (the term is used generically) are issued that can accumulate into redemption thresholds. These strategies are frequently called loyalty programs, which, as will be explained later, stretch the semantic or philosophical underpinnings of this overused phrase. Historians of this phenomenon will remember one of the earliest of these schemes, Green Stamps, introduced by the Sperry & Hutchinson company in 1896.[2] During the program's heyday in the 1950s and 1960s, grocery stores, in particular, issued stamps that patrons would "lick and stick" into books, later redeeming them for various household or gift items. The parent company waned and was bought out in 1999. The program has now been revamped as Greenpoints. Finders of old completed books of stamps can redeem them even today. But why the longevity of such strategies? Hopefully, satisfactory answers await further discussion.

THE DEVELOPMENT OF LOYALTY: A FRAMEWORK

Consider a new resident in a town who desires to become a supporter of the local symphony. It is instructive to conceptually trace the process of this individual's experience, from first encounter through continued attendance, to see how satisfaction may play a role in the beginnings of loyalty formation. Drawing on attribute-based models of attitude, whereby likes and dislikes are formed from attribute ratings, the consumer's initial set of expectations about the symphony's performance probably has little personal content and will be based on what the consumer knows about the reputation of the orchestra and the conductor. Thus, the conductor's reputation may provide one basis for initial impressions of how the symphony will perform.

The potential concertgoer's first one or two symphony experiences probably appear as shown in Figure 15.1, an extension of early work linking attitude concepts and satisfaction.[3] This portrayal appears as a three-phase process, but is actually a repetitive cycle in which postconsumption states become the preconsumption states for the next purchase round. In accord with what is known of anticipations of satisfying experiences, expectations of satisfaction are proposed as more abstract precursors of the consumption episode. This distinguishes, but is consistent with, the more objective predictions of performance level beliefs from the satisfaction level that one expects. It is suggested here that expected performance levels, even those that might imply superior quality, eventually must be translated to satisfaction "utils" by the consumer.

Viewing expectations as anticipated satisfactions, discussed in Chapter 3, is fairly new in the study of satisfaction; this may explain why the expectation component of the expectancy disconfirmation model does not appear with greater regularity and with stronger coefficients in studies of extended consumption episodes. Also as noted in Chapter 3, indirect evidence for this assumption is known to operate at the market (aggregate) level, where the various national consumer satisfaction indices recognize that later satisfaction is predicted by prior satisfaction and current performance expectations.[4] Presumably these expectations implicitly reflect the influence of prior satisfaction.

Figure 15.1 begins with the initial phases of purchasing experience in the leftmost column—before loyalty has a chance to develop.[5] In the traditional manner of attitude theory, the consumer's attitude, defined as a liking or disliking for the consumable, is portrayed as a function of beliefs or their future-oriented interpretation, expectations. In this first purchase cycle, it is unclear whether attitude will be based on objective attribute beliefs or on the satisfaction expected from those attribute levels. Generally, however, consumers will have predilections toward the product or service (or symphony), nonetheless. This may result in an intention to purchase based on their anticipated liking for the product or service.

After the consumer makes the first or first few purchases, the model assumes that this consumer's

426

Figure 15.1   The Cycle of Satisfaction-Based Loyalty

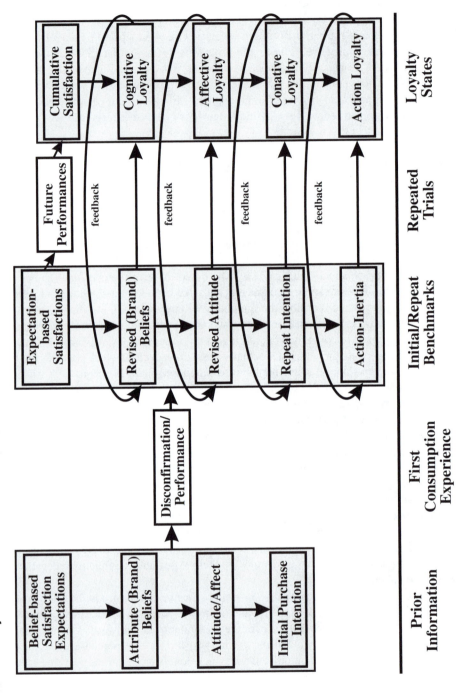

reaction follows the basic expectancy disconfirmation process, whereby satisfaction is a function of disconfirmation-based performance. The model suggests further that the resulting level of satisfaction or dissatisfaction is a major influence on the consumer's revised attitude, which is also influenced by the prior attitude and related affects. This influence of prior attitudes is explained by adaptation level adjustments. As previously discussed in Chapter 3, this perspective describes the final position of a concept as resulting from its initial position (the adaptation level) and the movement caused by a change agent (satisfaction in this case).

Repurchase intention (to be discussed) is similarly affected. Shown as resulting from the influence of attitude, revised intention is a function of the initial intention level and the movement caused by the change agent, namely, the revised attitude level. The continuation links are shown as feedback loops. Observed performance in the postconsumption phase is used to revise performance expectations in the following cycle. Experienced satisfaction, likewise, is shown as an influence on satisfaction expectations in the next cycle. Similar influences are evident for attitude and intention.

Note that the model predicts repurchase intention based primarily on attitude influences only. It is also possible for intention (and loyalty) to be influenced by social norms; that is, all residents of a particular city may be expected to support the local symphony. This alternative influence is recognized and has been shown to operate in tandem with attitudinal influences. It will be specifically addressed in later sections of this chapter.[6] For brevity, the present discussion focuses solely on the attitude → intention portion of the model.

To return to the new resident's symphony attendance experiences, the model in Figure 15.1 suggests that these reactions will accumulate over time. Positive encounters will create positive expectations that, in turn, will enhance the likelihood of interpreting the next encounter as positive. Assuming that most of the consumer's concert experiences are positive, either because of the artistic mastery of the conductor and musicians or because of the sheer enjoyment of attendance, the consumer may begin to experience the sensation of loyalty and later may decide to become a loyal season-ticket buyer. At this point, a phenomenon known as inertia may begin to operate whereby the (purchase) behavior becomes habituated (more on this later).

This scenario raises a number of questions about the psychological mechanisms that may have operated to turn this individual into a symphony supporter. More particularly, just what is this notion of loyalty, what stages are evident in its development, and what can one expect from loyal consumers when they have reached this state? To begin this discourse, it first becomes necessary to discuss the earliest mental leanings that could predispose this consumer to repeat purchase. This is a good prelude to the next section on psychological loyalty as these leanings are not necessarily encoded in the consumer's consciousness as a deep, reverent state. Rather, they are simply good intentions.

To a consumer behaviorist (or any other behaviorist in an applied area), this intention construal (or construct) should have been broached much sooner in this text. In an introductory attitude primer, for example, this would have certainly been performed by now. However, intentions tend to be conscious cognitions; people intend to engage in behaviors usually for a reason, and a number of "reasoned action" frameworks exist. Satisfaction, however, is not a pure cognition and is not always pursued as a goal. Often it just happens, sometimes as an afterthought. Behaviors can have intended consequences and satisfaction may be one of these. The reason for delaying discussion until now is that this is a proper location to discuss intentions in a satisfaction context because so many loyalty researchers have used intention as a proxy for loyalty. This usage is mostly a matter of convenience, however, because intention data are easy to collect, may have already been collected, and are sufficient for use as a practical agenda. Another reason is that loyalty is difficult to define operationally. Unfortunately, many of the studies reported here are based on hybrid loyalty measures composed of satisfaction, intention, word of mouth, and other concepts suggestive of loyalty. There would be little on which to base this chapter if this were not the case.

INTENTIONS AND BEHAVIOR: HISTORICAL PERSPECTIVE AS RELATING TO LOYALTY

The beginnings of a behavioral perspective (centered on observable actions) on loyalty appeared in the 1970s, after a period when the majority of researchers measured loyalty as a pattern of repeat purchasing. Indeed, numerous studies of the statistical properties of repeat buying (and switching) had been published at that time, including those that showed that elements of repeat-purchase cycles were stochastic—that is, they contained an unanalyzable random component.[7] In an effort to explain this and other mysteries of brand loyalty and switching, writers turned to behavior-based explanations for brand-specific purchase pattern sequences within a product category.

The reader may wonder why more philosophical approaches were not pursued. One is the very pragmatic notion of behavioral indices—true purchases that, of course, translate into revenues. Without going into the brain mechanics of holding action tendencies, one can talk of the various literatures addressing vectored thoughts. The vector implies that a thought leads to a change in status, such as achievement of a goal, which in the case here is simple acquisition of product or service outcome. It is also the case that this change may appear to be stationary (zero), such as when one intends to maintain the status quo. This, however, remains a change as the status quo is transferred over time—a change in its own right.

To this end, the author is aware of no major treatises on intentions, only grand theories and book-length compendia of articles espousing such.[8] This may be so because intentions exist in a netherworld of pre-actions. At the unenforceable limit, they may exist as personal musings, as in a New Year's resolution. At the far pole, they become promises, pledges, vows, or legally sanctioned commitments such as earnest money on a home purchase. Noncompliance consequences are outside the present discourse.

This discussion illustrates the two temporal boundaries of intentions, namely the promise stage and the compliance stage, and both are suitable as beginning points. Expectations as promises, anticipations, or hopes, some of which are volitional (promises) and others more externally mediated (anticipations), have already been discussed. The concern here is with the volitional categories. Not discussed are the standards for achievement, more commonly referred to as goals. At the compliance pole, a body of work on "action-control" held sway in the 1980s, spawning a number of attitude-based theories.[9] Some researchers have also focused on people's attempts to bring intentions to fruition, including the notion of "trying" after goals have been established.[10] This, too, was a worthy approach that now seems to have stabilized.

As the preceding suggests, there are three phases to the intention concept: initiation, implementation, and termination, the latter not necessarily connoting achievement.[11] Are all required for loyalty? Probably not, although it makes little sense economically if successful termination is not achieved. This may be only partially accurate, however, as devoted advocates may be valuable as champions and proselytizers. In the context of satisfaction-based loyalty, however, it may be best to focus on what it is about satisfying (and dissatisfying) experiences that fosters a sense of intention to reengage the consumable or to commit to avoiding it, in both cases repetitively in the future. Because the literature routinely does not distinguish the many nuances of intention measurement, one categorization is briefly elaborated here; later discussion will require that readers apply their own standards as to what meaning is intended.

This framework is based on "future connections"—that is, a relation between consumers and some action that they may take in the future.[12] In pure form, this cognition would be evaluation-free in order to distinguish it from attitude. The purpose, however, will be to introduce an evaluative overlay on this restriction as it is the valent nature of experience that gives the intention its approach or avoidance nature. Bear in mind, then, that intentions assume a valence; lack of emotional content is rarely motivating unless the behavior is a component of a broader goal acquisition that does have valence, such as routine daily rituals within a person's plans for the day. The reader will note that all the following variants have been discussed so far in other consumption contexts in this volume.

The first is intentions-as-expectations, as in "I expect that I will perform X." This can be construed as either volitional or nonvolitional because another causal agent could require consumers to engage in a behavior against their will or preference. Thus, students may adhere to a dress code in order to avoid disapproval despite their wishes to dress otherwise. Expectation-based intentions clearly qualify as intention prototypes although they may not have the motivational impact of more strongly held predispositions. This is why valence is necessary to distinguish mere expectations of the positive from hopes and mere negative expectations from dreads.

The second variant is intentions-as-plans. In fact, theories of planned behavior are among the most well-known of the conceptual carriers of this intention variant.[13] Plans are distinguished from expectations in that they are mostly volitional (plans can still be demanded of others) and typically involve some form of expected effort expenditure, particularly when obstacles must be overcome. Lastly, there exist intentions-as-wants or desires (see Chapter 4). Wants have "more desire" associated with them to the point of being necessities, but are intention-*related* only in the sense that others expect them to be pursued. Perhaps the best manner of detecting the various intentional variants in use is the method of measurement. The three verb forms of "I expect that . . . ," "I plan to...," and "I want..." will indicate the nature of the intention "intended."

In testing the three variants in the prediction of satisfaction with restaurants, the authors of this framework found that higher relations were obtained for the wants version and the lowest for expectations.[14] All were significant, of course, and differences were only a matter of degree. And, as has been found elsewhere, the satisfaction to intention relations were higher for action (patronizing) than for the restaurant itself (the object).

Intention as a Proxy for Loyalty

As noted, further discussion of the concept of intention is necessary because consumption researchers use future intention as a surrogate for loyalty (simplicity and convenience of measurement being the primary motivations). In a sense, what follows in this section is what would have been written some time ago before loyalty became something more than a philosophical tour de force. Briefly, the following topics are pursued. First, the central theme of the book is elaborated: namely, is satisfaction related to future intention in terms of the intensity of satisfaction, the nature of satisfaction, and moderators of the relationship? Then, the effect of measuring intention is explored, as some researchers would argue that there is no need to do this if all that matters is behavior as translated into revenues. Last, the relation between intention and behavior as a proxy for loyalty is entertained. This will prove to be problematic because intention may also be a component or a prototype of loyalty (see Figure 15.1). Discussion will prove to be more complex than is generally acknowledged.

The Relationship Between Satisfaction and Intention

Are satisfaction and intention related? The answer is yes; the real question is in what manner. Perhaps a good example of the ubiquity of this finding is the programmatic study of auto buyers.

Many of these data are proprietary, but the academic availability of data sets shows that the basic relation is robust. Autos, however, are somewhat unusual in that consumers regularly purchase new cars because of obsolescence, innovation, fashion, or social trends (e.g., the current hybrids). While many products, such as computers, follow this pattern, others do not because of the heavy influence of situational factors; home buying, for example, is subject to home owners' unexpected occupational changes.[15]

Generally, the severity of the satisfaction response is a main contributing factor beyond satisfaction per se. In this context, both extremely positive experiences, such as those of delight, and negative experiences often leading to extreme responses (grudge holding and purchase boycotts) result in correspondingly similar intention scores and changes.[16] Within the dissatisfaction category, recovery responses follow similar severity logic. Intention scores mirror the consumer's sentiments regarding the firm's performance.[17]

Researchers have observed a number of moderating influences that change the nature of the relationship between satisfaction and intention responses, which, as has been noted, is already quite strong. Based on a meta-analysis including both intention and repurchase findings (the results differed somewhat), these moderators have been found to include demographics, personal involvement with the product, length of experience with the vendor, and competitive intensity, among other variables. Other studies, not included, serve to both confirm and refute individual findings.[18] Generally, intention's effects on repurchase are fairly direct but interaction effects relating to nonlinearities are elusive.

What Effect Does the Query "Will You . . ." Have on Consumers?

Similar to the observer effect in many sciences, the act of measuring intentions has been shown to be disruptive of what would have occurred otherwise, a phenomenon also noted in other areas of satisfaction measurement itself.[19] Two issues are relevant here. The first is recall accuracy; the second is the supposed recalled intention on purchasing probabilities (and purchase). If intentions are not held in active memory, they must be retrieved, and the retrieval process itself is also subject to intervention inaccuracies. These include memory decay due to time (and not to changes in needs), memory fallibility, and simple accessibility (buried memories).[20] The other concern relating to measurement effects after reconstruction raises the very real possibility that the solidified intentions increase the likelihood that the intended purchase will actually occur. Evidence suggests that it does.[21]

The next phase of discussion reaches the crux of this chapter. Beyond mere intention to purchase (or not), the intention to be loyal will be addressed. This will prove just one step in understanding, however, as there are actually many more. Consumers must have a predilection to entertain something as committed as loyalty to a consumable. One would think that there is little downside to this as mass producers are not distressed over a lost customer, but service providers are, particularly if they wish to retain or gain customers. Nonetheless, the evidence on satisfaction and loyalty is accumulating rapidly. And, as a corollary, the theoretical basis for these data is also emerging nicely. Taken together, the following describes what is known.

Behavior as a Proxy for Loyalty

In a fitting segue from the previous section, a recent article titled "The Evolution of Loyalty Intentions" traces the development of cell-phone provider commitment over three time periods.[22] The authors base their analysis of intentions (behavior was not measured) on perceived value, brand personality (referred to as brand equity), and affective commitment (see Figure 15.1). The relations are largely supported, but of modest magnitude. The point here is that this study in an applied setting demonstrates one of the linkages to be discussed, that affective leanings translate into conative (intentional) leanings—one of the steps in the figure. This is a worthy start to what needs to be shown. No mention is made of operationalizing the focus of the study, namely loyalty itself.

It would be helpful to begin with a brief history of psychological, as opposed to behavior-based loyalty. This attempt will present a semantic conundrum because the early loyalty researchers observed behavior and inferred loyalty. The problem is that the term *behavioral* (as in the subtitle to this book) implies something more than observations of behavior and, in fact, was used as a "bridge" term in the days of rat psychology. This problem will be compounded when, of necessity, loyalty programs are discussed as current renditions of repeat purchasing loyalty models.

Proposed among the early writings was a model of multibrand loyalty, which would seem to be a contradiction in terms—but only if monogamy is viewed as the only permissible display of loyalty. These early articles attempted to explain the concept in psychological terms, arguing that brands could be viewed as substitutes if they fell within a latitude of acceptance on the basis of quality. Single-brand loyalty occurred when no competitive brand was in this region. At the time, this "new" loyalty was defined as the nonrandom purchase over time of one brand from a set of brands by a consumer using a deliberate evaluation process.[23] The authors of this view distinguished (1) true focal brand loyalty (loyalty to the particular brand of interest), (2) true multibrand loyalty to several brands including the focal brand, (3) nonloyal repeat purchasing of the focal brand, and (4) happenstance purchasing of the focal brand by loyal or nonloyal buyers of another brand. Happenstance purchasing includes any repeat-purchase sequence due to factors other than true psychological loyalty, such as unavailability of the consumer's favorite brand, surrogate purchasing, and temporary constraints. These patterns and others provided here are summarized Table 15.1.

Table 15.1 clearly shows the folly of inferring loyalty solely from repeat-purchase patterns. Given a pattern of repeat purchasing of a focal brand, true single-brand loyalty exists in only one of four situations. Alternatively, if a pattern of other-brand repeat purchasing seems to imply nonloyalty to the focal brand, this conclusion will be in error in two of four cases, one of which includes multibrand loyalty that includes the focal brand.

According to this perspective, one way to detect true single-brand loyalty is to examine the belief, affect, and intention (conative) structure of the consumer's orientation toward the focal brand. This requires that all three of these decision-making phases must be in place for true brand loyalty to exist. Put in other terms, three conditions must exist for true brand loyalty: (1) the brand information held by the consumer (i.e., the consumer's beliefs) must point to the focal brand as being superior to what is known of competitive offerings; (2) the consumer's degree of liking for the focal brand must be higher than that for other offerings, so that a clear affective preference exists for the focal brand; and (3) the consumer must intend to buy the focal brand, as opposed to the alternative brands, when a purchase decision arises.[24] This framework is, in effect, the predecision or prior information phase of Figure 15.1, which is reinforced over repeat-purchase cycles.

As noted in the first edition of this book, relatively little transpired after this perspective was published. A number of papers on various specifics of loyalty (e.g., switching costs) appeared, but the essential elements remained unchanged. An integrated model appeared in the mid-1990s.[25] The authors assumed, in accord with the prior literature, that loyalty requires consistency across the cognitive, affective, and conative dimensions of the consumer's focal brand orientation. They

Table 15.1

Multibrand Loyalty Categories

Repetitive purchase of	Psychological loyalty to			
	Focal brand	Multiple brands	Other brand	None
Focal brand	True loyalty	Multibrand loyal	Nonloyal repeater	Happenstance buyer
Other brand	Happenstance other brand buyer	Multibrand loyal	Other brand loyal	Happenstance buyer

proposed a notion of relative attitude, the degree to which the consumer's evaluation of one alternative brand dominates that of another. That is, it is extent of domination and not the absolute levels of the attitude scores that matters. An alternative's score can be very high, but have poor relative attitude if other brands' scores are also high. At the limit, all alternatives could have maximum scores (be ideal), in which case all are perfectly substitutable. This would describe one instance of low relative attitude and of multibrand loyalty. Single-brand loyalty emerges as one brand outdistances all others. High relative attitude could also exist for mediocre brands if the competitive brands were of universal low quality. This framework has been referenced, but does not achieve the goal of discussing loyalty without attitudinal considerations.

A DEFINITION OF LOYALTY

While prior frameworks were encouraging at the time, none provided a unitary definition without reliance on two or three staged components—namely, cognition, affect, and behavioral intention. This lack is not constraining, however, as the following discussion will continue to rely on these as precursor conditions to a more encompassing loyalty state. Other writers outside of the consumption arena have provided philosophical discourse, some dating back to Aristotle. In fact, one philosopher has said that "the great thinkers about morality have tended to avoid the subject of loyalty," thus suggesting that morality is somehow a parallel or, perhaps, orthogonal concept to loyalty. This same author refers to a well-cited tome by Royce, written in 1908 and reprinted regularly. Royce referred to loyalty as a "willing and practical and thoroughgoing devotion of a person to a cause."[26]

This historic definition does not serve the purpose intended here, most notably because it does not address a consumer's devotion to a product or service in the marketplace, which requires a modernized perspective acknowledging the strides made in the behavioral sciences. These advances would include the future promise of functional magnetic resonance imaging (fMRI) research, which is not sufficiently advanced as yet. Until another is available, this author will continue to rely on the unitary definition given in the first edition of this book: "*Customer loyalty* is a deeply held commitment to rebuy or repatronize a preferred product or service consistently in the future, *despite* situational influences and marketing efforts having the potential to cause switching behavior."[27] A consumer who fervently desires to rebuy a product or service and will have no other exemplifies this kind of loyalty. If the qualifier "against all odds and at all costs" were added, the definition would describe *ultimate* loyalty.

Note that no distinction is made between *proactive* loyalty and *situational* loyalty. In proactive loyalty, the consumer frequently and regularly rebuys the brand, settling for no other. In situational loyalty, a special situation (e.g., a social event) is needed to initiate consideration of the product category. Once primed, the consumer will have no other brand. Buying a favorite brand of soft drink, consumed regularly, constitutes proactive loyalty. Buying the same brand only for entertaining guests qualifies as situational loyalty. In either case, the consumer considers no alternative.

Why would consumers be so naive, unaware, or fervent that they seek out one—and only one—branded object or set of brands to fulfill their needs, especially when the present era of global competition seemingly allows consumers to move to better alternatives as soon as they materialize? Product improvements, refinements, and innovations are now accelerating to the point that new product introductions are most likely at record levels. In fact, authors have noted the decline or "erosion" of the loyal segments of companies' consumer bases.[28] What this means is that, for consumer to become and remain loyal, they must feel that a firm's products continue to offer the best choice. Moreover, they must naively shun communications from competitive firms and other innovators arguing that the loyalist's consumable is no longer the most efficient, the lowest priced, or the highest quality.

Although this level of loyalty may seem irrational, it remains true that consumers do exhibit loyalty, that firms with loyal customers benefit handsomely, and that those firms who can attain a loyal customer base will wish to do so. To put this consumer display of loyalty in perspective, an elaboration of the author's previous attempt in the first edition, shown in the third column of Figure 15.1, brings what is known of consumer loyalty up to date.

THE PHASES OF LOYALTY ELABORATED

As noted in the earlier sections of this chapter, the framework used here follows the cognition-affect-conation historical pattern, but differs in the sense that consumers can become "loyal" or "locked" at each loyalty phase. Specifically, consumers are thought to first become loyal in a cognitive sense, then later in an affective sense, still later in a conative sense, and finally in a behavioral sense, described as action-inertia.

Cognitive Loyalty

In this first loyalty phase, the brand attribute information available to the consumer suggests that one brand is preferable to its alternatives. This stage is referred to as *cognitive* loyalty or loyalty based on brand belief only. Cognition can be based on prior or vicarious knowledge and recent experience-based information. Loyalty at this phase is directed toward the brand because of this information (attribute performance levels). This consumer state, however, is of a very shallow nature. If the transaction is routine, so that satisfaction is not processed (e.g., trash pickup, provision of utilities), the depth of loyalty is no deeper than mere performance and all the performance-only models apply here (see Chapter 2). If satisfaction is processed, it becomes part of the consumer's experience and begins to take on affective overtones.

Affective Loyalty

At the second phase of loyalty development, a liking or attitude toward the brand develops based on cumulatively satisfying usage occasions. Commitment at this phase is referred to as *affective* loyalty and is encoded in the consumer's mind as cognition *and* affect (see Chapter 12 for the many levels of intensity of consumer affect). Whereas cognition is directly subject to counterargumentation, affect is not as easily dislodged. Here, the brand loyalty exhibited is directed at the degree of affect (liking) for the brand.[29] Like cognitive loyalty, however, this form of loyalty remains subject to switching, as evidenced by data showing that large percentages of brand defectors claim to have been previously satisfied with their brand, a phenomenon known as the "satisfaction trap."[30] Thus, it would be desirable if consumers were loyal at a deeper level of commitment.

Conative Loyalty

The next phase of loyalty development is the *conative* (behavioral intention) stage, as influenced by repeated episodes of positive affect toward the brand. Conation, by its definition, implies a brand-specific commitment to repurchase. Conative loyalty, then, is a loyalty state containing what at first appears to be the deeply held commitment to buy, noted in the definition of loyalty quoted above. However, this commitment is to one's intention to rebuy the brand and is more akin to motivation. In effect, the consumer desires to repurchase, but like any good intention, this desire may be anticipated but unrealized action. This loyalty stage may be solidified by factors that may not be conducive to long-term commitments such as promises, pledges, or vows (as in a marriage). In a sense, these bonds share some similarities with those in the cognitive stage but differ in terms of an additional level of *social* commitment that was not present at the earliest phase. This social bond is the distinguishing characteristic. The literature has not converged on this distinction, however.[31]

Action Loyalty

The mechanism by which intentions are converted to actions is referred to as "action control."[32] In the action control sequence, the motivated intention in the previous loyalty state is transformed into *readiness to act*. The action control paradigm proposes that this readiness is accompanied by an additional *desire to overcome obstacles* that might prevent the act. Action is seen as a necessary result of engaging both these states. If this engagement is repeated, an "action-inertia" develops, thereby facilitating repurchase.

The reader will note the correspondence between the two action control constructs, readiness to act and the overcoming of obstacles, and the loyalty definition presented earlier. Readiness to act is analogous to the "deeply held commitment to rebuy or repatronize a preferred product or service consistently in the future," while "overcoming obstacles" is analogous to rebuying "despite situational influences and marketing efforts having the potential to cause switching behavior." This latter notion of ignoring or deflecting suitors will be pursued in greater detail shortly.

Thus, completing the earlier cognitive-affective-conative frameworks with a fourth phase, action, brings the attitude-based loyalty model to the behavior of interest—the action state of inertial rebuying. Cognitive loyalty focuses on the brand's performance aspects, affective loyalty is directed toward the brand's likeableness, conative loyalty is expressed in the consumer's socially committed intention to rebuy the brand, and action loyalty is commitment to the action of rebuying.

Tests of the Phases

Are the Phases Distinct?

Since the publication of this phase-specific model, two bodies of supporting data have become available. The first exists as ad hoc tests showing that loyalty can be sustained at any of the four levels. The second addresses the model specifically, operationalizes the four stages, and tests for either a stage-by-stage correlational or partially sequential pattern of relations. Either set of data provides a starting point for later tests yet to come.

The numerous ad hoc tests result from directed efforts to address specific programs of research. This specific focus tends to support the four-phase framework and does not rule out other explanations for the simple reason that they are not entertained. Thus, readers will find repeat purchase patterns based on favorable performance (cognitive) variables, favorable attitude (affective) variables, favorable intention (conative) variables, and repeat purchasing. These perspectives are entrenched in their respective literatures and have been discussed in previous sections of this book. Sometimes two or more are entertained or contrasted; action-inertia is a frequent comparative model because of the ease with which these data are available.

Meta-analytic studies provide a useful beginning exposure to the nature of these approaches.[33] Here, the authors condense the observation of repeat purchasing into two overarching explanations. The first explanation is "well-practiced" behavior or habit, and the second explanation of "not well-learned" behaviors is the attitude-intention model—essentially the link between attitudinal loyalty and conative loyalty. The data on which these analyses are based show strong relations between past and future behavior and both behavior measures to attitude and intention. Attitude and intention are found to be correlated in the magnitude range of 0.5 and higher if extended models are used.

Other studies focus on individual stages of this chain of events, beginning with "automated cognitive processes" rather than being guided by "elaborate decision processes." This means simply that cognition logic repeats itself, as when a consumer expresses a convenience motivation: "I use the same bank because it is on my way to work."[34] In similar fashion, affect may repeat itself when a consumer says, "I just like it like that." Examples of this form of decision making are legion and can be found in the meta-analyses cited in the preceding paragraph as well as in studies that measure only affect influences. Even in what appear to be purely cognitively based repetitive behaviors, as in banking, affect can be found to dominate these types of decisions if that is the only phenomenon of interest in a given study.[35]

The initiation and emergence of conative loyalty has already been discussed in the previous section on intention. While the focus there was on the link between intention and behavior link, it becomes tedious to tease out the intention-specific motivations from studies that measure intention as part of a chain culminating in behavior (or intention as a proxy for behavior). Because of this difficulty, the reader is redirected to this earlier section. The last phase of the model, action loyalty, will also include loyalty sequences of repeat purchasing that are motivated by conative leanings. A common example of actions-by-intent is the phrase "I always play bridge on Saturday night" or "Saturday night is my bridge night." It does not matter that this card player likes the other players or always wins at bridge or that this activity has become a habit. What matters here are the intentions. An easy test of this proclivity is that the person could miss a bridge night and not have it impact the intention sentiment, which would subconsciously include missed events beyond these best intentions.

Lastly, other studies discuss inertial behavior, habituation, or nonconscious loyalty.[36] There are subtleties here that are difficult to surmount. How does "conscious" loyalty differ from nonconscious loyalty? Clarifying this distinction is the purpose of this chapter and more will be said on this later.

Are the Phases Sequential?

To date, the author is aware of five fairly recent tests of the cognitive-to-action loyalty framework.[37] In the first, SERVQUAL was used to measure cognitive loyalty, relative attitude was used to measure affective loyalty, and the traditional intention "will you" and "how often do you" measures were used for the final two stages. The test was cross-sectional and all relations were significant, the highest being affect-conation and the lowest conation-action. In the second two-article study, the authors' main focus was on loyalty stage measurement. Scale-items were constructed according to the model; what transpired were trans-stage scales tapping sustainers and vulnerabilities (to be discussed). No sequential testing was performed.

In the third study, four-item scales demonstrating high reliabilities were used to measure the four stages. A sequentially ordered path analysis was used to measure the best fit across all order-combinations of the four stages (twenty-four in all) across two e-product categories (books and air travel). Reports of the findings concluded that the best order was the hypothesized cognition-to-action sequence for both products. The measures used were reported in an appendix and are recommended. The fourth study, like the second, focused on measurement—in particular that of communal versus noncommunal programs. This study, also, contained no sequential test and further discussion appears in a following section on the necessity of a sense of community for the development of loyalty.

Lastly, the fifth study supports the findings of the other two that tested for sequentiality. Using measures similar to those used in the first sequential study, a stage-by-stage and overall test confirmed the hypothesis that the cognition-to-action chain operated as proposed and that the link between cognitive and affective loyalty was strongest while the link between conative and action loyalty was weakest—but significant nonetheless. Of interest is that moderator tests of the influence of demographic and strategic (e.g., recovery perceptions) variables showed effects in intuitively plausible directions. Until more data become available, these early measurement and model tests are encouraging in suggesting that consumers demonstrate a hierarchical orientation to the development of the four loyalty stages.

As noted, little additional work has appeared to corroborate or refute this extended perspective. This is unfortunate because the weaknesses inherent in these four loyalty phases require specification if marketers are to protect their loyal customer base. Two different sources of such weakness are discussed next.

OBSTACLES TO LOYALTY

Consumer Idiosyncrasies

It should be acknowledged that some aspects of consumer consumption are antithetical to loyalty. For example, variety seeking has been frequently cited as a trait that will not permit loyalty to develop until there is no variety to sample. This will be particularly true at the cognitive level and even at the conative level. Until the variety-seeking consumer reaches the inertial action stage, the lure of new experience will be too tempting to ignore. Many product and service providers, such as dining establishments, fall into this pattern, finding that even their regular clientele will try new and different alternatives. It follows that the number of available alternatives and knowledge of those alternatives are both instrumental in fostering the consumer's tendency to seek variety.[38]

For some, variety seeking is related to demographics, for others it is an acquired disposition related to, for example, price, and for others it is a function of the industry, as in the availability of alternatives noted in the preceding example. For simplicity, just a few demographics are noted. Youthfulness, for example, is negatively related to stability of preference, perhaps due to the early desire for experiential stimuli. This phenomenon will be correlated with generational differences. In contrast, income and education tend to enhance stability. Beyond these basic relations, factors such as the desire for technical versus functional features or hedonic versus utilitarian value will dominate such decisions, which tend to be idiosyncratic across contexts.[39]

Other reasons for apparent consumer disloyalty include multibrand loyalty, withdrawal from the product category (e.g., smoking cessation), and changes in need. This last phenomenon can occur in two different forms. In the first, as the consumer matures, new needs supplant the old. For example, the toys and games that children favor will change as they grow up; loyalty to sports bubblegum cards cannot be expected to endure. A second form of need-based disloyalty may occur when a competitive innovation fulfills the consumer's needs more efficiently, or so it may seem.[40] While it is also possible that the consumer's needs have changed, so that the competitive offering is now the logical choice, competitors' messages frequently tout the ability of their product to fulfill needs better. This shift brings discussion to another obstacle to loyalty, the role of switching incentives.

Switching Incentives

Previously, it was suggested that true loyalty is, in some sense, irrational. Competitors take advantage of this position, using persuasive messages and incentives to lure consumers away from their preferred offering. These verbal and physical enticements are the obstacles that brand or service loyalists must overcome. As may be evident at this point, the easiest form of loyalty to break down is the cognitive variety; the most difficult is the action state. Thus, the cognitive-to-action loyalty sequence brings the analysis closer and closer to the emergence of full loyalty, but still fails to satisfy the definition of ultimate loyalty as each phase is subject to attack, as follows.

Cognitive Loyalty

The four-stage loyalty model reveals different vulnerabilities depending on the nature of the consumer's commitment. These are summarized in Table 15.2. It has been noted that cognitive loyalty is based on purely functional characteristics, primarily costs and benefits, and is thus subject to functional shortfalls. For example, in the area of services, it has been shown that deteriorating service, apart from dissatisfaction, is a strong inducement to switch. Price, in particular, is a powerful competitive weapon for commonly purchased items. Thus, cognitive loyalty is actually "phantom loyalty," as it is directed to benefits and costs and not to the brand. Costs (including prices), in particular, are a major component of brand switching at the cognitive level.[41]

Here it is necessary to address the commonly observed breakdown in the satisfaction-loyalty link. Specifically, the low correlations between these two concepts can be explained by two occurrences. The first is apparent disloyalty (switching) in the face of satisfaction and the second is apparent loyalty when encountering very low levels of satisfaction (dissatisfaction). The first is easily explained by cognitive loyalty, which is overcome by attractive alternatives, as noted in the preceding discussion. The second is also easily explained by a phenomenon that has come to be known as "cognitive lock-in."[42]

Lock-in can be achieved via many channels. The most obvious is through a supply monopoly such as toner cartridges for printers, blades for razors, and video game cartridges. At the interpersonal level, consumers have been known to become loyal to particular provider employees such as salespeople (to be discussed).[43] And it is also known that normal consumer failings such as the sunk cost phenomenon and ordinary consumer learning and familiarity (exchange-specific assets) are strong motivators to stay with an otherwise dissatisfying provider. Working in parallel with these influences is simple fear of what a new, unknown provider will bring. These are all reasons for firms to "ensnare" consumers so that they are held through "captive loyalty."[44]

Table 15.2

Loyalty Phases With Corresponding Vulnerabilities

Stage	Identifying marker	Vulnerabilities
Cognitive	Loyalty to "information" such as price, features, etc.	Actual or imagined better competitive features/price via communication (e.g., advertising) and vicarious or personal experience. Deterioration in own-brand features/price. Variety-seeking and voluntary trial.
Affective	Loyalty to a liking: "I buy it because I like it"	Cognitively induced *dis*satisfaction. Enhanced liking for competitive brands perhaps conveyed through imagery and association. Variety-seeking and voluntary trial. Deteriorating performance.
Conative	Loyalty to an intention: "I'm committed to buying it"	Persuasive counterargument competitive messages. Induced trial (e.g., coupons, sampling, point-of-purchase promotions). Deteriorating performance.
Action	Loyalty to action "inertia," coupled with the overcoming of obstacles	Induced unavailability (e.g., stocklifts). Increased obstacles generally. Deteriorating performance.

Source: Richard L. Oliver, "Whence Consumer Loyalty," *Journal of Marketing* 63 (Special Issue 1999): 36, with permission from *Journal of Marketing*.

Affective Loyalty

Barring lock-in, affective loyalty can become susceptible to dissatisfaction with the cognitive elements of a purchase, thereby inducing attitudinal shifts. A concurrent effect of dissatisfaction observed in the literature is the increased attractiveness of alternative suppliers. Thus, affective loyalty is first subject to the deterioration of its cognitive base, causing dissatisfaction, which has deleterious effects on the strength of the consumer's attitude toward a brand and, hence, on affective loyalty. It is also possible for competitive communications to use imagery and association to enhance the image of alternative brands while degrading the image of the present brand.[45]

One unmistakable hallmark of a failing of attitudinal loyalty is the consumer's emotional display beyond the normal sadness or anger resulting from performance shortfalls, particularly in services. Stayers have strong, warm emotional bonds with the brand, while switchers express negative affects ranging from externally directed anger to internally directed guilt. And, of course, all dissatisfaction-related emotional and behavioral responses are found. Were it not for lock-in, switching is one of the most probable outcomes of attitudinal failings.[46]

Conative Loyalty

Although conative loyalty brings the consumer to a stronger level of loyalty commitment, it has its vulnerabilities nonetheless. Although a consumer at this phase can weather some small number of dissatisfactory episodes, the consumer's motivation to remain committed can be "worn down" by barrages of competitive messages and social failings, particularly if they enhance the perceived severity of experienced dissatisfaction, a phenomenon called "prejudice." As discussed in Chapter 1, the automotive industry and other fashion-driven enterprises are kept alive by the "organized creation of dissatisfaction" by marketing communications and social pressure from the consumer's environment. In fact, studies have shown that social norms vastly dominated satisfaction (or dissatisfaction) in the prediction of switching intentions.[47] Additionally, competitive product trial, via samples, coupons, or point-of-purchase promotions, may be particularly effective here as the consumer has only committed to the brand, but has not committed to avoiding trial of new offerings. Thus, the conatively loyal consumer has not developed the resolve to intentionally avoid consideration of competitive brands. And this avoidance is precisely what "vows" are intended to do.

At this juncture and perhaps before action loyalty manifests itself, the firm has achieved *product superiority*. Here, the firm has engendered enhanced liking—even an established preference—for its brand because of quality (information) and continued ability to satisfy. Additionally, the consumer is committed to its repurchase in the future. But the consumer has not reached the state of resistance, resilience, and the overcoming of obstacles and adversity necessary for ultimate loyalty to emerge. This is especially true in today's economy because of the plethora of seemingly superior alternatives that invade the consumer's senses.

Action Loyalty and the Beginning of Fortitude

When reaching the action phase of brand attachment, however, the consumer has both generated the focused desire to rebuy a brand and only that brand and has also acquired the skills necessary to overcome threats and obstacles to this quest. This consumer would be expected to routinely "tune out" competitive messages, to engage in effortful search for the favored brand, and to possibly even shun the trial of competitive brands. Marketers with action-loyal segments need not expend great sums on retention as, theoretically, their consumers would be governed by inertial repurchasing. Aside from deteriorating performance, a potential switching inducer at all stages, only insurmountable unavailability would cause this consumer to try another brand.

With the emergence of the action phase, it appears that the formula for loyalty has reached its ultimate end; later this state will be referred to as *consumer fortitude*. The action-loyal consumer has a deep commitment to repurchase, so much so that habitual, routine behavior may be guiding itself in the common requirements of everyday life. But everyday habituation is not the loyalty of interest to the firm. Rather, the marketer's quest is for a version of loyalty fitting the description of devotion. The state of consumer fortitude is achieved when the consumer fervently desires the consumable in a prohibitive, exclusive relationship. This should be a natural occurrence experienced by the consumer and not one created by the marketer.

However, it is the province of the competition to gain the consumer's attention to its communications. One major tactic by which this is accomplished, common in all loyalty phases, is the creation of dissatisfaction with the current brand (or firm, or the firm's loyalty program), discussed shortly. In fact, the role of satisfaction in loyalty formation and defection can now be more fully specified. In the same way that satisfaction is a building block for loyalty, primarily at the affective loyalty stage, dissatisfaction is its downfall—for the competition can strike through the creation or facilitation of dissatisfaction at every stage of loyalty, even that of action-inertia.

One might ask why emphasis has now shifted to the creation of dissatisfaction as a competitive weapon if the role of satisfaction is just one of many in the development of loyalty. An answer to this question relates to the well-known disproportional influence of negative information. As noted previously, research on disconfirmation-based satisfaction models shows that a unit of negative disconfirmation has a much greater effect on dissatisfaction than a unit of positive disconfirmation has on satisfaction (see Chapter 3). This is the bane of satisfaction-based loyalty; the satisfaction concept itself, in the form of competitively induced dissatisfaction creation, can be a switching incentive. There must be more to the attainment of ultimate loyalty; the reader is asked to bear with the following discussion until the topic of community is introduced.

INTERPERSONAL LOYALTY: ADDITIONAL EFFECTS IN SERVICES

Historically, loyalty effects have been discussed largely in the context of product marketing. With the possible exceptions of fan clubs, considered by many to be more faddish than fashion, and politics, where the politician of the moment tends to be in vogue, industries having a large service component were still thought to be governed by loyalty to the core deliverable. Thus, consumers' loyalty to Starbucks was thought to be loyalty to its product and business model and not to its baristas (service providers). With recognition of the strong interpersonal component of services, however, loyalty now takes on additional dimensions of a much more binding and even overriding nature. Little research had been available in this new area, but this oversight has reversed itself with a number of papers beyond those on the generic topic of service delivery, primarily with regard to service contact personnel.[48]

In particular, various social-bonding dimensions and their subcomponents have been identified. Beginning with distinctions among various relationships that consumers may have with company contacts and between the four stages of loyalty presented here and elsewhere (the cognition to action-behavior sequence), a number of dimensions emerged from the relationship literature in psychology.[49] These include, but are not limited to, accommodation, altruism, advocacy, identification, interdependence, fidelity, and sacrifice. Other insights and dimensions will become evident when the current discussion turns to the communal aspects of loyalty later in the chapter. Finally, there are normative considerations such as expectations of trust and fair play (see Chapter 8). As would be expected, all these factors serve to cement the loyalty relationship far more substantially than could be expected with product marketing.

LOYALTY PATTERNS

Is there a universally loyal consumer? The answer in the first edition of this book was "no" and the answer in this edition is still "no." Reviews of research at the time showed that loyalty patterns can be found that appear to represent loyal consumers on a product- or service-category-specific basis; moreover, specific brands and stores can be shown to have loyal segments.[50] Additionally, studies of consumer decision-making styles found clusters of consumers who claimed to "find a good brand and stick with it." Unfortunately, these same studies did not find (or did not attempt to find) the product categories that are purchased repeatedly over time. Thus, in the main, the perspective taken here is that consumers are not intrinsically loyal; some, in fact, eschew loyalty.[51] The reason for this conclusion is that studies investigating the correlates of loyalty generally find that loyal or repeat-buying segments do so because of price, service, or quality. In other words, they are loyal to the relative benefits of the product in a cognitive loyalty sense. As noted in the preceding discussion, this is the weakest of the loyalty modes, as its strengths are also its vulnerabilities.

In today's economy, it is more fruitful to take another direction by identifying those consumers who show idiosyncratic loyalties. The word *idiosyncratic* suggests that groups of individuals, regardless of their predispositions (demographic or psychographic), display loyalty, even fervent loyalty, toward particular consumables at a given phase in their lives. The most the marketer can hope for is "time-horizon" loyalty. Because the product-specific tenure of both brand managers and consumers has a finite duration, loyal segments can be found in just about any product or service category at a given span of time. This harks back to the "logic" of loyalty mentioned earlier. Why should one become loyal to everyday consumables? The answer awaits further discussion. For now, what loyalty categories are "out there?"

Only brief mention will be made of the ubiquitous two-by-two frameworks (although a very important example will be proposed shortly). For example, given two categories of satisfaction (satisfied and dissatisfied) and two of loyalty (loyal and disloyal), the greatest level of "true" loyalty should exist for the satisfied and loyal group and the lowest for the dissatisfied and disloyal group. A variation of this framework was shown in the prior edition where the off-cells were referred to as "spurious" (satisfied and disloyal) and "latent" (dissatisfied and loyal). The reader will immediately recognize these as falling into the "satisfaction trap" and "voice" groups. Illustrated next are some alternative cell-based typologies of greater complexity and insight.

THREE LOYALTY CATEGORIZATIONS

Of the many loyalty typologies that have been proposed, three are of interest—two in the consumer domain and one in the professional business area.[52] The first uses familiar terms that go beyond the "promoter/detractor" scale in the prior chapter. Here, truly loyal consumers are referred to as "apostles" in the biblical sense. They are emotionally committed, have bonds to the consumable "beyond satisfaction," and remain with the provider despite many available and attractive alternatives. Next are "satisfied loyalists" who are "reasonably satisfied," have moderately high commitment, and have no reason to switch to other available competitors. In the middle of the scheme are "purchased loyalists," who have been "bought with reward incentives. These are program (and maybe programmatic) buyers who see value in the program and are just moderately committed to the consumable and the firm, which typically has many competitors offering similar goods or service. Further down the continuum are the "detached loyalists," who recognize the high switching costs associated with moving to a competitor that may be qualitatively different (e.g., cable versus satellite TV). Their satisfaction is low and may be of the nature of a tolerant state. Last, there are "prisoners" or captive consumers who must patronize because of a total lack of alternatives. These are consumers of monopolistic public utilities, local governments, and purchasing environments restricted by social strata or geography. To refer to these alienated consumers as resentful would be an understatement, and the issue of satisfaction is moot.

In the second (and third) typology, the authors have proposed ladders to give the nature of loyalty an upward trajectory. The first, using a consumer approach, is based on three dimensions of experience, namely the degree of differentiated offerings, relationship bonding, and the totality of customer provision (this framework relies on this author's "Whence" paper among others). When each of these dimensions is divided into high and low categories and combined with three "characterization levels," the resulting twenty-four categories are given monikers ranging from "platinum loyalty" to "global disloyalty." The framework is richer than can be portrayed here, but does suffer from some nonlinearities in its progression. For example, there are only three "disloyalties" among the twenty-four loyalty rungs. Readers will recognize many "program levels" embedded in the many descriptive phrases, including the "diamond," "platinum," and "gold" levels of play used by a well-known casino operator.

In a business-to-business study, using electronic business equipment and software, the author proposes a ladder based on a Benefits-of-Customer-Retention scale. The scale does not expand to negative switching states as it is based only on positive behaviors of business customers. These include resistance to competition, resistance to adverse commentary, proneness to positive recommendation, favorable repurchase likelihood, stockout tolerance, and enthusiasm. When aligned on an eight-rung ladder, the positions range from an unwillingness to switch to a "superior" competitor at the low end to enthusiastic advocacy at the upper end.

The point of these three illustrations is that any number of variables can be combined to display consumer segments with differentiated orientations to the firm's offering. It is up to individual vendors to correctly identify the relevant variables, cluster their constituents on these variables, and compose the dimensional profiles. The next step, of course, is to formulate strategy to stabilize deterioration, assuage dissent, encourage satisfaction and loyalty, and solidify those segments most profitable to the firm.

LOYALTY PROGRAMS

It is now an opportune time to discuss the emergence of loyalty programs that have sprung up since the time of the Green Stamps promotion described in the introduction to this chapter. While there will always be those who refer to American Airlines AAdvantage program in 1983 as seminal, precedents included independent firms administering and redeeming stamps for retailers and United Airlines' offer of discount coupons for future flights in 1979. These programs proliferated and became worldwide and more fluid in indentifying what the coupons could be redeemed for. One of these programs, Australia's Fly Buys (begun in 1994), allowed a plethora of retail purchasing (constituting approximately 20 percent of the continent's retail spending) to be converted to air travel and accommodations.[53] This latter program is heavily researched.

The main question has not changed since the beginning of purchasing studies, when researchers first thought that repeat purchasing was an indicator of loyalty: Is repetitive purchasing linked to the mind-state of "true loyalty" Brain imaging or fMRI is of little help here. While it is true that science has identified the reward centers and pathways in the brain, loyalty, as a devotional phenomenon, may not be rewarding in the classical sense. In fact, one entire line of thought regarding loyalty in the definition provided in this chapter is the existence of loyalty *despite* dissatisfying experience or frustration.

Not broached here are individual (genetic) predispositions to loyalty as it is unlikely that they exist for the consumables in everyday life. Nor are conditioning events occurring in infancy or childhood, such as might exist for beliefs of faith, entertained. Rather the focus is on adolescence and beyond, as these are the times that demarcate the "consumer years." The question that must be answered, then, is that of mechanical incentives or rewards and loyalty apart from habit formation, but including inertial states that tend to persist until their exuberance wears off. In this sense, loyalty can exist, go into remission, reassert itself, and decay. It is not clear that loyalty programs are quite so "malleable."

The evidence for the success of such programs can be assessed along the progression stages in Figure 15.1. Do purchasing rewards pass the test of cognitive through action sequencing with the attendant behavioral building blocks? The answer given here is "no." Can reward programs be made to provide sufficient structure so that the consumer can become loyal to the program and to the behavior of pursuing its rewards? Possibly "yes." The interesting aspect of this analysis is that insights may be gained into the pursuit of the goal of true consumer loyalty.

Philosophy and Evidence

Two bodies of evidence are available attesting to the success of loyalty programs. The first is purely strategic from a profit standpoint; the second addresses the quest here, namely the ability of programs to build cadres of loyal buyers. The first is not the central focus of this book and will be only tangentially discussed. However, it cannot be denied that "devotional" loyalty (not loyalty programs) and profit are related—and will be later in this chapter. Perhaps it is fitting to suggest here, the last chapter in this book, that the greater goal of understanding behavior and its repetition is to benefit the firm. It is possible that a large component of a firm's customer base remains loyal, but unprofitable, and various methods of profitability analysis have been proposed to identify the size of this component.[54]

So the intent here is to explore the correctness inherent in loyalty programs from a behavioral standpoint. As noted, the success of the program from a profit standpoint is of secondary importance: "correct" programs are not universally profitable and "incorrect" programs are not necessarily unsuccessful. Exceptions to both cases persist, however, because profitable programs are easily defended, maintained, and "tweaked to perfection," while unprofitable programs are abandoned without the benefit of further diagnosis. Interestingly, one nonbehavioral goal thought to provide profit to the firm is the capturing of customers' personal information for the purposes of data dredging or market research.[55]

Cognition in Loyalty Programs

Most rewards programs are based on lock-in principles. Consumers are given participation points that accumulate over time. Programs that give immediate rewards, such as discounts, without long-term implications merely condition the consumer to expect future discounts; not having one becomes a penalty, as research by this author and others has shown.[56] Moreover, the reward must have value in and of itself or must add value to the basic consumable. Kewpie doll or carnival prizes are too fleeting a reward to the consumer to have lasting value, excepting that momentary "bragging rights" seem to have universal appeal. In contrast, higher-order values (e.g., attainment) do have lasting value in terms of either self-esteem or social approval. Thus, card levels (silver, gold, platinum) or club achievement identification (million-dollar, million-mile) will work. Tangibles (upgrades, free flights) work for the moment and are good future "carrots."[57] But few of these have lasting implications for the firm.

Loyalty to the prize (actually its receipt) simply does not engender loyalty to the firm. The firm becomes an instrument, an enabler. Sports is a good example of the many forms of "loyalty to," and an industry that is now in the early throes of programmatic "loyalty." What is the object of the loyalty target? Is it the sport itself, the statistics (including wins and losses), team identity, local spirit, the crowd of fans, becoming one of the fans, the camaraderie (which introduces the next loyalty requirement, to be discussed), or the new incentives that teams are deploying, including preferred seating, season ticket holding, game jerseys and balls, and free hot dogs? And in the entertainment venue of music, one of the most addictive pursuits due to its biological origin. Is it the melody, the artists, the high-ticket sales, the "being there" (e.g., at Woodstock), the free or discounted CDs, or, again, the fans?

If sports and music need some level of minimal incentives, tangible or not, what of truly mundane consumables such as air travel? And what of ordinary everyday purchasing where credit card programs dominate? These programs provide simple rewards similar to Green Stamps but without the need to physically fill books. The essential value of a reward is similar to all valued consumables. As promotions, they should take on the characteristic of a desired, wanted, or needed item and therefore become subject to all of the satisfaction criteria set forth here and elsewhere. But simple wanting satisfies only at the cognitive level. Loyalty "icons" must give pleasure in anticipation, in receipt, in use, in ownership, and in further or future desire. If rewards are viewed as a collection or accumulation, this in and of itself must be of value, satisfying value.

Affect in Loyalty Programs

This discussion would be incomplete if the next level of affective loyalty were omitted. Does a program enhance the liking that the consumer expresses toward its parent firm? This is where loyalty programs begin to falter. Unless the program rewards can transfer the pleasure of the reward to the pleasure of consuming the sponsor's deliverable, the program becomes disjoint and available to any competitor or substitution. Money is money; one program's rewards are easily imitated. What if the program becomes the product? When consumers begin buying Crackerjack for the prizes and discard the product, the product becomes the packaging, of little essential value. People begin taking airline flights for the next flight they will obtain or to complete the requirements for a free flight of even greater value or to stave off expiration. "To complete my collection" becomes the mantra for repetitive consumption. What becomes of satisfaction? Unfortunately, the data speaking to engendering true loyalty via satisfaction are dismal indeed.[58]

The next two phases, conative and action loyalty, remain as goals, but are easily hidden or mimicked. In some sense then, the loyalty progression in Figure 15.1 bifurcates at affective loyalty into a true psychological progression where the stages are in synchrony or into a false appearance of loyalty where consumers go through the motions of being committed to something about the program and then repeat-purchase. At this point, without a psychologically behavioral measurement metric, the mechanical and psychological loyalty patterns appear identical. The firm cannot know which is which until true loyalty is allowed to emerge. This can be observed with any of a variety of tests such as termination of the program, comparison to a control market without the program, or lack of defections to competitors with equal or better programs.

The data are universally discouraging with a small number of exceptions. What is clear is that programs increase purchasing in the classic carrot-and-stick fashion. What is not clear is whether revenues net of the additional costs are profitable, and these data are not available except anecdotally. It is also clear that heavy current purchasers are most favorably affected and benefit at the cost of less frequent purchasers (the free-rider phenomenon).[59] And, strategically, programs are necessitated, and costs incurred, when faced with close competitors with programs. Results of those firms that "tough it out" are not known.

Excess Returns to Loyalty

Yet another potential benefit may accrue if firms focus on the notion of excess returns to loyalty. This results from an analysis of repeat purchase observations and market share. Picture a graph with share on the horizontal axis and repeat purchase likelihood on the vertical and focus on the upper right (100 percent and 1.0) and lower left (0 percent and 0) corners. A forty-five-degree line would connect these two extremes. Logic dictates that firms with zero share have no repeat purchasers and those with 100 percent share contain all of repeat purchasing, by definition. Firms between these extremes fall near the line with a margin of error. Excess returns occur when the repeat purchase rate is above that expected by chance, such as would be seen for niche brands (e.g., Ben & Jerry's) and for superloyal brands (e.g., Harley-Davidson in the U.S. cruiser market).[60] Excepting very large share brands, brands with share increases attributed to increases in distribution, and online equivalents of offline brands, loyalty programs have little additional effect beyond the share effect dictated by this well-known norm. Incidentally, by this same benchmark as well as others, the loyalty of brands generally appears to be mature, slightly declining, or "eroding."[61]

Given this normative explanation, the only behavioral rationale for "excess success" is the notion of an increase in the consumer's value proposition. Some consumers are reported as citing greater value for the money with loyalty programs. This, perhaps, is true if by value they mean more product, benefits, and so on. Others see the ancillary psychic benefits of knowing that part of their additional purchasing dollar is going to a charity, for example.[62] In a sense, this is added value, but as at least one pundit has said, "why not just donate directly?" In short, this author sees no true loyalty-enhancing value to loyalty programs despite the fact that they make great strategic sense under the right circumstances. What has not been addressed is the additional *social* value of a program *if* it is compatible with a consumption community, discussed next.

NEW PERSPECTIVES ON LOYALTY GENERATION AND MAINTENANCE: CONSUMPTION COMMUNITIES

Three new perspectives on customer loyalty are proposed, stated as questions: (1) Can the consumer elect to be self-isolated from alternative consumable overtures so that competitive information is blocked or screened? (2) Can the consumer be socially integrated in an exclusive environment that envelops and directs the consumer's choices in a satisfying way? (3) Can the consumer effect a self-identity that corresponds only to selected brands *and* the community in the manner of ecovillage residents adopting a unique lifestyle, largely centered around a "green" theme? These issues speak to the "community" of loyalty, singular in the case of self-isolation, communal in the case of the village, and both in the case of a preclusive lifestyle.

Dimensions of the Framework

Table 15.3, admittedly in 2×2 format, illustrates the dimensions on which these new issues are based. The vertical dimension reflects the degree of "individual fortitude," or the degree to which the consumer fights off competitive overtures based on allegiance to the brand and not on marketer-generated information. Despite the artificial break in this continuum into high and low categories, loyalty commitment develops with the advancement of stages in the Figure 15.1 model. At the lowest levels of fortitude, the consumer has only brand-related information. At the deepest levels of fortitude, the consumer has developed both the action inertia discussed previously and also a fierce defense against competitive encroachment that approaches "blind faith."

The horizontal dimension of Table 15.3 illustrates low and high phases of community and social support.[63] Here, the community provides the impetus to remain loyal either because it is enticing in a passive sense or because it proactively promotes loyalty. This dimension is crossed with that of individual fortitude so that the high-high cell contains the apex of loyalty and the low-low cell the weakest case of more vulnerable "loyalty," basic product superiority.

Product superiority, the weakest form of loyalty in this new framework, has already been discussed in cognitive, affective, conative, and action terms. This reflects the traditional view of loyalty as resulting from high quality and/or product superiority, both of which are believed to generate a strong sense of brand-directed preference. At some point in the cognitive-affective-conative-action chain, consumers will cross the threshold from low consumer fortitude to high, based largely on their degree of immunization against competition. The perspective taken here, however, provides further conceptual content in the high-fortitude (and low–social support) cell. In addition to the consumers' desire to rebuy based on superiority, this framework suggests that they will also wish to rebuy based on determination or "determined self-isolation"; that is, the consumer desires an exclusive relation with the brand and does not wish to be courted by other suitors.

The low-fortitude, high–social support cell, labeled "village envelopment," is analogous to the popular concept of "it takes a village." Here, the consumer is sheltered from outside

Table 15.3

Four Loyalty Strategies

		Community/social support	
		Low	High
Individual fortitude	Low	Product superiority	Village envelopment
	High	Determined self-isolation	Immersed self-identity

Source: Richard L. Oliver, "Whence Consumer Loyalty," *Journal of Marketing* (American Marketing Association), Special Issue 1999: 38. Reprinted with permission.

influences, nurtured in the use of selected and protected brands, and provided integrated and routinely updated consumption systems. Although discussed in greater detail later, the common computer platform and networking environment supported by most businesses is an example of this concept. The distinguishing feature here is that the consumer is a passive acceptor of the brand environment.

Lastly, the "immersed self-identity" cell contains the combined influences of fortitude and social support. Here, consumers intentionally target (or are targeted by) the social environment because it is consistent with and supports their self-concept. In effect, the consumers immerse their self-identity in the social system of which the brand is a part. This is a synergistic, self-sustaining situation. Consumers fervently desire the product or service association, affiliate with the social setting knowing that it will be supportive of this association, and, at the limiting extreme, are rewarded by the social system for their patronage. Religious institutions are good exemplars of this situation, although other secular social settings, such as fan clubs and alumni organizations, are equally illustrative.

It should be noted that the defining characteristics of these new perspectives are not directly under the control of management, but can be facilitated by it. Transcending the cognitive-affective-conative-action sequence, they tap into the socioemotional side of loyal consumption and closely access its "meaning," as discussed next. Recall that the low-low cell has been previously discussed as cognitive-affective-conative-action loyalty.

Self-Isolation as a Sustainer of Loyalty

Crossing the threshold from a belief in product superiority to brand-directed determinism and personal fortitude is a somewhat nebulous process. The transitioning mechanism is not well understood, even for areas of life in which determinism is frequently observed (e.g., romance, religion, politics). One potential threshold transition phase is attachment. Attachment is something more than satisfaction as it requires states of satisfaction reinforcements over time until the "glue is set." This is an apt description because glue, being a chemical/mechanical adhesive, has resilience until the breaking strength is breeched. Brand attachments, particularly those of "human brands," are not necessarily monogamous, can withstand bouts of dissatisfaction, and display commitment without being "ultimate."[64] Still, this consumer may very likely be immune from competitive overtures, is unlikely to be swayed from determined repurchasing, may defend the brand fiercely, and most probably promotes the brand to others.

At this point, when consumers voluntarily remove themselves from competitive overtures, effectively tuning out persuasive arguments to switch, they may be approaching or have achieved a state not unlike the concept of love. Love has many manifestations, but in the present context the variant of interest is the love of consumables, referred to in a study cited in the previous paragraph as "passion."[65] In the context of consumption, the sensual component of the phenomenon can be put aside in order to concentrate on two other aspects: adoration or focused attention, and unfailing commitment.

Adoration

It is an aspect of "love" that alternatives to the love object are not processed. In fact, it has been reported that there is "no better predictor of relationship failure than high attentiveness to alternatives." In marketing, this same phenomenon has been observed in studies, for example, in the context of channel relationships and automobile selection. Other insights from the relationship literature include the observations that partners find their relationship better in an idealistic sense than comparable others, that they perceive the outcomes they currently receive as better than they could obtain elsewhere, and that the alternatives to the present situation, even when it is less than ideal, are even less desirable.[66]

For marketers of products, especially those marketing commodities as opposed to, say, major durables, this love aspect of loyalty may be elusive. The more common the item and the more likely that replacements are *exact* duplicates of the original, the less likely loyalty is to emerge for there is no unique value proposition. For consumables falling between commodity status and those that "love back," it may be that simple brand identification may serve some lesser but important function in a loyalty response. This aspect of loyalty would suggest that consumers might derive some psychic "romance" (as opposed to love) from identification with the brand. The symbolism of the corporate logo should imply to others a certain uniqueness possessed by the consumer and not by others. For some consumers, this identity is discretionary, such as when they wear team-specific sports-related attire. For others, the identity is meant for all to see at all times. The ultimate display is the tattoo—a timeless symbol of identification.[67]

Unfailing Commitment

Discussions of commitment can be found in many areas of study where individuals form attachments. For example, commitment is the most common dependent variable used in buyer-seller relationship studies (trust being a close second).[68] Generally, commitment is an implicit or explicit pledge of relational continuity. In a sense, it transcends even conative loyalty and action loyalty as it exists at a conscious level and is a goal in itself. Beyond the desire of reacquiring a preferred—even coveted—object, a consumer can also desire to be committed to that object. As discussed previously, conative commitment emerges from a prior liking, whereas love-generated commitment results from a true affection (as opposed to the attitude form of affect) for the product or service. This latter type of commitment is adoration- or devotion-based and maintained, in part, to stave off the sense of loss one experiences when loved ones are missed.

At this point, discussion has considered only an individual in isolation committed to a brand and, in effect, becoming a more determined naive loyalist. This single consumer, acting alone, derives immense "love" and psychic income from the cherished brand. Another consumer may be an aimless wanderer having no brand preference and engaging in happenstance consumption. What would happen if this second consumer chances on a social environment with built-in preferences? Might this consumer's gaze be directed toward brands the collective finds satisfying? And, if so, what effect will this have?

The Social Organization: The Village

In its pure form, the village is a social alliance whereby each consumer's primary motivation to become loyal is to be one with the group and the primary motivation of the group overseers is to please their constituency. In this situation, the consumer becomes a willing participant in the group because of the attention provided by its members. In the limiting case, the product or service is not the consumable. Rather, it is the camaraderie provided by the social organization. Good examples of this are book clubs, car clubs, bridge clubs, collectors' clubs, dance clubs, fan clubs, and Internet communities of all varieties.[69]

This concept goes by many names in its various literatures, but is perhaps best exemplified as the aforementioned "consumption community," based on the widely observed notion that individuals feel a sense of community when they share the same consumption behaviors. More to the point, when they espouse and own the same brand, these groupings are known as "brand communities."[70] The previous club examples are somewhat weaker forms of the social collective envisioned here as they largely assume only that the mere knowledge of shared consumption is sufficient to generate a consumption community. And at perhaps the weakest extreme is the notion of a "third place" (after home and job) whereby like-minded consumers congregate, sharing life stories, including consumption, as typified by the corner bar.[71] Thus, it appears that the social dimension of the proposed framework, much like the fortitude dimension, is a continuum and that some of the examples given drift to either the weaker or stronger side.

Implicit in the concept of the consumption community, and leaning to the stronger side, is that it encompasses both a sense of belongingness and what is referred to as "communality."[72] Communality, as distinguished from several other close relatives, is described as resembling a kinship, one marked by nonessential conversation, disclosure, and helping behavior. Thus, in the social consumption village, the consumer submits to the judgment and recommendations of the group collective voluntarily and willingly. This subjugation is performed in order to reap the rewards of membership and the friendships and protectiveness of the collective. Other descriptors used in the various papers cited include the following, all of which are shared: acceptance, belonging, consciousness, emotional connections, experiences, goals, identification, mutual influence, involvement, knowledge (beliefs), responsibility, rituals, traditions, and values. All these concepts are useful in the construction of a brand connectedness or community survey; brief examples will be given shortly.

Examples in the consumer environment are legion. Residential communities for the elderly are exemplars, as are military posts (e.g., the commissary). In the former case, many consumption activities, such as tours to locations of interest, are preselected for residents. Other examples include educational facilities (e.g., boarding and parochial schools), the fraternity and sorority system, medical facilities, managerial services that coordinate office environments, scouting, and cooperatives of all varieties. Producers with unique product lines requiring proprietary accessories (Apple Computer), buying clubs (Sam's), and goal-oriented programs (Weight Watchers) are other examples. In all manifestations of the consumption community, the loyalty exhibited stems from two primary sources, brand exposure and repetition, and the apparent endorsement by the collective.

In the absence of a contained environment, marketers can approximate this concept with the notion of "family." Consumers everywhere can be contacted with literature referring to buyers of like products as "family." GM's Saturn division used this concept when it had a first-year "reunion" and dealers have been hosting annual events ever since. Harley-Davidson has established a tradition of hosting five-year anniversaries (the 105th occurred in 2008), organizing major routes throughout America by which Harley riders converge on Milwaukee, the corporate home. Over 100,000 bikers typically participate, all part of the Harley "family." Other marketers use status themes such as airline VIP or Executive Clubs to achieve the same effect. And, in the absence of any contact whatsoever, companies can use "transcendent experience" or "flow" to stimulate virtual communities, a strategy made more possible with the Internet.[73]

Individual and Social Integration: Fully Bonded Loyalty

The final, lower right cell in Table 15.3 encompasses a blend of personal identity with the cultural milieu surrounding the consumable. This situation is distinguished from the previous example of the village because, in the present case, the cultural and social environment may assume a passive or stationary, although enticing, role. Here, consumers are drawn to the consumable environment as opposed to the situation where the environment defines consumption for the consumers, although this does occur. The main distinguishing feature of this cell is that consumers find a natural match with both the consumable and its environment.

This is a particularly healthy situation for the firm as its product or service is now inextricably embedded within its consumers' psyche and lifestyle, part of their self-identity and social identity. That is, the consumers cannot conceive of themselves as whole without it. At the extreme, the object is present intensionally and extensionally. Here, the consumer would say that the object is "part of me" or an "extension of me."[74] They live it. Strong examples include religious sects and cults, although consumables in the more ordinary consumption domain are also candidates. Common examples include products, services, and even images supported by fans with various levels of group identification. Sports teams, popular (and not-so-popular) bands, well-known—even deceased—entertainers (e.g., Elvis Presley), alma maters, political organizations, and activity and lifestyle themes (e.g., extreme sports enthusiasts, millennials) qualify. Typically, even in fan clubs, the identity of the consumer is not known to the team or artist. The allure of the larger consumption icon is sufficient to hold the consumer in the loyalty state. Many fans go to great lengths to support their icon: they travel extensively, wear special uniforms (e.g., *Star Trek* devotees, Halo 3 video gamers) and head gear (e.g., Jimmy Buffett's Parrot Heads, the Green Bay Packers' cheeseheads), and paint their bodies. Other forms of display insignia include logos on outerwear, badges, bumper stickers, affinity (credit) cards, and tattoos. One manifestation of this state is undying devotion, through good times and bad," such as exists when sport franchises are perennial losers.[75]

Clearly, consumers' willingness to rebuy or repatronize cannot reach the ultimate extreme until they are willing to adore and commit unfailingly to (i.e., to love) a product or service. Beyond this, the necessary additional adhesion stems from the social bonding of a consumption community and the synergy between community and consumers. In essence, the consumers want to be loyal, the social organization wants them to be loyal, and, as a result, the two may become symbiotic. These are stringent criteria for the firm that wishes to have a loyal customer base. A reasonable question, then, is which companies will be able to attain this state.

It should be apparent that a fully immersed self-identity (the lower right cell in Table 15.3), as an ultimate loyalty state, cannot be achieved by all marketers. This requires product superiority at the minimum, plus customers who can become determined defenders of the brand, plus a supportive social environment. As these requirements are unattained or unattainable, the depth of the loyalty state will become more shallow and precarious.

What does it take to bring all these requirements into being? There are five essential criteria. First, the product must be of some unique configuration that makes it desirable (i.e., superior). Second, a profitably sized segment of the firm's customers must find it to be desirable in this manner. Third, the consumable must be subject to adoration, at least in the eyes of the firm's potentially loyal consumers. Fourth, the product must have the capacity to be embedded in a social network, for, if a firm's consumers cannot be networked at least perceptually, they cannot feel that they are part of a village. Lastly, the company must be willing to expend resources to create, populate, and maintain the village. This does not have to be a physical or even an electronic (e.g., Internet) village, but can be maintained through communication at the corporate or local levels.

THE RELATION BETWEEN SATISFACTION AND LOYALTY

In the author's article "Whence," six plausible relations, shown graphically in Figure 15.2, linked satisfaction and loyalty. It is now time to discuss the appropriateness of each in light of the evidence offered. Panel 1, which suggests that satisfaction and loyalty are two manifestations of the same concept, is easily dismissed. From the many avenues of discourse presented and the definitions here, it should be clear that the two concepts are distinctly separate. Satisfaction is a fairly temporal postusage state for one-time consumption or a repeatedly experienced state for ongoing consumption that reflects how the product or service has fulfilled its purpose. From the perspective of the firm, satisfaction is *delivered* to the consumer. Loyalty, in contrast, is an *attained* state of enduring preference to the point of determined defense and shares elements of attachment, as previously discussed.

Panels 2 and 3 suggest that satisfaction is an essential ingredient for the emergence of loyalty, panel 2 arguing that it is core, panel 3 only that it is necessary. There is merit in these perspectives as no perspective discussed here entertains loyalty development without early or concurrent satisfying episodes. Even in the village concept, it is presumed that the menu offered to the constituents is satisfying or, at least, satisfactory. Excepting those villages with severe exit barriers (e.g., cults), members would express dissatisfaction or leave the group if aspects of its consumption system were unsatisfactory. While it may be that satisfaction is not a core element of loyalty, particularly after loyalty has set, it is difficult to entertain loyalty development without satisfaction. The endurance of loyalty is another matter, however.

Panels 2 and 3 do diverge from the discussion presented here in terms of the degree to which loyalty totally encompasses satisfaction (i.e., that satisfaction is entirely contained within loyalty). It is simple to demonstrate common consumption situations where satisfaction exists without loyalty (a satisfying meal, regardless of the entree) and where loyalty exists without satisfaction (unequivocal "blind faith"; "my country, right or wrong"). In this sense, Panel 5 is more accurate in that it shows satisfaction and loyalty in an overlapping posture, but the percent of overlap is small in relation to the content of each construct. Panel 5 fails, as well, on the criterion of the independence of satisfaction and loyalty for the situations described.

In an apparent contradiction to the previous conclusion, the data largely support interpretations 2, 3, and 5 since tests measuring both satisfaction and loyalty tend to be cross-sectional, thereby ruling out temporal explanations; the associations, when found, tend to be robust, however, with some of a curvilinear nature.[76] In defense of the many researchers who have addressed this conundrum, there are a number of methodological obstacles to overcome if a more definitive conclusion is desired. The time-dependent nature of the relationship has to be discussed, for example; two

Figure 15.2   **Six Representations of Satisfaction and Loyalty**

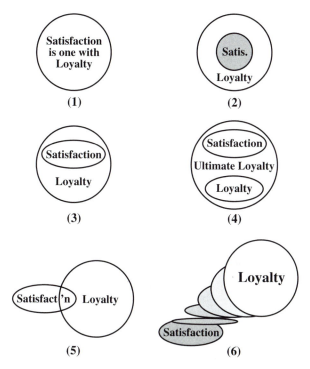

Source: Richard L. Oliver, "Whence Consumer Loyalty," *Journal of Marketing* 63 (Special Issue 1999): 34. Reprinted with permission from the American Marketing Association.

other obstacles are measurement and loyalty sensitivity. No matter how well one conceptualizes the satisfaction and loyalty concepts, there will always exist an apparent halo across the two that cannot help but be more prominent as the time interval across measures is compressed, the limiting case being one survey administration. Longer time intervals, including extended consumption episodes, introduce intervening confounds in the classic manner.

Sensitivity is also a problem as some consumables do not lend themselves to loyalty attainment; this problem is particularly acute if the sample contains unidentified segments, some amenable to the formation of loyalty and some not. For all these reasons, the data on the relationship between loyalty and satisfaction are variable, some indicating a relation and some not. What, then, is the explanation? Because the alternative configurations in Figure 15.2 are not rigorously specified, tests tend to concentrate on and report correlation-based findings. This author will have a conclusion to this conundrum which, rightly or wrongly, must suffice.

For now, it can be said that moderator analyses offer some insights as these approach the sensitivity issue indirectly. Of the many tests available, some failing for the use of errant measures typically culled from previously collected data, only a few address mediation. Of these, the satisfaction-loyalty link tends to be weak for business and e-commerce transactions because many purchase alternatives are readily available, for low purchase involvement, for low strength of the relationship, and for selected demographics, particularly age, since younger persons tend to be satisfied, but not necessarily loyal.[77] Of these, the most compelling is involvement. As one would expect, more involved consumers have higher satisfaction to loyalty "conversions" and, at the same time, higher dissatisfaction defection rates. This, of course, does not account for lock-in, sometimes measured as perceived switching costs.

This leaves panels 4 and 6, the first suggesting that a superordinate concept, referred to as ultimate loyalty, encompasses both satisfaction and loyalty. For the same reasons discussed for panels 2 and 3, the containment element of this description can be dismissed, but the notion of ultimate loyalty as superordinate seems valid. In the attitude theme of loyalty, four forms of "lesser" loyalty—cognitive, affective, conative, and action—were entertained. In their own way, these are variants of loyalty. It is not until community and immersion develop that ultimate loyalty becomes possible. The consumption literature has not yet addressed this philosophically terminal loyalty form.

This brings discussion to Panel 6, which suggests that satisfaction becomes transformed into loyalty much like a caterpillar becomes transformed into a butterfly. After this metamorphosis, the two creatures are not the same, sharing virtually no common characteristics except for their biological origins. This is truly an extreme position, for it suggests that loyalty can never return to mere satisfaction. Indeed, a number of writers have empirically suggested that there is a threshold at which loyalty can revert to dissatisfaction in the face of repeatedly unsatisfactory purchase episodes. Sometimes referred to as "catastrophe models," these arguments posit discontinuous jumps between an ordinarily continuous relationship, which is what many assume. Of note is one study in which satisfaction is treated as a "hygiene" factor (see Chapter 5) that must be attained before loyalty can emerge.[78] The model also allows for loyalty to revert to dissatisfaction, whereby the consumer becomes open to competitive advances.

The reason for the ambivalence as to which conception is most accurate is that, even in the perspective taken here, there remain variants of loyalty. In addition to the cognition-to-action sequence, it is suggested that there are now different degrees of loyalty depending on how many of the synergistic factors presented here are involved. Immersion-based loyalty is supported by the convergence of product, personal, and social forces; the consumer displaying this state has logical, personal, and communal loyalty sustainers. At the same time, competition is easily thwarted by these same forces. Removing any or one of them lowers the consumer's resistance to competitive persuasion. Loyalty supported only by the social environment permits the consumer to look beyond its borders. Loyalty supported only by fortitude is susceptible to relapse such as self-doubt, second thoughts, competitive onslaught, and repetitively unpleasant dissatisfying experiences. And, as discussed throughout this chapter, loyalty supported only by product information is subject to competitive counterinformation.

Thus, panel 6 comes closest to the perspective taken here except that satisfaction does not transform into loyalty as much as it is a seed requiring nurturance—personal determination and social support. Without these additional factors, satisfaction, much like the seed, stays dormant. The consumer remains satisfied, but does not progress beyond that state. Even a flash of sustenance—like the flash of delight—will not begin the transformation process. Once the seed sprouts, it will grow if the requisites are there. Only the full-grown version contains the strength to fight off all comers and can survive despite lapses in its base form, namely dissatisfaction.

IS BRAND LOYALTY AN ANACHRONISM?

Before discussing the research directions suggested by the issues raised in this chapter, it would be of interest to explore the claim of many that modern economic conditions are not conducive for loyalty to emerge. Much of this argument relies on the "irrationality of loyalty" position discussed earlier (see note 28). Increasing regional and global competition, price competition, and market fragmentation are all cited as reasons why rational consumers will be swayed to patronize the product or service with a preferred (lower) price, better features, or more personally customized features as competitors' products are introduced to the market. However, this argument overlooks the reasons that would cause consumers to *prefer* to be loyal.

For example, there is, arguably, a basic instinct of human nature to be loyal. Loyalty is noble. It suggests that an individual has conviction, trust, and fidelity.[79] Furthermore, maintaining loyalty is easy; it is the familiar path. Consumers weary of consuming can repurchase without great effort, provided the consumable has not changed for the worse. Thus, the forces arguing for waning loyalty are counterbalanced by those favoring loyalty. Loyalty behavior is in an apparent state of equilibrium. There is some evidence, at least in the categories studied, that the loyalty response shows some variability, as any human behavior does, but the stationary trend remains intact.[80]

At this point, the reader is left with all the author can provide with regard to the consumption psychology of loyalty. This is the ultimate pursuit of the consumer, from the perspective of the firm, and is a fitting last chapter to this book. But there remains yet another topic. Regardless of its attainability, one can reasonably ask where the firm stands.on what will be argued is a somewhat elusive loyalty scale. While lower and upper boundaries are not yet well defined, firms can still place their consumer constituents on a scale for competitive benchmarking purposes, as follows.

MEASURING LOYALTY

Despite the difficulty of tapping the loyalty concept via testing, a starting point is provided here. If only purchase data or logs are available to the researcher, then that is what will be used. In other cases, scales can be constructed. Convenience scales—that is, those previously collected—are not recommended. Typically, these will measure related concepts such as intention, recommendations, word of mouth, or other pseudomeasures. These are truly patchwork efforts of methodological desperation. Researchers may wish to embed these measures within a larger framework leading up to (antecedent to) or following (consequent to) satisfaction or loyalty. It has been the central premise of this chapter, however, that loyalty is a unique concept, requiring unique measures, examples of which follow. The following discussion includes seed items for the self-isolation and community subcomponents separately. A method of combining these will be idiosyncratic to the researcher's purpose and context.

Basic Loyalty Scales: Staying and Switching

According to the definition proposed at the beginning of this chapter, a loyalty measure must refer not only to a consumer's attraction to a brand but also to the consumer's vulnerability to switching. Thus, there will be two major dimensions to any loyalty scale net of social influences. Generally, the number of items that can be included in a loyalty scale is restricted only by the length constraints imposed by the researcher. Examples of items that might be used to "anchor" each of the loyalty phases will be illustrated.

Attraction Elements

The earlier discussion of loyalty sustainers describes attractions that operate at each phase of the loyalty sequence. These would provide specific areas that should be included in a loyalty scale if each of the four stages is to be represented. For example, items tapping the cognitive stage would relate to brand quality or superiority, while those at the affective stage would relate to the degree of liking, prior satisfaction, and involvement. At the conative stage, brand commitment, social commitment, and purchase intention would be represented; at the action stage, statements reflecting purchase history would be needed. Examples of each follow; also shown is a summary representation of fortitude. Generally, these items would be posed in five-point agree/disagree format.

- Cognitive: Brand X has more benefits than others in its class.
- Affective: I have grown to like brand X more than I like other brands.
- Conative: I intend to continue buying brand X in the future.
- Action: When I have a need for a product of this type, I buy only brand X.
- Fortitude: Brand X is the only brand for me; I love it.

To flesh out these items, measurement suggestions follow. For example, cognitive frameworks are very common, including those discussed in Chapter 2. They typically are attribute- or dimension-driven and will include lists that must be culled, factored, or otherwise reduced. Affective frameworks will appear similar to attitude scaling, incorporating attribute evaluations, valences, or other goodness/badness qualifiers either embedded in the attribute descriptions or measured in parallel. Satisfaction (and dissatisfaction) is central to this stage and should be reflected in the scaling unless a pure form of satisfaction exists within the network of concepts being tested. This should be measured separately and the context will dictate the degree of overlap intended.

Among the concepts that might be tapped in the conative section are commitment, social or otherwise, and involvement. Items from general scales tapping measuring these constructs can be selected for inclusion, subject to reliability testing. The action elements would be reflective of repetitive activity with overtones of why (in terms of loyalty logic) the repetitions are pursued. Despite earlier discussion, simple inertia (habit) is not the behavior of interest; measurement must go beyond this, leading to the concept of fortitude and its attendant "brand love" connection. The romance literature may be helpful up to a point. Other insights may appear within the brand personality literature. One well-constructed effort in the attraction area has been used in other works.[81]

Vulnerability (Detraction) Elements

Switching vulnerabilities are listed in the rightmost column of Table 15.2. Generally, these include competitive benefits, such as lower cost and higher quality, at the cognitive stage. Potential dissatisfaction with the current brand would operate at the affective level, while an eroding commitment to the brand would impact the conative stage. Finally, less frequent or multibrand purchasing would demonstrate vulnerabilities at the action level, as would barriers such as unavailability. Additionally, susceptibility to persuasion and a willingness to engage in product trial should enhance vulnerability at a number of stages. As with the attraction items, seed items are presented here to stimulate further efforts in the measurement of loyalty. Note that all are worded in the *anti*-switching direction.

- Cognitive: No amount of ___ (e.g., cost savings) will cause me to switch from buying Brand X.
- Affective: Even if the provider dissatisfied me on occasion, I would continue to buy Brand X.
- Conative: I cannot be persuaded or swayed from my commitment to continue buying Brand X.

- Action: I would surmount any obstacles to find and buy Brand X.
- Fortitude: No other brand could even come close to matching my allegiance to Brand X.

The Social Support of the Community

If the reader were to sample the various writings on a sense of community, all the descriptors used in these studies would be candidates for inclusion here. Given the recent history in the study of consumption communities, a small number of investigations have attempted to provide early measures of this phenomenon.[82] Sample items are presented below with dimensions specified. The list concludes with typical overall loyalty anchor statements.

- Identification: I see myself as part of the Brand X community.
- Integration: I enjoy the status of being a member of the Brand X community.
- Engagement: I am motivated to participate in the Brand X community's activities.
- Connections: I have pleasant experiences interacting with members of the Brand X community.
- Compliance: My actions are judged to be compatible with those of the Brand X community.
- Influence: I am an influential member of the Brand X community.
- Continuance: It would be difficult for me to leave the Brand X community.
- Immersion: All my friends agree that there is only one brand, Brand X.
- Loyalty:
  - I am a loyal buyer and user of Brand X.
  - I will continue to remain loyal to Brand X for many years to come.

THE TRANSLATION OF LOYALTY INTO PROFITS

The study of satisfaction as a precursor of loyalty, and the exploration of the concept of loyalty itself bring discussion to what many marketers consider the ultimate goal of satisfaction efforts—profit. Until recently, few data were available to establish the much talked-about relationship between satisfied consumers and a firm's profits. In fact, all the new information to be presented has appeared since 1990! While many people working in the satisfaction field had assumed that the relationships between satisfaction and loyalty and between loyalty and profits are inherently intuitive and self-evident, others provide anecdotal evidence to the contrary.

Data suggesting that the satisfaction-loyalty relation is less than perfect (the satisfaction "trap") were presented earlier. However weak this relationship, it is likely to be stronger than that between loyalty and profits, since both satisfaction and loyalty are behavioral constructs that can be linked theoretically. Unfortunately, loyalty and profit cross the conceptual plane. The first, as noted, is behavioral—at least in the individual-specific approach taken in this book. In contrast, profit is an economic outcome to the firm. To study this loyalty-profit relation, researchers must either break down profit into its customer-specific basis or aggregate loyalty up to the firm level so that aggregate loyalty figures can be related to profitability on an interfirm basis.

Unfortunately, results from the first or individual-level analysis can be calculated only within a given firm, since firm to firm comparisons must consist of aggregate data and, perhaps for this reason, are not widely reported.[83] The fairly recent benchmarking data from the national consumer satisfaction indexes are a welcome exception. Reports of the value of a retained customer or a customer's lifetime value are becoming more common, but they largely assume that current prices, margins, competitive offerings, and purchase rates will continue into the future.[84] Thus, data on aggregate loyalty may be more revealing and are, in fact, thought to be more predictive of the future. The reason is that aggregate data smooth out the vicissitudes of individual observations.

There is an additional problem in relating satisfaction or loyalty to a firm's profits. Namely, profit is a function of revenues and costs. While loyalty will be shown to reduce some of the firm's marketing costs, the main effect of loyalty is chiefly on revenues, but in an indirect manner. One reason for the less direct influence is that producer revenues do not fully recognize final prices to the consumer, a determinant of demand. Retailing and utility provision are obvious exceptions to this statement. With regard to the cost side of the profit equation, it must be acknowledged that a firm's cost structure is typically complex. In addition to direct costs of production and merchandising, numerous indirect and overhead costs affect the final profit picture of a given firm. Despite these complexities in the satisfaction-profit relationship, the various rationales behind expected satisfaction and loyalty effects on a firm's profitability will be examined.

THE BIG PICTURE: SATISFACTION MATTERS

The reader may remember when stock market valuation models contained only financial and accounting data. They still do. It may seem strange indeed that the customer is not represented beyond mere sales (revenue) data in these calculations. True, backward trends are analyzed and forward forecasts (redundancy intended) are made and these models are marginally improving, especially since many are based on mostly hard data such as the aging of the population and generational mobility. More to the point, the day of omitting marketing data is over (or should be). Equally hard data on customer satisfaction across industries and countries over time are now available, and the breadth of such data will grow as economies become universally globalized.[85] Moreover, it is now recognized that these same customer satisfaction data statistically and significantly add to the explanation of changes (variation) in stock valuations.[86] Why did it take so long?

Picture a half-filled bucket of customers with a leak in it.[87] The strategy of generating new customers, either from competitors or from new consumers of the product class, represents additional customer volume flowing into the bucket. However, the leak represents the exit of current customers who develop a lack of interest in the product or who leave because of dissatisfaction. The firm has two options to solve this leakage problem.

First, it can erect leaving or switching barriers, previously discussed as lock-in and analogous to plugging the hole. For example, a book club may ask consumers to pledge to buy ten books at retail prices over the coming year after hooking them with very low-cost introductory offers, thus maintaining sales in the face of potential declining interest. The ubiquitous frequent-flyer programs are another example of strategy aimed at maintaining brand repatronage despite occasional to frequent dissatisfactory performances. The second option is quite the opposite. Here, the firm can create satisfaction, allowing loyalty to emerge, so that the consumer does not wish to lose interest or switch. The current consumer base will thus avoid exit, positioning itself away from the leak.

The concern of this book has been the second approach. The erection of exit barriers is an anachronism in modern economies. When deprived of free will, as in the prisoner cell in the loyalty typologies, consumers who wish to exit will purchase reluctantly and exit at the earliest opportunity. Rather than fulfilling needs with satisfaction, the firm that creates barriers will fulfill these same needs with frustration, thus failing to reap the additional benefits of satisfaction on profit and growth. What, then, are the primary benefits of creating satisfaction to retain customers?

How Satisfaction Indirectly Influences Profits

A number of authors have proposed compelling arguments and presented data strongly supporting the links that translate satisfaction into profits, despite the other financial and accounting influences that affect profitability. In a sense, this is a ceteris paribus argument by which one holds external influences constant and examines the satisfaction-profitability link in isolation. In actuality, the profitability sequence has five stages:

$$Quality \rightarrow satisfaction \rightarrow loyalty \rightarrow market\ share \rightarrow profitability \rightarrow stockholder\ value$$

Here, quality refers to exceptional performance and all its variants, including the positive disconfirmation of quality expectations, although the literature at the macro level frequently does not distinguish between performance excellence and exceeding expectations. More accurately, the relations appear as shown in Figure 15.3, where profitability and its correlates of share and stock value can be shown to follow from the mediated effects of quality and satisfaction through loyalty, and from direct effects due to quality, satisfaction, and loyalty. Because the quality → satisfaction relation were discussed in Chapter 6 and some particulars of the satisfaction → loyalty sequence, most at the micro level, were addressed earlier in this chapter, the present focus will center on other links of each of these variables to profitability.

Quality and Profits

The quality-profit link is largely a macro relationship. In accord with the quality literature, high quality allows firms to charge higher premiums, thereby reaping greater margins. At the same time, quality reduces failures and operating costs and commensurately lowers the necessity for recovery efforts and the attendant costs of recovery. Moreover, firms with higher quality have better reputations among consumers, better channel member receptivity, and hence better word of mouth, better awareness, and lower costs of attracting new customers. This effect appears to be cumulative, as quality breeds market expectations of quality (see Chapter 3). When the market's expectations of quality are high, the firm's reputation is enhanced and customer attraction is facilitated. Additionally, the macro version of the direct expectation effect becomes operative as the effects of high expectations will favorably influence satisfaction. Examples showing this direct quality-profit link are reported in a number of studies.[88]

Satisfaction and Loyalty and Satisfaction and Profits at the Macro Level

Because these two relationships are frequently reported together, they are collapsed in this discussion.[89] The potential nonlinear nature of the satisfaction-loyalty link has been proposed; the effects at the macro level, because of the aggregation involved, can be viewed as essentially linear, particularly due to the many interpretations of loyalty available to researchers. For example, retention is often used as a catchall phrase. These literatures have been summarized and the results are consistent; satisfaction has direct effects on profit through its influence on retention as well as on numerous other facilitating concepts, including word of mouth, marketing cost reductions, and human capital attraction. Besides having such direct effects, satisfaction is also a mediator. Satisfied consumers will increase purchasing for those goods where volume discretion or cross-buying is possible, will tolerate lower price elasticities (i.e., the percentage change in purchases due to price hikes will fall off much less sharply than percentage increases in price), will be more

Figure 15.3 **Direct Effects on Profitability and Related Firm Performance Criteria by the Components of the Satisfaction Sequence**

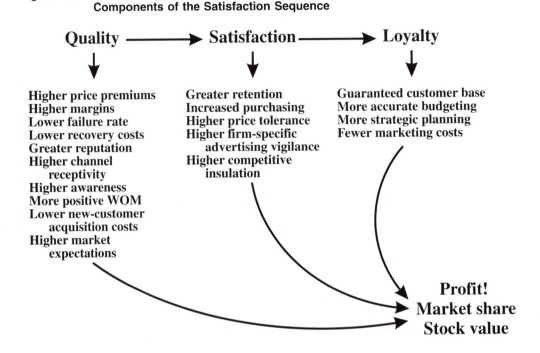

vigilant to communications from the focal firm, and will be more insulated from competitive encroachment through reduced attention to competitive overtures.[90] Research has noted that these effects may be particularly poignant in the services industry, where companies find that they must earn their loyalty, rather than simply produce it, due to the higher variation in service versus product delivery.[91]

Loyalty and Profits

Perhaps the greatest effect of loyalty on profit is the direct influence of a steady stream of future customers. In a manner similar to discounted cash flows, guaranteed future customers allow firms to budget offensive and defensive competitive efforts, to time tactical market moves, and to weather severe attacks by competitors until appropriate strategy can be mapped. Moreover, loyal customers in the pristine case require little, if any, marketing attention; efforts can be redirected toward product improvement and service enhancement.[92] In the limiting condition, if a firm had an optimal number of perfectly loyal customers who, by definition, could not be swayed away, the firm's marketing costs would be zero. Imagine.

Market Share and Shareholder Wealth

In the previous edition of this book, market share was omitted from the current topic. Despite the somewhat specious argument that market share is associated with profit through the mechanism of repeat purchase and sheer volume (e.g., loyalty programs), early studies suggested a negative relation between market share and satisfaction, attributed to the inability of firms to uniquely satisfy large numbers of diverse customers with the limited product and service variations that are normally feasible. Indeed, it has been found that the more differentiated an industry (i.e., the greater the number of competitors and variations in the offerings), the more satisfied are consumers of this industry. Paradoxically, this same level of differentiation allows consumers greater variety of choice, thereby encouraging greater switching and lower retention—one of the potential conundrums that lowers the relation between satisfaction and loyalty mentioned earlier.[93]

Of interest is that the one word *share* has now come to describe at least three characteristics of both behavioral and mechanistic phenomena in business. The first is the well-worn marketing concept of market share, the percentage of like-product sales purchased from one supplier. The second is the financial description of shares of stock or its macro translation into shareholder wealth, while the third is more recent and pertains to share of wallet, a micro concept suggesting multibrand loyalty and the percentage of purchasing in a category attributed to one brand among others purchased. This latter variable is now used as yet another proxy for behavioral loyalty.

The behavioral measure is discussed first as it is probably furthest removed from the bottom line. Here, the findings parallel those discussed throughout this chapter. Once again, though with the appropriate caveats and moderators, satisfaction is positively associated with wallet share. Direct relations, nonlinear relations, and moderated relations have all been found (e.g., loyalty program memberships, demographics). In particular, high levels of both satisfaction and loyalty appear to strengthen the relationship between satisfaction and share of wallet but can lead to erroneous, nonsignificant conclusions if the statistical variance is limited at these extremes.[94]

The criterion of interest, of course, is the effect of aggregate satisfaction on firm performance in the markets. One early effort at identifying this effect began with a micro approach, aggregating it into a macro model.[95] Some time passed before the accounting findings in the late 1990s resulted in more behaviorally oriented explanations, namely that satisfaction and loyalty are now viewed as cornerstones of a firm's financial performance. Research shows, for example, that the relation between satisfaction and shareholder value is positive, subject to variation across industries and firms; that the more quantitatively amenable criteria of cash flow growth and variability are consequent to satisfaction and predictive of shareholder value; and that customer lifetime value, the previously discussed derivative of favorable satisfaction-based loyalty, is indeed predictive of shareholder wealth.[96] These findings no doubt will be further explored and hopefully buttressed by new work in the field.

CONCLUSION

Thus ends the author's discourse of the determinants and consequences of customer satisfaction. Beginning with a definition and discussion of satisfaction's essentials (e.g., performance, expectations), the process of satisfaction formation has been traced through various literatures, theories, findings, and speculations in order to arrive at a greater understanding of what this phenomenon means to businesses and to individual consumers generally. To the extent possible, this author has tried to incorporate both the classic historical writings as well as the latest and newest research on satisfaction as it is understood today. New findings and conclusions will be forthcoming, since research on the topic is unfolding as this final section is written. In closing, the author's wish to the reader is that all your desires be satisfied. But, as Aristotle once said, "It is the nature of desire not to be satisfied . . ." And so it is with the topic of satisfaction.

NOTES

1. These examples are from the first edition. There is no limit to the number of fan identification themes that could be presented. Some exist without formal names excepting the product itself. For example, are Coca-Cola loyalists termed "Cokies" and Snapple fans called "Snappies?"—after all, Snapple's competitor at the time, SoBe, had followers referring to themselves as "Sobeings." Rock bands and individual members sometimes have clubs and subclubs, such as U2 and its lead guitarist, Edge.

2. See Lach, "Redeeming Qualities."

3. Oliver, "Cognitive Model of the Antecedents and Consequences of Satisfaction Decisions."

4. Cassel and Eklöf, "Modelling Customer Satisfaction and Loyalty on Aggregate Levels"; Grønholdt, Martensen, and Kristensen, "Relationship Between Customer Satisfaction and Loyalty"; and M. Johnson, Anderson, and Fornell, "Rational and Adaptive Performance Expectations in a Customer Satisfaction Framework."

5. Much of this section and later discussion draws from the author's article; see Oliver, "Whence Consumer Loyalty." Reprinted with permission from *Journal of Marketing*, published by the American Marketing Association, Special Issue 1999, pp. 33–44.

6. As a prelude to further discussion of social influence as it pertains to loyalty and to illustrate the operation of both attitude and expectations as precursors to consumption, see Bagozzi and Dholakia, "Antecedents and Purchase Consequences of Customer Participation in Small Group Brand Communities."

7. Bass, "Theory of Stochastic Preference and Brand Switching."

8. E.g., Gollwitzer and Bargh, *Psychology of Action*. Technically, motivation is the force behind an action-tendency, is antecedent to it, and does not necessarily translate into an intention.

9. Kuhl, "Volitional Mediators of Cognition-Behavior Consistency"; Kuhl and Beckmann, *Action Control*.

10. Bagozzi and Dholakia, "Goal Setting and Goal Striving in Consumer Behavior"; Bagozzi and Warshaw, "Trying to Consume"; Mischel, "From Good Intentions to Willpower."

11. Heckhausen and Beckmann, "Intentional Action and Action Slips." See, also, Gollwitzer, "Volitional Benefits of Planning."

12. Söderlund and Öhman, "Behavioral Intentions in Satisfaction Research Revisited"; Söderlund, "Retrospective and the Prospective Mind and the Temporal Framing of Customer Satisfaction."

13. E.g., see Ajzen, "Theory of Planned Behavior." This theory and others are variants of theories of reasoned action, which are more expectations-oriented. See Feather, *Expectations and Actions*; and Fishbein and Ajzen, *Belief, Attitude, Intention and Behavior*. The operation of these frameworks in predicting both intention and behavior is adequate and more accurate for intention than behavior; see Sutton, "Predicting and Explaining Intentions and Behavior."

14. Söderlund and Öhman, "Behavioral Intentions in Satisfaction Research Revisited."

15. Mittal and Kamakura, "Satisfaction, Repurchase Intent, and Repurchase Behavior"; Mittal, Kumar, and Tsiros, "Attribute-Level Performance, Satisfaction, and Behavioral Intentions Over Time." For a historical account, see McNeil, "Federal Programs to Measure Consumer Purchase Expectations."

16. Andreassen, "From Disgust to Delight"; Aron, "Consumer Grudgeholding"; Finn, "Reassessing the Foundations of Customer Delight"; Mittal, Ross and Baldasare, "Asymmetric Impact of Negative and Positive Attribute-Level Performance on Overall Satisfaction and Repurchase Intentions"; Otto et al., "When Consumers Get Upset"; Patterson and Spreng, "Modelling the Relationship Between Perceived Value, Satisfaction and Repurchase Intentions in a Business-to-Business, Services Context"; Sen, Gürhan-Canli, and Morwitz, "Withholding Consumption."

17. Feinberg et al., "Myth and Reality in Customer Service"; Halstead and Page, "Effects of Satisfaction and Complaining Behavior on Consumer Repurchase Intentions"; Mattila, "Impact of Relationship Type on Customer Loyalty in a Context of Service Failures"; Maxham, "Service Recovery's Influence on Consumer Satisfaction, Positive Word-of-Mouth, and Purchase Intentions"; Palmer, Beggs, and Keown-McMullan, "Equity and Repurchase Intention Following Service Failure."

18. The main study is by Seiders et al., "Do Satisfied Customers Buy More?" Also see Kumar, "Impact of Performance, Cost, and Competitive Considerations on the Relationship Between Satisfaction and Repurchase Intent in Business Markets"; Lu and Lo, "Television Audience Satisfaction"; Mittal and Kamakura, "Satisfaction, Repurchase Intent, and Repurchase Behavior"; Yi and La, "What Influences the Relations Between Customer Satisfaction and Repurchase Intention?"; and Zboja and Voorhees, "Impact of Brand Trust and Satisfaction on Retailer Repurchase Intentions."

19. Ofir and Simonson, "In Search of Negative Customer Feedback"; Shiv and Huber, "Impact of Antici-pating Satisfaction on Consumer Choice"; Simonson, "Influence of Anticipating Regret and Responsibility on Purchase Decisions."

20. Chapman, "Measuring Intent"; Krishnan and Shapiro, "Prospective and Retrospective Memory for Intentions"; Mazursky and Geva, "Temporal Decay in Satisfaction-Purchase Intention Relationship"; Morwitz, "Why Consumers Don't Always Accurately Predict Their Own Future Behavior."

21. Chandon, Morwitz, and Reinartz, "Do Intentions Really Predict Behavior?"; Fitzsimons and Mor-witz, "Effect of Measuring Intent on Brand-Level Purchase Behavior"; Morwitz and Fitzsimons, "Mere-Measurement Effect."

22. Johnson, Herrmann, and Huber, "Evolution of Loyalty Intentions."

23. This perspective appeared in the following: Jacoby and Chestnut, *Brand Loyalty*; and Jacoby and Kyner, "Brand Loyalty vs. Repeat Purchasing Behavior." Since that time, a test of "true" and multibrand loyalty has appeared which nicely supports the multibrand (or secondary brand) model. See Yim and Kan-nan, "Consumer Behavioral Loyalty." The incidence of multisupplier "loyalty" in B2B markets is shown in Du, Kamakura, and Mela, "Size and Share of Customer Wallet."

24. In the original works, this synchrony of belief, affect, and intention was required to conform to the tenets of the attitude theories of the time that included a fairly strict mathematical combinatorial rule for the manner in which the stages were combined. The discussion here relaxes that interpretation.

25. Dick and Basu, "Customer Loyalty." For examples of its application, see Baker, Nancarrow, and Tinson, "Mind Versus Market Share Guide to Brand Equity"; Olsen, "Comparative Evaluation and the Relationship Between Quality, Satisfaction, and Repurchase Loyalty"; and Sivadas and Baker-Prewitt, "Examination of the Relationship Between Service Quality, Customer Satisfaction, and Store Loyalty."

26. The first quotation is from Fletcher, *Loyalty*, p. 177; the second from Royce, *Philosophy of Loyalty*, p. 9.

27. Oliver, *Satisfaction*, p. 392 (italics in original).

28. East and Hammond, "Erosion of Repeat-Purchase Loyalty"; Keiningham et al., *Loyalty Myths*. The original idea of the "polygamous" consumer was originally put to me by an ex-colleague, Gerry Linda of Gerald Linda & Associates, a Chicago consultancy, who questioned why I would study this "anachronism."

29. Many sources could be cited here, particularly in the area of relationship marketing, where affect takes on the additional dimension of trust. Three articles of note are Dean, "Impact of the Customer Orientation of Call Center Employees on Customers' Affective Commitment and Loyalty"; Gustafsson, Johnson, and Roos, "Effects of Customer Satisfaction, Relationship Commitment Dimensions, and Triggers on Customer Retention"; and Verhoef, "Understanding the Effect of Customer Relationship Management Efforts on Cus-tomer Retention and Customer Share Development." See, also, Taylor, Hunter, and Longfellow, "Testing an Expanded Attitude Model of Goal-Directed Behavior in a Loyalty Context," where utilitarian and hedonic loyalty were used as proxies for cognitive and affective loyalty.

30. Reichheld with Teal, *Loyalty Effect*, pp. 234–239.

31. See, for example, Fullerton, "When Does Commitment Lead to Loyalty?"; Gundlach, Achrol, and Mentzer, "Structure of Commitment in Exchange"; and Pritchard, Havitz, and Howard, "Analyzing the Commitment-Loyalty Link in Service Contexts."

32. Kuhl and Beckmann, *Action Control*.

33. Ouellette and Wood, "Habit and Intention in Everyday Life"; Sutton, "Predicting and Explaining Intentions and Behavior."

34. Aarts, Verplanken, and van Knippenberg, "Predicting Behavior from Actions in the Past"; R. Anderson and Srinivasan, "E-Satisfaction and E-Loyalty."

35. For banking, see Barnes, "Closeness, Strength, and Satisfaction." Examples in other contexts include Bruyneel et al., "Repeated Choosing Increases Susceptibility to Affective Product Features"; and Chaudhuri and Holbrook, "Chain of Effects from Brand Trust and Brand Affect to Brand Performance."

36. Chintagunta, "Inertia and Variety Seeking in a Model of Brand-Purchase Timing"; Huang and Yu, "Are Consumers Inherently or Situationally Brand Loyal?"; Seetharaman and Chintagunta, "Model of Inertia and Variety-Seeking with Marketing Variables."

37. See, respectively, Sivadas and Baker-Prewitt, "Examination of the Relationship Between Service Quality, Customer Satisfaction, and Store Loyalty"; McMullan and Gilmore, "Conceptual Development of Customer Loyalty Measurement," and McMullan, "Multiple-Item Scale for Measuring Customer Loyalty Development"; Harris and Goode, "Four Levels of Loyalty and the Pivotal Role of Trust"; Rosenbaum, Ostrom, and Kuntze, "Loyalty Programs and a Sense of Community"; and Evanschitzky and Wunderlich, "Examination of Moderator Effects in the Four-Stage Loyalty Model."

38. Capraro, Broniarczyk, and Srivastava, "Factors Influencing the Likelihood of Customer Defection"; Keiningham et al., *Loyalty Myths*; Ping, "Antecedents of Satisfaction in a Marketing Channel"; Sambandam and Lord, "Switching Behavior in Automobile Markets"; Sharma and Patterson, "Switching Costs, Alternative Attractiveness and Experience as Moderators of Relationship Commitment in Professional Consumer Services"; van Trijp, Hoyer, and Inman, "Why Switch?"

39. Chiu et al., "Relationship Marketing and Consumer Switching Behavior"; Homburg and Giering, "Personal Characteristics as Moderators of the Relationship Between Customer Satisfaction and Loyalty"; Keaveney and Parthasarathy, "Customer Switching Behavior in Online Services"; Lipke, "Pledge of Allegiance"; Odekerken-Schröder et al., "Impact of Quality on Store Loyalty."

40. Athanassopoulos, "Customer Satisfaction Cues to Support Market Segmentation and Explain Switching Behavior"; Keiningham et al., *Loyalty Myths*, where much similar material can be found.

41. Bell, Auh, and Smalley, "Customer Relationship Dynamics"; Burnham, Frels, and Mahajan, "Consumer Switching Costs"; de Ruyter, Wetzels, and Bloemer, "On the Relationship Between Perceived Service Quality, Service Loyalty and Switching Costs"; Kalyanaram and Little, "Empirical Analysis of Latitude of Price Acceptance in Consumer Package Goods"; Keaveney, "Customer Switching Behavior in Service Industries"; J. Lee, Lee, and Feick, "Impact of Switching Costs on the Customer Satisfaction-Loyalty Link"; M. Lee and Cunningham, "A Cost/Benefit Approach to Understanding Service Loyalty"; Sivakumar and Raj, "Quality Tier Competition"; Yang and Peterson, "Customer Perceived Value, Satisfaction, and Loyalty."

42. Balabanis, Reynolds, and Simintiras, "Bases of e-Store Loyalty"; Büschken, *Higher Profits Through Customer Lock-In*; E. Johnson, Bellman, and Lohse, "Cognitive Lock-In and the Power Law of Practice"; M. Jones, Mothersbaugh, and Beatty, "Why Customers Stay"; Wirtz, Mattila, and Lwin, "How Effective Are Loyalty Reward Programs in Driving Share of Wallet?"; Zauberman, "Intertemporal Dynamics of Consumer Lock-In."

43. Auh, "Effects of Soft and Hard Service Attributes on Loyalty"; Barnes, "Closeness, Strength, and Satisfaction"; Macintosh and Lockshin, "Retail Relationships and Store Loyalty"; Vilares and Coelho, "Employee-Customer Satisfaction Chain in the ECSI Model."

44. Chiou and Dröge, "Service Quality, Trust, Specific Asset Investment, and Expertise"; Colgate and Lang, "Switching Barriers in Consumer Markets"; Ellen, Bearden, and Sharma, "Resistance to Technological Innovations"; Patterson and Smith, "Cross-Cultural Study of Switching Barriers and Propensity to Stay with Service Providers"; Roos, Edvardsson, and Gustafsson, "Customer Switching Patterns in Competitive and Noncompetitive Service Industries"; Wieringa and Verhoef, "Understanding Customer Switching Behavior in a Liberalizing Service Market."

45. Heide and Weiss, "Vendor Consideration and Switching Behavior for Buyers in High-Technology Markets"; Keaveney, "Customer Switching Behavior in Service Industries"; and M. Morgan and Dev, "Empirical Study of Brand Switching for a Retail Service."

46. Colgate et al., "Back from the Brink"; Dubé and Maute, "Antecedents of Brand Switching, Brand Loyalty, and Verbal Responses to Service Failure"; Ganesh, Arnold, and Reynolds, "Understanding the Customer Base of Service Providers"; M. Jones et al., "Positive and Negative Effects of Switching Costs on Relational Outcomes"; Roos, "Switching Processes in Customer Relationships"; Taylor, Hunter, and Longellow, "Testing an Expanded Attitude Model of Goal-Directed Behavior in a Loyalty Context."

47. Bansal and Taylor, "Service Provider Switching Model"; Oliva, Oliver, and MacMillan, "Catastrophe Model for Developing Service Satisfaction Strategies"; Roos and Gustafsson, "Understanding Frequent Switching Patterns."

48. Bove and Johnson, "Customer Loyalty to One Service Worker"; Goodwin and Gremler, "Friendship Over the Counter"; Palmatier, Scheer, and Steenkamp, "Customer Loyalty to Whom?"; Price and Arnould, "Commercial Friendships"; Reynolds and Beatty, "Customer Benefits and Company Consequences of Customer-Salesperson Relationships in Retailing."

49. Agnew et al., "Cognitive Interdependence"; Butcher, Sparks, and O'Callaghan, "Evaluative and Relational Influences on Service Loyalty"; Gutek et al., "Distinguishing Between Service Relationships and Encounters"; Iacobucci and Ostrom, "Commercial and Interpersonal Relationships"; T. Jones and Taylor, "Conceptual Domain of Service Loyalty," especially Table I; Reis and Rusbult, *Key Readings on Close Relationships*; Sternberg and Hojjat, *Satisfaction in Close Relationships*.

50. McDonald, "Roles of Demographics, Purchase Histories, and Shopper Decision-Making Styles in Predicting Consumer Catalog Loyalty"; Snyder, "Demographic Correlates to Loyalty in Frequently Purchased Consumer Services"; Sproles and Kendall, "Methodology for Profiling Consumers' Decision-Making Styles"; Tranberg and Hansen, "Patterns of Brand Loyalty."

51. De Wulf, Odekerken-Schröder, and Iacobucci, "Investments in Consumer Relationships"; Noble and Phillips, "Relationship Hindrance"; Sheth and Shah, "Till Death Do Us Part"; Wendlandt and Schrader, "Consumer Reactance Against Loyalty Programs."

52. Curasi and Kennedy, "From Prisoners to Apostles"; Mascarenhas, Kesavan, and Bernacchi, "Lasting Customer Loyalty"; Narayandas, "Measuring and Managing the Benefits of Customer Retention."

53. For histories, see, variously, Bellizzi and Bristol, "Assessment of Supermarket Loyalty Cards in One Major US Market"; Kearney, "Frequent Flyer Programs"; and Sharp and Sharp, "Loyalty Programs and Their Impact on Repeat-Purchase Loyalty Patterns."

54. Dyson, Farr, and Hollis, "Understanding, Measuring, and Using Brand Equity"; van Raaij, Vernooij, and van Triest, "Implementation of Customer Profitability Analysis"; Zeithaml, Rust, and Lemon, "Customer Pyramid."

55. Lacey and Sneath, "Customer Loyalty Programs."

56. Mägi, "Share of Wallet in Retailing"; Oliver and Shor, "Digital Redemption of Coupons"; Roehm, Pullins, and Roehm, "Designing Loyalty-Building Programs for Packaged Goods Brands."

57. Keh and Lee, "Do Reward Programs Build Loyalty for Services?"; Kendrick, "Promotional Products vs. Price Promotion in Fostering Customer Loyalty"; Lewis, "Influence of Loyalty Programs and Short-Term Promotions on Customer Retention"; van Heerde and Bijmolt, "Decomposing the Promotional Revenue Bump for Loyalty Program Members Versus Nonmembers"; Yi and Jeon, "Effects of Loyalty Programs on Value Perception, Program Loyalty, and Brand Loyalty."

58. Bellizzi and Bristol, "Assessment of Supermarket Loyalty Cards in One Major US Market"; Cigliano et al., "Price of Loyalty"; Dowling and Uncles, "Do Customer Loyalty Programs Really Work?"; Gómez, Arranz, and Cillán, "Role of Loyalty Programs in Behavioral and Affective Loyalty"; Leenheer et al., "Do Loyalty Programs Really Enhance Behavioral Loyalty?"; McIlroy and Barnett, "Building Customer Relationships"; O'Brien and Jones, "Do Rewards Really Create Loyalty?"; Rosenspan, "Delusions of Loyalty"; Shugan, "Brand Loyalty Programs."

59. Liu, "Long-Term Impact of Loyalty Programs on Consumer Purchase Behavior and Loyalty."

60. Bhattacharya, "Is Your Brand's Loyalty Too Much, Too Little, or Just Right?"; Ehrenberg, Uncles, and Goodhardt, "Understanding Brand Performance Measures"; Sharp and Sharp, "Loyalty Programs and Their Impact on Repeat-Purchase Loyalty Patterns"; Uncles, Dowling, and Hammond, "Customer Loyalty and Customer Loyalty Programs."

61. Danaher, Wilson, and Davis, "Comparison of Online and Offline Consumer Brand Loyalty"; Dekimpe et al., "Decline and Variability in Brand Loyalty"; East and Hammond, "Erosion of Repeat-Purchase Loyalty"; Fader and Schmittlein, "Excess Behavioral Loyalty for High-Share Brands"; Ferguson and Hlavinka, "COLLOQUY Loyalty Marketing Census"; Stern and Hammond, "Relationship Between Customer Loyalty and Purchase Incidence."

62. Bolton, Kannan, and Bramlett, "Implications of Loyalty Program Membership and Service Experiences for Customer Retention and Value"; Horne and Worthington, "Affinity Credit Card Relationship."

63. Early discussions of consumption communities include Friedman, Vanden Abeele, and De Vos, "Boorstin's Consumption Community Concept," based on Boorstin, *Americans*; McMillan, "Sense of Community"; McMillan and Chavis, "Sense of Community."

64. Aaker, Fournier, and Brasel, "When Good Brands Do Bad"; Thomson, "Human Brands"; Thomson, MacInnis, and Park, "Ties That Bind"; Van Vugt and Hart, "Social Identity as Social Glue."

65. Ahuvia, "Beyond the Extended Self" and "For the Love of Money"; Thomson, MacInnis, and Park, "Ties That Bind"; and Richins, "Measuring Emotions in the Consumption Experience." Passion appears in Thomson et al.

66. Miller, "Inattentive and Contented," p. 758; Ping, "Does Satisfaction Moderate the Association between Alternative Attractiveness and Exit Intention in a Marketing Channel?"; Sambandam and Lord, "Switching Behavior in Automobile Markets"; Murray, Holmes, and Griffin, "Benefits of Positive Illusions."

67. Bagozzi and Dholakia, "Antecedents and Purchase Consequences of Customer Participation in Small Group Brand Communities"; Bhattacharya, "When Customers Are Members"; Hunt, Bristol, and Bashaw, "Conceptual Approach to Classifying Sports Fans"; Laverie and Arnett "Factors Affecting Fan Attendance."

68. Fullerton, "When Does Commitment Lead to Loyalty?"; Wilson, "Integrated Model of Buyer-Seller Relationships"; Hess and Story, "Trust-Based Commitment."

69. Algesheimer, Dholakia, and Herrmann, "Social Influence of Brand Community"; Bagozzi and Dholakia, "Intentional Social Action in Virtual Communities"; Hart et al., "Are Loyalty Schemes a Manifestation of Relationship Marketing?"; Holland and Baker, "Customer Participation in Creating Site Brand Loyalty";

Liebermann, "Membership Clubs as a Tool for Enhancing Buyers' Patronage"; Stauss et al., "Retention Effects of a Customer Club"; Thorbjørnsen et al., "Building Brand Relationships Online."

70. McAlexander, Schouten, and Koenig, "Building Brand Community"; Muniz and O'Guinn, "Brand Community."

71. Rosenbaum, "Exploring the Social Supportive Role of Third Places in Consumers' Lives"; Rosenbaum, Ostrom, and Kuntze, "Loyalty Programs and a Sense of Community"; Rosenbaum et al., "A Cup of Coffee with a Dash of Love."

72. Goodwin, "Communality as a Dimension of Service Relationships."

73. Bagozzi and Dholakia, "Intentional Social Action in Virtual Communities"; Mathwick and Rigdon, "Play, Flow, and the Online Search Experience"; McAlexander, Kim, and Roberts, "Loyalty"; Schouten, McAlexander, and Koenig, "Trancendent Customer Experience and Brand Community."

74. Belk, "Possessions and the Extended Self."

75. Bristow and Sebastian, "Holy Cow!"

76. See Helgesen, "Are Loyal Customers Profitable?"; Ngobo, "Decreasing Returns in Customer Loyalty?"

77. See the meta-analysis of Seiders et al., "Do Satisfied Customers Buy More?" Other studies of note are Balabanis et al., "Bases of e-Store Loyalty"; Ball, Coelho, and Vilares, "Service Personalization and Loyalty"; Barnes, "Closeness, Strength, and Satisfaction"; Bennett and Rundle-Thiele, "Customer Satisfaction Should Not Be the Only Goal"; Chandrashekaran et al., "Satisfaction Strength and Customer Loyalty"; Chiou, Dröge, and Hanvanich, "Does Customer Knowledge Affect How Loyalty Is Formed?"; Homburg and Giering, "Personal Characteristics as Moderators of the Relationship Between Customer Satisfaction and Loyalty"; Iwasaki and Havitz, "Path Analytic Model of the Relationships Between Involvement, Psychological Commitment, and Loyalty"; Patterson, "Demographic Correlates of Loyalty in a Service Context"; Suh and Yi, "When Brand Attitudes Affect the Customer Satisfaction-Loyalty Relation"; Verhoef, Franses, and Hoekstra, "Effect of Relational Constructs on Customer Referrals and Number of Services Purchased From a Multiservice Provider"; Warrington and Shim, "Empirical Investigation of the Relationship Between Product Involvement and Brand Commitment"; and Yi and Jeon, "Effects of Loyalty Programs on Value Perception, Program Loyalty, and Brand Loyalty."

78. For the catastrophe and hygiene studies, see Oliva, Oliver, and MacMillan, "Catastrophe Model for Developing Service Satisfaction Strategies"; Oliva, Oliver, and Bearden, "Relationships among Consumer Satisfaction, Involvement, and Product Performance"; and Agustin and Singh, "Curvilinear Effects of Consumer Loyalty Determinants in Relational Exchanges," respectively. Others include Balabanis, Reynolds, and Simintiras, "Bases of e-Store Loyalty"; Bolton, "Dynamic Model of the Duration of the Customer's Relationship with a Continuous Service Provider"; Corstjens and Lal, "Building Store Loyalty Through Store Brands"; and Mittal and Kamakura, "Satisfaction, Repurchase Intent, and Repurchase Behavior."

79. Fletcher, *Loyalty*.

80. Dekimpe et al., "Decline and Variability in Brand Loyalty."

81. Harris and Goode, "Four Levels of Loyalty and the Pivotal Role of Trust." The study by Thomson, MacInnis, and Park, "Ties That Bind," used specific emotion items including "passionate," but did not report longer-stemmed full-length descriptors.

82. Algesheimer, Dholakia, and Herrmann, "Social Influence of Brand Community"; Rosenbaum, Ostrom, and Kuntze, "Loyalty Programs and a Sense of Community."

83. Net contributions of individual consumers are easily assessed based on the margins provided by individual purchases. See Helgesen, "Are Loyal Customers Profitable?"; and Zeithaml, Rust, and Lemon, "Customer Pyramid." Our concern at this point is with the aggregate profits of a firm's customer base.

84. Gupta et al., "Modeling Customer Lifetime Value"; Libai, Narayandas, and Humby, "Toward an Individual Customer Profitability Model"; and Malthouse and Blattberg, "Can We Predict Customer Lifetime Value?"

85. E. Anderson and Fornell, "Foundations of the American Customer Satisfaction Index"; Cassel and Eklöf, "Modelling Customer Satisfaction and Loyalty on Aggregate Levels"; and M. Johnson et al., "Evolution and Future of National Customer Satisfaction Index Models."

86. Ittner and Larcker, "Are Nonfinancial Measures Leading Indicators of Financial Performance?"; Keiningham et al., "Value of Different Customer Satisfaction and Loyalty Metrics in Predicting Customer Retention, Recommendation, and Share-of-Wallet"; and N. Morgan and Rego, "Value of Different Customer Satisfaction and Loyalty Metrics in Predicting Business Performance."

87. This example is from Rust, Zahorik, and Keiningham, *Return on Quality*, p. 86.

88. D. Aaker and Jacobson, "Financial Information Content of Perceived Quality"; E. Anderson, "Cross-

Category Variation in Customer Satisfaction and Retention"; E. Anderson, Fornell, and Lehmann, "Customer Satisfaction, Market Share, and Profitability"; Capon, Farley, and Hoenig, "Determinants of Financial Performance"; Fornell, "National Customer Satisfaction Barometer."

89. E. Anderson and Mittal, "Strengthening the Satisfaction-Profit Chain"; Bernhardt, Donthu, and Kennett, "Longitudinal Analysis of Satisfaction and Profitability"; Eklöf, Hackl, and Westlund, "On Measuring Interactions Between Customer Satisfaction and Financial Results"; Loveman, "Employee Satisfaction, Customer Loyalty, and Financial Performance."

90. A comprehensive overview can be found in Luo and Homburg, "Neglected Outcomes of Customer Satisfaction." For specifics, see E. Anderson, "Customer Satisfaction and Price Tolerance"; Homburg, Koschate, and Hoyer, "Do Satisfied Customers Really Pay More?"; Kalyanaram and Little, "Empirical Analysis of Latitude of Price Acceptance in Consumer Package Goods"; Krishnamurthi and Papatla, "Accounting for Heterogeneity and Dynamics in the Loyalty-Price Sensitivity Relationship"; Ngobo, "Drivers of Customers' Cross-Buying Intentions"; and Srinivasan, Anderson, and Ponnavolu, "Customer Loyalty in e-Commerce."

91. Edvardsson et al., "Effects of Satisfaction and Loyalty on Profits and Growth"; Hallowell, "Relationships of Customer Satisfaction, Customer Loyalty, and Profitability"; Storbacka, Strandvik, and Grönroos, "Managing Customer Relationships for Profit."

92. D. Aaker, "Value of Brand Equity"; Gupta and Lehmann, "Customers as Assets"; Reichheld and Sasser, "Zero Defections"; Reinartz and Kumar, "On the Profitability of Long-Life Customers in a Noncontractual Setting"; Rucci, Kirn, and Quinn, "Employee-Customer-Profit Chain at Sears."

93. E. Anderson, "Cross-Category Variation in Customer Satisfaction and Retention"; Fornell and Johnson, "Differentiation as a Basis for Explaining Customer Satisfaction across Industries"; M. Johnson and Fornell, "Framework for Comparing Customer Satisfaction across Individuals and Product Categories."

94. Mägi, "Share of Wallet in Retailing"; Leenheer et al., "Do Loyalty Programs Really Enhance Behavioral Loyalty?"; Cooil et al., "Longitudinal Analysis of Customer Satisfaction and Share of Wallet"; Keiningham, Perkins-Munn, and Evans, "Impact of Customer Satisfaction on Share-of-Wallet in a Business-to-Business Environment"; Wirtz, Mattila, and Lwin, "How Effective Are Loyalty Reward Programs in Driving Share of Wallet?"

95. Rust and Zahorik, "Customer Satisfaction, Customer Retention, and Market Share."

96. E. Anderson, Fornell, and Mazvancheryl, "Customer Satisfaction and Shareholder Value"; Berger et al., "From Customer Lifetime Value to Shareholder Value"; Fornell et al., "Customer Satisfaction and Stock Prices"; Gruca and Rego, "Customer Satisfaction, Cash Flow, and Shareholder Value"; Gupta and Zeithaml, "Customer Metrics and Their Impact on Financial Performance"; Mittal et al., "Dual Emphasis and the Long-Term Financial Impact of Customer Satisfaction."

BIBLIOGRAPHY

Aaker, David A. "The Value of Brand Equity." *Journal of Business Strategy* 13, no. 4 (July–August 1992): 27–32.

Aaker, David A., and Robert Jacobson. "The Financial Information Content of Perceived Quality." *Journal of Marketing Research* 31, no. 2 (May 1994): 191–201.

Aaker, Jennifer, Susan Fournier, and S. Adam Brasel. "When Good Brands Do Bad." *Journal of Consumer Research* 31, no. 1 (June 2004): 1–16.

Aarts, Henk, Bas Verplanken, and Ad van Knippenberg. "Predicting Behavior from Actions in the Past: Repeated Decision Making or a Matter of Habit?" *Journal of Applied Social Psychology* 28, no. 15 (August 1998): 1355–1374.

Agnew, Christopher R., Paul A.M. Van Lange, Caryl E. Rusbult, and Christopher A. Langston. "Cognitive Interdependence: Commitment and the Mental Representation of Close Relationships." *Journal of Personality and Social Psychology* 74, no. 4 (April 1998): 939–954.

Agustin, Clara, and Jagdip Singh. "Curvilinear Effects of Consumer Loyalty Determinants in Relational Exchanges." *Journal of Marketing Research* 42, no. 1 (February 2005): 96–108.

Ahuvia, Aaron C. "Beyond the Extended Self: Loved Objects and Consumers' Identity Narratives." *Journal of Consumer Research* 32, no. 1 (June 2005): 171–184.

———. "For the Love of Money: Materialism and Product Love." In *Meaning, Measure, and Morality of Materialism*, ed. Floyd Rudmin and Marsha Richins, 188–198. Provo, UT: Association for Consumer Research, 1992.

Ajzen, Icek. "The Theory of Planned Behavior." *Organizational Behavior and Human Decision Processes* 50, no. 2 (December 1991): 179–211.

Algesheimer, René, Uptal M. Dholakia, and Andreas Herrmann. "The Social Influence of Brand Community: Evidence from European Car Clubs." *Journal of Marketing* 69, no. 3 (July 2005): 19–34.

Anderson, Eugene W. "Cross-Category Variation in Customer Satisfaction and Retention." *Marketing Letters* 5, no. 1 (January 1994): 19–30.

———. "Customer Satisfaction and Price Tolerance." *Marketing Letters* 7, no. 3 (July 1996): 265–274.

Anderson, Eugene W., and Claes Fornell. "Foundations of the American Customer Satisfaction Index." *Total Quality Management* 11, no. 7 (September 2000): S869–S882.

Anderson, Eugene W., Claes Fornell, and Donald R. Lehmann. "Customer Satisfaction, Market Share, and Profitability: Findings from Sweden." *Journal of Marketing* 58, no. 3 (July 1994): 53–66.

Anderson, Eugene W., Claes Fornell, and Sanal K. Mazvancheryl. "Customer Satisfaction and Shareholder Value." *Journal of Marketing* 68, no. 4 (October 2004): 172–185.

Anderson, Eugene W., and Vikas Mittal. "Strengthening the Satisfaction-Profit Chain." *Journal of Service Research* 3, no. 2 (November 2000): 107–120.

Anderson, Rolph E., and Srini S. Srinivasan. "E-Satisfaction and E-Loyalty: A Contingency Framework." *Psychology & Marketing* 20, no. 2 (February 2003): 123–138.

Andreassen, Tor Wallin. "From Disgust to Delight: Do Customers Hold a Grudge?" *Journal of Service Research* 4, no. 1 (August 2001): 39–49.

Aron, David. "Consumer Grudgeholding: Toward a Conceptual Model and Research Agenda." *Journal of Consumer Satisfaction, Dissatisfaction and Complaining Behavior* 14 (2001): 108–119.

Athanassopoulos, Antreas D. "Customer Satisfaction Cues to Support Market Segmentation and Explain Switching Behavior." *Journal of Business Research* 47, no. 3 (March 2000): 191–207.

Auh, Seigyoung. "The Effects of Soft and Hard Service Attributes on Loyalty: The Mediating Role of Trust." *Journal of Services Marketing* 19, no. 2 (2005): 81–92.

Bagozzi, Richard P., and Utpal M. Dholakia. "Antecedents and Purchase Consequences of Customer Participation in Small Group Brand Communities." *International Journal of Research in Marketing* 23, no. 1 (March 2006): 45–61.

———. "Goal Setting and Goal Striving in Consumer Behavior." *Journal of Marketing* 63, (Special Issue): 19–32.

———. "Intentional Social Action in Virtual Communities." *Journal of Interactive Marketing* 16, no. 2 (Spring 2002): 2–21.

Bagozzi, Richard P., and Paul R. Warshaw. "Trying to Consume." *Journal of Consumer Research* 17, no. 2 (September 1990): 127–140.

Baker, Colin, Clive Nancarrow, and Julie Tinson. "The Mind Versus Market Share Guide to Brand Equity." *International Journal of Market Research* 47, no. 5 (2005): 525–542.

Balabanis, George, Nina Reynolds, and Antonis Simintiras. "Bases of e-Store Loyalty: Perceived Switching Barriers and Satisfaction." *Journal of Business Research* 59, no. 2 (February 2006): 214–224.

Ball, Dwayne, Pedro S. Coelho, and Manuel J. Vilares. "Service Personalization and Loyalty." *Journal of Services Marketing* 20, no. 6 (2006): 391–403.

Bansal, Harvir S., and Shirley F. Taylor. "The Service Provider Switching Model (SPSM): A Model of Consumer Switching Behavior in the Services Industry." *Journal of Service Research* 2, no. 2 (November 1999): 200–218.

Barnes, James G. "Closeness, Strength, and Satisfaction: Examining the Relationships Between Providers of Financial Services and Their Retail Customers." *Psychology & Marketing* 14, no. 8 (December 1997): 765–790.

Bass, Frank M. "The Theory of Stochastic Preference and Brand Switching." *Journal of Marketing Research* 11, no. 1 (February 1974): 1–20.

Belk, Russell W. "Possessions and the Extended Self." *Journal of Consumer Research* 15, no. 2 (September 1988): 139–168.

Bell, Simon J., Seigyoung Auh, and Karen Smalley. "Customer Relationship Dynamics: Service Quality and Customer Loyalty in the Context of Varying Levels of Customer Expertise and Switching Costs." *Journal of the Academy of Marketing Science* 33, no. 2 (Spring 2005): 169–183.

Bellizzi, Joseph A., and Terry Bristol. "An Assessment of Supermarket Loyalty Cards in One Major US Market." *Journal of Consumer Marketing* 21, no. 2 (2004): 144–154.

Bennett, Rebekah, and Sharyn Rundle-Thiele. "Customer Satisfaction Should Not Be the Only Goal." *Journal of Services Marketing* 18, no. 7 (2004): 514–523.

Berger, Paul D., Naras Eechambadi, Morris George, Donald R. Lehmann, Ross Rizley, and Rajkumar Venkatesan. "From Customer Lifetime Value to Shareholder Value: Theory, Empirical Evidence, and Issues for Future Research." *Journal of Service Research* 9, no. 2 (November 2006): 156–167.

Bernhardt, Kenneth A., Naveen Donthu, and Pamela A. Kennett. "A Longitudinal Analysis of Satisfaction and Profitability." *Journal of Business Research* 47, no. 2 (February 2000): 161–171.

Bhattacharya, C.B. "Is Your Brand's Loyalty Too Much, Too Little, or Just Right? Explaining Deviations in Loyalty from the Dirichlet Norm." *International Journal of Research in Marketing* 14, no. 5 (December 1997): 421–435.

———. "When Customers Are Members: Customer Retention in Paid Membership Contexts." *Journal of the Academy of Marketing Science* 26, no. 1 (Winter 1998): 31–44.

Bolton, Ruth N. "A Dynamic Model of the Duration of the Customer's Relationship with a Continuous Service Provider: The Role of Satisfaction." *Marketing Science* 17, no. 1 (1998), 45–65.

Bolton, Ruth N., P.K. Kannan, and Matthew D. Bramlett. "Implications of Loyalty Program Membership and Service Experiences for Customer Retention and Value." *Journal of the Academy of Marketing Science* 28, no. 1 (Winter 2000): 95–108.

Boorstin, Daniel J. *The Americans: The Democratic Experience*. New York: Random House, 1973

Bove, Liliana, and Lester W. Johnson. "Customer Loyalty to One Service Worker: Should It Be Discouraged?" *International Journal of Research in Marketing* 23, no. 1 (March 2006): 79–91.

Bristow, Dennis N., and Richard J. Sebastian. "Holy Cow! Wait 'til Next Year! A Closer Look at the Brand Loyalty of Chicago Cubs Baseball Fans." *Journal of Consumer Marketing* 18, no. 3 (2001): 256–275.

Bruyneel, Sabrina, Siegfried Dewitte, Kathleen D. Vohs, and Luk Warlop. "Repeated Choosing Increases Susceptibility to Affective Product Features." *International Journal of Research in Marketing* 23, no. 2 (June 2006): 215–225.

Burnham, Thomas A., Judy K. Frels, and Vijay Mahajan. "Consumer Switching Costs: A Typology, Antecedents, and Consequences." *Journal of the Academy of Marketing Science* 31, no. 2 (Spring 2003): 109–126.

Büschken, Joachim. *Higher Profits Through Customer Lock-In: A Roadmap*. Mason, OH: TEXERE (Thomson), 2004.

Butcher, Ken, Beverly Sparks, and Frances O'Callaghan. "Evaluative and Relational Influences on Service Loyalty." *International Journal of Service Industry Management* 12, no. 4 (2001): 310–327.

Capon, Noel, John U. Farley, and Scott Hoenig. "Determinants of Financial Performance: A Meta-Analysis." *Management Science* 36, no. 10 (October 1990): 1143–1159.

Capraro, Anthony J., Susan Broniarczyk, and Rajendra K. Srivastava. "Factors Influencing the Likelihood of Customer Defection: The Role of Consumer Knowledge." *Journal of the Academy of Marketing Science* 31, no. 2 (April 2003): 164–175.

Cassel, Claes, and Jan A. Eklöf. "Modelling Customer Satisfaction and Loyalty on Aggregate Levels: Experience from the ECSI Pilot Study." *Total Quality Management* 12, nos. 7–8 (December 2001): 834–841.

Chandon, Pierre, Vicki G. Morwitz, and Werner J. Reinartz. "Do Intentions Really Predict Behavior? Self-Generated Validity Effects in Survey Research." *Journal of Marketing* 69, no. 2 (April 2005): 1–14.

Chandrashekaran, Murali, Kristin Rotte, Stephen S. Tax, and Rajdeep Grewal. "Satisfaction Strength and Customer Loyalty." *Journal of Marketing Research* 44, no. 1 (February 2007): 153–163.

Chapman, Kenneth J. "Measuring Intent: There's Nothing 'Mere' about Mere Measurement Effects." *Psychology & Marketing* 18, no. 8 (August 2001): 811–841.

Chaudhuri, Arjun, and Morris B. Holbrook. "The Chain of Effects from Brand Trust and Brand Affect to Brand Performance: The Role of Brand Loyalty." *Journal of Marketing* 65, no. 2 (April 2001): 81–93.

Chintagunta, Pradeep. "Inertia and Variety Seeking in a Model of Brand-Purchase Timing." *Marketing Science* 17, no. 3 (1998): 253–270.

Chiou, Jyh-Shen, and Cornelia Dröge. "Service Quality, Trust, Specific Asset Investment, and Expertise: Direct and Indirect Effects in a Satisfaction-Loyalty Framework." *Journal of the Academy of Marketing Science* 34, no. 4 (October 2006): 613–627.

Chiou, Jyh-Shen, Cornelia Dröge, and Sangphet Hanvanich. "Does Customer Knowledge Affect How Loyalty Is Formed?" *Journal of Service Research* 5, no. 2 (November 2002): 113–124.

Chiu, Hung-Chang, Yi-Ching Hsieh, Yu-Chuan Li, and Monle Lee. "Relationship Marketing and Consumer Switching Behavior." *Journal of Business Research* 58, no. 12 (December 2005): 1681–1689.

Cigliano, James, Margaret Georgiadis, Darren Pleasance, and Susan Whalley. "The Price of Loyalty." *McKinsley Quarterly* 69, no. 4 (November 2000): 68–77.

Colgate, Mark, and Bodo Lang. "Switching Barriers in Consumer Markets: An Investigation of the Financial Services Industry." *Journal of Consumer Marketing* 18, no. 4 (2001): 332–347.

Colgate, Mark, Vicky Thuy-Uyen Tong, Christina Dwai-Choi Lee, and John U. Farley. "Back from the Brink: Why Customers Stay." *Journal of Service Research* 9, no. 3 (February 2007): 211–228.

Cooil, Bruce, Timothy L. Keiningham, Lerzan Aksoy, and Michael Hsu. "A Longitudinal Analysis of Customer Satisfaction and Share of Wallet: Investigating the Moderating Effect of Customer Characteristics." *Journal of Marketing* 71, no. 1 (January 2007): 67–83.

Corstjens, Marcel, and Rajiv Lal. "Building Store Loyalty Through Store Brands." *Journal of Marketing Research* 37, no. 3 (August 2000): 281–291.

Curasi, Carolyn Folkman, and Karen Norman Kennedy. "From Prisoners to Apostles: A Typology of Repeat Buyers and Loyal Customers in Service Businesses." *Journal of Services Marketing* 16, no. 4 (2002): 322–341.

Danaher, Peter J., Isaac W. Wilson, and Robert A. Davis. "A Comparison of Online and Offline Consumer Brand Loyalty." *Marketing Science* 22, no. 4 (Fall 2003): 461–476.

Dean, Alison M. "The Impact of the Customer Orientation of Call Center Employees on Customers' Affective Commitment and Loyalty." *Journal of Service Research* 10, no. 2 (November 2007): 161–173.

Dekimpe, Marnik G., Jan-Benedict E.M. Steenkamp, Martin Mellens, and Piet Vanden Abelle. "Decline and Variability in Brand Loyalty." *International Journal of Research in Marketing* 14, no. 5 (December 1997): 405–420.

de Ruyter, Ko, Martin Wetzels, and Josée Bloemer. "On the Relationship Between Perceived Service Quality, Service Loyalty and Switching Costs." *International Journal of Service Industry Management* 9, no. 5 (1998): 436–453.

De Wulf, Kristof, Gaby Odekerken-Schröder, and Dawn Iacobucci. "Investments in Consumer Relationships: A Cross-Country and Cross-Industry Exploration." *Journal of Marketing* 65, no. 4 (October 2001): 33–50.

Dick, Alan S., and Kunal Basu. "Customer Loyalty: Toward an Integrated Conceptual Framework." *Journal of the Academy of Marketing Science* 22, no. 2 (Spring 1994): 99–113.

Dowling, Grahame R., and Mark Uncles. "Do Customer Loyalty Programs Really Work?" *Sloan Management Review* 38, no. 4 (Summer 1997): 71–82.

Du, Rex Yuxing, Wagner A. Kamakura, and Carl F. Mela. "Size and Share of Customer Wallet." *Journal of Marketing* 71, no. 2 (April 2007): 94–113.

Dubé, Laurette, and Manfred Maute. "The Antecedents of Brand Switching, Brand Loyalty, and Verbal Responses to Service Failure." In *Advances in Services Marketing and Management*, ed. Teresa A. Swartz, David E. Bowen, and Stephen W. Brown, 5:127–151. Greenwich, CT: JAI Press, 1996.

Dyson, Paul, Andy Farr, and Nigel S. Hollis. "Understanding, Measuring, and Using Brand Equity." *Journal of Advertising Research* 36, no. 6 (November–December 1996): 9–21.

East, Robert, and Kathy Hammond. "The Erosion of Repeat-Purchase Loyalty." *Marketing Letters* 7, no. 2 (March 1996): 163–171.

Edvardsson, Bo, Michael D. Johnson, Anders Gustafsson, and Tore Strandvik. "The Effects of Satisfaction and Loyalty on Profits and Growth: Products Versus Services." *Total Quality Management* 11, no. 7 (September 2000): S917–S927.

Ehrenberg, Andrew S.C., Mark Uncles, and Gerald J. Goodhardt. "Understanding Brand Performance Measures: Using Dirichlet Benchmarks." *Journal of Business Research* 57, no. 12 (December 2004): 1307–1325.

Eklöf, Jan A., Peter Hackl, and Anders Westlund. "On Measuring Interactions Between Customer Satisfaction and Financial Results." *Total Quality Management* 10, nos. 4–5 (January 1999): S514–S522.

Ellen, Pam Scholder, William O. Bearden, and Subhash Sharma. "Resistance to Technological Innovations: An Examination of the Role of Self-Efficacy and Performance Satisfaction." *Journal of the Academy of Marketing Science* 19, no. 4 (Fall 1991): 297–307.

Evanschitzky, Heiner, and Maren Wunderlich. "An Examination of Moderator Effects in the Four-Stage Loyalty Model." *Journal of Service Research* 8, no. 4 (May 2006): 330–345.

Fader, Peter S., and David C. Schmittlein. "Excess Behavioral Loyalty for High-Share Brands: Deviations from the Dirichlet Model for Repeat Purchasing." *Journal of Marketing Research* 30, no. 4 (November 1993): 478–493.

Feather, Norman T., ed. *Expectations and Actions: Expectancy-Value Models in Psychology.* Hillsdale, NJ: Lawrence Erlbaum, 1982.

Feinberg, Richard A., Richard Widdows, Marlaya Hirsch-Wyncott, and Charles Trappey. "Myth and Reality in Customer Service: Good and Bad Service Sometimes Leads to Repurchase." *Journal of Consumer Satisfaction, Dissatisfaction and Complaining Behavior* 3 (1990): 112–114.

Ferguson, Rick, and Kelly Hlavinka. "The COLLOQUY Loyalty Marketing Census: Sizing Up the US Loyalty Marketing Industry." *Journal of Consumer Marketing* 24, no. 5 (2007): 313–321.

Finn, Adam. "Reassessing the Foundations of Customer Delight." *Journal of Service Research* 8, no. 2 (November 2005): 103–116.

Fishbein, Martin, and Icek Ajzen. *Belief, Attitude, Intention and Behavior: An Introduction to Theory and Research*. Reading, MA: Addison-Wesley, 1975.

Fitzsimons, Gavan J., and Vicki G. Morwitz. "The Effect of Measuring Intent on Brand-Level Purchase Behavior." *Journal of Consumer Research* 23, no. 1 (June 1996): 1–11.

Fletcher, George P. *Loyalty: An Essay on the Morality of Relationships*. New York: Oxford University Press, 1993.

Fornell, Claes. "A National Customer Satisfaction Barometer: The Swedish Experience." *Journal of Marketing* 56, no. 1 (January 1992): 6–21.

Fornell, Claes, and Michael D. Johnson. "Differentiation as a Basis for Explaining Customer Satisfaction across Industries." *Journal of Economic Psychology* 14, no. 4 (December 1993): 681–696.

Fornell, Claes, Sunil Mithas, Forrest V. Morgeson III, and M.S. Krishnan. "Customer Satisfaction and Stock Prices: High Returns, Low Risk." *Journal of Marketing* 70, no. 1 (January 2006): 3–14.

Friedman, Monroe, Piet Vanden Abeele, and Koen De Vos. "Boorstin's Consumption Community Concept: A Tale of Two Countries." *Journal of Consumer Policy* 16, no. 1 (1993): 35–60.

Fullerton, Gordon. "When Does Commitment Lead to Loyalty?" *Journal of Service Research* 5, no. 4 (May 2003): 333–344.

Ganesh, Jaishankar, Mark J. Arnold, and Kristy E. Reynolds. "Understanding the Customer Base of Service Providers: An Examination of the Differences Between Switchers and Stayers." *Journal of Marketing* 64, no. 3 (July 2000): 65–87.

Gollwitzer, Peter M. "The Volitional Benefits of Planning." In *The Psychology of Action: Linking Cognition and Motivation to Behavior*, ed. Peter M. Gollwitzer and John A. Bargh, 287–312. New York: Guilford Press, 1996.

Gollwitzer, Peter M., and John A. Bargh, eds. *The Psychology of Action: Linking Cognition and Motivation to Behavior*. New York: Guilford Press, 1996.

Gómez, Blanca García, Ana Gutiérrez Arranz, and Jesús Gutiérrez Cillán. "The Role of Loyalty Programs in Behavioral and Affective Loyalty." *Journal of Consumer Marketing* 23, no. 7 (2006): 387–396.

Goodwin, Cathy. "Communality as a Dimension of Service Relationships." *Journal of Consumer Psychology* 5, no. 4 (1996): 387–415.

Goodwin, Cathy, and Dwayne D. Gremler. "Friendship Over the Counter: How Social Aspects of Service Encounters Influence Consumer Service Loyalty." In *Advances in Services Marketing and Management*, ed. Teresa A. Swartz, David E. Bowen, and Stephen W. Brown, 5:247–282. Greenwich, CT: JAI Press, 1996.

Grønholdt, Lars, Anne Martensen, and Kai Kristensen. "The Relationship Between Customer Satisfaction and Loyalty: Cross-Industry Differences." *Total Quality Management* 11, nos. 4–6 (July 2000): S509–S514.

Gruca, Thomas S., and Lopo L. Rego. "Customer Satisfaction, Cash Flow, and Shareholder Value." *Journal of Marketing* 69, no. 3 (July 2005): 115–130.

Gundlach, Gregory T., Ravi S. Achrol, and John T. Mentzer. "The Structure of Commitment in Exchange." *Journal of Marketing* 59, no. 1 (January 1995): 78–92.

Gupta, Sunil, Dominique Hanssens, Bruce Hardie, Wiliam Kahn, V. Kumar, Nathaniel Lin, Nalini Ravishanker, and S. Sriram. "Modeling Customer Value." *Journal of Service Research* 9, no. 2 (November 2006): 139–155.

Gupta, Sunil, and Donald R. Lehmann. "Customers as Assets." *Journal of Interactive Marketing* 17, no. 1 (Winter 2003): 9–24.

Gupta, Sunil and Valarie Zeithaml. "Customer Metrics and Their Impact on Financial Performance." *Marketing Science* 25, no. 6 (November–December 2006): 718–739.

Gustafsson, Anders, Michael D. Johnson, and Inger Roos. "The Effects of Customer Satisfaction, Relationship Commitment Dimensions, and Triggers on Customer Retention." *Journal of Marketing* 69, no. 4 (October 2005): 210–218.

Gutek, Barbara A., Anita D. Bhappu, Mathhew A. Liao-Troth, and Bennett Cherry. "Distinguishing Between Service Relationships and Encounters." *Journal of Applied Psychology* 84, no. 2 (April 1999): 218–233.

Hallowell, Roger. "The Relationships of Customer Satisfaction, Customer Loyalty, and Profitability: An Empirical Study." *International Journal of Service Industry Management* 7, no. 4 (1996): 27–42.

Halstead, Diane, and Thomas J. Page, Jr. "The Effects of Satisfaction and Complaining Behavior on Consumer Repurchase Intentions." *Journal of Consumer Satisfaction, Dissatisfaction and Complaining Behavior* 5, (1992): 1-11.

Harris, Lloyd C., and Mark M.H. Goode. "The Four Levels of Loyalty and the Pivotal Role of Trust: A Study of Online Service Dynamics." *Journal of Retailing* 80, no. 2 (2004): 139–158.

Hart, Susan, Andrew Smith, Leigh Sparks, and Nikolaos Tzokas. "Are Loyalty Schemes a Manifestation of Relationship Marketing?" *Journal of Marketing Management* 15, no. 7 (July 1999): 541–562.

Heckhausen, Heniz, and Jürgen Beckmann. "Intentional Action and Action Slips." *Psychological Review* 97, no. 1 (January 1990): 36–48.

Heide, Jan B., and Allen M. Weiss. "Vendor Consideration and Switching Behavior for Buyers in High-Technology Markets." *Journal of Marketing* 59, no. 3 (July 1995): 30–43.

Helgesen, Øyvind. "Are Loyal Customers Profitable? Customer Satisfaction, Customer (Action) Loyalty and Customer Profitability at the Individual Level." *Journal of Marketing Management* 22, nos. 3–4 (April 2006): 245–266.

Hess, Jeff, and John Story. "Trust-Based Commitment: Multidimensional Consumer-Brand Relationships." *Journal of Consumer Marketing* 22, no. 6 (2005): 313–322.

Holland, Jonna, and Stacey Menzel Baker. "Customer Participation in Creating Site Brand Loyalty." *Journal of Interactive Marketing* 15, no. 4 (Autumn 2001): 34–45.

Homburg, Christian, and Annette Giering. "Personal Characteristics as Moderators of the Relationship Between Customer Satisfaction and Loyalty: An Empirical Analysis." *Psychology & Marketing* 18, no. 1 (January 2001): 43–66.

Homburg, Christian, Nicole Koschate, and Wayne D. Hoyer. "Do Satisfied Customers Really Pay More? A Study of the Relationship Between Customer Satisfaction and Willingness to Pay." *Journal of Marketing* 69, no. 2 (April 2005): 84–96.

Horne, Suzanne, and Steve Worthington. "The Affinity Credit Card Relationship: Can It Really Be Mutually Beneficial?" *Journal of Marketing Management* 15, no. 10 (October 1999): 603–616.

Huang, Ming-Hui, and Shihti Yu. "Are Consumers Inherently or Situationally Brand Loyal? A Set Intercorrelation Account for Conscious Brand Loyalty and Nonconscious Inertia." *Psychology & Marketing* 16, no. 6 (September 1999): 523–544.

Hunt, Kenneth A., Terry Bristol, and R. Edward Bashaw. "A Conceptual Approach to Classifying Sports Fans." *Journal of Services Marketing* 13, no. 6 (1999): 439–452.

Iacobucci, Dawn, and Amy Ostrom. "Commercial and Interpersonal Relationships: Using the Structure of Interpersonal Relationships to Understand Individual-to-Individual, Individual-to-Firm, and Firm-to-Firm Relationships in Commerce." *International Journal of Research in Marketing* 13, no. 1 (February 1996): 53–72.

Ittner, Christopher, and David F. Larcker. "Are Nonfinancial Measures Leading Indicators of Financial Performance? An Analysis of Consumer Satisfaction." *Journal of Accounting Research* 36 (Supplement 1998): 1–35.

Iwasaki, Yoshi, and Mark E. Havitz. "A Path Analytic Model of the Relationships Between Involvement, Psychological Commitment, and Loyalty." *Journal of Leisure Research* 30, no. 2 (1998): 256–280.

Jacoby, Jacob, and Robert W. Chestnut. *Brand Loyalty: Measurement and Management.* New York: Wiley, 1978.

Jacoby, Jacob, and David B. Kyner. "Brand Loyalty vs. Repeat Purchasing Behavior." *Journal of Marketing Research* 10, no. 1 (February 1973): 1–9.

Johnson, Eric J., Steven Bellman, and Gerald L. Lohse. "Cognitive Lock-In and the Power Law of Practice." *Journal of Marketing* 67, no. 2 (April 2003): 62–75.

Johnson, Michael D., Eugene W. Anderson, and Claes Fornell. "Rational and Adaptive Performance Expectations in a Customer Satisfaction Framework." *Journal of Consumer Research* 21, no. 4 (March 1995): 695–707.

Johnson, Michael D., and Claes Fornell. "A Framework for Comparing Customer Satisfaction across Individuals and Product Categories." *Journal of Economic Psychology* 12, no. 2 (June 1991): 267–286.

Johnson, Michael D., Anders Gustafsson, Tor Wallin Andreassen, Line Lervik, and Jaesung Cha. "The Evolution and Future of National Customer Satisfaction Index Models." *Journal of Economic Psychology* 22, no. 2 (April 2001): 217–245.

Johnson, Michael D., Andreas Herrman, and Frank Huber. "The Evolution of Loyalty Intentions." *Journal of Marketing* 70, no. 2 (April 2006): 122–132.

Jones, Michael A., David L. Mothersbaugh, and Sharon E. Beatty. "Why Customers Stay: Measuring the Underlying Dimensions of Services Switching Costs and Managing Their Differential Strategic Outcomes." *Journal of Business Research* 55, no. 6 (June 2002): 441–450.

Jones, Michael A., Kristy E. Reynolds, David L. Mothersbaugh, and Sharon E. Beatty. "The Positive and Negative Effects of Switching Costs on Relational Outcomes." *Journal of Service Research* 9, no. 4 (May 2007): 335–355.

Jones, Tim, and Shirley F. Taylor. "The Conceptual Domain of Service Loyalty: How Many Dimensions?" *Journal of Services Marketing* 21, no. 1 (2007): 36–51.

Kalyanaram, Gurumurthy, and John D.C. Little. "An Empirical Analysis of Latitude of Price Acceptance in Consumer Package Goods." *Journal of Consumer Research* 21, no. 3 (December 1994): 408–418.

Kearney, Terrence J. "Frequent Flyer Programs: A Failure in Competitive Strategy, with Lessons for Management." *Journal of Consumer Marketing* 7, no. 1 (Winter 1990): 31–40.

Keaveney, Susan M. "Customer Switching Behavior in Service Industries: An Exploratory Study." *Journal of Marketing* 59, no. 2 (April 1995): 71–82.

Keaveney, Susan M., and Madhavan Parthasarathy. "Customer Switching Behavior in Online Services: An Exploratory Study of the Role of Selected Attitudinal, Behavioral, and Demographic Factors." *Journal of the Academy of Marketing Science* 29, no. 4 (Fall 2001): 374–390.

Keh, Hean Tat, and Yih Hwai Lee. "Do Reward Programs Build Loyalty for Services? The Moderating Effect of Satisfaction on Type and Timing of Rewards." *Journal of Retailing* 82, no. 2 (2006): 127–136.

Keiningham, Timothy L., Bruce Cooil, Lerzan Aksoy, Tor Wallin Andreassen, and Jay Weiner. "The Value of Different Customer Satisfaction and Loyalty Metrics in Predicting Customer Retention, Recommendation, and Share-of-Wallet." *Managing Service Quality* 17, no. 4 (2007): 361–384.

Keiningham, Timothy L., Tiffany Perkins-Munn, and Heather Evans. "The Impact of Customer Satisfaction on Share-of-Wallet in a Business-to-Business Environment." *Journal of Service Research* 6, no. 1 (August 2003): 37–50.

Keiningham, Timothy L., Terry G. Vavra, Lerzan Aksoy, and Henri Wallard. *Loyalty Myths: Hyped Strategies That Will Put You Out of Business—and Proven Tactics That Really Work.* Hoboken, NJ: Wiley, 2005.

Kendrick, Alice. "Promotional Products vs. Price Promotion in Fostering Customer Loyalty: A Report of Two Controlled Field Experiments." *Journal of Services Marketing* 12, no. 4 (1998): 312–326.

Krishnamurthi, Lakshman, and Purushottam Papatla. "Accounting for Heterogeneity and Dynamics in the Loyalty–Price Sensitivity Relationship." *Journal of Retailing* 79, no. 2 (2003): 121–135.

Krishnan, H. Shankar, and Stewart Shapiro. "Prospective and Retrospective Memory for Intentions: A Two-Component Approach." *Journal of Consumer Psychology* 8, no. 2 (1999): 141–166.

Kuhl, Julius. "Volitional Mediators of Cognition-Behavior Consistency: Self-Regulatory Processes and Action versus State Orientation." In *Action Control: From Cognition to Behavior*, ed. Julius Kuhl and Jürgen Beckmann, 101–128. Berlin: Springer-Verlag, 1985.

Kuhl, Julius, and Jürgen Beckmann, eds. *Action Control: From Cognition to Behavior.* Berlin: Springer-Verlag, 1985.

Kumar, Piyush. "The Impact of Performance, Cost, and Competitive Considerations on the Relationship Between Satisfaction and Repurchase Intent in Business Markets." *Journal of Service Research* 5, no. 1 (August 2002): 55–68.

Lacey, Russell, and Julie Z. Sneath. "Customer Loyalty Programs: Are They Fair to Consumers?" *Journal of Consumer Marketing* 23, no. 7 (2006): 458–464.

Lach, Jennifer. "Redeeming Qualities." *American Demographics* 22, no. 5 (May 2000): 36–38.

Laverie, Debra A., and Dennis B. Arnett. "Factors Affecting Fan Attendance: The Influence of Identity Salience and Satisfaction." *Journal of Leisure Research* 32, no. 2 (2000): 225–246.

Lee, Jonathan, Janghyuk Lee, and Lawrence Feick. "The Impact of Switching Costs on the Customer Satisfaction-Loyalty Link: Mobile Phone Service in France." *Journal of Services Marketing* 15, no. 1 (2001): 35–48.

Lee, Moonkyu, and Lawrence F. Cunningham. "A Cost/Benefit Approach to Understanding Service Loyalty." *Journal of Services Marketing* 15, no. 2 (2001): 113–130.

Leenheer, Jorna, Harald J. van Heerde, Tammo H.A. Bijmolt, and Ale Smidts. "Do Loyalty Programs Really Enhance Behavioral Loyalty? An Empirical Analysis Accounting for Self-Selecting Members." *International Journal of Research in Marketing* 24, no. 1 (March 2007): 31–47.

Lewis, Michael. "The Influence of Loyalty Programs and Short-Term Promotions on Customer Retention." *Journal of Marketing Research* 41, no. 3 (August 2004): 281–292.

Libai, Barak, Das Narayandas, and Clive Humby. "Toward an Individual Customer Profitability Model: A Segment-Based Approach." *Journal of Service Research* 5, no. 1 (August 2002): 69–76.

Liebermann, Yehoshua. "Membership Clubs as a Tool for Enhancing Buyers' Patronage." *Journal of Business Research* 45, no. 3 (July 1999): 291–297.

Lipke, David J. "Pledge of Allegiance: Generational Shifts Challenge Familiar Views of the Mature Consumer and Brand Loyalty." *American Demographics* 22, no. 11 (November 2000): 40–42.

Liu, Yuping. "The Long-Term Impact of Loyalty Programs on Consumer Purchase Behavior and Loyalty." *Journal of Marketing* 71, no. 4 (October 2007): 19–35.

Loveman, Gary W. "Employee Satisfaction, Customer Loyalty, and Financial Performance: An Empirical Examination of the Service Profit Chain in Retail Banking." *Journal of Service Research* 1, no. 1 (August 1998): 18–31.

Lu, Xiaoling, and Hing-Po Lo. "Television Audience Satisfaction: Antecedents and Consequences." *Journal of Advertising Research* 47, no. 3 (September 2007): 354–363.

Luo, Xueming, and Christian Homburg. "Neglected Outcomes of Customer Satisfaction." *Journal of Marketing* 71, no. 2 (April 2007): 133–149.

Macintosh, Gerrard, and Lawrence S. Lockshin. "Retail Relationships and Store Loyalty: A Multi-Level Perspective." *International Journal of Research in Marketing* 14, no. 5 (December 1997): 487–497.

Mägi, Anne W. "Share of Wallet in Retailing: The Effects of Customer Satisfaction, Loyalty Cards and Shopper Characteristics." *Journal of Retailing* 79, no. 2 (2003): 97–106.

Malthouse, Edward C., and Robert C. Blattberg. "Can We Predict Customer Lifetime Value?" *Journal of Interactive Marketing* 19, no. 1 (Winter 2005): 2–16.

Mascarenhas, Oswald A., Ram Kesavan, and Michael Bernacchi. "Lasting Customer Loyalty: A Total Customer Experience Approach." *Journal of Consumer Marketing* 23, no. 7 (2006): 397–405.

Mathwick, Charla, and Edward Rigdon. "Play, Flow, and the Online Search Experience." *Journal of Consumer Research* 31, no. 2 (September 2004): 324–332.

Mattila, Anna S. "The Impact of Relationship Type on Customer Loyalty in a Context of Service Failures." *Journal of Service Research* 4, no. 2 (November 2001): 91–101.

Maxham, James G., III. "Service Recovery's Influence on Consumer Satisfaction, Positive Word-of-Mouth, and Purchase Intentions." *Journal of Business Research* 54, no. 1 (October 2001): 11–24.

Mazursky, David, and Aviva Geva. "Temporal Decay in Satisfaction–Purchase Intention Relationship." *Psychology & Marketing* 6, no. 3 (Fall 1989): 211–227.

McAlexander, James H., Stephen K. Kim, and Scott D. Roberts. "Loyalty: The Influences of Satisfaction and Brand Community Integration." *Journal of Marketing Theory and Practice* 11, no. 4 (Fall 2003): 1–11.

McAlexander, James H., John W. Schouten, and Harold F. Koenig. "Building Brand Community." *Journal of Marketing* 66, no. 1 (January 2002): 38–54.

McDonald, William J. "The Roles of Demographics, Purchase Histories, and Shopper Decision-Making Styles in Predicting Consumer Catalog Loyalty." *Journal of Direct Marketing* 7, no. 3 (Summer 1993): 55–65.

McIlroy, Andrea, and Shirley Barnett. "Building Customer Relationships: Do Discount Cards Work?" *Managing Service Quality* 10, no. 6 (2000): 347–355.

McMillan, David W. "Sense of Community." *Journal of Community Psychology* 24, no. 4 (October 1996): 315–325.

McMillan, David W., and David M. Chavis. "Sense of Community: Definition and Theory." *Journal of Community Psychology* 14, no. 1 (January 1986): 6–23.

McMullan, Rosalind. "A Multiple-Item Scale for Measuring Customer Loyalty Development." *Journal of Services Marketing* 19, no. 7 (2005): 470–481.

McMullan, Rosalind, and Audrey Gilmore. "The Conceptual Development of Customer Loyalty Measurement: A Proposed Scale." *Journal of Targeting, Measurement and Analysis for Marketing* 11, no. 3 (2003): 230–243.

McNeil, John. "Federal Programs to Measure Consumer Purchase Expectations, 1946–1973: A Post-Mortem." *Journal of Consumer Research* 1, no. 3 (December 1974): 1–10.

Miller, Rowland S. "Inattentive and Contented: Relationship Commitment and Attention to Alternatives." *Journal of Personality and Social Psychology* 73, no. 4 (October 1997): 758–766.

Mischel, Walter. "From Good Intentions to Willpower." In *The Psychology of Action: Linking Cognition and Motivation to Behavior*, ed. Peter M. Gollwitzer and John A. Bargh, 197–218. New York: Guilford Press, 1996.

Mittal, Vikas, Eugene W. Anderson, Akin Sayrak, and Pandu Tadikamalla. "Dual Emphasis and the Long-Term Financial Impact of Customer Satisfaction." *Marketing Science* 24, no. 4 (Fall 2005): 544–555.

Mittal, Vikas, and Wagner A. Kamakura. "Satisfaction, Repurchase Intent, and Repurchase Behavior: Investigating the Moderating Effect of Customer Characteristics." *Journal of Marketing Research* 38, no. 1 (February 2001): 131–142.

Mittal, Vikas, Pankaj Kumar, and Michael Tsiros. "Attribute-Level Performance, Satisfaction, and Behavioral Intentions Over Time: A Consumption-System Approach." *Journal of Marketing* 63, no. 2 (April 1999): 88–101.

Mittal, Vikas, William T. Ross Jr., and Patrick M. Baldasare. "The Asymmetric Impact of Negative and Positive Attribute-Level Performance on Overall Satisfaction and Repurchase Intentions." *Journal of Marketing* 62, no. 1 (January 1998): 33–47.

Morgan, Michael S., and Chekitan S. Dev. "An Empirical Study of Brand Switching for a Retail Service." *Journal of Retailing* 70, no. 3 (Fall 1994): 267–282.

Morgan, Neil A., and Lopo Leotte Rego. "The Value of Different Customer Satisfaction and Loyalty Metrics in Predicting Business Performance." *Marketing Science* 25, no. 5 (September–October 2006): 426–439.

Morwitz, Vicki G. "Why Consumers Don't Always Accurately Predict Their Own Future Behavior." *Marketing Letters* 8, no. 1 (January 1997): 57–70.

Morwitz, Vicki G., and Gavan J. Fitzsimons. "The Mere-Measurement Effect: Why Does Measuring Intentions Change Actual Behavior?" *Journal of Consumer Psychology* 14, nos. 1–2 (2004): 64–74.

Muniz, Albert M., Jr., and Thomas C. O'Guinn. "Brand Community." *Journal of Consumer Research* 27, no. 4 (March 2001): 412–432.

Murray, Sandra L., John G. Holmes, and Dale W. Griffin. "The Benefits of Positive Illusions: Idealization and the Construction of Satisfaction in Close Relationships." *Journal of Personality and Social Psychology* 70, no. 1 (January): 79–98.

Narayandas, Das. "Measuring and Managing the Benefits of Customer Retention: An Empirical Investigation." *Journal of Service Research* 1, no. 2 (November 1998): 108–128.

Ngobo, Paul-Valentin. "Decreasing Returns in Customer Loyalty: Does It Really Matter to Delight the Customers?" In *Advances in Consumer Research*, ed. Eric J. Arnould and Linda H. Scott, 26:469–476. Provo, UT: Association for Consumer Research, 1999.

———. "Drivers of Customers' Cross-Buying Intentions." *European Journal of Marketing* 38, nos. 9–10 (2004): 1129–1157.

Noble, Stephanie M., and Joanna Phillips. "Relationship Hindrance: Why Would Consumers Not Want a Relationship with a Retailer?" *Journal of Retailing* 80, no. 4 (2004): 289–303.

O'Brien, Louise, and Charles Jones. "Do Rewards Really Create Loyalty?" *Harvard Business Review* 73, no. 3 (May–June 1995): 75–82.

Odekerken-Schröder, Gaby, Kristof De Wulf, Hans Kasper, Mirella Kleijnen, Janny Hoekstra, and Harry Commandeur. "The Impact of Quality on Store Loyalty: A Contingency Approach." *Total Quality Management* 12, no. 3 (May 2001): 307–322.

Ofir, Chezy, and Itamar Simonson. "In Search of Negative Customer Feedback: The Effect of Expecting to Evaluate on Satisfaction Evaluations." *Journal of Marketing Research* 38, no. 2 (May 2001): 170–182.

Oliva, Terence A., Richard L. Oliver, and William O. Bearden. "The Relationships among Consumer Satisfaction, Involvement, and Product Performance: A Catastrophe Theory Application." *Behavioral Science* 40, no. 2 (April 1995): 104–132.

Oliva, Terence A., Richard L. Oliver, and Ian C. MacMillan. "A Catastrophe Model for Developing Service Satisfaction Strategies." *Journal of Marketing* 56, no. 3 (July 1992): 83–95.

Oliver, Richard L. "A Cognitive Model of the Antecedents and Consequences of Satisfaction Decisions." *Journal of Marketing Research* 17, no. 4 (November 1980): 460–469.

———. *Satisfaction: A Behavioral Perspective on the Consumer*. New York: Irwin/McGraw-Hill, 1997.

———. "Whence Consumer Loyalty." *Journal of Marketing* 63 (Special Issue 1999): 33–44.

Oliver, Richard L., and Mikhael Shor. "Digital Redemption of Coupons: Satisfying and Dissatisfying Effects of Promotion Codes." *Journal of Product & Brand Management* 12, no. 2 (2003): 121–134.

Olsen, Svein Ottar. "Comparative Evaluation and the Relationship Between Quality, Satisfaction, and Repurchase Loyalty." *Journal of the Academy of Marketing Science* 30, no. 3 (Summer 2002): 240–249.

Otto, Sean D., Brian L. Parry, Collin R. Payne, Jonathan C. Huefner, and H. Keith Hunt. "When Consumers Get Upset: Modeling the Cost of Store Avoidance." *Journal of Consumer Satisfaction, Dissatisfaction and Complaining Behavior* 17 (2004): 42–53.

Ouellette, Judith A., and Wendy Wood. "Habit and Intention in Everyday Life: The Multiple Processes by Which Past Behavior Predicts Future Behavior." *Psychological Bulletin* 124, no. 1 (July 1998): 54–74.

Palmatier, Robert W., Lisa K. Scheer, and Jan-Benedict E.M. Steenkamp. "Customer Loyalty to Whom? Managing the Benefits and Risks of Salesperson-Owned Loyalty." *Journal of Marketing Research* 44, no. 2 (May 2007): 185–199.

Palmer, Adrian, Rosalind Beggs, and Caroline Keown-McMullan. "Equity and Repurchase Intention Following Service Failure." *Journal of Services Marketing* 14, no. 6 (2000): 513–528.

Patterson, Paul G. "Demographic Correlates of Loyalty in a Service Context." *Journal of Services Marketing* 21, no. 2 (2007): 112–121.

Patterson, Paul G., and Tasman Smith. "A Cross-Cultural Study of Switching Barriers and Propensity to Stay with Service Providers." *Journal of Retailing* 79, no. 2 (2003): 107–120.

Patterson, Paul G., and Richard A. Spreng. "Modelling the Relationship Between Perceived Value, Satisfaction and Repurchase Intentions in a Business-to-Business, Services Context: An Empirical Examination." *International Journal of Service Industry Management* 8, no. 5 (1997): 414–434.

Ping, Robert A., Jr. "Antecedents of Satisfaction in a Marketing Channel." *Journal of Retailing* 79, no. 4 (2003): 237–248.

———. "Does Satisfaction Moderate the Association between Alternative Attractiveness and Exit Intention in a Marketing Channel?" *Journal of the Academy of Marketing Science* 22, no. 4 (Fall 1994): 364–371.

Price, Linda L., and Eric J. Arnould. "Commercial Friendships: Service Provider–Client Relationships in Context." *Journal of Marketing* 63, no. 4 (October 1999): 38–56.

Pritchard, Mark P., Mark E. Havitz, and Dennis R. Howard. "Analyzing the Commitment-Loyalty Link in Service Contexts." *Journal of the Academy of Marketing Science* 27, no. 3 (Summer 1999): 333–348.

Reichheld, Frederick F., and W. Earl Sasser. "Zero Defections: Quality Comes to Services." *Harvard Business Review* 68, no. 5 (September–October 1990): 105–111.

Reichheld, Frederick F., with Thomas Teal. *The Loyalty Effect: The Hidden Force Behind Growth, Profits, and Lasting Value.* Boston: Harvard Business School Press, 1996.

Reinartz, Werner J., and V. Kumar. "On the Profitability of Long-Life Customers in a Noncontractual Setting: An Empirical Investigation and Implications for Marketing." *Journal of Marketing* 64, no. 4 (October 2000): 17–35.

Reis, Harry T., and Caryl E. Rusbult, eds. *Key Readings on Close Relationships.* Washington, DC: Taylor & Francis, 2004.

Reynolds, Kristy E., and Sharon E. Beatty. "Customer Benefits and Company Consequences of Customer-Salesperson Relationships in Retailing." *Journal of Retailing* 75, no. 1 (Spring 1999): 11–32.

Richins, Marsha L. "Measuring Emotions in the Consumption Experience." *Journal of Consumer Research* 24, no. 2 (September 1997): 127–146.

Roehm, Michelle L., Ellen Bolman Pullins, and Harper A. Roehm Jr. "Designing Loyalty-Building Programs for Packaged Goods Brands." *Journal of Marketing Research* 39, no. 2 (May 2002): 202–213.

Roos, Inger. "Switching Processes in Customer Relationships." *Journal of Service Research* 2, no. 1 (August 1999): 68–85.

Roos, Inger, Bo Edvardsson, and Anders Gustafsson. "Customer Switching Patterns in Competitive and Noncompetitive Service Industries." *Journal of Service Research* 6, no. 3 (February 2004): 256–271.

Roos, Inger, and Anders Gustafsson. "Understanding Frequent Switching Patterns: A Crucial Element in Managing Customer Relationships." *Journal of Service Research* 10, no. 1 (August 2007): 93–108.

Rosenbaum, Mark S. "Exploring the Social Supportive Role of Third Places in Consumers' Lives." *Journal of Service Research* 9, no. 1 (August 2006): 59–72.

Rosenbaum, Mark S., Amy L. Ostrom, and Ronald Kuntze. "Loyalty Programs and a Sense of Community." *Journal of Services Marketing* 19, no. 4 (2005): 222–233.

Rosenbaum, Mark S., James Ward, Beth A. Walker, and Amy L. Ostrom. "A Cup of Coffee with a Dash of Love: An Investigation of Commercial Social Support and Third-Place Attachment." *Journal of Service Research* 10, no. 1 (August 2007): 43–59.

Rosenspan, Alan. "Delusions of Loyalty: Where Loyalty Programs Go Wrong." *Direct Marketing* 60, no. 10 (February 1998): 24–27, 61.

Royce, Josiah. *The Philosophy of Loyalty*. 1908. Nashville: Vanderbilt University Press, 1995.

Rucci, Anthony J., Steven P. Kirn, and Richard T. Quinn. "The Employee-Customer-Profit Chain at Sears." *Harvard Business Review* 76, no. 1 (January–February 1998): 82–97.

Rust, Roland T., and Anthony J. Zahorik. "Customer Satisfaction, Customer Retention, and Market Share." *Journal of Retailing* 69, no. 2 (Summer 1993): 193–215.

Rust, Roland T., Anthony J. Zahorik, and Timothy L. Keiningham. *Return on Quality: Measuring the Financial Impact of Your Company's Quest for Quality*. Chicago: Probus, 1994.

Sambandam, Rajan, and Kenneth R. Lord. "Switching Behavior in Automobile Markets: A Consideration-Sets Model." *Journal of the Academy of Marketing Science* 23, no. 1 (Winter 1995): 57–65.

Schouten, John W., James H. McAlexander, and Harold F. Koenig. "Transcendent Customer Experience and Brand Community." *Journal of the Academy of Marketing Science* 35, no. 3 (September 2007): 357–368.

Seetharaman, P.B., and Pradeep Chintagunta. "A Model of Inertia and Variety-Seeking with Marketing Variables." *International Journal of Research in Marketing* 15, no. 1 (February 1998): 1–17.

Seiders, Kathleen, Glenn B. Voss, Dhruv Grewal, and Andrea L. Godfrey. "Do Satisfied Customers Buy More? Examining Moderating Influences in a Retailing Context." *Journal of Marketing* 69, no. 4 (October 2005): 26–43.

Sen, Sankar, Zeynep Gürhan-Canli, and Vicki Morwitz. "Withholding Consumption: A Social Dilemma Perspective on Consumer Boycotts." *Journal of Consumer Research* 28, no. 3 (December 2001): 399–417.

Sharma, Neeru, and Paul G. Patterson. "Switching Costs, Alternative Attractiveness and Experience as Moderators of Relationship Commitment in Professional Consumer Services." *International Journal of Service Industry Management* 11, no. 5 (2000): 470–490.

Sharp, Byron, and Anne Sharp. "Loyalty Programs and Their Impact on Repeat-Purchase Loyalty Patterns." *International Journal of Research in Marketing* 14, no. 5 (December 1997): 473–486.

Sheth, Jagdish N., and Reshma H. Shah. "Till Death Do Us Part . . . But Not Always: Six Antecedents to a Customer's Relational Preference in Buyer-Seller Exchanges." *Industrial Marketing Management* 32, no. 8 (November 2003): 627–631.

Shiv, Baba, and Joel Huber. "The Impact of Anticipating Satisfaction on Consumer Choice." *Journal of Consumer Research* 27, no. 2 (September 2000): 202–216.

Shugan, Steven M. "Brand Loyalty Programs: Are They Shams?" *Marketing Science* 24, no. 2 (Spring 2005): 185–193.

Simonson, Itamar. "The Influence of Anticipating Regret and Responsibility on Purchase Decisions." *Journal of Consumer Research* 19, no. 1 (June 1992): 105–118.

Sivadas, Eugene, and Jamie L. Baker-Prewitt. "An Examination of the Relationship Between Service Quality, Customer Satisfaction, and Store Loyalty." *International Journal of Retail & Distribution Management* 28, no. 2 (2000): 73–82.

Sivakumar, K., and S.P. Raj. "Quality Tier Competition: How Price Change Influences Brand Choice and Category Choice." *Journal of Marketing* 61, no. 3 (July 1997): 71–84.

Snyder, Don R. "Demographic Correlates to Loyalty in Frequently Purchased Consumer Services." *Journal of Professional Services Marketing* 8, no. 1 (1991): 45–55.

Söderlund, Magnus. "The Retrospective and the Prospective Mind and the Temporal Framing of Customer Satisfaction." *European Journal of Marketing* 37, no. 10 (2003): 1375–1390.

Söderlund, Magnus, and Niclas Öhman. "Behavioral Intentions in Satisfaction Research Revisited." *Journal of Consumer Satisfaction, Dissatisfaction and Complaining Behavior* 16 (2003): 53–66.

Sproles, George B., and Elizabeth L. Kendall. "A Methodology for Profiling Consumers' Decision-Making Styles." *Journal of Consumer Affairs* 20, no. 2 (Winter 1986): 267–279.

Srinivasan, Srini S., Rolph Anderson, and Kishore Ponnavolu. "Customer Loyalty in e-Commerce: An Exploration of Its Antecedents and Consequences." *Journal of Retailing* 78, no. 1 (Spring 2002): 41–50.

Stauss, Bernd, Klaus Chojnacki, Alexander Decker, and Frank Hoffman. "Retention Effects of a Customer Club." *International Journal of Service Industry Management* 12, no. 1 (2001): 7–19.

Stern, Philip, and Kathy Hammond. "The Relationship Between Customer Loyalty and Purchase Incidence." *Marketing Letters* 15, no. 1 (February 2004): 5–19.

Sternberg, Robert J., and Mahzad Hojjat, eds. *Satisfaction in Close Relationships*. New York: Guilford Press, 1997.

Storbacka, Kaj, Tore Strandvik, and Christian Grönroos. "Managing Customer Relationships for Profit: The Dynamics of Relationship Quality." *International Journal of Service Industry Management* 5, no. 5 (1994): 21–38.

Suh, Jung-Chae, and Youjae Yi. "When Brand Attitudes Affect the Customer Satisfaction-Loyalty Relation: The Moderating Role of Product Involvement." *Journal of Consumer Psychology* 16, no. 2 (2006): 145–155.

Sutton, Stephen. "Predicting and Explaining Intentions and Behavior: How Well Are We Doing?" *Journal of Applied Social Psychology* 28, no. 15 (August 1998): 1317–1338.

Taylor, Steven A., Gary L. Hunter, and Timothy A. Longfellow. "Testing an Expanded Attitude Model of Goal-Directed Behavior in a Loyalty Context." *Journal of Consumer Satisfaction, Dissatisfaction and Complaining Behavior* 19 (2006): 18–39.

Thomson, Matthew. "Human Brands: Investigating Antecedents to Consumers' Strong Attachments to Celebrities." *Journal of Marketing* 70, no. 3 (July 2006): 104–119.

Thomson, Matthew, Deborah J. MacInnis, and C. Whan Park. "The Ties That Bind: Measuring the Strength of Consumers' Emotional Attachments to Brands." *Journal of Consumer Psychology* 15, no. 1 (2005): 77–91.

Thorbjørnsen, Helge, Magne Supphellen, Herbjørn Nysveen, and Per Egil Pedersen. "Building Brand Relationships Online: A Comparison of Two Interactive Applications." *Journal of Interactive Marketing* 16, no. 3 (Summer 2002): 17–34.

Tranberg, Hugo, and Flemming Hansen. "Patterns of Brand Loyalty: Their Determinants and Their Role for Leading Brands." *European Journal of Marketing* 20, nos. 3–4 (1986): 81–109.

Uncles, Mark D., Grahame R. Dowling, and Kathy Hammond. "Customer Loyalty and Customer Loyalty Programs." *Journal of Consumer Marketing* 20, no. 4 (2003): 294–316.

van Heerde, Harald J., and Tammo H.A. Bijmolt. "Decomposing the Promotional Revenue Bump for Loyalty Program Members Versus Nonmembers." *Journal of Marketing Research* 42, no. 4 (November 2005): 443–457.

van Raaij, Erik M., Maarten J.A. Vernooij, and Sander van Triest. "The Implementation of Customer Profitability Analysis: A Case Study." *Industrial Marketing Management* 32, no. 7 (October 2003): 573–583.

van Trijp, Hans C.M., Wayne D. Hoyer, and J. Jeffrey Inman. "Why Switch? Product Category-Level Explanations for True Variety-Seeking Behavior." *Journal of Marketing Research* 33, no. 3 (August 1996): 281–292.

Van Vugt, Mark, and Claire M. Hart. "Social Identity as Social Glue: The Origins of Group Loyalty." *Journal of Personality and Social Psychology* 86, no. 4 (April 2004): 585–598.

Verhoef, Peter C. "Understanding the Effect of Customer Relationship Management Efforts on Customer Retention and Customer Share Development." *Journal of Marketing* 67, no. 4 (October 2003): 30–45.

Verhoef, Peter C., Philip Hans Franses, and Janny C. Hoekstra. "The Effect of Relational Constructs on Customer Referrals and Number of Services Purchased From a Multiservice Provider: Does Age of Relationship Matter?" *Journal of the Academy of Marketing Science* 30, no. 3 (Summer 2002): 202–216.

Vilares, Manuel José, and Pedro Simões Coelho. "The Employee-Customer Satisfaction Chain in the ECSI Model." *European Journal of Marketing* 37, nos. 11–12 (2003): 1703–1722.

Warrington, Patti, and Soyeon Shim. "An Empirical Investigation of the Relationship Between Product Involvement and Brand Commitment." *Psychology & Marketing* 17, no. 9 (September 2000): 761–782.

Wendlandt, Mark, and Ulf Schrader. "Consumer Reactance Against Loyalty Programs." *Journal of Consumer Marketing* 24, no. 5 (2007): 293–304.

Wieringa, Jaap E., and Peter C. Verhoef. "Understanding Customer Switching Behavior in a Liberalizing Service Market." *Journal of Service Research* 10, no. 2 (November 2007): 174–186.

Wilson, David T. "An Integrated Model of Buyer-Seller Relationships." *Journal of the Academy of Marketing Science* 23, no. 4 (Fall 1995): 335–345.

Wirtz, Jochen, Anna S. Mattila, and Mary Oo Lwin. "How Effective Are Loyalty Reward Programs in Driving Share of Wallet?" *Journal of Service Research* 9, no. 4 (May 2007): 327–334.

Yang, Zhilin, and Robin T. Peterson. "Customer Perceived Value, Satisfaction, and Loyalty: The Role of Switching Costs." *Psychology & Marketing* 21, no. 10 (October 2004): 799–822.

Yi, Youjae, and Hoseong Jeon. "Effects of Loyalty Programs on Value Perception, Program Loyalty, and Brand Loyalty." *Journal of the Academy of Marketing Science* 31, no. 3 (Summer 2003): 229–240.

Yi, Youjae, and Suna La. "What Influences the Relations Between Customer Satisfaction and Repurchase

Intention? Investigating the Effects of Adjusted Expectations and Customer Loyalty." *Psychology & Marketing* 21, no. 5 (May 2004): 351–373.

Yim, Chi Kin (Bennett), and P.K. Kannan. "Consumer Behavioral Loyalty: A Segmentation Model and Analysis." *Journal of Business Research* 44, no. 2 (February 1999): 75–92.

Zauberman, Gal. "The Intertemporal Dynamics of Consumer Lock-In." *Journal of Consumer Research* 30, no. 3 (December 2003): 405–419.

Zboja, James J., and Clay M. Voohrees. "The Impact of Brand Trust and Satisfaction on Retailer Repurchase Intentions." *Journal of Services Marketing* 20, no. 5 (2006): 381–390.

Zeithaml, Valarie A., Roland T. Rust, and Katherine N. Lemon. "The Customer Pyramid: Creating and Serving Profitable Customers." *California Management Review* 43, no. 4 (Summer 2001): 118–142.

NAME INDEX

H

SUBJECT INDEX

503

ABOUT THE AUTHOR

Richard L. Oliver (PhD, University of Wisconsin-Madison) is Professor Emeritus of Management (Marketing) at Vanderbilt University's Owen Graduate School of Management. He has research interests in consumer psychology with a special focus on customer satisfaction, loyalty, and postpurchase processes. He holds the position of Fellow of the American Psychological Association for his extensive writings on the psychology of consumer satisfaction. He is also a highly distinguished teacher, having earned "excellence in teaching" awards at both Vanderbilt and Washington University.